D1714991

The Fourfold Gospel

The Fourfold Gospel

A Formational Commentary on Matthew, Mark, Luke, and John

Volume 1: From the Beginning to the Baptist

John DelHousaye

PICKWICK *Publications* • Eugene, Oregon

THE FOURFOLD GOSPEL
A Formational Commentary on Matthew, Mark, Luke, and John
Volume 1: From the Beginning to the Baptist

Pickwick Publications
An Imprint of Wipf and Stock Publishers
199 W. 8th Ave., Suite 3
Eugene, OR 97401

www.wipfandstock.com

PAPERBACK ISBN: 978-1-5326-8364-0
HARDCOVER ISBN: 978-1-5326-8365-7
EBOOK ISBN: 978-1-5326-8366-4

Cataloguing-in-Publication data:

Names: DelHousaye, John.

Title: The fourfold gospel : a formational commentary on Matthew, Mark, Luke, and John : Volume 1 : from the beginning to the Baptist / by John DelHousaye.

Description: Eugene, OR: Pickwick Publications, 2020. | Includes bibliographical references and index.

Identifiers: ISBN 978-1-5326-8364-0 (paperback) | ISBN 978-1-5326-8365-7 (hardcover) | ISBN 978-1-5326-8366-4 (ebook)

Subjects: LCSH: Bible. Gospels—Commentaries. | Mystagogy. | Bible. Gospels—Criticism, interpretation, etc. | Bible. Gospels—Hermeneutics | Bible. Gospels—Theology

Classification: BS2555.3 D45 2020 (print) | BS2555.3 (ebook)

Manufactured in the U.S.A. 08/05/20

To Tiffany, a lifelong gift from Christ,
who insisted on this publication.

Not on bread alone will the human being live, but on every word coming through God's mouth. . . . And opening his mouth, he began teaching them . . .

—Matthew 4:4; 5:1

Contents

Preface

For twenty years or so, Jesus and I met nearly every morning in the Gospels. He kindly heard my questions and hopes; I tried to listen, but the noise was almost overwhelming (tinnitus eventually added to the challenge). But we met, teacher to student, physician to patient, savior to sinner. He loved me, and I began to love him because I knew more of the beloved, the Spirit, who is love, and the unrelenting Lover. The Gospels have witnessed faithfully to this reality for two millennia, but must be seen and heard by each generation.

We enter God's Kingdom (or, as John puts it, "eternal life") through what Jesus calls the "faith of a mustard seed," which is very small yet real. This is necessarily so: beliefs are not reality—they are often simplified or distorted—but direct our way in a strange world that would otherwise overwhelm us. All genuine human knowledge, I suspect, is but a drop in a still, dark sea. We are sponges to what we heard as children, learned in school, and see modeled around us. Everything is our teacher. Humans generally believe what is easiest to understand ("processing fluency"). These organizing filters deepen each day with each meeting of our mind and stimuli, so that reality and interpretation are nearly indistinguishable; they become a culture's definition of sanity, the ability to think and behave normally. "He is out of his mind," declared Jesus's own family (Mark 3:21). In the Gospels, the crowds—many of whom had grown up hearing Scripture read and expounded in the synagogue, praying, and hoping in a messiah—are confused and do not trust Jesus. Even the disciples struggle to understand. After Christendom was underway, Antony of Egypt (c. 251–356), who left his culture to hear Jesus in the desert, said: "A time is coming when men will go mad, and when they see someone who is not mad, they will attack him saying, 'You are mad, you are not like us.'"[1] Christianity's historical

1. Ward, *Sayings of the Desert Fathers*, 6.

impact, particularly in the West, may disguise the reality that understanding Jesus is still difficult—indeed impossible—without the illumination of the Holy Spirit. That many today reject the gospel should not surprise. The Gospels suggest starting over in Jesus, who is one with our inherent God awareness (see Rom 1:21). The Jesuit theologian Karl Rahner (1904–1984) predicts that third-millennium Christians will have a "genuine experience of God emerging from the very heart of our existence," or they will no longer be Christians.[2]

The Gospels invite the reader into a strange world, full of demons and the devil, but I suggest they are strangers to our beliefs about them. Several fields of knowledge have been drawn to the same mysteries, offering their own frames. But how well does the university understand evil and oppression, which are unavoidable in human experience? Anselm of Canterbury (1033–1109) describes this path as *fides quaerens intellectum* ("faith seeking understanding").[3] Jesus comes to each of us in the darkness, and, without explanation, says, "follow me." Mirroring this summons, the Gospels offer a narrative depiction of reality—a necessary simplification, a model.[4] The faith of a mustard seed allows readers to participate in the story, to begin a pilgrimage, while allowing space for illumination and growth.

2. Rahner, *Theological Investigations*, 20:149; see Egan, *Ignatius Loyola*, 13–14; Carroll, "Moving Mysticism to the Center," 41–52.

3. Anselm, *Proslogion,* 1–6.

4. Bruner, "Narrative Construction of Reality," 1–20; see Powell, *What Is Narrative Criticism*, 23.

Acknowledgments

Many have given financially to Phoenix Seminary, which allowed time for research and writing. Many students read and improved the material by sharing their own readings and stories. Lorne Zelyck and Travis Buchanan, who are now professors, encouraged me through their friendship and expertise. Corinne Bellars, who became my teaching assistant, was the first student to voice excitement about the medieval Quadriga (PaRDeS) and its potential for reaching her generation. (I also thank everyone who questioned this approach, seeking grounding and clarity.) Brian Arnold, John Meade, Jonathan Logan, Justin Smith, Malcolm Hartnell, Norm Wakefield, Paul Wegner, Peter Gurry, Steve Tracy, and Wayne Grudem have been invaluable colleagues. Our library staff, Doug Olbert, Jim Santeford, and Mitch Miller, helped secure resources for this project. Ted Wueste, who directs the Spiritual Formation Society of Arizona, has been a soul friend in this material. My father has modelled Bible study and shepherding; my mother, spiritual direction; and my brother, cultural engagement. I am also grateful for many friends at Redemption Church Alhambra, who are sharing this journey with my family—Tiffany (to whom this first volume is dedicated, my bride and co-minister), Livia, Joslyn, and Tate.

Abbreviations

א	*Codex Sinaiticus*
Ag. Ap.	*Against Apion*
Alleg. Interp.	*Allegorical Interpretation*
Ant.	*Jewish Antiquities*
Apol.	*Apology of Socrates*
b.	Babylonian Talmud
Barn.	*Barnabas*
BDAG	*Greek-English Lexicon*
Ber.	*Berakhot*
CA	*Catena Aurea*
C. Ar.	*Orations Against the Arians*
CD	Damascus Document
CD	*Church Dogmatics*
Cels.	*Contra Celsum*
Chron.	*Chronicle*
Col	Colossians
Comm. Isa.	*Commentarium in Isaiam libri XVIII*
Comm. Jo.	*Commentarii in evangelium Joannis*
Comm. Matt.	*Commentarium in Matthaeum libri IV*
	Commentarium in evangelium Matthei
Comm. Mich.	*Commentarium in Michaeum libri II*
Confusion	*On the Confusion of Tongues*
Contempl. Life	*On the Contemplative Life*
D	Codex Bezae Cantabrigensis

Dan	Daniel
Demon.	*Demonax*
Dial.	*Dialogues*
	Dialogue with Trypho
Dom. or.	*The Lord's Prayer*
Deut	Deuteronomy
Eccl	Ecclesiastes
11QT^{a}	Temple Scroll ^{a}
Embassy	*On the Embassy to Gaius*
Eph	Ephesians
Eph.	*To the Ephesians*
ESV	English Standard Version
Exod	Exodus
Ezek	Ezekiel
Flaccus	*Against Flaccus*
1 Apol.	*First Apology*
1–2 Chr	1–2 Chronicles
1–2 Clem.	*1–2 Clement*
1–2 Cor	1–2 Corinthians
1 En.	*1 Enoch*
1–2 Kgs	1–2 Kings
1–2 Macc	1–2 Maccabees
1–2 Pet	1–2 Peter
1QapGen ar	Genesis Apocryphon
1QIsaa	Isaiah^{a}
1QM	War Scroll
1QpHab	Pesher Habakkuk
1QS	Rule of the Community
1–2 Sam	1–2 Samuel
1 Thess	1 Thessalonians
1–2 Tim	1–2 Timothy
4QD^{a}	Damascus Documenta
4QFlor	Florilegium
4QTest	Testimonia

Gal	Galatians
Gen	Genesis
Hag	Haggai
Heb	Hebrews
Hist. eccl.	*Ecclesiastical History*
Hom. Luc.	*Homilae in Lucam*
Hos	Hosea
Isa	Isaiah
Jas	James
Jer	Jeremiah
Joseph	*On the Life of Joseph*
Josh	Joshua
Jub.	*Jubilees*
Judg	Judges
J.W.	*Jewish War*
KJV	King James Version
Leg.	*Laws*
Lev	Leviticus
Life	*The Life*
LXX	Septuagint
m.	Mishnah
Mal	Malachi
Matt	Matthew
Meg.	*Megillah*
Mic	Micah
Mor.	*Moralia*
ms	manuscript
mss	manuscripts
MT	Masoretic Text
Nah	Nahum
NAS	New American Standard
Nat.	*Natural History*
Ned.	*Nedarim*
NIV	New International Version

NRSV	New Revised Standard Version
NT	New Testament
Num	Numbers
OG	Old Greek
P	Papyrus
PL	*Patrologia Latina*
Pelag.	*Adversus Pelagianos dialogi III*
Phaed.	*Phaedo*
Phlm	Philemon
Posterity	*On the Posterity of Cain*
Praep. ev.	*Preparation for the Gospel*
Protr.	*Exhortation to the Greeks*
Prov	Proverbs
Ps/Pss	Psalms
Pss. Sol.	*Psalms of Solomon*
Resp.	*Republic*
Rev	Revelation
Rhet.	*Rhetoric*
Šabb.	*Shabbat*
Sanh.	*Sanhedrin*
Sib. Or.	*Sibylline Oracles*
Sir	Sirach
Smyrn.	*To the Smyrnaeans*
Song	Song of Songs
Spec. Laws	*On the Special Laws*
S.T.	*Summa Theologiae*
Strom.	*Miscellanies*
T. Dan	*Testament of Dan*
T. Jud.	*Testament of Judah*
T. Levi	*Testament of Levi*
T. Sol.	*Testament of Solomon*
T. Zeb.	*Testament of Zebulun*
Tim.	*Timaeus*
Tob	Tobit

Trin.	*The Trinity*
Vat	Codex Vaticanus
Vir. ill.	*De viris illustribus*
Vit. Ant.	*Life of Antony*
W	Codex Washingtonianus
Wis	Wisdom of Solomon
Yebam.	*Yebamot*
Zeph	Zephaniah

1

Entering the Gospels

The Gospels invite their readers, whether they are hearing about Jesus for the first time or are old disciples, into their story, which was typical in contemporary rhetoric and Jewish religious life.[1] We often encounter the invitation to "look" (*idou*, ἰδού) at what is presented:[2]

> Look: an angel of the Lord appeared to him in a dream . . . (Matt 1:20; 2:13, 19)
>
> Look: magi from the eastern regions came to Jerusalem . . . (2:1)
>
> Look: the star that they saw in the east was going before them . . . (2:9)

The evangelists often employ the present tense, which is obscured in translation, to draw the reader into the story.[3] The English Standard Version renders παραγίνεται ὁ Ἰησοῦς ἀπὸ τῆς Γαλιλαίας ἐπὶ τὸν Ἰορδάνην as "Jesus

1. For the rhetorical background, see Neufeld, *Mockery and Secretism*, 5. Peter Flint notes, "The *yaḥad* [responsible for many of the Dead Sea Scrolls] saw itself as part of the biblical world, divinely ordained heirs of the Scriptures, and in continuity with figures and events of the past that formed their own sacred history" (Embry et al., *Early Jewish Literature,* 1:104). Non-sectarian Jews who heard Scripture read in the synagogue presumably felt the same way because festivals like Passover and Unleavened Bread were designed to represent the Exodus to each generation.

2. BDAG glosses the verb as "to perceive by sight of the eye" (468).

3. The culprit has been the syntactical category "historical present." Joel Marcus, for example, notes that Mark ostensibly writes, "the Spirit casts" (1:12) but claims "the sense is past" (*Mark 1—8*, 167n12). Aspect, a Russian calque, refers to the point of view the reader (hearer) is to take. Grammarians often speak of two general points of view—a view from the *outside* and a view from the *inside.* We call the view from the outside perfective aspect. There is *remoteness* between the observer and the action seen. The outside view provides context. We call the view from the inside imperfective aspect. The observer and the action seen are *proximate* to one another. The inside view provides detail. This distinction is meaningful because each involves a choice of the writer (speaker).

came from Galilee to the Jordan"; a more natural translation is "Jesus *appears* from the Galilee at the Jordan" (Matt 3:13). Instead of merely summarizing an action, the story slows down for us to inhabit the scene. Matthew and John came to Jesus; Mark and Luke, later disciples, also came imaginatively with the Holy Spirit; and now we, their readers, are summoned. The proclaimed becomes the proclaimer.

Mystagogy

The Gospels may be received like a film with moving, connected images of Jesus Christ, who elicits action from the center. Jesus is the protagonist and focal point of nearly every scene. But they go even further, inviting readers to see *with* Jesus:

> Look: the heavens were opened [to him], and he saw [the] *Spirit* of God descending like a dove [and] coming *upon* him. (Matt 3:16)

This way of discipleship came to be called *mystagogy*, "the gradual initiation of the believer into the mystery of the indwelling Christ by a master who is capable of communicating some experience of this mystery."[4] The apostle Paul bases his teaching on the presupposition that his readers possess "the mind of Christ," who, despite their immaturity, are nevertheless enabled by the Holy Spirit to perceive with Jesus (1 Cor 2:16).

Meditating in the Gospels invites a life centered on Christ. We begin to see our own every-day scenes—work, rest, worship—differently. Ludolph of Saxony (c. 1295–1378), a Carthusian monk who wrote an entire discipleship manual, *The Life of Christ* (*Vita Christi*), from this approach, claims, "Of all the many kinds of spiritual exercise, I believe this is the one that is the most necessary, the most beneficial, and the one that can lead you to the greatest heights."[5] Queen Isabella (1451–1504) was so taken by the work that she ordered the Franciscan poet Fray Ambrosio Montesiano (c. 1444–1514) to translate it into Castilian for all her people. Ignatius of Loyola (1491–1556), the founder of the Jesuits, was deeply impacted by the *Life of Christ* and incorporated the method into his *Spiritual Exercises*, a month-long retreat that helped novitiates in his order to discern the Lord's calling.[6] After a pre-

4. Kavanaugh, *John of the Cross*, 32.

5. Ludolph of Saxony, *Life of Christ*, 1:11.

6. The *Exercises*, which last for four or five hours per day, focus on four themes from the Gospels—week one: sin; week two: the life of Jesus up to Palm Sunday; week three: the Passion of Jesus; and week four: the Resurrection and Ascension. We discern the

paratory prayer seeking "the grace that all our energies and activities be sincerely directed to His glory and worship" for the first *Exercise*, Ignatius evokes the imagination of the reader:

> *The first prelude* consists of a certain mental re-creation of the place. It should be observed in this regard that during any meditation or contemplation of a corporal entity, for example of Christ, we shall see with a sort of imaginary vision a physical place representing what we are contemplating, for instance a temple or a mountain where we could find Christ Jesus or the Virgin Mary, and everything else that is related to the theme of our contemplation.[7]

Especially among the Orthodox, the Gospel Book, a codex conjoining Matthew, Mark, Luke, and John, is read like an icon. Theodore the Studite (759–826) describes the Gospels as "written in ink"; icons, "in gold."[8] Icons are to be read, not just seen. The reader is invited to look at and through the surface to the source, like we do with words, moving from the signifier to the signified. The focal point is not outside, the view of the reader, but inside the icon. After prayer and fasting, ancient iconographers painted an eye on the empty canvas. Andreas Andreopoulos notes, "The icon, therefore, is not only something for us to look at but also something that looks at us, through a window *from* the other world."[9] We may imagine two neighbors talking to one another through an apartment window. When Jesus speaks, he is addressing whoever is in the scene but also us: "let the reader understand" (Mark 13:14). When we respond, there is, of course, the awkward reality of talking to a page! But in faith we are also responding to God. "For the Fathers of the Church," observes Andrew Louth, "the Scriptures function as a *place of encounter* between the Word of God and humankind."[10] "The person who thirsts for God," assures Bernard of Clairvaux (1090–1153), "eagerly studies and meditates on the inspired word, knowing that there he is certain to

---

many wounds of sin in our lives and the world around us, which, like the ministry of the Baptist, prepare us to hear the call of the King, the heart of the *Exercises*. The third and fourth week immerse the retreatant into the mystery of the cross and resurrection. See Wolff, *Spiritual Exercises*, 4. In some modern representations, the retreatant begins with the unconditional love of God for all humanity and every individual, and then turns to the rejection of that love (Lonsdale, *Eyes to See, Ears to Hear*, 130–31).

7. Wolff, *Spiritual Exercises*, 18.

8. Cited in Andreopoulos, *Metamorphosis*, 11.

9. Andreopoulos, *Metamorphosis*, 27.

10. Andreopoulos, *Metamorphosis*, 12 (emphasis his). "In cognitive linguistics reading a text is understood as entering mental spaces" (van Tilborg and Counet, *Jesus' Appearances and Disappearances*, 95).

find the one for whom he thirsts."[11] Like Abraham with the mysterious visitors, "we are called to show hospitality to God as he graciously comes to us through the pages of the Bible."[12] Bernard meditates on Christ as the ultimate image of the Bible, a book of mental images.[13]

Christians inherited this iconography from Jews, who approached God through temple gates. The temple was patterned after the tabernacle (a sacred tent), which had an altar in front of the Holy of Holies (a Hebrew idiom for the superlative, "the Holiest of Places"), a small room that housed the ark of the covenant. The ark, a gold-covered wooden chest, had a lid that was covered by two cherubim (winged angels with the faces of a lion, ox, human being, and eagle), who, in turn, held up God's throne (or chariot).[14] We are told that God spoke to Moses "from between the Cherubim" (Num 7:89). They protected the entrance to the Garden of Eden after Adam and Eve sinned; their images were embroidered into a veil that restricted access to the Holy of Holies. The Gospels relate that the boy Jesus and his parents made an annual pilgrimage to the temple at Passover. One year, his parents accidentally left without him. After returning and much searching, they found Jesus there. "How is it that you were seeking me?" he said. "Did you not know that I must be in my Father's place?" (Luke 2:49). In a later debate, an adult Jesus says, "The one who swears by the temple swears by it and by the one who dwells in it," referring to his Father, the God of Israel (Matt 23:21). After the Romans destroyed the temple (AD 70), Jews continued to approach God through prayer and Scripture, a presupposition we find in the Gospels. On the cross, Jesus recites a psalm: "Father, *into your hands I entrust my spirit*" (Ps 31:15).[15] Tempted to feed the stomach, he recites at the devil: "*Not on bread alone shall the human being live, but on every word coming through God's mouth*" (Deut 8:3; cited at Matt 4:4). Like the synagogue, the church was not dependent on the temple because Jesus himself is Immanuel, "God with us" (Matt 1:23). We may approach the Triune God in Christ through the prayerful study of the Gospels. Jesus foresaw the temple's destruction, but presented himself as a place of divine encounter. The psalmist cries, "As a deer thirsts for fountains of water so my soul thirsts for you, God" (42:1). His thirst comes from being far away from the temple. But Jesus responds: "If anyone is thirsty, come to me and drink"

11. McGinn, *Essential Writings of Christian Mysticism*, 28.

12. Boersma, *Scripture as Real Presence*, 1, 56. He describes this way of reading the Bible as sacramental—the words point to and make God present.

13. Bernard of Clairvaux, *Selected Works*, 43.

14. 1 Kgs 6:22–29; 2 Kgs 19:15; Ezek 10:1–2; 2 Chr 28:18.

15. Awkwardly, there are three versifications in the textual tradition. The citation is 31:5 in most English Bibles, 30:6 in OG, and 31:6 in MT.

(John 7:37–38). An icon usually consists of three panels, so that the outer ones can fold inward, becoming protected and portable.

Sacred Time

Soon after the Ascension, Christians began to gather on the first day of the week, Sunday, to commemorate the resurrection. They partook of the Lord's Supper (Eucharist, communion, mass) and sang directly to him (Eph 5:19), knowing that the crucified yet resurrected Lord was with them: "Look, I stand at the door and knock" (Rev 3:20). By the end of the first century, selections from the Gospels were being read with other Scripture (Justin, *1 Apol.* 67). Today, in many traditions, the Gospel Book is taken in procession out to the people who stand during its reading.

Alongside these weekly gatherings, patterned after the synagogue, a festal calendar developed with two parts. The *temporale*, a Latin word referring to the passing of time, focuses on Easter and Christmas, the two great independent feasts. The *sanctorale*, as the name suggests, is concerned with feasts of individual saints. The Jerusalem church commemorated events of Holy Week at the traditional sites where they happened, and pilgrims brought the liturgical practice home.[16] Not everyone could live in Jerusalem, but any Christian could identify with Christ in sacred time. Palm Sunday, Maundy Thursday, Good Friday—all prepared the worshiper for Easter Sunday. Following the chronology of Acts, the church related Easter and Pentecost as one sequence of events, with Ascension celebrated on the Thursday ten days before Pentecost.[17] In the West, the Sunday after Pentecost was designated Trinity Sunday.[18] Lent, a forty-day preparation for Holy Week, developed from the proximate period of catechesis for those seeking to be baptized on Easter, which marked their initial assimilation into the life and death of Christ.[19] The beginning was observed on Ash Wednesday. Christmas, Epiphany, and the twelve intervening days were a Christianization of Pagan mid-winter festivals. Analogous to Lent, the preparatory season of Advent developed in Gaul eventually consisting of four Sundays before Christmas. There are also two seasons of "Ordinary Time" between the feasts, which allow the church to rest and digest the extraordinary moments and meditate on scenes from Christ's public ministry. They

16. Davies, *Dictionary of Liturgy and Worship*, 133.

17. Davies, *Dictionary of Liturgy and Worship*, 134.

18. The observance began in the tenth century and was formally recognized by Rome in the fourteenth century (Davies, *Dictionary of Liturgy and Worship*, 134).

19. Davies, *Dictionary of Liturgy and Worship*, 134.

offer space to integrate the life of Christ into the everyday. The Christian calendar places every season, week, and day in Christ. Simple awareness of our place in the year may deepen our devotion.

Sacred Space

Inspired by the work of Ammonius of Alexandria, Eusebius of Caesarea (c. 260–c.340) divided the Gospels into units and then ten tables (canons) according to parallel and unique material.[20] In medieval manuscripts, these canons are usually surrounded by an arcaded frame.[21] Carl Nordenfalk claims Eusebius was inspired by the Church of the Holy Sepulcher in Jerusalem, the traditional site where Jesus was executed and raised from the dead.[22] This wedding between text and architecture continued into the Middle Ages with the great cathedrals, which, in turn, inspired Hugh of St. Victor (1096–1141) and others to see the soul of every Christian as a microcosm of the building.[23]

Along with seating a bishop, a cathedral is an *imago mundi*, a miniature cosmos to image God's fuller creation. Mircea Eliade (1907–1986) notes, "The faithful enter progressively into a world of values and meanings which, for some, becomes more 'real' and precious than the world of everyday experience."[24] The Gospels likewise open into superreality. The Lord Jesus Christ, architect of creation, is seated in our soul, and we may approach him through Scripture and prayer.

Sensory experience, which informs the soul, comes through the main entrance, *the West Door*, in the narthex, which is not a part of the church proper. The narthex is a public space, like the Court of the Nations in the temple where the moneychangers sat, and is where distraction happens. Just inside the church is the baptismal where human beings are reintroduced to the Trinitarian life of God. Past the narthex are three aisles. The left aisle leads to *the chapel of creation* at the transept (or cross beam). Here, we worship the Creator by meditating on heaven and earth. Ewert Cousins summarizes the medieval worldview: "God, in creating the universe, imprinted

20. There are around 1,165 units: 355 in Matthew, 235 in Mark, 343 in Luke, and 232 in John. There is some variation in the mss. See Scrivener, *Plain Introduction*, 52. For a short biography of Ammonius, see Jerome, *Vir. ill.* 55.

21. See Friedländer, "Eine Zeichnung des Villard de Honnecourt und ihr Vorbild," 349–52. Apparently, the earliest example is the Rabula Codex (AD 586).

22. Nordenfalk considered the tables of the Echmiadzin Gospels (fols. 1–5) as the closest to the archetype developed in Caesarea Palestine (*Die spätantiken Kanontafeln*).

23. This section was originally inspired by Carruthers, *Craft of Thought*.

24. Eliade, *History of Religious Ideas*, 3:99.

certain spiritual meanings into physical symbols, which could be discerned by a heightened spiritual sensibility nourished by Scripture and tradition."[25] All that is true in science assists. (Meditation on the Gospels in cathedral schools contributed to the first universities in Europe.) The right aisle takes us to the other side of the transept, *the chapel of the imago Dei*.[26] Scripture claims that human beings are created in God's image (Gen 1:26–27), but does not fully explain that mystery. We therefore share in God's mystery (1 John 3:1–2). Christian orthodoxy presents God as one in essence and three in person. Essence points to what God is; person, who. The Jewish scholar Abraham Heschel (1907–1972) gave a series of lectures at Stanford University entitled, *Who is Man?* intentionally departing from the "What" of the psalmist (Ps 8:4). In this regard, he is like the church fathers who maintain that God cannot be known in his essence, but can be related to as a person. He notes: "As a thing man is explicable; as a person he is both a mystery and a surprise. As a thing he is finite; as a person he is inexhaustible."[27] We also learn about God through other people, who are stamped with the *imago Dei*. We may not be persons in the exact way God is, but Scripture invites the analogy of personhood. The Western Christian tradition has understood the soul as a diverse unity of will, understanding, and memory, which Augustine treats as an analogy of the Triune God (*On The Trinity*).[28] Christians were the first to use the term "person" in this sense.[29] Human beings are also embodied, like the Son after the Incarnation, and interpersonal. It was "not good" for Adam to be alone. Eve arises from Adam's rib. The yin of Eve and yang of Adam become "one flesh." As Richard of St. Victor (c. 1120–1173) notes, from this union of love arises a third person, a child. But like everything related to God, no universally agreed upon, complete understanding of personhood exists.

It is good to spend time in these chapels, but eventually we must make our way down the long central aisle to the Holy Altar, where the Gospels are placed in a gold case behind a veil when not being read, facing east and the rising sun: "God is light" (1 John 1:5); "And the light in the darkness shines,

25. Bernard of Clairvaux, *Selected Works*, 10.

26. This heuristic (metaphor) goes back at least to Philo. Teresa of Ávila describes the soul as "like a castle made exclusively of diamond or some other very clear crystal. In this castle are a multitude of dwellings, just as in heaven there are many mansions" (*Interior Castle*, 36).

27. Heschel, *Who is Man?*, 28.

28. This schema dominated in the Christian tradition in the West until Aquinas, who allowed for only two spiritual faculties—intellect and will (Kavanaugh, *John of the Cross*, 35). However, we find the tripartite language in subsequent writers.

29. Zizioulas, *Being As Communion*, 27–49.

and the darkness did not overcome it" (John 1:4). The Father and Son are enthroned above the altar and indwell our souls through the Holy Spirit. Our Scripture, music, and liturgy echo their warm conversation.[30] There is the cross where our Lord Jesus Christ, the Messiah, died in our place that we might inhabit this space. There is the bread and wine.

We can unpack the person as cathedral more with Aristotle's four causes of being—formal, efficient, material, and final. (We do not intend scientific precision with this language, but appropriate it merely as a heuristic to approach a complex reality.)

Formal Cause: Mind of Christ

The formal cause is the pattern by which something is formed. Disciples are being formed into the image of the invisible God, Jesus Christ, who offers his body as temple. We are beginning to understand the role of mirror neurons, which fire after we see another human being do something with intention.[31] If we are attracted to the action, we imitate. This is fundamental to our shared humanity, and it finds its perfection in the imitation of Christ (*imitatio Christi*): "For to this you were called. For Christ also suffered on behalf of you, leaving behind for you an example, so that you might follow after his footsteps" (1 Pet 2:21). Ludolph notes, "Christ's whole earthly life, which he chose to assume for us, offers instruction for our behavior."[32] This imitation is not forced or external, but results from sharing a common mind or intellect. The same Spirit who led Christ leads us. Since the Spirit's work is internal, Christians have no distinct culture, dress, or ethnicity. As everyone is the same—sharing a common humanity—yet different in Adam, so it is in Christ. Thomas Merton (1915–1968) notes, "Each one of us has a peculiar vocation to reproduce the likeness of Christ in a mode that is not quite the same as anybody else's, since no two of us are quite alike."[33] We are all saved by entering Christ's journey back to God, but everyone's path and pace are unique.[34]

30. Duby, *Age of the Cathedrals*, 73. Catherine De Hueck notes, "all music is an echo of God's music" (*Essential Writings*, 53).

31. Kurt Thompson notes, "Virtually all intentional human behavior is ultimately mimicked" (*Anatomy of the Soul*, 42).

32. Ludolph of Saxony, *Life of Christ*, 1:14.

33. Merton, *Life and Holiness*, 28.

34. Albert Peyriguère claims "every soul has 'its own' road known only to God and which God alone can reveal" (*Voice from the Desert*, 22).

Efficient Cause: Holy Spirit

The efficient cause refers to things apart from the thing being changed or moved, which interact as an agency of the change or move—like the builder of a cathedral. The Holy Spirit takes this role through our intellect, which organizes our worldview and expands our awareness: "When you think about the really big questions in life—be they religious, scientific, or psychological—your brain is going to grow."[35]

Material Cause: Memory

The material cause refers to what composes the thing being changed or moved. Memory or recollection (*mnēmē*, μνήμη) is like the stones of a cathedral. As children, we discover a sense of self in family stories and culture. Our reactions to these stories are held by synapses that signal neurons to send the same message repeatedly, leading to mental states and habits: "neurons that fire together wire together."[36] These stones (memories) of our old personhood in Adam can be repurposed, but the structure must be reformed in Christ. Through the mind of Christ, the soul is gradually rebuilt by remembering our new story. We see our past as a journey toward and now with Christ. Imagination, the formation of new memories, "gives us the opportunity to envision new possibilities," as we focus on Christ.[37]

Final Cause: Will

The final cause answers the question why a thing is changing or moving. Will is like the worship of the cathedral. Jesus lives for the will of the Father, as the Lord's Prayer teaches us, and models this perfection in Gethsemane by submitting to the Passion: "not my will, but your will be done." A fully formed soul enjoys a union of wills with the Triune God, which is to love God and one another. Augustine treats the will as the most fundamental and mysterious element of the soul, intersecting with the tension between divine sovereignty and human responsibility (free will). Love requires an I and a You. Our formation depends on a distinction between us and God

35. Newberg and Waldman, *How God Changes Your Brain*, 16.

36. Burtis Breese notes that images are "never exact duplicates of former experiences. . . . We always know the difference between the image and the actual sensory experience, except in the case of hallucinations" (*Psychology*, 262). The quoted axiom is attributed to Donald Hebb.

37. Van Der Kolk, *Body Keeps the Score*, 17.

and the rest of creation. Eve did not lose her individuality or will when she became one with Adam (a common evil in spousal abuse), but became a member of a family whose well-being ultimately depended on conformity to God's Truth, Goodness, and Beauty.

Sacred Movement

The Gospels relate a journey from God to God. The Son "comes" from the Father and returns to the Father, and we are invited to follow. "He became a sojourner and an alien so that he might lead us to his homeland," notes Ludolph, who offers this invitation: "Watch him with love and devotion, and enter into his travels with all the compassion in your heart."[38] *See* and *follow* speak to the inseparability of space and time in storytelling.[39] Unlike an image, which can be observed, at least superficially, in a moment, a text demands time from a reader. A movable icon, we follow Jesus through the stages of his birth, adolescence, public ministry, death, resurrection, and ascension, the completion of the journey, although this sequence is only so from the perspective of "historical time." Although the Passion follows Christ's baptism, both events invite the reader into the same reality—entrance into the "sacred" or "liturgical time" and space before God in Paradise.[40] This journey to God traditionally has been presented in three stages: purgative, illuminative, and unitive.[41] The Lutheran pastor Johann Arndt (1555–1621) notes:

> Just as our natural life has its stages, its childhood, manhood, and old age, so too our spiritual and Christian life is set up. It has its beginning in repentance, through which a person does penance every day. A greater enlightenment follows after this like middle age, through the contemplation of divine things, through prayer, through the cross, through which all God's gifts are increased. Finally comes the perfection of old age, being established in complete union through love, which St. Paul calls

38. Ludolph of Saxony, *Life of Christ*, 1:420.

39. Mikhail Bakhtin refers to this as "chronotope" (space-time). See his "Forms of Time and of the Chronotope," 15–24.

40. Sebastian Brock, a respected authority on the Syrian Christian tradition, notes: "historical time is concerned only with the sequence of time, whereas sacred, or liturgical, time is concerned with the quality of events; this means that events separate in historical time can come together in sacred time" (*Spirituality in the Syriac Tradition*, 61).

41. The concept goes back to Origen, and the language was codified by Bernard of Clairvaux.

"the perfect age of Christ" and being "a perfect man in Christ" (Eph 4:13).[42]

However, the Gospels place baptism at the beginning, which signifies our union with Christ, not the end of the journey. A careful reading of the Gospels and Paul's letters, as John Calvin rightly emphasized in his *Institutes*, shows that union is a gift and empowerment that makes the rest of the journey possible (see Gal 2:20; Rom 6). Arndt's "complete union," then, may be described as *the subjective appropriation of an objective reality.* To illustrate this process I offer a very mild allegory of three mountain scenes in Matthew with a traditional courtship progression in North American culture.

Purgative Mountain (Matt 5:1)

John the Baptist calls the reader to repent because of the nearness of God's Kingdom (Matt 3:2) and to produce fruit worthy of that repentance (v. 8). He looks forward to a baptism "of the Holy Spirit," a purification from sin. Jesus fulfills this divine plan of salvation by undergoing John's baptism and is led by the Spirit to be tempted in the wilderness, as Israel was after their redemption from Egypt (4:1–10). He is able to overcome by digesting "every word through the mouth of God" (v. 4). After defeating the devil, Jesus echoes John's call to repentance (v. 17). Calling his first disciples and attracting a crowd, Jesus went up "the mountain" like Moses, "opened his mouth," and offered what came to be called the Sermon on the Mount. These words discipled new believers in the early church, leading them to purify their heart by surrendering to the Father's will in prayer.

Purgation removes all that is incompatible with God. But the goal is not negative, merely an emptying, the relinquishment of genuine needs—as if Jesus were merely crucified and not enthroned in Paradise. The purgative stage of the journey awakens love for God.[43] We may detach from idols to worship and love the one true, living God. Similarly, when a man and woman become engaged, it is necessary for both to leave potentially rival relationships to commit to one another.

42. Translated by McGinn, *Essential Writings of Christian Mysticism*, 277.

43. This is the *nada* (nothing) path of John of the Cross (Kavanaugh, *John of the Cross*, 65–69).

Illuminative Mountain (Matt 17:1)

In the Sermon on the Mount, Jesus promises that the pure in heart will see God (Matt 5:8). This was partially fulfilled for Peter, James, and John at the mount of Transfiguration when they were allowed to see the two great mysteries of our faith, the metamorphosis of the Son's Incarnated body at the resurrection and what came to be called the hypostatic union, the union of Christ's humanity and deity in one person (*hypostasis,* ὑπόστασις). Moses similarly ascended a mountain with witnesses and God speaks after six days (Exod 24:16).

By meditating on these mysteries we begin to understand the significance of our union with Christ. This knowledge gradually replaces what was eliminated in the purgative stage. Although our bodies age, become diseased, and die, as members of Christ's body we anticipate their own metamorphoses at the resurrection. We do not become God, but our union with Christ's humanity offers the benefits of his deity, like eternal life and the fruit of the Spirit. Another goal of the illuminative stage is for all sensible reality to become pure sacrament—to follow the command, "study the birds," and then, by grace, to begin to see what Jesus sees. When a man and woman are attracted to one another, it is natural for them to desire more intimate knowledge. Indeed, we cannot love who we do not know. Sometimes, love fades as two people get to know each other. However, to taste God's love naturally leads to a desire to know God more correctly and to love more fully.[44]

Unitive Mountain (Matt 28:16)

Matthew ends with final instructions from Jesus on a mountain for the disciples to reproduce themselves, bringing people into the mystery of the Triune life of God through baptism and teaching them to observe everything they learned, including the lessons of the previous two mountains (see Matt 17:9). This is all done with God, Immanuel: "I am with you always, to the end of the age" (Matt 28:20; see 1:23).[45] It is natural for a wife and husband to unify. The wife does not become the husband, and the husband remains distinct from the wife, but they are, according to Scripture, "one flesh." This

44. This is the core teaching of Catherine of Siena (*Dialogue,* xiv–xv).

45. The motif of mature Christian as missionary is developed by Gregory the Great, particularly his biography of Benedict, and Richard of St. Victor's *Four Degrees of Violent Love.*

mysterious, ontological reality naturally leads to a relational reality through knowledge and fidelity.

This threefold schema risks being too linear. For some, experientially, the accent may be on one of these elements; for others, they may be evenly distributed through a season. But there is a beginning to the journey—the transition from being outside Christ to "in Christ." There is something of a middle, a liminal space, and an end of sorts, although it is fair to ask with Gregory of Nyssa (c 335–c. 394) if union with Christ is ever exhaustibly grasped by a finite human being. The end of the Bible, Revelation's retelling of the creation story, is better understood as a new beginning.

Guides

The cathedrals were not built by elites, but through the collective labor of peasants, who nevertheless had a sense of participating in something larger than themselves: "We who cut mere stones must always be envisioning cathedrals" was a medieval quarry worker's creed.[46] Sons often picked up where their fathers left, and their sons did the same. Patrons shared their wealth. The evangelists similarly laid the foundation for a comprehensive worldview that builds through the reflection of each generation. I have learned from nearly every generation since the Ascension. Some of my teachers are

> Ignatius of Antioch (c. 35–c. 110), Papias of Hierapolis (c. 60–130), Polycarp (c. 70–c. 160), Clement of Rome (fl. c. 96), Justin Martyr (c. 110–165), Tatian (c. 120–after 174), Clement of Alexandria (c. 150–c. 215), Tertullian (155–222), Origen (c. 185–c. 254/5), Irenaeus of Lyon (d. c. 195), Cyprian of Carthage (c. 200–258), Antony of Egypt (c. 251–356), Eusebius of Caesarea (c. 260–c.340), Macrina the Elder (before 270–c. 340), Pachomius (c. 287–346), Athanasius (c. 295–d. 373), Ephrem the Syrian (c. 306–373), Epiphanius (c. 310/320–403), Cyril of Jerusalem (c. 310–386), Martin of Tours (316–397), Macrina the Younger (c. 327–379), Basil of Caesarea (c. 330–379), Gregory of Nazianzus (c. 330–389/390), Monica (c. 331–387), Gregory of Nyssa (c 335–c. 394), Ambrose (c. 340–397), Evagrius of Pontus (346–399), Jerome (c. 347–420), John Chrysostom (c. 349–407), Theodore of Mopsuestia (c. 350–428), Augustine (354–430), John Cassian (c. 365–c. 435), Vincent of Lérins (d. c. 445), Patrick (c. 387/90–c. 460/1), Prosper of Aquitaine (c.

46. Duby, *Age of the Cathedrals*, 93. The quotation is from Hunt and Thomas, *Pragmatic Programmer*, xx.

390–455), Simeon Stylites (c. 390–459), Theodoret of Cyrus (c. 393–c. 457), Leo the Great (c. 400–461), Benedict of Nursia (c. 480–c. 547), Gregory the Great (c. 540–604), John Climacus (579–649), Maximus the Confessor (c. 580–662), Eligius (588–650), Cuthbert (c. 634–687), Willibrord (c. 658–739), Bede (c. 672–735), John of Damascus (c. 676–749), Theodore the Studite (759–826), Rabanus Maurus (c. 780–856), Johannes Scotus Eriugena (c. 815–c. 877), Symeon the New Theologian (949–1032), Anselm (1033–1109), Peter Abelard (1079–1142), William of Saint-Thierry (c. 1075–1148), Bernard of Clairvaux (1090–1153), Hugh of St. Victor (1096–1141), Hildegard of Bingen (1098–1179), Andrew of St. Victor (c. 1110–1175), Richard of St. Victor (c. 1120–1173), Guigo the Carthusian (d. 1188), Joachim of Fiore (c. 1135–1202), Zachary of Besançon (d. c. 1155), Dominic (1170–1221), Mary of Oignies (1177–1213), Francis of Assisi (1181–1226), Bonaventure (1221–1274), Thomas Aquinas (1224–1274), Meister Eckhart (c. 1260–c. 1328), Duns Scotus (1265–1308), William of Ockham (c. 1288–c. 1348), Ludolph of Saxony (c. 1295–1378), Gregory of Palamas (1296–1359), Richard Rolle (c. 1300–1341), Johannes Tauler (c. 1300–1361), John Wycliffe (mid 1320s–1384), Julian of Norwich (1342–c. 1423), Catherine of Siena (1347–1380), Margery Kemp (1373–1440), Thomas À Kempis (c. 1380–1471), Nicholas of Cusa (1401–1464), Catherine of Genoa (1447–1510), Desiderius Erasmus (1466–1536), Matthias Grünewald (c. 1470–1528), Michelangelo (1475–1564), Raphael (1483–1520), Martin Luther (1483–1546), Huldrych Zwingli (1484–1531), Thomas Cranmer (1489–1556), Ignatius of Loyola (1491–1556), William Tyndale (c. 1494–1536), Philipp Melanchthon (1497–1560), Francis Xavier (1506–1552), John Calvin (1509–1564), Teresa of Ávila (1515–1582), Theodore Beza (1519–1605), John of the Cross (1542–1591), Galileo Galilei (1546–1642), Matteo Ricci (1552–1610), Johann Arndt (1555–1621), Francis Bacon (1561–1626), François de Sales (1567–1622), Johannes Kepler (1571–1630), Jacob Boehme (1575–1624), John Cotton (1585–1652), René Descartes (1596–1650), Roger Williams (1603–1683), Rembrandt (1606–1669), John Milton (1608–1674), Brother Lawrence (1611–1691), Henry Moore (1614–1687), Blaise Pascal (1623–1662), George Fox (1624–1691), John Bunyan (1628–1688), Philipp Jakob Spener (1635–1705), Isaac Newton (1642–1727), Gottfried Wilhelm von Leibniz (1646–1716), Madame Guyon (1648–1717), François Fénelon (1651–1715), Jean Pierre de Caussade (1675–1751), George Berkeley (1685–1753), Johann Sebastian Bach

(1685–1750), William Law (1686–1761), Jonathon Edwards (1703–1758), John Wesley (1703–1791), George Whitefield (1714–1770), Jeremy Bentham (1748–1832), William Godwin (1756–1836), Seraphim of Sarov (1759–1833), William Carrey (1761–1834), Georg Wilhelm Friedrich Hegel (1770–1831), William Wordsworth (1770–1850), Samuel Taylor Coleridge (1772–1834), Sojourner Truth (c. 1797–1883), Ferdinand Victor Eugène Delacroix (1798–1863), Alfred, Lord Tennyson (1809–1892), Johann C. K. von Hoffmann (1810–1877), Søren Kierkegaard (1813–1855), Theophan the Recluse (1815–1894), Fyodor Dostoyevsky (1821–1881), Louis Pasteur (1822–1895), Ellen G. White (1827–1915), Leo Tolstoy (1828–1910), Martin Kähler (1835–1912), William James (1842–1910), Gerard Manley Hopkins (1844–1889), Vincent van Gogh (1853–1890), Ebina Danjo (1856–1937), Charles de Foucauld (1858–1916), Rudolph Otto (1869–1937), Georges Rouault (1871–1958), Thérèse of Lisieux (1873–1897), Burnett Hillman Streeter (1874–1937), Evelyn Underhill (1875–1941), Pope John XXIII (1881–1963), Albert Schweitzer (1875–1965), Pierre Teilhard de Chardin (1881–1955), Albert Peyriguère (1883–1959), C. H. Dodd (1884–1973), Karl Barth (1886–1968), T. S. Eliot (1888–1965), Ludwig Wittgenstein (1889–1959), Reinhold Niebuhr (1892–1971), Catherine De Hueck Doherty (1896–1985), Henri de Lubac (1896–1991), A. W. Tozer (1897–1963), C. S. Lewis (1898–1963), Oscar Cullmann (1902–1999), Karl Rahner (1904–1984), Hans Urs von Balthasar (1905–1988), Dietrich Bonhoeffer (1906–1945), Bede Griffiths (1906–1993), Mircea Eliade (1907–1986), Simone Weil (1909–1943), Mother Teresa (1910–1997), George Eldon Ladd (1911–1982), W. D. Davies (1911–2001), Louis Bouyer (1913–2004), Thomas Merton (1915–1968), Brevard Childs (1923–2007), Thomas Keating (1923–2018), Jaroslav Pelikan (1923–2006), Birger Gerhardsson (1926–2013), Masao Takenaka (1925–2006), Pope Benedict XVI (b. 1927), Raymond Brown (1928–1998), Martin Luther King, Jr. (1929–1968), Thomas Oden (1931–2015), Morna Hooker (b. 1931), Basil Pennington (1931–2005), John Mbiti (1931–2019), Henri Nouwen (1932–1996), Benedicta Ward (b. 1933), Benedict Groeschel (1933–2014), Dallas Willard (1935–2013), Pope Francis (b. 1936), Donald Hagner (b. 1936), Anscar Chupungco (1939–2013), N. T. Wright (b. 1948), Wayne Grudem (b. 1948), Darryl DelHousaye (b. 1949).

There is a danger in reading the Gospels from only one point of view. Each individual is partially blinded by bias; every generation, its own idolatry. But when Christians from different times and places offer similar interpretations, idiosyncratic readings can be isolated. Indeed, without any clear indication of literary dependence, when two or more very different people see the same thing, it may reveal a deeper, spiritual unity. I do not necessarily agree with everything claimed by these guides—to do so would strip my understanding of coherence and, in a way, dishonor them by not recognizing the tensions and contradictions of our tradition—but each has uniquely pointed me to Christ.

Preparation

When I visited Jerusalem as a child, I noticed that the steps to the temple ("stairs of ascent"), one of the few remaining elements of the ancient complex, were uneven. Our guide shared they were intended to slow worshipers from mindlessly rushing into God's presence. Ludolph writes:

> The sinner who already faithfully believes in Christ and has been reconciled to him through penance should strive to stay close to this physician by devoutly meditating on his most holy life as much as possible. But take care to do this with deliberation and not hurry through the reading of Christ's life; rather, take a small selection in turn each day. With such devout reflections you can celebrate a daily Sabbath for Christ.[47]

Teresa of Ávila notes, "While there's not a thing we can do to direct the work of the Beloved, there is much we can do to open ourselves to receiving his favors" through prayer and meditation.[48] With all of Scripture, the Gospels require a human response to God's initiative in salvation.

Breathing

Following Jesus is an embodied process. It is very difficult to read for comprehension when the body is stressed.[49] A symptom is shallow, quick breaths. But attending to our breathing stimulates the parasympathetic nervous system, allowing a "rest-and-digest" response to our environment and space for the Spirit. Jesus, it can be inferred, controlled his breathing, a manifestation of his spirit or life principle, until surrendering it to the

47. Ludolph of Saxony, *Life of Christ*, 4.

48. Teresa of Ávila, *Interior Castle*, 126.

49. Cohen et al., *Behavior, Health, and Environmental Stress*, 215.

Father on the cross (Mark 15:37; Luke 23:46).[50] Every moment of discipleship is accompanied by breathing in and breathing out; we cannot breathe apart from Christ (Col 1:15–20), and, unless Christ returns in our lifetime, someday we will exhale in him a final breath before the Father. Breathing is analogous to the ministry of the Spirit, who gives life, so that the gentle activity may become sacramental because it conveys life in God's common grace and mirrors a spiritual quickening. The Hebrew and Greek words translated "spirit" may also be rendered "breath." It may be helpful, then, to breath slowly and deeply with the awareness that we are breathing with Jesus and that each breath is a gift. Imagine his first breath in Bethlehem and last on the cross. Let the exhalation be a little longer than the inhalation. We may even wed Jesus's prayer word, "Abba" (dad), to the exhalation.[51]

Literacy

Jesus learned to read, although educating the masses was not a priority outside of Judaism. Jews were the only culture to gather weekly to hear a word from their God, but there was also encouragement to read and study Scripture. According to rabbinic tradition, the Hasmonean Queen, Salome Alexandra (141–67 BC), encouraged primary education, which was implemented by her brother, Simeon ben Shetach (c. 120–40 BC), a Pharisee.[52] Josephus (37–after 100) claims, "Above all we pride ourselves on the education of our children."[53] A rabbinic commentary tells a story about Rabbi Akiva (c. AD 50–135) going to an "elementary teacher" and saying, "Master, teach me Torah." On a tablet, the teacher wrote down *aleph, bet*, the first two letters of the Hebrew alphabet, and so forth until he could read Leviticus and then the rest of Torah.[54] We see the impetus for reading Scripture in Ezra (fl. 480–440 BC), the paradigmatic scribe "skilled in the Law of Moses that the Lord the God of Israel had given. . . . For Ezra had set his heart to study the law of the Lord, and to do it, and to teach the statutes and rules in Israel" (Ezra 7:6, 10 ESV). A pattern in the Pharisaic agenda was to apply anything transferable from specific roles—priest, prophet, king, scribe—to

50. See the subtle rewording of Christ's death in Matthew (27:50) and John (19:30).

51. For more discussion, see Laird, *Into the Silent Land*, 36–45.

52. Specifics about the extent and nature of primary education in first-century Judaism are debated. See Hezser, *Jewish Literacy*.

53. Josephus, *Ag. Ap.* 1.60 (Thackeray, LCL). He goes on to claim that every Jew knew the Law (2.18, 178).

54. Goldin, *Fathers According to Rabbi Nathan*, 41 (A6).

the people.[55] Luke's portrait of Jesus fits this background. When his parents discover "the boy Jesus" in the temple, he is "sitting in the middle of the teachers and listening to them and questioning them. Now all who were listening to him were amazed by his understanding and his answers" (Luke 2:46–47); and then, at the beginning of his public ministry we read: "And he came to Nazareth where he had been brought up, and he went according to his custom on the day of the Sabbaths into the synagogue. And he stood up to read" (Luke 4:16).

This emphasis continues in the Christian tradition. Pachomius (c. 287–346), the father of communal monasticism, required literacy from novitiates:

> They shall give him twenty psalms or two of the Apostle's epistles, or some other part of the Scripture. And if he is illiterate, he shall go at the first, third, and sixth hours to someone who can teach and has been appointed for him. He shall stand before him and learn very studiously and with all gratitude. Then the fundamentals of the syllable, the verbs, and nouns shall be written for him, and even if he does not want to, he shall be compelled to read.[56]

Thomas Cranmer (1489–1556), the archbishop of Canterbury, prefaced the Great Bible with this directive: "When ye be at home in your houses, ye apply yourselves from time to time to the reading of holy Scriptures."[57] Illiteracy in England begins to drop dramatically after 1500. In 1800, only a minority of humanity could read; today, a majority do.

Reading, the decoding of a series of abstract symbols into complex ideas, is wondrous.[58] There is no primary location in the brain for the activity, as there is for seeing, listening, and touching; the act requires interconnectivity. Reading about something, in fact, stimulates the same neurological regions of the brain as if we had directly experienced it, but also allows distance for processing.

Communities create and agree upon codes that can be decoded by readers, so that writers can communicate to later generations. This is especially important for the marginalized and otherwise forgotten voices. Writing, if preserved, is more stable than oral tradition, allowing for retrieval of lost wisdom, renewal, and critique. Mahatma Gandhi (1869–1948) read the Sermon on the Mount and remarked, "If it weren't for Christians, I'd be a

55. See DelHousaye, "Jewish Groups at the Time of Jesus," 100–106.

56. Cited in Lee, *Pagans and Christians*, 205 (rule 49).

57. Cranmer, *Writings of the Rev. Dr. Thomas Cranmer*, 75.

58. For this paragraph, I am indebted to Wolf, *Proust and the Squid*.

Christian."[59] The church preserves the Gospels, in part, so that our children might know Jesus despite our failure.

Every human culture has language, but reading is not universal; the skill requires teachers and has different levels of mastery. After Rabbi Akiva learned to read Hebrew and read all the Scriptures, he went before Rabbi Eliezer and Rabbi Joshua and said, "My masters . . . reveal the sense of Mishnah to me."[60] *Mishnah* (מִשְׁנָה) describes "study by repetition," which transforms reading into a meditative loop or habituation. The Psalter opens with a blessing over anyone whose "joy is in the *torah* (instruction, law) of the Lord, and on his *torah* he will meditate day and night" (Ps 1:2). Rabbi Hananiah ben Tradion, a martyr, offers this gloss:

> If two sit together and no words of *torah* (are spoken) between them, they are a session *of scoffers,* of whom it is written: *Nor sit in the seat of scoffers.* [Ps 1:1] But if two *sit* together and the words of *torah* (are spoken) between them, the *Shekinah* (divine presence) rests between them.[61]

When this happens, Scripture becomes an essential ingredient in every human experience. Some dismiss the rabbis as legalistic and miss the genius of their study: by repeating and contextualizing the Law of Moses, the written Torah or Pentateuch, they were able to relate every aspect of human existence to God. Scripture and their tradition, the Oral Torah, came together in the Mishnah (c. AD 200), the first major work of rabbinic Judaism. It is their rewritten Bible, and we shall attend to these readings often.

Like breathing, reading is most beneficial, presuming the text is worthy and the occasion is more than mere communication, when it is done slowly and deeply. Rabbi Akiva would ask, "This 'aleph [the first letter of the Hebrew alphabet] . . . why was it written? That *bet* [the second], why was it written."[62] Jesus says, "until the heaven and the earth pass away, not one *yod* or one *vav* will ever pass away from the Law, until all things come into being" (Matt 5:18). A *yod* and *vav* are not only the smallest Hebrew letters but also stand-ins for vowels or breaths.[63] Citing the verse, Bernard says, "We are commanded to gather up the tiniest fragments lest they be lost."[64] The skill attends not just to the tacit meaning of words, but also to what the

59. Cited in Stedman, *Surprising Reasons to Believe in God*, 74.

60. Goldin, *Fathers According to Rabbi Nathan*, 41 (A6).

61. M. Avot 3:2 (*Ethics of the Fathers*, 40 [Goldin]).

62. Goldin, *Fathers According to Rabbi Nathan*, 41 (A6).

63. Nodet, "Pas un *yod,* pas un *waw,*" 614–16.

64. IV. 6 (1:4).

author is doing with language—connoting, alluding, creating, subverting, extending. We should, with Jesus, presume every word, even letter, matters. There is also the often ambiguous space between words (syntax), inviting reflection: What, for example, is the conjoined meaning of the preposition and object of preposition "in Christ"?

Lectio Divina

Sexual intimacy can be beautiful and fruitful or ugly and exploitive, depending on the context. So it is with the sacredness of reading. People forget how potentially intimate reading can be, unless we harden our heart. Francis of Assisi (c. 1181–1226) knew this, so that whenever he found a piece of writing on the floor, regardless of the content, he would reverently pick it up "and put it in a sacred or discrete place."[65] Scripture is a place to meet God.

Lectio Divina ("divine reading") is a Benedictine practice of reading Scripture that is couched in a set of habituations called *askēsis* (ἄσκησις, "discipline"). Through *hēsuchia*, *kavanah*, and *horarium*, we allow the Spirit to form us. Like prayer, there is an active and passive element to this expression of faith. All we do is approach Scripture conscious of the ultimate author until, as John Cassian (c. 365–c. 435) notes, "ascending" thoughts predominate and the mind is fixed on God alone.[66] Reading Scripture—digging for every treasure and listening for its ultimate author, with the grace of the Spirit—leads to what he calls the "prayer of fire," the contemplation of God himself, the fire of love.[67] At the beginning, the Jesuits encourage offering a short prayer of invocation—to invite the Holy Spirit to guide the *Lectio Divina*.

Hēsuchia ("quietness")

The psalmist exhorts: "Be still and know that I am God." (Ps 45:10).[68] The verb translated "be still" (*scholazō*, σχολάζω) describes a "release from routine or pressing obligation" and to "stand empty."[69] Ephrem the Syrian (c.

65. The anecdote is from the twenty-ninth chapter of *The Life of Saint Francis* by Thomas of Celano. The translation is from Armstrong et al., *Francis of Assisi*, 1:251.

66. Wakefield, *Groundwork*, 37.

67. Drobner, *Fathers of the Church*, 376.

68. The verse is Ps 45:10 in Alfred Rahlf's Greek text and 46:10 in the Hebrew Masoretic Text, which is followed by most modern translations.

69. BDAG, 982. The former meaning is attributed to Philo. For the latter, see Matt 12:44.

306–373) speaks of a "resting-place," so that knowledge can be assimilated: "Blessed is the one," he hymns, "who has perceived that heaven above is quiet, And the earth below is troubled, and has quieted himself amidst the waves."[70] We enter the space between the opening verses of Genesis—watching God's Spirit softly hovering over the still, dark sea. There was silence before God spoke everything into existence. Ignatius of Antioch (c. 35–c. 110) reminds us that Christ came from this silence, spoke, and returned: "The one who truly possesses the word of Jesus," the yang, may hear his "silence" (*hēsuchia*, ἡσυχία), the yin, that "he may be perfect, that he may act through what he says and be known through his silence" (*Eph.* 15:2).[71] Silence and speaking are not contraries, but are complementary sides of God' disclosure. We have to be quiet before we can hear. Quietness is a "calm through the whole" person that Benedicta Ward (b. 1933) describes as "a still pool of water, capable of reflecting the sun."[72] To the newly baptized—those who are participating in the mysterious death and life of Christ—Clement of Alexandria (c. 150–c. 215) exhorts:

> Cultivate quietness in words and quietness in actions—in speaking and walking. But avoid the inclination toward outbursts. For then the mind will remain grounded, and will not, from excessive agitation, become weak and narrow in understanding and darkened (in) seeing. Nor will it be vanquished by gluttony or vanquished by boiling rage or vanquished by the other passions, lying as easy prey for them. For the mind, which is seated on high before a quiet throne, may control the passions (by) focusing on God.[73]

In 1975, Herbert Benson, a well-known cardiologist and professor at Harvard Medical School, popularized the Relaxation Response, an "inducible, physiologic state of quietude." He tells the ironic story of discovering this effect of meditation in the same room where Walter Cannon (1871–1945) discovered the "flight-or-flight" response to stress.[74] *Hēsuchia* occurs when our sympathetic and parasympathetic nervous systems are balanced.[75] Sadly, the increasingly frenetic pace and distractions of modern life are making quietness more elusive. But Jesus promises:

70. Ephrem the Syrian, *Hymns on Faith*, 69 (hymn 3).
71. For the Greek text of my translations, see Holmes, *Apostolic Fathers*, 194, 196.
72. Ward, *Sayings of the Desert Fathers*, xxvi.
73. For the Greek text of my translation, see Clement, *Clement of Alexandria*, 370.
74. Benson and Klipper, *Relaxation Response*, 8–9.
75. Thompson, *Anatomy of the Soul*, 193.

"Peace I leave to you, my peace I give to you. Not as the world gives I give to you" (John 14:27).

Kavanah ("mindfulness")

In the Jewish tradition, prayer was more than speaking to God.[76] It included the preparation of the heart through *kavanah* (כַּוָּנָה, "focusing"), a reverential, loving attention to God's presence. The God of Israel was transcendent yet personal and therefore could be known through encounter. The Mishnah exhorts:

> One may stand to pray [the *Amidah*] only in a solemn frame of mind. The early pious ones used to tarry one hour [before they would] pray, so that they could direct their hearts to the Omnipresent. [While one is praying] even if the king greets him, he may not respond. And even if a serpent is entwined around his heel, he may not interrupt. (*Ber.* 5.1)[77]

Physiologically, it takes time to quiet oneself before God. The "early pious ones," probably a reference to the Essenes, would stand facing the horizon to greet the sun in the morning before their labor (Philo, *Contempl. Life* 27–28; Josephus, *J.W.* 2.128–29).

We find this antecedent to speaking in the Christian tradition. Augustine (354–430) counsels, "When you pray to God in psalms and songs, the words spoken by your lips should also be alive in your hearts."[78] Francis de Sales (1567–1622) writes, "when you make ready to pray, you must say with your whole heart, 'God is indeed here.'"[79] Jesus commands, "Watch and pray"—focus and then speak (Matt 26:41).

Benson observes, "When the mind is focused, whether through meditation or other repetitive mental activities, the body responds with a dramatic decrease in heart rate, breathing rate, blood pressure (if elevated to begin with), and metabolic rate—the exact opposite effects of the fight-or-flight response."[80] Jon Kabat-Zinn, a professor of medicine at the University of Massachusetts, defines mindfulness as an awareness that emerges

76. DelHousaye, "Praying with *Kavanah*," 87–100.

77. The translation is by Tzvee Zahavy and Alan J. Avery-Peck in Neusner, *Mishnah*, 8.

78. Augustine, *Rule*, 13.

79. Francis de Sales, *Introduction to the Devout Life*, 50.

80. *Relaxation Response*, 9.

through careful, nonjudgmental attention in the present moment.[81] It begins with an intention, a purposeful state of mind. In the Christian tradition, our intention is simple: to be with God.

Daniel Siegal, professor of psychiatry at the UCLA School of Medicine, describes three dimensions of attention: orienting, alerting, and executive.[82] Orienting is selecting an object—in our case, a passage from the Gospels—on which to focus. *Lectio Divina* works best with relatively short units—a verse or at most a paragraph. Alerting is sustaining our focus on this text, which is helped by reading aloud and, if short, repeating. The mind is prone to wander. When this happens, the executive dimension allows us to refocus on the passage, which is called attunement.

Horarium ("division of hours")

Benedict (c. 480–c. 547), author of the famous *Rule*, expected his monks to spend a sizable portion of their day in *lectio Divina*.[83] They divided their time between "prayer and work" (*ora et labora*). Although encouraged to pray throughout the day, regular times were set to ensure God was not forgotten. Monks spent the first three hours of the day *vacare Deo* ("being free for God"). John Chryssavgis offers this explanation: "If in our prayers we long for His Presence and wait for Him with patience, confidence, humility, and trust, then He will come into the center of our lives and establish there His kingdom."[84]

Three hours every morning may not be realistic, depending on our life situation. We do what we can. John Chrysostom (c. 349–407) counsels:

> But what is the answer to these charges? "I am not," you will say, "one of the monks, but I have both a wife and children, and the care of a household." Why, this is what has ruined everything—your supposing that the reading of Scripture appertains to those only [monks], when you all need it more than

81. Blanton, *Contemplation and Counseling*, 2. The Buddhist tradition refers to this as *sati*, a "discriminating attention that should be cultivated all day long" (Harrison, *Foundations of Mindfulness*, 2). The author helpfully adds, "Buddhism is not meditation. Meditation is not Buddhism" (3). Bikkhu Bodhi describes this "careful attention" as *yoniso manasikāra* (*In the Buddha's Words*, 19).

82. Blanton, *Contemplation and Counseling*, 6.

83. Stewart, *Prayer and Community*, 36.

84. Chryssavgis, *In the Heart of the Desert*, xi.

> they do. For they that dwell in the world and each day receive wounds, these have most need of medicine.[85]

In another homily, he exhorts:

> What can it be, then, that I ask of you? Let each one of you, on some day of the week, even on the Sabbath itself, take in his hands the selection of the Gospels that is going to be read to you [at our next meeting]. Read it frequently as you sit at home in the time intervening, and often ponder with care the thoughts stored up in it and examine them well. Note what is clear and what is obscure, and which thoughts seem to be contradictory, though they really are not. And when you have finally sampled all of it, thus prepared come to the sermon.[86]

I have found it helpful to keep a specific time each day for *Lectio Divina*. It has been my first activity for decades, as long as the constraints of life permit.

Guigo the Carthusian

After making external and internal space for the Spirit to respond to our *lectio* ("reading"), this sacred time is traditionally extended into three other periods—*meditatio, oratio,* and *contemplatio*. Guigo the Carthusian (d. c. 1188) summarizes the process:

> Reading [*lectio*] is the careful study of the Scriptures, concentrating all one's powers on it. Meditation [*meditatio*] is the busy application of the mind to seek with the help of one's own reason for knowledge of hidden truth. Prayer [*oratio*] is the heart's devoted turning to God to drive away evil and obtain what is good. Contemplation [*contemplatio*] is when the mind is in some sort lifted up to God and held above itself, so that it tastes the joys of everlasting sweetness.[87]

Called "the angelic," Guigo saw reading, meditation, prayer, and contemplation as four rungs on a ladder to heaven. The reader moves through the literal, allegorical, moral, and anagogical senses of Scripture. The taste or experiential dimension is the fruit of the Spirit.

85. Second homily on Matthew (Prevost, 13 [lightly updated]).

86. Translation is from Chrysostom, *Commentary on Saint John*, 104 (eleventh homily).

87. Guigo the Carthusian, *Ladder of Monks*, 68.

Meditatio ("meditation")

Meditatio, according to Guigo's contemporary Richard of St. Victor (c. 1120–1173), is the examination of an object—in this case, moving from the signifier (the word) to the signified (referent) or surrendering to the horizon of our understanding (ambiguity). My tradition calls this "Bible study." We find a preponderance of word studies in the commentaries of the church fathers—many of which are inaccurate because of the limited understanding of the biblical languages. Nevertheless, these attempts witness to a noble desire of taking Scripture's language seriously. It is also striking how often the writer says something to the effect of Paul's admission to the Romans:

> O the depth of the wealth and wisdom and knowledge of God! How unsearchable are his judgments, and inscrutable are his ways! *For who has known the mind of the Lord, or who has been his counselor?* [Isa 40:13] Or *who first gave to him, (that) it might also be paid back to him?* [Job 41:11] For all things are from him and through him and to him. To him (be) the glory forever! Amen. (Rom 11:33–36)

Richard's predecessor, Hugh of St. Victor (1096–1141), claims, "The beginning of learning lies in reading, but its consummation lies in meditation."

Oratio ("prayer")

Oratio is speaking to God, the natural fruit of meditation: we voice our desire to obey what is learned or to understand better what is concealed or to ascribe what makes God the only suitable recipient of our worship (prayer is theology in the second person). When Thomas Aquinas faced a seemingly insurmountable theological conundrum, he would pray in the chapel at night and often wake up the next morning with a solution. However, most importantly, prayer completes Scripture's intended cycle of communication: the Bible began as God's Word to us, which, internalized, becomes our response to God.

Contemplatio ("contemplation")

For Richard, meditating on something becomes *contemplatio* in the wonder of it, "a penetrating and free gaze of a soul."[88] We do not look at the sun, as

88. Cited in Stewart, "Fourfold Sense of Scripture," 124.

Origen and Augustine note, but its light allows us to see everything else. As God's Word, Scripture reflects a light that illumines what Paul calls "the eyes of the heart" (Eph 1:18). We take this awareness into the rest of our day, seeing all creation through a biblical lens. Unlike *meditatio*, which actively focuses on all the details of the text, *contemplatio* is largely passive—simply opening ourselves to however God responds to our *oratio*. It brings our *Lectio Divina* into the rest of the day.

Quadriga

From *Lectio Divina*, medieval theologians codified a fourfold way of studying Scripture called the *Quadriga*, a "chariot drawn by four horses."[89] Cassian integrated Origen's exegesis with the devotion of the desert fathers in the *Conferences*. In one dialogue, Abba Nesteros describes four senses: "historical," "tropological," "allegorical," and "anagogical." He uses Paul's allegorical reading of Jerusalem in Galatians (4:25–26) as a point of departure. The city can be interpreted

> historically, as the city of the Jews; allegorically as the Church of Christ, anagogically [Lat. "leading up"] as the heavenly city of God "which is the mother of us all," tropologically, as the soul of man, which is frequently subject to praise or blame from the Lord under this title.[90]

The *glossa ordinaria* ("ordinary gloss" or "standard commentary"), a collection of patristic sayings that was copied alongside the Latin translation of Scripture (Vulgate) offers this definition:

> History, which speaks of things done; allegory, in which one thing is understood from another; tropology, that is, moral speech, which deals with the ordination of morals; anagogy . . . through which we are led to higher things to be drawn to the superior things.[91]

89. I want to acknowledge the direct and indirect influence of Henri de Lubac's *Exégèse medieval, les quatre sens de l'Ecriture*, which is now available in English translation (*Medieval Exegesis*). As Susan Wood notes, what remains after his exhaustive study is to "undertake the work of biblical exegesis" for today (*Spiritual Exegesis*, viii). See also van Liere, *Introduction to the Medieval Bible*, 110–39.

90. *Conferences* 14.8 (*NPNF2* 11:438).

91. Cited in Leithart, "Quadriga or Something Like It," 114. This version of the *glossa* was from the school headed by Anselm of Laon.

Augustine of Denmark (d. 1282) converted the *Quadriga* into what became a famous hexameter for easy memorization:

> The letter teaches facts, allegory what you are to believe, The moral meaning what you ought to do, anagogy what you should strive for.[92]

Bonaventure

Bonaventure (1221–1274) summarizes the *Quadriga* in *Retracing the Arts to Theology*:

> In its [Scripture's] literal sense, it is *one*, still, in its spiritual and mystical sense, it is *threefold*, for in all the books of Sacred Scripture, in addition to the *literal* meaning which the words clearly express, there is implied a threefold *spiritual* meaning: namely, the *allegorical*, by which we are taught to believe concerning the Divinity and humanity; the *moral* [tropological] by which we are taught how to live; and the *anagogical* by which we are taught how to keep close to God.[93]

In *The Soul's Journey Into God*, he relates the spiritual senses to Origen's three stages of the soul's journey (without attribution):

> By Scripture we are taught that we should be purged, illumined and perfected . . . according to its threefold spiritual meaning: the tropological, which purifies one for an upright life; the allegorical, which illumines one for clarity of understanding, and the anagogical, which perfects through spiritual ecstasies and sweet perceptions of wisdom.[94]

In context, he correlates the senses with the theological virtues: the tropological builds love—What to do; allegorical, faith—What to believe; anagogical, hope—What to expect. According to this schema, the *anagogical* marks the soul's perfection. There is nothing beyond this *sensus mysticus*: the reader receives light that "is reflected back to God whence it came."[95] Bonaventure relates Scripture to the light God created on the first day before the sun, moon, and stars, which emanates from Christ and illumines the

92. *Littera gesta docet, quid credas allegoria, Moralis quid agas, quo tendas anagogia.* Cited in Drobner, *Fathers of the Church*, 141.

93. Hyman and Walsh, *Philosophy*, 464.

94. Translation is by Cousins in Bonaventure, *Soul's Journey*, 91 (4.6).

95. Goppelt, *Typos*, 7.

spiritual senses of the soul. Purified and illumined, the soul can delight in *visio Dei* ("the vision of God"). In the preface of his *Breviloquium*, he refers to the Bible's end as "theology." Bonaventue models the *Quadriga* in commentaries on Luke and John.

Aquinas

Thomas Aquinas (1224–1274) is known for his great summas, but he also synthesized patristic readings of the Gospels as foundational to his theologial project in the *Catena Aurea* ("golden chain"). He adopted the *Quadriga*, but not without a critical reflection we also find in his near contemporary, the brilliant Moses Maimonides (1135–1204).[96] Gradually, people were beginning to recognize differences in worldview between themselves and the biblical writers. Aquinas cites Gregory the Great (c. 540–604) approvingly: "For with the same word it at once narrates a fact and sets for a mystery," and yet insists that "All other senses of Holy Scripture are based on the literal," the signified of the signifier.[97] For this, he appeals to semantics and context. The literal sense, though, acknowledges metaphor and anthropomorphism. When Scripture mentions God's arm, the literal meaning is not that God has a body part, but the power to act. Allegory is not a solid foundation for theology.

However, because God through the Holy Spirit is the ultimate author of every Scripture and the final compiler of the biblical canon, the literal meaning of words can also signify other things.[98] So, for example, when the New Testament presents Jesus as the Passover lamb, it is not rejecting the reality of the earlier, literal lambs that were sacrificed for the occasion. They, not the word "lamb," are signs or types of Christ, the antitype. This secures the unique value of the Old Testament and unifies the seeming disparity. God, whose mind grasps all things simultaneously, uniquely has the power to invest meaning into anything, and intentionally relates all things to Christ. Aquinas's anagogical approach follows the same logic: God can signify Jesus's resurrection as a type for his followers. The moral sense is *imitatio Christi*: "Whatever our Head has done is a type of what we ought to

96. *Guide for the Perplexed*, 65–66 (ch. XXVVI). Both intellectuals benefitted from Muslim reflection on Aristotle.

97. *Summa Theologiae* I.1.10, *ad* 1. See Goppelt, *Typos*, 7; van Liere, *Medieval Bible*, 127, 130–33.

98. *Quod auctor sacrae Scripturae est Deus* ("The author of Holy Scripture is God," *S.T. Art.* 10). This claim is made in the same context of his view of *sensus literalis* ("literal sense").

do." We follow Old Testament saints in the way they followed him, a criterion that echoes Augustine.

Reformation

Martin Luther (1483–1546) and John Calvin (1509–1564) rejected the *Quadriga*, but a growing chorus of Protestant voices invite its retrieval.[99] A careful reading of their exegesis shows that they, in fact, operated by the same impulses; it is probably scholastic abuses of the Quadriga, particularly defending dogma through allegory, that is more at issue. In any case, the historical critical method, initiated by the Dutch Enlightenment, is a dead end.[100] We cannot enter the mind of the human author, but the mind of Christ may enter us. By reducing the interpretation of Scripture to the "literal" sense, the Bible became like any other book.[101]

The *Quadriga* responds well to the postmodern turn in Western philosophy and culture, but without relinquishing a unified witness to the world.[102] Roland Barthes (1915–1980) opines:

> The Text is plural. Which is not simply to say that it has several meanings, but that it accomplishes the very plural of meaning: an irreducible (and not merely and acceptable) plural. The Text is not co-extensive of meanings but a passage, an overcrossing; thus it answers not to an interpretation, even a liberal one, but to an explosion, a dissemination.[103]

This claim is rooted in the analogy between the fecundity of God, a medieval assumption, and that of God's Word. Meister Eckhart (c. 1260–c. 1328) exclaims, "the holy Scriptures make me wonder, they are so full."[104] Like God, Scripture is both revelatory and inexhaustibly mysterious and should lead to obedience and worship.

99. Davis, *Meditation and Communion with God*; Leithart, "Quadriga or Something Like It," 110–25. It continues in the Orthodox and Roman Catholic traditions. See Pentiuc, *Old Testament in Eastern Orthodox Tradition*, 178.

100. See the helpful distinction van Liere, *Medieval Bible*, 110–11.

101. We see this universalizing in the hermeneutical theory of Friedrich Schleiermacher (1768–1834), who influenced liberal readings of Scripture in the late nineteenth century and for most of the twentieth.

102. DelHousaye, "Post-Structuralist Criticism," 257–73.

103. Cited in Gu, *Chinese Theories of Fiction*, 150.

104. Cited in Fox, *Breakthrough*, 25.

PaRDeS

The rabbis developed a similar approach to Scripture they called *PaRDeS* (פַּרְדֵּס), a reference to the Garden of Eden or Paradise.[105] The Hebrew word, which is spelled only with consonants, serves as an acronym: the "*P*" stands for *peshat* (פְּשָׁט), the plain sense of words; "*R*", *remez* (רֶמֶז), which means "hint," is the allegorical sense; "*d*", *derash* (דְּרַשׁ), "interpreting" or "searching," the homiletical sense;[106] "s", *sod* (סוֹד) or "secret," the innermost meaning of Scripture, the intent of the divine author. Gershom Scholem (1897–1982) suggests the rabbis borrowed from the *Quadriga*, although one might speak of mutual stimulation.[107] The exchange primarily occurred in and around Paris, the intellectual center of Europe at the time. Andrew of St. Victor (c. 1110–1175) consulted with Jewish authorities when interpreting the Old Testament.[108] Rashi (1040–1105), the great French rabbi whose commentary on the Talmud accompanies nearly all printed editions, like Hugh of St. Victor and Aquinas, prioritizes the literal sense.[109] A millennium after rabbinic Judaism and Christianity parted ways, there was a momentary reunion. We find these isolated senses in Philo, who sought a middle way between the literal and allegorical, and was appropriated by later Christian writers (*Migr.* 89–94). Both faiths turned to a unifying vision of biblical interpretation that would spark devotion to the God of Abraham, Isaac, and Jacob.

Peshat ("straight")

Peshat primarily attends to the meaning of words, the medium. In everyday conversation, people use words for communication. They are a vehicle for meaning. The reader (hearer) moves from the signifier to the signified.[110] If a woman hears "fish" (signifier), the soul (or, more specifically, mind) decodes the word and recalls whatever she had pulled out of a river on a fishing pole or some other association. This may or may not overlap with the signified of the author. If there is overlap, basic communication has been achieved.

105. On this approach, see Michael Fishbane's two studies: *Biblical Interpretation* and *The Garments of Torah*.

106. Before then, *derash* was viewed as an exegetical and theological method and *midrash*, a literary genre (Del Agua, "Die 'Erzählung des Evangeliums,'" 140–54).

107. "The Meaning of the Torah in Jewish Mysticism," in his *On the Kabbalah and its Symbolism*, trans. Ralph Manheim (New York: Schocken Books, 1965), 61–62.

108. See van Liere, *Medieval Bible*, 130–33.

109. Rashi's home and resting place, Troyes, is around 100 miles from Paris.

110. Not every signifier has a signified; there are "function words."

However, there cannot be perfect overlap because no two minds are the same, nor should there be: by definition, communication acknowledges the reality of difference. This philological (semantic) emphasis encouraged a return to the biblical languages—Hebrew (Aramaic) and Greek—a touchstone for the Renaissance (beginning around 1300).

Remez ("hint")

Remez attends to the message of the whole Bible.[111] Although written over millennia, with many hands, God is the ultimate author of Scripture. We find this way of reading in Origen who, according to Robert Daly, insisted "that all of the bible must be kept in mind when interpreting any particular passage."[112] Each unit is a microcosm of the whole. Of course, human authors stamp some of themselves and their communities onto texts, but that was not the goal of the biblical author. When Paul wrote letters, he was not inviting us into his mind ("way of thinking"), but God's.[113] Jeremiah and James, for example, may be approached as individual books, but they are also chapters in God's book, who speaks through the prophet and brother of Jesus. The Bible is God's communication to all generations, speaking to us through what has already been said because God does not change. Augustine writes, "the Old Testament is simply the New Testament covered with a veil, and the New is simply the Old, unveiled."[114] As Brevard Childs (1923–2007) notes, interpretation may go in both directions.[115] What David conveys in the Psalms helps us to understand the public ministry of Jesus Christ, while that same ministry illumines the ultimate intention behind the Spirit's inspiration of the king.[116] For this reason, cathedrals often juxtapose scenes from the Old and New Testaments.[117]

111. In the last two centuries, a remarkable amount of time and energy has gone into retrieving the religious and social backgrounds of biblical authors. This scholarship has deepened our understanding of *peshat*, but has pushed expertise into increasingly narrow fields of enquiry. It is not unusual for a scholarly community to focus entirely on a single book or theme.

112. Cited in van Balthasar, *Origen*, xvii.

113. The apostle emphasizes this point even when giving his own opinion (1 Cor 7:40).

114. Cited in Duby, *Age of the Cathedrals*, 106.

115. "A strong case can be made that Biblical Theology of both testaments must issue in theological reflection which also moves in the reverse direction from the New Testament back to the Old" (Childs, *Biblical Theology*, 17).

116. DelHousaye, "Across the Kidron," 110–26.

117. There are sixty-eights scenes at Saint-Denis (Duby, *Age of the Cathedrals*, 107).

The Gospels are remarkably allusive to earlier Scripture, which is in keeping with virtually all Jewish literature from the period. When Josephus composed the history of his people in the *Antiquities*, it was "on the basis of our sacred books" (*Ag. Ap.* 1.1). Readings that do not attend to this intertextuality are greatly impoverished.

Derash ("searching")

Derash attends to the application of Scripture, the moment. The rabbis distinguish between *haggadah* (הַגָּדָה) and *halakah* (הֲלָכָה). *Haggadah* is narrative or story; *halakah,* behavior or right participation in that story.[118] There is something similar at work in the Gospels. On the one hand, we are called to imitate Christ. "Meditate on the life of Christ," Ludolph urges, "with a thirst to put into practice what you read there—it does little good to read unless you seek to imitate."[119] He adds, "In Christ's life is found the perfection of all virtues."[120] *The Imitation of Christ* by Thomas À Kempis (c. 1380–1471) may be the most widely read devotional book after the Bible. Jesus also engages in *halakah*, making several remarkable demands on would-be disciples. But, as we have shown, the Gospels also call us into union with Christ whose Spirit empowers our conformity to the Father's will. Seeking a personal relationship with Jesus, disciples developed what came to be called spiritual disciplines or "ways of being present to God."[121] They are "skills of perceiving and responding to God's invitations."[122] Adele Calhoun notes, "The simple truth is that wanting to keep company with Jesus has a staying power that 'shoulds' and 'oughts' seldom have."[123] We walk with Jesus, a kind of knowing by doing.[124]

This participation also has a communal dimension: "What is most personal is also what is most universal."[125]As we noted, Jews uniquely gathered every week to hear Scripture. After the reading, someone would apply the ancient words to the contemporary life of the people, a practice that continued in the church.

118. Vande Kappelle, *Wisdom Revealed*, 134.

119. Ludolph of Saxony, *Life of Christ*, 1:4.

120. Ludolph of Saxony, *Life of Christ*, 1:12.

121. Calhoun, *Spiritual Disciplines Handbook*, 11.

122. Howard, *Brazos Introduction*, 231.

123. Calhoun, *Spiritual Disciplines Handbook*, 18.

124. For meaning through doing, see Swanwick, *Developing Discourse*, 144.

125. Nouwen et al., *Spiritual Direction*, ix.

The New Testament authors relied heavily on the "anointing" of the Holy Spirit for personal application.

In both Testaments, God teaches a people through concrete example. God rests before we are asked to do the same and so forth. Paul invited the Ephesians to imitate God (Eph 5:1). Old Testament anthropomorphisms anticipate the Incarnation.[126]

Sod ("secret")

Sod attends to the Bible's ultimate author, the messenger.[127] Communication may reveal something of a speaker's heart. Learning about God, we come to love God more deeply. It is the purpose of Scripture, commentary, and theology:

> Every doctrine is connected with every other doctrine, and every doctrine is a kind of lens or prism with which to view THE Christian doctrine: the reality that God, Holy Mystery, has revealed God's true self to women and men in the warp and woof of history, through the presence of the Spirit and in the life, death/resurrection, and especially the person of Jesus of Nazareth, and calls them into friendship and partnership.[128]

Sod may therefore include our prayer to God, thereby completing a cycle of communication. Through the Gospels, Jesus offers space to know God. We are invited to be immersed into Christ's life, death, and resurrection, to project ourselves into the narrative with an open heart. Finding our place in God's story is essential, but that is only the signifier. The signified or ultimate reality to which the story points is life in God. We may filter all of our theology through Christ's life (Heb 1:1–4).

Jesus of Nazareth

Jesus Christ (c. 4 BC–AD 33) was born in Bethlehem in what then was called Judea (modern southern Israel);[129] after some time in Egypt (perhaps

126. Micheline Chaze notes, Dieu condescend donc à se comporter comme l'homme afin de lui enseigner, de la conuier et souvent de lui enjoindre, à faire de même (*L'Imitatio Dei*, 4).

127. *Sod* may have been the final sense, originating in *kabbalah*, which parallels the development in the Christian tradition (Schwartz, *Reimagining the Bible*, 38).

128. Bevans, *Introduction to Theology*, 2.

129. For contemporary use of "Judea," see Matt 2:1, 5; Josephus, *Ant.* 1.134.

Alexandria), he grew up in Nazareth, a small agricultural village in southern Galilee (modern northern Israel).[130] (As far as we know, Jesus never set foot outside the Roman Empire.) Around age thirty, he began to proclaim God's kingdom and to call Israelites to faith and repentance. He did remarkable things. Pilate, the Roman Prefect of Judea, executed Jesus on a cross as "king of the Judeans."[131] His disciples claimed he was raised from the dead, offering the same victory over death for those who call on his name. People trusted the message, and they became part of a church that gathered as a family for worship and to embody the gospel on earth.

Jesus did not write down his message. (It may be significant that the only time he is remembered writing is in the dirt.) Memories of his words and actions became part of Christian teaching and preaching—what may be called Jesus tradition. Although some of it may have been written during his ministry, there are no surviving documents that are earlier than what we possess in the New Testament.

Jesus tradition is expressed in Paul's letters and James, which may have been composed before the Gospels (c. AD 50–64). Much, but not all, of the tradition was written down in the four canonical Gospels. They informed early Christian evangelism, worship, and discipleship (catechesis).[132] The autographs (originals) have not survived, but the Gospels were copied by hand until the modern printing press.[133] This transmission process introduced errors and a few changes, but also many witnesses to the originals that inspire confidence. (Significant textual problems will be addressed.) With successful evangelism, the Gospels were translated into many languages, including English (beginning in the seventh century).

Each link in this chain—Jesus, tradition, publication of the Gospels, copying, and translation—has its own questions that drive scholarship in various disciplines.[134] Since the Enlightenment, a contested issue has been the relationship between the Jesus at the beginning to the Jesus at the end.[135]

130. Some critical scholars doubt Jesus was born in Bethlehem or that his family fled to Egypt. They interpret these claims as having a rhetorical (theological) intent—to link the historical Jesus with ancient Israelite Scripture. Everyone agrees he grew up in Nazareth because the church would not invent such a location because of its insignificance.

131. Tacitus, a non-Christian historian, claims Jesus was executed during the reign of Tiberius (AD 14–37) while Pontius Pilate was ruling Judea (AD 26–36).

132. See Bauckham, *Gospels for All Christians*, 1–7.

133. The autographs were probably written on papyrus, the most popular writing surface at the time, which begins to disintegrate after contact with moisture.

134. Powell, *Fortress Introduction*, 11.

135. Most scholars who study the Gospels are Christians, but are perhaps especially skeptical of historical claims. I value their work, and submit my own for their

The deist Hermann Reimarus (1694–1768), for example, claimed the disciples stole Jesus's body from the tomb, invented the story of the resurrection, and turned him into a universal savior who would return in glory.[136] Is the Jesus of history, the flesh-and-blood Jew who walked around Galilee, the same as the object of Christian faith? This is an essential question for every human being: the Gospels want us to believe that Jesus is God, who became a human being, who died in our place because of sin, but was raised from the dead so that we might have eternal life in him. If this Christ of faith is the Jesus of history—one and the same—then this extraordinary claim is grounded in historical reality, not myth.

The Gospels present Jesus as undergoing transfiguration, a metamorphosis, at his resurrection. This allows a spiritual union between God and human beings. In the fourth Gospel, Jesus looks forward to the Father and Son indwelling believers through the Holy Spirit. The transfiguration included Jesus's body, like a butterfly emerging from a chrysalis. The evangelists emphasize the empty tomb. The resurrected Jesus is not immediately recognized by his disciples, but is embodied; he can be touched, and he eats with them. Jesus Christ has changed but is the same person, even bearing scars from his earthly journey (John 20:27).

The gospel or basic message about the significance of Jesus's life and ministry had circulated broadly around the Mediterranean before the end of the first century, which made it difficult for anyone to change it.[137]

At least since the third century, Christians have encountered Jesus in the Eucharist *and* made pilgrimages to the Holy Land. There was no perception of an either/or. Similarly, the Christ who came to the apostles in the Gospels is who I know in faith and practice. The Jesus of my academic work is more complex, but not different from whom I met as a child through Sunday school teachers. An analogy: The perception I have of my parents changes with every season of life; they also change, but not into different people.

A deeper understanding of the Gospels is an increasingly correct interpretation of their truth claims, which present a reality greater than our immediate experience. What is needed for our time is not simply a recovery of the "historical Jesus," but Jesus's way of seeing that makes his

---

evaluation. For more context and a slightly different viewpoint, see the introduction in the opening volume of John P. Meier's magnum opus, *A Marginal Jew*. For a similar position, see van der Watt, *Quest for the Real Jesus*. He asks, "Is there a 'real Jesus' as an ontic reality beyond the images that people have been making of him since the time he lived—and also beyond the image he had of himself?" (12).

136. The so-called *Wolfenbüttel Fragments* were published posthumously (Bond, *Historical Jesus*, 8).

137. Williams, *Can We Trust the Gospels?*, 23.

self-understanding possible.[138] He felt beloved by the Father, and he wants us to know God's love. We are beloved. If we know this, deep in our bones, everything changes. His story becomes our story, and our story is his, and what evil cruelly broke apart comes back together. The field of mental health recognizes the importance of integrating all our experiences, even the most painful ones, into a coherent, sequential narrative.[139] We come to see that Jesus suffered with us in those experiences.

What Is a Gospel?

I have always enjoyed the mystery of being. We call a certain fruit an "apple." But what *is* it? What is "fruit" as opposed to some other classification? What are the Gospels? When people ask ontological questions of a text, they often enquire into its genre, a French word from the Greek noun *genos* (γένος) that refers to entities united by common traits.[140] The calque is more specifically applied in English to literary and other artistic works, and refers to an intellectual tradition that was refined in Greek culture in the centuries before Christ and re-emerged in the Renaissance after the rediscovery of Aristotle's *Poetics.*[141] It simply asks, "What is this?" But answers are not always clear.

Aristotle

Aristotle (384–322 BC) studied reality through comparison; within this bold research project, he found underlying patterns of communication, with some variation, in the epic and drama of his culture.[142] Isolating these patterns, a mass of Greek literature became intelligible to him.[143]

Aristotle recognized the evolution of genres, but believed they were static after reaching their *telos* (τέλος, "perfection").[144] Yet history shows a dynamic process of new genres surfacing from older ones, where the sum is greater than the parts (to quote the philosopher in a different

138. For the Enlightenment's destruction of the "symbolic system that acted as a counterweight to an overly literalistic reading of the Bible," see Patella, *Word and Image*, 7.

139. Van Der Kolk, *Body Keeps the Score*, 47.

140. BDAG, 194–95.

141. The word genre entered English discourse in the late eighteenth century.

142. We also find nascent genre theory in Plato's *Republic.*

143. Aristotle, *Poetics*, xii.

144. Adams, *Genre of Acts*, 30–31.

context). For example, the comedy of the philosopher's day, exemplified by Aristophanes (c. 446–c. 386 BC), parodied well-known historical figures, like Socrates, and employed mythology through the chorus. But a century later, Menander employed average, fictional characters, and reduced the role of the chorus to occasional entertainment. Critics now distinguish between Old and New Comedy.

Genres (patterns of expression and communication) emerge in a tension between freedom and constraint. They are constrained by, among other things, the background, ability, and interests of the author, the mode of communication, and the expectations and capacity of the reader.[145] If the work is to communicate, at least elements must be recognizable to both parties.[146] This is especially important if the writer seeks to persuade, the function of rhetoric. John (20:30–31) and Luke (1:1–4) are explicit, but all four Gospels want to convince their readers about Jesus Christ.

Students of culture, like Aristotle, eventually recognize new genres or subgenres and do something like this part of our study: they aid communication by relating the patterns to others and highlighting their uniqueness.[147] But any critic knows that no art is without antecedent.[148]

Aristotle distinguished between comedy and tragedy by also attending to function, famously charting the cathartic effect of the latter. The union of form and function ground the interpretive value of genre criticism: awareness of genre guides reading expectations. Such classification is a point of departure for interpretation. If someone reads a love letter like an assembly guide for a couch, at least some meaning is lost.

After genres become culturally established, they inform audience expectation, like imitations of a profitable film. Love stories become or deviate from boy meets girl, boy loses girl, boy regains girl. Films that deviate too far from the formula risk rejection, although modest developments are praised. In ancient Athens, genre was a sort of contract between patron, artist, and audience.[149] A similar dynamic happens between producers, directors, and movie-watchers today.

145. *Quidquid recipitur ad modum recipientis recipitur,* "Whatever is received is received according to the capacity of the receiver."

146. Mikhail Bakhtin emphasizes social life as the center of language. His influence may be seen in this definition of genres as "types of rhetorical actions that people perform in their everyday interactions with their worlds" (Devitt, *Writing Genres*, 2).

147. Smith, *Why* βίος?, 3.

148. Kathleen Jamieson notes how authors use "antecedent rhetorical forms" to address rhetorical situations ("Generic Constraints," 162–70).

149. For example, dramatists like Aristophanes wrote plays that were performed at festivals attended by thousands. A wealthy citizen recruited and funded the chorus.

The four Gospels are different from one another; John is especially unique. But they are closer to one another than any other document from antiquity. All are narratives about Jesus, who emerges publicly from John the Baptist, preaches and performs miracles, engages in disputes with religious leaders, is arrested and executed by the Romans, but raised from the dead by God. They all describe salvation in Christ.

Origen

Aristotle's vision was furthered in Alexandria, Egypt, which was named by his famous pupil. Demetrius of Phaleron encouraged Ptolemy I to establish the museum where scholars lived together and researched, among other things, medicine, engineering, mathematics, philosophy, and literature. The library became the largest deposit of knowledge in the ancient world.[150] Such benefaction allowed the intensive study of texts.

Alexandrian scholars determined that science and poetry describe the same reality, but differently. Science required precision of language and logic; poetry, polyvalence and symbolism. Prose was ideal for the particular, like accurately describing a historical event. But poetry caught something of the universal, inspiring wonder. To understand direct claims on reality they developed the literal interpretation of texts; for indirect claims, like epic or hymn, the allegorical.

From this milieu came Origen (c.185–c.254), the most important Christian thinker and biblical interpreter before Augustine.[151] He glossed most of the Bible and would begin with the literal sense of Scripture, the clear meaning of words, which included a discussion of genre. So, for example, he opens a commentary on the Song of Songs with

> It seems to me that this little book is an epithalamium, that is to say, a marriage-song, which Solomon wrote in the form of a drama . . . For we call a thing a drama, such as the enaction of a story on the stage, when different characters are introduced and

150. There were perhaps 500,000 volumes (Strabo 13.608, 17.793–794). Authors deposited the original copies of their works in the library. The head librarian was one of the most powerful men in the city. For more discussion, see Kennedy, *Cambridge History of Literary Criticism*, 1:200–214.

151. We know his life from Eusebius (*Hist. eccl.* 6), Jerome (*Vir. ill.* 54), Photius (*Bibliotheca* 118), and an oration by his student Gregory Thaumaturgus. For a discussion of Origenian biblical scholarship, see Martens, *Origen and Scripture*, especially 243–46.

> the whole structure of the narrative consists in their comings and goings among themselves.[152]

This classification is based on a pattern of traits in light of a library catalogue. The epithalamium (ἐπιθαλάμιος) was commonly employed in the Greco-Roman social world.[153] Origen did not stop at the literal level, but read the drama as playing out between God and the soul, leading to union.

Origen does not identify the Gospels accordingly, but focuses on the uniqueness of their contents. This is significant because the Alexandrian had no philosophical issue with literary antecedents. He reads the Gospels as if they were a hybrid of prose and poetry. Not everything is taken literally (historically): the devil did not actually take Jesus to the temple's pinnacle; the parables are fictional, and disciples should not physically tear out their eye when facing temptation. He writes:

> The chief concern of the evangelists was related to the mysteries; they did not so much care to report the accurate history of the events as to set forth the mystery of those things that derive from historical facts . . . The evangelists sometimes changed historical circumstances to the benefit of the spiritual purpose, so that they reported that something happened in a determined place and time, although in fact it happened in another place and time.[154]

Origen is aware of the same story occurring in different places in the Gospels. But he also rejected interpreting everything metaphorically: "We are quite convinced," he says, "of the historical truth of certain passages," like the claim of Jesus's resurrection. So Origen read the Gospels literally ("bodily") and metaphorically (allegorically, "spiritually"). They addressed reality, some of which touched history, like the empty tomb, but also mysteries requiring a poetic imagination. The Alexandrian created a continuum, from maintaining that every detail in the Gospels is historical to attributing the totality to myth, that helpfully plots the work of scholars today. Evangelicals and conservative Catholics typically begin on the historical side; atheists commit to the mythological. Most critical studies fall somewhere between these polarities.

152. Origen, *Song of Songs*, 21–22 (Lawson).

153. Sappho, Anacreon, Stesichorus, Pindar, Catullus—all play with the form.

154. The comment (*Comm. John* 10.5.19) is cited with discussion in Hill, "Truth Above All Demonstration," 57.

Since Origen, we have come to see that there was nothing *exactly* like the Gospels before Christ.[155] Some, therefore, like the modern scholar Rudolf Bultmann (1884–1976), claim the Gospels are *sui generis.* Karl Ludwig Schmidt (1891–1956) made the definitive study for this position, *The Place of the Gospels in the General History of Literature*. Schmidt claimed the Gospels are the fixed record of popular oral tradition (*Kleinlitteratur*).[156] The first storytellers about Jesus did not appropriate literary genres. Any seeming parallel is analogous, not genetic. He challenged the prevailing view of the nineteenth century that the Gospels were a kind of Greco-Roman *bios* (βίος, "life"), which has become popular again in recent decades.[157]

In sum, our study will address three questions: What are the Gospels? How novel or derived is their genre? And most importantly: How should we read them? This requires a close reading of where the evangelists and their early interpreters discuss the matter.

The Gospels themselves reveal some of their literary environment. They are written in Greek, a language with a rich textual heritage.[158] They often cite Ancient Israelite Scripture, a monumental literary achievement. They also bear the marks of orality or storytelling.[159] We may ask: Where do the Gospels fall in this context? Were the first readers shocked by their novelty, like the villagers with Jesus's preaching at Capernaum? Would they have recognized them as being similar to Scripture read in the synagogue (Mark 1:27)? Did they draw comparisons with contemporary biographies?

155. Vern Poythress notes: "The genre 'Gospel' is distinct from other genres in its time. God brought into being this specialized genre in the context of the early church, without any exact parallels preceding it, because the events and their meaning were unparalleled. It has some similarities to Hellenistic history writing, to Hellenistic biographies, and to Old Testament history writing. But the genre 'Gospel' is also distinctive" (*Inerrancy and the Gospels*, 44).

156. His position is largely adopted by Rudolf Bultmann (*History of the Synoptic Tradition*, 373–74).

157. Aune, "Gospels as Ancient Biography," 46–76; Bird, *Gospel of the Lord*, 20; Burridge, *What Are the Gospels?* Bauckham, who follows Burridge, nevertheless acknowledges: "We still lack an adequate typology of the Greco-Roman *bios*" (*Testimony of the Beloved Disciple*, 95).

158. Evidence for an original Hebrew Matthew is strong (see below), but that edition is no longer extant. The canonical edition is in Greek.

159. Bailey, "Informal Controlled Oral Tradition," 34–54; Longenecker, "Humorous Jesus?," 179–204.

Euangelion ("good news")

Justin Martyr, a second-century Christian teacher in Rome, refers to the *euangelia* (εὐαγγέλια) or "gospels" (pl. of *euangelion,* εὐαγγέλιον).[160] The familiar title Gospel, which is now pervasive when referring to these writings, is a calque from the Old English gōd-*spell* ("good news"), which is a literal translation of the Latin *evangelium* from the Greek *euangelion* (εὐαγγέλιον).[161] Presumably, Justin appropriated Mark's opening: "The beginning of the gospel (τοῦ εὐαγγελίου) of Jesus Christ," which could be read as a title for the entire book and therefore applicable to all four Gospels that had been collected together into a codex (book) by that time.[162]

Mark delimits his opening unit by repeating *euangelion* through the mouth of Jesus: "The season has been fulfilled, and the Kingdom of God has drawn near. Repent and believe in the gospel (*euangelion*)" (1:15). John the Baptist has just promised the forgiveness of sins and empowerment of the Holy Spirit (1:4, 5, 8). "Forgiveness" (*afesis,* ἄφεσις) is liberation; "sin" (*hamartia,* ἁμαρτία), a destructive, evil power leading to death.[163] Jesus associates himself with sinners at his baptism (1:9–11) and models victory over Satan in the wilderness (1:12–13). So, for Mark, the *euangelion* is freedom from the effect and influence of evil.

Philosophy, which had taken an ethical turn in the period, correlated unhappiness with *akrasia* (ἀκραςία) or a lack of self-control. Paul had described the predicament to Roman Christians, offering Christ as the solution.[164] He also emphasizes forgiveness and empowerment. His letter to the Romans had been circulating in Mark's community for probably nearly a decade. Sixty of the seventy-six occurrences of *euangelion* in the New Testament occur in Paul's letters, including the phrase "beginning of the gospel" that opens Mark's

160. "Τὰ ἀπομνημονεύματα τῶν ἀποστόλων, ἃ καλεῖται εὐαγγέλια . . . the apostles, in the memoirs composed by them, which are called Gospels" (Justin Martyr, *1 Apol.* 66). Gundry claims that earlier occurrences of εὐαγγέλιον in the Apostolic Fathers do not necessarily refer to a book ("How Soon a Book?," 321–25).

161. We find this spelling in the Lindisfarne Gospels (c. 950), the first citation in the Oxford English Dictionary. A calque reveals holes in the host language and therefore the need for borrowing. Marcion (c. 110–160) used εὐαγγέλιον for his edited version of Luke (von Harnack, *Marcion*, 184).

162. Justin seems to have known the western order of the Gospels: Matthew, John, Luke, and Mark. This may have been a process of elimination: Luke and John do not begin with titles, and Matthew echoes the contemporary title for Genesis (Βίβλος γενέσεως).

163. BDAG, 50–51.

164. See Rom 7—8:1; Stowers, *Rereading of Romans*, 279.

Gospel (Phil 4:15).[165] There is little reason to doubt that a Pauline understanding of *euangelion* impacted Mark's presentation.[166]

After Mark's first use of *euangelion*, he cites Isaiah: "prepare the Lord's way, make straight his paths (40:3). The Greek translation of the prophet uses the verb εὐαγγελίζω (*euangelizō*), which shares the same root as *euangelion*, to announce the restoration of God's people in the same passage:

> On a high mountain, ascend, the one who brings good news (*ho euangelizomenons*, ὁ εὐαγγελιζόμενος) to Zion; lift up your voice with strength, the one who brings good news (*ho euangelizomenons*, ὁ εὐαγγελιζόμενος) to Jerusalem; lift up, do not fear, say to the cities of Judea, "behold, your God!" (40:9)[167]

God announces good news through Isaiah to the exiles in Babylon: "Comfort, comfort my people!" (Isa 40:1). At the beginning of the chapter, God announces their "sin is pardoned" (*hamartia*, ἁμαρτία, v. 2); the end, "power to the faint" (*ischus*, ἰσχύς, v. 29). In Mark, the Baptist uses the related adjective *ischuros* (ἰσχυρός) to describe Jesus's ministry (1:7). We find a similar announcement in Isaiah's Servant Song: "How lovely upon the mountains are the feet of him who brings good news, who proclaims peace, who brings good news of welfare, who proclaims salvation, who says to Zion, 'Your God reigns'" (52:7). This passage was applied to the coming messiah in contemporary Judaism (*Pss. Sol.* 11:1).[168] According to Isaiah, God had raised Cyrus (d. 530 BC), the most powerful man in the world, to redeem his people so that they could return from exile (44:24—48:22). Yet this national restoration (42:18—43:21) is paired with a spiritual one—healing from sin (43:22—44:23). For this, he speaks of a mysterious servant of God (49:1—53:12):

> He was despised and rejected by men; a man of sorrows, and acquainted with grief; and as one from whom men hide their faces he was despised, and we esteemed him not. Surely he has borne our griefs and carried our sorrows; yet we esteemed him

165. 1 John uses the related term ἀγγελία to describe the revelation of God as light (1:5) and the instruction to love one another (3:11).

166. Smith, *Influence of the Epistles on the Synoptic Gospels*. Some go too far with this scenario: see, e.g., Patella, *Lord of the Cosmos*.

167. The verb describes a messenger travelling to inform those in one place of what happened somewhere else, often with the expectation of a joyful response. The Philistines, traditional enemies of Israel, "bring good news" (εὐαγγελίζω) of Saul's death on the battlefield back to their country (1 Sam 31:9 OG).

168. James Dunn notes the link (*Jesus, Paul, and the Gospels*, 46). See also 11QMelch 2.15–24.

> stricken, smitten by God, and afflicted. But he was wounded for our transgressions; he was crushed for our iniquities; upon him was the chastisement that brought us peace, and with his stripes we are healed. (53:3–5 ESV)

The servant had been "anointed" for this, the literal meaning of messiah or Christ (52:14).[169] This foreshadows the arrest, trial, and death of Jesus Christ, which occupy nearly half of Mark's Gospel.

King Cyrus and the Suffering Servant are distinct yet related in Isaiah's vision. God even refers to the Persian as "my christ" (*Christou mou,* χριστῷ μου) or messiah (Isa 45:1 OG). Similarly, Mark suggests a typology with Caesar and Jesus. When Julius Caesar was deified in death, Augustus (r. 27 BC–AD 14) became "son of God."[170] Watching Jesus die, the Roman centurion says, "Truly this man was God's son" (Mark 15:39).[171] The Priene Calendar inscription honors Caesar Augustus:

> It seemed good to the Greeks of Asia, in the opinion of the high priest Apollonius of Menophilus Azanitus: "Since Providence, which has ordered all things and is deeply interested in our life, has set in most perfect order by giving us Augustus, whom she filled with virtue that he might benefit humankind, sending him as a savior, both for us and for our descendants, that he might end war and arrange all things, and since he, Caesar, by his appearance (excelled even our anticipations), surpassing all previous benefactors, and not even leaving to posterity any hope of surpassing what he has done, and since the birthday of the god Augustus was *the beginning of the gospel* [*euangeliōn*] for the world that came by reason of him," which Asia resolved in Smyrna.[172]

It is difficult to isolate Mark's politics. Emperor worship was especially popular in the east, particularly Egypt. The evangelist may open his Gospel by claiming Jesus, not Caesar, is God's Son. Yet in the subsequent narrative, Jesus does not attack the *Pax Romana* but Satan's Kingdom (Mark 3:22–27). When asked about paying taxes (tribute), Jesus says: "Give back the things

169. I am grateful to my colleague John Meade for drawing my attention to this interpretation. He, in turn, acknowledges the work of Peter Gentry: "Atonement," 20–47.

170. Adkins and Adkins, *Handbook to Life in Ancient Rome*, 20.

171. We may also use the terms "bracketing" and "envelope structure." In any case, biblical writers often create a frame by placing similar material at the beginning and end of a unit.

172. The translation is slightly altered from Evans, "Mark's Incipit," 67–81.

that are Caesar's to Caesar, and the things of God to God" (Mark 12:17). In Mark, Jesus gives lives back to God.[173]

Justin assumes others used the title (ἃ καλεῖται εὐαγγέλια, "which *are called* Gospels"), and this is confirmed by slightly later writers (Clement of Alexandria and Irenaeus). We also find *euangelion* in the subscriptions for Mark, Luke, and John in Codex Vaticanus (c. 300–350). While a title is not necessarily a genre, Origen uses it this way, which is significant because, as was noted, he knew of other genres.[174]

Kerygma ("preaching")

The early form critic Martin Dibelius (1883–1947) pronounced: "At the beginning of all Christian activity there stands the sermon."[175] As Mark narrates, the initial form of the gospel is *kerygma* (κήρυγμα) or "preaching."[176] God proclaims the gospel through Isaiah, the Baptist, and then Jesus, who makes twelve apostles "to preach" (Mark 3:14). The evangelist probably composed his work to be read as a whole in the context of corporate worship.[177] The Gospel could be performed in about an hour, which might have been viewed as being longer than a typical sermon but still within the bounds of a gathering.[178]

Martyrdom Sermons

The synagogue and church memorialized martyrs. The Gospels may be placed in this trajectory, from the Hasmonean rebellion (167–160 BC) to the Edict of Milan (AD 313).[179] Martin Kähler (1835–1912) describes them as "passion narratives with extended introductions."[180] As narrative, the

173. For critique of those who find anti-imperialistic rhetoric under every rock, see Kim, *Christ and Caesar*, 1–2; for broader discussion, Reasoner, *Roman Imperial Texts*, 9–11; Winn, *Introduction to Empire*.

174. "Now we have no written work of Paul which is commonly called a gospel. But all that he preached and said was the Gospel" (Origen, *Comm. Jo.* 6 [*ANF* 9:300]).

175. Dibelius, *From Tradition to Gospel*, 37.

176. McDonald, *Kerygma and* Didache, 1–6.

177. Shiner, *Proclaiming the Gospel*; Boomershine, *Messiah of Peace*.

178. People generally read between 200 and 250 words per minute. Mark is approximately 11,304 words long. It is longer than Hebrews (approx. 4,953 words), which identifies itself as a "word of exhortation" or sermon (13:22).

179. Cohen, *Sanctifying the Name of God*, 16–17.

180. Kähler, *So-Called Historical Jesus*, 80n11.

Gospels describe Jesus's suffering and death in great detail (see Gal 3:1). We find a similar form in 1 Maccabees, an invitation to celebrate Hanukkah that provides the historical background for the festival. Judas Maccabeus rescues his people, eventually dying on their behalf. 4 Maccabees, a sermon probably written at the time of Christ, discusses how reason may reign over passion in difficult trials.[181] Didacticism and biography comingle as the narrator focuses on Eleazer, a righteous man who is tortured and killed by Antiochus Epiphanes (c. 215 BC–164 BC). Eleazar prays:

> You have known, God, [that] while being able to save myself I am dying with burning tortures because of the Law. Be merciful to your people. Let our punishment suffice on behalf of them. Make my blood their purification, and take my life in exchange [or as a ransom] for theirs. (16:27–29)

The author adds: "They have become, as it were, a ransom for the sin of our nation. And through the blood of those devout ones and their death as an atoning sacrifice, divine Providence preserved Israel that previously had been mistreated" (17:21–22). The hearers (readers) should follow his example—not necessarily dying, but living for more than pleasure. Jesus similarly announces: "the son of man [a veiled self-reference] did not come to be served, but to serve and to give up his life (as) a ransom in exchange for many" (Mark 10:45). A ransom is paid in exchange for a life, typically someone who has been kidnapped or incriminated. Unlike 4 Maccabees, the Gospels do not celebrate reason as much as faithfulness, the most significant virtue in contemporary Judaism. Not surprisingly, the Gospels influenced the subsequent martyrdom tradition. *The Martyrdom of Polycarp* (c. 70–c. 155–160) echoes several scenes from the Gospels.[182] Yet Kähler was intentionally hyperbolic. The passion occupies only about 15 percent of the narrative. The Gospels include but cannot be reduced to this classification.

"Concerning the first *logos* (λόγος)" is how Luke describes his own work (Acts 1:1). He also uses the word to describe the eyewitness sources he appropriates into his narrative (Luke 1:2). Most scholars believe he refers to Mark; several, Matthew as well; a few, including myself, John too. So Luke probably refers to one or more of the other Gospels as *logoi*. In the Gospels, *logos* is to *euangelion* as form is to content.[183] A *logos* is typically first expressed orally, often translated "speech" or "sermon," but can be refined as literature.[184]

181. deSilva, *4 Maccabees*, 11–18.

182. Holmes, *Apostolic Fathers*, 298–333.

183. See, e.g., Matt 7:28; 13:19, 20, 21, 22, 23; Luke 4:32; probably 1:2. John and Luke does not use εὐαγγέλιον in their Gospels. But see Acts 15:7 and 20:24.

184. Many books today begin as lectures, sermons, or speeches.

Luke illustrates the process. After "the reading from the Law and from the Prophets, the synagogue-heads sent a word to Paul and Barnabas at Antioch in Pisidia, saying, 'if there is any word of exhortation (*logos paraklēseōs*, λόγος παρακλήσεως) in you for the people, speak" (Acts 13:15; see also Luke 4:16–30). *Logos paraklēseōs* appears to have been a common expression for preaching in the synagogue. The discourse began orally from Paul's mouth, but was later converted into literature by Luke (13:16–47).[185] Expansion is natural to this literary phase, and it fits the common view that Luke appropriated and expanded one or more of the earlier Gospels.

Biblical Prose

All four Gospels are written in prose, which, as we noted, was contrasted with poetry, the other primary mode of communication.[186] In the opening sentence, Luke identifies his Gospel as a kind of prose—"narrative" or story (*diegesis,* διήγησις). We are therefore not surprised to find a plot constrained by time, topic, and causality.[187] After his preface (1:1–4), which is patterned after Greco-Roman works, Luke begins to imitate the prose of Scripture.[188] We find the same phenomenon in Matthew and Mark. (John is similarly dependent on earlier Scripture, but has a more idiosyncratic style.) This form of prose is distinctive and indigenous to Israel. Other cultures produced psalms, proverbs, and oracles, but not a narrative history of one God in relationship with a people over time. The story moves from creation, fall, exodus, exile, and hope of restoration, with attention to Israel's disobedience and flawed leaders, like Abraham, Jacob, Moses, and David. God remains while everything else passes by like an assembly line. For any story to be ultimately true, it must relate to God's one story. Justin Martyr discloses that the Gospels were read alongside Israelite Scripture. The overlap in style makes sense, but also the content: although Jesus is presented as unique from biblical personalities, his significance is ultimately found in relation to God.

185. The author of Hebrews describes his piece as a "word of exhortation" (*logos paraklēseōs*, λόγος παρακλήσεως; 13:22).

186. See van Oyen, *Reading the Gospel of Mark as a Novel.*

187. Kingsbury, *Conflict in Luke*, 34.

188. Adela Collins notes: "The author of Mark has taken the model of biblical sacred history and transformed it, first, by infusing it with an eschatological and apocalyptic perspective and, second, by adapting it to Hellenistic historiographical and biographical traditions" (*Mark*, 1).

Bioi ("lives")

Contemporary writers were composing *bioi* (βίοι) or "lives" of important people.[189] Plutarch (46–120) wrote fifty *bioi* that often relate the circumstances of the subject's birth, public career, and death. But his main concern was to reveal character through action, so that a sympathetic reader could imitate virtue and avoid vice:

> For it is not Histories that I am writing, but Lives (*bioi*); and in the most illustrious deeds there is not always a manifestation of virtue or vice, nay, a slight thing like a phrase or a jest often makes a greater revelation of character than battles when thousands fall, or the greatest armaments, or sieges of cities. Accordingly, just as painters get the likenesses in their portraits from the face and the expression of the eyes, wherein the character shows itself, but make very little account of the other parts of the body, so I must be permitted to devote myself rather to the signs of the soul in men, and by means of these to portray the life of each, leaving to others the description of their great contests.[190]

The Christian writer Sulpicius Severus (c. 363–c. 425) expresses the intended effect on readers "stirred to no little emulation by the pictures of great men thus set before them."[191] The central character tends to be static, unlike modern interest in development.

Plutarch emphasizes the rhetorical dimension of the genre. Aristotle found three rhetorical genres in Athenian social life: judicial (legal), deliberative (political), and epideictic (ceremonial).[192] The latter's function is to praise or blame. It blended with biography in funeral orations where the audience was exhorted to imitate or avoid the character of the deceased.[193] The genre is similar to the Jewish martyrdom sermon. A good death naturally created interest in the life that caused it. Plutarch and others met the need.

The Gospels are a kind of epideictic rhetoric.[194] They commemorate Jesus Christ in a ceremonial context, as Justin Martyr notes:

189. The genre had been developing for centuries. There is *Bios of Euripedes* by Satyrus (third century) in Alexandria. It continued into the Christian era with lives of holy men. See Hägg, *Art of Biography*.

190. Plutarch, *Lives*, 224–25.

191. Preface to his *Life of Martin of Tours* in Noble and Head, *Soldiers of Christ*, 4.

192. Aristotle, *Rhet.* 1.3.1–6 (1358b).

193. Roberts, *Greek Rhetoric*, 27. Lecturing on this topic at Harvard, John Quincy Adams said, "Every line of praise upon the fathers should be received as a line of duty for the children" (cited in Lockwood, *Reader's Figure*, 19).

194. For Matthew, see Neyrey, *Honor and Shame*, 70–89; for Mark, Bryan, *Preface*

> And on the day called Sunday there is a gathering together in the same place of all who live in a given city or rural district. The memoirs of the apostles [Gospels] or the writings of the prophets are read, as long as time permits. Then when the reader ceases, the leader through a sermon exhorts and urges the imitation of these good things. (*1 Apol.* 67.3)[195]

Aristotle claims "The epideictic style is especially suited to written compositions; for its function is reading."[196] Rhetors must consider if they are facing sympathetic or hostile readers. A sympathetic reader happily identifies with the subject, finding his or her life praiseworthy, but a hostile reader is quicker to blame what the author finds praiseworthy. Were the evangelists writing for insiders or outsiders? Does Luke intend for Theophilus to become a Christian or to deepen his understanding of the faith? Is John writing for his readers *to begin* or *to keep* believing? Justin presumes a private function for the Gospels, a way for believers to imitate Christ, but he also uses them to address Caesar. If the Gospels are a kind of preaching, they must have a "semi-public" function.[197] Jesus privately taught his disciples after public rejection, but promises a universal audience for the gospel: "Wherever the gospel is preached, into the whole world, even what she did will be told in memory of her" (Mark 14:9).

The Gospels fall along a continuum of public and private discourse with none on the edges. If Mark is primarily for outsiders, it may explain why Jesus is always teaching, but relatively little of the content is given: the hearer (reader) must repent and believe to receive the actual teaching. What is given is often evangelistic and polemical. Perhaps Matthew writes primarily for insiders, referring to "their synagogues," as if Judaism and Christianity had parted ways, and offering five blocks of extensive teaching, beginning with the Sermon on the Mount. John's rhetoric is similarly introverted, while Luke's is extroverted like Mark.

The Gospels clearly resemble *bioi*.[198] Indeed, this may be the most comprehensive genre classification. Matthew, Luke, and John (in his own way)—all convey the birth, life, and death of Jesus for the emulation of their readers. Biographies were written by individuals, not committees, which is

---

to Mark, 60; for Luke, Mallen, *Reading and Transformation of Isaiah*, 164; and for John, Brant, *John*, 12.

195. Justin Martyr, *Apologies of Justin Martyr*, 100.

196. Aristotle, *Rhet.* 3.12.5 (1413b—1414a).

197. Ian Henderson discusses the "semi-public quality of the gospel rhetorics" (*Jesus, Rhetoric and Law*, 20).

198. James Bailey and Lyle Vander Broek claim Luke is closest to the genre (*Literary Forms in the New Testament*), 95.

consistent with tradition.[199] Nevertheless, the Gospels are more than biographies. As we noted, there is a disproportionate emphasis on Christ's death and much more teaching, especially in Matthew and John, than we would find in Plutarch. There is also something of a subversion of the Greco-Roman hero paradigm: humility was not celebrated in *bioi*; association with sinners was not praiseworthy; how was the emotional breakdown in Gethsemane and subsequent crucifixion for sedition a good death? Jesus was not great in the sense usually presumed in biography.[200] Paul meditates on the scandal of the cross for outsiders, but his letters reveal that even professing Christians struggled to identify with their founder's suffering and death.

Apomnēmoneumata ("recollections")

Justin Martyr refers to the Gospels as "memories" or "recollections" (*apomnēmoneumata*, ἀπομνημονεύματα).[201] The language evokes Xenophon's (c. 430–c. 354 BC) memories of Socrates, who underwent a good death and was the subject of many *bioi*.[202] Socrates is a fitting antecedent: everyone in retrospect saw that he was right and the Athenians were wrong. Unlike Plato's dialogues, Xenophon mainly composed with anecdotes and sayings, which are amenable to passing information from one generation to another. Papias, an early bishop of Hierapolis (c. 60–130) and probably Justin's source, describes Mark as a loose collection of anecdotes (*chreia*, χρεία) from Peter's teaching about Jesus.[203] They were the basic form for *bioi* because, as Plutarch notes, it is through anecdotes, more than seismic events, that a person's character is revealed.

Creation Stories

Where the evangelists suggest genre, they emphasize beginnings. This echoes foundation stories like Vergil's *Aeneid*, which explain the origin

199. Burridge, "About People, by People, for People," 125–30.

200. Jean-Noël Aletti isolates this as the primary difficulty for identifying the Gospels as this genre (*Birth of the Gospels as Biographies*, 4).

201. Justin Martyr, *1 Apol.* 66. The Greek is from *Justini Philosophi et Martyris*, 2:70.

202. Kennedy, *Progymnasmata*, 77n13.

203. Papias is cited in Eusebius, *Hist. eccl.* 3.39.15. There is discussion over the translation of χρεία as "anecdote" or "need" according to older interpretation. But the rhetorical terminology is becoming more recognized (Black, "Use of Rhetorical Terminology," 31–41).

of a community.[204] Creation stories typically function to show the superiority of the community over others by remembering a founding hero.[205] They define who is in and out. Some are open; others closed. "Everlasting Rome" was created through a suffering hero, the Trojan Aeneas. Vergil (70–19 BC) creatively appropriated Homer's epic.[206] If being a Christian is different than being a Roman or Jew, a new story is required. The Gospels tell Christians where they come from and why they exist.[207] Although few artifacts remain, these stories have passed from the first to present generation; and they will outlive us. But they are also evangelistic, emphasizing mercy over superiority. Some find a "third race" (*tertium genus*) mentality in Matthew, but the issue is debated.[208]

Spolia

The term *spolia* has been used in the discourse of art history since the sixteenth century to describe the reuse of materials from older buildings into new ones.[209] Such construction was probably done for many reasons: aesthetics, economic and material constraints, but also to associate the old with the new. By new, I mean something less than *ex nihilo* but more than parody.[210]

The proclamation of the death and resurrection of Christ was a new message, but people begin to process new patterns of communication by recognizing what is familiar in them. (Jesus communicates the mystery of God's Kingdom by appropriating a well-known genre, the parable.) Origen offers this advice to his student Gregory:

> Take with you from the philosophy of the Greeks both those parts that are able, as it were, to serve as encyclical or propaedeuctic studies for Christianity, and also those elements of geometry

204. Miles, "*Aeneid* as Foundation Story," 231–50. His distinction between foundation story and creation story is unnecessarily specific. Callimachus's major work was *Aetia*, a collection of origin stories. Ovid opens *Metamorphoses* with the origin of the world and, following Hesiod, the descent of humanity.

205. Perkell, *Reading Vergil's Aeneid*, 231.

206. Humphries, *Aenead*, vii–xiii.

207. Dennis MacDonald claims Mark imitated Homer (*Homeric Epics and the Gospel of Mark*).

208. See Matt 21:43; Hare, *Theme of Jewish Persecution*, 170.

209. Frey, *Spolia in Fortifications and the Common Builder*. Spolia were a part of the building of old St. Peter's Basilica at the time of Constantine.

210. Bale, *Genre and Narrative Coherence*, 72–73.

> and astronomy that may be useful for the interpretation of the Holy Scriptures . . . Perhaps something of this sort is hinted at in the passage of Exodus where God in person directs the sons of Israel to ask from their neighbors and those dwelling in their tents vessels of silver and gold and clothing [Exod 12:35–36]; thus they are to spoil the Egyptians, and so find material for the preparation of what will be required for the worship of God. For out of the things which the sons of Israel spoiled the Egyptians the furniture of the Holy of Holies was made, the ark with its cover, and the cherubim and the mercy-seat.[211]

The Gospels, I suggest, exemplify this spirit—they are like *spolia*.[212] We find pieces of Hebrew Scripture, Jewish martyrdom tradition, and Greco-Roman biography, but recontextualized and unified in a unique person and genre.

Jesus invites this balance: "every scribe who has been trained for the Kingdom of the heavens is like a master of the household, who casts out of his treasure box things new and old" (Matt 13:52).

The Evangelists

The composers of the Gospels are called "evangelists" (εὐαγγελιστής). Tradition unanimously associates Matthew, Mark, Luke, and John with their respective Gospels. Irenaeus offers the earliest summation of all four:

> Matthew published a Gospel in writing also among the Hebrews in their own tongue, while Peter and Paul were preaching the Gospel and founding the church in Rome. But after their departure Mark, the disciple and interpreter of Peter—he also transmitted to us in writing the things which Peter used to preach. And Luke too, the follower of Paul, set down in a book the Gospel which Paul used to preach. Afterwards John, the disciple of the Lord, the same who leant back on his breast—he too set forth the Gospel, while residing at Ephesus in Asia.[213]

However, none of the Gospels explicitly identify their authors. Traditioning is often a communal activity; it is possible that anonymous disciples contributed to the final form of the Gospels (see John 21:24). However, Luke and John emphasize the importance of eyewitness testimony; it is unlikely

211. Cited in Grafton and Williams, *Christianity and the Transformation of the Book*, 24.

212. See Larsen, *Gospel of John as Genre Mosaic.*

213. *Haer.* 3.1.1 (translation from Bettenson and Maunder, *Documents*, 29–30).

that anonymous gospels would become authoritative, especially in light of the internecine conflict that is evident in the New Testament. There would need to be popularly recognized voices behind the Gospels. Some doubt the traditional attributions because the evangelists were not elites with adequate rhetorical training.[214] But we find similar prowess among artisans and tradesmen of the period.[215] They also may have used scribes (language professionals) for their final written drafts. When Scripture was read in the Jewish synagogue, it was often prefaced by their title or name "as verification of their authenticity and authority."[216] Since the church originated in this context, it is reasonable to presume Christians adopted the practice.

Introducing Matthew

Matthew introduces the four Gospels and the entire New Testament. The opening genealogy, which rehearses God's salvation history with Israel, bridges the testaments. It is the second longest Gospel (c. 18,345 words, 969 verses).[217]

Author

Our earliest title, *According to Matthew* (κατα μαθθαιον), attributes the Gospel to a certain Matthew.[218] Tradents, those who hand down tradition, unanimously identify him with the repentant tax collector made apostle by Jesus Christ (10:3).[219] Mark offers this anecdote: "And going along, he saw Levi, the son of Alphaeus, sitting at the tax office and says to him: 'Follow me!' And getting up, he followed him" (2:14). This is the only scene in the Gospels that uniquely mentions the apostle. No other book is attributed to him in the New Testament. Our biographical material is therefore limited. "Levi, the son of Alphaeus" may translate a Hebrew or Aramaic patronymic, a name derived from one's father, *Levi ben* (or *bar*) *Alphaeus* (see Matt 16:17). Levi was a common name in Palestine. The fuller identification distinguished

214. For a skeptical view, see Renan's comment on John (*Life of Jesus*, 14).

215. Alexander, *Preface to Luke's Gospel*, 176–84.

216. Edwards, *Gospel According to Luke*, 4.

217. Textual variants lead to slightly different counts.

218. The title occurs in the subscription in Vat. We find the same inscription in א.

219. Tertullian praises the truthfulness of his Gospel because he was a companion of the Lord (*On the Incarnation* 22). Unfortunately, whatever the Muratorian Fragment (or Canon) would have related about Matthew is lost. But there is no reason to assume it conveyed an alternative tradition.

him in a crowd.[220] The little story is paradoxical. The name Levi suggests a priestly ancestry.[221] If so, he would have been at the core of Judaism. But tax collection was a broadly despised profession, placing him at the margin—if not outside—of the faith. He is the paradigmatic sinner, Jesus's focus: "he will save his people from their sins" (Matt 1:21).

Matthew retells Mark's story: "And going along from there, Jesus saw a human being sitting at the tax office, who is called Matthew. And he says to him: 'Follow me.' And rising, he followed him" (9:9). The versions are nearly identical, except for the name of the would-be apostle, which suggests the names refer to the same person, a not uncommon phenomenon in the early church. The apostle Peter was known by the names Simon and Kephas. Paul had the birth name Saul. Perhaps Jesus renamed Levi Matthew, which means "gift of Yahweh."

Matthew is also mentioned in the apostolic lists (Matt 10:2–4; Mark 3:13–19; Luke 6:12–16; Acts 1:13–14). He is one of the Twelve, but not part of the "inner circle" of Peter, James, and John, who saw the Transfiguration and were closer to the Lord's suffering in Gethsemane. This adds verisimilitude to the claim: if the church wanted to invent an apostolic authority behind their preferred Gospel, presumably they would attach a more prominent name. Nevertheless, Matthew was an eyewitness of Jesus's historical ministry, including some of the resurrection appearances, and would have been present at the Great Commission. His memories of Jesus must have been precious to the early church. However, it does not necessarily follow that the primary source of the Gospel wrote it down. Like Peter and Paul, he may have used the services of scribes.

Matthew's Gospel focuses on the two primary goals of Jewish scribal activity: "First, they had to copy the books of Scripture as exactly as possible, with care for every detail . . . But second, they needed to make the text of Scripture adaptable and relevant to the contemporary situation."[222] Matthew offers two Jesus sayings that do not occur in the other Gospels:

> "Do not think that I came to abolish the Law or the Prophets! I did not come to abolish, but to fulfill. For amen I say to you: until the heaven and the earth pass away, under no circumstances shall one *yod* or one *vav* pass away from the Law until all things happen." (5:17–18)[223]

220. James, another apostle, also had a father named Alphaeus, but was probably a different man (see Mark 3:18; Matt 10:3).

221. The Hebrew etymology is uncertain: "joining" or "priest."

222. Crawford, *Rewriting Scripture*, 3.

223. Luke has a similar saying: "But it is easier for heaven and earth to pass away

> "Have you understood all these things? They say to him, "Yes." And he said to them: "For this (reason), every scribe who has been trained for the Kingdom of the heavens is like a master of the household, who casts out of his treasure box things new and old." (13:51–52)

We find this balance—a firm grasp on the old while embracing the new covenant reality—throughout Matthew's Gospel, which is especially interested in the fulfillment of Scripture.

Papias, an early second century bishop in Asia Minor (Hierapolis), passes on this tradition from the apostle John: "So Matthew arranged the sayings [of the Lord] in the Hebrew language. And each person interpreted [or translated] them as he was able."[224] Papias may refer to oral or written tradition. Orators (preachers) arranged material, as did writers for publication. However, that Matthew first wrote his Gospel in Hebrew (or Aramaic) was broadly held in the early church.[225] Jerome (c. 347–420) writes:

> Matthew, also called Levi, apostle and former publican, composed a gospel of Christ at first published in Judea in Hebrew for the sake of those of the circumcision who believed, but this was afterwards translated into Greek, though by what author is uncertain. The Hebrew itself has been preserved until the present day in the library at Caesarea which Pamphilus so diligently gathered. I have also had the opportunity of having the volume described to me by the Nazarenes of Beroea, a city of Syria, who use it. In this it is to be noted that wherever the Evangelist, whether on his own account or in the person of our Lord the Savior quotes the testimony of the Old Testament he does not follow the authority of the translators of the Septuagint but the Hebrew. Wherefore these two forms exist *Out of Egypt have I called my son*, and *for he shall be called a Nazarene*.[226]

A version of Matthew in Hebrew is preserved in a polemical treatise by Shem Tob ben-Isaac ben-Shaprut (Ibn Shaprut), a Jewish physician.[227] The very late date of the treatise (fourteenth century) should give us pause. Elements also seem to depend on a Latin translation.[228] Yet Craig Evans notes, "Shem Tob may actually preserve an independent textual tradition

than for one *vav* from the Law to fall away" (16:17).

224. Cited in Eusebius, *Hist. eccl.* 3.39.16.

225. Irenaeus of Lyon, *Haer.* 3.1.1; Origen, cited in Eusebius, *Hist. eccl.* 6.25.4.

226. *Vir. ill.* 3 (*NPNF*2 3:362, slightly updated).

227. For the text, see Howard, *Hebrew Gospel of Matthew*.

228. See William Horbury's appendix in Davies and Allison, *Matthew*, 3:729.

of Matthew, possibly related to the 'Gospel in Hebrew letters' (in Papias)."[229] It is remarkable to consider that Matthew's original words are preserved only in a polemical treatise against Christianity. But, with the exception of Jerome and Origen, few Christians took the time to learn Hebrew until the Renaissance. After Matthew had been translated (and apparently edited) into Greek, which must have taken place even before Papias's comment, there would have been little use for the Hebrew original. Josephus originally composed *Jewish War* in Aramaic to be translated into Greek. Perhaps Matthew composed in his first language with the intent that its final form would be in Greek.

Date

Irenaeus claims Matthew wrote his Gospel while Paul and Peter were still alive—in the fifth and sixth decades of the first century (*Haer.* 3.1.1). Paul appeals to Matthew as Scripture, although his citation of Jesus echoes Luke's wording as well (1 Tim 5:18; Luke 10:7/Matt 10:10). Peter appropriates Matthew's version of the Transfiguration in his second letter.[230] James, which was probably written around that time, appeals to teaching that is found in the Sermon on the Mount. Some Jesus sayings presuppose the temple, which was destroyed in AD 70 (5:23; 23:16–21, 23).[231] This presumably reflects Matthew's memory of what Jesus said around AD 30 and does not necessarily date the entire Gospel, but the teaching would be less relevant to the first readers after the temple's destruction. Although we cannot be certain, the evidence supports Irenaeus's claim. Matthew must have been written and circulated by the time Ignatius of Antioch (c. 35–c. 110) describes Jesus with a line unique to it: "baptized by John in order that all righteousness might be fulfilled by him" (*Smyrn.* 1:1; see Matt 3:15).[232]

229. Skarsaune and Hvalvik, *Jewish Believers in Jesus*, 267. The Hebrew text is not dependent on the Vulgate or Byzantine Greek (268).

230. However, critical scholars view 1 Timothy and 2 Peter as pseudonymous.

231. Of course, the final editor(s) may have appropriated earlier tradition, but this is not demonstrable. If Matthew is providing a discipleship manual, why, if we assume he is writing after the destruction of the temple, does he include teaching that is no longer applicable?

232. Holmes, *Apostolic Fathers*, 249. For allusions, see his letters to the Ephesians (14.2; 17.1) and Philadelphians (3.1), which can be read in Holmes, *Apostolic Fathers*, 195, 197, 239.

Provenance

We do not know where Matthew was first published. The Gospel probably surfaced in Antioch on the Orontes in Syria, although Galilee is another possibility.[233] Matthew uniquely mentions the early impact of Christ's healing ministry in Syria: "And his fame went out into all of Syria, and they [the Syrians] brought to him all who have it bad with various diseases and who are oppressed with sufferings" (4:24), perhaps to include his readers. Matthew bears some relationship with the Didache, which probably has a Syrian origin.[234] The rabbis considered the region to be part of the land of Israel.[235] Ignatius, a bishop of Antioch, relies heavily on the Gospel. The Syrian Orthodox Church claims Peter as their founder whose leadership is emphasized in Matthew (see 16:13–20 in contrast with Mark 8:27–30). Paul assumes Peter's influence there in Galatians.

Unique Contribution

Matthew imitates the style of ancient Israelite Scripture, which suggests he intended this work to be read with the Law and Prophets.[236] His style and diction are similar to retellings and expansions of Scripture in the Second Temple period.[237]

We may also describe his Gospel as a discipleship manual. Matthew's Jesus instructs his followers to make disciples of all people groups (28:19). The Sermon on the Mount is transcultural, relaxing purity and sacrificial law to reach and include non-Jewish disciples (5:8; 6:1–18). Another discourse delegitimizes the competing mission of the Pharisees (ch. 23) while promising a judgment for all people based on their treatment of Jesus's missionary disciples (25:31–46).

233. A decade after the destruction of the temple (AD 80), many Pharisaic rabbis relocated to Usha in Galilee. There seems to have been hostility between the two surviving expressions of Second Temple Judaism. The disciples of both traditions were competing for followers in the same region. But this theory is tied somewhat to a later dating of the Gospel.

234. The Didache is the *Grundtext* or "original text" (c. 100) of three Syrian church manuals: *Apostolic Tradition* (c. 215), *Didascalia Apostolorum* (early third century), and *Apostolic Constitutions* (late fourth century).

235. Freyne, *Jesus*, 76. Josephus similarly describes the mixing of the two peoples because of the proximity of their countries (*J.W.* 7.43).

236. Deines, "Did Matthew Know He Was Writing Scripture?," 101–9.

237. Matthew is especially close to the author of Prayer of Azariah and the Song of the Three Young Men in Additions to Daniel in the Apocrypha.

Structure

Matthew generally follows Mark's narrative, but begins and ends his own way. (We suggest that Matthew appropriated Mark's Gospel below.) He adds a birth story (chs. 1–2) and accounts of guarding Jesus's tomb (27:62–66), bribing the guards (28:11–14), and the Great Commission (28:16–20). Matthew also supplements Mark with five lengthy discourses:

1. The Sermon on the Mount (chs. 5–7)
2. Mission Instructions to the Twelve (ch. 10)
3. Parables of the Kingdom (ch. 13)
4. Discipleship and Discipline (ch. 18)
5. Eschatology (chs. 24–25)

Respectively, they emphasize the Kingdom's foundation, mission, mystery, family, and destiny.[238] Benjamin Bacon suggests Matthew organized his Gospel into a new Pentateuch, a pattern we find in the five books of the Psalter.[239] There are also two major turning points in the story, signaled by the repetition of "from that time Jesus began . . ." (4:17; 16:21), allowing a three-part outline: the Person (1:1—4:16), Proclamation (4:17—16:20), and Passion of Jesus Messiah, along with his resurrection (16:21—28:20).[240] There are many other proposals.[241] Complex narratives, like we have with the Gospels, resist overly precise structural analysis.

Matthew bookends his Gospel with God's presence. In fulfillment of Isaiah's prophecy, Jesus is to be called "Immanuel," which, in Hebrew, means "God is with us" (1:23).[242] Yet he is never called Immanuel in the narrative. But the resurrected Jesus closes the Gospel with "*I am with you* every day until the completion of the age" (28:20). This motif is in Matthew's addition to Mark, which suggests a special importance to the evangelist. (When Marcel Proust conceived the structure of his masterpiece, *Remembrance of Things Past,* he wrote the first and final chapters together.) He emphasizes

238. Smith, "Literary Evidence of Fivefold Structure in the Gospel of Matthew," 549. With slight variation, each discourse ends with the comment "When Jesus finished all these sayings" (7:28; 11:1; 13:53; 19:1; 26:1).

239. Bacon, "Five Books of Moses against the Jews," 56–66.

240. Kingsbury, *Matthew,* 1–24. But see 26:16.

241. David Bauer notes, "There is presently no consensus regarding the structure of Matthew's Gospel" (*Structure of Matthew's Gospel,* 135).

242. The Great Isaiah Scroll (1QIsaa) actually reads "his name will be called Immanuel" (Embry et al., *Early Jewish Literature,* 1:118).

our subjective response to God's work of salvation in Christ. Discipleship brings us to Jesus, who brings God to us.

Purpose

Matthew may write, in part, to persuade a skeptical Jewish audience, possibly a nearby synagogue. He often refers to "their synagogue" (4:23; 9:35; 9:35; 10:17; 12:9; 13:53). Rebuking the Pharisees and scribes, Jesus mentions "your synagogues" (23:34). Presumably, they rejected the historical claims of the virginal conception and resurrection, which Matthew rebuts at the beginning and ending of his Gospel.

This raises an important yet difficult question: How did Matthew understand the relationship between the synagogue and church? On the one hand, Jesus acknowledges the validity of Mosaic teaching in the synagogue: "On the seat of Moses have sat the scribes and the Pharisees. So everything they might preach to you practice and keep" (23:2–3). He says: "Do not think that I came to abolish the Law or the Prophets!" (5:17). But in both places, Jesus criticizes the leaders of the synagogue for hypocrisy; throughout the Gospel, he rejects their interpretation of Scripture: "Have you not read?" (12:3, 5; 19:4; 21:16, 42). Matthew presents Israel suffering in exile because of their sins (1:11–12). Jesus is firstly a Jewish Messiah, who came to save "the lost sheep of the house of Israel" (10:6). He describes this salvation as a new exodus and return from exile. The story of the exodus is repeated and completed in Jesus, who comes out of Egypt and is tempted in the wilderness. Where Israel failed he overcomes. In fulfillment of Isaiah's prophecy, Jesus dies in the place of his people, but is resurrected after three days, taking all the faithful into God's presence. But Matthew seems to be writing in a context where many, if not most, Jews had followed the Pharisees and not Jesus. They are illegitimate and under God's condemnation: "But woe to you, scribes and Pharisees, hypocrites! For you shut the kingdom of the heavens before people. For *you* do not enter. Nor do you allow to enter those who are [otherwise] entering. Woe to you, scribes and Pharisees, hypocrites! For you travel over sea and dry land to make one proselyte. And when he becomes (one), you make him twice as much a son of Gehenna than you" (23:13–15; see also vv. 29–35). Anticipating his rejection and execution, Jesus says, "the kingdom of God will be taken away from you and will be given to a nation producing the fruits of it" (21:43). In another controversial passage, Matthew has "all the people" say to Pilate, the executioner of Jesus, "His blood be on us and on our children" (27:25). The request is ironic because the blood—that is, the life of Jesus—is God's means of forgiveness for sin. Jesus sacrifices his life in the place of his people, but the same "righteous blood" also condemns the unrepentant. Matthew does not appear to be motivated by anti-Semitism, but, like Paul, a heartfelt desire for his own people to see Jesus as Messiah and be saved (see Rom 9:1–5).

Reception

Matthew came first in the codices before settling at the head of the canon, and is the most cited of the four Gospels in the early church.[243] Matthew has Christ's definitive sermon on discipleship—what Augustine famously titled *De sermone Domine in monte* ("The Sermon on the Mount"); within that discourse was the most cited saying in the second century: "love your enemies."[244] We find echoes of the sermon in several New Testament letters (1 Corinthians, James, 1 Peter) and early Christian writings (the Didache), suggesting it was fundamental to conversion. Ignatius of Antioch appropriates Matthew on the way to martyrdom in Rome. This suggests it was known to his readers in Asia Minor. Papias, as we noted, cites John's discussion of Matthew in the region. This is especially important because one apostle is affirming the work of another. Polycarp (c. 70–c. 160) uses Matthew.[245] Justin Martyr (c. 110–165), who came from Ephesus, uses Matthew as part of a harmony in Rome. So Matthew is appropriated throughout the Mediterranean before Marcion's rejection (c. 110–160). The papyri evidence dissemination in Egypt before the mid-third century.

Introducing Mark

The second canonical Gospel is Mark, the shortest (approx.. 11, 304 words). Matthew and Luke may have seen it as unfinished.[246]

Author

According to the early form critics, Paul Wendland and Karl Ludwig Schmidt, the second Gospel is largely the product of anonymous contributors in the early church, but evidence is overwhelming to the contrary.[247]

243. See Massaux, *Influence of the Gospel of Saint Matthew.*

244. Swartley, *Love of Enemy and Nonretaliation in the New Testament*, 8.

245. Polycarp, *Phil.* 2.3; 7.2; 12.3.

246. Becker, "Reception of 'Mark' in the 1st and 2nd Centuries C.E.," 15–36.

247. Schmidt, *Place of the Gospels*; Wendland, *Die hellenistisch-römische Kultur.*

We find *kata Markan* "According to Mark" at the head of the Gospel in our early Alexandrian codices, Sinaiticus and Vaticanus, which are dated to the mid-fourth century.[248] There are no alternative names in the manuscript tradition. Clement of Alexandria and Origen know the title. Presumably, they represent a common assumption of Egyptian Christians in the second century that a certain Mark is the author of the Gospel. African Christians remember Peter being married to the cousin of Mark's father, Aristopolus. There is a pervasive tradition in the early church that Mark appropriated Peter's memories of Jesus for his Gospel. Eusebius quotes Papias, a representative of Asia Minor:

> Mark, having become Peter's interpreter [or translator], wrote accurately what he remembered, although not in an order, the things either said or done by the Lord [or Christ]. For he neither heard the Lord nor followed him [as a disciple], but later, as I said, Peter, who would teach in anecdotes [or according to needs], but not [with the thought] of producing an orderly arrangement of the sayings of the Lord, so that Mark did not err in this manner, having written down some of the things as he recalled [them]. For he made [it a] singular concern not to omit what he heard or to falsify anything in them. (Cited in Eusebius, *Hist. eccl.* 3.39.15)[249]

The bishop is probably invoking the opinion of John, a contemporary of Mark.[250] He and Polycarp, bishop of Smyrna, were "hearers" of the apostle.[251] Eusebius also cites from Clement of Alexandria:

> And so a great light of piety shone upon the minds of the hearers of Peter that they were not satisfied with merely a single hearing or with unwritten teaching of the divine gospel, but with all sorts of entreaties they besought Mark, who was a follower

James Crossley still holds this view (*Date of Mark's Gospel*, 17).

248. The beginning and ending of Mark do not survive in the Alexandrian papyri, where a title may have been. Something like "According to Mark" was probably attached to the Gospel by the end of the first century. A title originally would have been unnecessary for a Gospel because the author would have been well-known to his intended readership. But as soon as his work was copied, sent to other churches and put in an archive, a title became necessary to distinguish it from other works.

249. For the translation "anecdotes," see Renan, *Life of Jesus*, 10.

250. Streeter, *Four Gospels*, 18–19. It is ambiguous if Papias intends to distinguish the Elder from John, the son of Zebedee, mentioned in the previous list. Eusebius cites Papias to show that two different men are meant. He may be attempting to marginalize the book of Revelation, which he attributes to the Elder.

251. Eusebius, *Chron.*

> of Peter and whose gospel is extant, to leave behind with them in writing a record of the teaching passed on to them orally; and they did not cease until they had prevailed upon the man and so became responsible for the Scripture for reading in the churches. (*Hist. eccl.* 2.15.1)[252]

Justin Martyr, a Christian philosopher in Rome, describes the second Gospel as "memories" of Peter.[253] The anonymous author of the Anti-Marcionite Prologue (c. 160–80) notes: ". . . Mark declared, who is called 'stump-fingered' because he had short fingers in comparison to the size of the rest of his body. He was Peter's interpreter. After the death/departure (*post excessionem*) of Peter himself he wrote down (*descripsit*) this same gospel in the regions of Italy."[254] Irenaeus notes, "Peter and Paul proclaimed the gospel in Rome and founded the community. After their death/departure (*exodus*), Mark, the disciple and interpreter of Peter, handed on his preaching to us in written form."[255]

Mark did not follow Jesus as a disciple, but may have been the young man who flees naked at Christ's arrest. Tradition claims the Last Supper and Pentecost took place in his mother's home (Acts 12:12). He joined Paul and Barnabas, his uncle, for their first mission, but turned back (Acts 13:13; Col 4:10). Although Barnabas wanted to give Mark another chance, Paul refused, leading to the end of their partnership (15:37–41). He then went with Barnabas to Cyprus. At some point, he joined Peter, whose mission overlapped with Paul's, perhaps leading to a reconciliation in Rome (see 1 Pet 5:13). Paul writes: "After picking up Mark, bring him with you, because he is useful to

252. Eusebius goes on to quote Clement: "When Peter had preached the Word publicly at Rome, and by the Spirit proclaimed the gospel, those present, who were numerous, urged Mark, inasmuch as he had followed him for a long time and remembered what had been spoken, to write down what was said; and after he had done this he gave it out to those who requested it. When Peter discovered this, he neither energetically prevented it not urged it on" (*Hist. eccl.* 6.14.5–7 [Lake, LCL]). He also cites Origen: "And second, that according to Mark, who did as Peter instructed him, whom he also acknowledged as a son in the catholic epistle" (6.25.5). See also Clement of Alexandria, *Adumbrationes ad 1 Peter* 5.13.

253. Justin Martyr describes the Gospels as "the memories of the apostles." The phrase occurs twice in his *First Apology* (66; 67) and thirteen times in *Dialogue with Trypho*. In the *Dialogue*, he mentions "the memories of the apostles and their successors" (103). By way of exception, he mentions "his memories" (106) referring to Peter. Justin reveals he has the second Gospel in mind when he refers to the sons of Zebedee as "Boanerges, which is 'sons of thunder'"—a clear allusion to Mark (3:16).

254. Cited in Hengel, *Studies in the Gospel of Mark*, 3.

255. Irenaeus of Lyon, *Haer.* 3.1.1 (*ANF* 1:414).

me for righteousness" (2 Tim 1:11). According to tradition, Mark eventually went to Africa to establish churches in Alexandria.[256]

Date

Mark is often dated between 60–75—that is, before or after the temple's destruction (AD 70).[257] But a more reliable date is around Peter's martyrdom. According to Jerome, Peter came to Rome in 42, "the second year of Claudius."[258] We have reliable tradition that Peter and Paul died during the Neronian persecution (64).[259] Jerome claims Mark was martyred in the eighth year of Nero (c. 62).[260]

Provenance

Jerome notes that Mark wrote down Peter's memories for Christians in Rome, which explains the many Latinisms in the Gospel.[261] It also correlates with the overlapping emphases and language we find in Paul's letter to the Romans. Michael Patella notes:

> Mark's Gospel presents Jesus as the Son of God, who battles Satan and reclaims and redeems creation from him. This ongoing battle is evident within the earthly ministry and reaches its climax and decisive victory in the passion, death, and resurrection. Jesus conquers death, and disciples who enter into his life through baptism share in his triumph and gain eternal life. Insofar as Mark evidences this participationist theology of Jesus's life, we can see a strong Pauline character to Mark's Gospel.[262]

256. See Oden, *African Memory of Mark*, 34–35, 193, 209.

257. See Crossley, *Date of Mark's Gospel*, 61–62.

258. *Vir. ill.* 1 (*NPNF*2 3:361).

259. 1 Clem. 5:1–7; 6:1; Ignatius, *Romans* 4.2–3; Irenaeus of Lyon, *Haer.* 3.3.2; Eusebius, *Hist. eccl* 3.1.3.

260. Jerome, *Vir. ill.* 8. For more, see the *Martyrium Marci.*

261. For example, at 12:42, Mark adds the following parenthesis: "And a destitute widow, coming, cast two *lepta* (which is [the equivalent of] a *quadrans*)." The Roman *quadrans* only circulated in the western part of the Roman Empire. For a Roman provenance, see Streeter, *Four Gospels*, 12 and the whole study by Incigneri, *Gospel to the Romans*. It has been argued that Mark was written in Galilee either during the Jewish Revolt or sometime afterward. It is more likely that Mark has appropriated tradition that began its life in Galilee, that is, the anecdotal memories of Peter. Still others propose a Syrian provenance.

262. Patella, *Lord of the Cosmos*, 1. See the collections of essays in Bird and Willitts,

There are three key moments in Mark's Gospel: Baptism, Transfiguration, and Crucifixion—all of which must be shared by the disciple in Christ.

Unique Contribution

Mark employs irony throughout his presentation, telling his story at two levels: the surface that could be understood by anyone, but also a deeper message for disciples (see 4:10–12).[263] Mark's Jesus wants us to see beyond appearances—originally, the wealth and power of the Roman Empire—so that we might pick up our crosses and follow him.[264]

Structure

Mark's Gospel is chiastic with Jesus's first passion prediction (8:31–33) at the center, surrounded by Peter's confession (8:27–30) and the Transfiguration (9:1–10).[265] Immediately before this pivot is a strange story, unique to Mark, about a man who is initially only partially healed from his blindness (8:22–26). Even Peter, who makes the right confession and sees the deity of Christ, cannot grasp the paradoxical reality that there is no glory before the cross: "Get behind me, Satan!" (8:33).[266]

Purpose

The chiasm suggests that Mark is concerned about the ultimate identity of Jesus Christ. The Gospel begins with the Father's acknowledgment of the Son at his baptism, which is acknowledged at the end in the centurion's confession (15:39).

Francis Maloney rightly calls attention to Mark's "good news of human failure."[267] If Mark published his Gospel during the Neronian persecution

Paul and the Gospels.

263. van Oyen, *Reading the Gospel of Mark as a Novel*, 7.

264. Raymond Brown notes, "Readers can learn much about Jesus from the traditions of his parables and mighty deeds; but unless that is intimately combined with the picture of his victory through suffering, they cannot understand him or the vocation of his followers" (*Introduction to the New Testament*, 126).

265. Scott, "Chiastic Structure," 17–26.

266. Saban, *Gospel According to Mark*, 157.

267. Maloney, *Mark*, 191.

in Rome, he is responding to a remarkable exigence. The Roman historian Tacitus notes:

> But all the endeavors of men, all the emperor's generous patronage and the propitiation of the gods, did not suffice to allay the scandal or banish the belief that the fire had been ordered. And so, to get rid of this rumor, Nero set up (*subdidit,* "fraudulent substitution") as the culprits and punished with the utmost refinement of cruelty a class hated for their abominations [e.g. infanticide, cannibalism, incest; see Athenagoras, *Legatio pro Christianis,* iii], who are commonly called Christians. Christus, from whom their name is derived, was executed at the hands of the procurator Pontius Pilate in the reign of Tiberius. Checked for the moment, this pernicious superstition again broke out, not only in Judea, the source of the evil, but even in Rome, that receptacle for everything that is sordid and degrading from every quarter of the globe, which there finds a following. Accordingly, arrest was first made of those who confessed [to being Christians]; then, on their evidence, an immense multitude was convicted, not so much on the charge of arson as because of hatred of the human race. Besides being put to death they were made to serve as objects of amusement; they were clothed in the hides of beasts and torn to death by dogs; others were crucified, others set on fire to serve to illuminate the night when daylight failed. Nero had thrown open his grounds for the display, and was putting on a show in the circus, where he mingled with the people in the dress of a charioteer or drove about in his chariot. All this gave rise to a feeling of pity, even towards men whose guilt merited the most exemplary punishment; for it was felt that they were being destroyed not for the public good but to gratify the cruelty of an individual. (*Annals,* 15.44)[268]

Another historian Suetonius writes, "punishment was inflicted [by Nero] on the Christians, a set of men adhering to a novel and mischievous superstition" (*Nero* 16).[269] The women who flee at the end of his Gospel may represent a beleaguered community, who had just lost their leaders, Peter and Paul, and needed an exhortation to faithfulness.[270]

268. Cited in Bettenson and Maunder, *Documents,* 1–2.

269. Cited in Bettenson and Maunder, *Documents,* 2.

270. Strauss, *Mark,* 747.

Reception

Mark's Gospel was not as widely discussed in early Christian literature.[271] After reading Matthew, there was little left in Mark that was unique. Origen wrote commentaries on all the Gospels, but Mark. Augustine famously describes Mark as "the abbreviator and follower of Matthew," a pronouncement that furthered its neglect.[272] In the fifth century, Victor of Antioch "arranged in an orderly commentary the scattered explanations of Mark by the teachers of the church"—Origen, Titus of Bostra, Theodore of Mopsuestia, Chrysostom, and Cyril of Alexandria—what came to be called a *catena*.[273] The seventh-century *Commentarius in Evangelium secundum Markum* is the first formal, full-length commentary on Mark.[274] The author observes that Mark "tells the same story as Matthew does."[275] The Venerable Bede (c. 672–735) wrote a commentary—much of which Aquinas appropriated in his *Catena*. Only sparse commentaries followed. However, after the discovery in the nineteenth century that Mark was the earliest Gospel, studies have exploded.

Introducing Luke

Luke is the first of a two-part work, often referred to as Luke-Acts.[276] Luke's Gospel is approximately 19,404 words long; Acts, 18,374—respectively, the longest and second longest books in the New Testament. Luke, not Paul, is the largest contributor to the New Testament—nearly 30 percent.[277] The author makes bridges between Jesus and Paul, the apostles and the early church, then and now.

271. Streeter notes: "It is the Gospel least valued, least quoted, and most rarely commented on by the Fathers" (*Four Gospels*, 10).

272. *Marcus Matthaei tanquam breviator et pedisequus.*

273. The citation is from the preface in Cahill, "First Markan Commentary," 266.

274. See Cahill, *First Commentary on Mark* (PL 30:589–644).

275. Cahill, "First Markan Commentary," 264. Euthymius Zigabenus, a twelfth-century monk of Constantinople, makes a similar point: "the second gospel is in close agreement with the first, excepting where the first is fuller" (cited in Lightfoot, *Gospel of St. Mark*, 2).

276. This hyphenated title appears to begin with Benjamin Bacon. Patricia Walters challenges the single author hypothesis (*Assumed Authorial Unity of Luke and Acts*), but I find Robert Tannehill's *The Narrative Unity of Luke-Acts* compelling.

277. Paul is often assumed to be the largest contributor to the New Testament. But 28 percent is Luke's contribution in contrast to 24 percent from the apostle.

Author

Irenaeus (d. c. 195), writing in Lyon (France), identifies the author of the third Gospel as *Loukas* (Λουκᾶς), "the companion of Paul."[278] The association is repeated by Origen, who knew tradition from Egypt, where Papyrus Bodmer 14 was discovered, which uses the inscription "Gospel According to Luke."[279] There are no alternative claims for authorship in subsequent tradition until the modern period. In an environment where later works were falsely attributed to apostles, this modest claim rings true.

Paul mentions Luke three times in his letters. He is "the beloved physician" (Col 4:14) and "fellow worker" in spreading the gospel (Phlm 24). Only Luke is with him at the end of his life (2 Tim 4:11). In Acts, Luke implies their paths crossed in Syria. Paul and Barnabas come to Antioch before he begins to include himself in the narrative—the so-called "we passages."[280] From that point, Luke writes from experience. He acknowledges not being an eye-witness of Jesus's historical ministry, but relied on those who were (Luke 1:2).

Luke might have been a member of the ethnically diverse church in Antioch before travelling with Paul. His two books emphasize Gentile inclusion in God's mission. He may have been a Gentile, although this is uncertain. Michael Card suggests Luke was a slave.[281] Slaves were often given shortened forms of their master's name; Λουκᾶς is short for *Lucius*.

Date

Luke probably appropriates the other Gospels as sources, and therefore is the last to publish. His presentation of the temple's destruction is the most vivid and specific (21:20–24), suggesting he writes after AD 70. However, it is unclear if Paul has been executed (c. AD 64) by the time of Act's publication. The *Anti-Marcionite Prologue to the Gospel of Luke*, dated from the second to the fourth century, claims Luke "died at the age of eighty-four years." If Luke

278. Irenaeus of Lyon, *Haer.* 3.1.1; 3.14.1.

279. For Origen, see Eusebius, *Hist. eccl.* 6.25.6, 14. The manuscript, which can be dated to around 200, was donated to the Vatican Apostolic Library in 2006. It contains the earliest ending of Luke and is also the oldest extant manuscript that contains two Gospels.

280. Beginning at 16:10–17; see 20:5–21:18; 27:1–28:16. The masculine participle at 1:3 presumes the author is male. The voice is mistakenly classified as the narrator, a literary term. The purported author addresses Theophilus in the first person at the beginning of the works.

281. Card, *Gospel of Amazement*, 17.

joined Paul's team as a young man, he may have composed Luke later in life. Andrew Gregory notes: "I have found no external evidence to demonstrate that *Luke* was used before the middle of the second century."[282] This is an argument from silence, but is consistent with our scenario.

Provenance

It is not clear where Luke published his Gospel. His narrative ends in Rome. Paul mentions Luke's presence towards the end of his life (2 Tim 4:11). If Luke appropriates Mark's Gospel, it could be further evidence of a Roman provenance. However, tradition locates the Gospel in Achaea (Greece).[283]

Unique Contribution

Luke is the most socially aware of the Gospels. Even before the Nazareth Manifesto (Luke 4:16–30), Luke foregrounds poverty in his presentation of the gospel. Mary and Joseph are poor, offering "a pair of turtledoves or two young pigeons" when presenting the infant Jesus at the temple (2:24). John the Baptist requires the sharing of an extra tunic and food (3:11). In Acts, he emphasizes the generosity of the first church (2:42–47; 4:32–37). Perhaps editing Matthew, Luke has Jesus pronounce blessing on the "destitute" and woe against the rich (6:20, 24). The evangelist has two unique parables that feature a selfish, wealthy man under God's judgment: the Rich Fool (12:13–21) and the Rich Man and Lazarus (16:19–31). In these cases, the rich are not condemned simply because they are rich, but for the missed opportunity to bless others with their wealth.

Luke also takes a special interest in women.[284] "Among all the writers of the New Testament," Justo González notes, "it is Luke who includes the most frequent references to women and their place in the history of salvation."[285] Unlike Matthew, he tells the Nativity from Mary's perspective, including the Magnificat (1:46–55) and features the prophetess Anna (2:36–38).[286] In Acts, he emphasizes that both men and women will prophesy (1:14; 2:17–18). The raising of a widow's son (7:11–17), the gratitude of a forgiven, sinful woman (7:36–50), and the healing of a woman with a disabling spirit (13:10–17) only

282. Gregory, *Reception of Luke and Acts*, 353.

283. Streeter, *Four Gospels*, 12.

284. Witherington, *Women in the Earliest Churches*, 128–57.

285. González, *Story Luke Tells*, 45.

286. However, only Matthew includes women in his genealogy.

occur in the third Gospel, along with the mention of female financial supporters (8:1–3). John also mentions Martha and Mary, but the sisters receive a special anecdote that inaugurated the tension in the Christian tradition between the active and contemplative life (10:38–42). He also relates two unique parables that feature women: the Lost Coin (15:8–10) and Persistent Widow (18:1–8). Jesus offers a special word to lamenting women on the way to the cross (23:27–31). Ben Witherington observes "that Luke will stress again and again that women are the oppressed that Jesus came to liberate."[287] Luke does not include women in the male apostolic circle, but he does present them as full disciples—indeed, Mary is the ideal student sitting at the feat of her master—and sharers in the prophetic ministry of the Holy Spirit, which are sentiments Paul also expressed (Gal 3:28; 1 Cor 11:5).

Structure

Luke is the only evangelist to write a sequel. However, the church separated the books to allow Acts to introduce Paul's letters. Yet Luke originally envisioned them as one work (see Acts 1:1). "Change and development are expected" in Luke's narrative, Robert Tannehill explains, but "unity is maintained because the scenes and characters contribute to a larger story that determines the significance of each part."[288] The big story is God's "controlling purpose" (providence).[289]

Luke may structure his narrative after Psalm 22.[290] The psalm moves from suffering—"they pierced my hands and feet"—to proclamation—"All the ends of the earth will remember and turn to the Lord, and all the families of the peoples will worship before you" (vv. 16, 27). Jesus says, "Thus it stands written: The Christ is to suffer and to rise from those who are dead on the third day" (Luke 24:46). This is the focus of the Gospel. Jesus continues: "And repentance for the forgiveness of sins is to be preached in his name to all the peoples beginning from Jerusalem" (v. 47), the focus of Acts (24:46–47). Of course, this may be a happy, unintended similarity. But it was common to base a sermon or "word of exhortation" on a primary Scripture.[291]

287. Witherington, *Women in the Earliest Churches*, 128.

288. Tannehill, *Narrative Unity*, xiii.

289. Tannehill, *Narrative Unity*, xiii. This is a common interpretation. See, e.g., Cadbury, *Making of Luke-Acts*, 303.

290. Schubert, "Structure and Significance of Luke 24," 173.

291. Luke, who may be the author of Hebrews, does the same in that work with Psalm 110.

We find a geographical chiasm that unites Luke-Acts.[292] A decree goes out from Caesar in Rome at Christ's birth (Luke 2:1); Acts ends with Paul entering Rome "proclaiming the Kingdom of God" (Acts 28:30). Inside this envelope, Jesus ministers to Samaritans (Luke 9:51—10:37); later, the disciples do the same (Acts 8:1–25). At the end of the Gospel, which is the center of Luke's two-volume work, Jesus is executed and resurrected at Jerusalem (Luke 22–24); Jesus sends the disciples from this city: "you will be my witnesses in Jerusalem and in all Judea and Samaria and to the end of the earth" (Acts 1:8).

Purpose

This geographical flow reveals Luke's interest in mission as reconciliation—between Jews, Samaritans, and Gentiles (Romans), rich and poor, and so forth. It is therefore not surprising to find the Parable of the Prodigal Son at the center of his Gospel. At the center of Luke-Acts is the Ascension, which he narrates twice (Luke 24:50–53; Acts 1:6–11). He is the only evangelist to do so. The son of God takes a position of authority over the temple and Roman Empire. Embodying his people, the Son sits as co-regent at the right hand of the Father (see Pss 2 and 110).

Reception

Despite being the largest contributor to the New Testament, his work receives less attention than Matthew, John, and Paul's Letters.[293] Luke is appropriated by later non-canonical gospels, such as the one attributed to the Ebionites and Thomas.[294] Marcion (c. 110–160) infamously edited his own version.[295] Tertullian (c. 155–222) claims he "expunged all the things that oppose his view . . . but retained those things that accord with his opinion" (*Against Marcion* 4.6.2). Although we cannot be sure, he probably chose Luke because of his close relationship to Paul, who, according to the heretic, was the only apostle who understood the gospel. Apparently, he believed Luke had been

292. A chiasm is "an ordered set of inclusios" (Barton, *Reading the Old Testament*, 17). Sometimes, the parallelism is disrupted by a single line that receives the emphasis in the middle, but that is not the case here.

293. Just, *Luke*, xvii.

294. Gregory, *Reception of Luke and Acts*, 294.

295. His version is no longer extant, but is partially preserved in later Christian writings, especially Tertullian's *Adversus Marcionem*, Epiphanius's *Panarion*, and the Pseudo-Origenic *Adamantius*. See Roth, *Text of Marcion's Gospel*.

enlarged and wanted to restore the original edition. He omitted the opening chapters and much of the end, leaving a "torso."[296]

We possess collections of sermons on Luke from Origen, Ambrose of Milan, Cyril of Alexandria, the Venerable Bede, and fragments of Titus of Bostra in the catenae.[297]

Introducing John

John complements the other Gospels with many distinctive passages. It is the second shortest Gospel after Mark (15,635 words).

Author

The Gospel closes by attributing its content to the "witness" (*marturia*, μαρτυρία) of a certain disciple "who wrote these things" (21:24). No name is given, but the claim evokes the beginning of the story when two disciples leave John the Baptist to follow Jesus and become eyewitnesses (1:37). One is Andrew, who goes on to summon Simon Peter, his brother (1:40–42); the other remains unnamed. If the first readers were familiar with the Synoptic tradition, which is likely, this leaves James or John, the sons of Zebedee (Mark 1:16–20 pars.). Herod Agrippa I executed James sometime between AD 37 and 44 (Acts 12:1–5), which is probably too early for him to be the author. John, the son of Zebedee, is the most likely candidate.

Luke may associate the fourth Gospel with John. With Peter, he responds after being arrested: "[Peter:] 'If it is right before God to hear you or God, you judge.' [John:] 'For we cannot stop speaking about what we saw and heard' (γὰρ ἡμεῖς ἃ εἴδαμεν καὶ ἠκούσαμεν μὴ λαλεῖν, Acts 4:19–20). English translations attribute both sayings to Peter. But Paul Anderson notes that the latter has a distinctively Johannine vocabulary.[298] In John's Gospel, the Baptist witnesses: "What he has seen and heard, this he witnesses" (ὃ ἑώρακεν καὶ ἤκουσεν τοῦτο μαρτυρεῖ, John 3:32; see also 1 John 1:3).

Polycarp, whose life overlaps with the apostolic period, associates John with the Gospel, and this becomes a uniform tradition among the early fathers: Theophilus of Antioch, Clement of Alexandria, Irenaeus, Origen,

296. For a different perspective, see Lieu, *Marcion and the Making of a Heretic*.

297. Just, *Luke*, xviii.

298. Anderson, *Fourth Gospel and the Quest for Jesus*, 116–17. There are no quotation marks in our earliest witnesses to the New Testament, so that, without introductory formulas, the extent of a citation must be inferred.

Hippolytus, and Tertullian.[299] The Muratorian Canon, perhaps the oldest list of New Testament books, notes:

> The fourth of the Gospels, that of John, (one) of the disciples. When his fellow-disciples and bishops urged him, he said: Fast with me from today for three days, and what will be revealed to each one let us relate to one another. In the same night it was revealed to Andrew, one of the apostles, that, whilst all were to go over (it), John in his own name should write everything down.[300]

This appears to be a historical commentary on an ambiguous antecedent at the end of the Gospel: the "we" who affirm the testimony (21:24) are "fellow-disciples and bishops," while the unnamed would-be disciple with Andrew at the beginning of the story (1:41) is John.

John may have composed his Gospel orally, like Peter's involvement with Mark, so that a disciple (or scribal group) wrote his memories and interpretations down before or after his death.[301] The epilogue may presuppose his passing (21:21–23).

John, a revered interpreter and witness to the historical Jesus, invites us into their intimate friendship. The epilogue identifies him as "the disciple whom Jesus loved . . . who also reclined at the supper on his chest, and said: "Lord, who is the one who betrays you?," which evokes the first mention of this character (13:23), who also witnesses the crucifixion (19:26–27), the empty tomb (20:1–10), and the resurrected Jesus (21:7, 20)—the most essential historical realities of the gospel (1 Cor 15:3–5).[302] John is not indifferent to history: "the Logos became flesh" in a particular time and place, and he was in a privileged position to understand the significance of these events. But he firstly describes himself in relationship with Jesus, a beloved follower, a love that began in the Father (3:16) and was expressed by the Son on the cross (13:1). The loving Son came from the loving Father, and John, the beloved, was following the Son back to God. The love John enjoyed was

299. Apparently, the Allogoi are the only group to deny Johannine authorship, claiming Cerinthus was behind the Gospel (Wiles, *Spiritual Gospel*, 8).

300. Schneemelcher and Wilson, *New Testament Apocrypha*, 1:34–35. Some have criticized the title for being anachronistic.

301. Brant, *John*, 6. At the end of Romans, we find "I, Tertius, wrote this letter" (16:22). By this, the scribe probably does not take responsibility for the contents but the mechanics of writing. Peter similarly concludes his first letter, "By Silvanus, a faithful brother as I regard him, I have written briefly to you" (5:12).

302. Through Mark, Peter included John and his brother James in the inner circle of disciples who witnessed the raising of Jairus's daughter, the Transfiguration, and Jesus's despair in Gethsemane (Mark 5:37; 9:2; 14:33).

not exclusive, but available to the "world" (*kosmos*, κόσμος) or those presently alienated from God. John reclined on the chest of the Son, who, in turn, knew the Father this way (1:1, 18), and offers this fellowship along the way back to anyone who believes the message (20:31). We too may become beloved, even God's children (John 1:12; 1 John 3:1–2).

Date

Most studies date the fourth Gospel between 80 and 110.[303] Our earliest textual witness to the New Testament, The Rylands Library Papyrus, a fragment of John (18:31–33, 37–8), is dated to the early part of the second century, if not earlier, providing a *terminus ad quem*. Finding a *terminus a quo* is more difficult. There has been a bias to date John late because of its high Christology, but we find the same affirmations in Paul's letters that are some of the earliest writings in the New Testament (c. 50–c. 64).[304] If John reworked Mark's presentation, then it may be dated after AD 64, around the time of Peter's martyrdom. The fourth Gospel remembers Jesus predicting the crucifixion of Peter, perhaps because this event was in the past (21:15–19). Some believe John is responding to rabbinic opposition in the nineties of the first century when the *Birkat Ha-Minim* was added to the synagogue liturgy, but it is difficult to know how pervasive that excommunication was. Nevertheless, the threat against the blind man's family (9:22) suggests a "parting of the ways" was underway.

Provenance

Irenaeus follows a tradition from Polycarp, who heard some of the apostles: "Afterwards, John, the disciple of the Lord, who had leaned upon his breast, did himself publish a gospel during his residence at Ephesus in Asia" (*Haer.* 3.1.1). John may have relocated to the city before or during the Jewish rebellion that began in AD 66.[305] This tradition may originate in the identification of the evangelist with the author of Revelation, which contains letters to seven churches in the province of Asia Minor, including Ephesus,

303. See, e.g., Lincoln, *Gospel According to Saint John*, 18. Brant suggests "a decade or so after AD 70" (*John*, 5).

304. For more discussion, see Lewis, *John*, 4–5. See Phil 2:1–11; Col 1:15–20, which may actually reflect earlier understandings of Jesus originating in the Palestinian church.

305. James, the brother of the Lord, was executed around this time (Josephus, *Ant.* 20.200–203).

but Polycarp knew John. Irenaeus writes: "I can even describe the place where the blessed Polycarp used to sit and teach—his going out, too, and his coming in—his general mode of life and personal appearance, together with the sermons that he delivered to the people; also how he would speak of his familiar conversation with John . . .[306]

The Gospel's presentation fits especially well in a Jewish, Alexandrian context.[307] The striking parallels with Philo will be discussed in the commentary. Alexandria had a large Jewish population and prominent synagogues, a possible background for the internecine conflict in John.[308] The Gospel was known among Christians in Egypt by the early second century.[309]

In any case, intellectuals demanded a lot from metaphysical claims in these major cities. Western philosophy originated in Asia Minor and deepened in Alexandria. Since Diogenes (c. 403–323), philosophers or "lovers of wisdom" had taken their views to the people. Plato sought the good life—"one that is fitting to the place of humanity in the cosmos and reflects an understanding of how things really are."[310] After the local synagogue, John's primary competitors were Stoics, Epicureans, and, to a lesser degree, skeptics.[311]

Unique Contribution

Each Gospel is unique, but John is especially recognized for this. Eusebius of Caesarea cites a lost work of Clement of Alexandria: "John, last of all, conscious that the outward facts (*ta sōmatika*, τὰ σωματικά) had been set forth in the Gospels, was urged on by his disciples, and, divinely moved by the Spirit, composed a spiritual Gospel (*pneumatikon . . . euangelion*, πνευματικὸν . . . εὐαγγέλιον)."[312] The adjective "spiritual" (*pneumatikos*, πνευματικός) usually refers to the inner life of a human being or the divine

306. Fragments (*ANF* 1:372, slightly updated). The tradition is furthered by Jerome (*Vir. ill.* 17).

307. See Perry, "Is John an Alexandrian Gospel?," 99–106.

308. Perry, "Is John an Alexandrian Gospel?," 104.

309. The Rylands Library Papyrus is from the region. John was also appropriated by an apocryphal gospel whose fragments were found in Egypt (Egerton Papyrus 2) and can be dated to the middle of the second century. Clement of Alexandria often cites the Gospel. Origen wrote an entire commentary on John. An Alexandrian provenance may help to explain Luke's marginal appropriation of the fourth Gospel, along with Roman writers like Justin Martyr.

310. Ward, *God*, 111.

311. Under the direction of Arcesilaus of Pitane (c. 315–241 BC), the Academy had embraced radical skepticism down to the time of Cicero (106–43 BC).

312. Eusebius, *Hist. eccl.* 6.14.7 (Lake, LCL).

spirit.[313] A more literal translation of *ta sōmatika* is "bodily things," which presumes the outer dimension. The Alexandrian also claims John is moved by the Holy Spirit (*pneuma*, πνεῦμα). *Pneumatikos* may refer to understanding given by the Spirit (Col 1:9) and also the fruit of that revelation, such as "spiritual songs" (Eph 5:19; Col 3:16). Clement recognizes this in the fourth Gospel (see 2:18–22). John and the other apostles came to a right understanding after receiving the Holy Spirit, and John is rightly a "spiritual Gospel." So both senses are in play. William Barclay notes:

> What Clement meant was that John was interested not so much in the mere facts as in the meaning of the facts, that is was not facts he was after but truth. John did not see the events of Jesus' life simply as events in time; he saw them as windows looking into eternity, and he pressed towards the spiritual meaning of the events and the words of Jesus' life in a way that the other three Gospels did not attempt.[314]

I do not completely disagree, except that Barclay, like so many other interpreters, flirts with a false dichotomy between the synoptic Gospels as factual history (the husk) and John as timeless meaning (the kernel).[315] Clement valued all four Gospels. I suggest his language is complementary: the *body* works, the *spirit* enlivens. A body without spirit is dead (James 2:26). John is actually more conscious of time than the other evangelists,[316] and we find "timeless truth" in the synoptic parables, none of which is directly appropriated by the fourth Gospel. The Parable of the Tenants (Mark 12:1–12; Matt 21:33–46; Luke 20:9–19) focuses on the Son's identity, a mystery unpacked by the Johannine Jesus. John is the Mary to the synoptic Martha. They are sisters who should be distinguished but not separated. Since John is an eyewitness, he enjoyed the freedom to integrate history and significance, event and interpretation.

The fourth Gospel presents the gospel as the offering of "eternal life."[317] Jesus came from God to offer this life to human beings. He prays to the Father: "Now this is eternal life: they know you, the only true God and Jesus Christ, whom you sent" (17:3). Knowledge, in this context, is an imparted intimacy between Father and Son. The Father knows the Son, and the Son knows the Father, and the Son has made God known to us, so

313. BDAG, 837.

314. Barclay, *Gospel of John*, 12.

315. See Blomberg, *Historical Reliability of John's Gospel*.

316. Bauckham, *Testimony of the Beloved Disciple*, 93–112.

317. See John 3:15, 16, 36; 4:14, 36; 5:24; 39:1; 6:27, 33, 40, 47, 54; 6:68; 10:28; 12:25, 50; 17:2, 3.

that we may know God.[318] We know the Father (7:28; 8:55; 14:7; 16:3; 17:3, 25), Son (10:14; 14:7, 9; 17:3), and Holy Spirit (14:17), that they are in one another (10:38; 14:20) and we are in them (14:20). The dynamism of these relationships is love.

Richard Bauckham notes that John begins with the synoptic expression "Kingdom of God" (3:3) but switches to "eternal life."[319] Receiving eternal life in the Trinitarian God is entering the Kingdom. Abiding in Christ actualizes this relationship: "I am the way and the truth and the life. No one comes to the Father except through me" (14:6).

We find paradox and irony in Mark, but John emphasizes this approach to truth: The Logos is distinct from God and is God (1:1); he became flesh (a human being, 1:14); people believe when they see the signs (2:23) and then do not believe (12:37); they know Jesus and where he comes from (7:28), and then they do not (8:14, 19); if Jesus bears witness of himself, his testimony is not true (5:31); and then it is (8:13–14); Jesus did not come to judge (3:17; 12:47), and he then takes that role (9:39);[320] The Father loves the world, and the Son loves "his own" in the world (3:16; 13:1); the humiliation of the cross reveals the Son's glory (13:31–32).[321] These formal contradictions are not accidental, but "are part of the author's way of making us reflect more deeply on the multitude of meanings of the words involved."[322] A paradox may be described as two truths that must be held together in a creative tension, if a fuller reality is to be understood.[323] Jesus is revelation and mystery (21:25). The metaphysical implication of paradox is that reality is not static. Parmenides was wrong. Yes, apparently Creator can *become* part of creation, the Incarnation. Yes, God can also *be* a human being, the hypostatic union of Christ. John's language encouraged Tertullian to formulate the truth of distinction-within-unity (*adversus Praxean*).[324] So, yes, God can *be* three persons and one essence. We also learn that what it means to be human is not static: we are not God, but union with Christ, the God-man, unites us to God because the humanity of the Son cannot be separated from his deity: "Beloved, we are already children of God, but it has not yet been revealed what we will be. But we know that when he is

318. Kim, *Spirituality of Following Jesus*, 143.

319. Bauckham, *Gospel of Glory*, 192.

320. I have taken some of these paradoxes from Williams, *Can We Trust the Gospels?*, 123–25. For paradox in Mark, see Sweat, *Theological Role of Paradox*.

321. For this paradox, see Meeks, *Prophet King*, 297.

322. Williams, *Can We Trust the Gospels?*, 125.

323. Some use the expression "coincidence of opposites."

324. Pollard, *Johannine Christology*, 69.

revealed, we will be like him (Christ) because we will see him as he is" (1 John 3:2). The human body, so much at the core of *what* we are, changed in the resurrection. The resurrected body of Christ is the only fully realized representative of this transformation.

We also find a tension between human responsibility and divine sovereignty.[325] John emphasizes the latter: whatever a human being can become, it cannot happen apart from the gift of eternal life.

Structure

Raymond Brown divides John into four parts: a prologue (1:1–18), a book of signs (1:19—12:50), a book of glory (13:1–20:31), and an epilogue (21:1–25).[326] The first book offers six signs;[327] the second, the culminating, seventh sign of Jesus's death and resurrection, the hidden glory of God. Following Marc Girard, Brandon Crowe finds a chiasm:

A Water changed to wine (2:1–12)

B Healing of a moribund child (4:43–54)

C Healing of a disabled man (5:1–18)

D Multiplication of bread (6:1–15)

C' Healing of a disabled man (9:1–6)

B' Resuscitation of a dead man (11:1–44)

A' The sour wine, the water, and the blood (19:17–37)[328]

The first and last signs, which focus on water and the relationship between wine and blood, form *inclusio*. Mary is present in only these two accounts (2:4; 19:26). The first offers the earliest mention of Jesus's "hour" of death

325. Robert Kysar notes, "in the text [John 6] there seems to be present a tension between human and divine responsibility for faith" (*Voyages with John*, 45).

326. There are other proposals. Brian Peterson sees the evangelist following the structure of Ezekiel, beginning with the prophet's vision of the glory of Yahweh (Ezek 1–3) and vision of the Lord departing the temple (Ezek 8–11), which corresponds to John 1–12 and his visions of the revival of the nation and its unification (Ezek 37) and of the temple and the Lord's return (Ezek 40–48) corresponding to John 13–21 (Peterson, *John's Use of Ezekiel*). We could also label the two main parts "Jesus's public career" (1:19—12:50) and "departure from the world" (13:1—20:31; Lincoln, *Gospel According to Saint John*, 5). I follow Brown's analysis in his *Introduction*, 334–35.

327. Some (C. H. Dodd; Raymond Brown) detect the appropriation of an earlier written source, the so-called "Book of signs."

328. Girard, "La composition structurelle," 315–24; Crowe, "Chiastic Structure," 67.

and resurrection (2:4) and demonstration of glory (2:11).[329] The pivot is the multiplication of bread, which anticipates Jesus's provocative invitation to eat his flesh and drink his blood (6:26–59). Consequently, the signs point to our eternal life-giving participation in the body of Christ—our manna for the journey back to God. They are intended to foster belief (20:30–31). If Mark emphasizes the purgative and illuminative stages of the journey back to God, John goes further into the unitive stage.

John also structures the book of signs around seven discourses, which focus on Christ's true identity and mission.[330] He is the son of God from God—what Bauckham calls "agency Christology."[331] Seeded throughout the narrative are "I am" claims that flesh out his identity and mission: "I am" (4:26; 6:20; 8:24, 28, 58; 13:19; 18:5), "I am the bread of life" (6:35, 41, 48), "I am the light of the world" (8:12; see 9:5), "I am the gate" (10:7, 9), "I am the good shepherd" (10:11, 14), "I am the resurrection and the life" (11:25), "I am the Way and the Truth and the Life" (14:6), and "I am the true vine" (15:1). The absolute "I am" invites a link with Yahweh's self-revelation (Deut 32; Isa 40—55); the predicates emphasize the mediation of the Son, offering light, guidance, protection, life, truth, and nourishment from God—all revealing the goodness and love of God for humanity (3:16). Like the first Exodus, God has not abandoned his people. He mercifully comes to those in need: "I have surely seen the oppression of my people who are in Egypt, and I have heard their cry from under the taskmasters. For I know their sufferings" (Exod 3:7 LXX).

The book of glory is comprised of the "Upper Room Discourse" (13:1—17:26) and Passion story (18:1—20:31), which are linked by the Son's expressed love for his own (13:1; 19:30). His death and resurrection as the Passover Lamb inaugurate a new exodus.

Purpose

Like Matthew, John conveys his purpose at the beginning and end of his Gospel:

> Whoever received him (the Logos, Christ), he gave them the right to become God's children—to those who believe in his name. (1:12)

329. Crowe, "Chiastic Structure," 72.

330. John 3:1–21; 4:1–26; 5:19–47; 6:22–59; 7:14–36; 8:12–59; 10:1–21.

331. Bauckham, *Gospel of Glory*, 193.

> These things have been written that you may believe that Jesus is the Christ, the son of God, and that, believing, you may have life in his name. (20:31)

We are called to "receive" and "believe" in the Son of God from God, which leads to a state of "abiding" in Christ. We receive the bread and wine. Although the Son returned to the Father, they are present in the indwelling Holy Spirit—what came to be called *perichoresis* (John of Damascus).[332]

Reception

The ambiguity of John's presentation has invited the greatest diversity of interpretation.[333] Everyone claims him. Tatian generally followed John's order for his *Diatessaron*, the first harmony of the Gospels.[334] Several churches in Asia Minor made John their primary Gospel.[335] Heracleon, a purported disciple of the gnostic Valentinus, wrote the earliest known commentary (c. 180). Irenaeus depended heavily on Johannine thought to defend the deposit of faith. Origen and Cyril wrote commentaries. Bede, at the time of his death, was translating John into English.

John establishes a dialectic in the Christian tradition between scholasticism—knowledge about Creator and creation—and mysticism—awareness of God's presence. John was the first Christian to be called *theologos* (Θεολόγος) or "theologian" (Eusebius, *Chron.*). The title is derived from the verb *theologeō* or "one who speaks for God." John writes as an enlightened child of God, who "beheld" the glory of the Son, who "exegeted" God to him (John 1:9, 12, 14, 18).

We also find a tradition that claims John wore the "sacerdotal plate," the dress of the high priest (Polycrates).[336] This may result from confusing a priest named "John" in Acts (4:5–6) for the apostle, but the fourth Gospel opens the door to this tradition by claiming its primary disciple "was known to the high priest" (John 18:15).[337] The mystery deepens when John stands

332. Humble, *Divine Round Trip.*

333. Keefer, *Branches of the Gospel of John*, 1.

334. Tatian transposes chapters 5 and 6.

335. Metzger, *Canon of the New Testament*, 263. He makes the stronger claim that they *only* used John's Gospel.

336. We find similar tradition about Mark and James (or Jacob), the brother of the Lord.

337. It was not unusual to conflate common names with the same person in patristic literature. The reference to a priest named John in Acts cannot refer to the apostle who is distinguished as a different character in the context (v. 13).

like a priest with Mary, a symbol of the church, at the foot of the cross as the Paschal lamb is being sacrificed (John 19:25–27). His disciples continued to celebrate an annual Passover on Nisan 14, leading to the Quartodeciman controversy when other churches preferred to celebrate on the following Sunday (Polycarp, Melito of Sardis), appealing to tradition from Peter and Paul. Initially, bishops were able to respect these differences, but then it became ugly. Perhaps we can integrate these traditions by noting that John was received in the early church as the theologian and priest for the temple of Christ's body. These roles should be inseparable. John offers the meaning of the mutual abiding of God and humanity in the body of Christ.[338]

Thomas Aquinas, who solidified the "classical Christian view" of God, claims John "refutes all heresies" (*Commentary on John* 1.10).[339] Augustine and Aquinas wrote longer commentaries on John than the Synoptic Gospels.[340] Teresa of Ávila alludes to John throughout her *Interior Castle*, which focuses on the journey inside the soul towards complete union with God.

The Roman church, at the Toledo Council (AD 589), added the *filioque* clause to the Nicene Creed—"We believe in the Holy Spirit, . . . who proceeds from the Father *and the Son*"—in part because of John's perichoretic language (14:26; 15:26; 20:22–23), contributing to the 1054 schism between the eastern and western lungs of the church.

Martin Luther cherished John because of its emphasis on belief (the noun "faith" interestingly never occurs in the Gospel). Along with the letters of Paul and Peter, John was "the true kernel and marrow" of the New Testament.[341]

Unfortunately, like Matthew, John was appropriated for anti-Semitic propaganda. His portrayal of "the Jews" is largely negative.[342] But John was himself a Jew and uses the epithet ironically (see Rev 2:9; 3:9).[343] "Jew" is probably an insensitive and inaccurate translation since the term came to represent an entire ethnic group and religious identity.[344] The Greek *Ioudaios* described "those of Judea"—"Judeans" (see 7:1–2). The key to John's use is looking carefully at the first occurrence of the term: "And this is the witness from John when the Judeans [or Jews] from Jerusalem sent [to him]

338. Paul is also a rich source for this central mystery; the two should be appreciated for their individual approaches to the mystery, but not divided.

339. Ludolph of Saxony, *Life of Christ*, 1:26.

340. Brant, *John*, 18.

341. See Martin Luther's *Preface to the New Testament* (1522).

342. See, e.g., 1:19; 2:18, 20; 3:25; 5:10, 15, 16, 18; 6:41, 52.

343. Keener, *Gospel of John*, 1:194–214.

344. On this development, see Cohen, *Beginnings of Jewishness*.

priests and Levites to question him" (1:19). He goes on to identify this group more particularly: "And they were sent from the Pharisees" (1:24). John consistently presents the south, specifically its religious leaders, as hostile and dangerous. I therefore prefer "Judean" as a translation. In most cases, John uses the term specifically for the religious leaders in Jerusalem.[345] One Johannine scholar defines *Ioudaioi* as "those who reject the revelation of God in and through Jesus."[346]

The Fourfold Gospel

The Gospels may be read independently but also as one book—what may be called the Fourfold Gospel.[347] Our earliest titles—*According to Matthew, According to Mark, According to Luke,* and *According to John*—in Codex Vaticanus presume one gospel in four perspectives.[348]

The Codex

The autographs and first copies of the Gospels were probably written on scrolls. Pliny the Elder (c. 23–79) notes they extended to twenty sheets of papyrus (a paper-like surface made from pith) pasted together—around thirty feet.[349] Luke's Gospel, the longest, filled a scroll.[350] He depicts Jesus reading from a scroll of Isaiah (Luke 4:17). However, by the third century, the four Gospels were being collected together in various orders into a codex, the forerunner of the printed book. Leaves of papyrus or vellum (treated animal skin) were stitched together between a cover.[351] Christians were early adopters of this technology, but do not explain why.[352] It could be accidental. Yet the persistent and broad appropriation of the modality suggests a preference,

345. Brown notes: "'The Jews' include Jewish authorities but cannot be confined to them" (*Introduction*, 339).

346. Skinner, *Reading John*, 65.

347. Several works have adopted this title: Simpson, *Four-Fold Gospel*; Butler, *Fourfold Gospel*; Watson, *Fourfold Gospel*.

348. Comfort, *Commentary*, 1.

349. Pliny the Elder, *Nat.* 13.23. See Comfort, *Encountering the Manuscripts*, 386.

350. Carsten Thiede discusses the transition from scrolls to codices in the Roman catacomb art (*Rekindling the Word*, 85).

351. Around AD 105, Cai Lun invents paper in China. But this medium was not available in the West.

352. The Romans probably invented the codex in the first century (Llewelyn, *New Documents*, 254).

especially since most Pagan writings continued to be copied on scrolls.[353] The codex had three advantages over the scroll that were especially amenable to the faith: travel, volume, and comparative study.

Travel

Martial (c. 38–c. 102), a Roman writer, is the first to mention the codex:[354]

> You who desire for my little books to be with you everywhere and long to have them as companions on a long journey, buy these, which parchment confines within small pages. (*Epigram.* 1.2)

Avid readers could travel with Martial, whereas scrolls were cumbersome as can be seen in 2 Timothy: "When you come, bring . . . the scrolls, especially the parchments" (4:13).[355] Seneca (c. 4 BC–AD 65) notes, "A multitude of books [scrolls] only gets in one's way" (*Letters* 2.3). Unless stored in a *capsa*, the rolled papyrus was easily crushed. Sheet against sheet was more durable.

Christianity began as a missionary movement. By the third century, it had spread to the borders of Persia in the east; Spain in the west; North Africa in the south; and Britannia in the north. Ancient Israelite Scripture and new sacred writings from the apostles were used for evangelism, catechesis, and worship.

Volume

The codex allows larger collections of texts—a library in hand. We have several pages from an early codex (c. 225) that contained Luke and John.[356] Chester Beatty I, a larger, slightly later (mid third-century) codex, has all four Gospels, but in the "western" order (Matthew, John, Luke, and Mark), and Acts.[357] The editor may have intended a Christian Pentateuch.[358] After

353. This preference continued through the third century (Hadas, *Ancilla to Classical Reading*, 11).

354. He notes that Homer, Virgil, Cicero, Livy, and Ovid were available in this format (*Epigram.* 14.184, 186, 188, 190, 192, respectively; Llewelyn, *New Documents*, 254).

355. The parchments may refer to a codex or codices, although the wording more likely distinguishes the material from papyrus.

356. 102 pages, whole or fragmentary, survive; the remains are called Papyrus 75. The ending Luke and beginning of John occur on the same page.

357. Stanton, *Jesus and Gospel*, 71–75; Royse, *Scribal Habits*, 103.

358. In the Roman Domatilla Catacombs, a mural shows the apostle Paul with a *capsa* (cylindrical container) of five scrolls.

Christianity became established in a city, a library was often collected and expanded. The great Alexandrian codices, Vaticanus and Sinaiticus, contain most of the Old and New Testaments as well as other documents; because of their great size, they probably served as reference works.

Study

The codex was ideal for cross-referencing. Instead of unrolling one scroll at a time, the reader could flip through its sheets. This was especially helpful for the Gospels and Paul's Letters because of their similar yet distinct passages.[359]

The inclusion of these four Gospels into a single codex presupposes something about their complementary authority. The church could have selected one "authorized version," like Tatian's *Euangelion* or Marcion's torso of Luke.

Tetramorph Gospel

Irenaeus speaks of a "tetramorph" or fourfold gospel.[360] They are "fourfold in form but held together by one Spirit" (*Haer.* 3.11.8). The father maintains a clear delimitation: there had to be four—and only four—Gospels like the four zones or compass points of the world, the four winds, and the four covenants with Adam, Noah, Moses, and Christ.[361] The symbolism represents completeness or perfection. He contrasts this singular collection with unreliable gnostic gospels.

Irenaeus pairs each evangelist with a face of the tetramorph angel seen by Ezekiel:

Matthew = Human

John = Lion

Luke = Ox

Mark = Eagle[362]

359. Concerning Paul, the arguments in Galatians and Rome are similar; there are two slightly different elder lists in 1 Timothy and Titus; and so on. Papyrus 46, a twin of Papyrus 45, contains Paul's Letters.

360. Irenaeus of Lyon, *Haer.* 3.11.8. The adjective "tetramorph" signifies the combination of four different elements in one unit.

361. Irenaeus of Lyon, *Haer.* 3.11.8–9.

362. Skeat, "Irenaeus and the Four-Gospel Canon," 194–99.

According to contemporary Jewish interpretation, the faces looked East, South, North, and West. They witness to the singular gospel for all creation. Jesus used Ezekiel's vision to explain his revelatory ministry (John 1:51). Above the *tetramorph* angels (Cherubim) was an exalted being, who had a "likeness with a human appearance," the pre-incarnate Christ. The Fourfold Gospel similarly reveals heavenly realities, presenting the crucified yet resurrected Lord who is enthroned.

Irenaeus is not idiosyncratic. He had lived and lectured in Rome (c. 177) and mediated a conflict between the churches in Asia Minor and Victor of Rome. "We may be certain," claims Burnett Streeter, "that what he says about the Gospels represents the official view at Rome and Ephesus."[363] The churches in both cities had strong ties with the apostles.

As we noted, Justin Martyr describes the Gospels as "the memories of the apostles," but also "of those who followed them."[364] This presumes the same arrangement as Irenaeus—Matthew, John, Luke, and Mark—the western order.[365] Tertullian uses this order to distinguish the apostles from their associates (*Adv. Marcionem* 4.2, 5). Although some argue Justin did not know John, he presumes Jesus's discussion with Nicodemus (*1 Apol.* 61.4–5).[366] In context, Justin cites Luke (22:44, 42), who is not an apostle. He describes Mark's Gospel as "memories" of Peter, but perhaps aware they were written down by Mark.[367] In any case, the father assumes the Fourfold Gospel.[368]

363. Streeter, *Four Gospels*, 8. This view may have become predominate soon after Papias, who prefers tradition.

364. Justin Martyr, *Dial.* 103.56–58.

365. Papyrus 45 et al. Streeter claims they "put the least important Gospel last" (*Four Gospels*, 11). But Augustine was able to make the same point from the canonical order, viewing the eyewitnesses as holding the first and last positions (*Harmony* 3). For more discussion, see Skeat, "Codicological Analysis," 27–43; Elliott, *New Testament Textual Criticism*, 616.

366. In my opinion, he also owes much to John's prologue, particularly the Logos. See Romanides, "Justin Martyr and the Fourth Gospel," 115–34.

367. As we noted, Justin mentions "his memories" in reference to Peter: καὶ γεγράφθαι ἐν τοῖς ἀπομνημονεύμασιν αὐτοῦ γεγενημένον καὶ τοῦτο (106). He reveals he has the second Gospel in mind when he refers to the sons of Zebedee as "Boanerges, which is 'sons of thunder'"—a clear allusion to Mark 3:16.

368. Justin also seems to be aware of tradition we find in Papias, a bishop near Ephesus, in the city of Hierapolis, who relates opinions he received from John the Elder, probably the apostle responsible for the Fourth Gospel. John affirms Mark and Matthew, despite their perceived shortcomings. Papias does not mention Luke, but uses the distinctive vocabulary of his preface.

Subsequent generations of ecclesial authorities followed Irenaeus's approach to the Gospels, although the referents of the allegory and order shifted. Augustine preferred:

Matthew = lion

Mark = human

Luke = ox

John = eagle

But Jerome's classification became normative for the Christian tradition:

Matthew = human

Mark = lion

Luke = ox

John = eagle

The Book of Kells (c. AD 800), the most precious document in Ireland, offers a beautiful depiction of the Tetramorph Gospel in Jerome's order (folio 27v).[369] Cornelius Boel (c. 1576–c. 1621) adopted the symbolism in the title page (frontispiece) to the first edition of the Authorized (King James) Version (1611).

The analogies are mysterious and have invited much reflection over the centuries.[370] Aquinas offers this summation:

> Matthew might be said to speak of Christ chiefly with respect to the mystery of the Incarnation, and thus he is depicted in the figure of a man. Luke, with respect to the mystery of the Passion, and therefore he is depicted as a bull, which is an animal to be immolated. Mark, with respect to the victory of the Resurrection, and thus he is depicted as a lion. But John, who soars to the heights of his divinity, is depicted as an eagle.[371]

We may go a little further. Matthew opens with an allusion to the genealogy of Adam, the first human being. Mark alludes to Cyrus (and possible Caesar), who was associated with a lion. Arthur Just notes, "Luke frames his Gospel with priestly themes, beginning with Zechariah's Levitical offering in the temple and concluding with the priestly victim, Jesus, the calf

369. See also the Book of Durrow (c. 680), the Gospel of St. Willibrord (c. 690), the Book of Lindisfarne (c. 700), the Gospel of St. Chad (early eighth century), and the Canterbury Codex Aureus (c. 750).

370. For more discussion, see Burridge, *Four Gospels, One Jesus?*

371. Aquinas, *Selected Writings*, 12.

offered in sacrifice on the cross."[372] (The ox is traditionally associated with the Nativity Scene inspired by Luke's birth narrative.) John opens with the most soaring passage of the New Testament. (The ancients believed only the eagle could look into the sun.) The associations may be forced, but the key point is that *each face is distinctive yet harmonious with the others*. The Fourfold Gospel, Irenaeus notes, is "held together by one spirit," an allusion to Ezekiel: "And each was proceeding according to its face—wherever the spirit was proceeding they were proceeding, and they were not turning" (1:12 OG).[373] The Muratorian Canon (or fragment) similarly claims: "Though various rudiments are taught in the several Gospel books, yet that matters nothing for the faith of believers, since by the one and guiding Spirit everything is declared in all."[374] This tradition invites us to attend to both unity and diversity.[375] We read the whole Fourfold Gospel and then each Gospel in light of the whole and then the whole in light of each Gospel and so on. This reading strategy anticipates the diversity we find in the Christian tradition, but also its borders. Everything is meaningful in Christ, but Christ does not mean everything.

Harmonies

The early church often harmonized readings of the Gospels. Justin Martyr writes:

> And the angel of God, who was sent to the same virgin at that time, brought her good news, saying: "Look—you will conceive in the Holy Spirit [Luke 1:35], and shall give birth to a son. And he shall be called the Son of the Highest, and you shall call his name Jesus [Luke 1:31]. For he shall save his people from their sins [Matt 1:21]." (*1 Apol.* 33)

The apologist cites the unique presentations in Luke (1:35) and Matthew (1:21) as one angelic announcement. In both cases, the message is essentially the same, although the angel addresses Joseph in Matthew and Mary in Luke. It is unclear if he conflates the sayings or is working from a harmony. In any case, Matthew and Luke are read together.

Tatian (c. 160–c. 175), one of Justin's students, produced what came to be called the *Diatessaron* ("through the four") in Syria or, more likely,

372. Just, *Luke*, 1.

373. Irenaeus of Lyon, *Haer.* 3.1.2; 3.11.8.

374. Schneemelcher and Wilson, *New Testament Apocrypha*, 1:35.

375. There is an *argumentum* for its use in miniscule 908.

Rome where he opened a school.[376] He trimmed nearly 30 percent of the Gospels through conflation and harmonization.[377] The Syrian Church used the *Diatessaron* for communal worship until the fifth century when it was supplanted by the individual Gospels in the Peshitta.[378]

Ammonius of Alexandria (fl. 200–230) labored to produce a harmony of the Gospels, a *dia tessarōn euangelion* ("through-the-four Gospel"). He relates parallel passages with Matthew as a base text.[379] This required delimiting the Gospels into units. His work perished, but Eusebius, as we noted, adapted his arrangement into ten groups—the Eusebian canons.

Some units occur in all four Gospels—what may be called *quadruple tradition.* For example, all four evangelists record the Feeding of the Five Thousand (Matt 14:13–21; Mark 6:32–44; Luke 9:10b–17; John 6:1–15). This is fairly rare. When all four Gospels narrate the same event or teaching, it is especially prominent in the Christian tradition. Other units occur only in the Synoptic Gospels—or *triple tradition.* Matthew, Mark, and Luke narrate the Parable of the Sower (Matt 13:1–9; Mark 4:1–9; Luke 8:4–8), which does not occur in John. This overlapping material is probably the result of Matthew and Luke appropriating Mark as a source. These units may reveal the unique interests and style of the evangelists, what is called redaction criticism, by attending to how Matthew or Luke departs from Mark's wording.[380] Around 200 verses occur in Matthew and Luke, but not Mark or John—*double tradition.* For example, Matthew and Luke relate the content of Jesus's temptations (Matt 4:1–11; Luke 4:1–13; compare with Mark 1:12–13). The overlap is often attributed to a shared, hypothetical source called Q, but it is more

376. Streeter, *Four Gospels*, 9. Tatian does not describe his work as a *diatessaron.* Ulrich Schmid suggests he viewed it as an independent gospel ("Diatessaron of Tatian," 115–42). For a more traditional presentation, see Petersen, *Tatian's Diatessaron.* Carmel McCarthy notes: "The fact that the Diatessaron never fell under suspicion of heresy suggests that it might have been produced in Rome before Tatian returned home to the East. Since there is no evidence of a Syriac version of the separate Gospels earlier than the Diatessaron, it might seem more logical that Tatian would have made his harmony in Rome in Greek and then taken it eastwards with him" (*Saint Ephrem's Commentary*, 5).

377. McCarthy, *Saint Ephrem's Commentary*, 7.

378. Aphrahat (c. 270–c. 345) appears to quote from the *Diatessaron* in his sermons, the *Demonstrations.* Near one of the earliest church buildings to be recovered, the Dura-Europas Church (c. 235), a harmony was discovered. Its relationship to Tatian is unclear (Petersen, *Tatian's Diatessaron*, 196). Some believe the *Diatessaron* was known by Muhammad—what he called *Injil.*

379. Eusebius explains this in a letter to a certain Carpianus, printed in *Patrologia Graeca* vol. 22, columns. 1276–1277. See Oliver, "Epistle of Eusebius," 138–45.

380. Craig Keener, for example, notes: "Where possible, Matthew has made Mark's Jesus 'more Jewish'" (*Matthew*, 8). Luke has a special interest in the quality of the heart (cf. Mark 4:20; Luke 8:13–15; Acts 8:13, 21).

likely that Luke appropriates Matthew. If correct, then such overlap may reveal the special interests of Luke, who is editing the first Gospel for a different reader.[381] All four Gospels present *unique tradition*. Only Matthew has a parable about a household master who casts out of his treasure box things new and old (13:51–52). Mark uniquely relates a healing where a man's sight is partially restored (8:22–26). Luke alone offers the great parables about The Good Samaritan (10:30–35) and Prodigal Son (15:11–32). John offers several unique traditions. These unique contributions may reveal the special interests of the evangelists. So, for some events in Jesus's earthly ministry, we have four perspectives; others, three, two, or one. Overlap and uniqueness are helpful signals for interpreting the *Fourfold Gospel*.

Harmonization?

Until recently, most Jews and Christians accepted the infallibility of Scripture, holding to something like a dictation view of inspiration: "no prophecy ever came by the will of a human being; instead, human beings, carried by the Holy Spirit, spoke from God" (2 Pet 1:21 in the context of the Transfiguration). Yet early Christians knew there were differences between the Gospels. Non-Christians, like Celsus and Julian the Apostate, used them to attack the veracity of the gospel message.[382] This led to various attempts at harmonization. Augustine gives enormous concentration to the problem of diversity in his *Harmony of the Gospels* (*De Consensu Evangelistarum*). He explains the differences of order and detail through the prism of his *tetramorph*, finding a place for the unique contributions of the human author. By way of analogy, the Gospels are like four brothers of a good father: all remember him with affection, but in his own way.[383]

The uniqueness of the presentations of Matthew, Mark, Luke, and John foster imagination and reflection; they speak to one another, along with the rest of Scripture, encouraging the reader to find truth in the tension.

Today, criticisms are lodged against the truthfulness of the Gospels by Muslim apologists, skeptics, and atheists, but also Christians, who are embarrassed by traditional notions of inspiration.[384] The way forward, I

381. For example, Luke also emphasizes the heart in this material (cf. Matt 7:16–20; Luke 6:43–45).

382. Streeter, *Four Gospels*, 9.

383. Emil Brunner uses a similar metaphor (*Our Faith*, 8).

384. In Islam, we find the conviction (*tahrif*) that Jews and Christians tampered with Scripture.

believe, is to acknowledge—even celebrate—the diversity but also to seek out the unifying truth.

Canon

By the second century, the *Fourfold Gospel* was read in the church as a distinct, authoritative collection. We find various orders, but always the same four.[385] They will enter the canon together. The Muratorian Canon, our earliest discussion of what became the New Testament, only discusses the four Gospels.[386] Clement of Alexandria, a catechist on the eastern side of the Roman Empire, cites from other gospels, but refers to the four "accepted" Gospels that were handed down to him.[387] Origen also engages with a broader tradition, but describes the same collection as "not spoken against."[388] His apology, *Contra Celsum*, assumes his interlocutor treated the Gospels as official interpretations.[389] Serapion, the patriach of Antioch (writing c. 200–210), goes further, rejecting the apocryphal *Gospel of Peter*: "We, brothers, receive both Peter and the other apostles as Christ, but we reject the writings that falsely go under their names, since we are experienced and know that such were not handed down to us."[390] Athanasius (c. 295–d. 373) similarly writes,

> mention is nowhere made of the apocrypha; rather they are a fabrication of the heretics, who write them down when it pleases them and generously assign to them an early date of

385. According to my friend Lorne Zelyck, who specializes in this, there is no evidence that apocryphal gospels ever circulated with the canonical Gospels: The Gospel of Judas is bound with the Letter of Peter to Philip, 1 Apocalypse of James, Book of Allogenes (Codex Tchacos)—all of which are found in the Nag Hammadi Codices. Gospel of Mary and Sophia of Jesus Christ are bound with the Apocryphon of John and Acts of Peter (P. Berol. 8502). Gospel of Peter is bound with the Apocalypse of Peter and Enoch (P. Cair. 10759). Gospel of Thomas and Gospel of Philip and Book of Thomas the Contender are bound together in Nag Hammadi Codex 2; a version of Sophia of Jesus Christ and Dialogue of the Savior are bound together in Nag Hammadi Codex 3. The rest are all fragments, and "it is difficult to determine what texts they were bound with" (personal correspondence 6 January 2015).

386. The discussion of Matthew and Mark is missing, but subsequent references make their inclusion clear.

387. See, e.g., *Rich Man's Salvation* 5. Clement is able to respond: "We do not have this word in the four Gospels handed down to us" (*Strom.* 3.13.92).

388. Origen, *Comm. Matt.* 1.

389. Nicol, *Four Gospels*, 43.

390. Cited in Eusebius, *Hist. eccl.* 6.12.3–6. Eusebius cites from a pamphlet addressed to Christians in Rhossus.

> composition in order that they may be able to draw upon them as supposedly ancient writings and have in them occasion to deceive the guileless."[391]

The Council of Laodicea (middle of the fourth century) only allowed the Old and New Testament writings to be read in church.[392] At the Council of Nicea (325), the four Gospels were placed at the head of the room, although no decision was made about the canon. Athanasius, in his thirty-ninth *Festal Letter* (367), mentions all twenty-seven books of the New Testament, beginning with the Gospels in the canonical order with the titles in Codex Vaticanus: "fourfold Gospel: According to Matthew, According to Mark, According to Luke, According to John," εὐαγγέλια τέσσαρα· κατὰ Ματθαῖον, κατὰ Μάρκον, κατὰ Λουκᾶν, κατὰ Ἰωάννην. In 381, Jerome was commissioned by Pope Damasus to produce a revised translation of the New Testament for the people. Two years later he presented the Gospels as the first installment.[393] With the rest of the New Testament, the four Gospels were ratified at the Third Council of Carthage (397).[394]

Roman Catholic, Orthodox, and Protestant traditions—all acknowledge Matthew, Mark, Luke, and John as Scripture. In light of this, I suggest this means of discernment: *truth claims about Jesus should be tested against the Fourfold Gospel.* Origen states, in contrast to gospels like the one attributed to Thomas, "Our doctrines about the person of our Lord and Savior should be drawn from these approved Gospels" (*Hom. Luc.* 1.2). Teachers—those who were given the responsibility of making disciples of Jesus—must intensely study the Gospels. Justin, Clement, Origen—all served as catechists. Ignorance of the Gospels is ignorance of Jesus. We may not always find the Jesus we want, but the canon was coming into being at the same time many were creating Jesus in their own image.[395]

391. Kirchhofer, *Quellensammlung zur Geschichte*, 7–9.

392. Schneemelcher and Wilson, *New Testament Apocrypha,* 1:10.

393. Streeter, *Four Gospels*, 44. Jerome did not publish the "Vulgate," a single edition of the Bible, but submitted individual books and groupings after editing them.

394. Westcott, *Canon of the New Testament*, 440, 541–42. Some claim the list was determined earlier at the Synod of Hippo Regius in North Africa (393), but the acts of the council were lost. For more discussion, see Gallagher and Meade, *Biblical Canon Lists*, 52–56.

395. Raymond Brown asks, "If Christian groups can eliminate from the canon what they do not agree with, how has Scripture the ability to make them rethink?" (*Introduction*, 770).

Alternatives

Copying the four Gospels together into a single codex and Tatian's chiseling on only these documents imply a judgment about what was not included. The unique path of the *Fourfold Gospel* may be seen by unsuccessful alternatives.

Marcion

According to Irenaeus, Marcion of Sinope (c. 85–160)

> mutilates the gospel that is according to Luke, removing all that is written respecting the generation of the Lord [the birth narrative], and setting aside a great deal of the teaching of the Lord, in which the Lord is recorded as most dearly confessing that the Maker of this universe is his Father. He likewise persuaded his disciples that he himself was more worthy of credit than are those apostles who have handed down the gospel to us, furnishing them not with the gospel, but merely a fragment of it.[396]

Tertullian similarly claims Marcion "expunged [from Luke] all the things that oppose his view . . . but retained those things that accord with his opinion."[397]

Marcion came to Rome from Pontus around 139, and he ingratiated himself to the church by donating 200,000 sesterces, although the donation was later returned after leaders found fault with his theology. He returned to Asia Minor and continued to preach an alternative gospel, although Tertullian claims he repented late in life.[398]

Marcion's gospel is no longer extant, but most of it can be reproduced from quotations by later apologists opposing it. There is a family resemblance to modern reconstructions of the "historical Jesus" like Thomas Jefferson's *The Life and Morals of Jesus of Nazareth* (1820), which excluded the miracles, the resurrection, and references to the Son's deity, or the work of the Jesus Seminar in the 1980s. This tendency has morphed into what may be called the ideological Jesus, who is always relevant, cares about our agenda, and agrees with us against our enemies. He is fun to preach *to* our community, or, if we are a reformer, *against*.

396. Irenaeus, *Haer.* 1.8.1, emphasis added. My translation.

397. Tertullian, *Marc.* 4.6.2.

398. Tertullian, *Praescr.* 30.3.

Apocryphal Gospels

Writing gospels (or gospel-like treatises) became something of a cottage industry in the early church. They are called apocryphal gospels. Although some may betray a gnostic influence, many reflect a regional piety with elaborations like Jewish targums or religious novels today.[399] The intent was probably not to distort the gospel, but to satisfy curiosity or to refute heresy. These gospels may be divided into four categories, focusing on Jesus's origins, ministry, sayings, or death and resurrection.[400] We also find what I call missionary digests of Jesus sayings.

Infancy Gospels

The Infancy Gospel of Thomas (not to be confused with The Gospel of Thomas) presents self-contained narratives about a youthful Jesus.[401] The many surviving copies suggest it was popular.[402] This gospel ends with a retelling of Luke's depiction of Mary and Joseph leaving Jerusalem without Jesus, who remained in the temple (see Luke 2:41–51), and begins with a story when Jesus was five:

> He was playing by the ford of a stream; and he gathered the flowing waters into pool and made them instantly pure. These things he ordered simply by speaking a word. He then made some soft mud and fashioned twelve sparrows from it. It was the sabbath when he did this. There were also a number of other children playing with him. When a certain Jew saw what Jesus was doing while playing on the Sabbath, he left right away and reported to his father, Joseph, "Look, your child is at the stream and he has taken mud and formed twelve sparrows. He has profaned the Sabbath!" When Joseph came to the place and looked, he cried out to him, "Why are you doing what is forbidden on the Sabbath?" But Jesus clapped his hands and cried to the sparrows, "Be gone!" And the sparrows took flight and went off, chirping.

399. We find the most literary activity in Egypt, Syria, Asia Minor (around Ephesus), and Rome.

400. Bart Ehrman and Zlatko Pleše have conveniently collected them into a single volume, *Apocryphal Gospels*. I have slightly reworked their genre classifications.

401. The Infancy Gospel of Thomas C provides three additional chapters of similar material, which suggests the work was fluid.

402. Ehrman and Pleše, *Apocryphal Gospels*, 3. A more accurate title is *Paidika*. Until the discovery of the Gospel of Thomas, scholars confused the two works leading to the inaccurate identification of Thomas as the author (Cousland, *Holy Terror*, 1–2).

> When the Jews saw this they were amazed; and they went away and reported to their leaders what they had seen Jesus do.[403]

The evangelists never depict Joseph speaking with Jesus; it is always Mary. The controversy over Sabbath is reminiscent of conflict anecdotes in the four Gospels. Especially relevant is the healing of the blind man on the Sabbath—when Jesus made mud from his saliva (John 9:6). John portrays Jesus recapitulating the creation story, healing on the Sabbath because the "Father is working until now" (5:17–24). *The Infancy Gospel of Thomas* similarly has Jesus gather waters and create living things. While probably not historical, the miraculous story nevertheless witnesses to an important Christology. But in the canonical Gospels, Jesus only breaks the Sabbath to help others in need. The twelve sparrows, however, may symbolically anticipate the Great Commission.

Throughout this gospel, Jesus becomes irritated and can be vindictive: "A child ran up and banged into his shoulder. Jesus was aggravated and said to him, 'You will go no further on your way.' Right away the child fell down and died."[404] It is difficult to integrate this with the canonical portrait of a Savior calling others to turn the other cheek and to love their enemies.

The gospel aims to establish Jesus as a wonder-worker, even as a small child. According to contemporary biographical sensibilities, characters were static and showed their greatness from the beginning. But in the canonical Gospels, the infant Jesus is passive and vulnerable; others must intervene on his behalf. Luke even claims Jesus "was advancing in wisdom and in stature and in grace with God and before people" (2:52). A perennial challenge in the Christian tradition is holding together the humanity and deity of Christ.

The Proto-Gospel of James (c. 145) is a retelling of the birth narratives in Matthew and Luke, but also relates the circumstances of Mary's birth, contributing to the traditions of her immaculate conception (being born without original sin), which became dogma in 1854 by Pope Pius IX in his bull *Ineffabilis Deus,* and her perpetual virginity.[405] Her parents, Joachim and Anna, are righteous yet childless, which pushes the father into self-imposed exile and lamentation from the mother (chs. 1–3). An angel of the Lord announces Mary's conception and birth (ch. 4). Like Samuel, she is dedicated to the temple where she serves, being fed by an angel, until the age of twelve

403. Ehrman and Pleše, *Apocryphal Gospels*, 11.

404. Ehrman and Pleše, *Apocryphal Gospels*, 11.

405. The author appropriates the Annunciation (ch. 11), Mary's visit with Elizabeth (ch. 12), the journey to Bethlehem (ch. 17) from Luke and Joseph's discovery of Mary's pregnancy (ch. 13), the visit of the Magi (ch. 21) from Matthew. The gospel also appropriates John, but to a much lesser degree (ch. 19).

when, because of the defilement of menstruation, she had to leave. Joseph, a widower, becomes her guardian. The gospel presents Jesus's "brothers" as sons of Joseph from a previous marriage, although this view was condemned by Pope Innocent I (405) and in the sixth-century Gelasian Decree.[406] As a result, this gospel was far more popular in the east.

While faithful in some ways to the birth narrative in Luke, the gospel rejects the implication that Mary was poor (see especially 2:24); her father is the richest man in Israel.[407] It also exaggerates Zechariah's importance: instead of a "priest" (Luke 1:5), he is a "chief priest" (8.3) and is murdered.

The Gospel of Pseudo-Matthew (sixth century) is a Latin reworking of *The Proto-Gospel of James*, but with additional tradition. Expanding on Matthew's depiction of the infant Jesus's flight to Egypt, it depicts Jesus performing several miracles—taming wild animals, making a palm tree droop to offer its fruit to Mary, causing idols in a temple to bow before him.[408] The gospel did better in the west than *The Proto-Gospel of James* because it did not appropriate the claim that Joseph had children from a previous marriage; apocryphal letters from Jerome approving the gospel were added.[409]

This gospel presents Mary as the monastic ideal, spending all her time in the temple praying and working: "She was stable and unmovable; and she daily progressed, becoming better and better" (6.2).[410] There may be echoes of Benedict's Rule, which was popularized by Pope Gregory the Great (c. 540–604). Mary celebrates her perpetual virginity: "I determined in my heart that I would never know a man" (7.2).

The History of Joseph the Carpenter uniquely focuses on Jesus's earthly father, who is presented as a forty-year old widower with children from a previous marriage. The prologue states, "This is the departure from the body of our father Joseph, the carpenter, the father of Christ according to the flesh, who lived one hundred and eleven years, and whose entire life our Savior related to the apostles on the Mount of Olives."[411] Jesus somewhat mysteriously never discusses Joseph in the canonical Gospels.

406. Ehrman and Pleše, *Apocryphal Gospels*, 31–32. Joseph was a widower (Proto-Gospel of James 8.3).

407. The author imitates Luke's imitation of the Greek translations of Hebrew Scripture and typology from 1 Sam 1–4.

408. *The Latin Infancy Gospels (J Composition): Arundel Form* is a reworking of the Proto-Gospel of James and the Gospel of Pseudo-Matthew, witnessing to the popularity of these traditions.

409. Ehrman and Pleše, *Apocryphal Gospels*, 74.

410. The author presents her as a temple (3.2; 9.1).

411. Ehrman and Pleše, *Apocryphal Gospels*, 163.

Jewish-Christian, Ministry Gospels

The so-called Jewish-Christian gospels were thought to be derived and distorted from Matthew's original Hebrew Gospel.[412] According to Origen, a gospel "according to the Hebrews," identified by scholars as *The Gospel of the Nazarenes*, offers this expansion on Matthew's presentation of the Rich, Young Ruler:

> The other of the two rich men said to him, "Master, what good thing must I do that I may live?" He said to him, "Man, fulfill the law and the prophets." He answered him, "That have I done." He said to Him, "Go and sell all that you possess and distribute it among the poor, and then come and follow me." But the rich man then began to scratch his head and it pleased him not. And the Lord said to him, *"How can you say, 'I have fulfilled the law and the prophets?' For it stands written in the law: 'Love your neighbor as yourself.' And look: many of your brothers, sons of Abraham, are clothed in excrement and dying of hunger—and your house is full of many good things and nothing at all comes forth from it to them!* And he turned and said to Simon, his disciple, who was sitting by him, "Simon, son of Jonah, it is easier for a camel to go through the eye of a needle than for a rich man to enter into the kingdom of heaven."[413]

Running contrary to other apocryphal gospels that are hostile to Judaism, Jesus betrays an enduring concern for the vulnerable of his first people, as we find in Luke (12:13–21; 16:19–31). This gospel provides more background and justification for the man healed from a withered hand in the synagogue (see Matt 12:9–14), who says to Jesus: "I was a mason and earned (my) living with (my) hands; I beseech you, Jesus, to restore me to health that I may not shamefully have to beg for food."[414]

The Gospel of the Ebionites was partly a harmony of the Synoptic Gospels.[415] However, like Mark, it did not contain an infancy narrative but began with Jesus's baptism. The community responsible for the document were probably vegetarian—meat had a close association with Pagan sacrifice, and this diet may have led to an adaptation:

412. Ehrman and Pleše, *Apocryphal Gospels*, 197.

413. Origen, *Comm. Matt.* 15.14; see Matt 19:16–22. The translation is my own from Ehrman and Pleše, *Apocryphal Gospels*, 204. The title *Gospel of the Nazarenes* was first used in Latin by Paschasius Rabertus (790–865).

414. Jerome, *Comm. Matt.* 12.13. I slightly updated the translation from Schneemelcher and Wilson, *New Testament Apocrypha*, 1:160.

415. Ehrman and Pleše, *Apocryphal Gospels*, 210.

> And John was baptizing, and Pharisees came out to him and were baptized and all of Jerusalem. And John was having a garment of camel hair and a leather belt around his waist; and his food was wild honey that tasted like manna, like a cake (*ekkris*, ἐγκρίς) cooked in olive oil.[416]

Mark (1:6) and Matthew (3:4) claim the Baptist ate locusts (*akris*, ἀκρίς), which this gospel puns with "cake" (*egkris*, ἐγκρίς). They also have Jesus say, "I have no desire to eat the meat of this Passover lamb with you."[417]

The Gospel according to the Hebrews is perhaps the most mysterious of these Jewish gospels, especially Jesus's presentation of the Holy Spirit: "my mother, the Holy Spirit, took me by one of my hairs and carried me away to the great mountain, Tabor" (Origen, *Commentary on John* 2.12).[418] Mount Tabor is the traditional site for the Transfiguration.[419] To complement the locution of the Father at the baptism in the Synoptic Gospels, this gospel states:

> Then, when the Lord came up from the water, the entire fountain of the Holy Spirit descended and rested on him; and it said to him, "My Son, in all the prophets I have been expecting you to come, that I might rest on you. For you are my rest, you are my firstborn Son, who rules forever.[420]

Although "Spirit" in Greek is neuter (*pneuma*, πνεῦμα), the Hebrew (and Aramaic) equivalent is feminine, as Jerome notes expounding this passage.[421] Origen takes no issue with maternal imagery, but he interprets the saying metaphorically, alluding to Jesus's willingness to call those who

416. Epiphanius, *Panarion* 30.13.4–5. The translation is mine from Ehrman and Pleše, *Apocryphal Gospels*, 213. Paul seeks a mutually honoring position with Jewish believers in Rome who ate only vegetables (Rom 14:2).

417. Epiphanius, *Panarion* 30.22.4; trans. Ehrman and Pleše, *Apocryphal Gospels*, 215.

418. I slightly updated the translation in Schneemelcher and Wilson, *New Testament Apocrypha*, 1:160. Origen gives a shorter form of the saying in *Homilae in Jeremiam* (15:4). We find a similar saying in Jerome, who knew the gospel: *Modo me tulit mater mea, Spiritus sanctus*, "A moment ago my mother, the Holy Spirit, took me up" (*Comm. Mich.* 7.7; *Comm. Isa.* 40.9; *Ezech.* 16.13). Bel and the Dragon reads: "So the angel of the Lord took hold of the crown of his head, and carried him by his hair; with a great blast of his breath he set him down in Babylon, right over the den" (36 Theodotion; translation is by Peter Flint in Embry et al., *Early Jewish Literature*, 1:91). For more discussion, see Edwards, *Hebrew Gospel*, 56–59.

419. In Ezekiel (8:3), the Spirit lifts the prophet by the hair.

420. Jerome, *Comm. Isa.* 11.1–3; Ehrman and Pleše, *Apocryphal Gospels*, 213.

421. Jerome, *Comm. Isa.* 40.9–11 and *Ezech.* 16.13.

obey his Father brothers. In the canonical Gospels, Jesus interacts with the Spirit interpersonally, as he does the Father, but uses the masculine pronoun (John 16:7–8). But we might remember that Christian orthodoxy does not posit God as male or female; the kataphatic language allows the way of analogy. Nicolaus Zinzendorf (1700–1776) was able to cultivate a more intimate relationship by calling the Holy Spirit "mother," not in the sense of assigning a gender to God, a heresy, but to appreciate the distinctive role of the One who comforts like a mother (see Isa 66:13).

The Gospel according to the Egyptians is quoted only by Clement of Alexandria, who did not place it on par with "the four Gospels handed down to us" but used it for clarification (*Miscellanies* 3.92.2—93.1). However, other fathers disparaged the gospel. Clement focuses on a conversation between Jesus and a female disciple named Salome, who is mentioned by but does not speak in Mark:

> When Salome asked, "How long will death have power?" the Lord replied, "For as long as you women bear children." (Clement of Alexandria, *Strom.* 3.45.3).
>
> [Salome replied,] "Then I have done well not to bear children" . . . The Lord answered, "Eat every herb, but not the one that is bitter." (Clement of Alexandria, *Strom.* 3.66.1–2).
>
> [Jesus said,] "I came to destroy the works of the female." (Clement of Alexandria, *Strom.* 3.63.1).
>
> "When you (pl.) trample on the garment of shame and when the two become one and the male with the female is neither male nor female." (Clement of Alexandria, *Strom.* 3.92.2—93.1).[422]

The fathers generally condemned the pleasure of sex, but they acknowledged the goodness and necessity of procreation. Clement resolves the tension by allegorizing the sayings. Jesus allows some disciples "to become eunuchs" for the Kingdom—that is, to be celibate like himself and the apostle Paul (Matt 19:12), but he does not go this far in the canonical Gospels. He blesses children and the marriages that produce them (Matt 19:1–15; John 2:1–12), but he also claims there will be no marriage after the resurrection (Matt 22:30).[423] Anticipating this eschatological destiny, Paul reminds the Galatians that "there is no male and female" in Christ (Gal 3:28) and recommends celibacy to the Corinthians (ch. 7). There is a balance in the New

422. See Mark 15:40; 16:1; Gospel of Thomas 61; *Pistis Sophia* 132. My translations are from the Greek in Ehrman and Pleše, *Apocryphal Gospels*, 227.

423. For more discussion, see DelHousaye, "Jesus and the Meaning of Marriage," 80–89.

Testament between the already and not yet elements of God's Kingdom. Since so little is preserved from this gospel, it is difficult to know if and how that dynamic tension was managed by the author. Jesus's initial response is harsh, but it is a moral question that people have asked throughout human history: parents bring children into a life of joys and the potential for eternal beatitude, but also into a world of suffering and death.

Papyrus Egerton 2 (c. 200) contains three retellings of events in the canonical Gospels—the exhortation to "search the Scriptures" (John 5:39–47; 10:31–39), a failed attempt to stone Jesus after he restored a leper (John 10:31–42; Matt 8:1–4 pars.), and the question about tribute (Matt 22:15–22 pars.)—but also a unique, fragmentary account (*EG* 2v.6–16) of Jesus performing a miracle by the Jordan River:

> Then Jesus, as he walked, stood on the bank of the Jordan River; and reaching out his right hand, he took salt and scattered it upon the river. Then he poured out much water upon the ground. He prayed, and it was filled before them. Then it brought forth a crop of great abundance, produced by an everlasting gift for all these people.[424]

The document emphasizes conflict between Jesus and other leaders and may have functioned to guide the debate with outsiders.

Papyrus Oxyrhynchus 840 is a single parchment leaf, written front and back, and contains a single event that is otherwise unprecedented in Jesus tradition.[425] The front reads,

> . . . earlier, before acting unjustly, he argues everything wisely. But watch out lest you somehow also suffer like them. For human evildoers receive (their judgment) not only among the living; they also wait for punishment and great torment." And taking them along he brought them into the sanctuary itself and began walking in the temple. A Pharisee, a certain high priest named [Levi], came and met them and said to the Savior, "Who permitted you to trample this sanctuary and to behold these holy vessels, when you did not wash nor did your disciples immerse their feet? Although defiled you trampled this temple, a place that is clean, where no one else walks or dares to behold these holy vessels without washing and changing his clothes." Immediately the Savior stood with his disciples and answered him . . .

The back reads:

424. I have simplified the presentation of Zelyck's translation, *Egerton Gospel*, 143.

425. Ehrman and Pleše, *Apocryphal Gospels*, 267.

> You therefore who are here in the temple, are you clean?" That one says to him, "I am clean, for I washed in the pool of David, and by one set of steps I went down [into the *miqveh*] and by another I came up; and I put on clothes that are white and clean. And then I came and looked upon these holy vessels." The Savior answered him and said: "Woe to you blind who do not see. You washed in these waters that have been poured out, in which dogs and swine have wallowed night and day. And when you washed you scrubbed the outer skin, which even prostitutes and flute girls anoint, wash, scrubb, and beautify for human lust. But inside they are full of scorpions and every evil. But I myself and my disciples, whom you say have not bathed, have been dipped in waters of eternal life, which come from . . . But woe to those . . ."[426]

Jesus expresses indifference towards ritual purity in the canonical Gospels and attacks the Pharisees' hypocrisy. They never depict Jesus immersing in a *miqveh* (or purification baptismal), the ground of the conflict. The anecdote presumes the common belief that vision began in the heart and therefore required purification. Like sees like. Some of the elements of the story are less historically credible, like a Pharisaic high priest.

Sayings Gospels

The Gospel according to Thomas does not narrate events in the life of Christ but is a list of 114 teachings. It was probably composed in Syria, possibly Edessa. We have a complete Coptic translation from the Nag Hammadi library, the second tractate in Codex II, as well as Greek fragments from three papyri (Oxyrhynchus 1, 654, 655). The several differences between the witnesses suggest *Thomas* may have been a fluid document.

The opening is reminiscent of gnostic writings, "These are the hidden sayings that the living Jesus spoke and Judas Thomas the Twin recorded," suggesting dissatisfaction with "public" teaching about Jesus—presumably churches that used the canonical Gospels.[427] Many of the sayings are derivative of the canonical Gospels, but some are unique.[428] I reserve comment on the former; here are examples of the latter:

> Jesus said, "I have cast fire upon the world, and see, I am guarding it until it blazes." (10)

426. My translation is from the Greek in Ehrman and Pleše, *Apocryphal Gospels*, 273.

427. Translation is from Meyer, *Gospel of Thomas*, 23.

428. Zelyck, *John among the Other Gospels*, 85–103.

> Jesus said, "Become passers-by." (42)
>
> Jesus said, "It is I who am light which is above them all. It is I who am the all. From me did the all come forth, and unto me did the all extend. Split a piece of wood, and I am there. Lift up the stone, and you will find me there." (77)
>
> Jesus said, "He who is near me is near the fire, and he who is far from me is far from the kingdom." (82)[429]

The ending is reminiscent of the conversation with Salome in *The Gospel according to the Egyptians*:

> Simon Peter said to them, "Let Mary leave us, for women are not worthy of life." Jesus said, "I myself shall lead her in order to make her male, so that she too may become a living spirit resembling you males. For every woman who will make herself male will enter the kingdom of heaven."[430]

Unless Peter had a change of heart later in life, the claim about women is contradicted in his first letter (3:7).

At the core of the Sermon on the Mount is teaching on charity, prayer, and fasting (Matt 6:1–18). Jesus repudiates the distortions of the Pharisees, but nevertheless recommends these disciplines to his disciples. But in *Thomas*, he says, "If you fast, you will give rise to sin for yourselves; and if you pray, you will be condemned; and if you give alms, you will do harm to your spirits" (14).[431] If genuine, the original context for the saying may have allowed integration—"If you fast [like the Pharisees] . . . ," but it is a glaring contradiction as it stands.

Early studies concluded *Thomas* was a gnostic gospel, but the sayings appear to lack a consistent perspective. Nevertheless, the "gospel" of this gospel focuses on knowledge. The search for truth is initially troubling, but ultimately brings rest (2; Papyrus Oxyrhynchus 654.8–9). We discover that God's Kingdom is outside but also inside of us, that we are God's children and one with the savior (3, 108).[432] We find these motifs in the New Testament (Luke 17:21; John 15; Gal 2:20), but in the context of Jesus's penal substitutionary sacrifice for the forgiveness of sins. Paul warns against overly ascetic teaching that forbids marriage and emphasizes knowledge over humility and love (1 Tim 1:5; 4:3).

429. The translations are by Thomas Lambdin in Robinson, *Nag Hammadi Library in English*, 127, 131, 135.

430. Robinson, *Nag Hammadi Librar in English*, 138.

431. Robinson, *Nag Hammadi Library in English*, 128.

432. Meyer, *Gospel of Thomas*, 11.

Passion and Resurrection Gospels

Like Paul's letters, several gospels focus on the death and resurrection of Jesus Christ. We will focus on *The Gospel of Peter* and the *The Gospel of Judas.*

Eusebius excludes a gospel related to Peter from Scripture (*Hist. eccl.* 3.3.2; 3.25.6). Although we cannot be certain it is the fragment available to us, discovered in the grave of a monk in Upper Egypt in the late nineteenth century, most scholars accept that this is the gospel rejected by Serapion already discussed.[433]

We find three significant differences from the canonical Gospels. First, it is not Pilate who orders the crucifixion but the Jewish "King Herod" (2). Second, one of the robbers does not revile Jesus but the Roman soldiers, who respond by *not* breaking his legs to extend the suffering (13–14). Finally, whereas the Gospels do not depict the resurrection but respect the mystery, this gospel ends with the guard seeing

> three men emerge from the tomb, two of them supporting the other, with a cross following behind them. The heads of the two reached up to the sky, but the head of the one they were leading went up above the skies. And they heard a voice from the skies, "Have you preached to those who are asleep?"[434]

The Gospel according to Judas claims Judas is the only true disciple, who helps Jesus discard his body to free his inner, divine self. Christ offers this praise: "you will exceed all of them [other apostles]. For you will sacrifice the man that clothes me."[435] There are other differences with the canonical Gospels; some minor—Jesus laughs throughout *Judas*—but also more significant ones.[436] This gospel opens like the *Gospel of Thomas*: "The secret account of the revelation that Jesus spoke in conversation with Judas Iscariot during a week three days before he celebrated Passover."[437] In place of Peter's confession (Matt 16:13–20; Mark 8:27–30; Luke 9:18–21), Judas says, "You are from the immortal realm of Barbelo," a Sethian gnostic term.[438] This group viewed themselves as "descendants of Seth," the third son of Adam, who was revered as the mediator of divine knowledge. In

433. Ehrman and Pleše, *Apocryphal Gospels*, 375.

434. The translation is by Ehrman and Pleše, *Apocryphal Gospels*, 383.

435. The Coptic text is the second tractate in Codex Tchacos, which was apparently discovered in the 1970s but was not published until 2006. Translation is from Kasser et al., *Gospel of Judas*, 43.

436. For laughter, see Kasser et al., *Gospel of Judas*, 21, 24, 42.

437. Kasser et al., *Gospel of Judas*, 19.

438. Kasser et al., *Gospel of Judas*, 23.

Sethian writings, the creator god is called by the Semitic name Yaldabaoth, and he is presented as a demonic figure and enemy of humanity. He sleeps with Eve and fathers Cain and Abel. Only Seth is Adam's son, and his descendants alone can reach enlightenment. There is no evidence that Sethian Gnosticism was popular in Galilee where Jesus grew up. In fact, the earliest documents of the ideology date to about AD 100, seventy years after Jesus's ministry.

Irenaeus rejected this gospel:

> They declare that Judas the traitor was thoroughly acquainted with these things, and that he alone, knowing the truth as no others did, accomplished the mystery of the betrayal; by him all things, both earthly and heavenly, were thus thrown into confusion. They produce a fictitious history of this kind, which they style the Gospel of Judas.[439]

Judas, in turn, attacks the orthodox community. The disciples have a vision of themselves presiding over a temple, which represents the church. They describe themselves as sacrificing "their own children, others their wives, in praise [and] humility with each other; some sleep with men; some are involved in [slaughter]; some commit a multitude of sins and deeds of lawlessness."[440] Jesus provides an allegorical interpretation of the vision, which includes criticizing the disciples for planting "trees without fruit, in my name, in a shameful manner."[441] He adds: "The cattle you have seen brought for sacrifice are the many people you lead astray."

Missionary Digests

As we noted, missionaries often brought the *Fourfold Gospel* in a codex for the discipleship of new believers, but this was not always the case, especially when there was a language barrier. Because of this constraint, missionaries presented a digest of Jesus's life and teaching, which allows us to sense what was important to them.

In 635, a bishop from Sassanian Mesopotamia named Alopen brought the gospel to China.[442] A delegation went along the Silk Road for nearly six months. A religious exchange produced several texts that western scholars called *The Jesus Sutras*, which were sealed up in a cave at Dunhuang around

439. Irenaeus of Lyon, *Haer.* 31.1 (*ANF* 1:358).

440. Kasser et al., *Gospel of Judas*, 26.

441. Kasser et al., *Gospel of Judas*, 26.

442. Palmer, *Jesus Sutras*, 5.

1005.[443] The first tractate is in the form of a gospel, perhaps patterned after *Teachings of the Apostles*, a popular Syrian Christian work in the east that is no longer extant. In any case, this gospel opens with a paraphrase of the Sermon on the Mount. Here are a few of the more unique lines:

> [Jesus said,] "Pay no attention to outsiders but worship the One Sacred Spirit. The One will become visible to you, and then you should worship only the One."
>
> [Jesus said,] "All ultimately belongs to the One Sacred Spirit. At birth everyone is given a heavenly soul and the Five Attributes, and at the appropriate time food, drink, or clothing is provided."
>
> [Jesus said,] "Look for the best in others and correct what is worst in yourself."
>
> [Jesus said,] "Yet all who have faith will be saved. Those who have no faith this is because the evil spirits make it impossible for them to see."[444]

The sutra also relates Jesus's death and resurrection.

The other sutras are less obviously Christian. The perennial danger in missions is syncretism. For Martin Palmer, the translator of the *Sutras*, it is a matter of celebration: "It [the *sutras*] united the wisdom and moderation of Taoism and the humanism and compassion of Christianity—the Path of the Buddha and the Way of Jesus."[445] The issue would erupt again between Matteo Ricci, a Jesuit, and Franciscan missionaries a thousand years later. Ricci appropriated Chinese thought to contextualize Jesus, while others took the position of Tertullian, "What does Athens have to do with Jerusalem?" This tension has yet to be resolved.

Agrapha ("not written")

The New Testament and early fathers occasionally have Jesus say something that is not recorded in the canonical Gospels. These additional sayings came to be called *agrapha* ("not written").[446] A single saying is an *agraphon*. The term is somewhat ambiguous because they were ultimately recorded, just not in the Gospels. (Traditionally, it is only applied to sayings, not anecdotes,

443. Palmer, *Jesus Sutras*, 50.

444. Palmer, *Jesus Sutras*, 60, 61, 65.

445. Palmer, *Jesus Sutras*, 5.

446. The term seems to have been used first by J. G. Körner, a German biblical scholar in 1776. Many *agrapha* are collected in Schneemelcher and Wilson, *New Testament Apocrypha*, 1:88–91.

longer stories, or discourses, but I have allowed some flexibility for the sake of presentation.) We also find *agrapha* in less authoritative Christian literature, heretical writings, and even Muslim literature.

New Testament

In Acts, Paul cites Jesus to the Ephesian elders, "It is more blessed to give than receive" (20:35), although the saying does not occur in the Gospels.[447] Luke's placement may suggest Jesus gave this teaching after his resurrection, like other sayings in Acts.[448] The church in Jerusalem distinguished themselves by their radical generosity towards one another (Acts 2:42–47; 4:32–37). But Paul uses a formula, "We . . . must remember the words of the Lord Jesus" (20:35), that suggests the saying came from Jesus's earthly ministry (see Acts 11:16). If so, it may have been remembered as the punchline of an anecdote whose setting is now lost or, more likely, as part one of his mission discourses like the sending of the Twelve (Luke 9:1–6) or Seventy-Two (10:1–12) who offer peace and healing for hospitality. In Matthew's version of the former, Jesus says, "Freely you received, freely give" (10:8), but this similar saying does not occur in Luke's Gospel. The elders are the fruit of that mission, suggesting a coherence of context.

Paul also grounds his eschatology with Jesus's teaching:

> For we say this to you *by the word of the Lord*: we who are living, who remain until the coming of the Lord, will in no way precede those who fell asleep. For the Lord himself with a loud command, with the voice of an archangel and with a trumpet of God, will come down from heaven and the dead in Christ will rise (from those who are dead) first. [John 5:25–29] Then *we* who are living, who are remaining, will be seized together with them in the clouds into a meeting with the Lord. [Matt 25:6] And so we will be with the Lord forever. (1 Thess 4:15–17)

He speaks "by the word of the Lord" (*en logo kuriou*, ἐν λόγῳ κυρίου). The unit reads like a Jesus saying converted from the second person: "*You* who are living, who remain until the coming of the Lord, will in no way precede those who fell asleep . . ." The material is unique but fits well with apocalyptic teaching in the Gospels (John 5:25–29; Matt 25:6). Paul may allude to the parable

447. This example is especially significant because, in my view, Luke was aware of all four canonical Gospels.

448. See Acts 1:5, 7–8; 9:4–6 (repeated 22:7–8; 26:14); 9:10–12, 16 (repeated 22:10; 26:15–18); 10:13 (repeated 11:7), 15 (repeated 11:9); 18:10; 22:18, 21; 23:11.

of Ten Virgins (Matt 25:1–13), which focuses on wakefulness in light of the Parousia, in the next section of the letter: "let us not sleep" (5:6).

Paul claims in his first letter to the Corinthians, "as it stands written: *What eye did not see and ear did not hear, and did not rise up in the heart of a human being—what God prepared for those who love him*" (2:9). This is probably an *agraphon*. The apostle alludes to Jesus in the immediate context (v. 8). The *Gospel of Thomas* has Jesus say: "I shall give you what no eye has seen, what no ear has heard, what no hand has touched, what has not arisen in the human heart" (17).[449] Since the *Gospel of Thomas* appears to have been composed in the second century, it is likely the apostle is citing from a now lost work, partially preserved in the heterodox gospel.[450] Clement of Alexandria writes: "Lo, I make new things," says the Word [Jesus], "which eye has not seen, nor ear heard, nor has it entered into the heart of man" (*Strom.* 2.4). In the Gospels, Jesus promises revelation to his disciples. Especially significant is the parables discourse. Jesus cites Isaiah, who warns against the hardness of Israel: "*Seeing they do not see, and while hearing, they do not hear or understand*" (Matt 13:13; Isa 6:9–10 OG), and then to the disciples he says: "But blessed are your eyes because *they see* and your ears because *they hear*. For amen I say to you: many prophets and righteous people longed to see what you see, and did not see; and to hear what you hear, and did not hear" (Matt 13:16–17). In the same letter, Paul cites Jesus's words concerning divorce (7:10) and at the Last Supper (11:22), but we find clearer parallels in the canonical Gospels (Matt 19:1–12; Luke 22:17–19).

Paul may cite Jesus in Ephesians, "For everywhere the light is shining. Therefore, he[451] says: 'Awake, O Sleeper! And rise from those who are dead. And Christ will shine upon you'" (5:14), as Clement of Alexandria concludes (*Protr.* 9.84.2). The father even quotes the subsequent line: "The sun of resurrection, begotten before the day star, who has given life with his own beams." Epiphanius claims the saying comes for the Apocalypse of Elijah, but our extant version lacks the line (*Haer.* 42.12.3).[452] It seems more logical that Jesus would be the closer authority for Paul. The call to wakefulness echoes the Jesus Tradition in 1 Thessalonians.

These examples are not controversial because they occur in the New Testament, although we cannot be certain that Paul is citing Jesus in 1

449. Meyer, *Gospel of Thomas*, 31. The saying is attested in Papyrus Oxyrhynchus 654.

450. If I had to guess, it was a document that Paul used for catechesis in the churches he founded. It is also possible that Paul worked with a missionary digest. Melito of Sardis (Eusebius, *Hist. eccl.* 4.26.13) describes "extracts" (*eklogai*).

451. Or "it says."

452. See Charlesworth, *Pseudepigrapha*, 2:721–53.

Corinthians (2:9) and Ephesians. They actually contribute to arguments for the historical reliability of the Gospels because Paul is authoritatively citing a similar-sounding Jesus only twenty years or so after the resurrection.

The Fathers

Ignatius of Antioch quotes Jesus, "Take hold of me; handle me and see that I am not a disembodied demon" (*Smyrn.* 3:2).[453] Jesus makes similar claims in the Gospels (see Luke 24:36–43), especially in response to Thomas: "Bring your finger here and see my hands and bring your hand and put (it) into my side and do not be unbelieving, but believing" (John 20:27). The disciples mistook Jesus for a ghost (Mark 6:49). The *agraphon* may therefore be genuine, following the resurrection.

The *Epistle of Barnabas* has Jesus say, "Those who desire to see me and to gain my Kingdom must receive me through oppression and suffering" (7.11).[454] This too sounds like the Jesus of the Gospels (see Mark 8:34—9:1; Acts 14:22). Paul confidently writes, "All who desire to live god-like in Christ Jesus will suffer" (2 Tim 3:12).

The anonymous sermon, traditionally titled 2 Clement, has several *agrapha*—many of which are close in wording to sayings in the Gospels:

> [Jesus said,] "I will acknowledge before my Father the one who acknowledges me before others." (3:2; see Mark 8:38)
>
> [Jesus said,] "Not everyone who says to me, 'Lord, Lord' will be saved, but only the one who does righteousness." (4:2; see Matt 7:21–23)
>
> [Jesus said,] "Even if you were cuddled up with me next to my breast but did not do what I have commanded, I would cast you away and say to you, 'Leave me! I do not know where you are from, you who do what is lawless." (4:5; see Matt 7:21–23)
>
> For the Lord said, "You will be like sheep in the midst of wolves." But Peter replied to him, "What if the wolves rip apart the sheep?" Jesus said to Peter, "After they are dead, the sheep should fear the wolves no longer. So too you: do not fear those who kill you and then can do nothing more to you; but fear the one who, after you die, has the power to cast your body and soul into the hell of fire." (5:2–4; see Matt 10:16–25)

453. Holmes, *Apostolic Fathers*, 251.

454. My translation from Holmes, *Apostolic Fathers*, 404.

> For the Lord says in the Gospel, "If you do not keep what is small, who will give you what is great? For I say to you that the one who is faithful in very little is faithful also in much." (8:5; see Luke 16:10)[455]

Two *agrapha* are more distinctive:

> For the Lord himself, when he was asked by someone when his kingdom was going to come, said, "When the two shall be one, and the outside like the inside, and the male with the female, neither male nor female . . . When you do these things," he says, "the kingdom of my Father will come" (12:2–6)

> For the Lord says, "My name is continually blasphemed among all the nations," and again, "Woe to him on whose account my name is blasphemed." (13:2)[456]

We find two versions of the first *agraphon*—in Clement's citation from *The Gospel of the Egyptians* (*Strom.* 3.13.92) and *The Gospel of Thomas* (22). The gist meets what critical scholars call the criterion of multiple attestation, suggesting that Jesus said something like this. In the second *agraphon*, Jesus sounds like YHWH in the Old Testament (Isa 52:5, cited at Rom 2:24). There are several places in the New Testament where Scripture is spoken by the preincarnate Christ (e.g., Heb 10:5–7).

Justin Martyr (c. 110–165), who appropriates the *Fourfold Gospel*, also cites Jesus, saying, "And whoever will be angry is in danger of the fire" (*First Apology* 16), and "In whatever things I apprehend you, in those I will judge you" (*Dialogue with Trypho* 47). We find a similar saying in *The Book of Steps* (fourth or fifth century), a Syriac work on spiritual direction: "As you are found, so will you be led away [to judgment]" (Serm. III 3; XV 4).[457] Justin emphasizes the teaching in the Sermon on the Mount, and these sayings may be part of that tradition not entirely recorded by Matthew and Luke (see Matt 5:21–26; 7:21–23).

Irenaeus records a long saying of Jesus:

> The blessing thus foretold undoubtedly belongs to the times of the kingdom, when the righteous will rise from the dead and reign, when creation, too, renewed and freed from bondage, will produce an abundance of food of all kinds from the dew of heaven and from the fertility of the earth, just as the elders,

455. All the translations from 2 Clement are from Ehrman and Pleše, *Apocryphal Gospels*, 359, 361.

456. Holmes, *Apostolic Fathers*, 153, 155.

457. Cited in Schneemelcher and Wilson, *New Testament Apocrypha*, 1:91.

> who saw John the disciple of the Lord, recalled having heard from him how the Lord used to teach about those times and say: "The days will come when vines will grow, each having ten thousand shoots, and on each shoot ten thousand branches, and on each branch ten thousand twigs, and on each twig ten thousand clusters, and in each cluster ten thousand grapes, and each grape when crushed will yield twenty-five measures of wine. And when one of the saints takes hold of a cluster, another cluster will cry out: 'I am better, take me, bless the Lord through me.' Similarly, a grain of wheat will produce ten thousand heads, and every head will have ten thousand grains, and every grain ten pounds of fine flour, white and clean. And the other fruits, seeds, and grass will produce in similar proportions, and all the animals feeding on these fruits produced by the soil will in turn become peaceful and harmonious toward one another, and fully subject to humankind." Papias, a man of the early period, who was a hearer of John and a companion of Polycarp, bears witness to these things in writing in the fourth of his books, for there are five books composed by him. And he goes on to say: "These things are believable to those who believe." "And," he says, "when Judas the traitor did not believe and asked: 'How, then, will such growth be accomplished by the Lord?' the Lord said: 'Those who live until those times will see.'"[458]

The language is consistent with the Jewish messianic hope in a messianic kingdom:

> Then all the earth will be tilled in righteousness, and all of it will be planted with trees and filled with blessing; and all the trees of joy will be planted on it. They will plant vines on it, and every vine that will be planted on it will yield a thousand jugs of wine, and of every seed that is sown on it, each measure will yield a thousand measures, and each measure of olives will yield ten baths of oil. (1 En. 10:18–19)[459]

This background suggests escalation with Christ's vision: 10,000 is the largest Greek number. The *agraphon* may stand behind the enigmatic teaching of a millennial kingdom in Revelation (20:1–6).

Clement of Alexandria, who has been referenced already for his citations from the Jewish-Christian gospels, offers other sayings: "For 'ask,' he says, 'for the great things, and the small things will be added 'to you'"

458. Irenaeus of Lyon, *Haer.* 5.33.3–4. Translation is from Holmes, *Apostolic Fathers*, 753.

459. Nickelsburg and VanderKam, *1 Enoch*, 30.

(*Strom.* 1.24.158); "Be approved moneychangers, disapproving some things, but holding fast that which is good" (*Strom.* 1.28.177); "He that marvels will reign, and he that has reigned will rest" (*Strom.* 2.9.45 and 5.14.96; see *G.Th.* 2); "For not grudgingly, he said, did the Lord declare in a certain gospel: 'My mystery is for me and for the sons of my house" (*Strom.* 5.10.64). We also find sayings similar to Matthew's Great Commission:

> For this reason Peter indicates that the Lord said to the apostles: "If then anyone in Israel wishes to believe in God after repenting through my name, his sins will be forgiven. But after twelve years go out into the world, so that no one can say, "We did not hear." (*Strom.* 6.5.43)

> "I chose you twelve, judging you to be disciples worthy of me, you whom the Lord desired; and considering you faithful apostles, I am sending you into the world to proclaim the gospel to people throughout the earth, that they might know that there is one God, and to reveal the things that are about to take place through faith in me, the Christ, so that those who hear and believe may be saved, but those who hear and do not believe may bear witness and have no excuse to say, "We did not hear." (*Strom.* 6.6.48)[460]

Origen, who favored the *Fourfold Gospel*, still has Jesus say, "He who is near me is near the fire. He who is far from me is far from the kingdom" (*In Jer. hom. lat.*III 3; see also Didymus, *In Psalm.* 88.8; *GTh.* 82);[461] "I was weak because of the weak, and I was hungry because of the hungry, and I was thirsty because of the thirsty."[462]

These examples are generally considered to be less authoritative than the New Testament *agrapha*, although their provenance is more secure coming from recognized authorities. Several are reminiscent of the canonical Gospels, but we also find some strikingly unique sayings. We see the impact of canonization after this period where *agrapha* largely disappear in patristic writings.

460. Both translations from *Miscellanies* are from Ehrman and Pleše, *Apocryphal Gospels*, 363.

461. Cited in Schneemelcher and Wilson, *New Testament Apocrypha*, 91.

462. Ehrman and Pleše, *Apocryphal Gospels*, 365.

Textual Variants

The study of *agrapha* intersects with textual criticism in that some witnesses to the Gospels add Jesus tradition. At Luke 6:4, Codex Bezae Cantabrigensis, a fifth-century diglot of Greek and Latin featuring the Gospels and Acts, reads:

> On the same day, [Jesus] saw a man working on the sabbath. He said to him: "Man, if you know what you are doing, you are blessed. But if you do not know, you are accursed and a transgressor of the Law!"[463]

In Mark, Jesus expresses an enduring purpose for sabbath—a restful blessing to people (2:27). He does not simply "work" on the sabbath, but does so when there is an immediate need to feed or heal. Nevertheless, he also retains authority over the sabbath. Jesus does not condemn the man, but requires clarification of intent. If he was working for a sanctioned purpose, momentarily giving up his right to rest, he is blessed; but if he was flagrantly transgressing the Law, defying God, he is accursed. The saying may be genuine, but it is also possible that later disciples wanted Jesus to be more conservative concerning the sabbath, perhaps opposing Paul (see Rom 14), and put words into the Lord's mouth. The same codex adds at Luke 22:27, 28: "For I came into your midst not as one who reclines at the table, but as the one who serves; and you have grown in my service as one who serves."[464] The saying correlates with the Gospels, especially when Jesus washed the feet of the disciples.

Several late manuscripts read at Luke 9:55b–56a: "And he said, 'You do not know of what sort of spirit you are; for the son of man did not come to destroy human souls but to save them.'"[465] This saying reverses the warning about fearing God more than people because the ultimate Judge can destroy body and soul (Matt 10:28). Jesus uniquely functions as our savior against the backdrop of the Father's wrath. Paul confidently says, "Faithful is the word, deserving full acceptance: Christ Jesus came into the world to save sinners" (1 Tim 1:15). Perhaps the "word" presupposes this or a similar saying.

Famous examples are the longer endings of Mark, the drops of blood (Luke 22:43–44), and the Pericope Adulterae (John 7:53—8:11), which are discussed in their traditional places. These have an uncertain provenance, although the communities that produced the copies of the Gospels clearly valued these traditions.

463. The codex moves the contents of Luke 6:5 to after 6:10.

464. Ehrman and Pleše, *Apocryphal Gospels*, 357.

465. Ehrman and Pleše, *Apocryphal Gospels*, 357.

Apocryphal Works

In *Acts of Philip,* Jesus says, "Unless you make the lower into the upper and the left into the right, you will not enter into my kingdom."[466]

We find *agrapha* in the *Oxyrhynchus Logia* (third century), the same codex providing our earliest text of *Gospel of Thomas*. Some emphasize asceticism:

> [Jesus said,] "If you do not fast to the world, you will not find the Kingdom."
>
> [Jesus said,] "I stood in the midst of the world, and I appeared to them in the flesh. I found them all drunk; I found none among them thirsting, and my soul was afflicted for the sons of men; for they are blind in their heart and do not see that they came empty into the world, (and) empty they seek to leave the world again."[467]

Muslim Literature

There are many sayings attributed to Jesus (or anecdotes about him) in Islam, which views him as a great prophet, second only to Muhammad, but not divine.[468] They emphasize asceticism: "The highest asceticism was displayed by Christ when he threw away the brick he used as a pillow after the devil asked him why he kept it if he had renounced the world."[469] The following two anecdotes illustrate this:

> Jesus passed by three men. Their bodies were lean and their faces pale. He asked them, saying: "What have you brought to this plight?" They answered: "Fear of the fire." Jesus said: "You fear a thing created, and it behooves God that he should save those who fear." Then he left them and passed by three others whose faces were paler and their bodies leaner, and asked them, saying: "What have you brought to this plight?" They answered: "Longing for Paradise." He said: "You desire a thing created, and it behooves God that he should give you that which you hope for." Then he went on and passed by three others of exceeding paleness and leanness, so that their faces were as mirrors of light,

466. Cited in Schneemelcher and Wilson, *New Testament Apocrypha,* 1:213.

467. Cited in Schneemelcher and Wilson, *New Testament Apocrypha,* 1:121.

468. For discussion, see Triebel, "Das koranische Evangelium," 269–82.

469. Attributed to al-Ghazzali; cited in Faddiman and Frager, *Essential Sufism,* 182, slightly modified.

> and he said: "What has brought you to this?" They answered: "Our love of God." Jesus said: "You are the nearest to him, you are the nearest to him."[470] Jesus (upon whom be peace!) saw the world revealed in the form of an ugly old hag. He asked her how many husbands she had possessed; she replied that they were countless. He asked whether they had died or been divorced; she said that she had slain them all. "I marvel," he said, "at the fools who see what you have done to others, and still desire you."[471]

We see Jesus's demotion in the following anecdote:

> One day Jesus was walking in the desert with a group of self-seeking people. They begged him to tell them the Secret Name by which he restored the dead to living. Jesus said: "If I tell you, you will abuse its power." The people promised they would use the knowledge wisely and begged him again. "You do not know what you ask," he said, but he told them the Word. Soon after, the group was walking in a deserted place when they saw a heap of whitened bones. "Let us try out the word," they said to each other, and they did. The moment the Word was pronounced, the bones became clothed with flesh and transformed into a wild beast, which tore them to shreds.[472]

We also find adaptations from the canonical Gospels:

> A man of piety was following Christ. A thief seeing this thought to himself: "If I sit in the company of the pious ones, perhaps God may for his sake forgive me." Prompted by humility in his heart, the thief started condemning himself for the impious life he had led. He considered himself unfit to sit by the side of such a saint. On the other hand, the pious man, seeing the thief seated by his side, reprimanded him lest his shadow corrupt him. Immediately Christ heard the Divine Voice say: "Tell the pious one and the thief that I have washed clean the scrolls of both. The virtues of the pious and the sins of the thief are washed clean. Now they must start life again. The virtues of the pious are washed away because of pride, and the sins of the thief are washed away because of his humility and repentance."[473]

470. Cited in Nicholson, *Mystics of Islam*, 11.

471. Fadiman and Frager, *Essential Sufism*, 55, slightly modified.

472. Attributed to Rumi; cited in Fadiman and Frager, *Essential Sufism*, 86, slightly modified.

473. See Luke 18:9–14. Fadiman and Frager, *Essential Sufism*, 63, slightly modified.

An Arabic inscription in the ruined city of Fathpur-Sikri in North India has Jesus say, "The world is a bridge. Pass over it. But build not your dwelling there!"[474] The saying echoes *The Gospel of Thomas,* "Be passers-by," and may be closer to Jesus than many Christians are comfortable to admit. But in the canonical Gospels, the asceticism of Jesus is placed in a creative tension with a celebratory ministry.

The church has struggled to find the right place for these extracanonical gospels and sayings of Jesus. We find three positions. Irenaeus would have us focus on the canonical Gospels, and there are good reasons for this. All four originate from the first century and from apostles or those who knew them. We know they were valued and protected by true disciples of Jesus Christ. They have official sanction, and they have nurtured countless Christians. Nevertheless, despite his preferences for the *Fourfold Gospel*, Irenaeus also used an agraphon to defend his interpretation. Furthermore, as we find in Paul's letters, anything Jesus *said* had absolute authority.[475]

Another position is to relativize all the sources—to place *The Gospel of Thomas* or *Judas* on par with Matthew and so on. But these other gospels have an ambiguous provenance, and they are largely derivative. We find a consistent pattern of dissatisfaction with the canonical portrait of Jesus: some wanted their Lord to be vindictive, vegetarian, more ascetic, less Jewish, and so on. Whereas Marcion attempted to narrow the official portrait of Jesus Christ, many of these authors intended to expand it. Like Procrustes, this could not be accomplished without distorting the witness of the apostles and their associates from the first century.

Except for the Jewish-Christian gospels, we find increasing hostility towards the Jews (e.g., *The Gospel of Peter*). There is hostility towards other expressions of Judaism in the canonical Gospels, but it is an "in-house" conflict—Jews challenging other Jews to follow God's messiah. But this distinction cannot be maintained after the "parting of the ways" when the church became primarily Gentile. Anti-Semitism is one of the great failures of the Christian tradition.

The canonical Gospels respect the transcendence of the subject matter, like not depicting the resurrection, whereas a lot of this material seeks to satisfy curiosity rather than cultivate reverence. The apocryphal gospels were not copied with the canonical Gospels in our manuscripts, differentiated then as they should be now.

In a few places, these other writings may preserve an authentic *agraphon*, but they lack context for understanding. When Jesus has become a

474. Jeremias, *Unknown Sayings of Jesus*, 99.

475. Schneemelcher and Wilson, *New Testament Apocrypha*, 1:19.

mouthpiece for an ideology that did not exist in first-century Palestine, like various expressions of Gnosticism, as we find in *Judas*, that material should be discarded. When Jesus contradicts himself, that is, when the teaching cannot be integrated with earlier, authoritative tradition, as we find in *Thomas*, it should be discarded.

Another option is to follow the wisdom of the early fathers, who prioritized the four Gospels for faith and practice, but they did not immediately discount tradition from other sources. If an *agraphon* in the writings of a reputable authority enhances our understanding of Jesus, such tradition is helpful. However, as Serapion wrote, such material should not be treated as Scripture. Discernment is necessary. Two themes, I suggest, are especially helpful from this material, although they are also conveyed in the New Testament. First, Jesus came to reconcile all things. Therefore, it should not be surprising to find the union of opposites in the Kingdom, the breaking down of false dichotomies because of the limits of our present understanding. This opens the door for recognizing and worshiping the Triune God. Second, the whole of Christian literature emphasizes that the present life is a journey, a recapitulation of Israel's passage from the enslavement of Egypt to the joy of the Promised Land. Travel is difficult and requires a disciplined way of life.

In sum, with the *Fourfold Gospel* we have a plurality of voices, but not *all voices*. The early church recommends these books as our most reliable witnesses to Jesus based on their own judgements according to *antiquity* and *apostolicity*.

The Synoptic Problem and John

When reading the four Gospels together, the careful reader is struck by their similarities and differences. Matthew, Mark, and Luke are called the Synoptic Gospels (or Synoptics).[476] The adjective comes from the Greek *syn* ("together") and *optic* ("seen"). These three Gospels present Jesus with similar content and order. In contrast to John, Clement of Alexandria suggests they wrote "the outward lives" of Christ (*ta sōmatika*). Did one or more appropriate one or more as a source? There is no universally agreed upon answer to this question, which is called the Synoptic problem, but I have found one scenario to be the most plausible.[477]

476. The term may originate with Johann Griesbach (1745–1812).

477. For more discussion, see Goodacre, *Synoptic Problem*; Stein, *Synoptic Problem*.

Some believe the Gospels were written independently of one another, attributing the overlap to the Holy Spirit.[478] Many Fathers held something like a dictation view of inspiration, as Peter declared: "no prophecy ever came by the will of a human being; instead, human beings, being carried by the Holy Spirit, spoke from God" (2 Pet 1:21). The contemporary exegete Philo similarly claims:

> a prophet does not utter anything whatever of his own, but is only an interpreter, another Being suggesting to him all that he utters, while he is speaking under inspiration, being in ignorance that his own reasoning powers are departed, and quitted the citadel of his soul.[479]

Moses Maimonides claims that Moses acted like a secretary taking dictation for the Torah. As we noted, Christian contemporaries felt the same way, approaching the inerrancy of Scripture as a theological necessity. Although this has been criticized by those who do not accept the possibility of special revelation, there is no proof either way. I accept the Holy Spirit's role in the inspiration of Scripture as part of a sacramental worldview. But we should avoid the same reductionist error, claiming there is no human involvement in God's Word. Throughout Scripture, the Holy Spirit works through human personalities. Each Synoptic Gospel reflects a distinctive style and viewpoint, as Irenaeus's use of the four faces attests. Luke, without affirming or denying inspiration, claims to have studied eyewitness testimony (1:1–4).

Some attribute the overlap to oral tradition.[480] Stories about Jesus presumably were told from the beginning of the movement. Our earliest writings may not go back to the first decade of the movement, although we cannot be sure. In any case, the fact that people became disciples of Jesus soon after his departure presumes they were told something of his life and teaching. Discipleship required continuity in how the story was told.[481] Paul expresses concern over what exactly Jesus said (1 Cor 7:25). This Jesus tradition may explain the similarities and differences between the Synoptics. Even if an evangelist used another Gospel, other versions of the tradition might contribute to his presentation. We often find continuity

478. Farnell, "Views of Inspiration," 33–64.

479. Philo, *Works of Philo*, 630 (*Spec. Laws* 4.49).

480. Reicke, *Roots of the Synoptic Gospels*; Rist, *Independence of Matthew and Mark*.

481. Richard Bauckham notes: "the Twelve are listed as the official body of eyewitnesses who formulated and authorized the core collection of traditions in all three Synoptic Gospels. They are named, not as the authorities for this or that specific tradition, but as responsible for the overall shape of the story of Jesus and much of its content" (*Jesus and the Eyewitnesses*, 97).

in the core saying of Jesus, the topic of the anecdote, and diversity in the setting. Although some of the differences may be attributed to authorial style and interest, many appear to be incidental—the kind of variation typical of oral tradition.

Without denying the variables of inspiration and tradition, the extensive structural and verbal overlap in the Synoptics suggests a literary relationship. This is consistent with the common Greco-Roman practice of *aemulatio* and, in a Jewish context, rewritten Scripture. *Aemulatio* or *zēlōsis* (ζήλωσις), a way of composing that respects one's predecessors by appropriating and updating their compositions, was common:

> Classical rhetoricians felt it important to imitate authoritative texts to the best of their ability, with as little personal contribution as possible. Originality was esteemed less highly than copying, repeating and discovering how others thought. Ultimately, this provided the incentive for one's own thinking.[482]

Discussing Josephus, Steve Mason notes:

> Whereas we are bothered by conflicting accounts of the same events because we want to know *what really happened*, the Greco-Roman educational system aimed to produce men proficient in rhetoric, and this training emphasized the skill of telling the same story in very different ways.[483]

Josephus writes, "The industrious man is not the one who merely remodels another person's arrangement and order, but the one who, by speaking of recent things, also establishes the body of the history in a distinctive way."[484] We see *aemulatio* throughout his *Antiquities*. The historian adopted the twenty-book structure of *Roman Antiquities* by Dionysius of Halicarnassus. For the first half of *Antiquities*, he relies primarily on Scripture, but also appropriates earlier texts and tradition, like Philo's *On the Creation of the World* and tradition about Moses' birth (2.205). Josephus rearranges and condenses his sources, reserving elements for a later work. For example, he amalgamates *Kings* and *Chronicles*. The Jewish writer eliminates the most

482. Gahan, "'Imitatio and Aemulatio,'" 380; Kytzler, "Imitatio und aemulatio," 209–32; van Ruiten, "Book of Jubilees as Paratextual Literature," 65. In the first and second centuries, we find "old comedies" in the style of Aristophanes; "new comedies" after Plautus and Terence. Seneca emulates Euripides to test the knowledge (literacy) of his audience.

483. Embry et al., *Early Jewish Literature*, 1:254.

484. Josephus, *J.W.* 1.15. Translation is by Steve Mason in Embry et al., *Early Jewish Literature*, 1:336.

embarrassing elements of his people's history, like the golden calf and the breaking of the first tablets of the Law (3.99).[485]

We find a similar phenomenon in the Old Testament, with Deuteronomy as a "second Law" and 1–2 Chronicles re-presenting Israel's sacred history from a post-exilic perspective. Some of the Dead Sea Scrolls, called "rewritten Bible," expand, abridge, and re-arrange biblical texts.[486] Jubilees re-presents the biblical story from the opening of Genesis to Exodus 19.[487] They are not commentaries in the sense of citing a Scripture with a lemma, as we find in the *pesharim* of the Dead Sea Scrolls, but compositions—the earlier text is appropriated and transformed. Peter did not view inspiration and *aemulatio* as contradictory if, as most scholars believe, he appropriated Jude in his second letter.

Matthew fits within this Jewish interpretive tradition.[488] Luke probably appropriated Josephus as a source. In any case, he acknowledges *aemulatio* in his preface.

There is probably enough ambiguity in the problem that a final solution, convincing to all, will not be had. But a highly plausible scenario is suggested by the evidence. Andrew Gregory summarizes a popular criterion: "Direct literary dependence may be considered established and the direction of such dependence determined only when one text can be shown to presuppose redactional material that is present in the other."[489] If an evangelist put his face on the material and that unique portrait turns up in another Gospel, the latter has appropriated the former.

485. I derived this list from H. St. J. Thackeray's introduction to Josephus's *Antiquities*, viii–xiii.

486. See, e.g., Genesis Apocryphon (1QapGen ar) and the Temple Scrolla (11QT a). The description "rewritten Bible" is attributed to Geza Vermes (*Complete Dead Sea Scrolls*, 429–504). Sidnie Crawford describes the genre as "characterized by a close adherence to a recognizable and already authoritative base text . . . and a recognizable degree of scribal intervention into that base text for the purpose of exegesis" (*Rewriting Scripture*, 13, see also 40). Van Ruiten discusses the literature and makes the link ("Book of Jubilees as Paratextual Literature," 69–70). See also Zsengellér, *Rewritten Bible after Fifty Years*.

487. Van Ruiten, "Book of Jubilees as Paratextual Literature," 72.

488. Puéch, "4Q525 et la péricope des Béatitudes," 80–106; Stendahl, *School of St. Matthew*.

489. *The Reception of Luke and Acts*, 59. Michael Goulder employs the same criterion ("Luke's Knowledge of Matthew," 144).

Matthean Priority?

At least from the time of Origen, it was believed that the Gospels were written in the canonical order. Concerned with the relationship between Matthew and Mark, where the overlap is most pervasive, Augustine suggests Mark abridges Matthew.[490] He emulated the First Gospel, but found ways to shorten the presentation. After modern scholars began to argue for Markan priority, it was refined as the Griesbach hypothesis.[491]

Abridgments, like the *Diatessaron*, were common and accepted if they did not distort the original work.[492] Reading (performing) Mark requires about one and a half hours; Matthew, more than two. We might envision Mark editing Matthew to fit a worship service. One could read Mark as Matthew's story without the large blocks of teaching, like the Sermon on the Mount, which may have been used in the different context of discipleship (catechesis). But, as John Calvin noted, having created a harmony of the Synoptics, Mark's presentation of events is often longer than Matthew's.[493] Why would an abridger do this?[494]

Markan Priority

Most scholars reverse Augustine's solution—Matthew appropriated Mark.[495] This is the theory of Markan priority. It is often easier to interpret Matthew altering Mark's presentation than the reverse.[496] Rhetorically, Matthew's presentation is more refined.[497] (Augustine did not read Greek

490. *Harmony* 2.4. In book 4, Augustine describes Mark as a "unifier"—bringing the kingly and priestly emphases of Matthew and Luke respectively together.

491. The primary work of Johann Jakob Griesbach (1745–1812) on this topic is *Synopsis Evangeliorum*. William Farmer had championed this view more recently (*Synoptic Problem*).

492. See Keener, *Historical Jesus*, 134–35.

493. Cf. Mark 5:1–20; Matt 8:28–34; Luke 8:26–39. See Farmer, *Gospel of Jesus*, 129.

494. Goodacre, *Synoptic Problem*, 163. Perhaps the expansions reflect the values of an oral performance where emphases must be repeated because the hearer cannot re-read the page.

495. Mark Goodacre notes, "the consensus of scholarly opinion has pronounced strongly in favour of the priority of Mark" (*Synoptic Problem*, 56). Occasionally, someone argues Mark was written after Matthew and Luke (Voelz, *Mark 1:1—8:26*, 88).

496. See, e.g., Head, *Christology and the Synoptic Problem*. Around 90 percent of Mark's Gospel is duplicated in Matthew, although the content is often abridged. Over 50 percent is found in Luke, often closer to Mark's wording.

497. Alex Damm, comparing the Synoptics with contemporary rhetoric, notes: "A text that consistently and in numerous ways improves another text along rhetorical

well, and this may have prevented him from appreciating the difference.) He also appears to clarify Mark's wording where it might be misunderstood, as in the following:

> Jesus "was unable to do any powerful work there [in Nazareth] except, having laid hands on a few of the sick, he healed (them)," adding that "he was marveling because of their unbelief." (Mark 6:5–6)
>
> "And he did not perform many acts of power there because of their unbelief" (Matt 13:58).

It also easier to view the material unique to Mark as being passed over by Matthew (and Luke) than the reverse. For example, Mark unusually presents Jesus at first only partially healing the blind man at Bethsaida (8:22–26). Mark Goodacre has observed that Matthew and Luke depart from Mark's wording the most at the beginning of a passage but then come closer towards the end—what he calls "editorial fatigue."[498] For example, Matthew departs from Mark's presentation of the healing of the leper (Mark 1:40–45) at the beginning by noting "many crowds followed him" (Matt 8:1), but parallels Mark's wording of Jesus's response after cleansing him, "See that you say nothing to anyone" (Matt 8:4/Mark 1:44), which stands in tension with the very public setting.[499]

But what could lead Matthew, an apostle, to use Mark?[500] As we noted, Mark was remembered for writing down Peter's memories of Jesus. The form itself invites refinement and expansion.[501] Matthew likely published his Gospel in Antioch, where Peter was revered as a "pillar" of the church.[502] Some claim Matthew wanted to displace Mark, seeing problems with it. But this does not comport with the extensive overlap.[503] Mark often presents Jesus as a teacher, but provides little teaching. Matthew offers five large discourses, beginning with the Sermon on the Mount, which probably reflect his own tradition. He may also have wanted to adapt Mark to a Jewish audience.

---

lines is probably posterior to a text that rarely improves its alleged source, or that systematically removes marks of effective composition" (*Ancient Rhetoric*, 168).

498. Goodacre, *Synoptic Problem*, 71–76.

499. Goodacre, *Synoptic Problem*, 72.

500. Over 600 of Mark's 661 verses occur in Matthew.

501. See Larsen, *Gospels before the Book*.

502. Paul acknowledges this, despite his disagreement with the apostle over pulling away from table fellowship with Gentile Christians, in Galatians, written around AD 50.

503. See Doole, *What Was Mark for Matthew?*

Q?

Matthew and Luke overlap with material not found in Mark—some thirty-six units or 230 verses.[504] If Matthew and Luke wrote independently of one another, then presumably they are drawing on a common source. Scholars refer to this hypothetical document as Q (from German *Quelle* "source").[505] According to what has been called the Holtzmann/Streeter hypothesis, Q was written in Greek and is almost wholly preserved in Matthew and Luke, although the latter is more faithful in wording.[506] This paradigm dominated critical scholarship on the Gospels for much of the twentieth century.[507] Although great effort has gone into recovering the original document, no ancient writer refers to it; not a single copy or fragment survives.

The Farrer Hypothesis

A simpler explanation is that Matthew or Luke appropriated the other. The Jerusalem School of Synoptic Research maintains that Luke was written first. Mark and then Matthew follow Luke, although all three Gospels are dependent on an earlier Greek translation of a Hebrew biography of Jesus, which is no longer extant.[508] But this solution also rests on a hypothetical source.

Austin Farrer (1904–1968) claims Luke used Mark and Matthew—the Farrer hypothesis.[509] Luke "indicates in his prologue that other Gospels

504. Hagner, *New Testament*, 132.

505. Christian Hermann Weisse (1801–1866) claims that Matthew and Luke followed a common source of Jesus sayings (*Die evangelische Geschichte*). The precise origin of the expression *Quelle* is difficult to determine. Johannes Weiss (1863–1914) apparently shortened *Quelle* to Q.

506. Heinrich Julius Holtzmann (1832–1910) argues that Matthew and Luke used an *Urmarkus* ("Document A") in addition to another source ("Document B"), which is roughly equivalent to Q. Holtzmann later abandoned the *Urmarkus* hypothesis. His standard works are *Die synoptischen Evangelien*; *Lehrbuch der historisch-kritischen.* Burnett Hillman Streeter (1874–1937) extends Holtzmann's classification into a four-document hypothesis: (1) Mark, (2) Q, (3) "M", and (4) "L." The latter two sources comprise material unique to Matthew and Luke respectively. See his *Four Gospels*. When scholars reference Q, they actually cite the chapter and verse of Luke. For example, Q 6:20 is Luke 6:20.

507. See, e.g., Mack, *Lost Gospel*. For recent defenses of the Q hypothesis, see the essays in Tuckett, *From the Sayings to the Gospels*.

508. Lindsey, "New Approach," 87–106; Lindsey, "Modified Two-Document Theory," 239–63.

509. Farrer, "On Dispensing with Q," 55–88. James Ropes suggested this in 1934, without offering a comprehensive argument (*Synoptic Gospels*). See also Goulder, "Is Q a Juggernaut?," 667–81; Poirier and Peterson, *Marcan Priority without Q*.

were written before his," as Bonaventure notes.[510] Furthermore, Matthew and Luke occasionally agree in their wording against Mark—the so-called "minor agreements."[511] Streeter believed textual criticism would resolve this problem. Some argue the overlap is accidental—independent improvements on Mark's presentation. The simpler explanation is that Matthew's editing of Mark influenced Luke.

Why might Luke rearrange Matthew? Luke's aim "to write in an orderly sequence" (1:3) may refer to the rhetorical arrangement of material into series.[512] Matthew presents Jesus's teaching in large blocks, which break up Mark's narrative. The Sermon on the Mount extends for three chapters (5–7). Luke abridges Matthew's presentation, offering the so-called Sermon on the Plain (6:17–49), relocating material in smaller sections throughout his Gospel—like the Lord's Prayer (compare, for example, Matt 6:9–13 with Luke 11:1–4).

Marian Tradition

Around 25 percent of Luke is unique, raising the possibility of other sources. Luke appeals to eyewitness testimony of the Twelve for the material between Jesus's baptism and ascension (Acts 1:22) and intimates a reliance on Mary, who is present from before the birth to after the ascension (Luke 2:19, 51; Acts 1:14).[513] But unique to the Nativity, he claims twice that Mary "was remembering all these words, considering them in her heart" (2:19, 51). Both occurrences are part of uniquely Lukan material: The Shepherds and the Angels (2:8–20) and The Boy Jesus in the Temple (1:41–51). Joseph never speaks in either Gospel, but Mary does in Luke, with the story presented from her perspective.[514] Poetry was a culturally acceptable mode of female

510. Farrer, "Dispensing with Q," 56. Bonaventure attributed the prologue to Jerome, but scholars have identified it as part of the Monarchian prologues originally published in the late fourth or early fifth century (*Works of St. Bonaventure*, 14).

511. See, e.g., Matt 8:2/Luke 5:12/Mark 1:40. I follow Goulder's solution ("Luke's Knowledge of Matthew," 143).

512. Culy et al., *Luke*, 4. Peter uses καθεξῆς in a way that initially seems to be chronological (11:4) and yet his order of narration differs from Luke's order (10:1–48).

513. Minear, "Luke's Use of the Birth Stories," 111–30.

514. Luke implies eyewitness testimony of women elsewhere: note their juxtaposition to the Twelve at the beginning of Luke 8 and then see 24:10. See Bauckham, *Jesus and the Eyewitnesses*, 131.

literary expression.[515] Jesus's family was part of the early church.[516] Luke has Mary at Pentecost (Acts 1:14).[517] Some balk at this, but evidence suggests Luke had access to Jesus's family, specifically Clopas (see Luke 14:13–35). On this point, I agree with Raymond Brown.[518]

Other male and female disciples (Mary and Martha) may have served as eyewitnesses (Luke 8:1–3; 23:50—24:49; Acts 1:14).

Josephus

Luke may appropriate Josephus as a source.[519] This is suggested by their similar prefaces, the census of Quirinius, overlapping vocabulary, and focus on the destruction of the Second Temple of which the historian was an eyewitness. At least by the time of Origen, Christians were making explicit use of the historian's works. There is no reason why Luke could not have been an early adopter. Steve Mason suggests he heard Josephus read in Rome.[520] If this scenario is correct, Luke uses Josephus primarily for historical information.

John

John offers the most unique presentation. Some believe John writes independently; others, mindful of one or more of the Synoptics.[521] The fourth

515. For example: "Sappho," Corinna, Erinna, Nossis; Hannah's Prayer (1 Sam 2:1–10).

516. Paul mentions James, "the brother of the Lord" (Gal 1:19; 2:9, 12; 1 Cor 15:7), in contexts where fiction does not work.

517. Even if one prefers to date the publication of Luke towards the end of the first century (or later), the author could still be appropriating tradition originating from Mary. Papias valued oral tradition from those who knew Jesus (frag. 3).

518. Brown, *Virginal Conception*, 61.

519. F. Crawford Burkitt is confident of this scenario (*Gospel History*, 105–10). G. J. Goldberg suggests both authors appropriated a common source for part of the post-resurrection tradition ("Coincidences of the Emmaus Narrative," 59–77).

520. Mason, *Josephus*, 279.

521. Gregory, *Reception of Luke and Acts*, 56. C. H. Dodd detects a Jesus tradition independent of the Synoptics (*Historical Tradition in the Fourth Gospel*, 8). Zbyněk Garský argues that John offers an allegorical interpretation of the Synoptics (*Das Wirken Jesu in Galiläa bei Johannes*). Renan expresses either/or thinking I wish to avoid: "If Jesus spoke as Matthew represents, he could not have spoken as John relates" (*Life of Jesus*, 16).

Gospel may be read, at least in part, as a supplement to Mark.[522] John clarifies Bethany as the location for the Baptist's ministry (John 1:28; see Mark 1:5). In Mark, when Jesus stands before the Sanhedrin, he is accused of threatening to destroy the temple, although there is nothing in the preceding narrative to suggest this (14:58). But in John the temple demonstration is brought forward (fronted), with Jesus saying something that could be misconstrued as a threat (2:19–22). As an eyewitness (21:24–25), John apparently exercises the freedom to adjust Mark's chronology. We also find a pattern of John introducing characters that are not mentioned in Mark—Lazarus (11:1–2; 12:1, 9), Nicodemus (3:1), and Caiaphas (11:39; 18:13–14, 24), but assuming knowledge of those mentioned in Mark.[523] John may also have been inspired by Matthew, especially the Father-Son relationship (11:25–27).[524] These observations correlate with the Muratorian Canon, which claims that John incorporates the memories of the other apostles into his presentation.

The beloved disciple is consistently contrasted with Peter, who, at the Last Supper, is farther away from Jesus and must ask the disciple to ask Jesus to identify the betrayer (13:24). The beloved outruns Peter to the tomb and is the first to see (20:4). Yet Peter is the first to enter. Similarly, when the resurrected Lord encounters them fishing, the beloved is the first to recognize Jesus, but Peter jumps into the water (20:7). John sees; Peter acts. They may represent two modes of being, referred to in the Greco-Roman world as the contemplative life and the active life. Without falling into a false dichotomy, it is probably fair to say that Mark's Gospel, which is based on Peter's recollections, focuses on the active life of Jesus, while the fourth Gospel further explores its contemplative dimension.

522. For an extensive argument, see Barrett, *Gospel According to St. John*. For a detailed comparison and analysis of two passages, see Mackay, *John's Relationship with Mark*.

523. Bauckham, *Gospels for All Christians*, 165–67. The "beloved disciple" could be added to the list, although Mark mentions John the son of Zebedee, who is traditionally identified as the author of the fourth Gospel. Joseph of Arimathea is an exception (see John 19:38; Mark 15:43).

524. Viviano, "John's Use of Matthew," 209–37.

Luke's Appropriation of John

However, there is more overlap between John and Luke.[525] Some claim John appropriates Luke; others, the reverse.[526] The latter is more likely because the Fourth Gospel does not claim to appropriate other sources, but is based on eyewitness testimony, whereas Luke acknowledges sources. He may have taken notes from John's preaching or appropriated "Johannine tradition."[527] But a literary influence is more likely because of the pervasiveness of the overlap.[528]

Mark Matson focuses on the Passion.[529] For example, with John Luke does not record the flight of the disciples (Mark 14:49–52; Matt 26:55b–56) or the Barabbas exchange (Mark 15:10–11; Matt 27:17–20). In contrast to the other Synoptics, but with John, Luke relates Judas to Satan/the devil (Luke 22:3; John 13:2, 27), has Pilate declare Jesus innocent three times (Luke 23:4, 15, 22; John 18:38; 19:4, 6), and places two angels at the tomb (Luke 24:4; John 20:12).[530]

Luke often follows Mark's (and Matthew's) order, but his deviations generally follow John, as if deferring to the latter's chronology.[531] Paul Anderson suggests Johannine influence behind Luke's commitment to "orderly sequence" (Luke 1:4).[532]

When the other Synoptics and John present similar yet different accounts of an event, Luke conflates or harmonizes them (compare Luke 5:1–11 with Mark 1:16–20 par. and John 21:1–19).[533] John and Luke record

525. For an earlier list, see Schniewind, *Parallelperikopen bei Johannes und Lukas*. Parker offers several verbal parallels ("Luke and the Fourth Evangelist," 317–36).

526. Anton Dauer finds Lukan redaction in John (*Johannes und Lukas*) but does not even consider the reverse. For more discussion, see DelHousaye, "John's Baptist," 32–48.

527. E. Osty, "Les points de contact entre le récit de la Passion dans S. Luc et dans S. Jean," *RSR* 39 (1951) 146–54, 154; cited in Shellard, *New Light on Luke*, 204.

528. Cribbs, "St. Luke and the Johannine Tradition," 422–50; Cribbs, "Study of the Contacts," 1–93.

529. Matson, *In Dialogue with Another Gospel?*

530. See also the charts in Shellard, *New Light on Luke*, 204–6.

531. Shellard, *New Light on Luke*, 207; Gregory, "Third Gospel?," 129.

532. Anderson notes: "at least three dozen times, Luke appears to depart from Mark and to side with the Johannine rendering of an event or teaching" (*Fourth Gospel*, 112). He believes Luke appropriates Johannine tradition, not the canonical form.

533. This overlap may result from a common tradition. But John seems to clarify an implication of Mark's presentation—that Jesus calls strangers to his mission—by describing earlier encounters between Jesus and the first disciples, like Peter. Luke reflects this adjustment by having Jesus heal Peter's mother-in-law before the call, although this could be explained by his motif of counting the cost.

only one feeding miracle. He conflates Peter's confession (Mark 8:29; John 6:69; Luke 9:20).[534]

Luke also sharpens implications of John's presentation. The Fourth Gospel has the resurrected Jesus cook breakfast; Luke has him eat.[535]

When Luke records a triple tradition, the percentage of verbal overlap is high, between 51 and 75 percent. But in cases of quadruple traditions, the percentage drops to around 25 or 12 percent.[536] Matson also notes overlap around the presentation of the Baptist, the miraculous catch of fish, and the healing of the centurion's son.[537]

Luke appropriates the fourth Gospel like he does Josephus, as a historical source,[538] but he also adopts Johannine themes.[539] Especially significant is the difference between the baptisms of John and Jesus. Although only Luke depicts the Ascension, Jesus claims he must depart so that the Spirit might come in the Upper Room Discourse. John also provides a "mini Pentecost" (20:22). Mark and Matthew jump to Galilee after the resurrection, but Luke remains committed to Judea with John, emphasizing a similar pneumatology. Both are sympathetic to Samaritans, women, Gentiles, and emphasize the Holy Spirit.[540] The contrast between Peter and John in the Fourth Gospel resurfaces in Luke with Mary and Martha.

If our solution is correct, Luke is the first (extant) unifier of what came to be called the New Testament, anticipating Polycarp. He expresses perhaps our earliest validation of Matthew, Mark, and John as reliable presentations of Jesus's life and ministry. He also makes Paul an essential part of the story, indirectly holding a place for his letters, along with the three pillars—Peter, James, and John.

There is no universally-held solution to the Synoptic Problem. We may only argue in degree of plausibility. A majority of those who study the matter hold to Markan priority, but are less sure from there. Instead of bringing all the evidence forward, out of context, we shall read through the parallel and unique material of the Gospels, making observations along the way. The reader may choose a position or withhold judgment. The issue should not divide Christians or be a matter of doctrine. Indeed, no single hypothesis

534. Anderson, *Fourth Gospel*, 114.

535. Gregory, *Reception of Luke and Acts*, 59.

536. Shellard, *New Light on Luke*, 209.

537. Matson, *In Dialogue with Another Gospel?*, 91–163.

538. Without discussing Josephus, Matson arrives at a similar conclusion (*In Dialogue with Another Gospel?*, 448).

539. Shellard, *New Light on Luke*, 148–88.

540. Anderson, *Fourth Gospel*, 115.

answers every question. With that said, I recommend this history of publication: Mark was the first Gospel, which was appropriated by Matthew and John. Luke appropriates all three of the earlier Gospels and weds the story to a history of the early church (Acts).

Format of Commentary

To my knowledge this is the first modern commentary on the *Fourfold Gospel* using the Quadriga.[541] I borrowed the acronym *PaRDeS* ("paradise") from the rabbis, both as a framing device and perennial reminder of Jesus's invitation to Paradise, the Garden of Eden (Luke 23:43). Augustine came to God reading Scripture in a garden (*Confessions,* Book 8). Daily *lectio Divina* allows for a taste of our ultimate desire and space for spiritual growth in Christ. Monastic libraries had individual books of the Bible for study with glosses (commentary) in smaller script along the margin.[542] Some of these interpretations are very early, and were occasionally misunderstood as being part of Scripture. We maintain a clear distinction between Scripture and gloss. After a translation of part of the Gospels, the reader will, in many cases, work through glosses headed by P, R, D, and S. Not every gospel portion is amenable to all four senses, at least to my eyes. We invite the reader to work through the headings with the intention of receiving and giving to God. It should go without saying that our glosses are not intended to be the final word. We could only reproduce a fraction of Christian reflection on the Gospels. We also yield to the illumination of the Spirit in the mind and heart of the reader.

With Hugh of St. Victor, Aquinas, and the Reformers, we prioritize the *peshat* or literal sense (*sensus literalis*). Usually, this is the longest gloss. The main purpose of a commentary is to explain what a book is about. This is firstly fidelity to the text. A good commentary serves the reader by offering fresh insight and wisdom but also eliminating misunderstandings. The literal sense includes citation and allusion to the Old Testament as well as literary/rhetorical devices like hyperbole.

I prepared a fresh translation of the Gospels from the Greek that focuses on syntactical and semantic clarity. I attempted a word-for-word correspondence whenever possible, which often left barely suitable North American English on the page. If the signified of a word or phrase was too exotic for English, I opted for a transliteration, like *psychē* for ψυχή, with an explanatory footnote at its first occurrence. Some words come from

541. See Steinmetz, "Superiority of Pre-Critical Exegesis," 27–38.

542. Rosewell, *Medieval Monastery*, 30.

first-century Mediterranean social and religious lexica (like "kingdom of God," "tax collector," and "prefect") and therefore require a fuller exposition in the commentary proper. I have done my best, when facing an ambiguity, to keep my opinion in the footnotes and not the translation, although this is not always possible.

The four Gospels are broken down into 300 units (the length of Noah's ark in cubits, the worth in denarii that Mary poured on Jesus's feet) and combined according to a shared narrative or theme. Our first rule of interpretation is to cut at the joints—determining where a thought unit begins and ends.[543] The earliest manuscripts of the Gospels lack punctuation or versification. Stephen Langton (c. 1150–1228), Archbishop of Canterbury, created the chapter divisions around 1205, using the Vulgate. His system was inserted into Greek manuscripts of the New Testament in the fifteenth century.[544] Langton's decisions are often sagacious, but occasionally obscure the flow of the text. He did not seem to be aware of *inclusio* or chiasm, important framing devices in both Testaments. Often, at the beginning of P, a brief explanation for the unit's delimitation is given.

Eusebius notes a perennial and valid complaint against gospel harmonies: by prioritizing one narrative structure, like Matthew or John, the others are lost. The Gospels have similar beginnings and basically all end with Jesus's suffering, death, and resurrection. But the "middles" appear to be more thematic than strictly chronological. Some chapters reflect the order of Christ's life, our path to God; others are grouped according to theme and form: callings, miracles (signs), conflicts, parables, and eschatology. The exegetical principle is that reading like with like reveals patterns for theological reflection (Scripture interpreting Scripture). This arrangement, of course, is not intended to improve upon the individual Gospels. The *Fourfold Gospel* is a tool for study and meditation.

543. We find the use of *petuchah* and *setumah* already in Qumran manuscripts.

544. Byzantine scholars had introduced "headings" (*kephalai*) by the fifth century, but they reflected thought units while the philosophy of chapter divisions seems to be primarily spatial—the equivalent of a page. Robert Estienne divided these chapters into numbered verses in 1551.

2

Beginnings

This chapter allows the Gospels to introduce themselves. Wide are the paths of misunderstanding, but a good start anticipates a fruitful end.[1] We also jump ahead to the end of the fourth Gospel for its purpose statement. *Lord, may we bring everything—heart, energy, time, and mind—to the task at hand. Set us on the right path. Amen.*

1A: The Gospel Begins (Mark 1:1)

[1:1] (The) beginning of the gospel of Jesus Christ, son of God . . . [Isa 52:7]

P: The opening verse may title the immediate section or the whole Gospel.[2] Many translations place a period at the end (NIV, NRSV, ESV), but our earliest Greek witnesses lack punctuation.[3] On the one hand, *kathōs* (καθώς), which is translated "as" at verse 2, never begins a clause that introduces a quotation in the New Testament.[4] A repetition of *gospel* may delimit the opening unit: "Repent and believe in the gospel," says Jesus (1:15). On the other hand, the grammatical argument is not especially strong. *Kathōs* begins several clauses in the New Testament, including one that cites Scripture, albeit not explicitly (Gal 3:6).[5] There is no compelling reason why *gospel* cannot serve a dual purpose—to delimit *inclusio* and refer to the whole

1. Clements describes the beginning of a narrative as boundary and intimations of purpose (*Mothers on the Margin?*, 271).

2. Boring, "Mark 1:1–15," 43–82. David Aune agrees with Boring and also addresses the strained claim that the incipit is an interpolation (*Jesus*, 5–6).

3. They are probably following the lead of Aland et al., *Novum Testamentum Graece*, which adds a period following the verse.

4. Elliott, *New Testament Textual Criticism*, 187.

5. See John 15:9; Acts 7:17; Phil 1:7; 1 Tim 1:3.

story. There is a family resemblance to a biblical form called an incipit ("it begins"), an independent syntactical unit that titles a work:

> παροιμίαι Σαλωμῶντος υἱοῦ Δαυιδ ὃς ἐβασίλευσεν ἐν Ισραηλ (Prov 1:1)
>
> Proverbs of Solomon, son of David, who reigned in Israel
>
> ῥήματα Ἐκκλησιαστοῦ υἱοῦ Δαυιδ βασιλέως Ισραηλ ἐν Ιερουσαλημ (Eccl 1:1)
>
> Words of (the) Preacher, son of David, king of Israel in Jerusalem
>
> ᾆσμα ᾀσμάτων ὅ ἐστιν τῷ Σαλωμων (Song 1:1)
>
> Song of songs, which is by Solomon

Mark's first word *beginning* (*archē,* ἀρχή) is anarthrous (lacking an article) like these examples. So we the see the opening verse as serving a dual purpose—enlightening the immediate context and the entire Gospel.[6]

Now we may attend to the contents of the verse. The word *gospel* (*euangelion,* εὐαγγέλιον) was unpacked in our discussion of genre. Mark is celebrating freedom from the effect (fragility, death) and the influence of evil (temptation, sin). The phrase *of Jesus Christ* (*Iēsou Christou,* Ἰησοῦ Χριστοῦ) is ambiguous. The Greek genitive may present *Jesus* as the source or object of the gospel—subjective genitive or objective genitive, respectively. On the one hand, the "good news" will soon come *from Jesus's* mouth (1:15), who speaks in every chapter but the last (unless we include the "longer ending"). On the other, the *gospel* is also *about* Christ, the apostolic message or *kerygma.*[7] The good news is *about* the death and resurrection of Christ. Mark devotes at least half his story to this. However, some grammarians speak of a "plenary genitive," which allows *Jesus Christ* to function as both subject and object, a syntactical pun.[8] The genitive simply juxtaposes words and leaves their relationship to be deciphered by the hearer (reader). Jesus will *subjectively* interpret the significance of his *objective* ministry (10:45).

There is also ambiguity concerning the original wording of the verse. On the one hand, *son of God* (υἱοῦ θεοῦ) is absent in Codex Sinaiticus, one of our earliest witnesses to Mark's wording (early fourth century).[9] This is

6. Kingsbury, *Christology of Mark's Gospel,* 56.

7. See Mark 13:10; 14:9; 10:29.

8. For the syntax, see Wallace, *Greek Grammar,* 120–21; for this interpretation, Aune, *Jesus,* 335.

9. For this and other reasons, Peter Head rejects its originality ("Text-Critical Study of Mark 1.1," 621–29).

also the case with our earliest witness (late third or early fourth century).[10] The shorter reading is usually preferred. It is perhaps easier to imagine the epithet being added than lost, especially after Mark followed Matthew in a codex. The incipit opening the first Gospel refers to Jesus as "the son of David" and "the son of Abraham" (Matt 1:1), which might have encouraged a scribe to add a similar epithet to Mark's incipit. On the other, Codex Vaticanus, a contemporary witness from the same region has the epithet. If Matthew appropriated Mark, which is likely, then the epithet *son of God* may have inspired "son of David" and "son of Abraham" (Matt 1:1). Major translations retain *son of God,* although some alert the reader with a footnote of the textual variant. In any case, the variant is not essential: if added, the original hearers (readers) only had to wait a moment to hear, "You are my beloved Son" (v.11).[11]

D: The earliest, surviving application of this verse was to ward off evil spirits, an emphasis in Mark (see 1:21–28). The papyrus fragment we call Oxyrhynchus 5073 was part of an amulet.[12] The text adds an article to *Christ* (τοῦ Χριστοῦ)—*the Christ.* The amulet presupposes power in the name and role of Jesus. It is, despite the troubling associations with magic, an enacted gospel, an expression of faith—at least that of a mustard seed. There is more power in the name of Jesus *the* Christ than any opponent.

S: *Lord Jesus, thank you for not only proclaiming good news but being the gospel. Thank you for saving all who call on your name. May we wear you, like an amulet, upon our hearts. Amen.*

1B: Genesis (Matt 1:1)[13]

[1:1] (The) *book of genesis* of Jesus Christ [Gen 5:1], *son of David* [Prov 1:1; Eccl 1:1], son of Abraham.

P: Only Mark and Matthew title their Gospels. Mark's "beginning" (*archē,* ἀρχή) and Matthew's *genesis* (*genesis,* γένεσις) were also titles for

10. P. Oxy. 5073. See Comfort, *Commentary on the Manuscripts*, 178.

11. See Malik, "The Earliest Corrections," 207–54. Wasserman and Gurry applied the Coherence-Based Genealogical Method and found that the shorter reading was not transmitted well and that the witnesses to this reading only agreed coincidentally (*New Approach to Textual Criticism*, 43–50).

12. Sanzo, *Scriptural Incipits on Amulets*, 99.

13. Providing a subhead description for gospel units probably goes back at least as far as our earliest textual witness for this unit, P1 (mid-third century), which may have read, "Was born [Jesus Christ, the son of David,] from [the Holy Spirit coming upon] his mother [Mary, the wife of Joseph]" (Comfort and Barrett, *Text of the Earliest New Testament*, 40).

the first book of the Pentateuch in the first century. Both employ an ancient, global means of characterization through patronymic: *Jesus Christ* is firstly a *son* of someone.[14] Mark immediately relates Jesus to God the Father; Matthew follows Mark in these ways but wants to give the backstory first.[15] *Son of David* was a popular messianic title, signifying a descendant of the king, a warrior, who would free Israel from Roman oppression and establish an eternal kingdom on earth.[16] It evokes the longest, most extensive biography in the Old Testament (1 Sam 16:1–31; 2 Sam; 1 Kgs 1:1—2:12, rewritten in 1 Chr 11:1—29:30). Matthew allows the opening words to anticipates the subsequent genealogy (1:2–16) but also the whole Gospel, which resolves with Jesus commissioning the disciples, saying "all authority in heaven and earth has been given to me" (28:18).[17] *Son of Abraham* evokes the patriarchal stories in Genesis.

R: The opening words (*Biblos geneseōs*, Βίβλος γενέσεως) occur nowhere else in Scripture before Matthew, except twice in Genesis (2:4; 5:1 LXX).[18] The first occurrence anticipates the intimate creation of Adam among creation: "This is the book of *genesis* (βίβλος γενέσεως) of heaven and earth . . . God formed the human being, dust from the earth, and breathed into his face (the) breath of life (2:4, 7 LXX); the second opens a genealogy of his descendants—"This is the book of *genesis* (βίβλος γενέσεως) of human beings. On the day God made Adam, he made him according to the image of God" (5:1 LXX)—that emphasizes the consequence of the Fall. Adam lives 930 years and dies (Gen 5:4). Despite the remarkably long lifespans, reaching a ceiling with Methuselah (969 years), all of Adam's descendants die, except Enoch, "who walked with God and was not, for God took him" (5:24). Adam Christology will be more explicit in Luke and Paul's letters, but there is an embryonic form of it here. Like Adam, Jesus is not begotten by a human father (1:16, 18); unlike Adam, yet similar to

14. See Homer's *Iliad* and *Odyssey.*

15. If Mark's "son of God" is not original (see P above), then it may be due to a scribe wanting to align the second Gospel more closely to the opening of the first.

16. Horsley, "Jesus und imperiale Herrsschaft," 89–93. For this title in the New Testament, see Mark 10:47, 48; 12:35; Matt 1:1, 20; 9:27; 12:23; 15:22; 20:30; 21:9, 15; 22:42; Luke 3:31; 18:38, 39. Paul claims Jesus's Davidic ancestry in the early 50s (Rom 1:3). The Jewish-Christian historian Hegessipus (c. 110–180) claims Jesus's ancestors were questioned by the Roman government for their Davidic ancestry. Christian expectation in the second coming largely conforms to the traditional view of a Davidic Messiah.

17. Aune, *Jesus*, 8.

18. The original Hebrew read *sefer toledot* (MT). The LXX Greek is a literal translation. Technically, Genesis 5 offers a "linear" not "segmented" genealogy, which speeds the narrative along. For a similar incipit, see 1 En. 14:1.

Enoch, Jesus overcomes death.[19] The genitive *of Jesus Christ* (*Iēsou Christou*, Ἰησοῦ Χριστοῦ) is ambiguous. On the one hand, this *book of genesis* is *about* Christ. His birth resolves the genealogy (1:16–17); his resurrection, the narrative of the Gospel. But the genitive may also be taken as conveying the agency of the understood action: Jesus brings a new genesis or "regeneration" (19:28).[20] As we noted with a similar ambiguity in Mark's opening, both senses may be at play ("plenary genitive").

Matthew evokes the covenants or special relationships that God made with *Abraham* and *David*, as John Chrysostom notes: "in him [Christ] was fulfilled the promises to both."[21] God says to *Abraham* when his name was still Abram: "In you all the families of the earth will be blessed" (Gen 12:3). *Abraham's* calling begins God's solution to the Fall. God's blessing for all people will be traced back to this divine-human encounter. Jesus will express his kinship with all of *Abraham's* children throughout the world at the Great Commission when he sends his eleven "brothers" (disciples) to retrieve them. The covenant language reoccurs in God's further promising to *David*: "I will raise up your seed (offspring) after you, who will come from your body, and I will establish his kingdom . . . Your throne will be established forever (2 Sam 7:12, 16; see Gal 3:16). Proverbs and Ecclesiastes open with incipits that identify the speaker with the epithet *son of David*.[22] We are therefore not surprised when Jesus, who is greater than Solomon, speaks proverbially.

D The incipit has been described as a "demiurgical act," the first scene of worldview creation, and this makes demands on readers.[23] For those unfamiliar with Ancient Israelite Scripture, the language is opaque (as the subsequent genealogy will be as well). Matthew opens *in medias res* ("in the middle things"), presupposing a cursory level of education. In this case, knowledge—biblical literacy—must precede formation, so that there is something to give the Spirit.

Jesus is a *son* or "descendant" *of Abraham* whose name in Hebrew means "father of a multitude."[24] Jews, Christians, Muslims—all claim *Abra-*

19. Noted by Rabanus Maurus (c. 780–856) who is cited in Aquinas, *CA* on Matthew 1.

20. Quarles, "Matthew 27:51–53," 283.

21. Aquinas, *CA* on Matthew 1.

22. The Hebrew *ben Dawīd* (בֶּן־דָּוִד) is translated *huiou Dauīd* (υἱοῦ Δαυιδ) in Greek, the wording in Matthew's incipit.

23. Fusillo, "From Petronius to Petrolio," 417.

24. For the semantic range of *huios* "son/descendant" (Heb. *ben*; Ar. *bar*), see Davies and Allison, *Matthew*, 1:158. Very few Jews took Abraham's name out of reverence. See Gen 17:4–5; Gal 3:7–9; Rom 4:16; *t. Ber.* 1:12.

ham as father, although he was not a Jew, Christian, or Muslim but was from Mesopotamia ("between two rivers," the Tigris and Euphrates), the cradle of civilization.[25] His father Terah was a polytheist from the city of Ur (which lies 186 miles southeast of modern Baghdad). In this culture, every city had a god with a temple ("house"). But *Abraham* hears God and leaves.[26] Today, over half the world's population self-identify as children of Abraham. Many claim descent through his son Ishmael; others, Isaac; and still others embrace a spiritual link, following the apostle Paul (Rom 4). They do not identify with Abram, the Mesopotamian and polytheist, but the one called out by God. Muslims believe Abraham initiated the first *Hajj* or pilgrimage, the largest annual gathering of human beings on earth. Jews have been a nomadic people, but many are settling in Israel. And yet God has begun an even greater gathering in Christ.

S: Matthew's incipit presupposes the two greatest distinctives of Israel's God: creative and interpersonal. He relates Jesus Christ to a God who spoke the heavens and earth into existence; but unlike deism, which presupposes a deity that lacks interest in creation, the God of Israel meets people through promises. *Father, we thank you for our lives, our very being, and for the promises that find their fulfillment in your Son, Jesus Christ. Amen.*

2: The Logos (John 1:1–18)

John opens with something like a prologue (*prologos*, πρόλογος "pre-speech"), which Aristotle describes as "a foretaste of the theme . . . intended to inform the hearers of it in advance instead of keeping their minds in suspense."[27] The unit functions as the "interpretive key" for the rest of the Gospel.[28] He delimits the unit with *inclusio*, which emphasizes friendship: "the Logos was beside God . . . the one who is at the chest of the Father—that

25. 3500–3000 BC. From here, "the impetus to develop civilized structures radiated out to India, China, and the Mediterranean basin" (Starr, *History of the Ancient World*, 28). The Sumerians imposed abstract order on nature. They developed place-value notations (the root of our number system leading to the measurements of weight: the chief weight, a talent of 60 minas, remained the standard quantity down to the writing of this Gospel—see Matt 18:24), fields (geometry), and time (the "year" was solar, but defined in twelve lunar months, which required an intercalary month about every three years). Scribes began writing literature down by 2600 BC.

26. Gen 12:1–3. Muslims believe he removed all the idols in Canaan at this time.

27. Aristotle, *Rhet.* 3.14 [1415a] (*Basic Works*, 1438).

28. Skinner, *Reading John*, 29.

one explained him" (1:1, 18).[29] Four subunits further present the Logos as distinct from John the Baptist:

A Creation through The Logos (1:1–5)

B Origin of The Baptist (1:6–8)

A' Mission of The Logos (1:9–14)

B' Mission of The Baptist (1:15–18)

Unlike Mark and Matthew, John does not begin with the proper name Jesus or the messianic title Christ, both of which occur later (1:17), but *logos* (λόγος). We transliterate the Greek because it is especially difficult to find a sufficient English replacement. Meditating on the meaning(s) of *logos* is a rite of passage for the thinking disciple. We begin to understand the connectivity of all creation with our Creator, the Triune God ("In the beginning *God*").

The simplistic dichotomy between Athens and Jerusalem, between reason and faith, obscures the stimulating encounters between Jewish and Greek thought before the Hasmonean rebellion in Judea, a synthesis that continued in nearby Alexandria, Egypt, at the time of Christ; and before this encounter is the ancient Israelite integration of the transcultural wisdom tradition.[30] The appropriation of wisdom precedes civilization, but is also an earmark of every successful culture, often beginning as an oral pool of know-how passed from one generation to the next for survival. The earliest wisdom texts feature a king, the protector of a people, preparing his son to take his place.[31] The biblical wisdom tradition draws from human observation while disciplining these claims under the revelation of YHWH, the covenant-making God of Israel (Prov 1:7).

Wisdom (*Sophia*, σοφία) is the only divine attribute to be personified in Hebrew Scripture (*Hochmah*, חָכְמָה). The New Testament presents her as a type of Christ (Col 1:15–20; Heb 1:1–4), as do Justin Martyr (*Dialogue* 61), Irenaeus (*Against Heresies* 4.20.3, spec. vv. 27–31), and other church fathers. In Proverbs, Wisdom is a beautiful yet scorned woman, who makes four appearances.[32] In the first, she cries out:

> How long, O simple ones, will you love being simple? How long will scoffers delight in their scoffing and fools hate knowledge? If you turn at my reproof, behold, I will pour out my spirit to you;

29. *Inclusio* is a repetition of a key word or phrase at the beginning and end of a unit. See Kim, *Sourcebook*, 23.

30. The benchmark study remains Hengel, *Judaism and Hellenism*.

31. Crenshaw, *Old Testament Wisdom*, 1–10.

32. See Prov 1:20–33; 3:13–20; 8:1–36; 9:1–18.

> I will make my words known to you. Because I have called and you refused to listen, have stretched out my hand and no one has heeded, because you have ignored all my counsel and would have none of my reproof, I also will laugh at your calamity; I will mock when terror strikes you, when terror strikes you like a storm and your calamity comes like a whirlwind, when distress and anguish come upon you. Then they will call upon me, but I will not answer; they will seek me diligently but will not find me. Because they hated knowledge and did not choose the fear of the LORD, would have none of my counsel and despised all my reproof, therefore they shall eat the fruit of their way, and have their fill of their own devices. For the simple are killed by their turning away, and the complacency of fools destroys them; but whoever listens to me will dwell secure and will be at ease, without dread of disaster. (1:22–33 ESV)

She addresses the immature and oblivious.[33] Her response is similar to a jilted lover. In the second appearance (3:13–20), her incomparable value is extolled. The son of David describes her as a "tree of life" (v. 18). In the fourth (9:1–18), Wisdom invites the immature to eat her bread and drink her wine (v. 5). The third appearance (8:1–36) is the most theologically significant and controversial:

> I, wisdom, dwell with prudence, and I find knowledge and discretion. The fear of the LORD is hatred of evil. Pride and arrogance and the way of evil and perverted speech I hate. I have counsel and sound wisdom; I have insight; I have strength. By me kings reign, and rulers decree what is just; by me princes rule, and nobles, all who govern justly. I love those who love me, and those who seek me diligently find me. Riches and honor are with me, enduring wealth and righteousness. My fruit is better than gold, even fine gold, and my yield than choice silver. I walk in the way of righteousness, in the paths of justice, granting an inheritance to those who love me, and filling their treasuries. The LORD possessed [*qanah,* קָנָה; OG *ktīzō,* κτίζω] me at the beginning of his work, the first of his acts of old. Ages ago I was set up, at the first, before the beginning of the earth. When there were no *depths* [Gen 1:2] I was brought forth, when there were no springs abounding with water. Before the mountains had been shaped, before the hills, I was brought forth, before he had made the earth with its fields, or the first of the dust of the world. When he established *the heavens,* I was there; [Gen 1:1] when he drew a circle on the face of *the deep,* [Gen 1:2] when he

33. The unit is delimited by *inclusio*—the "simple" (vv. 22, 32).

> made firm the skies above, when he established the fountains of *the deep,* [Gen 1:2] when he assigned to the sea its limit, so that *the waters* might not transgress his command, when he marked out the foundations of the earth, then I was beside him, like a master workman, and I was daily his delight, rejoicing before him always, rejoicing in his inhabited world and delighting in the children of man. And now, O sons, listen to me: blessed are those who keep my ways. Hear instruction and be wise, and do not neglect it. Blessed is the one who listens to me, watching daily at my gates, waiting beside my doors. For whoever finds me finds life and obtains favor from the LORD, but he who fails to find me injures himself; all who hate me love death." (8:12–36 ESV, emphasis added)

The Old Greek translates the Hebrew *qanah* with *ktīzō,* which may be rendered "create,"[34] although "possess" is a more common sense in the Bible.[35] Scripture uses a different word, *bara* (בָרָא), to describe God creating the heavens and the earth (Gen 1:1). The sense may be "generate."

Sirach (200–175 BC), an influential Jewish writing in the wisdom tradition, now in the *Apocrypha,* picks up the discussion from Proverbs. Wisdom is also personified as a woman (24:3–22); the motif of rejection continues, but with a twist. Seeking a home among the Nations (Gentiles), she cries: "Come to me, you who desire me, and eat your fill of my fruits. For the memory of me is sweeter than honey, and the possession of me sweeter than honeycomb" (24:19–20). She went everywhere (24:2–6); ignored, God assigns her to dwell in the temple at Jerusalem (24:10–12). She is identified with the Mosaic Law and is only available to Israel.[36] This interpretation may have been challenged by other Jewish writings that claim she is rejected even there and must return to heaven.[37] Sirach explicitly presents Wisdom as "created" (*ktīzō,* κτίζω) by God (1:4, 9; 24:9), which encouraged Arius (c. 250–c. 336) to claim, "There was [a time] when he [Jesus Christ] was not."[38] Yet John makes no statement about the Logos's origin.

34. See NRSV, JPS, and Clifford, *Proverbs*, 96.

35. The ESV translates accordingly—God appropriated Wisdom to create everything (see 3:19). Interestingly, the Greek translations of Aquila, Symmachus, and Theodotion read *ktaomai* (κτάομαι "to possess"). This represents a Jewish perspective on Wisdom from the first and second centuries.

36. This claim is at the center of the book (24:23; Embry et al., *Early Jewish Literature,* 2:4; see Grabbe, *Wisdom of Solomon*, 70–71).

37. 1 En. 42:1–2; see Nickelsburg and VanderKam, *1 Enoch*, 4–5.

38. See "The Arian Syllogism" [c. 440], in Theodoret, *Hist, eccl.* 1.5. In a letter (c. 321) to Eusebius, Bishop of Nicomedia, he admits: "We are persecuted because we say that the Son has a beginning, but God is without beginning."

In Hellenistic philosophy, *logos* describes the mysterious, dynamic force and rational purpose behind all things that opposes chaos and nihilism. Ancients perceived *logos* from the rhythmic dance of the sun and moon and patterns across nature's spectrum.[39] *Why do the veins of a palmate leaf mirror those on my hand?* The first surviving use of *logos* in Greek literature is in a metaphysical poem by Parmenides (c. 515 BC–c. 450), "One Being." With *logos*, he intuited that reality (truth) is one—an unmoving, unchanging, solid, homogenous sphere. Around the same time, Siddhartha Gautama (563–483 BC), the Buddha ("enlightened one"), came to a similar realization: "I consider the doctrine of sameness as the absolute ground of reality."[40] Yet we live in a moving world of seeming difference: today is not the same as yesterday; *the veins on my hand are not the same as those on a leaf.* To resolve this tension, a distinction was made between "the way of truth (reality)," the oneness and changelessness of being, and "the way of seeming," our shifting perceptions. The physical senses are trapped in the latter and therefore oblivious to ultimate reality. The Ephesian philosopher Heraclitus (fl. 504–501 BC) claims the *logos* is not self-evident as part of human experience:

> The Logos, (which is) as I describe, proves incomprehensible, both before it is heard and even after it is heard. For although all things happen according to the Logos, many act as if they have no experience of it, even when they do experience such words and action as I explain, as when I separate out each thing according to its nature and state how it is; but as to the rest, they fail to notice what they do after they wake up, just as they forget what they do when they sleep.[41]

He writes: "Nature (*fusis*, φύσις) likes to hide." Yet the philosopher also claimed knowledge of truth (reality) is possible for anyone who focuses on the "real nature" of things by paying attention to their universal aspect or place in the subtle web of reality.[42]

Parmenides and Heraclitus, a part of the so-called Pre-Socratics, provided the ontology for Plato (d. 348/7 BC) who focused his dialogues on "the Greek insight that Reason, the *logos*, is nature steering all things from

39. Galileo Galilei (1546–1642) claims that the universe is written in the language of mathematics. Carl Friedrich Gauss (1777–1855) claims the logic that holds together mathematics also pervades the universe. Johannes Kepler (1571–1630) detects a rational architecture underlying the structure of the solar system.

40. Shaku, *Zen for Americans*, 21.

41. Geldard, *Remembering Heraclitus*, 32.

42. For more discussion, see Miller, "Logos of Heraclitus," 161–76.

within."[43] To know reality requires union or participation in the *logos*.[44] The philosopher was also influenced by the Orphics, who believed the soul was divine and therefore united to "the One God who dwells in all."[45] As a fragment of God, the soul was destined for reunion with God. But until the soul was purified, it was fated to follow the round of reincarnation.[46] Orphic theology moves along a continuum of personal and impersonal conceptions of God.[47] The Stoic philosopher Epictetus (c. A.D. 50–125) presents the *logos* as a rational principle that orders and unites the universe. Marcus Aurelius (121–180) identifies the *logos* with God, but a God who is essentially the consciousness of the world and wholly material.[48] In the first century, Platonic and Stoic thought was espoused in schools around the Mediterranean.

The Wisdom of Solomon, a book of Jewish wisdom, now in the Apocrypha, from a generation or two before John, conflates the Greek term *logos* with Wisdom:

> O God of my ancestors and Lord of mercy, who have made all things by your word (*logos*), and by your wisdom have formed mankind. . . . With you is wisdom, she who knows your works and was present when you made the world; she understands what is pleasing in your sight and what is right according to your commandments. (9:1–2, 9 NRSV)

Wisdom is presented as a "kindly spirit" that "holds all things together" (1:6, 7; see Col 1:15–20), but also enters those who seek her: "In every generation she passes into holy souls and makes them friends of God and prophets" (7:7; see John 15), perhaps a gloss on Proverbs ("I will pour out

43. Plato, *Collected Dialogues of Plato*, xiii.

44. Being cannot come from not-being. Indeed, not being or "it is not" cannot exist. Parmenides therefore embraced a static view of the universe. Epicurus (c. 341–c. 270 BC) took a similar view. Aristotle argues that the existence of all finite and transitory things can be understood as a movement from potential to actual existence. However, the world exists eternally, so that the movement of all things is an unceasing movement. The source of this movement is the unmoved or eternally actual First Mover, the actuality of which draws finite things from potential into actual existence. Thomas Aquinas goes further, arguing that God is not only the first cause of all motion in the finite order, he is also the concurrent cause of all the operations of the natural order. Alfred North Whitehead (1861–1947) argues that everything but God is an actual entity occasioned by something; but God, although an actual entity, is not an actual occasion.

45. Cited in McGreal, *Great Thinkers*, 3. Graffiti from Olbia attest to followers in the fifth century BC (Burkert, *Greek Religion*, 296).

46. Smart, *World Philosophies*, 126.

47. de Jáuregui, *Orphism and Christianity*, 322–23.

48. Frank McLynn describes his theology as "largely abstract and pantheistic" (*Marcus Aurelius*, 233).

my spirit to you" 1:23). Wisdom "is a breath (*atmis,* ἀτμίς) of the power of God and a pure emanation (*aporroia,* ἀπόρροια) of the glory of the Almighty" (7:25). So Wisdom comes from God, not creation.[49] Ontologically speaking, Wisdom and God are one in essence. She also images God's attributes: "a reflection (*apaugasma,* ἀπαύγασμα) of eternal light, a spotless mirror of the working of God, and an image (eikōn, εἰκών) of his goodness" (7:26; see Heb 1:1–4).

Philo (c. 20 BC–AD 50), who is described by Ernest Renan as "the elder brother of Jesus," also equates Wisdom with *logos*.[50] Human wisdom is the varying capacity to perceive reality and act accordingly. Practicing wisdom imitates God because God is ultimate reality. Wisdom bridges the human and divine. Philo presents the *logos* as an intermediary between the absolutely transcendent and unknowable God and the human soul.[51] In *Who Is the Heir?*, a commentary on Genesis 15:2–8, he notes:

> To His Word (*logos*), His chief messenger, highest in age and honour, the Father of all has given the special prerogative, to stand on the border and separate the creature from the Creator. This same Word both pleads with the immortal as suppliant for afflicted mortality and acts as ambassador of the ruler to the subject. He glories in this prerogative and proudly describes it in these words 'and I stood between the Lord and you' (Deut. v.5), that is neither uncreated as God, nor created as you, but midway between the two extremes, a surety to both sides.[52]

In the immediate context of the quote, he compares Aaron, the high priest, who stands between the living and the dead, and the cloud, which separates the Egyptian army from Israel (201–4). Earlier in the commentary, Philo claims the *logos* was given the task of division in creation (133–140). In another passage, preserved by the church historian Eusebius, in *Preparation for the Gospel*, Philo presents the *logos* as "second God":

> Why does he say, as if speaking about another god, "in the image of God I made man" (Gen 9:6), but not "in his own image"? Excellently and wisely this oracular utterance is given. For nothing

49. *Aporroia* may describe "a stream" sourced by ground water.

50. Renan, *Life of Jesus*, 4.

51. Samuel Sandmell notes: "Logos is the knowable aspect of God, because *To On* ["the One who Is"] reaches down into the intelligible world in the form of the Logos" (*Philo of Alexandria*, 94). Lester Grabbe describes the *logos* as "an emanation" that "comes from him [God] like a stream of light which reaches toward the world and makes him emanant and accessible to humanity" (*Wisdom of Solomon*, 76).

52. 205–6 (Colson and Whitaker, LCL).

> that is mortal can be likened to the highest God and Father of the universe, but to the second god (*pros ton deuteron theon,* πρὸς τὸν δεύτερον θεόν), who is his *logos.* For it was necessary that the rational element in the soul of man should be marked by the divine *logos,* since the God anterior to the *logos* (*ho pro tou logou theos,* ὁ πρὸ τοῦ λόγου θεὸς) transcends every rational nature. It was unlawful that anything that has come into being should be thought a likeness of him who exists beyond the *logos* in the most excellent and transcendent state.[53]

Alan Segal notes: "*Logos* is equivalent with the intelligible world; but, because it can be hypostasized, the *logos* can also be viewed as a separate agent and called *a* god."[54] Elsewhere, Philo calls the *logos* God's first-born (*prōtogonos,* πρωτόγονος) or oldest Son.[55] The language is similar to John's "the only one" (*monogenēs,* μονογενής [1:14]).[56]

In sum, reflection on Wisdom forks in the centuries around the cross. Some viewed Wisdom as the first of God's creation; others, as an emanation from the eternal God. The latter has the most in common with Greek philosophy. This divergence contributed to the early confusion about the Son's origin. Arius and Athanasius, who defended the eternality and deity of Christ, are both Alexandrians. However, the prologue of John has more in common with the eternal emanation branch of Jewish thought, so that the Arian interpretation is a misreading at the literal level. Philo and The Wisdom of Solomon anticipate the Orthodox language of hypostasis (*hypostasis,* ὑπόστασις), the underlying reality or substance of something. Unique in all reality, God the Son has both a human *hypostasis* and a divine *hypostasis.* The Son is fully human and divine. Not created, the Son is eternally proceeding (begotten) from the Father—what came to be called the eternal generation of the Son.[57] The Nicene-Constantinopolitan creed (AD 381) allows us to confess:

53. Eusebius, *Praep. ev.* 7.13. The translation (slightly adapted) is taken from Runia, *Philo in Early Christian Literature*, 152–53).

54. Segal, *Two Powers in Heaven*, 23, emphasis his.

55. Philo, *Confusion* 63; *Posterity* 63.

56. While John and Philo may share a similar trajectory of thought, there is no clear evidence of literary dependence. Jerome says of Philo: "Concerning him there is a proverb among the Greeks 'Either Plato philonized or Philo platonized,' . . . so great is the similarity of ideas and language" (*Vir. ill.* 11 [*NPNF*2 3:365]). In the first century BC, Publius Nigidius in Rome and Eudorus in Alexandria revived the Pythagorean tradition. While Philo draws upon both traditions, he is firstly a pious exegete of Scripture.

57. Ludolph finds this doctrine in John's prologue (*Life of Christ*, 1:26–28).

> The Son of God, the Only-begotten, Begotten of the Father before all ages, Light of Light, Very God of Very God, Begotten, not made; of one essence with the Father; by whom all things were made.[58]

Bonaventure offers this description: "From that Eternal Light which is at the same time measureless and most simple, most brilliant and most hidden, there emerges a coeternal, coequal, and consubstantial splendor, who is the power and wisdom of the Father."[59]

Does this position compromise monotheism? Neither Philo nor Wisdom was considered heretical by contemporary Jews.[60] Josephus describes Philo as "a man held in the highest honor" (*Ant.* 18.259). This leads to an important twofold conclusion: on the one hand, the deity of the *logos* is not a Pagan accretion or an early Christian misunderstanding but the fruit of Jewish biblical interpretation and meditation.[61] On the other, as Justin Martyr and other early Christians note, the wisdom typology reveals the universal mission of the Logos before the Incarnation. Aware of the fourth Gospel, Justin claims:

> We have been taught that Christ is the firstborn of God, and we have declared above that he is the Logos of whom every race of men were partakers. And those who lived according to reason

58. τὸν Υἱὸν τοῦ Θεοῦ τὸν μονογενῆ, τὸν ἐκ τοῦ Πατρὸς γεννηθέντα πρὸ πάντων τῶν αἰώνων· φῶς ἐκ φωτός, Θεὸν ἀληθινὸν ἐκ Θεοῦ ἀληθινοῦ, γεννηθέντα οὐ ποιηθέντα, ὁμοούσιον τῷ Πατρί, δι οὗ τὰ πάντα ἐγένετο.

59. Bonaventure, *Soul's Journey*, 126. We find the same description in Ludolph of Saxony's *Life of Christ*, 1:36.

60. Philo was selected by the Jews of Alexandria to represent their grievance with the prefect Flaccus before the emperor, Gaius Caligula (*Flaccus*; *Embassy*). The great city was the location of the largest Jewish community outside of Palestine at the time, which retained close ties with Jerusalem. Philo made a pilgrimage to the temple (*Providence* 2.64), and his brother, Alexander, provided the funds to plate the temple gates (Josephus, *J.W.* 5.205; *Ant.* 18.159–160). The exegete-philosopher was thoroughly enmeshed in Second Temple Judaism. Less is known about the circumstances behind the publication of the Wisdom of Solomon. But the text was broadly read.

61. Norman Solomon claims Jewish theology "ceased" with Philo until Saadia Gaon and others in the tenth century (*Talmud*, xliv). The *logos* as emanation of God anticipates the mystical side of Judaism, Kabbalah ("receiving"), where God is understood and worshiped through emanations (*sefirot*), which have their own integrity (particularity) but share in the common nature of God. Alan Segal demonstrates two strands of rabbinic discussion on "the two powers." One approaches them dualistically (Zoroastrianism, Gnosticism). This conflicts with the ethical monotheism of Scripture, and is therefore rejected. But the other strand views the two powers as being complementary to one another, so that the second power is presented as the principal hypostatic manifestation of God (Segal, *Two Powers in Heaven*, x).

> (*logos*) are Christians, even though they have been thought atheists; as among the Greeks, Socrates and Heraclitus, and men like them; and among the barbarians, Abraham, and Ananias, and Azarias . . .[62]

The apologist presumes humans have their own *logos* or "reason," a constituent of the soul, which is informed by a "living spirit" *zōtikon pneuma* (ζωτικόν πνεύμα) from God (2 *Apol.* 10; 13). With the Stoics, Justin claims that living according to reason provides a glimpse of God. But he notes that philosophers had only a "seed" of the *logos spermatikos* (λόγος σπερματικός "seed-bearing word"), which left them vulnerable to metaphysical and moral confusion, whereas followers of Christ have access to full reality.

Creation Through the Logos (1:1–5)

[1:1] *In the beginning* was the Logos. And the Logos was beside the God,[63] and the Logos was God. [2] It was *in the beginning* beside the God. [Gen 1:1] [3] All things through it came to be,[64] and apart from it not one thing came to be that is.[65] [4] In it (the Logos) was life, and the life was the *light* of people. [5] And the light in *the darkness* shines, and *the darkness* did not overcome (or comprehend) it. [Gen 1:4; Isa 9:2, cited at Matt 4:15–16]

P: Some limit the opening of John's Gospel to the first five verses, but most follow Jerome, as we do, and place the break at verse 18.[66] Nevertheless, the subunit offers a complete story—from a time before creation, to creation, focusing on *life* and *light*, to a conflict with and victory over *the darkness*. John distinguishes yet associates the *Logos* (λόγος), often

62. 1 *Apol.* 46 (*ANF* 1:178).

63. This could be amplified as "the Word was at God's side," a position earlier given to Wisdom (Prov 8:22–30; see Lincoln, *John*, 92). Scripture also maintains that God created by speaking—with a word. The Psalmist claims: "By the word of the Lord were the heavens made" (33:6).

64. This is the first of many occurrences of what is called the "divine passive"—God is the understood agent. "Came to be" (*ginomai*, γίνομαι) actually means "God brought into existence." The creation story uses the same verb (LXX) when God said: "Let there be light" (1:3).

65. The claim is repeated negatively for emphasis.

66. Tatian switches to Luke's birth narrative here. Ludoph of Saxony also treats the first five verses as a unit (*Life of Christ*, 1:26). Bonaventure divides his commentary into two very uneven parts: 1:1–5, The Word in se ["in itself"] and 1:6—21:25, The Word united to the flesh (Bonaventure, *John*, 23). Michaels classifies the relatively small unit as a "preface or preamble" (*John*, 45).

translated as "Word," with *the* (that is, the one true) *God* (*ho theos*, ὁ θεός), the Creator of *all things* (the universe).

John introduces ambiguity with a pun. The verb *katalambanō* (καταλαμβάνω) signifies *overcome*, which fits the context (so ESV): the present tense *shines* celebrates the survival of light in a dark place. If the reader is familiar with the gospel, then he or she might think of the death and resurrection of Christ. But the verb can also mean *comprehend*, which also fits: the informed reader knows that Jesus is misunderstood. The two meanings are complementary: people attack what they do not understand.

R: Diogenes Allen (1932–2013) notes: "The biblical view of creation is so familiar to us that its role as the foundation of all Christian theology may not be apparent."[67] John encourages us to meditate on this presupposition. Whereas Mark ("beginning") and Matthew are implicit ("the book of *genesis*"), John is explicit: *In the beginning.* Those familiar with Scripture hear the opening line of Genesis twice.[68] But the creation story is now retold through God's self-revelation in the Logos, a strategy that we saw above with Wisdom in Proverbs. *All things* (*panta*, πάντα) *through the Logos came to be* is John's way of expressing *creatio ex nihilo* ("creation from nothing"), another clarification and theological leap:

> The Christian view of God's will in creation offended Roman and Greek sensibilities. God, in the Greek view, dwelt in a realm above the earth, but he did not stand outside the world, the *kosmos*. Earth and heaven are part of the same cosmos, which has existed eternally. The world is not the creation of a transcendent God. The cosmos has its own laws, and all that exists—the physical world, animals, man, and the gods—are subject to nature's laws. "Certain things are impossible to nature," said Galen, and "God does not even attempt such things at all." Rather, "he chooses the best out of the possibilities of becoming."[69]

67. Allen, *Philosophy*, 1.

68. *Came to be* represents "created" and *all things*, "the heavens and the earth." Pious Jews regularly heard the story in the synagogue, but not a few Greeks—an umbrella term for non-Jews living in a predominately Hellenistic (Greek) social world (see Rom 1:14)—appreciated its rhetorical power. Longinus, the traditional name for the Hellenized author of *On the Sublime*, likely published around this time, cites the creation story as an example: "A similar effect was achieved by the lawgiver of the Jews—no mean genius, for he both understood and gave expression to the power of the divinity as it deserved—when he wrote at the very beginning of his laws, and I quote his words: 'God said'—what was it?—'Let there be light.' And there was. 'Let there be earth.' And there was."

69. Wilkin, *Christians as the Romans Saw Them*, 91.

Plato's Demiurge is typical of ancient cosmology in that it shaped everything from pre-existing matter (*creatio ex materia*). But in line with earlier Jewish reflection, the *Shepherd of Hermas* (first or early second century) makes the doctrine part of a revelatory command: "First of all: believe that (the) *God is one*, the one who created all things and fit (them together) and made from what is not into all things that are and who contains all things, but who is alone uncontained."[70] Tertullian, who was critical of *Hermas*, maintains the same position: "What we worship is the one God, who, out of nothing, simply for the glory of his majesty, fashioned this enormous universe" (*Apology* 17). The Fourth Lateran Council presents God as the "Creator of all things, visible and invisible, . . . who, by His almighty power, from the beginning of time has created both orders in the same way out of nothing."[71]

The retelling commences to the first day of creation—when God says, "Let there be light," which introduces the first separation and distinction—*light* and *darkness* (Gen 1:3–4). The first light precedes the sun, moon, and stars, and therefore emanates from a different body (Gen 1:3–4; cf. vv. 14–19). In New Jerusalem, there is no need for "sun or moon to shine on it, for the glory of God gives its light, and its lamp is the lamb" (Rev 21:23). This light is morally and aesthetically "good" (Gen 1:4). Deepening an implication of the creation story, John claims the *darkness* is not only contrastive but antagonistic to the *light* (Gen 1:2–3). *Light* and *darkness* invite a second binary—*life* and death, a pairing we find throughout Scripture.[72] Death is a dark place; living is remaining in the *light* of God's presence (see John 8:12). *Light* and *life* are on the same ontological side as the *Logos* and *God*. John sees a kinship between the opening *darkness* of the creation story and the resulting death from the Fall (Gen 2:18; 3:19). The initial overcoming of darkness anticipates the overcoming of mortality in *the Logos*. The language also evokes Isaiah, who depicts the renewal of creation: "O *people* living in *darkness* a great *light*—behold a great *light*! O those dwelling in the land and in the shadow of death—light will shine upon you" (9:1 OG; see also Matt 4:16). The prophet identifies *the people* as the "Galilee of the nations" or "Gentiles" (8:23 OG).

D: It is difficult to overstate the pedagogical significance of this passage. John models thinking before the Father, in the Son, by the Spirit. The language is our *light*. Tatian and Ludolph begin their great projects here.

70. Πρῶτον πάντων πίστευσον ὅτι εἷς ἐστιν ὁ θεός ὁ τὰ πάντα κτίσας καὶ καταρτίσας καὶ ποιήσας ἐκ τοῦ μὴ ὄντος εἰς τὸ εἶναι τὰ πάντα καὶ πάντα χωρῶν μόνος δὲ ἀχώρητος ὤν (26:1).

71. Cited in Copan and Craig, *Creation Out of Nothing*, 148.

72. Job 3:20, 28; 33:30; Pss 49:20; 54:14; Prov 13:9; see also Sir 22:9.

Augustine, who knew reality was too complex for anyone to learn in a lifetime, offers this foundational belief:

> It is enough for the Christian to believe that the only cause of all created things, whether heavenly or earthly, whether visible or invisible, is the goodness of the Creator, the one true God; and that nothing exists but Himself that does not derive its existence from Him; and that He is the Trinity—to wit, the Father, and the Son begotten of the Father, and the Holy Spirit proceeding from the same Father, but one and the same Spirit of Father and Son.[73]

This is faith leading to understanding (*fides quaerens intellectum*). For these givens, we depend on God's self-communication in Scripture and our surrender to them, as Lesslie Newbigen (1909–1998) notes: "For we know a person only as he chooses to reveal himself, and only as our own spirit is sensitive and trustful to respond to his revelation."[74] According to one calculation, *all things came to be* around fourteen billion years ago. But the laws of physics break down in the "singularity," requiring ignorance, speculation, or revelation.

However, if we accept this faith of a mustard seed, we begin to see the universe differently. It is like a child growing up in Barcelona under the shadow of the *Sagrada Familia*. The unfinished basilica had always been part of her life, the destination of endless school field trips, becoming almost invisible until, one day, she looks up into the vault of the nave and *sees with faith*. In addition to *life* (1:4; 8:12), *light* will have three other associations in the Gospel—Truth (1:9; 3:21), Goodness (3:19, 20), and a Beauty that offers a distinct pleasure in its perception (1:5, 9; 5:35).[75] Alaksandr Solzhenitsyn observes in his Nobel Prize Lecture (1970):

> So perhaps that ancient trinity of Truth, Goodness and Beauty is not simply an empty, faded formula as we thought in the days of our self-confident, materialistic youth? If the tops of these three trees converge, as the scholars maintained, but the too blatant, too direct stems of Truth and Goodness are crushed, cut down, not allowed through—then perhaps the fantastic, unpredictable, unexpected stems of Beauty will push through and soar to that very same place, and in so doing will fulfil the work of all three?[76]

73. Cited in Runes, *Treasury of Philosophy*, 73.

74. Newbigin, *Missionary Theologian*, 18.

75. See Maritain, *Art and Scholasticism and the Frontiers of Poetry*.

76. Cited in Worley, "Splendor of Holiness," 65. David Bentley Hart suggests beauty

Everyone, even his persecutors in the gulag, are surrounded by the same trees, the faint tracings of our original temple. Clement of Alexandria notes, "The one true God is the sole author of all beauty, whether it is Hellenic or whether it is ours" (*Strom.* 1.28).

We have focused on the subjective appropriation of faith, but John's language is also boldly metaphysical: everything is dark *except for a spotlight on the Logos* (1:5, 7–9; see also Heb 1:1–4). There are severe limits to human understanding. Like Parmenides and Heraclitus, we are immersed in the way of seeming, oblivious to ultimate reality. Our reality is dominated by *darkness* and *death*. God's people were given some light through Scripture but this led only to partial understanding, as the author of Hebrews notes: "Progressively and partially speaking long ago to (our) fathers in the prophets, in these end of days God spoke to us in (his) Son (1:1–2). Jews and Gentiles, at most, had only the *spermatikos logos* until the Incarnation. However, before disciples can appropriate God's self-revelation, a uniquely Christian metaphysics, they must first become like children—that is, unlearn their partial truths and idolatries. Theologians came to describe this as the apophatic and kataphatic way to truth.

The apophatic way begins with God's mystery, a truth we find in Scripture. Commenting on Job, Manfred Oeming and Konrad Schmid note: "God is—God."[77] Their point is that Job must shed his expectations about God and allow God to reveal God. Philo, who helped us understand John's use of *logos*, rejects any immediate knowledge of God's being (or nature), who is beyond all predicates of human language:

> For [God] has not displayed his nature to anyone; but keeps it invisible to every kind of creature. Who can venture to affirm of him who is the cause of all things either that he is a body, or that he is incorporeal, or that he has such and such distinctive qualities, or that he has no such qualities? Or who, in short, can venture to affirm anything positively about his essence, or his character, or his constitution, or his movements? But only he can utter a positive claim about himself, since only he has an accurate knowledge of his own nature, without the possibility of mistake. (*Alleg. Interp.* 3.206)[78]

Maimonides carries this tradition into scholastic Judaism: "The description of God by means of negations is the correct description—a description that is not affected by an indulgence in facile language. . . . With every

is found in the gratuitous presence of good whose existence is not necessary.

77. Oeming and Schmid, *Job's Journey*, 24.

78. Philo, *Works of Philo*, 162 (Yonge [slightly updated]).

increase in the negations regarding God, you come nearer to the apprehension of God."[79] This *via negative* is appropriated by Clement of Alexandria and Origen and is seminal to the spirituality of the desert fathers. The Egyptian monk John of Lycopolis is typical: "he who has been granted a partial knowledge of God—for it is not possible for the whole of such knowledge to be received by anyone."[80] Minucius Felix (d. c. 250) writes: "God is invisible, because too bright for our sight; intangible, because too fine for our sense of touch; immeasurable, because he is beyond the grasp of our senses; infinite, limitless" (*Letter to Octavius* 18). Gregory of Nazianzus (c. 330–389/390) would have us meditate on God's shadow, not being.[81] "It is obvious to everyone," notes Theodore the Studite (759–826), "that the Godhead is incomprehensible and uncircumscribable, and I may add boundless, limitless, formless, and whatever adjectives signify the privation of what the Godhead is not."[82] Research in the field of neuroscience has found that "the more one contemplates God, the more mysterious God becomes."[83]

The kataphatic way, a *via postiva,* begins with accepting the Logos as our teacher and following the course of revelation, the gradual unveiling of God's Truth, Goodness, and Beauty. Gregory of Nyssa describes the outer world as the "the garment and drapery of God."[84] He writes:

> Hope always draws the soul from the beauty which is seen to what is beyond, always kindles the desire for the hidden through what is constantly perceived. Therefore, the ardent lover of beauty, although receiving what is always visible as an image of what he desires, yet longs to be filled with the very stamp of the archetype."[85]

Johannes Scotus Eriugena (c. 815–c. 877) saw everything as a "graduated revelation of God."[86] The medieval church envisioned the universe in concentric circles. The tenth, outermost circle, the empyrean heaven, was a quintessence of pure light. Gothic cathedrals opened to this reality through the medium of stained glass.

In sum, Christian revelation is not exclusive of mystery, but the world's mysteries are no longer exclusive of the revelation of Christ.

79. Cited in Matt, *Essential Kabbalah*, 7.
80. Ward, *Lives of the Desert Fathers*, 56.
81. Gregory of Nazianus, *De Filio*, 170; discussed in Carnes, *Beauty*, xi.
82. Theodore the Studite, *On the Holy Icons*, 100 (1.2 [Roth, 100]).
83. Newberg and Waldman, *How God Changes Your Brain*, 5.
84. Cited in Harpur, *Love Burning*, 8.
85. Gregory of Nyssa, *Life of Moses*, 114 (231).
86. Cited in Harpur, *Love Burning*, 57.

S: Scripture offers no divine biography. The one true *God* is without *beginning*. The Greeks relate that Zeus became supreme by banishing his father Kronos ("Time"), who had emasculated his father Ouranos ("Heaven"). Who or what came before Ouranos? Genesis simply presumes *God's* existence and work. God is not proven by argument but given as the first presupposition for what follows. However, those familiar with the opening of Genesis may be surprised that in place of "In the beginning *God*," John writes *was the Logos*. On the one hand, by citing the Scripture, the evangelist makes a claim on the God of Israel: There is only one *God*, the *God* of Moses who *created all things*, the *God* of Abraham, Isaac, and Jacob, who covenanted with a people. And yet the *Logos*, the antitype (or fulfillment of Wisdom), shares in the being of this *God*. The *Logos* does this God's work.

This self-revelation has metaphysical implications: *God* is the ground of *sameness and difference*.[87] Ideologies tend to pit one against the other—*cogito ergo sum* vs. the postmodern decentering of personhood—because humans are especially vulnerable to false dichotomies.[88] There is much suffering in the world because *sameness and difference* are unnaturally separated. A minority is excluded even though we all share a common nature. Nature shows meadows of the same flower in which every flower is different. So we may not be surprised when *the Logos* reveals a *God* who is the same yet different.

Origin of the Baptist (1:6–8)

[6] There was a human [or a human came into being], *who has been sent from God*.[89] [Mal 4:5] His name was John. [7] This one came for a witness, that he might witness about the light, that all might believe through him. [8] That one was not the light, but (he came) that he might witness about the light.

87. John writes, ὁ λόγος ἦν πρὸς τὸν θεόν, καὶ θεὸς ἦν ὁ λόγος. The first occurrence of *God* has an article (τὸν θεόν). The second is anarthrous (θεὸς). The presence of an article often serves to identify the signified, a kind of proper noun. In this case, John is signifying the God of Scripture. The absence of an article may emphasize quality: *the Logos*, although distinct from *God*, shares the same quality as *God* (Harris, *John*, 19).

88. This problem occupied Plato. See Gerson, "Plato on Identity," 305–32.

89. The perfect participle conveys a stative (enduring) quality to the act of sending. The verb translated "came" may also be rendered "came into being," like v. 3 (see Gen 2:7 LXX). John uses *erchomai* (ἔρχομαι), which emphasizes direction in the subsequent clause. Sent from God may imply preexistence. Luke claims John "leaped" in his mother's womb over the Incarnation (Luke 1:41). Origen posits this preexistence in the soul. Another possibility is the "mind" of God. But the sense could also be his physical generation, with the sending taking place around that time. The subsequent clause depicts his birth (= Luke 1:57–66, esp. v. 63).

P: The contemporary biographer Plutarch developed his characters through *synkrisis* (σύνκρισεις), the rhetorical juxtaposition of places and things.[90] This was a well-established trope. Isocrates wrote an encomium for Evagoras by comparing him to Cyrus. Without denigrating the Persian king, Evagoras is even greater (*Evag.* 39).[91] Similarly, *John* is *from God* but does not share in God's nature or creative work. The earlier occurrence of the verb *ginomai* (γίνομαι), which is often translated "was" (ESV) or "came" (NIV), signified "coming into being" (1:2). This may be another pun: John *came* but was also created. Foregrounding the distinction anticipates conflict between the disciples of *John* and Jesus in the Gospels, which may have reflected social reality (3:25–36; see also Matt 9:14; Acts 19:1–10).

R: The Christian Old Testament ends with a divine promise through the prophet Malachi (mid 5th cent. BC): "Behold, I will send (*apostellō*, ἀποστέλλω) you Elijah, the Tishbite, before the great and glorious day of the Lord comes, who will turn the heart of a father to his son and the heart of a human to his neighbor, lest I come and strike the earth grievously" (3:22–24 LXX = MT 4:5–6).[92] The evangelist appropriates *sent from God*. Elsewhere, the Gospels present Elijah as a type of John.[93] The language is also reminiscent of prophetic commissioning (Isa 6:8–13; Jer 1:4–19).

D: There is a striking simplicity to *John's* burden, compared to the Logos who holds the universe on his shoulders. He is a *witness*, a bystander to the unfolding cosmic drama.

S: The prologue cites Genesis and Malachi, the first and last books of the Old Testament. At the end of the New Testament, Jesus says: "I am the Alpha and the Omega, the first and the last, the beginning and the end" (Rev 22:13).

90. Duff, "Plutarchan synkrisis," 141–61; Erbse, "Die Bedeutung der Synkrisis," 389–424. Zeba Crook notes the absence of any attempted definition in ancient literature (*Reconceptualising Conversion*, 118). Quintilian discusses the rhetorical effect of comparing the merits of two persons (*Inst.* 2.4.21).

91. See Crook, *Reconceptualising Conversion*, 118.

92. Even at the time of Jesus these final verses concluded "The Book of the Twelve" (or "Minor Prophets" LXX) and therefore the entire prophetic corpus.

93. Luke claims John the Baptist came in the Spirit of Elijah (Luke 1:17). Jesus says he *is* Elijah (Matt 11:14).

Mission of the Logos (1:9–14)

[9] It (the Logos) was the true[94] light[95] that enlightens every human by coming into the world. [10] He[96] was in the world, and the world came into being through him. But the world did not recognize him. [11] To his own (places)[97] he came, but his own (people) did not receive him. [12] Yet whoever received him, he gave them the right[98] to become God's children—to those who believe into his name, [13] who, not by bloods or by a bodily intent[99] or by the intent of a husband, but by God they were begotten.

P: The evangelist rehearses the opening subunit (1:1–5), emphasizing the biblical, wisdom motif of rejection. He vacillates between the *world* (*kosmos*, κόσμος) referring to creation and more specifically to its people. Like John, they are part of creation. He repeats yet narrows the cycle to refer to the historical ministry of the Logos, who *came to his own (places)*, the neuter form of the adjective *idios* (τὰ ἴδια), *but his own (people)*, the masculine form of *idios* (ἴδιοι), *did not receive him*. As the fulfillment of Wisdom, indeed all Scripture, the Israelites should have *recognized* and *received* the Logos. *Yet* (*de*, δέ) anticipates a pivot in the Gospel: in the first half (chs. 1–12), rejection and unbelief predominate; then Jesus focuses on the nucleus of his New Covenant Community (chs. 13–21).[100] The claim *whoever received him, he gave them the right to become God's children—to those who believe in his name* is central to John's presentation (see 20:30–31). The call *to believe into*

94. The adjective describes a genuine form over a counterfeit. People are often drawn to false, imperfect lights. Paul claims Satan disguises himself as an "angel of light" (2 Cor 11:14). The deception begins in the human heart. A darkened heart sees only a darkened world (see Matt 6:22–23). This conviction should be set in equipoise to the universal import of the Logos and "blind" acceptance of the empirical method. Parmenides believes that "the way of truth" was not accessible through human investigation, but was given through revelation. Plato adopts this worldview, but Aristotle goes in the opposite direction.

95. A darkened heart cannot see this light in the way it may see the sun or the controlled fire from a lamp. God is predicated as light in Scripture, thereby moving the emphasis from the material to the spiritual realm. John claims the Logos enlightens every human being, not in the sense that everyone will be saved, but that all who know the truth in their hearts will be judged (3:19–20). The Qumran community referred to themselves as "the children of light" (4QD[a] 1).

96. The switch to the masculine begins here, although it is not explicit until the end of the clause.

97. *To his own places*: The plural could also be translated "possessions" (see John 16:32; 19:27).

98. Authority semantically overlaps with its implementation—power.

99. Or "flesh"—human, physical impulse.

100. Köstenberger, *John*, 38; Lincoln, *John*, 102.

Christ's *name* is unique to John in Scripture (e.g., 2:23; 3:18; 1 John 3:23; 5:13). However, the language is similar to the Lukan (Petrine) and Pauline appropriation of Joel: *Everyone who will call on the name of the Lord will be saved.*[101] *Name* (*onoma*, ὄνομα) signifies "all that a person represents."[102] John may have been inspired by Matthew's presentation: "you will call his name Jesus. For he will save his people from their sins" (1:21). Belief, for John, is *receiving* Jesus.[103] The verb *lambanō* (λαμβάνω) can signify the acceptance of a truth claim (12:48; 17:8), but also receiving Christ himself—"The one who eats my flesh and drinks my blood remains in me, and *I* also in him" (6:56)—thereby ontologically transforming the recipients. Believers *become God's children*. God *begets* them like an earthly father, but supernaturally: *not by bloods or by a bodily intent or by the intent of a husband*. The unusual expression *bloods* (*haimatōn*, αἱμάτων), often not fully translated, may refer to the ancient theory of conception, which included the mixing of blood from the male sperm and the female.[104] In any case, we have God's "seed" (*sperma*, σπέρμα) in us (1 John 3:9). Faith is also a movement *into* (*eis*, εἰς) everything Christ is. This is the first of thirty-six pairings of the verb *pisteuō* (πιστεύω), "to believe," and the preposition *eis* (εἰς), which is most naturally translated "into."[105] We find this expression elsewhere in the New Testament, but not with such regularity. This twofold movement points to the mystery of mutual indwelling. If we "remain" in the Son, the Spirit of the Son and Father resides in us (Prov 1:23; John 14:15, 23).

D: We are really *God's children*, and this happens through receiving Christ in faith, the *res*, which is represented by communion (Eucharist), the *sacramentum*. Martin Luther retained the sacramentalism of the Catholic Church, but also took John's language seriously, claiming "Christ is present in the faith itself" (*in ipsa fide Christus adest*).[106] *On The Liberty of*

101. Joel 2:32; see Acts 2:21; 9:21; 11:15; 15:1, 11; 16:30; 1 Cor 1:2; Rom 10:13–14.

102. See John 2:23; 3:18; Acts 5:40–41; 3 John 7; Köstenberger, *John*, 38. The citation is from Lincoln, *John*, 103.

103. As the em dash indicates, the participial phrase τοῖς πιστεύουσιν εἰς τὸ ὄνομα αὐτοῦ functions as a clarifying statement of the main clause.

104. In the ancient world, a woman's power was primarily her unique connection to sexuality and birth (Squillace, *Odyssey*, xxxii). In Jewish literature, the plural can refer to a woman's menstruation and the breaking of the hymen, which collectively anticipate pregnancy (Goldin, *Fathers According to Rabbi Nathan*, 9 [A1]). God's response to Cain incorporates a plural: "The voice of your brother's bloods is crying to me from the ground" (Gen 1:10). In this context, it is probably a reference to his potential descendants.

105. 1:12; 2:11, 23; 3:16, 18 (x2), 36; 4:39; 6:29, 35, 40; 7:5, 31, 38, 39, 48; 8:30; 9:35, 36; 10:42; 11:25, 26, 45, 48; 12:11, 36, 37; 12:42, 44 (x2), 46; 14:1 (x2), 12; 16:9; 17:20.

106. Braaten and Jensen, *Union with Christ*, viii; Mannerma, *Christ Present in Faith*, 27.

a Christian has a summation: "Faith does not merely mean that the soul realizes that the divine word is full of all grace, free and holy: it also unites the soul with Christ."[107]

The historical ministry of the Logos to Israel is a microcosm of what will become a universal mission (macrocosm). The Logos had planted seeds in their Scripture, so that they might understand and receive the gospel; similarly, as we saw with the early apologists, there was a seedbed in Greco-Roman philosophy.[108] Presumably, then, the Logos had gone farther.

Plato and the Orphics were influenced by Indian thought.[109] Before Greek philosophy and Buddhism, Indian philosophers ruminated on what they called *Brahman* ("holy power"), which sustains and vivifies all things but is accessible only through *Atman* ("Self"), the essence of the human being.[110] *Brahman* and *Atman* are one.[111] (Buddha departed from this thinking by denying the ultimate reality of *Atman* but retained a place for *Brahman*.) *Brahman* is mystery beyond words. Yet imbedded in the *Upanishads* is the suggestion that *Brahman* is a personal being—Brahmā Prajāpati, the "father of creatures."[112] There is a similar mystery in Chinese reflections on the *tao* or "the way." Everything, it was observed, follows certain patterns and processes that escape precise definition and yet pointed to ultimate reality.[113] Most Confucians recommended the "way of heaven," a surrendering to the *tao* like the Stoics to an impersonal *logos*.[114] Yet Mozi (c. 470 BC–c. 391 BC) goes in a more personal direction: "Heaven wants righteousness and dislikes unrighteousness."[115] It became common practice to translate the Logos in John's prologue as *tao*. Andrew Sung Park notes, "Had the Johannine author lived in Asia, he or she would have used

107. See McGrath, "Newman on Justification," 99–100.

108. Peter Abelard (1079–1142) also claims the works of pre-Christian philosophers contain prefigurations of Christ (McGreal, *Great Thinkers*, 87).

109. The Orphic belief in reincarnation and practice of vegetarianism suggest an Indian origin (Burkert, *Greek Religion*, 296–98).

110. Olivelle, *Upanishads*, lv.

111. Pausanias writes, "I know that the Chaldaeans and Indian sages were the first to say that the soul [ψυχή] of man is immortal [ἀθάνατός], and have been followed by some of the Greeks, particularly by Plato the son of Ariston" (*Description of Greece* 4, 32, 4 [Jones and Ormerod, LCL). Plato claims, "The soul [ψυχή] is most like that which is divine, immortal, intelligible, uniform, indissoluble, and ever self-consistent and invariable, whereas body is most like that which is human, mortal, multiform, unintelligible, dissoluble, and never self-consistent" (*Collected Dialogues*, 63 [*Phaed.* 80a–b]).

112. Smart, *World Philosophies*, 21.

113. Lao-Tzu, *Te-Tao Ching*, xviii.

114. Chan, *Source Book in Chinese Philosophy*, 211.

115. Cited in Chan, *Source Book in Chinese Philosophy*, 218.

the term *Tao* instead of *Logos* for his or her apologetic work."[116] Another scholar describes the *Tao* as "the functional equivalent of the apophatic God in Christian theological tradition."[117]

How might we appropriate the *spermatikos logos* of India, China, and other great intellectual traditions? This is a perennial tension in missiology. Contextualization is essential for evangelism; the Logos has gone ahead of us, preparing a culture to receive him. Indeed, anything true, good, and beautiful points to God. And yet syncretism is a real danger. Sadly, a history of missions shows an ever-swinging pendulum.[118] Translating Logos as *tao* or *Brahman* may assist the apophatic side of our witness. Thoughtful human beings everywhere have been humbled by the limits of their understanding. Socrates knew only that he knew nothing.[119] However, *Brahman* or *tao* is insufficient for the kataphatic side of our proclamation. The prologue eventually identifies the Logos as Jesus Christ, God's supreme, enlightening self-revelation with all its offensive particularity.

S: God is at work in a hostile world reclaiming its goodness.[120] *Lord, you are welcome among us and in our hearts. Come, Lord Jesus. Come quickly!*

116. Park, "Theology of *Tao* (Way)," 43. He shows that the signified is closer to *Tao* than Hellenistic notions.

117. Smith, *Indescribable God*, 161.

118. See Gort, "Syncretism and Dialogue," 37.

119. Plato, *Apol.* 21d. See Diogenes Laërtius's biography of Socrates in *Lives and Opinions of Eminent Philosophers* (2.32).

120. See Westerholm, *Understanding Matthew*, 7–16.

[14] And the Logos became embodied [or flesh] and was a tabernacle[121] among us.[122] And we perceived his glory—glory[123] as the only one[124] from the Father,[125] full of grace[126] and truth.[127]

P: *The Logos* is God (1:1) and instrumental in creation—that is, not a part of creation—and yet, surprisingly, unites to creation through embodiment—a doctrine that came to be called the Incarnation: The eternal *Logos*, Son of the Father, *became flesh*. Bonaventure describes the event: "By the action of that power, instantly his body was formed, his soul created, and at once both were united to the divinity in the Person of the Son, so that the same Person was God and man, with properties of each nature maintained."[128]

Intellectual currents were going in the opposite direction. For all the similarities concerning the *logos*, there is no incarnation in Philo.[129] The Orphic slogan *sōma sēma*, "the body is a tomb," captures popular sentiment. Why would a deity take on anything as fragile as our mortality? The Egyptians believed Horus, the god of heaven, was continuously manifested in Pharaoh. But when one Pharaoh died, the deity transferred to the next.[130]

121. Or "dwelt." The root and context suggest an allusion to the biblical tabernacle. Jesus as temple (God's dwelling place) is a prominent theme in John.

122. Or "in us." John alludes to the story of Israel's redemption, when God "pitched his tent" among his people and went before them (Exod 24:16; 25:7–8; 29:46; 40:35; Zech 2:14 [OG 2:10]). He invites the reader to follow after Jesus's glory. God's Son will present himself as "the light of the world" (8:12; 9:3; 11:9). The Shekinah is the source of the Son's light. A tabernacle signifies the human body, which houses God's Spirit (see the Greek at 2 Pet 1:13). Becoming flesh and tabernacle is synonymous parallelism.

123. *Anadiplosis*, emphasizing the *glory* or "splendor" of the incarnate Logos.

124. Only (*monogenēs*, μονογενής) signifies being the only one of its kind within a specific relationship, often describing an "only son." Josephus presents Isaac as Abraham's "only son" (*Ant.* 1.222). See also *PsSol* 18:4; *TestSol* 20:2; Luke 7:12; 9:38. The claim is repeated in 1 John 4:9. Although the Logos is God's unique Son, through the Son, God desires to adopt every human being as his child.

125. Note how God switches to Father.

126. Or "divine favor" or "benefaction."

127. The evocative phrase *grace and truth*, which reoccurs at 1:17, may also be found in a non-canonical psalm, Hymn to the Creator (11QPSa 26:9–15), which overlaps thematically with John's prologue: "Grace and truth surround his presence; truth and justice and righteousness are the foundation of his throne. Separating light from darkness, he established the dawn by the knowledge of his mind" (Embry et al., *Early Jewish Literature*, 1:159).

128. Bonaventure, *Soul's Journey*, 127.

129. Hamerton-Kelly observes that the incarnation was not part of Jewish wisdom speculation (*Pre-Existence, Wisdom, and the Son of Man*, 209).

130. Bauer, *History of the Ancient World*, 65.

When Jesus died, it would have made sense for God to raise up another human in his place (cf. John 20:28). Greek and Indian mythologies describe a god taking a visible form. In the *Bhagavad Gita*, God or the "Supreme Being" (*svayam Bhagavan*) takes the form of Lord Krishna, who encourages the human Arjuna about engaging his cousins in battle. Deities also take the form of animals and mixed creatures (polymorphism). In Greek mythology, Zeus takes the form of a swan and, depending on the version, rapes or seduces Leda. In these scenarios, the god does not *become* an animal or human being.[131] So the Incarnation, as Augustine noted, has no parallel (*Confessions* 7.9.14), or, in the words of Dorothy Sayers, "Jesus Christ is unique—unique among gods and men."[132]

R: Jesus is the antitype of the *tabernacle*, a tent housing God's interpersonal, covenanting presence. John's community is on a journey—somewhere between their Egypt and the Promised Land. The *glory* of the first temple was hidden under a covering of animal skins.

D: The truth of the Incarnation led to the doctrine of *theosis* (deification). Irenaeus claims that God "became what we are in order to make us what he is himself."[133] Clement of Alexandria writes: "Yea, I say, the Word of God became a man so that you might learn from a man how to become a god."[134] Athanasius of Alexandria reasons: "The Word was made flesh in order that we might be made gods . . . Just as the Lord, putting on the body, became a man, so also we men are both deified through his flesh, and henceforth inherit everlasting life."[135] Augustine embraces the language: "But he himself that justifies also deifies, for by justifying he makes sons of God. 'For he has given them power to become the sons of God' [John 1:12]. If then we have been made sons of god, we have also been made gods."[136] However, Scripture and tradition maintain a distinction between Creator and creation. Eschewing pantheism, John of Damascus (c. 676–749), viewed by the Orthodox Church as the last father, and Gregory Palamas (1296–1359) distinguish between God's essence (*ousia*, οὐσία) and energies (*energeia*,

131. James Cameron blurs the distinction between *avatāra* and the Incarnation in his film, *Avatar* (2009). A human protagonist enters into an avatar, a genetically engineered body, to communicate to a humanlike species, the Na'vi, on a faraway moon, Pandora. By the end of the film he becomes a Na'vi. Technically, his title is incorrect.

132. Sayers, *Man Born to Be King*, Introduction.

133. Irenaeus of Lyon, *Haer.* 5.1. The Greek has not survived. The Latin translation reads, *Factus est quod sumus nos, uti nos perficeret quod et ipse.*

134. Clement of Alexandria, *Protr.* 1.

135. Athanasius of Alexandria, *C. Ar.* 1.39; 3.34 (*NPNF2* 4:306–447).

136. Augustine, *On the Psalms* 52.

ἐνέργεια).[137] God's *ousia* is uncreated and incomprehensible.[138] Turning toward God, our soul is like a sword thrust into fire. The fire's energy interpenetrates the steel, which begins to glow (reflect). Despite taking some of its properties, the sword does not become the fire. Orthodox theologian John Zizioulas (b. 1931) regards *theosis* as participation in the subsistence of Christ.[139] Although the Creator took on creation in the Incarnation, the church interpreted the event at the Council of Chalcedon (AD 451) with the doctrine of the hypostatic (mystical) union:

> So, following the saintly fathers, we all with one voice teach the confession of one and the same Son, our Lord Jesus Christ: the same perfect in divinity and perfect in humanity, the same truly God and truly man, of a rational soul and a body; consubstantial with the Father as regards his divinity, and the same consubstantial with us as regards his humanity; like us in all respects except for sin; begotten before the ages from the Father as regards his divinity, and in the last days the same for us and for our salvation from Mary, the virgin God-bearer, as regards his humanity; one and the same Christ, Son, Lord, only-begotten, acknowledged in two natures which undergo no confusion, no change, no division, no separation; at no point was the difference between the natures taken away through the union, but rather the property of both natures is preserved and comes together into a single person and a single subsistent being; he is not parted or divided into two persons, but is one and the same only-begotten Son, God, Word, Lord Jesus Christ.[140]

Jesus Christ, son of God, has two natures, divine and human, each retaining its own properties yet united "in one subsistence and in one single person" (εἰς ἓν πρόσωπον καὶ μίαν ὑπόστασιν). United to Christ's humanity, we may partake of his deity.[141] This embodied union will be realized at the general

137. This distinction goes back to the Cappadocian fathers. Basil defines *ousia* as what is common in the Godhead. His younger brother Gregory appropriated neo-Platonic framing.

138. John claims "God" (*theos*, θεός) in Scripture does not refer to the divine nature or essence, which is unknowable, but to the divine energies—the power and grace of God, which is perceptible. Generally, we do not find this distinction in the Western tradition, which views God as "pure activity," *actus purus*, and this has caused friction.

139. Hypostasis may refer to the essential or basic structure/nature of an entity—substantial nature, essence, actual being, reality (see Heb 1:3). However, Basil made the more precise denotation of having the term refer to the Three in their particular ontological realities.

140. Tanner, *Decrees of the Ecumenical Councils*, 1:86.

141. We are part of the transfigured (metamorphosed) body of Christ, which is part

resurrection of the dead, for those who are in Christ, but has begun already by the mutual indwelling of Holy Spirit (see John 14–16; Rom 8).

In the Incarnation, the likeness of God is rendered visible, thereby annulling the Old Testament ban on imaging the divine. As John of Damascus and other fathers argued against the iconoclasts, worship may now be imagistic, a restoration of the kataphatic. From this freedom developed rich artistic and aesthetic traditions. The Damascene writes:

> I do not worship matter; I worship the Creator of matter who became matter for my sake, who willed to take his abode in matter; who worked out my salvation through matter.[142]
>
> Since he who, being in the form of God, is, by the excellence of his nature exempt from quantity, quality, and magnitude, yet took upon him the form of a servant, and put on the fashion of a body, contracting himself to quantity and quality. So represent him in pictures, and present him to be gazed on openly, who willed to be gazed on. Paint his humiliation, his nativity, his baptism, his transfiguration, his agonies that ransomed us, the miracles that, although worked by his fleshly ministry, proved his divine power and nature, his burial, his resurrection, his ascension—paint all these things in colors as well as in speech, in pictures as well as in books.[143]

This invitation assisted the church's mission: people could identify with Jesus Christ in icons and the depiction of scenes from the Gospels. But, like the distinction between essence and energy, the kataphatic side of worship is only wholesome when balanced with apophatic mystery. Too easily a depicted Jesus becomes our little Jesus, subservient to our comfort and politics.

The phrase *grace and truth* may suggest a creative tension. We are always seeking this balance in ministry, which is found in Jesus's care for the Samaritan woman and others. *Truth* is necessary but often too painful without *grace*.

S: *Lord, you are beautiful. You are full of* grace and truth. *Why do we ever look away? The powers of the world are strong, but we desire to behold your face forever. Focus us. Amen.*

---

of his human nature, the beginning of new creation, which is nevertheless united to Christ's divine nature. Donald Fairbairn describes adoption in this context as "sharing in the communion that the natural Son has with God the Father" (*Life in the Trinity*, 10).

142. Cited in Nes, *Mystical Language of Icons*, 15.

143. Cited in Farrar, *Life of Christ*, 5. I updated and slightly edited the language.

Mission of the Baptist (1:15–18)

[15] John serves as witness to him and has cried out, saying:[144] "This was who[145] I spoke. The one who comes after me has come before my (face)[146] because he was before me." [16] For out of his fullness we all received—indeed, grace upon grace, [17] because the Law was given through Moses; Grace and Truth came (to be) through Jesus Christ. [18] No one has ever seen God;[147] the only God,[148] the one who is at the chest of the Father—that one explained him."

P: John came to *witness* (vv. 6–8) and now offers it (v. 15)—essentially, the superiority of the Logos—which is unpacked by the narrator (vv. 16–18).[149] Philo also develops the relationship between the *logos* and the Mosaic *Law*. Before *Moses*, the patriarchs lived according to *orthos logos* (ὀρθός λόγος) or impeccable reason, a reflection of the universal *spermatikos logos.*[150] But *the Law* became the ideal reflection of *logos* on earth. We find a similar claim in later rabbinic literature. In contrast, John places *the Law* in an anticipatory role (1:17).

The phrase *grace upon grace* (*charin anti charitos,* χάριν ἀντὶ χάριτος) is ambiguous. The preposition may also be translated "in exchange for." Augustine argues for a *grace* in which we live by faith that is given in exchange

144. The extent of John's citation is unclear. The Greek manuscripts lack quotation marks. We run into the same ambiguity with Jesus's teaching (e.g., 3:10–21).

145. For this Greek construction, see 1:45.

146. Has come before my (face) or "ranks before me" or even "has come into being before me." Our reading appropriates the spatial sense of *emprosthen* (ἔμπροσθεν)—before the presence of someone or something (see, e.g., Matt 5:24; 6:1; John 10:4; 12:37). For the image of light shining before people, see the startling command at Matt 5:16. The second reading, adopted by the ESV (et al.), follows the sense of rank. The final reading creates difficulties for Orthodoxy, because it suggests there was a time when the Son was not (Arius). But it is difficult to make sense of the idea of the Logos coming into existence before John's eyes or presence. Instead, the prophet claims Jesus, who is the light of his witness, has now arrived on the scene. He stands in front of John as the fulfillment of prophecy (see 1:23).

147. "Moses hid his face because he was afraid to look at God" (Exod 3:6). Later, he asks to see God, but is told: "no man can see Me and live!" (33:20). To even hear his voice is a miracle (Deut 5:24).

148. The *only God*, a more difficult reading vs. "the only Son," is found in our earlier mss (P66, P75, ℵ, and Vat).

149. As we noted, the extent of the Baptist's citation is not entirely clear. The repetition of fullness, however, appears to mark the resumption of the narrator, along with the switch to the first person (*we*). We find a similar citation of the Baptist in the Synoptic Gospels as delimited here (Mark 1:7; Matt 3:11).

150. Sandmell, *Philo of Alexandria*, 85, 97.

for the *grace* of eternal life.[151] Another image is grace piling upon grace—like waves breaking on the beach—which suggests that grace did not begin with Jesus but reached its *fullness*.[152]

R: The *Law through Moses* allusion may extend the Malachi citation (1:6). After the prediction of Elijah's (= Baptist's) return, God adds:[153] "Remember the *Law of Moses*, my servant, the commandments and ordinances, just as I commanded him in Horeb for all Israel" (Mal 3:24 OG = MT 4:4). The passage fits John's rhetoric: *Moses* is not *God*, but a servant. God does not offer *grace* here, but requires obedience. *Moses* originally "hid his face, for he was afraid to look at God" (Exod 3:6 ESV). However, through the journey, he is increasingly attracted to God's Beauty and Goodness:

> Moses said, "Please show me your glory [Beauty]." And he said, "I will make all my goodness pass before you and will proclaim before you my name 'YHWH.' And I will be gracious to whom I will be gracious, and will show mercy on whom I will show mercy. But," he said, "you cannot see my face, for a human will not see me and live." And YHWH said, "Look: there is a place by me where you will stand on the rock, and while my glory [Beauty] passes by I will put you in a cleft of the rock, and I will cover you with my hand until I have passed by. Then I will take away my hand, and you will see my back, but my face will not be seen." (Exod 33:18–23)

John echoes this passage when he claims, "we beheld his glory" (1:14). His community has seen more of God than the Law-giver. God has chosen to be revealed in the Son and to dispense *grace*. Jesus will soon pass before him (1:36).

D: The *we* (v. 16) may refer to John and the Baptist, the apostles, the "Johannine community," but most naturally includes "whoever received him" (1:12). Those who have trusted in the name of the Lord Jesus Christ offer their own witness. John describes a gracious reciprocity—those who received Jesus, a kind of hospitality, also *received his fullness*. Theodore the Studite writes on the adoration of the cross: "Indeed an unheard of exchange! We are given life instead of death, incorruptibility instead of corruption, glory instead of dishonor."[154] "Draw near to him who descends from the bosom of the Father into the Virgin's womb."[155]

151. For critique, see Carson, *John*, 131.

152. Bultmann, *John*, 78.

153. The MT reverses the order, putting the reference to Moses before Elijah.

154. PG. 99: 696B.

155. Ludolph of Saxony, *Life of Christ*, 1:7.

S: Jesus is the *only* (*monogenēs*, μονογενής) *God*. The adjective turns what is modified into something unique. Isaac is Abraham's *only* son, not in a biological sense, but concerning God's promise (Heb 11:17–19).[156] Here, Jesus is *monogenēs* in the hypostatic union and the unique mission that follows from that event (see John 3:16). *Lord Jesus, you took our emptiness that we might share in your fullness. Father, you are gracious to us through your Son. Please fill us with your truth, light, life, and grace. Amen.*

3A: To Believe (John 20:30–31)

[30] So many other signs Jesus did before (his)[157] disciples, which have not been written down in this scroll (or book), [31] but these things have been written, that you may believe that Jesus is the Christ, the son of God, and that, believing, you may have life[158] in his name.

P: John is selective. The length of his Gospel falls between Mark, the shortest, and Matthew and Luke, whose presentations probably filled an entire *scroll* (approx. 30 feet). But what he *wrote* is sufficient—perhaps for one reading/listening (see Rev 1:3).

This purpose statement echoes the prologue: "Yet whoever received him, he gave them the right to become God's children—to those who believe into his name, who, not by bloods or by a bodily intent or by the intent of a husband, but by God they came to be" (1:12–13). *Name* is filled out with two epithets, *Christ* (or Messiah), which also occurs in the prologue (1:17) and *the son of God*, a confession that is first made by the Baptist after he witnesses the descent of the Spirit (1:34) and then repeated by Nathanael after seeing very little (1:49). Further into the story, we learn that whoever believes in *the son of God* will not be condemned (3:18) and will be raised from the dead by him (5:25). Finally, Jesus claims to be *the son of God*, consecrated and sent for our salvation (10:36). He demonstrates the power of this title by raising Lazarus from the dead (11:4). At the heart of the climactic sign, Martha offers the confession of this passage: "I believe that you are *the Christ, the son of God*" (11:27). Others reject the claim (19:7). John, then, is following Mark's central confession.

156. The common English translation "only begotten" (KJV) is possible, despite recent arguments to the contrary (Dawson, "*Monogenēs* and the Social Trinity," 32–66). As we saw, Wisdom of Solomon presents the *logos* as an emanation from God (7:25), a precursor to the orthodox doctrine of the eternal generation of the Son.

157. The possessive pronoun is absent in Codices Vat and Alexandrinus and several other witnesses. The sense is little affected.

158. Witnesses, including א, read "eternal life." The clarification is probably not original but consistent with John's usage.

D: John can be read to initiate faith, to deepen faith, or, most likely, both.[159] Faith is a journey with a beginning, middle, and end. Martha's confession comes in an especially difficult season. She had begun to walk with Jesus, but he initially let her down. Most of us face similar disappointments. Jesus eventually raised Lazarus to live a little longer, but someday *life* will overcome all death and sadness in new creation. But this *life* is not merely granted at the end of the age, but is available today. Often, I lapse into survival mode and feel detached from life, vacillating between anxiety and boredom. The key to *life* and therefore joy is connecting to God and one another, which the Father and Son offer through the Spirit.

John uses the verb *graphō* (γράφω, "to write"), which stands behind the term *agraphon*—a saying of Jesus not written in the canonical Gospels. He may also acknowledge his very selective appropriation of other Gospels. He passes over most of the *signs* in the Synoptics, except for the Feeding of Five Thousand and Walking on Water, and does not include a single exorcism. Some make a big deal of this, hypothesizing that John is antagonistic towards the other evangelists, but selecting a few items from a larger body of material is a topos.[160] As editors know, what is omitted is often not inferior but tangential to a work's purpose. John, in fact, is seeking to elicit the same confession as the other evangelists. In response to the question, "Who do you say that I am," Peter replies in Matthew: "You are the Christ, the son of the living God" (16:16).[161]

S: *Lord Jesus Christ, son of God, may we come alive by meditating on your signs, entrusting ourselves to you, our Messiah. Amen.*

3B: To Be Certain (Luke 1:1–4)

[1:1] Since many attempted[162] to arrange for themselves a narrative concerning matters that are fulfilled among us, [2] like the eyewitnesses (who were) from the beginning and became ministers of the word (*logos*) handed over to us, [3] it also seemed appropriate for me, who has followed everything accurately for a significant period of time, to write in orderly sequence for

159. Our earliest witnesses present *believe* as a present subjunctive (πιστεύητε). However, a larger number opt for the aorist subjunctive (πιστεύσητε). The difference is aspectual. A present subjunctive would have us see belief as an unfolding process, which suggests perseverance or maturation. An aorist subjunctive invites an external, transcendent view of the action. A both/and approach is becoming popular (Tam, *Apprehension of Jesus in the Gospel of John*, 197).

160. See, e.g., 1 Macc 9:22; Lucian, *Demon.* 67.

161. σὺ εἶ ὁ χριστὸς ὁ υἱὸς τοῦ θεοῦ τοῦ ζῶντος.

162. Origen interprets "attempt" negatively (*Hom. Luc.* 1.1).

you, most excellent Theophilus, [4] that you may have certainty concerning the things you have been taught.[163]

P: Only Luke and John explicitly disclose their purpose for writing. Both evangelists emphasize the veracity of eyewitness testimony and the selectivity of their account.[164] Such disclosures are best suited at the beginning or ending of a work. Luke was inspired by John, but since he also wanted to acknowledge Theophilus, chose to share the background in a preface. Presumably, John is one of the *eyewitnesses* appropriated by Luke. John writes so that his readers may believe; with characteristic escalation, Luke wants Theophilus to be *certain*!

The unit has clear delimitation. It is a concentrated preface of one rhetorically balanced sentence (period).[165] Afterwards, the style changes. We find similar prefaces in Greco-Roman literature that convey intent (*skopos*), acknowledge assistance, and admit challenges of composition.

Luke moves from the general to the particular—a communal *we/us* to *me/Theophilus*. While focusing on their relationship, he is mindful of their place in a community, which may now have three generations: *eyewitnesses* (*autoptēs*, αὐτόπτης), first writers, and now Luke and *Theophilus*. Modern studies often identify the first person with a narrator, but that does not comport with the form; Luke is introducing himself.[166] But, like the other evangelists, he withholds his name, which is significant in his presentation: the beggar's name is Lazarus; the wealthy man (Luke 16:19–31)?

The evangelist wants *Theophilus* to be assured of the reliability of his sources. But the language of *following everything accurately* (*parakoloutheō akribōs*, παρακολουθέω ἀκριβῶς) may also describe Luke's own discipleship journey. The primary signification of the verb, according to a standard lexicon, is being closely associated with someone viewed as an authority figure.[167]

Some claim *Theophilus* (Θεόφιλος "friend of God") is imaginary, but this does not comport with the form of the preface or tradition.[168] Yet he is otherwise unknown to history. Like the early apologists (Quadratus, Aristides, and Justin Martyr), Luke may be attempting to persuade a Roman

163. Following the ESV. An alternative translation is "that you might recognize the truth of the words by which you were taught."

164. Luke and John use the word *polus* (πολύς "many").

165. Vv. 1–2 function as the protasis; vv. 3–4, apodosis. For background on the form, see Alexander, *Preface to Luke's Gospel*. She finds the most analogues with non-elitist, artisan, scientific literature.

166. A narrator may be appropriate after the preface, beginning with v. 5, but I am still unconvinced that Luke is not intending to be the storyteller.

167. BDAG, 767.

168. Alexander, *Preface to Luke's Gospel*, 73–75, 133, 188.

authority to accept the gospel. The evangelist often presents authorities in a positive light and wants to show Christians as peace-loving and obedient. It is their opponents, Jewish and Pagan, who disrupt the *Pax Romana*. He uses *most excellent* (*kratistos*, κράτιστος) in Paul's addresses to the procurators of Judea, Felix and Festus.[169] The verb *katēcheō* (κατηχέω), which I translated *were taught*, may also signify "be informed" with a negative connotation (Acts 21:21). So Luke may write to an outsider, making his Gospel a kind of apologetic (evangelistic) public document. It is more likely, however, that *Theophilus* was a prominent Christian, who patronized the writing of Luke and Acts.[170] As we noted, Luke probably appropriated the work of Josephus, who acknowledges his patron as "most excellent (*kratiste*, κράτιστε) Epaphroditus" in his preface to *Against Apion*. He encouraged the historian to complete the lengthy *Antiquities* (*Ant.* 1.8–9). If a would-be writer was poor, it was necessary to find someone who could provide, among other things, a place to live, papyri and ink, as well as scribes (also called stenographers, secretaries, and amanuenses), who would take down dictation and copy the autograph (original) for general publication. *Katēcheō* also signifies "instructing" (Acts 18:25)—what came to be called "catechesis" (*katēchēsis*, κατήχησις).[171] This aim is consistent with the large amount of teaching in Luke's Gospel.

R: The act of *fulfilling* (*plēroforeō*, πληροφορέω) evokes biblical prophecy, as his version of Christ's birth will show.

D: Some contextualize Luke's preface in history; others, rhetoric.[172] But with biography this is an unnecessary dichotomy. Plutarch dramatizes people known to history. He enjoys a constrained freedom. On the one hand, the biographer can please the reader with a good story; on the other, if he transgresses the communal memory of his subject, the project fails. (This is a perennial truth that may be seen in biographical films that fail or succeed.) Luke happily writes under a similar constraint. He retells the Jesus story from the *eyewitnesses* Peter, Matthew, and John—revered apostles. His version reflects a different rhetorical sensibility that might have been more amenable to *Theophilus* and those like him, but he is not seeking to reinvent how Jesus was remembered. Those who did were rejected.

169. Acts 23:26; 24:3; 26:25.

170. Marshall, *Gospel of Luke*, 39.

171. 2 Clem. 17:1; Alexander, *Preface of Luke's Gospel*, 139.

172. Work from the historical paradigm is legion. See, e.g., Marshall, *Gospel of Luke*, 39; Fitzmyer, *Luke*, 288.

Luke appeals to *eyewitnesses* (*autoptai*, αὐτόπται).[173] Aristotle claims their testimony establishes "whether a thing has occurred, or not occurred" (*Rhetoric* 1375–76a).[174] Lucian of Samosata (c. 125–d. after 180), skeptical of most truth claims, opines:

> As to the facts themselves, [the historian] should not assemble them at random, but only after much laborious and painstaking investigation. He should for preference be an eyewitness but, if not, listen to those who tell the more impartial story, those whom one would suppose least likely to subtract from the facts or add to them out of favor or malice.[175]

Preference for eyewitness testimony appears to be a broadly held conviction. Josephus criticizes those who "have published works under the title of histories without either visiting the sites or going anywhere near the action."[176] John of Lycopolis (c. 394) notes, "the ears are naturally less reliable than the eyes—and because very often forgetfulness follows what we hear, whereas the memory of what we have seen is not easily erased but remains imprinted on our minds like a picture."[177] Luke acknowledges not being an *eyewitness*, a humble disclosure that differs from later apocryphal gospels, but opts for the best alternative—carefully finding the most reliable eyewitness testimony (Lucian). By his generation, Peter (Mark), Matthew, and John had this reputation. However, these earlier writings did not measure up to the rhetorical polish expected by educated readers. Whoever Luke was he was an excellent stylist.[178] The Jewish-Christian scholar Eduard Norden (1868–1941) describes the preface as the best written sentence in the New Testament.[179] Ernest Renan praises the Gospel as "the most beautiful book ever written."[180]

Luke's preface situates the gospel in history. Thucydides notes, "most of the events of the past, through lapse of time, have fought their way past

173. Papias uses the same language for Polycarp's place in the chain of tradition. Polycarp "had been appointed to the bishopric of the church in Smyrna by the eyewitnesses and ministers of the Lord" (cited by Eusebius, *Hist. eccl.* 3.36.1–2). A similar value is at work in isolating the legitimate *hadith* of Muhammed.

174. Ancient historians believed history could be written only while events were still within living memory (Bauckham, *Jesus and the Eyewitnesses*, 8–9).

175. Lucian of Samosata, *How to Write History*, 6.60 (cited in Black, *Luke*, 40n3).

176. Josephus, *Ag. Ap.* 1.46 (Embry et al., *Early Jewish Literature*, 1:322).

177. Ward, *Lives of the Desert Fathers*, 55.

178. I suggest Luke's rhetorical prowess is most on display in Hebrews.

179. daß diese Periode, die allgemein als die beststilisierte des ganzen N.T. gilt (Norden, *Agnostos Theos*, 316n1).

180. C'est le plus beau livre qu'il y ait (*Les Evangiles*, 283).

credence into the country of myth" (1.21.8). Like the historian, Christians had a low view of myth (*mythos*, μῦθος).[181] For them, like many others in the first century, a myth signifies a false story about the divine.[182] Although perhaps the majority of the populace continued to believe in them, many had turned to philosophy with their deepest questions.[183] Today, people speak about the truth of myth by which they usually mean timeless, abstract essences or vitalities beyond scientific observation. But it would be anachronistic to apply this to the Gospels. When Luke appeals to *truth*, it is a claim on verifiable reality.

A rhetorically polished presentation of history is not necessarily myth. The aim simply enlarges the values of the writer. Luke writes to educate (and possibly to entertain), the goal of biography, to persuade, the goal of rhetoric, but also to record history for the next generation. Ambrose describes Luke's style as "historical mode" and notes: "As compared with the other Gospels, we see greater zeal devoted to the description of the events than to the expression of rules of behavior."[184]

If important events are not recorded, they are often forgotten or distorted. Herodotus claims to present what he "learned by inquiry" so that "the memory of the past may not be blotted out from among men by time."[185] Human memory can fail.[186] Luke wrote at the right time—something like a recent experience I had at a family reunion. Sitting near a cornfield in Iowa, my older family members shared memories about my great grandparents, who had died around forty years ago. Several times they corrected one another over dates, names, and places, the very details that are often the first

181. See 1 Tim 1:4. Paul emphasizes the truthfulness of God and his gospel (see Titus 1:2; Eph 4:21). Peter contrasts myths with his eyewitness testimony of the Transfiguration (2 Pet 1:16). For the problems labeling Hebrew Scripture myth, see Oswalt, *Bible among the Myths*.

182. Josephus, *Ag. Ap.* 2:256; Herodotus, *Persian War* 2:45; Plato, *Resp.* 330d; 377a; Plato, *Leg.* 636c; Plato, *Tim.* 26e; Arian, *Disc.* 3.24.

183. Veyne, *History of Private Life*, 19.

184. Cited in Just, *Luke*, 1.

185. Herodotus, *Hist.* 1.1 (Godley, LCL). He acknowledges the fragility of memory in relation to time. He is concerned with what happened and the causes leading to the event and can be very critical of Homer's mythological presentation. But he also does not necessarily believe his sources, upon which he is completely dependent. His task is "to say what is said" (7.152.3). Luke and Herodotus share the common value of wanting to preserve the great works of the past, but the former narrows his focus on what "Jesus began to do and to teach" (Acts 1:1). Unlike Herodotus, Luke accepts the veracity of his sources, and writes as a committed believer who had a lot to gain or lose depending upon the truthfulness of their claims.

186. One study claims an average 20 percent distortion soon after an event (McIver, "Eyewitnesses as Guarantors," 529–46).

to be forgotten. Yet by stimulating one another's memories, they were able to find the truth. Luke is probably writing from the same distance, but had access to multiple sources.

Historians were expected to construct a narrative without distortion or prejudice. Tacitus (c. 60–c. 120) writes: "My purpose is to relate a few facts about Augustus—more particularly his last acts, then the reign of Tiberius, and all which follows, without either bitterness or partiality, from any motives to which I am far removed" (*Annals* 1.1). Josephus also attempts "historical accuracy"—the careful, even laborious, collection of facts from reliable sources (*J.W.* 1.16). Desire, of course, does not always reflect reality; and these historians may have fallen short of their ideal.[187] Some feel the same about Luke, who makes claims that seem to contradict Josephus—specifically, the date of Quirinius' reign (Luke 2:2) and the chronological sequence of the insurrectionists, Theudas and Judas the Galilean (Acts 5:36–37)—and, with the other Gospels, our everyday experience. Having worked through Luke and Acts, my impression is that Luke is an earnest, careful historian. If Ananias and Sapphira died for lying about property, as Luke narrates (Acts 5:1–11), would he be quick to do the same with the gospel?

What typically divides scholars is worldview. If one rejects the supernatural at the level of presupposition, then much of Luke's presentation will read like fiction. The logic proceeds from making the criterion of judgment personal experience or the general patterns of nature. But might reality transcend such things? Science is helpful for understanding the everyday, not the supernatural.

The historian was expected to provide both truthful facts and their larger implications for the reader.[188] Despite the need to capture living memory from reliable eyewitness testimony, writing history took time. This required some distance between the events and discerning their context. The often proposed distance in time between Jesus's departure (33) and the publication of the first Gospel, twenty to forty years, is appropriate—not too short to undercut reflection, not too distant for the preservation of living memory. Although Luke was not a first-generation believer, he came at the right time to make the largest contribution to the New Testament. We also do a disservice to history by underreporting it. How underwhelming would the Gospels be if they only recorded Who, What, When, and Where? like a first-semester journalism course?

187. See Mason, *Josephus and the New Testament*.

188. Black, "Mark as Historian," 64–83.

Seeing truth, we should follow Luke's example and offer the way of vision to others. His preface suggests *Theophilus* values a rigorously historical presentation according to Greco-Roman conventions. Fundamentalists and evangelicals are often criticized for their "tendency to historicise biblical narratives," but, at least with Luke (and John—see 21:24–25), this is the intended approach of the authors. Christianity is grounded in history.[189]

Athanasius appropriates Luke's preface in his thirty-ninth Festal Letter:

> Since, however, we have spoken of the heretics as dead but of ourselves as possessors of the divine writings unto salvation, and since I am afraid that—as Paul has written to the Corinthians [2 Cor. 11:3]—some guileless persons may be led astray from their purity and holiness by the craftiness of certain men and begin thereafter to pay attention to other books, the so-called apocryphal writings, being deceived by their possession of the same names as the genuine books, I therefore exhort you to patience when, out of regard to the Church's need and benefit, I mention in my letter matters with which you are acquainted. It being my intention to mention these matters, I shall, for the commendation of my venture, follow the example of the evangelist Luke and say [cf. Luke 1:1–4]: Since some have taken in hand to set in order for themselves the so-called apocrypha and to mingle them with the God-inspired Scripture, concerning which we have attained to a sure persuasion, according to what the original eye-witness and ministers of the word have delivered unto our fathers, I also, having been urged by true brethren and having investigated the matter from the beginning, have decided to set forth in order the writings that have been put in the canon, that have been handed down and confirmed as divine, in order that everyone who has been led astray may condemn his seducers, and that everyone who has remained stainless may rejoice, being again reminded of that.[190]

Aquinas claims every generation must find new words to express the old faith because they must answer new heresies.[191] What does our audience seek? Many I encounter seek a gospel addressing, among other things, the explanatory power of science, the claims of other religious and secular worldviews, and the evils of church history. We no longer live in a world—at least in the west—that takes God's existence and activity for granted. Some believe we had our chance—Christendom came and went and for what? Yet the Gospels

189. Ausloos and Lemmelijn, *Book of Life*, 2.

190. Schneemelcher and Wilson, *New Testament Apocrypha*, 1:49.

191. Aquinas, *S.T.* 29.3 (*Summa Theologiae*, 69).

claim Jesus came, went (while remaining mysteriously present), and shall come again. Still, in the meantime, we have not always represented our Lord well. Following Luke, we must preserve the insights of those who have gone before us, but also translate them for the next generation.

Summation

In this chapter, we explored how the Gospels began their presentations of Jesus Christ. John (1:17), Matthew (1:1, 16), and Mark (1:1) refer to Jesus as the Christ or "Messiah." The Fourth Gospel also identifies the Messiah as the divine Logos (wisdom). Matthew explicitly and Mark implicitly focus on Jesus's Davidic ancestry—specifically, God's covenant with the King to establish his throne forever, despite the Babylonian captivity. Both the Logos and son of David identifications find their meaning in a Jewish context. What appears to be new is the linking of these two figures into a single person. This requires the eventual confession that Jesus is the God-man. While Jesus enters into our humanity, he does not originate with us but comes from God. John claims the divine Logos became flesh (1:14).

3

Birth

The previous chapter focused on how the Gospels began. Matthew and Luke chose to extend their introductions with a "birth story" (infancy narrative, Nativity).[1] Matthew gives forty-eight of his 969 verses—5 percent; Luke, 132 of 938 verses—15 percent. This comparatively short space did not satisfy the curiosity of some, leading to the production of several infancy gospels.

Although both evangelists provide birth stories, their presentations considerably differ. A common view is that Matthew and Luke independently appropriated Mark and Q, which lacked discussion of Christ's origin and therefore relied on conflicting tradition that only became apparent after their Gospels were read together.[2] Raymond Brown notes, "Some scholars have tried very hard to reconcile the differences between Matthew and Luke but with little convincing success."[3] However, these attempts did not incorporate the genre expectations of rewritten Scripture. *Aemulatio,* as we noted, respects one's predecessors by appropriating and updating their work. Matthew probably wrote the first birth story, which was incorporated by Luke and modified to reflect the contributions of John's Gospel, liturgical elements, and Mary's memories. This partially explains why Luke's birth story is longer. The two evangelists also have unique emphases: Matthew presents Jesus as the embodiment of God's people, who repeats and completes the

1. For a collection of essays on this topic, see Clivaz, *Infancy Gospels*. Helmut Koester notes: "they [Matthew and Luke] speak of the birth of the divine child that marks the beginning of the new age of the history of the world" (*Ancient Christian Gospels*, 304). Stephen Langton correctly recognized the thematic transition with his third chapter division in both Gospels.

2. See, e.g., Hurtado, *Lord Jesus Christ*, 318. C. K. Barrett claims, "there is no evidence to suggest any literary relationship between the two narratives" (*Holy Spirit*, 5).

3. Brown, *Coming Christ*, 8–9.

biblical story. Luke focuses on Christ's formation, a traditional emphasis of the Greco-Roman *bios* genre.

4A: Abraham to Jesus (Matt 1:2–17)

Matthew does not use the term γενεαλογία, which is transliterated as "genealogy" in English (see 1 Tim 2:4; Titus 3:9), but an element of the word, *genea* (γενεά, "generation"), occurs three times at the end of the unit (v. 17). A genealogy offers a very concentrated family history—centuries can be rehearsed in a few lines. The genre is especially important in cultures that ascribe honor to someone in light of their ancestry, like the social world of Matthew's first readers. As we shall see, the evangelist uses the genre to introduce the main themes of his Gospel.

The final part of the incipit, "son of David, son of Abraham" (Matt 1:1), anticipates the genealogy's content. As noted by Jerome, Matthew employs a latching technique whereby the repetition of a word unites two units.[4] Although the genealogy emphasizes David "the King" (v. 6), it begins with Abraham (אַבְרָהָם), the "father of a multitude" (v. 2). For those familiar with Genesis, the transition is not surprising: "book of *genesis*" also headed a genealogy that began with Adam to introduce Abraham into the story (Gen 5:1–32 LXX). Matthew adopts the language for the genealogy proper: "Adam . . . begot (*egennēsen*, ἐγέννησεν) . . . Seth" (Gen 5:3); "Abraham *begot* (*egennēsen*, ἐγέννησεν) *Isaac*" (Matt 1:2).

Matthew structures the genealogy with three series of fourteen generations (1:17). The first series culminates with David (v. 6), a distant father; the second, what has been called the Babylonian Captivity, which disrupted the kingdom (v. 11); the third, its reestablishment in Jesus Christ (v. 16).[5] There is also a thematic *inclusio*, suggesting typology with escalation: Isaac (v. 1) was remarkably conceived—Sarah being ninety or ninety-one years old—and Jesus, as the next unit will unpack, even more supernaturally (v. 16).

4. This may be due to Semitic influence; the same technique is found in James (e.g., 1:4, 5). Some fathers found great significance in the temporal inversion of the names David and Abraham. But Jerome makes the literal observation that the order sets up the genealogy (Aquinas, *CA*).

5. Josephus similarly divides his *Antiquities* with the close of the exile at the end of Book 10. Pseudo-Daniel A (4Q243—4Q244) moves from primeval history to a section that runs from the patriarchs to the exile (see Embry et al., *Early Jewish Literature*, 1:99).

Son of Abraham (1:2–6a)

[2] Abraham *begot* Isaac. Isaac begot Jacob.[6] Jacob begot Judah and his brothers. [3] Judah begot Perez and Zerah by Tamar. Perez begot Hezron. Hezron begot Ram. [4] Ram begot Aminadab. Aminadab begot Nahshon. Nahshon begot Salmon.[7] [5] Salmon begot Boaz[8] by Rahab. Boaz begot Obed[9] by Ruth. Obed begot Jesse. [6] Jesse begot David, the King.

P: *Begot* is an old-fashioned word, but the popular circumlocution "was the father of" (NIV, NRSV, ESV) obscures the active voice of the verb *gennaō* (γεννάω) that emphasizes sexual reproduction.[10]

R: Matthew summarizes a lot of Scripture by genealogy, appropriating the end of Ruth (4:13–17) and 1–2 Chronicles, the last book of the Hebrew Bible, which also rehearses Israel's history in this way, beginning with Adam (1:1—9:44).[11] The covenant is assumed through the choices of descendants: Isaac, not Ishmael (Abrahamic); Judah, not his brothers (Davidic).[12] *Isaac* was Abraham's immediate son through the promise that Sarai (later Sarah), his barren, elderly wife, would provide a son.[13] The son is remembered for almost being sacrificed (Gen 22), a typology recognized by the Gospels. Matthew may foreshadow the Passion, which breaks the rocks of the temple—one being, according to tradition, the place Abraham bound Isaac (27:51). *Judah* is neither the firstborn, Reuben (Gen 35:23), nor the main character in the

6. As with Sarah, Rebekah was barren, but (albeit less dramatically) supernaturally conceived (Gen 25:21). Like Tamar, she gives birth to twins, but only *Jacob* is mentioned.

7. The Chronicler reads "Salma"; Ruth, "Salmon." Matthew is clearly dependent upon the latter at this point.

8. The Chronicler does not relate Salmon with Rahab. The pairing occurs only here. Perhaps Matthew appropriates Jewish tradition. After saving the spies and being spared, she and her family had to remain "outside of the camp of Israel" (Josh 6:23). Despite some chronological tension—which is ameliorated when we recognize that genealogies throughout the Bible omit several generations—there is no contradiction in that no other mother of Boaz is mentioned.

9. The Chronicler does not relate Boaz with Ruth. For this, Matthew appropriates Ruth whose narrator claims God "made her conceive" (4:13).

10. The New King James Version updated the King James's "begat" to "begot," and is superior here (Brown, *Birth of the Messiah*, 58).

11. The "Chronicler" is a scholarly designation for the one (or those) responsible for bringing 1–2 Chronicles (Luther: *Die Chronika*) to closure. The Old Greek bears the earlier title *Paraleipomena*, "things omitted." The books were intended to supplement Samuel and Kings. They may have been at the end of Matthew's Scripture (see the R at Matt 23:35). He also appropriates the genealogy at the end of Ruth.

12. Chrysostom notes the significance of not mentioning Ishmael and Esau in the subsequent generation (Aquinas, *CA* on Matt 1).

13. See Gen 16:1; 17:15, 19, 21; Rom 9:7–10; Gal 4:28.

subsequent narrative, Joseph (Gen 37–48). The genealogy advances through him because he is David's ancestor. Jacob's last words to him are, "The scepter will not depart from Judah, nor the ruler's staff from between his feet" (Gen 49:10). Matthew focuses on the sin of Judah, who slept with *Tamar* presuming she was a prostitute. The twins, *Perez* ("breach") and *Zerah* ("Brightness"), were the result of that encounter (Gen 38:1–30).

D: We find a more explicit interpretation of this narrative (*haggadic*) theology in Paul's letter to the Romans (9:7–13): *God does not elect according to human expectation.*

S: Scripture reveals a God who surprises.

Son of David (1:6b–11)

[6b] David begot Solomon by the (wife) of Uriah. [7] Solomon begot Rehoboam. Rehoboam begot Abijah. Abijah begot 'Asaph.' [8] 'Asaph' begot Jehoshaphat. Jehoshaphat begot Joram. Joram begot[14] Uzziah. [9] Uzziah begot Jotham. Jotham begot Ahaz. Ahaz begot Hezekiah. [10] Hezekiah begot Manasseh. Manasseh begot 'Amos.' 'Amos' begot Josiah. [11] Josiah begot[15] Jechoniah[16] and his brothers[17] at (the time) of the Babylonian captivity.[18]

P: This section is comprised of Davidic kings. *Solomon*, according to the genealogy, is the first "son of David." He constructs the temple and is famous for his wisdom, but Scripture offers this sad commentary: "When Solomon was old his wives turned away his heart after other gods, and his heart was not wholly true to the Lord his God, as was the heart of David his father" (1 Kgs 11:4 ESV). Jesus, the true son of David, will surpass Solomon in wisdom and temple construction.[19]

14. Matthew skips three (or four) generations: Ahaziah, [Athaliah], Joash, and Amazaiah (1 Chr 3:11). A few manuscripts add: "Ochozias, And Ochozias begot Iōas, And Iōas begot Amasias, And Amasias begot." This would conform Matthew's genealogy to the biblical record. But these additions disturb the counting of v. 17, and clearly reflect a later harmonizing attempt.

15. A few mss add "Iōakim, And Iōakim begot."

16. Matthew skips a generation: Jochoniah is the son of Jehoiakim, who is the son of Josiah (1 Chr 3:15–16).

17. *And his brothers* parallels 1:2—Judah and his brothers, probably forming an *inclusio* around the rise and fall of Israel.

18. Jechoniah, a variant form of "Jehoiachin," was taken captive in 597 BC and released from a Babylonian prison approximately thirty-seven years later (2 Kgs 25:27–30). The Chronicler refers to Jechoniah as "the captive" (1 Chr 3:17).

19. 1 Kgs 4:29–54; Duling, "Solomon, Exorcism, and the Son of David," 235–52. The superscription of Proverbs reads: "Proverbs of Solomon, son of David, King of Israel" (MT). See 12:23.

Often obscured in translations, Matthew superimposes two names over similarly sounding ones: *Asaph* for Asa and *Amos* for Amon.[20] This is a rhetorical (literary) device called malapropism. We find a similar playfulness in rabbinic interpretation.[21] It brilliantly fuses the Prophets (*Amos*) and Psalms (*Asaph*) with the central biblical story.[22] Matthew wants to emphasize the genealogy as prophetic fulfillment. *Amos* prophesied God's judgment at the time of *Uzziah*. Jesus will also cite *Asaph* as "the prophet" (Matt 13:35; see 1 Chr 25:2; 2 Chr 29:30).

Composers of genealogies often make a point by breaking from the repetition. With *the wife of Uriah*, Matthew completes a list of four women who are explicitly mentioned: *Tamar*, *Rahab*, *Ruth*, and Bathsheba.[23] They anticipate Mary's supernatural yet initially disturbing pregnancy (v. 16), but differ from her because they are non-Israelites impregnated by Israelite men.[24] They show God's universal intent for the Abrahamic covenant.

The section terminates in the *Babylonian captivity* (586/7 B.C.), another break in the pattern. At that time, God's promises to Abraham (Gen 12:1–3; 15:1–21; 17:12–27) and David (2 Sam 7:1–17) appeared to be in jeopardy because of the unfaithfulness of God's people, represented by the kings (see Matt 1:21 for the continuation of this pattern). Some interpreters attempted to rewrite this dark history. The Damascus Document minimizes David's sin with Bathsheba: "The deeds of David rose up, except for the murder of Uriah, and God left them to him";[25] Josephus withholds the incident of the golden calf in *Antiquities*, his rewritten Scripture; The Prayer of Manasseh, part of the Apocrypha, depicts the evil king repenting and seeking God's mercy. With the Prophets, Matthew subverts this ideology: instead of whitewashing the past, as nations are prone to do, he pins all their hope for redemption on a messiah.[26]

20. Scribes "fixed" the spelling in later mss. However, the earlier, more difficult witnesses are preferred.

21. Keener, *IVP Bible Background Commentary*, 47.

22. See the inscriptions of Ps 50, 73–83.

23. Matthew does not name the more traditional matriarchs of Israel: Sarah, Rebekah, and Leah, Jacob's mother. Jerome claims "none of the holy women are taken into the savior's genealogy" because they were sinful (Aquinas, *CA* on Matthew 1).

24. Beare, *Matthew*, 64. Tamar, Rahab, and Bathsheba have unusual sexual backgrounds, and some interpret Ruth's actions toward Boaz in a provocative way—"uncovering the feet" (Ruth 3:6–9, 14) as a euphemism for sexual intercourse: see, e.g., Lüdemann, *Virgin Birth*, 64–65.

25. CD V, 5–6 (Vermes, *Complete Dead Sea Scrolls*, 130).

26. For messianic hope amidst communal critique, see Hos 3:5; Amos 9:11; Isa 55:3; Zech 3:8; Mic 4:8; 5:1–5; the latter is cited in Matt 2:5–6.

D: Because of Jesus, the Messiah, we can be honest about our own national stories. "Our citizenship is in the heavens," Paul reminds the Philippians, who may have been a little too proud of their Roman identity (Phil 3:20). We may interpret history differently, but a communal commitment to establishing facts is a vital aspect of truth (reality).

S: God's Spirit guided human history through women long before the virginal conception.[27]

"Son" of Joseph (1:12–16)

[12] After the Babylonian captivity, Jechoniah begot Shealtiel. Shealtiel begot Zerubbabel.[28] [13] Zerubbabel begot Abiud. Abiud begot Eliakim. Eliakim begot Azor. [14] Azor begot Zadok. Zadok begot Achim. Achim begot Eliud. [15] Eliud begot Eleazar.[29] Eleazar begot Matthan.[30] Matthan begot Jacob. [16] Jacob begot Joseph,[31] the husband of Mary. In her (womb) was begotten Jesus, the one called "Christ."

P: Matthew switches from the active *begot* to passive *was begotten* (v. 16), breaking the pattern of sexual reproduction.

R: *Zerubbabel*, the last name in the genealogy to occur in the Hebrew Bible, a "son of David," is enigmatic. He, along with the priest Joshua, brings permission from the Persian emperor to return to Palestine and rebuild the temple (Ezra 2:2; 3:2, 8; 4:2, 3; 5:2). The prophet Haggai calls him "governor" (1:1), and, with Zechariah (4:6–10), appears to give messianic significance to him. But nothing happens.

Matthew may emphasize a typology by naming *Joseph's* father *Jacob* like the biblical patriarchs. We saw a similar playfulness with the superimposing of the names "Asaph" and "Amos" (vv. 7–8, 10). However, it is not impossible that the evangelist is recording a historical reality as well: *Jacob*

27. Maloney, "Genealogy of Jesus," 20–21.

28. The Chronicler lists Zerubbabel as the son of Pedaiah, Shealtiel's brother (1 Chr 3:17). But Ezra claims Shealtiel is Zerubbabel's father (3:2). The simplest explanation is that Shealtiel died and his brother Pedaiah begot Zerubbabel through Levirate marriage (Deut 25:5–10). Matthew, then, appropriates Ezra as an additional source.

29. Eleazar or "Lazarus" was the third most popular name in Palestine at this time (Bauckham, *Jesus and the Eyewitnesses*, 85).

30. *Matthan* is probably a variant spelling of "Matthat" (Luke 3:24), which, in turn, is a shortened form of "Mattathias" or "Matthias" or "Matthew," the ninth most popular name in Palestine at this time (Bauckham, *Jesus and the Eyewitnesses*, 85). Mattathias set off the rebellion against the Seleucids, which was completed by his sons.

31. *Joseph* or "Joses" was the second most popular name in Palestine at this time (Bauckham, *Jesus and the Eyewitnesses*, 85).

was the eleventh most popular in Palestine at the time.[32] If so, the typology did not begin with Matthew, but *Joseph's* own family.

D: After *Zerubbabel*, Jesus's ancestors are lost to history.[33] These final generations before Christ lived and died between God's promises and their fulfillment. They had to trust their convictions and communal deposit about God and wait. After Christ's resurrection, there is more substance to our faith, but testing remains (James 1:2–4). The Nicene Creed allows us to confess: "From thence [heaven] he [Jesus Christ] will come to judge the quick and the dead." Since we do not know when this will happen, we cannot fully understand our place in salvation history. There have been many especially bleak seasons in church history, but at least a minority has always believed.

S: Matthew presents the Spirit, the soon to be revealed agent of *Mary's* pregnancy, as the creative and purifying power by which God achieves his purpose of restoring his people to himself.[34]

Numerical Significance (1:17)

[17] So all the generations from Abraham until David are fourteen generations; and from David until the Babylonian captivity, fourteen generations; and from the Babylonian captivity until the Christ, fourteen generations.[35]

P: The threefold unity of *fourteen generations* invites multiple interpretations.[36] This is probably an expression of *gematria*: Hebrew letters also had a numeric value; the three consonants of *David's* name (דוד) add up

32. Bauckham, *Jesus and the Eyewitnesses*, 85.

33. Matthew may have taken names from a public record in the temple, but such documents have not survived (Josephus, *Life* 6).

34. On the relationship between the Holy Spirit and purity, see Keener, *Spirit in the Gospels and Acts*, 91–117.

35. Some count only thirteen generations in the final section, but Matthew presumes Jesus as representing the final generation.

36. The author favors triadic arrangements (5:21–48; 6:1–18; 6:19–24). C. Kaplan suggests the pattern of fourteen reflects the division of a lunar month of twenty-eight days (fourteen waxing, fourteen waning). Abraham, then, would have begun the fourteen waxing generations with David as the full moon. Fourteen waning generations follow, leading to the eclipse of the Babylonian Captivity. Fourteen more waxing generations follow with the Messiah as the full moon ("Generation Schemes in Matthew," 465–71). M. J. Morton draws attention to the symbolic importance of the number forty-two (3 X 14) for the early church, noting that in Rev 13:5 a season of forty-two months is allowed for evil before God's final intervention ("Genealogy of Jesus," 219–24).

to fourteen.[37] The king is the fourteenth name in the genealogy.[38] We may also approach *fourteen* as a series of two sevens, the number of fullness. Jesus will offer seven beatitudes (5:3–10), seven petitions in the *Our Father* (6:9–13), seven parables in one section (13:1–9, 24–30, 31–33, 44, 45–46, 47–50, 51–52), and seven woes (23:13–29).[39] The structure will reinforce the verb *plēroō* (πληρόω "fulfill" or "fill up") in his citations from the Prophets (see, for example, 1:22; 2:17). For this intentional structure, Matthew had to omit several generations.[40] Genealogical conflation is common.[41] It would be anachronistic to require scientific precision from the evangelist whose interest is legitimating Jesus as a "son of David" and tracing his family though the patriarchal, monarchical, and exilic periods of Israel.[42] Nevertheless, regardless of the editing, the genealogy may be historically accurate: contemporary Jews traced their lineage back to David.[43]

S: Joachim of Fiore (c. 1135–1202), who perhaps went too far but was unafraid of Scripture's depth, also divided history into three ages—the Father, which continued until the incarnation; the Son, which would last forty-two generations like Matthew's genealogical frame, ending in 1260; and the age of the Holy Spirit (*Expositio in Apocalypsim*).[44] Logically, it followed that history would reflect its Creator, the Triune God.[45] While seven is complete in itself, three cycles of seven (forty-two) equates to three and a half years, which is an incomplete period or broken number in the prophetic tradition (see Dan 7:25; 12:7; James 5:17 on Elijah). We find another periodization of forty-two months in Revelation (11:2; 12:6, 14; 13:5), which Joachim applied to the his eschatology. After a second age (*status*) characterized by action, a contemplative third age would arise—*ecclesia contemplantium* ("church of contemplatives"). His thought was condemned by Aquinas and others because the third age, the freedom of the Spirit, appeared to make the church, the body of

37. Davies and Allison, *Matthew,* 1:165. We find *gematria* in roughly contemporary Jewish literature (Sib. Or. 5.12–51; T. Sol. 6.8; 11:6; see also b. Yoma 20a; b. Makk. 23b—24a; b. Ned. 32a; b. Sanh. 22a; Rev 13:8; Barn. 9).

38. Carlson, "Davidic Key," 665–83.

39. The Parables of the Seed and Leaven (13:31–33) are treated as one in this scheme.

40. For details, see Brown, *Birth of the Messiah,* 60–61. With oral genealogies, omissions generally happen in the middle because founders are important and the end is part of living memory (75n34).

41. For example, Gen 4:17–22 reduces millennia of cultural development into seven generations. There must also be conflation in Josephus's genealogy (*Life* 1).

42. Brown, *Birth of the Messiah,* 65.

43. Williams, *Can We Trust the Gospels?,* 34n16.

44. See Koester, *Revelation,* 438.

45. See McGinn, "Joachim of Fiore," 5–6.

Christ, less consequential. Yet that does not follow from the Triune pattern in which Father, Son, and Spirit are one and equal.[46]

Charles Lyell (1797–1875) argued in the first volume of his *Principles of Geology* that the earth's crust was much older than six thousand years, as some inferred from the Bible, and that it had not been shaped directly by God, but was formed by the slow, incremental effects of wind and water. He struggled to integrate these observations with faith, although he died a Christian.[47] And yet the books of Scripture and creation are consistent—pointing to a Father who delights in the faithfulness of generations, the slowly disclosed beauty of erosion, and a Spirit that works through wind and water.

4B: Jesus to Adam (Luke 3:23–38)

We find another genealogy in Luke's Gospel. Instead of heading the presentation, it is imbedded in the story (3:23–38). On one side of the unit, God affirms Jesus as "my beloved Son" (3:22); on the other, the devil challenges, "If you are the son of God . . ." (4:3). So Luke traces Christ's family back to Adam, the first "of God" (v. 37).

Luke's genealogy is an uninterrupted list of seventy-seven names, not including Jesus,[48] which appear to have been divided into eleven groups of sevens, allowing around 200 years for each group.[49] The pattern is most clear at the beginning and end of the genealogy. Matthew similarly structured his genealogy into three groups of fourteen generations (1:17). Typical of *aemulatio,* we find escalation in Luke's presentation: Matthew goes back to Abraham; Luke, all the way to Adam![50] However, Matthew opened the door for Luke by alluding to Adam with his opening words "(The) book of *genesis*" (Βίβλος γενέσεως).

The two genealogies overlap with biblical characters but otherwise differ considerably, an issue that perplexed later Christians and provided

46. See McGinn's defense ("Joachim of Fiore," 7–8).

47. His obituary in the *New York Times* (February 25, 1875) reads "But, though an evolutionist, Lyell was not a skeptic. He lived and died a Christian believer."

48. Following the textual decision of Nestle-Aland 28. Irenaeus counts only seventy-two generations from Adam (*Haer.* 3.22.3); Augustine, seventy-six (*Harm. Gosp.* 2.4.12–13).

49. The numbers have invited speculation. Seven may represent perfection. The eleven groups may anticipate Jesus as the head of the twelfth and final group, representing all of Israel or the final age.

50. Farrer suggests Luke corrects Matthew's genealogy in two ways: the artificial doubling of names to make fourteen generations and the missing generations in the monarchical period ("On Dispensing with Q," 87).

evidence for those wanting to discredit the gospel. Eusebius of Caesarea (c. 260–c.340) notes that many in his community found the genealogies to be in error, perhaps referring, in part, to Julian the Apostate's criticism in *Against the Galileans* (*Hist. eccl* 1.7.1). Some scribes, copying the Gospels, even altered the text. One imported part of Matthew's genealogy into Luke! Tatian avoids the problem by omitting both genealogies from his harmony.[51] Augustine writes to a certain Faustus, who had rejected the faith for this reason:

> Anyone can see as well as you that Joseph has one father in Matthew and another in Luke, and so with the grandfather and with all the rest up to David. Did all the able and learned men, not many Latin writers certainly, but innumerable Greek, who have examined most attentively the sacred Scriptures, overlook this manifest difference? Of course they saw it. No one can help seeing it. But with a due regard to the high authority of Scripture, they believed that there was something here that would be given to those who ask, and denied to those that snarl; would be found by those who seek, and taken away from those who criticize; would be open to those that knock, and shut against those that contradict. They asked, sought, and knocked; they received, found, and entered in. (*Reply to Faustus* 3.2)

Eusebius appropriates a solution in a letter to a certain Aristides from Julius Africanus (170–245). Julius distinguishes between natural and lawful parentage. Following Matthew's specific wording, Jacob "begot" Joseph, making him the natural father (1:16). Jacob's family traced themselves back to Solomon. Following Luke, Heli is Joseph's legal father. Through inference, Julius suggests Heli died without producing children. So Jacob practiced levirate marriage, begetting Joseph in Heli's name whose family traced themselves back to Nathan, another son of David (Deut 25:5–10). The two men were uterine brothers (having the same mother—Estha according to tradition—but different fathers). Augustine makes a similar argument: "Joseph had two fathers and consequently two lists of ancestors" (*Reply to Faustus* 3.3; 28.3). While complex, the scenario is not impossible. The Sadducean challenge presumes Levirate marriage was practiced in the first century (Luke 20:28–31).[52] Although some challenge the obligation of a uterine brother to marry his sister-in-law, the Pharisaic school of Shammai, which

51. Concerning Luke, it is explicit (4.29–30).

52. Philip Blackman notes, "theoretically the law of levirate marriage is still presumed to be obligatory" (*Mishnayoth*, 3:18).

was dominant at the time, included the relationship (*m. Yebam.* 1:1–4). Yet this solution may seem forced.[53]

A simpler, more natural explanation was offered by Annius of Viterbo (c. 1490) and followed by Martin Luther: Matthew provides Joseph's lineage and Luke, Mary's.[54] Matthew writes his birth story from Joseph's perspective and is concerned to show that he is a "son of David" (Matt 1:20). But Luke writes from Mary's perspective, implying that he appropriates her as a source. He also implies that Paul must circumcise Timothy because his mother was Jewish, despite having a Greek father (Acts 16:1–3). Paul himself presumes Jesus was a descendant of David from his mother's side: "born from a woman" (*genomenon ek gynaiokos,* γενόμενον ἐκ γυναικός [Gal 4:4])—"born from a descendant of David" (*genomenou ek spermatos Dauid,* γενομένου ἐκ σπέρματος Δαυὶδ [Rom 1:3]).[55] Ignatius of Antioch reflects this tradition: "For our God, Jesus the Christ, was conceived by Mary according to God's plan, both from the seed of David and of the Holy Spirit" (*Eph.* 18:2). To the Smyrnaeans, he claims that Jesus "is truly of the family of David with respect to human descent, Son of God with respect to the divine will and power, truly born of a virgin, baptized by John in order that all righteousness might be fulfilled by him, truly nailed in the flesh for us . . ." (1:1–2a). Justin Martyr claims Mary is of Davidic ancestry (*Dial.* 100). Following Matthew, Luke does not deny Joseph's Davidic ancestry (Luke 1:27), but probably considered it necessary to show that that heritage was also true on Christ's maternal side. Josephus, who may have been one of Luke's sources, is proudly aware of both his paternal and maternal heritage (*Life* 1). Also important is the ancestor *Levi* who is only mentioned in Luke's genealogy (v. 24). This was naturally a common name for a priest. Luke claims Mary is related to Elizabeth who is of priestly stock, from the tribe of Levi (1:5, 36). Through Mary, as Gregory of Nazianzus notes, Jesus is of both regal and priestly ancestry—the ideal Messiah (*Carmen* 18).

53. However, there may be a simpler explanation according to this line of inquiry. Matthew alludes to the Levirate situations of Tamar (v. 3) and Ruth (5). Yet here the Levirate law extends beyond brothers. Judah was a father and Boaz, a kinsman (Ruth 4:1–6). Jacob may have been the closest blood relative of Heli. Nazareth may have been largely a clan of extended family. This scenario would eliminate the need for the uterine hypothesis.

54. Unfortunately, Annius was a dishonest man, but, ironically, God may have given him truth in this matter. Tertullian anticipates this solution. He claims Matthew gives Mary's lineage; Luke, Joseph's (*De Carne Christi* 20–22). Unlike Luke's presentation, Mary is part of Matthew's genealogy (1:16), who also features four other women. But Matthew claims "Jacob begot Joseph," not Mary (1:16). For more discussion, see Gurtner, "Genealogies," 211–12.

55. The preposition *ek* (ἐκ) may describe birth from a woman (Matt 1:3, 5, 6).

From Joseph to Joseph (3:23b–24)

[23] And Jesus, who was beginning around thirty years (of age), who was, as was thought, son of Joseph, was himself (a descendant) of Heli [24] of Matthat of Levi of Melchi of Jannai of Joseph . . .

P: Only Luke provides a general age for Jesus at the time of his public ministry. *Thirty* marked a person's maturation—the usual time for marriage, family, and holding office.[56] Before, Christ "was growing in wisdom and in maturity" (1:52; see 2:40).

The repetition of *Joseph*, seventh from the first, initiates the pattern of the genealogy and may have served as a recitation or mnemonic device, suggesting that Luke is offering an oral, communal memory.[57]

The ambiguous Greek—Καὶ αὐτὸς ἦν Ἰησοῦς ἀρχόμενος ὡσεὶ ἐτῶν τριάκοντα—requires comment. The verb ἦν may be connected to the participle ἀρχόμενος, forming an imperfect periphrastic construction: "Jesus was beginning," but it more naturally introduces Christ's age (ὡσεὶ ἐτῶν τριάκοντα), so that the participle functions adverbially: "Jesus was about thirty years old when he began."[58] The second part of the verse—ὢν υἱός, ὡς ἐνομίζετο, Ἰωσὴφ τοῦ Ἠλὶ—is also ambiguous. The sense could be "being the son (as was thought) of Joseph (the son) of Heli." The qualification would then be answered at the end of the genealogy: Jesus was really the son of God (v. 38) as was just declared at his baptism (v. 22). However, the qualification may also be read as "being as was thought the son of Joseph, was himself of Heli."[59] It is important to remember that punctuation is interpretive and not a part of the early Greek manuscripts. This better appropriates the emphatic *autos* (αὐτὸς) at the verse's beginning. The genitive *of Heli* (τοῦ Ἠλὶ) conveys a relationship, but the word "son" in translations is not in the Greek. Rather, the relationship could be more general, allowing the translation "descended from."[60] If Joseph is removed, as the Greek may be read, only Mary is left. For this rhetorical move, Luke had to look no further than Matthew's genealogy: "Jacob begot Joseph, the husband

56. See Philo, *Joseph* 1.121. This conforms to Aristotle's criterion that a hero should not be too young because wisdom comes with age. See Ludolph of Saxony, citing Bede (*Life of Christ,* 1:419).

57. Goulder, *Luke*, 283; Haami, *Pūtea Whakairo*, 15.

58. Culy et al., *Luke*, 120.

59. Aquinas, *S.T.* IIIa, q. 31, a.3, Reply to Objection 2.

60. Cheney, *Life of Christ in Stereo*, 222. John Wesley and others suggest the translation "son-in-law." As the brotherless heir to *Heli*, her estate went to Joseph, who became his son. In other words, Mary's father adopted Joseph as his son-in-law. However, as we noted, the Greek does not require an immediate relation between Joseph and *Heli*. *Heli* is simply Mary's father.

of Mary. In her (womb) was begotten Jesus, the one called "Christ" (1:16). Both Gospels emphasize that Joseph is not the biological father of Jesus. *The Proto-Gospel of James,* probably written around the middle of the second century, identifies Mary's father as "Joachim" (Ιωακειμ).[61] Heli (Ηλὶ) is a shortened form of this name (hypocorism).[62]

R. David began to reign and Joseph entered Pharaoh's service at the age of *thirty* (2 Sam 5:4; Gen 41:46).

D: By relating Christ's age, Luke contextualizes the temptation at the acme of vulnerability but also wisdom in human life. Gregory the Great, reflecting on Benedict's life, notes that after fifty the fire of lust passes and the grace of age becomes a "teacher (doctor) of the soul" (*Dial.* 2.2).

S: *Father, by the grace of your Spirit, may we reach maturation in your Son, that we might not be infants in thinking but wise and strong. Amen.*

From Mattathias to Mattathias (3:25–26a)

[25] of Mattathias of Amos of Nahum of Hesli of Naggai [26] of Maath of Mattathias . . .

P: We find the same pattern of seven with *Mattathias.* A famous Mattathias instigated the Seleucid rebellion, living around the time of the first Mattathias (d. 167 B.C.), although he did not have a son named Joseph. But Mary's family may have appropriated the name to honor him. Jesus's brothers, Judas and Simon, were probably named after famous Seleucids (Matt 13:55). The second *Mattathias* may be an ancestor of both, although we cannot know. It was common for names to be repeated in a family (Luke 1:61).

From Semein to Shealtiel (3:26b–27a)

. . . of Semein of Josech of Joda, [27] of Joanan of Rhesa of Zerubbabel of Shealtiel . . .

P: The mnemonic pattern of sevens ends because Luke is no longer appropriating oral tradition but Scripture. Indeed, with *Shealtiel* and *Zerubbabel,* Luke and Matthew's genealogies overlap (see Matt 1:12–13).

R: First Chronicles (3:19) claims *Zerubbabel* was the son of "Pedaiah," a younger brother of Shealtiel, but Haggai (1:1) and Ezra (3:2, 8; 5:2) agree with Matthew (1:12) and Luke. The discrepancy may be explained by Levirate marriage.

61. See, e.g., 1:1.

62. See Ελιακιμ at 2 Chr 36:4 OG.

From Neri to David (3:27b–31)

[27b] . . . of Neri[63] [28] of Melchi of Addi of Cosam of Elmadam of Er [29] of Joshua of Eliezer of Jorim of Matthat of Levi [30] of Simeon of Judah of Joseph of Jonam of Eliakim [31] of Melea of Menna of Mattatha of Nathan of David . . .

P: Gabriel announces to Mary, "He will be great and will be called *the Son of the Most High*; and the Lord God will give (him) the throne of David, his father" (Luke 1:32). Zechariah also alludes to "the house of David" in his worshipful response (Luke 1:69).

Luke traces the ancestry through *Nathan*, Solomon's brother (2 Sam 5:14). The Bible does not offer a genealogy for *Nathan*.[64] Unless Luke invented the names, which is unlikely because of his historical interests (1:1–4), he is either dependent on family history or a text in the genre of rewritten Scripture. Paul speaks of endless genealogies (1 Tim 1:4).

From Jesse to Abraham (3:32–34a)

[32] . . . of Jesse of Obed of Boaz of Salmon of Nahshon [33] of Amminadab of Admin of Ram of Hezron of Perez of Judah [34] of Jacob of Isaac of Abraham . . .

P: This list overlaps with Matthew (1:2–3) because both evangelists are dependent on Scripture.[65] Mary and Zechariah allude to *Abraham* in their worshipful response to God's salvation (Luke 1:55, 73).

From Terah to Enoch (3:34b–37a)

[37a] . . . of Terah of Nahor [35] of Serug of Reu of Peleg of Heber of Shelah [36] of Cainam of Arphaxad of Shem of Noah of Lamech [37] of Methuselah of Enoch . . .

P: At this point, Luke extends beyond Matthew's genealogy.

R: The evangelist appropriates the Table of Nations in Genesis (chs. 10–11), where we find *Cainam* (v. 36) in the Greek but not the Hebrew,[66]

63. *Neri* otherwise is not mentioned in Scripture.

64. Farrer, "On Dispensing with Q," 88.

65. *Admin* is not mentioned in either the Hebrew or Greek biblical mss. Michael Goulder claims the name is an "artificial insertion," but such minor variations are common in the manuscript tradition (*Luke*, 286).

66. καὶ Αρφαξαδ ἐγέννησεν τὸν Καιναν καὶ Καιναν ἐγέννησεν τὸν Σαλα Σαλα δὲ ἐγέννησεν τὸν Εβερ (Gen 10:24; see also 11:24)

and where language is confused at the Tower of Babel (11:1–10), a section important to Luke: Jesus will send seventy (or seventy-two) missionaries, each representing a nation in anticipation of a global mission (10:1–11), and then the confusion of languages is reversed at Pentecost (Acts 2:1–13). With *Noah*, Luke moves to the earlier genealogy in the Bible where *Enoch* is famously seventh from Adam—conforming to his pattern (Gen 5:18–24, 32; see Jude 14).

From Jared to God (3:37b–38)

[37b] . . . of Jared of Mahalaleel of Cainan [38] of Enosh of Seth of Adam of God.

P: This is the only occurrence of the name *Adam* in the Gospels. His is the only name in the genealogy that receives elaboration—*of God* (*tou theou*, τοῦ θεοῦ).

R: *God* never calls *Adam* his son, although he and the woman are created in the divine image (Gen 1:26–27). Paul notes that Jesus is "the image of the invisible God" (Col 1:15). Rather, with the long list of concatenative genitives, Luke claims that Jesus is ultimately God's son: "Jesus . . . who was, as was thought, son of Joseph, was . . . (son) of God." Luke may intend a double irony: Joseph was not Jesus's ultimate father, and *Adam* was not the final son *of God*.

D: A study on our theme notes: "The New Testament genealogies point to the necessary embedment of Jesus in the course of human history and also to his eschatological finality."[67] God became one of us, John's prologue claims (1:14). Genealogies are another way of saying the same thing. There is a lot of joy and suffering in the biblical allusions, and we can only imagine the same for Christ's more immediate family history. And yet Matthew and Luke imply Jesus is the end of the mortal coil. He is the first (Luke) to reenter Paradise and the last (Matthew) to be born in exile.

S: *Lord Jesus Christ, son of God, you enter our tragedy so that ours might end in you. Amen.*

Greco-Roman Biography and Scripture

We discussed a few similarities between the Gospels and Greco-Roman biographies (*bioi*) and how they might inform our reading. Plutarch (46–120), the exemplar of the genre, often begins with circumstances around

67. Johnson, *Purpose of the Biblical Genealogies*, xxviii.

the subject's birth to anticipate greatness.[68] Similarly, in the Gospels we learn that Jesus is supernaturally conceived, heir to David's throne, and Messiah for God's people. However, the evangelists also describe a humble background: Joseph and Mary offer pigeons, the gift of the poor (Luke 2:24); Jesus grows up in Nazareth, an insignificant village (Matt 2:23; Luke 2:39–40; see John 1:46).

Aristotle claims "good fathers are likely to have good sons."[69] Matthew and Luke claim Joseph and Mary were unusually righteous. Joseph, a son of David, is more obedient than his ancestors (Matt 1:6–11); Mary, the priest Zechariah (Luke 1:20). They are not passive, but advance the story by embracing God's will. Rudolf Bultmann notes: "In the Israelite view of history the goal of history is promised, but the realization of the promise is conditional on the obedience of the people."[70]

The evangelists also evoke the origins of Moses and Samuel. With the exception of David, they are given the most biographical treatment in Scripture, so that their appropriation is not surprising. Matthew retells the Exodus story in Jesus, the messianic representative of God's people. Herod repeats Pharaoh's murderous intent (Matt 3:16, alluding to Exod 1:16), but the infant Jesus is protected in Egypt until returning to the Promised Land. Luke tells his story in the dress of Samuel, who anoints David (1 Sam 16:1–13).[71] Mary echoes Hannah's prayer, the first mention in Scripture of the Messiah (1 Sam 2:1–10). Biographies reveal character through conflict.[72] With Greek and Roman heroes, the subject's virtue is tested; Scripture focuses on God's faithfulness.

Matthew's Birth Narrative

Matthew's birth narrative is delimited by Joseph's emotional response to two crises—Mary's unexpected pregnancy (1:20) and Archelaus's danger to his

68. For example, concerning Alexander the Great, Plutarch relates that his mother Olympias, the night before the consummation of her marriage, "dreamed that a thunderbolt fell upon her body" (*Lives*, 474 [Clough]). His father Philip also had a strange vision. There was a rumor that Alexander's real father was Zeus. For more discussion, see Burridge, *What Are the Gospels*, 153–54.

69. Aristotle, *Basic Works*, 1357 (*Rhet.* 1.9.29 [1367b]).

70. Bultmann, "History and Eschatology," 7.

71. Rice, *Behold, Your House Is Left to You*, 61–88.

72. M. Kadushin notes, "Haggadah is an almost perfect reflection of the way in which the value-concepts [of the rabbis] function in day-to-day living, in speech and action" (*Rabbinic Mind*, 59).

family's well-being (2:22), and may be read as a diptych ("two panels").[73] Panel one (1:18–25) unpacks the mysterious disclosure in the genealogy: "Jacob begot Joseph, the husband of Mary. In her was begotten Jesus, the one called Christ" (1:16). The second focuses on Herod the Great's opposition to Israel's true king (ch. 2).[74] In this case, the magi propel the conflict (2:1–12). Joseph emerges as the primary character. He cares for Christ's body at birth; another Joseph, a rich man from Arimathea, at death (27:57–61).[75]

5: Unpacking of Virginal Conception (Matt 1:18–25)

[18] Now the *genesis* of Jesus Christ happened this way. [Gen 2:4] After his mother Mary was engaged to Joseph,[76] before they came together,[77] she was found having (a baby) in (her) womb by the Holy Spirit.

P: *Genesis* echoes the incipit "Book of *genesis*" (1:1); after a genealogy relating *Jesus* to David and Abraham (1:2–17), the evangelist explains why *Joseph* is not the direct father (see 1:16), introducing a plot complication. The unit is delimited by inclusio: *before they came together* is completed by "he did not know her (sexually) until she gave birth to a son" (v. 25).

The passive voice *found* may be intentionally ambiguous, not disclosing *who* discovered the pregnancy but emphasizing the shameful effect.[78] Mary is given no voice in the matter, and we find a general mistrust of female fidelity in contemporary Jewish literature (Josephus *J.W.* 2.120; Philo *Hyp.* 11.14.17). *By the Holy Spirit* introduces dramatic irony: nobody but presumably Mary (Luke will fill in this narrative gap) knew the agency of her pregnancy. Mary's virginity belonged to Joseph; the reasonable conclusion was that another man had stolen it.

Jews practiced two stages of marriage—the "betrothal ceremony" and "home-taking."[79] The groom's parents normally chose the bride (Gen

73. Prabhu, *Formula Quotations in the Infancy Narrative*, 11–12.

74. Like the whole Gospel and some of the parables, this story has a beginning, climax (killing of the children), and end.

75. There is also one Mary at the beginning and two at the end (27:61).

76. Unless a widower, *Joseph* may have been between eighteen and thirty years old. The Mishnah remembers Judah ben Tema saying, "eighteen to the wedding canopy . . . twenty to responsibility for providing for a family" (*Avot* 5:21 [Neusner]).

77. *Came together* or "have sexual intercourse."

78. Since the bride and groom were not allowed to spend time together, Mary's father may have had the shameful task of informing his son-in-law that he had failed on his side of the exchange (Lev 21:9). Kenneth Bailey suggests the community related the information (*Jesus Through Middle Eastern Eyes*, 44).

79. Our knowledge of marriage in the Second Temple period is limited, although it

21:21; 38:6). A legally binding contract with witnesses followed. Three gifts were often exchanged: the bride price (Gen 34:12), a compensation from the family of the groom to the family of the bride for "the loss of a skilled and fertile member";[80] the dowry, a gift to the bride or the groom from her father, which enabled them to start economically; and the groom's gift to the bride (Gen 24:53), a symbol of commitment. After the betrothal or *engagement*, the woman is considered legally to be a wife except in regard to sexual intercourse, which took place at the home-taking. There was typically a year between the stages, allowing planning for the weeklong celebration and acquiring the proper attire (m. Ketub. 5:2; Ned. 10:5). *Mary* became pregnant between these stages.

Matthew and rabbinic literature presume engagement is part of marriage, but this is not in the Mosaic Law where there is also no contractual discussion.[81] These developments evidence the influence of the scribes and Pharisees—what came to be called "tradition" (*paradosis*, παράδοσις).

R: As with the first occurrence of *genesis* (1:1), the narrator evokes the opening book of Scripture, but the emphasis moves from genealogy (Gen 5:1) to God's creative activity before human involvement: "This is the book of *genesis* (βίβλος γενέσεως) of heaven and earth, when it came to be, on the day God made the heaven and the earth" (2:4 LXX). At this time, "there was no man to work the ground" (Gen 2:5 ESV). The transition looks back to "the *Spirit* of God . . . hovering over the face of the waters" (Gen 1:2 ESV) and forward to the union and procreation of marriage: "Therefore a man shall leave his father and his mother and hold fast to his wife, and they shall become one flesh" (2:24).

D: The Nicene Creed allows us to confess: "he became incarnate by the Holy Spirit and the virgin Mary, and was made human." Today, some Christians do not take the claim of the virginal conception literally. Bruce Chilton suggests Joseph and Mary had sexual intercourse before the home-taking.[82] Much has been made of the supposed dearth of references to the doctrine in the New Testament, but two Gospels are emphatic on the point at the beginning of their presentations (see also Luke 1:34–35).[83] Others are

is generally a conservative social institution. There is continuity with practices recorded in Scripture, and rabbinic literature, albeit from a later time, contains helpful information (see Wilkins, *Matthew*, 73–74).

80. Martos, *Doors to the Sacred*, 353.

81. P. Zaas notes Matthew provides the earliest witness to this view ("Matthew's Birth Story," 125–28).

82. Chilton, *Rabbi Jesus*, 8–13.

83. Andrew Lincoln claims, "It has been confirmed that there are no other possible New Testament witnesses to the virgin birth apart from Matthew and Luke" (*Born of*

dismissive because of similar accounts in Greco-Roman literature. Zeus is presented as begetting Alexander, Hercules, and Perseus; Apollo, Asclepius, Ion, Plato, Pythagoras, and Augustus. Ironically, these connections may have been made first by early Christian apologists seeking analogies for evangelism.[84] But in these stories, "no stress is laid upon the virginity of the mother."[85] Despite the implication of Isaiah—"the virgin shall conceive" (7:14)—Jewish writings from the period that mention the Messiah do not anticipate a virginal conception. If anything, this claim might have been embarrassing, as it is for many today.[86] Paul makes no mention of the event in his letters. The simplest explanation, if one is open to the supernatural, is that the Holy Spirit is responsible for Mary's pregnancy.

The *Holy Spirit* did not create *in* the *womb* of a single woman, so that Jesus might have a mother and a father.

S: Because of the Father-and-Son relationship shown at Christ's baptism, it may be surprising that the Father is not the immediate agent of the pregnancy, which would have been more amenable to Greco-Roman mythology where gods take physical form and have sexual intercourse with women. Instead, Matthew attributes agency to the *Holy Spirit*.[87] God is not taking the place of the male principle—that is, providing semen—but is doing something *new*. Unlike Adam, the body of Christ is formed inside a human womb; and unlike all other human bodies, it is not from the union of a sperm and egg. Logic opens the door to the hypostatic union.

Spirit (*pneuma*, πνεῦμα) is not a very personal word.[88] The Greek noun is grammatically neuter, usually signifying "wind" or "breath." But Matthew presents the Spirit as a kind of parent—not a father like Joseph or God the Father and not a mother like Mary but perhaps analogous or transcendental to both. Spiritual parenting begins here as *generative*.

[19] Now her husband Joseph, being righteous and not wanting to expose her, intended to divorce her secretly.

P: *Joseph* and Mary presumably live in the same community, a gap filled in by Luke (1:26–27). The verb *deigmatizō* (δειγματίζω), which can be translated *expose* or "make an example of," involves public shaming. Jewish,

a Virgin?, 26).

84. Barrett, *Holy Spirit*, 6.

85. Barrett, *Holy Spirit*, 7.

86. Karl Barth's enthusiastic embrace of the doctrine was an embarrassment in its day.

87. Matthew employs a prepositional phrase (ἐκ πνεύματος ἁγίου, 1:18) that often describes ultimate agency. Secondary agencies are conveyed by διά: e.g., "by the Lord (ultimate agency) through the prophet" (ὑπὸ κυρίου διὰ τοῦ προφήτου, Matt 1:22).

88. Badcock, *Light of Truth*, 8–34.

Greek, and Roman law—all demanded for the sake of honor that a husband divorce an adulterer.[89] Adultery violated "the property rights of the woman's father or husband"; and, according to contemporary logic, produced a state of impurity that necessarily dissolved the marriage.[90]

R: According to appearance, Mary has committed adultery against Joseph, her legal husband, which breaks one of the Ten Commandments (Exod 20:14), requiring death for her and the male adulterer (Lev 20:10; Deut 22:21–24; see also John 7:53—8:11).[91] The New Testament responds by emphasizing the holiness of the agency and offspring (Matt 1:18, 20; Luke 1:35). *Being righteous* (*dikaios*, δίκαιος), that is, obedient to the covenant stipulations in the Mosaic Law, Joseph discovered "some indecency" in Mary and is therefore justified in divorcing her (Deut 24:1 ESV). Only in this Gospel does Jesus allow divorce for sexual immorality (5:32; 19:9).[92]

D: The evangelist distinguishes yet does not separate *Joseph's* desire and intention.[93] His intention is informed by piety, the options available within Second Temple Judaism, and his desire leads to the merciful option of a quiet divorce. By this, Joseph is willing to receive the shame of the sin, protecting Mary. We also should pursue the most compassionate option of justice.

S: Joseph is like God the Father who desires all people to be saved, and yet intends according to righteousness (1 Tim 2:4; 2 Pet 3:9). But God's desire finds the most merciful option. Instead of punishing the wicked, God receives the penalty and shame.

First Angelic Disclosure (1:20–21)

[20] But having pondered these things, look: an angel of the Lord appeared to him in a dream, saying, "Joseph, son of David: Do not be afraid to take

89. Hornblower and Spawforth, *Oxford Companion to Classical Civilization*, 5–6. In Mediterranean society, men who allowed their feelings to get in the way of divorce were viewed with contempt (Keener, *Matthew*, 91).

90. Bockmuehl, "Matthew 5.32," 291–95; Martos, *Doors to the Sacred*, 354.

91. There was no need to determine if Mary had committed adultery because she was pregnant (see Num 5:11–31). Technically, only Rome had the authority to carry out capital punishment (the discovery of a Gentile in the Court of the Israelites in the temple was the exception), but it is difficult to imagine anyone noticing mob justice.

92. The "betrothal view" holds that Jesus here refers to the unique Jewish practice that allowed for a marriage to be annulled if evidence of infidelity was manifest during the betrothal period (Jones, "Betrothal View of Divorce," 68–85). Others interpret the claim more generally as a reference to some form of adultery.

93. Wilkins, *Matthew*, 75.

(home) your wife Mary.[94] For what is generated in her (womb) is by the Holy Spirit.[95] [21] She *will give birth to a son, and you will call his name* Jesus because he will save his people from their sins." [Gen 16:11]

P: This is the first of five angelic disclosures in the story that advance the plot (1:20–21; 2:12a, 13–14, 19–20, 22b). Joseph and the magi will respond with obedience (1:24:25; 2:12, 14, 21, 23a), whereas Pilate ignores the warning given to his wife in a dream (27:19). After these disclosures, the narrator claims the fulfillment of Scripture (1:22–23; 2:15, 17–18, 23b). According to popular belief, the Mosaic Law was mediated by angels; it is therefore fitting for its fulfillment to have angelic witness (see Matt 5:17–20).[96] The *angel of the Lord* will return and roll back the stone at Christ's tomb, except that it is no longer a dream (1:20, 24; 28:2).

The epithet *son of David* links *Joseph* to the genealogy and therefore *Jesus* to *David* (1:1, 16, 20) through a kind of adoption. No ceremony is mentioned because, like Mary's pregnancy, *Joseph* may have been divinely appointed for this role. The angel may require him to raise *Jesus* as if he were their biological son (see Luke 3:23). It would have been irregular for a man to adopt a child of adultery between his wife and another man. However, by naming *Jesus*, Joseph takes the father's role (Luke 1:62–63).

The command was necessary because it was customary to name a son after an ancestor, a detail supplied by Luke concerning John (1:61). No one else was named *Jesus* in the genealogy. The *angel* reveals the unique significance of the Hebrew (or Aramaic) name *Jesus* (ישוע): "the Lord is salvation" or possibly "Lord, save!" It was common belief that people became their names (*nomen omen*). *He will save his people from their sins* is fulfilled at the cross (26:28). The penalty of *sin* (*hamartia*, ἁμαρτία) is spiritual death or separation from God, shown in the mortality and Babylonian captivity of the opening genealogy.[97] Scripture presents *sin* as a burden, a divine account, a path or direction, and stain or impurity.[98] According to the ancient logic of sacrifice,

94. While the Greek could be more literally translated "Mariam," we follow popular usage (see also Matt 1:20, 24; 28:2).

95. The Greek could also be translated: "For what is begotten in her by the Spirit is holy." This is the only occurrence in the New Testament where the noun *pneumatos* (πνεύματός) and the adjective *hagiou* (ἁγίου) are separated by a word other than an article. If so, Jesus can save his people from their sins because he *is holy* (v. 21).

96. For more discussion, see Bendoraitis, *'Behold, the Angels Came.'*

97. Grudem, *Systematic Theology*, 810.

98. Lam, *Patterns of Sin*. Karl Rahner emphasizes sin as a wound that harms everything. Kurt Thompson defines sin as "the state of being separated or disconnected from God or to behaviors that lead to or exemplify the condition" (*Anatomy of the Soul*, 183).

a typological frame, *Jesus* will hang in our place (8:17).[99] The genealogy also broadens *his people*: they are the immediate descendants of "Judah and his brothers," the Judeans or Jews (1:2; 2:6), but Jesus also has Gentile mothers.[100]

R: The epithet *angel of the Lord* occurs some sixty times in the Old Testament, referring to a messenger and mediating agency of God's will. The *angel* appeared to Moses at the burning bush (Exod 3:2), encouraged Gideon (Judg 6:11–16), and often comes to the aid of God's people (Exod 14:19; Judg 2:1; 1 Kgs 19:7; Ps 34:7). In some cases, this messenger even seems to *be* God (Gen 16:7–13; Exod 3:2–4; 14:19; 23:20; Num 20:16; Judg 6:11–22; Isa 63:9; Hos 12:4–5).

The *angel* echoes his first appearance in Scripture, a birth announcement to Hagar, Sarai's Egyptian servant: "Look, you are pregnant and shall give birth to a son; and you shall call his name Ishmael because the Lord listened to your affliction" (Gen 16:11 LXX).[101] Not only does the allusion contextualize the moment for Joseph and the reader, but reinforces the narrator's interest in including those initially outside the Abrahamic Covenant, the Gentiles, in Christ's *people*.

Dreaming immediately associates *Joseph* with the biblical patriarch, whose father's name was also "Jacob" (1:16). Similarly, the import of the *dream* will not be immediately received by Jacob's (Israel's) other sons: "Are you indeed to reign over us?" (Gen 37:8; see Matt 28:16–20). Like the Hebrew midwives (Exod 1:15–22), Joseph engages in subterfuge, pretending that Jesus is his son.

The *angel* mentions King *David*, who had a special relationship with *his people*. United to him, they enjoyed a portion of his divine inheritance but could also opt out. Anticipating the separation of Israel from Judah and Benjamin, during an argument between representatives of the tribes among David's supporters, Sheba, a "worthless man," cries out: "We have no portion in David, and we have no inheritance in the son of Jesse; every man to his tents, O Israel!" (2 Sam 20:1 ESV).

D: *Pondering* expresses free will. Josephus claims there were three main positions on the relationship between divine sovereignty and human responsibility in Judaism. The Essenes were deterministic; the Sadducees embraced free will; and the Pharisees maintained a tension (*J.W.* 2.164; *Ant.*

99. By "typological frame" I mean a contextualization and logic for understanding divine action.

100. McDaniel, *Experiencing Irony in the First Gospel*. The Syriac manuscipt Syrus Curetonianus replaces *his people* with "the world."

101. The Septuagint marks this by withholding the article in the first occurrence (ἄγγελος Κυρίου) and then supplying it with all subsequent references (ὁ ἄγγελος Κυρίου). The epithet in Matthew is also anarthrous.

13.5.9), which is evident throughout the New Testament. Aquinas claims God works through free will as an intermediary to share the dignity of cause with creatures (*S.T.* 22.2–3). Joseph's deliberation allows *him* to participate in the Kingdom of God. There is an intentional space between stimulus (divine) and response (human), allowing for moral action and God's judgment. Obedience is not inevitable in the Gospels.

Dreams were interpreted as divine-human encounters in Scripture and contemporary literature.[102] They are mediated revelation. Yet because of their ambiguity, we find a motif of an interpreting angel (see 1 En. 1–5). They can also be false (Jer 29:8–9). Jesus ben Sirach claims dreams are meaningless "unless they are sent by intervention from the Most High" (Sir 34:1–8). Dreams are still not entirely understood. They occur during rapid eye movement sleep (REM), which, for mature and senior adults, lasts twenty to 25 percent of their total sleep time, with the longest time occurring early in the morning. During REM the inhibiting effects of serotonin and norepinephrine disappear, and the neurotransmitter acetylcholine increases in the brain stem, activating a flood of memories and perceptions. There is also no activity in the frontal area of the brain, which is involved in planning and higher reasoning (suppression of the prefrontal cortex). Memories cohere into various narratives, but are experienced in the immediate present.[103] Defenses down, the deep sleeper is open to revelation yet vulnerable to meaninglessness or to deception, a *pseudo mediated revelation.* As a righteous person, Joseph took his problem to God in the day to receive an answer at night. God may do this by embedding the problem in a story, a meaningful context (EMDR therapy imitates this natural process. The therapist induces rapid eye movement from the patient, who often experiences relief from trauma. The painful event becomes integrated into a life story and joins others into the past.).[104] The *angel* does not contradict the moral fabric of Joseph's worldview: had Mary committed adultery, divorce would have been justified. This provides Joseph with discernment, along with the cultural expectation of an angelic interpretation.

Names matter. Nomen omen has received some empirical support, leading to a field of study called nominative determinism ("name-driven outcome"). Our sense of self directs attraction (implicit egotism). If human naming has power, all the more a name from God. Jesus will name

102. See, e.g., 1 Kg 3:5; 1 En. 13:8; 1QapGen ar. Jesus alludes to Jacob's Ladder (Gen 28:10–22; John 1:51). Cyrus asserts after one: "I am a man for whom the gods take thought, and show me beforehand all that is coming" (Herodotus, *Hist.* 1.209). But *he goes on to misinterpret the dream* (210–211).

103. Fuster, *Memory in the Cerebral Cortex*, 287.

104. Van Der Kolk, *Body Keeps the Score*, 250–64, especially 262.

his apostles; the good shepherd calls each sheep by name (John 10:3). Paul claims that a certain Onesimus, whose name means "useful" in Latin, had become "useless" to Philemon as a runaway slave but could fully realize his name as a brother sharing in the work of the gospel (Phlm 8–16).

S: The *angel* claims *he*, that is the bearer of the name, *Jesus* Christ, will save his people. The Son is presented as the primary agent of our salvation. The *Lord* probably signifies God the Father, opening to a Trinitarian action in the Incarnation: *son* and *Holy Spirit.*

Fulfillment of Scripture (1:22–23)

[22] Now all this has taken place so that what was spoken by the Lord through the prophet might be fulfilled, saying: [23] "Behold, *the virgin will have* (a baby) *in her womb,*[105] *and she will give birth to a son. And they will call his name Immanuel*, which is translated "*God with us.*" [Isa 7:14; 8:8, 10]

P: Matthew backs the angelic witness with Scripture introduced with a citation formula, the first of several in the birth story.[106] Placing these quotations in strategic places, he claims that God's plan for salvation is accomplished in Jesus.[107]

R: This quotation echoes and extends the earlier allusion to the angelic announcement to Hagar (1:21) in the Law (Gen 16:11), emphasizing a motif of birthing and naming and its ultimate fulfillment in Christ. As the opening genealogy reinforces, throughout Scripture God advances the plot through the birth of a child. The Prophets were read and expounded as a commentary on the Law in the local synagogue. Jesus speaks of "the Law and the Prophets" (Matt 7:12; 22:40).

This fulfillment moves beyond the historical context of the specific prophecy. Isaiah sees Assyria vanquish Israel and Aram before "a son" is grown (7:14–17). Most believe the prophet's own son is under discussion.[108] Furthermore, while the Greek noun *parthenos* (παρθένος) usually signifies a "virgin," it translates the Hebrew *alma* (עַלְמָה), which can more generally refer to a "young woman." However, as we have noted, Isaiah looks forward to a messiah who would rescue God's people from their sin. The

105. Matthew used the same language to describe Mary's pregnancy at 1:18.

106. "To fulfill" (1:22; 2:17; 4:15; 12:17 [13:14, Jesus speaking]; 13:35; 21:4); "it stands written" (2:5 [4:4, 7, 10; 11:10; 21:13, Jesus speaking]); see also 3:3; 15:7; 21:16, 42. It is possible that the angel is still speaking because there are no quotation marks in our Greek witnesses.

107. Viljoen, "Fulfillment in Matthew," 301–24.

108. Trypho represents an early Jewish tradition that interprets the line as referring to Hezekiah's son (Justin Martyr, *Dial.* 67).

verse has taken on additional meaning in its own book—what Richard of St. Victor (c. 1120–1173) calls a "double literal sense."[109] Shortly after the cited prophecy, we read:

> For to us a child is born, to us a son is given; and the government shall be upon his shoulder, and his name shall be called Wonderful Counselor, Mighty God, Everlasting Father, Prince of Peace. (Isa 9:6 ESV)

This description is too big for any merely human *son*. Matthew will allude to this section (4:15–16, citing Isa 9:1–2). Indeed, the motif of naming and the repetition of the word "God" links these passages. Although there is no mention of a virginal conception here, this "son is given" and called "Mighty God."[110] God and human beings are different in Isaiah: "I am the first and I am the last; besides me there is no god" (44:6). The Greek translator may have connected the dots (or was simply guided by the Spirit), selecting *parthenos*, which is still a legitimate rendering of *alma*, to emphasize the uniqueness of this birth apart from all others; in any case, the Christians did.

The point of the virginal conception, for Matthew, is that *Jesus Christ is like and unlike the rest of us*. We may seek to be more specific, but that is the central mystery—the hypostatic union of the God-man. He is like us in that we all have a mother. In the context of the genealogy and birth story, he is unlike us in the way of his conception, the uniquely creative work of the Holy Spirit, and calling—to save us from our sins. A sinner cannot save other sinners. Perhaps, then, the virginal conception, as the beginning of new creation, kept the Messiah in Paradise, outside the consequence of original sin, allowing him to be Immanuel. Aquinas claims we incur original sin through our father's semen.[111] Possible, although Scripture is not specific. We have since learned that the blood in a fetus is not from the mother, but begins to flow after the fertilization of the egg.[112] "Life is in the blood" (Lev 17:11, 14). Christ's blood is a pure offering, offering eternal life (Matt 26:28; 1 Pet 1:19).

D: What the *Lord* (YHWH) communicates through an angel in a dream correlates with what he said *through* a *Prophet*, providing discernment for

109. Van Liere, *Introduction to the Medieval Bible*, 134–37. This marks an advance on the impasse between Justin Martyr and a Jewish teacher he calls Trypho, who both argue for direct fulfillment of the specific verse (*Dial.* 67.1).

110. "Mighty God" is a natural way to translate the Hebrew *El gibor* (אֵל גִּבּוֹר). The Greek translation in Rahlf's edition is dynamic and did not attempt to render the epithet. However, a corrector in א provided a more direct translation.

111. Aquinas, *On Evil*, 225.

112. Dehaan, *Chemistry of the Blood*, 30–31.

readers. Matthew presumes they trust God's Word, a quality we find in Jesus (4:1–11).

Brother Reginald, Aquinas's close friend, testified under oath that he once heard a crucifix in chapel say to his friend, "You have written well of me, Thomas. What will you have as your reward?" Thomas replied, "Only yourself, Lord." For any maturing Christian, Christ and the Triune love into which he calls us becomes our treasure.

S: After the Exile, Jews believed God hid his face, retiring into mysterious transcendence—what theologians call *Deus absconditus*: "Truly, you are a God who hides himself, O God of Israel, the Savior" (Isa 45:15 ESV). The literary critic Joseph Hillis Miller, the son of a Baptist pastor, notes "the disappearance of God"—the gradual loss of faith by intellectuals and writers in the West.[113] More and more of creation and life experience is narrated apart from God, diminishing our most fundamental context for understanding. The doctrine of omnipresence does little to overcome atheism because God rarely confronts at this level. *Immanuel* did not come to restore omnipresence, but God's relational presence—the God who encountered Abraham, Isaac, Jacob, Moses, and the Prophets, the God who cleaved to a people like a husband to his wife. Until fully hardened, God is always confronting us in Christ as the gospel to all peoples (28:16–20).

Father and Holy Spirit, thank you for visiting your people in the Son, and for the Son and Father remaining with us in the Spirit. Away from our sin, you are with us. Amen.

Joseph's Obedience (1:24–25)

[24] After this, Joseph got up from sleep. He did as the angel of the Lord commanded him and took his wife (home). [25] And he did not know her (sexually) until she gave birth to a son, and he called his name Jesus.

P: *Joseph* becomes a surrogate father. Jewish law banned those of a "forbidden union," a *mamzer*, from entering the "assembly"—a term applied to the temple and synagogue.[114] As he intended to protect Mary from public shame, so with *Jesus*. But rumor may have followed *Jesus* into adulthood. Celsus (fl. 175–180) may record a version of this slander, claiming Mary was impregnated by a Roman soldier named Pantera.[115] Matthew encloses his

113. Miller, *Disappearance of God*.

114. See Deut 23:2 and the expansions at b. Yeb. 49a–b, 69a, 78b, 87b; Kidd. 67b, 73a.

115. Cited by Origen in *Cels*. 32.

presentation with two calumnies—the disciples stole the body (27:62–66) born from an adulterer.

R: Like Abraham, Joseph obeys immediately (Gen 22:3).

D: Let us imitate Joseph, who may have been hurt and confused by God's mysterious work, but obeyed and eventually came to see its beauty.

Children require a home, a responsibility that falls on Joseph.

Until (*heōs hou*, ἕως οὗ) *she gave birth to a son* may suggest that, after Mary's purification, the couple eventually "came together" (v. 18), but this scenario is not explicit, allowing the development of conflicting traditions.[116] Helvidius, apparently following Tertullian and Victorinus, connected this wording to Matthew's presumption that Jesus had brothers and sisters (12:46; see also Mark 3:31).[117] But Jerome responded with *The Perpetual Virginity of Blessed Mary*. He claims Matthew refers to Joseph's children from a different mother, Origen's position, or to cousins. Athanasius also distances Mary from the children, noting that Jesus entrusts her to a disciple, not a sibling (John 19:26–27).[118] Helvidius's work was lost, except when Jerome is quoting to refute it. By the seventh century, the perpetual virginity of Mary was being affirmed in ecumenical councils. We see popular support for the doctrine in the *Protoevangelium of James*, which claims that Joseph served as Mary's "guardian" (4.1). The doctrine became pervasive, even held by most of the Reformers and John Wesley. As we noted, the clause completes an inclusio that delimits the unit. The focus is not on the future, but between Mary's pregnancy and the birth.

Bias is partly responsible for this conflict: Helvidius placed marriage over virginity; Jerome, the opposite. However, the Gospels celebrate both paths: the Baptist, Jesus, and eventually the apostle Paul embrace virginity; most, if not all, of the other apostles were married. Indeed, God uses both paths in the Incarnation: contrary to the *Protoevangelium of James*, Mary and Joseph were legally married—a canonical Gospel has more authority than an apocryphal one; our tradition must not contradict the clear teaching of Scripture—so that Jesus would have an earthly father and the care and protection he brings. And yet Mary brought Jesus into the world as a virgin. Since Joseph is not mentioned in the Gospels after Jesus becomes an adult, it is reasonable to conclude that he died, so that Mary entered the church and served most of her life without a husband (Acts 1:14).

S: *Holy Spirit, we ask for discipline to subordinate our sexual desire to love and for the grace of family, married or unmarried. Amen.*

116. Brown, *Mary in the New Testament*, 86–87.

117. *PL* 23.207, 213.

118. Cited in Gambero, *Mary and the Fathers*, 104.

6: Herod's Opposition (Matt 2:1–23)

This relatively long yet concentrated unit is the second panel in Matthew's diptych. After resolving the first crisis, Mary's unprecedented pregnancy, the evangelist retells the Exodus story as fulfilled in Jesus. Along with several typological correspondences, he offers three fulfillment citations (2:15, 17–18, 23). The angel of the Lord who led Joseph in the first panel (1:20–21) makes two more appearances (2:13–14, 19–20).

[2:1] Now after Jesus was born in *Bethlehem of Judea*[119] in the days of Herod, the king, look: magi from the rising (suns)[120] came to Jerusalem,[121] saying, [2] "Where is the one who has been born king of the Jews? [Mic 5:2] For we saw his star in the dawn and have come to worship him."[122] [Num 24:17]

P: This unit is delimited by the *magi's* desire *to worship the king of the Jews* (2:2, 11), which establishes conflict with the Roman Senate who gave *Herod* the title *king of the Jews* in 37 BC. The title was applied earlier to David (1:6). *Herod* was not a Jew (or Judean) but an Idumean (Nabatean), a descendant of Esau according to Scripture.[123]

The *magi* (*magoi,* μάγοι) came east of *Jerusalem*—probably from Babylon, which had a thriving Jewish population where Scripture was copied and disseminated in centers of learning.[124] There was a pilgrim route between the cities (Josephus, *Ant.* 17.26). Matthew mentions the Babylonian exile (1:11, 12), allowing the *magi* to represent the Gentiles of that region like the women in the genealogy. A *magus* (μάγος) was a Babylonian or Persian sage or priest and expert in astrology. Yet Matthew is not explicit, and the ambiguity invited

119. Jesus is born in *Bethlehem of Judea*, not Bethlehem of Zebulon near Nazareth (Josh 19:10, 15).

120. This seems to be the sense of the plural (*anatolōn,* ἀνατολῶν), in light of the context, unless "eastern regions" is the emphasis.

121. *Came to Jerusalem*: If the magi came from Babylon, they traveled approximately 900 miles on a trade route that followed the Euphrates River north, then south through the Orontes valley of Syria into Palestine (Wilkins, *Matthew,* 94). Ezra took four months to make the journey, but with a group of four to five thousand people (Ezra 7:9).

122. The Greek *anatolē* (ἀνατολή) is often translated "east." But Michael Wilkins notes: "they didn't see the star rise in the eastern part of the sky, otherwise it would have caused them to travel east. Rather, while they were to the east of Jerusalem, the star rose, perhaps to the west of them, causing them to travel west to Jerusalem" (*Matthew*, 95).

123. Josephus, *J.W.* 1.123; *Ant.* 14.8. Idumea was a desert region just south of Judea. Johanan Hyrcanus (ca. 130 BC) forced their conversion to Judaism.

124. Hillel, the founder of rabbinic Judaism, came from Babylon.

other interpretations. The *Revelation of the Magi*, an eighth century work in Syriac, suggests they came from the land of silk (China).

R: The *magi* may have encountered Balaam's oracle in dialogue with Jews in Babylon—". . . a *star* shall come out of Jacob, and a scepter shall rise out of Israel; it shall crush the forehead of Moab and break down all the sons of Sheth" (Num 24:17, ESV)—which had been interpreted as Messianic and is applied to Jesus in the New Testament (Rev 22:16; 2 Pet 1:19).[125] Even non-Jews knew the oracle's implications. The Roman historian Seutonius (c. 75–160) notes:

> Throughout the whole of the East there had spread an old and persistent belief: destiny had decreed that at that time men coming forth from Judea would seize power [and rule the world]. (*Vespasian* 5; see also Tacitus, *Annals* 5.13)[126]

In the second century after Christ, many Jews, including the famous Rabbi Akiva, followed Simeon Bar Kokhba ("Son of a Star") as the Messiah.[127] The rabbi cited the same verse and said, "This is the Messianic King" (*y. Ta'an.* 4.5). But the rebellion failed; hundreds of thousands died and thousands were enslaved; and Akiva was executed. Rabbis changed the false Messiah's name to Bar Kozeba ("Son of lies"). The *magi* do not cite this Scripture, a Jewish activity; but it is hard to imagine that Matthew is not appropriating the oracle, which he pairs with Micah's prophecy (5:2)—*Bethlehem of Judea*—that shortly will be cited in full (Matt 2:6).[128]

Later tradition identified the *magi* as kings based on Psalm 72:11: "May all kings fall down before him, all nations serve him."[129]

D: Astrology is explicitly condemned in Scripture (Deut 18:11; Isa 2:6 [which mentions "diviners from the East!"]; 47:11–15; 48:13). But Philo attributes the prophetic function of stars to God himself: "And they [the stars] have been created, as Moses tells us, not only that they might send light upon the earth, but also that they might display signs of future events" (*Creation* 19:58.). The practice is inextricably bound up with predestination or Fate, the dominate worldview at the time. In the Greco-Roman world, astrology was

125. See CD VII, 18–26; 4QTest I, 9–13; 1QM XI, 6–7.

126. Cited in Wilkens, *Matthew*, 94.

127. His original name was Simon ben Kosiba (or Aramaic: Simeon bar Koziba).

128. Matthew and the translator of the Greek text available to us use slightly different words for *star—astēr* (ἀστήρ) and *astron* (ἄστρον), respectively. But the noun translated *dawn, anatolē* (ἀνατολή), is very similar to the verb "shall rise" (*anatellō*, ἀνατέλλω). Benedict Viviano argues Matthew's presentation is a *midrash* on Numbers 24:17 ("Movement of the Star," 58–64).

129. Wilkins, *Matthew*, 94.

viewed as a science and highly respected.[130] Some Roman soldiers joined the cult of Mithras, which had adopted astrology from Babylonia.[131]

Western tradition settled on three *magi*: Melchior, a Persian; Caspar, an Indian; and Balthasar, a Babylonian, presumably because of the three gifts.[132] Eastern churches maintain there were twelve—all with Persian names, the Gentile counterpart to the twelve sons of Israel (or apostles).[133] No matter the number or heritage, the magi, like the women in the genealogy, represent the peoples (Gentiles, the rest of humanity).

As the gospel went eastward, it was natural for Christians to find their ethnicities anticipated in the magi. Not only that, but what has been called an eastern way of thinking or philosophy or intellectual tradition was a *praeparatio evangelica*, in the way that western Christians claimed Socrates for Jesus. The magi, carriers of this wisdom, are the flesh-and-blood equivalent to John's appropriation of the Logos, except that, unlike a mere concept, they are also responsive to God.

The *magi* intend *to worship* (*proskuneō*, προσκυνέω) the *king of the Jews*. The verb has a broad range of meaning—from idolatry (Rev 9:20) to honoring a family member (Gen 37:9). It is difficult to know how much they knew of the child's special relationship with God. Emperor worship was especially prominent in the East, but this would still be less than a revelation into the hypostatic union or Triune God. They may also form *inclusio* with the centurion at the cross, who may have been contrasting Jesus with Caesar (Matt 27:54). I suggest the magi were responding to what had been revealed to them at that point—what theologians call progressive revelation. The verb signifies "surrender."[134]

Shaking the Powers (2:3–6)

[3] Now Herod, the king, after hearing, became troubled[135] and all Jerusalem with him. [4] And having assembled all the head priests and scribes of the people, he inquired from them where the Christ is to be born. [5] Now they said to him, "in *Bethlehem*[136] *of Judea*.[137] For it stands written through

130. Veyne, *History of Private Life*, 176.

131. Starr, *History of the Ancient World*, 605.

132. The names are variously spelled.

133. *Revelation of the Magi* 2.3.

134. BDAG, 883.

135. *Became troubled* or "began to shake."

136. *Bethlehem* is about ten miles ("a day's walk") from Jerusalem.

137. Matthew uses this language to summarize Jesus's birth at 2:1 to connect the

the prophet as follows: [6] *And you Bethlehem, land of Judah,*[138] *are by no means least among the rulers of Judah. For from you will come a ruler who will shepherd my people, Israel.* [Mic 5:1, 3 OG]

P: *All of Jerusalem* is the counterpart to the magi. *The head priests and scribes of the* Jewish *people* have prophetic knowledge, but they follow a different *king. Herod* handpicked the *high priest.*[139]

R: The conflict between Jesus, a descendant of Jacob, and *Herod*, a descendant of Esau (Idumean), goes back into Scripture: "I have loved Jacob, but Esau I have hated" (Mal 1:2–3 ESV). In context, God promises to tear down whatever the Edomites build (vv. 4–5).

Matthew cites from Micah, who looks forward to a new David, but describes him only as *the prophet.*[140] The final *shepherding* line echoes David's anointing when the tribes of Israel say: "In times past, when Saul was king over us, it was you who led out and brought in Israel [shepherding image]. And the LORD said to you, "You shall be shepherd of my people Israel, and you shall be prince over Israel" (2 Sam 5:2 ESV; see 1 Chr 11:1–2).

D: Herod's response exemplifies those who manipulate God's patience and mercy for their own benefit. Do we truly yearn for God's Kingdom or harbor a desire for the status quo?

S: God consoles *Israel.* They belong to God, and God will provide a *shepherd* or "pastor." Jesus will lead Israel out of Exile into God's relational presence.

A Secret Plot (2:7–8)

[7] Then Herod, secretly calling the magi, found out from them the time of the appearance of the star. [8] And sending them to Bethlehem, he said, "Go, search carefully for the child. And when you find him, tell me, so that I too may go and worship him."

---

event with prophecy.

138. A few mss read "Judea." However, א and Vat probably preserve the earlier, more difficult reading that evokes the patriarch's name.

139. About thirty years earlier (35 BC), Herod drowned his own appointee, the Hasmonean Aristobulus III, because he feared his popularity (Josephus, *Ant.* 15:50–56). E. P. Sanders notes, "From the time of Herod on the office became a kind of political football. The secular ruler controlled it and appointed whom he wished" (*Judaism*, 321).

140. Dennison, "Micah's Bethlehem," 4–11. Matthew may also return to Micah in the Passion. Immediately preceding the quotation, the prophet says: "They strike the ruler of Israel on the cheek with a staff" (4:14; see Matt 27:30).

P: Repeating the adverb *secretly* (*lathra*, λάθρᾳ), Matthew juxtaposes *Herod's* evil, disingenuous intention with Joseph, who, while alone, seeks to act rightly and mercifully (1:19).

D: If *worship* means surrender, *Herod* could not be a greater liar.

Three Gifts (2:9–11)

[9] Now hearing the king, they went and look: the star that they saw in the dawn was going before them until, having come, it was standing over where the child was. [10] Now seeing the star, they rejoiced with an exceedingly great joy. [11] And coming to the house, they saw the child with his mother, Mary. And falling, they worshiped him. And opening their treasure boxes,[141] they offered him gifts—gold and *frankincense and myrrh*. [Isa 60:6]

P: There are several interpretations of this *star* (*astēr*, ἀστήρ). Halley's Comet was visible in 12 and 11 BC, but this is probably too early. Chinese and Korean astronomers recorded a supernova from March to April 5 BC.[142] Johannes Kepler (1571–1630), who taught mathematics at a seminary, focused on the conjunction of Jupiter and Saturn, which normally occurs every 805 years, but happened three times in 7 and 6 BC, the most important date being May 27, 7 BC. The two planets joined with Mars to form a triangle. In Babylonian astrology, Jupiter represented the primary deity; Saturn, the Jews; the constellation Pisces, Palestine. (We should note that Judea was not called Palestine until after AD 135).[143] But the description of the star's movement—*standing over Bethlehem*—suggests a supernatural (perhaps angelic) phenomenon (Rev 7:11). *Angels*, both good (Job 38:7; Dan 8:10; Rev 1:16, 20; 2:1; 3:1) and fallen (Rev 8:10, 11; 9:1), are described as stars. Perhaps the angel who directs Joseph also guides the magi. The Syriac *Revelation of the Magi* claims Jesus is the *star*—putting him two places at once.[144] It is also possible that the magi were given a vision of what would otherwise be invisible.

141. *Treasure boxes* (*thēsauros*, θησαυρός) or "treasure." Josephus uses the term to signify the wooden chest the high priest Jehoida placed beside the altar to collect the people's offerings for renovating the temple (*Ant.* 9.163). The wealthy kept a strongbox, or *kalendarium*, which could only be opened with a key. *Gifts* also expressed obeisance (Gen 43:11–15; 1 Sam 9:7–8; 1 Kg 10:1–2).

142. Kidger, *Star of Bethlehem*.

143. Hughes, *Star of Bethlehem*; Barnett, *Jesus*, 20.

144. Each king saw Jesus differently (polymorphism; 14.3–8).

Comets and such signaled the death of one ruler and rise of another.[145] Heaven and earth were interconnected, so that instability in one realm was telling of the other. The Roman writer Pliny the Elder notes: "Augustus himself judged this comet highly propitious in that it appeared at the beginning of his principate," but also describes the dark side of the movement:

> Sometimes there is a comet in the western sky, generally a star, that inspires terror and is not easily propitiated. This comet appeared during the civil disturbance when Octavian was consul [43 BC], as earlier during the war between Pompey and Caesar [49 BC]; in our own era it appeared about the time of the poisoning as a result of which Claudius Caesar left the Empire to Domitius Nero [AD 54; Nero murdered Britannicus], and then, during Nero's principate, when it was almost continually visible and fierce in its appearance. Men think that the direction in which a comet begins to move, the star from which it draws its strength, the things it resembles and the places in which it shines, are all important factors.[146]

Nero slaughtered many nobles, hoping their deaths would substitute for his own.[147] Herod had little to fear from the west since he had been appointed by Rome. But danger was to the east. Earlier, during the Hasmonean conflict, Antigonus joined forces with the Parthians, an empire northeast of Israel, who had invaded Judea and besieged Jerusalem. Herod fled to Rome. When Jerusalem was recaptured in 37 BC, he built several fortress-palaces all along the eastern border for protection. Towards the end of the Gospel, astral phenomena anticipate Christ's death (27:45) and ascension (24:29).

The narrator does not explain the significance of the *gifts*, inviting several interpretations. The magi offer what is fitting for a king (*gold*) and priest (*frankincense*). *Myrrh* functioned as an anointing oil, particularly for embalming. Alexander the Great, buried in Alexandria, was embalmed with *frankincense and myrrh* and then "sealed in exquisitely beaten *gold* sheets."[148] Clement of Rome draws attention to the Phoenix bird, who, when passing away, makes "a coffinlike nest of frankincense and myrrh and the other spices" into which it sits and dies, but then, in a sense, is resurrected (1 Clem. 25:1–5). At the end of the Gospel, a woman will anoint Christ's body

145. See Seutonius, *Vesp.* 23; Lucan, *C. W.* 1.529. Dong Zhongshu (c. 195–c. 115 BC) claims regular and irregular events contain symbolic politico-cosmic meaning. Apparently, the first emperor of China was plagued by bad portents.

146. Pliny the Elder, *Nat.* 20 (2.92–93).

147. See Rogers, "Neronian Comets," 237–49.

148. Pollard and Reid, *Rise and Fall of Alexandria*, 16 (emphasis mine).

with *myrrh* to prepare his burial (Matt 26:6, 12). Yet *frankincense and myrrh* were also medicinal (see Matt 8:17).

The disciples will partially repeat the behavior of the magi at the Great Commission by *worshiping* (*proskuneō*, προσκυνέω) Jesus (28:17); but instead of offering *gifts*, they are commanded to make disciples of the Gentiles (see Eph 4:1–16). Offerings will be made at the completion of the mission (Matt 25:14–30).

R: The *star's* movement resembles the guiding fire and cloud of Exodus (13:21–22), except that Gentiles are the recipients. In an oracle about Jerusalem's restoration (Isa 60:1–22), the wealth of nations is partly *gold and frankincense* brought to David's city (60:6).[149]

D: Ludolph exhorts, "Go with the magi to Bethlehem and adore the infant king."[150] The *magi* express their *exceedingly great joy* through gratitude.[151] Someday, we will be able to offer *gifts* to our king.

S: Perhaps the *magi* were filled with the Holy Spirit, the source of their *exceeding joy* (see Matt 1:18, 20). I wonder if they had felt anything quite like it before. Pure in heart, they were able to see God—or at least what was seeable in that moment (Matt 5:8). They were led by the God of Exodus—the great I AM, the God of Abraham, Isaac, and Jacob—*to worship* the *child* Jesus. *Lord Jesus, may our joy deepen as we draw ever closer to you, knowing that you are already mysteriously with us. Amen.*

Joseph's Obedience (2:12)

[12] And having been warned in a dream not to return to Herod, they departed to their land through another way.

P: The magi may have ventured far south to Hebron, then followed the less traveled road to Gaza on the coast where another road could lead them northward. If so, they would have passed Nazareth, Capernaum, and Damascus.

D: Here is a kind of civil disobedience (see also Acts 5:29).

S: *Having been warned* is a divine passive. Perhaps they too were commanded by the Lord's angel. In any case, the magi are now being personally led by God.

149. For this motif, see Ps 72:10–11; Isa 66:20; Zeph 3:10; Hag 2:7–8.

150. Ludolph of Saxony, *Life of Christ*, 1:7.

151. Matthew employs *adnominatio*, the repetition of a cognate for emphasis: ἰδόντες δὲ τὸν ἀστέρα ἐχάρησαν χαρὰν μεγάλην σφόδρα.

Second Angelic Disclosure (2:12)

[13] And after they departed, look: an angel of the Lord appears in a dream to Joseph, saying: "When you get up, take the child and his mother and flee to Egypt. And stay there until I speak to you because Herod is about to seek the child to destroy it."

P: The *dream* and action of departure (*anachōreō*, ἀναχωρέω) latch the travel stories of the magi and *Joseph* together.[152] (Matthew keeps these subplots distinct; the magi see Jesus and Mary, but there is no mention of Joseph.) By not alerting *Herod*, *Joseph's* family has opportunity to escape.

R: *Egypt* evokes the Exodus story but the country is now a place of refuge, not slavery. *Herod* plays the role of Pharaoh.[153] (Around this time, rabbis were meditating and expanding on the story of Exodus. These traditions were eventually written down in *Mekilta*.[154])

D: *Children* require protection, a responsibility that falls on *Joseph*.

S: God is ahead of *Herod*.

Joseph's Obedience (2:14)

[14] And he got up and took the child and his mother by night and went to Egypt.

P: Again, Joseph responds with obedience (see 1:24–25). One tradition claims they resided "in the territory of Hermopolis in the Thebaid."[155] Another option is Alexandria, the chief seaport city of Egypt,[156] a meeting place of European and Asian culture.[157] (Theravada Buddhist monks had been active in the region long before the Incarnation.[158]) The city was founded by Alexander the Great (331 BC), after taking Egypt from the Persians.[159] Jewish

152. Romans paid careful attention to their dreams before starting off on a journey (Casson, *Travel*, 178).

153. Leithart, *Deep Exegesis*, 64–65.

154. There are two versions: *Mekilta de Rabbi Ishmael* and *Mekilta de Rabbi bar Yohai*.

155. Ward, *Lives of the Desert Fathers*, 70.

156. There were three other Greek cities in Egypt: Naukratis, Ptolemais, and Antinoopolis.

157. Dio Chrysostom mentions the presence of Greeks, Italians, Syrians, Libyans, Cilicians, Ethiopians, Bactrians, Scythians, Persians, Arabs, and Indians (*Discourses*, 32.40)

158. Sugirtharajah, *Postcolonial Reconfigurations*, 28. The great Alexandrian library probably had Indian literature (Bruns, *Christian Buddhism*, 27).

159. It is the first known city to bear the name of its founder instead of a god or

immigration to the region had intensified during the Babylonian captivity.[160] Alexandria had the largest Jewish community outside of Palestine.[161] They had their own quarter of the city, administration (elders and a president), and, by the time of Ptolemy III (246–221 BC), three synagogues.[162] Josephus notes they enjoyed equal rights with the Greeks, including Alexandrian citizenship for at least many (*J.W.* 2.487). The community became the center of Hellenized Jewish culture.[163] Presumably, Joseph would have been able to find employment to provide for his family.

Travel in the ancient world was difficult and dangerous. Later, Jesus will say: "But woe on women who have (a baby) in their stomach and who are nursing in those days! But pray that your flight may not be in winter or on a sabbath" (Matt 24:19–20).

R: God redeemed Israel from *Egypt* at *night* (Exod 12:31).

Fulfillment of Scripture (2:15)

[15] And he was there until the end of Herod, so that what was spoken by the Lord might be fulfilled through[164] the prophet, saying: "*Out of Egypt, I called my son.*" [Hos 11:1 MT]

R: Matthew cites Hosea, but, as with Isaiah (see 1:23), does not mention his name. In context, God punishes Israel for their sin by *sending them back to Egypt,* a new slavery—separation from God and home (8:13). The language matches their experience of Exile. But Matthew applies the passage to Jesus who represents Israel before God. The son of God is redeemed, inaugurating a new exodus or return from the Exile.[165] A textual variant in the manuscripts of Hosea supports this unitive reading. Matthew's wording is closest to the Masoretic (Hebrew) tradition. The Old Greek reads "Out of Egypt I called his [Israel's] children."[166] His citation of Isaiah was closer

mythical hero.

160. Jewish tombs can be dated from the late fourth century BC.

161. Philo claims a Jewish population of more than a million, which is probably hyperbolic but nevertheless attests to a large community (*Flaccus* 43). At the time of Augustus, the free population was 300,000, with a total population of 600,000 or more.

162. For more discussion, see Hachlili, *Ancient Synagogues.*

163. We may speak of the first of three summits of Jewish Exile Culture, between Babylon and the United States: Alexandria (second century BC to second century AD), Muslim Analusia (Spain), and Austria-Germany (1890s–1933).

164. A Syriac witness adds ". . . the mouth of Hosea."

165. This is a common observation. See, e.g., Estelle, *Echoes of Exodus*, 208–35.

166. ἐξ Αἰγύπτου μετεκάλεσα τὰ τέκνα αὐτοῦ.

to this tradition (1:23).[167] The biblical scroll or scrolls used by Matthew are probably no longer extant. In any case, "son" and "children" are distinct yet intimately connected through the messianism of the Old Testament and Matthew's storytelling.

S: God the Father *called* (*kaleō*, καλέω) God the *Son* as representative of God's people to repeat and complete the central story of salvation in the Old Testament. Jesus Christ is the "elect of God" (*eklektos tou theou*, ὁ ἐκλεκτός τοῦ θεοῦ).[168]

Massacre of the Innocents (2:16)

[16] Then Herod, seeing that he had been tricked by the magi, became exceedingly furious.[169] And sending (soldiers), he killed all the male children,[170] who were in Bethlehem and in all its regions from two years old and younger according to the time that he determined from the magi.

P: This is the darkest moment in either birth story of Jesus. (Luke's is generally less dangerous.[171]) Josephus, our primary source outside the New Testament for this region and time, does not record the event, but narrates a bizarre account of *Herod* arresting the best men in the region and commanding that they be killed upon his death, so that the people would mourn (*J.W.* 1.659). He also killed members of his own family to retain power. The historian cannot offer a complete account, but his portrait lends plausibility to this account. Macrobius (c. 395–423) remembers Augustus saying, "It is better to be Herod's pig, than his son" (*Saturnalia* 2.4.11). Later Christians claimed Herod murdered thousands of children, but Matthew does not offer a number; scholars estimate less than fifty families were affected.

R: The scene recapitulates Pharaoh's attempt to kill the *male* Hebrew babies, except that now it is perpetuated by a "king of the Jews" (Exod 1:8–22)! Egyptian sons die in the first; Jews in the second. The Hebrew midwives Shiphtah and Puah, who feared God, *trick* Pharaoh (Exod 1:17, 19); the *magi*, *Herod*. Both attempts fail to destroy the seed of God's promise to

167. Aquila is closer to Matthew's text, opting for "son" instead of "children."

168. John 1:34; Luke 23:35.

169. Herod knew he had been tricked because the best way back for the magi was through Jerusalem. The verb *empaizō* (ἐμπαίζω) may also signify "mock," as we find it applied to Jesus at the end of the Gospel (Matt 27:29, 31).

170. Matthew switches to the masculine to show that only the male children were in danger. Compare with the neuter at v. 13.

171. The *Protoevangelium of James* conflates the birth stories, so that John the Baptist is also in danger.

Abraham. Like Moses, Jesus is protected and is therefore able to lead God's people into a new exodus, but only for a time; like the innocents, he too will be summarily executed, but only for a time.

D: This event came to be called the Massacre of the Innocents. The Catholic Church claims the murdered children are the first Christian martyrs, remembering them on December 28.

Matthew plays with intermediate and ultimate agency. *Herod sent* others to carry out his murderous intention, but he ultimately *killed* the children.[172] Although *tricked by the magi*, they were ultimately warned by God. The unit addresses the ethical dilemma of collateral damage. Presumably, the children in Egypt and *Bethlehem* would not have died if God had not intervened to save a people. In both cases, the obstinate pharaoh or king is morally responsible; nevertheless, the vulnerable suffer because of God's initiation and continue to suffer wherever the gospel is lived and preached (Matt 5:1–16).[173] Jesus identifies with them and overcomes the dark side of divine intervention by dying alone on the cross.

S: Like Pharaoh, *Herod* cannot overcome God's providence but can cause harm in the pocket of free will. *Lord, you allowed a spiritual warfare that impacts all of creation, that often harbors the wicked and harms the vulnerable. "Why do you idly look at traitors and remain silent when the wicked swallows up the man more righteous than he?"*

Fulfillment of Scripture (2:17–18)

[17] Then was fulfilled what was spoken through Jeremiah, the prophet, saying: [18] *A voice in Rama was heard,*[174] *wailing and great mourning—Rachel, crying for her children. And she was not willing to be comforted because they are no more.* [Jer 31:15]

P: Matthew offers a preamble to the crucifixion scene, the lament of a woman over the death of *her children* (Matt 27:55–56, 61).[175] Jesus will cite another lament on the cross, forming *inclusio* (27:46, citing Ps 22:1).[176]

R: In retelling the Exodus story, *Rachel* plays the role of God's people *crying* out to God (Exod 3:7). For the first time, Matthew names the quoted

172. The verb to kill is singular in Greek.

173. This problem is explored in the fifth chapter of Albert Camus's *The Fall.*

174. Several mss add "a dirge and," which is probably taken from Jeremiah 38:15 in the Old Greek tradition. But Matthew seems to be following a textual tradition reflected in the MT, as he does at 2:15.

175. Strickert, "Rachel on the Way," 444–52.

176. Campbell, "Matthew's Hermeneutic," 46–58.

prophet. Jeremiah was associated with Lamentations, a lament expressing the trauma of the Babylonian Exile. He presents *Rachel* as weeping for the death of men in *Ramah*—descendants of her son, Benjamin, the smaller tribe comprising the Kingdom of Judea. At this point, she is understandably inconsolable. However, the quotation immediately precedes the promise of a New Covenant (31:31), which Jesus offers to the disciples in the night of his betrayal (26:28; see Luke 22:20).

S: *Jeremiah's* words are God's words (Jer 1:9), so that both cry out, "Oh that my head were waters, and my eyes a fountain of tears, that I might weep day and night for the slain of the daughter of my people!" (Jer 9:1 ESV).[177] *What was spoken*, a divine passive, reminds us of this dual authorship.[178] This Scripture, then, is also God's emotional response to the Massacre of the Innocents. *Lord, you are not indifferent to our suffering but hurt inside our hurt in stirrings we cannot fathom, but your tender response can be felt in our compassion toward others. Amen.*

Third Angelic Disclosure (2:19–20)

[19] But after Herod died, look: an angel of the Lord appears in a dream to Joseph in Egypt, [20] saying, "When you get up, take the child and his mother and journey to the land of Israel. For the ones seeking the child's life have died."

P: According to Aristotle, reversal is a key plot element. Matthew does not elaborate on *Herod's* death in 4 BC—indeed, the brief, anticlimactic *after Herod died* may be his own mocking gesture with the magi—but it was a matter of public record. Josephus ends the first book of *War of the Jews* describing the king's final miseries—aggravated by the betrayals of his own sons and depressed "with no pleasure in life":

> He had a fever, though not a raging fever, an intolerable itching of the whole skin, continuous pains in the intestines, tumors in the feet like dropsy, inflammation of the abdomen and gangrene of the private parts, engendering worms, in addition to asthma, with great difficulty in breathing, and convulsions in all his limbs.[179]

177. There seems to be intentional ambiguity in the passage concerning the speaker(s).

178. A few mss add " . . . by the Lord" to align the fulfillment citation with earlier ones (1:22; 2:15). But Matthew omits the phrase at 2:5 as well.

179. I slightly altered Thackeray's translation, *Jewish War*, 311–312 (Josephus, *J. W.* 1.656); see also 647.

Archeologists discovered Herod's tomb and sarcophagus; it was desecrated—smashed—during the rebellion leading up to the destruction of what would have been his greatest monument, the Second Temple.[180]

R: *The land of Israel* has a biblical ring. Through Ezekiel, God promises: "I will gather you from the peoples and assemble you out of the countries where you have been scattered, and I will give you the land of Israel" (Ezek 11:17 ESV). In context, God promises judgment on the wicked counselors of Jerusalem and for Israel's restoration.

D: Dating Herod's death is significant because it provides a *terminus ad quem* for the Incarnation. Josephus is our only witness, and his wording is interpreted differently—either 4 BC (traditional view) or 9 March AD 1.[181] In either case, Christ's birth is close to the traditional cleaving of the ages in the Gregorian calendar.

S: God waits for the natural *deaths* of his enemies.

Joseph's Obedience (2:21)

[21] And when he got up, he took the child and his mother by night and went to the land of Israel.

P: The return mirrors the escape (Matt 2:14), including the urgency and departing *by night*, allowing for a more literal recapitulation of the Exodus.

Fourth Angelic Disclosure (2:22)

[22] But after hearing that Archelaus rules over Judea in the place of his father Herod, he became afraid to go there. And having been instructed by a dream, he departed to the regions of Galilee.[182]

P: It was probably well-known to Matthew's first readers that Jesus grew up in Nazareth; he wants to explain how the family ended up there. Presumably, they would have returned to the house in Bethlehem, which was only five or so miles (9 kilometers) from Jerusalem (Matt 2:11).

Joseph's subjective response to God's will mirrors the beginning of the birth story—when he discovers Mary's pregnancy (Matt 1:20). In both

180. Netzer, *Architecture of Herod*, x.

181. For the revised dating, see Mahieu, *Between Rome and Jerusalem*.

182. Another of Herod's sons ruled Galilee, Herod Antipas. But he was more tolerant than Archelaus, which may explain his longer reign as tetrarch.

cases, God wants to alleviate his *fear*, but does not condemn the emotion (1:20; 2:22).

Josephus records that Herod "made *Archelaus*, his eldest son . . . his successor; and Antipas, tetrarch" (*J.W.* 1.662). Ineffectual, *Archelaus* only ruled from 4 BC to AD 6.

D: Matthew is not interested in revealing the totality of Joseph's spirituality, but it is significant that he was consistently guided by four *dreams*. (In this final instance, the angel is not mentioned but may be assumed.) I have encountered a pattern among disciples of a primary modality in their relating to God. For Matthew, the storyteller, it is through Scripture; for Joseph, who might have been illiterate, God's word is mediated through a dream. In any case, the repetition deepens the relationship, establishing a reliable, trusted history with God's relational presence.

S: *Lord, thank you for guiding Joseph and his family throughout their journey, for never leaving them. Amen.*

Fulfillment of Scripture (2:23)

[23] And having come, he resided in the city called Nazareth, so that what was spoken through the prophets might be fulfilled: "he will be called a Nazarene."

Nazareth was uninhabited from the eighth to the second centuries until it was resettled during the reign of the Hasmonean king John Hyrcanus (134–104 BC).[183] The Hasmonean family led a revolt against the Seleucid Empire and ruled until, because of internecine conflict, they lost power to the Romans in 63 BC (Josephus, *Ant.* 14.77–78). The scholar Seán Freyne claims these "settlers remained staunchly Jewish [Judean] and pro-Hasmonean and never willingly accepted the Herodians or their lifestyle."[184] Two of Jesus's brothers, Judas and Simon, were given Hasmonean names (Mark 6:3).[185]

The village overlooked the Jezreel Valley to the south, the natural and political border between Galilee and Samaria. Jesus could look south across the grand plain of Esdraelon, west, to Mount Carmel on the Mediterranean

183. Estimates of its population differ widely—from 1,600 to 200 (Meier, *Marginal Jew*, 1:317).

184. Freyne, *Jesus*, 44.

185. Judas (or Judah) Maccabee is credited for leading the Jewish revolt against the Seleucid rule under the reign of Antiochus IV Epiphanes. Maccabee is probably a Greek translation of the Aramaic *maqqaba* or Hebrew *maqqebet* for "hammer" (see 1 Macc 2:4). Simon Maccabeus, the brother of Judas, enlarged the territory of the Jews. For more background, see Honigman, *Tales of High Priests and Taxes*.

coast, east, to nearby Mount Tabor, and north, to Mount Hermon. Nazareth was also near a great highway connecting Egypt to Mesopotamia.[186] He could have watched exotic merchant caravans pass by.[187]

Nazareth spread out over terraced fields, a common farming method throughout Galilee.[188] Excavations have located vaulted cells for wine and oil storage, as well as a wine press and storage jar vessels. Capital resources included almonds, pomegranates, dates, oil, and wine.

Although the population of Nazareth was Jewish, Jesus probably came into regular contact with non-Jews. The village is near Gath-hepher, the birthplace of Jonah the prophet to the Gentiles (2 Kgs 14:25), and Sepphoris, one of the three largest cities in the region, which had been destroyed by the Romans in the wake of the rebellion following Herod the Great's death but was being rebuilt by his son Antipas as the "Ornament of the Galilee" a mere four miles (six kilometers) from Nazareth (Josephus, *Ant.* 18.27).[189] Like his father, Jesus was a *tektōn* (τέκτων). The popular translation "carpenter" may be too narrow; the word signifies a construction worker or "builder."[190] Presumably, they found work in Sepphoris where Jesus would have seen the devastation of violent revolt and disparity between rich and poor.

Archeologists have excavated a first-century home in Nazareth that the early church believed was used by Jesus's family.[191]

Jesus grew up in the extreme southerly part of lower Galilee (הַגָּלִיל, "the circle") between the Sea of Galilee and the Mediterranean.[192] He spent most of his ministry in the region, which is only about twenty-five miles (40 kilometers) in diameter. Any location could be reached in no more

186. Variously named, it came to be called *Via Maris* ("Way of the Sea") after Isa 9:1, which is cited in Matt 4:14.

187. Mark Chancey suggests most travelers avoided Galilee (*Myth of a Gentile Galilee*, 20).

188. Freyne notes that an excavated farm "shows considerable human development in terms of watch-towers, terracing, grape presses and a field irrigation system" (*Jesus*, 44).

189. Scholars dispute the extent of the destruction.

190. See Matt 13:55; Mark 6:3.

191. Dark, "Has Jesus' Nazareth house been found?," 54–63. They found limestone vessels, which suggests Jewish purity concerns (57).

192. Mark appears to be aware of this sense (6:6b). Galilee was divided into two sections: Lower and Upper. The southern boundary was the north edge of the Plain of Esdraelon; the eastern boundary, the Jordan River from as far north as Luke Hula southward through the Sea of Galilee; the northern boundary, Gischala (or Gush halab, "the valley of the olive"); the western boundary, Cabul. Since harvest-times differed between regions, it was necessary to define those regions precisely, in part, for tithing and taxation.

than a two-day walk. It was densely populated—about 300,000 people in 200 or more villages, as well as several large cities.[193] Large-scale commercial or manufacturing was rare. The population was primarily Jewish, but they were surrounded by Gentiles. If the Gospels offer a generally complete itinerary, Jesus largely avoided cities and focused on the Jewish population (see Matt 10:5–6).[194]

The high priest and Sanhedrin lacked *de jure* authority in Galilee, which was under Antipas's jurisdiction. There is some evidence of Galilean independence in religious matters. Rabbi Johanan ben Zakkai (d. c. AD 90) is remembered to have preached for seventeen years in the area with little success.[195] Nevertheless, the Pharisees enjoyed a *de facto* influence in many of the synagogues, and, as Jesus's ministry progresses, are able to frustrate his aims among the people. Archeological evidence suggests "there was a strong attachment to the mother-city, its temple and customs."[196] The region would later become the center of Jewish faith after the Second Uprising (AD 135), when the Romans renamed Judea and Galilee Palestine after the long-forgotten Philistines.

R: In the previous citation formula, Matthew departed from his pattern by naming the prophet (2:17); he does so again by referring to *the prophets* generally instead of a particular Scripture. The line, *he will be called a Nazarene*, does not occur anywhere else in the Bible. However, it parallels the first prophetic citation from Isaiah, "*he will be called Immanuel*" (Matt 1:23), except for the name. In that earlier unit, Matthew replaces the name "Immanuel" with "Jesus" while drawing attention to its Hebrew meaning "he will save his people" (1:21) and is probably doing the same here. Concerning a messianic son of David, Isaiah prophesies: "There shall come forth a shoot from the stump of Jesse [King David's father], and a branch (*netser*, נֵצֶר) from his roots shall bear fruit" (11:1 ESV). The Hebrew noun translated "branch" is very similar to *Nazareth* (*natserat*, נָצְרַת), suggesting a pun.[197] Jesus of Nazareth is Isaiah's messianic branch.

193. Josephus, *Life* 235. Most people lived in rural areas or in small villages, with only about 10 to 15 percent of the population in big cities of 10,000 or more. 80 to 90 percent of the population worked in agriculture (Holman, *Wealth and Poverty*, 19).

194. Richard Horsley insists he preached an alternative community to replace disintegrating village life, but our evidence is scanty (*In the Shadow of Empire*).

195. Hengel, *Charismatic Leaders*, 55.

196. Freyne, *Jesus*, 82.

197. Another possible pun is "Nazirite." The Nazirites were a class of people especially dedicated to God, who were ascetic and refused to cut their hair (Num 6:1–21). Luke presents the Baptist as a Nazirite (1:15). A difficulty with this proposal is that Jesus is nowhere else described this way. He regularly drinks wine with his disciples.

D: It is ironic that Jesus came from *Nazareth*, which is never mentioned in the Old Testament, let alone having any explicit messianic significance. Nathanael was originally dismissive (see John 1:46), and the epithet "Jesus of Nazareth" became something of a slur. The marginal town is an ingredient to Paul's theological reflection called the Kenosis or "emptying" (Phil 2:6–11). Jesus and his followers were dismissed as "Nazarenes" and "Galileans."[198]

S: *Lord, you oppose the proud but favor the humble. Amen.*

Luke's Birth Narrative

As we noted, Luke's birth narrative is longer than Matthew's. The opening chapter is the longest in the New Testament and is rhetorically more complex. After the preface (1:1–4), the evangelist offers an extended *synkrisis* (contrast) between John and Jesus:

A Declaration of John's Birth (1:5–25)

A' Declaration of Jesus's Birth (1:26–38)

B Meeting between Mary and Elizabeth (1:39–56)

C Birth of John (1:57–80)

C' Birth of Jesus (2:1–40)[199]

Formally, the story consists of two diptychs with a unique center—the only narrated occasion that Mary and Elizabeth meet, but also Jesus and John in utero, before their adult ministries.

We see the same strategy in John's Gospel (1:1–42; 3:22—4:1; 5:30–47; 10:40–42): the Baptist is great; Jesus is greater—what students of typology call "escalation." Tatian (c. 120–after 174) appears to have recognized the similarity by placing Luke's narrative immediately after John's prologue.[200] We suggest Luke appropriates the fourth Gospel. He betrays knowledge of the prologue in at least two places, adding the "glory" (*doxa*, δόξα) of Jesus to his version of the Transfiguration (John 1:14; Luke 9:32) and summarizing the Baptist's ministry in Acts:[201]

> Ἰωάννης ἐβάπτισεν βάπτισμα μετανοίας τῷ λαῷ λέγων εἰς τὸν ἐρχόμενον μετ᾽ αὐτὸν ἵνα πιστεύσωσιν, τοῦτ᾽ ἔστιν εἰς τὸν

198. Arrian, *Epict. diss.* 4.7.6.

199. Bovon, *Luke 1*, 29.

200. McCarthy, *Saint Ephrem's Commentary*, 44.

201. Anderson, *Fourth Gospel and the Quest for Jesus*, 113.

> Ἰησοῦν, John baptized with a baptism of repentance, speaking to the people concerning the one coming after him—that is, Jesus—that they might believe. (19:4) οὗτος ἦλθεν εἰς μαρτυρίαν ἵνα μαρτυρήσῃ περὶ τοῦ φωτός, ἵνα πάντες πιστεύσωσιν δι᾽ αὐτοῦ, This one came for a witness that he might witness concerning the light that everyone might believe through him. (John 1:7)

John does not speak this way in Luke's Gospel.

Luke has a special interest in the temple. The birth story begins and ends there. The whole Gospel is enclosed by *the hour of incense*—the ninth hour (c. 3:00 p.m.), the timing of the afternoon sacrifice and Jesus's death with crowds standing outside in both scenes (23:44–49).

7: Birth of John Foretold (Luke 1:5–25)

Zechariah and Elizabeth Without Child (1:5–7)

[5] This happened in the days of Herod, king of Judea: There was a priest whose name was Zechariah, who was from the priestly division of Abijah.[202] And his wife was from the daughters of Aaron[203] whose name was Elizabeth.[204] [6] Both were righteous, even blameless, before God, walking[205] in all the laws and right actions (required by) the Lord,[206] [7] but no child was given to them[207] because Elizabeth was barren and both were advanced in their days.

P: Luke opens the narrative proper with a chiasm (inverted parallelism) that emphasizes the central line—Zechariah's unbelief, a problem that advances the plot:

> A Zechariah and Elizabeth without child (1:5–7)

202. *Abijah* was the leader of the eighth of the twenty-four divisions of priests serving in the temple (1 Chr 24:10). He is a descendant of *Aaron* (v. 1). So *Zechariah* and *Elizabeth* originate from the same tribe.

203. Semitic expression, meaning from the tribe of Aaron.

204. For the Semitic expression, see also John 1:6. A more precise translation is *Elisabet*.

205. A common expression for "living" and "obeying."

206. *Blameless*: Paul uses the adjective to describe his obedience to the Law as a Pharisee (Phil 3:6). Noah and his family survived the flood because he was "blameless" (Gen 6:9). God commands Abraham to be "blameless" (Gen 17:1). This couple had reached the pinnacle of Jewish piety. Implicit in the claim is the indictment that many others were "unrighteous."

207. A divine passive—"God did not give a child to them."

B The Praying Crowd (1:8–10)

C Angelic Announcement (1:11–17)

D Zechariah's Unbelief (1:18)

C' Angelic Response (1:19–20)

B' The Praying Crowd (1:21–22)

A' Zechariah and Elizabeth with child (1:23–25).

R: Whereas the preface (1:1–4) follows contemporary rhetorical values, Luke begins to imitate the style of biblical story-telling, particularly 1 Samuel that opens with a similar problem: "There was a certain man of Ramathaim-zophim of the hill country of Ephraim whose name was Elkanah . . . He had two wives. The name of the one was Hannah, and the name of the other, Peninnah. And Peninnah had children, but Hannah had no children" (1:1–3 ESV).[208] This echo begins extensive interaction with the origin stories of Samuel and David, types of John the Baptist and Jesus, respectively. Whereas the conflict with *Herod, king of Judea*, is explicit in Matthew (see 2:1 and following), Luke is nuanced: the informed reader knows that *Hannah* will give birth to Samuel, who will anoint David against Saul. *Barrenness*, a biblical motif, also evokes the plight of Sarai (Gen 18), Rebecca (Gen 25), Rachel (Gen 30), and the mother of Samson (Judg 13). These women came to represent Israel in exile, but God promises a reversal through Isaiah: "Rejoice, barren one!" (54:1).[209]

D: Zechariah and Elizabeth follow the rules of the covenant, but their story falls short of a fairy tale, which is partly due to the corporate effect of a lingering exile. Many of God's people have asked, Why do *righteous* and unrighteous suffer *together*? But human ecology, by definition, is not an isolated phenomenon.

S: *God* sees *Zechariah* and *Elizabeth* as individuals but also as a couple (see Acts 5:1–11) and part of a community, and is like an all-seeing judge *waiting* to act (see Luke 18:1–8). Because of this, our immediate experience with God may not correlate with who God is and how God will ultimately respond to our situation. We may feel that God is indifferent to our plight. And yet God may, in fact, be pleased with us but not grant our deepest yearning until the right time.

208. See also 1 Sam 4:1 OG and the opening of *Letter of Aristeas*. Kenneth Litwak offers much on this theme (*Echoes of Scripture in Luke-Acts*).

209. See 1 Sam 2:5, 9; Isa 49:20–21, 23. That Luke intends this corporate sense is clear from the shift in the *Magnificat* from Mary's own self (1:48) to the people of God (1:54). For more discussion of this theme, see Beale and Kim, *God Dwells Among Us*, 66–67.

Praying Crowd (1:8–10)

[8] Now this happened:[210] while he was acting as priest before God in the order of his priestly division,[211] [9] according to the custom of the priesthood, it fell (to him) to enter the temple of the Lord to burn incense.[212] [10] And there was a whole crowd of people praying outside at the hour of incense.

P: There was a surplus of *priests* by the first century. So they were divided into twenty-four *divisions*, each serving a week twice a year. *Incense* was integral to the morning and evening sacrifices (Exod 30:7–8; m. Tamid 6:1—7:3). The *crowd's* presence suggests the latter—the ninth hour or around 3:00 p.m. They participated—that is, exercised their faith—through praying, with their requests rising with the smoke (see Luke 18:9–14; Rev 5:8; 8:3–4).[213] Afterwards, the priestly blessing was spoken over them. Jews and God-fearers (Gentiles drawn to the God of Israel but had yet to be circumcised) throughout the diaspora also directed their hearts toward the incense. Far away, Cornelius will pray at this time and hear, "Your prayers and your acts of mercy ascended as a memorial offering before God" (Acts 10:4).

R: We find a unit on the Altar of Incense in Exodus (30:1–10). It was placed before the veil that separated the Holy of Holies from everything else in creation, in front of the Ark with its Cherubim, echoing our displacement from the Garden of Eden (Gen 3:24) and mercy seat. In addition to its annual role in the Day of Atonement (Lev 16:18–19), Aaron (or a descendant) was to "burn fragrant incense on it" every morning and evening (vv. 7–8). The coals were taken from the Altar of Burnt Offerings because atonement was a prerequisite. The precise ingredients—stacte, onycha, galbanum, frankincense, along with salt—were to be a perfume only for God (Exod 30:34–38).

210. Or "Now it came about": Luke follows the paratactic construction of Scripture throughout his narrative—a literary barbarism from the perspective of Classical Greek, but followed throughout by the LXX (Gen 41:8).

211. While redundant, from a modern literary point of view, the repetition solidifies certain themes for the hearer, who cannot refer back to the page—another feature of Luke's pedagogy.

212. *It fell (to him)* is an expression for casting lots. The apostles will cast lots for Judas's replacement (Acts 1:24–26). The Mishnah describes the process in the temple: "[The superintendent] said to them, 'Those who are new to [the preparation of] the incense, come and cast lots'" (Tamid 5:2 [Neusner]). The Roman soldiers cast lots for Jesus's clothing (23:34; Mark 15:24) to fulfill Scripture (John 19:24). *Temple* signifies the place outside the holy of holies.

213. See Ezra 9:5–15; Dan 9:21; Jdt 9:1–14; Sir 50:12–21.

D: The *incense* offering was the apex of the morning and evening liturgy, the smoke connecting heaven and earth. In Revelation, we learn that angels collect the prayers of the saints in bowls (5:8).

S: *Before God*: According to the *Zohar*, a later rabbinic work, the *incense* offering was the most beloved by God (I 130:A).

Angelic Announcement (1:11–17)

[11] Now an *angel of the Lord* appeared to him, standing on the right side of the altar of incense.[214] [Gen 16:7, 11] [12] Seeing, Zechariah became troubled and terror fell on him.[215] [13] Now *the angel* said to him: "Do not fear, Zechariah![216] For your prayer was heard. And your wife, Elizabeth, *will give birth to a son for you, and you will name him*[217] John. [Gen 16:11] [14] And there will be joy and gladness *for you*, and many will rejoice at his birth. [15] For he will be great before the Lord. *And wine and alcohol he will never drink*, and he will be filled with the Holy Spirit, even from the womb of his mother. [Lev 10:9; Num 6:3; Judg 13:5][218] [16] And many sons of Israel[219] will turn to the Lord their God.[220] [17] And he will go before him [Mal 3:1; Isa 40:3] in the Spirit and power of Elijah, *to turn the hearts of the fathers to (their) children* [Mal 4:6] and the disobedient to the wisdom of the righteous[221] to make ready a people prepared."

214. The position of the angel—*at the right side*—signifies authority. The *altar of incense* is mentioned in the New Testament elsewhere only by the author of Hebrews, who is probably Luke (9:4).

215. The subjective (*troubled*) and objective (*fear*) elements of the experience are conveyed. The latter invades the priest's mind from the outside. His response reflects the *mysterium tremendum* (see Exod 15:16; Judg 6:22–23; 13:6, 22; 2 Sam 6:9; Isa 6:5; Dan 8:16–17; 10:10–11).

216. *Do not fear* is a biblical announcement of divine reassurance (Gen 15:1; Dan 10:12), often in birth announcements (Gen 21:17; 35:17; 1 Sam 4:20), and becomes a Lukan motif (v. 30; 2:10; 5:10; 8:40; Acts 18:9; 27:24).

217. The Greek may be woodenly translated "call his name."

218. *Even from the womb of his mother*: This claim reveals John's prophetic calling (Jer 1:4–5; Gal 1:15). Although the phrase can mean "from birth" (Ps 22:10 [21:11 OG]), the event of 1:41 confirms the sense "before birth" (Judg 13:7; Isa 44:2; 49:1).

219. *Sons of Israel* is a circumlocution for "Israelites."

220. *Will turn to the Lord* is another expression for repentance (Deut 30:2; 1 Sam 7:3; Hos 3:5; see Acts 15:19). This claim ties John to Malachi's prophecy about Elijah (Mal 4:5–6). Turning to the Lord would normally require directing one's heart toward the temple.

221. "Those who are right."

P: The *angel's* language echoes the opening of Mark, which cites Isaiah and (obliquely) Malachi:

> *Look—I send my messenger before your face who will prepare* (*kataskeuasei*, κατασκευάσει) *your way.* [Mal 3:1] [3]—*a voice of one crying out in the wilderness: "Prepare* (*etoimasate*, ἑτοιμάσατε) *the way of the Lord. Make his paths straight.*" [Isa 40:3]

The synonymous yet different verbs meaning "to prepare" in the two citations occur on the lips of the angel: *etoimasai kuriō laon kataskeuasmenon*, ἑτοιμάσαι κυρίῳ λαὸν κατεσκευασμένον (v. 17). Although Luke may appropriate Mark, Mark may have summarized the tradition behind Luke's presentation. In other words, Luke provides the origin of Mark's claim. As we noted, the citations presuppose the divine throne room. The *angel* relays the conversation to Zechariah. Luke may appropriate Matthew's "in (the) days of Herod the King" (ἐν ἡμέραις Ἡρῴδου τοῦ βασιλέως, 2:1). Matthew (1:19) presents Joseph as *dikaois* ("righteous"), as Luke does with Zechariah and Elizabeth (1:6). Luke may follow Matthew's angelic announcement to a would-be father (1:18–25), as the echoes also suggest: ἄγγελος κυρίου "angel of the Lord" (Matt 1:20; Luke 1:11); μὴ φοβηθῇς (Matt 1:20) and μὴ φοβου "do not be afraid" (Luke 1:13); τέξεται δὲ υἱόν, καὶ καλέσεις τὸ ὄνομα αὐτοῦ (Matt 1:21) and γεννήσει υἱόν [σοι][222] καὶ καλέσεις τὸ ὄνομα αὐτοῦ "will give birth [beget] to a son, and you shall call his name" (Luke 1:13).

Presumably, Mary, a relative of *Elizabeth*, provides this tradition. If Luke is aware of Matthew, who writes from Joseph's perspective, he may present Mary as a complementary witness and therefore a ground for his unique material.

The *angel* clarifies the relationship between *Elijah* and the Baptist: the latter comes *in the Spirit and power of Elijah*, but is not *Elijah* himself. This could be inferred from the earlier Gospels but there may have been confusion, especially with the rivalry of John's later followers.

R: The birth annunciation is a common form in Scripture, featuring the announcement of someone advancing God's salvation history and those directly impacted.[223] The *angel of the Lord* echoes the message to Hagar—"You will bear a son, you will call his name Ishmael" (Gen 16:11)—which is significant because Ishmael, like the Baptist, is not the immediate fulfillment of God's first annunciation (Gen 15:5) but Isaac and

222. Absent in D.

223. See Ashmon, *Birth Annunciations*. In addition to Scripture, he explores the Egyptian prophecies of Neferti, King Cheops and the Magicians and the three birth-myth of the god-king texts for Hatshepsut, Amenhotep III, and Ramses II; the Ugaritic texts Keretand Aqhat; the Hittite text Appu; and the Sumerian text Shulgi G.

ultimately Jesus. The language also echoes the announcement of Samson's birth, specifically abstaining from alcohol:

> And the people of Israel again did what was evil in the sight of the LORD, so the LORD gave them into the hand of the Philistines for forty years. There was a certain man of Zorah, of the tribe of the Danites, whose name was Manoah. And his wife was barren and had no children. And the angel of the LORD appeared to the woman and said to her, "Behold, you are barren and have not borne children, but you shall conceive and bear a son. Therefore be careful and drink no wine or strong drink, and eat nothing unclean, for behold, you shall conceive and bear a son. No razor shall come upon his head, for the child shall be a Nazirite to God from the womb, and he shall begin to save Israel from the hand of the Philistines." (Judg 13:1–5 ESV)

The superior joy of *the Holy Spirit* over *alcohol* is a Lukan theme (Acts 2;13).

D: The outpouring looks ahead to Pentecost (Acts 2). Paul appropriates this language (Eph 5:18), undergoing a Nazirite vow himself (Acts 18:18; see 21:20–26). According to tradition, Jacob, the brother of Jesus, lived this way.

S: *Was heard* is a divine passive—God hears the prayers of the righteous.[224] *The Holy Spirit* will *fill* the Baptist, and *joy*, a fruit of the Spirit, will become contagious in the community. *Come, Holy Spirit, give joy to our neighbors!*

Zechariah's Unbelief (1:18)

[18] And Zechariah said to the angel, "How will I know this? For I am old, and my wife is advanced in her days."

P: As we noted, Luke emphasizes the priest's unbelief by placing it at the center of the unit. The priest is an *old* man who has stopped dreaming—a tragedy overcome at Pentecost (Acts 2:17). Faith brings us into the blessings of the new covenant (Acts 16:31).

R: As a priest, Zechariah should have known the late blessing of a child to Abraham. Indeed, he echoes the patriarch's words: "Abraham fell on his face and laughed and said to himself, 'Will a child be born to a man who is a hundred years old? Will Sarah, who is ninety years old, bear a child?'" (Gen 17:17). Sarah expresses similar doubt (Gen 18:12–14). In both cases,

224. *Heard*: The verb is used in the LXX for God hearing petitions. For a parallel with Samuel, see 1 Sam 1:9–11. We find a parallel scene in Luke's depiction of Cornelius (Acts 10:1–8).

the righteous stumbled in faith (see v. 20). In Zechariah's case, *the failure is more serious becuase he is the spiritual leader of the people* (vv. 8–10, 21–22; James 3:1). God killed Nadab and Abihu because they performed the offering of incense inappropriately (Lev 10:1–2).

D: Those who lead should model faith for the people. Let us, who struggle with faith, choose silence ahead of judgment.

S: *Lord, speak to us. Amen.*

Angelic Response (1:19–20)

[19] And replying, the angel said to him, "I am Gabriel, who stands before God, and I was sent to speak to you and to proclaim these good announcements to you. [Isa 40:9; 52:7] [20] Now pay attention: You will be silent and not be able to speak until these days come to pass because you did not believe in my words that will be fulfilled in their season."

P: Luke may clarify the identity of the "Angel of the Lord" in Matthew's presentation—*Gabriel.* The scene is similar to Raphael's appearance to Tobit in response to prayer (Tob 12:11–15). There is probably a correlation between the prayers of the people and the sending of an angel. Tobit claims: "At that very moment, the prayers of both of them were heard in the glorious presence of God. So Raphael was sent to heal both of them" (3:16–17 NRSV).

R: *The angel* echoes Isaiah's announcement of the end of Exile (Isa 40:9; 52:7), as we saw in the opening of Mark.

D: God's discipline—in this case, *silence*—is not merely retributive but reformative (see Heb 12:11). We should all be "slow to speak" but "quick to hear" (James 1:19). Like the Pythagoreans, *Zechariah* begins an apophatic season of quiet learning.

S: *The angel stands before God,* who is seated in the heavens. *Gabriel* is like the Seraphim and Cherubim who do nothing but worship unless summoned for such tasks.[225] *Lord, may we live the angelic life. Amen.*

Praying Crowd (1:21–22)

[21] And the people were waiting for Zechariah and were marveling over him because he was delayed in the temple. [22] Coming out, he was unable

225. Some Jews believed there were seven *archangels* or "head angels" (e.g., Gabriel and Michael), who enjoy direct access to God (Tob. 12:11–22), along with an extended hierarchy of rulers, powers, and authorities.

to speak to them. And they perceived that he had seen a vision in the temple.[226] And he was making signs to them but was remaining mute.

P: *Zechariah* is unable to offer the priestly blessing.

D: We are not to speak on God's behalf, unless we first listen and obey.

Zechariah and Elizabeth With Child (1:23–25)

[23] And it came about when the days of his temple service were completed, he went to his home. [24] After these days, his wife Elizabeth became pregnant[227] and was hiding herself for five months, saying: [25] "So the Lord has done to me in the days that he concerned himself to take away my shame among people."

P: Luke introduced *Elizabeth* at the beginning of the narrative (1:5) and gives her a small part here. She may have waited *five months*, so that her showing would offer proof to an otherwise unbelievable situation.

R: Elizabeth's response echoes Rachel: "God has taken away my reproach" (Gen 30:23 ESV). The Septuagint translates "reproach" with *oneidos* (ὄνειδός), which Luke adopts here. It is an ancient word going back to Homer, which describes a loss of standing because of disparaging speech.[228] *Shame* was the first consequence of sin (Gen 2:25; 3:7, 11). However, in this case, *Elizabeth* is "righteous—even blameless—before God" (1:6).

D: This allows a distinction between guilt, the recognition of doing wrong, and toxic shame, the feeling that something is wrong with *us*. *Elizabeth* most likely began to feel shame soon after marriage as a teenager.

What is our *shame among people*? How does it impact our thinking and behavior? It manifests in automatically negative self-judgments, feelings of inadequacy, depression, and a desire *to hide*. Jesus despised and transcended shame, so that we might find freedom in him (Heb 12:2).

S: *May the Lord do to us in the days that he concerns himself to take away our shame among people. Amen.*

226. Cornelius also received a vision (Acts 10:3).

227. Sexual intercourse created an impurity that was inappropriate for priestly service.

228. This is the only occurrence of the word in the New Testament.

8: Birth of Jesus Foretold (Luke 1:26–38)

Introduction of Mary (1:26–27)

[26] Now in the sixth month the angel Gabriel was sent from God to Nazareth,[229] a city of Galilee, [27] to a virgin engaged to a man with the name Joseph, from the house of David.[230] And the name of the virgin was Mary.

P: The transition is stark—from the Jewish center of the universe, the temple in Judea, above which is the throne of *God*, to a small *city* in *Galilee*; from a male, elderly priest to a young woman. This chiasm is similar to the previous one, but without the crowds (contrast with 1:8–10, 21–22):

A Introduction of Mary (1:26–27)

B Gabriel's Announcement (1:28–33)

C Mary's Question (1:34)

B' Gabriel's Response (1:35–37)

A' Mary's Submission (1:38).

Like Zechariah (1:18), *Mary* questions the announcement at the center of the unit, which fosters suspense, but the escalation of the situation, a virginal conception, makes her wonder entirely appropriate, so that no discipline follows.

Luke appropriates and clarifies elements of Matthew's presentation, who does not relate where the Angel of the Lord speaks to Joseph; *Nazareth* is not mentioned until the end of his birth narrative (2:23).[231] Joseph is *from the house of David* (Matt 1:20) and engaged (*mnēsteuō*, μνηστεύω) to a *virgin* (*parthenos*, παρθένος) (Matt 1:18, 23, 25).

D: Muslims believe *Gabriel* came to Mohammad and, over a twenty-three year period, dictated to him the *Qur'an*.

229. The Greek may be woodenly translated "named Nazareth."

230. *From the house of David* may refer to Joseph or Mary.

231. We find various spellings for "Nazareth" in the Greek mss. According to several, Matthew and Luke use the same spelling: Ναζαρὲθ. The two accounts share nine significant words: ἄγγελος, παρθένον / παρθένου, ἐμνηστευμένην, ἀνδρὶ, Ἰωσὴφ, Δαυὶδ, Μαριάμ, μετὰ.

Gabriel's Announcement (1:28–29)

[28] And he came and said to her, "Greetings, favored one—*the Lord is with you!* [Blessed are you among women!]."[232] [Judg 6:12] [29] But the (virgin) was greatly confused by the message and was considering what sort of greeting this might be.

P: Mary's angelic encounter is more direct than Joseph's (Matt 1:20). Like Zechariah, she undergoes the *mysterium tremendum.*

R: The scene echoes and therefore probably cites from the call of Gideon: "the angel of the LORD appeared to him and said to him, "The LORD is with you, O mighty man of valor" (Judg 6:12; see also the motif at 2 Sam 7:3; 2 Chr 15:2). The implication is that God is calling Mary into a redemptive work requiring courage and faith.

D: Matthew (1:23) and Luke (1:28) share an interest in God's presence. The verb translated *favored one*, *charitoō* (χαριτόω), is related to "grace" (*charis*, χάρις). Grace or favor is God being present to us. Without being overly self-conscious, we should never become entirely used to this privilege. Mary is shocked by the attention. She is also, like many of us, unaware of God's favor in her life. Favor must be revealed before it can be appropriated. Scripture criticizes the simplistic correlation between favor and positive circumstances. If anything, favor led to more suffering in Mary's life, beginning with the birthing of Jesus, before the joy.

S: *Lord, who are we that you would be mindful of us, to be the apple of your eye. And yet through the mediation of Mary, our God-bearer (*theotokos*), we are your beloved. Amen.*

[30] And the angel said to her, "Do not be afraid, Mary! For you found favor in God's presence. [31] Look: *you will become pregnant in (your) womb,* and you will give birth to a son; *and you will call his name* Jesus. [Gen 16:11] [32] He will be great and will be called *the Son of the Most High*; and the Lord God will give (him) *the throne* of David, his father, [2 Sam 7:13; Ps 82] [33] and he will rule over *the house of Jacob* forever; and concerning his kingdom, there will be no end." [Isa 14:1]

P: *The angel* reassures and explains. The promise anticipates the Ascension—*son of the Most High*—which is heavily emphasized by Luke by describing the event twice at the center of his two-book project (Luke 24:50–53; Acts 1:6–11).

Luke elevates Jesus through *synkrisis*. In the earlier unit (1:15), Gabriel claims: "For he [John] will be great before the Lord. *And wine and alcohol he will never drink.* And he will be filled in the Holy Spirit, even from the womb

232. This eulogistic fragment is not in our earliest mss. It anticipates Elizabeth's response (1:42).

of his mother." But Jesus "will be great" without qualification—an attribute normally reserved for God.

The scene overlaps with and complements Matthew's presentation (1:18–25). Both evangelists relate Jesus to *David* and have an angel say *Do not be afraid* (Matt 1:20), echoing Hagar's reassurance (see below), except for their focus on different parents.

R: Gabriel announces the fulfillment of the David Covenant: "I will establish the throne of his kingdom forever" (2 Sam 7:13). *House of Jacob*, referring to the twelve tribes, is a common epithet but especially in Isaiah (2:6; 8:17; 10:20; 29:22; 46:3; 48:1; 58:1). One passage looks forward to the inclusion of "sojourners" who "will join them and will attach themselves to the house of Jacob" (14:1). Reinforcing this theme, *the angel* echoes the announcement to Hagar, Sarai's Egyptian servant: "Look, you are pregnant and shall give birth to a son; and you shall call his name Ishmael because the Lord listened to your affliction" (Gen 16:11 LXX).[233] Gentile inclusion is a Lukan emphasis. Finally, the angel narrows the sense of an otherwise problematic psalm for monotheism:

> God has taken his place in the divine council; in the midst of the gods he holds judgment: "How long will you judge unjustly and show partiality to the wicked? Selah Give justice to the weak and the fatherless; maintain the right of the afflicted and the destitute. Rescue the weak and the needy; deliver them from the hand of the wicked." They have neither knowledge nor understanding, they walk about in darkness; all the foundations of the earth are shaken. I said, "*You are gods, sons of the Most High, all of you;* nevertheless, like men you shall die, and fall like any prince." Arise, O God, judge the earth; for you shall inherit all the nations! (Ps 82 ESV, emphasis added)

Instead of "*You are gods, sons of the Most High*," Gabriel announces Jesus as *the Son of the Most High*.

D: The Christian tradition reinterpreted the psalm as a description of deification or *theosis*, the taking on the divine nature through adoption and union with Christ.[234] Irenaeus is exemplary:

> Do we cast blame on him [God] because we were not made gods from the beginning, but were at first created merely as

233. Compare Luke's καὶ ἰδοὺ συλλήμψῃ ἐν γαστρὶ καὶ τέξῃ υἱὸν καὶ καλέσεις τὸ ὄνομα αὐτοῦ Ἰησοῦν with the LXX: ἰδοὺ σὺ ἐν γαστρὶ ἔχεις καὶ τέξῃ υἱὸν καὶ καλέσεις τὸ ὄνομα αὐτοῦ Ισμαηλ ὅτι ἐπήκουσεν κύριος τῇ ταπεινώσει σου (Gen 16:11). See also von Heijne, *Messenger of the Lord*, 136–37.

234. Fairbairn, *Life in the Trinity*, 8.

> men, and then later as gods? Although God has adopted this course out of his pure benevolence, that no one may charge him with discrimination or stinginess, he declares, "I have said, Ye are gods; and all of you are sons of the Most High." . . . For it was necessary at first that nature be exhibited, then after that what was mortal would be conquered and swallowed up in immortality. (*Against Heresies* 4.38)

S: Gabriel uses full language for *God*. *Most High* was a common epithet (e.g., Gen 14:18; Ps 7:17; 1QapGen ar II, 4) that Luke appropriates more than any other New Testament writer (1:32, 35, 76; 6:35; 8:28; Acts 7:48; 16:17), referring specifically to God the Father. Outside of monotheism, it referred to the king of the gods like Zeus. In this context, the Father is given prominence by virtue of his role in resurrecting and glorifying the Son to his right hand. He is also *the Lord God*, a very common pleonastic expression in the Old Testament that combines the names *Yahweh* and *Elohim* (or *Adon*).[235] *Elohim* describes God in the broadest sense, as Creator and sovereign over all things, and *Yahweh* in the narrower sense of the One cleaving to Israel in an intimate, covenant relationship.

Mary's Question (1:34)

[34] But Mary said to the angel, "How will this be since I do not know a husband (sexually)?"

P: We may wonder why *Mary* is not rebuked for questioning like Zechariah (v. 18). Her question is inevitable: How does a virgin give birth to a child, at least in the first century? Zechariah had precedents like Abraham and Sarah, but the virginal conception was new.

D: *This* (*touto*, τοῦτο) is neuter in Greek, which allows a broad antecedent: although *Mary* focuses on the pregnancy disclosure, *the angel* has announced the solution to every problem, the answer to all prayer, and the fulfillment of every promise—and how it intersects with her otherwise small, quiet existence. The obstacle of a virginal conception, seen within the whole context of God's redemptive history, is not so great. When participating in the Kingdom, we may see our own little impossibilities that way.

235. The epithet begins in Genesis 2 (vv. 4, 5, 7, 8, 9, 15, 16, 18, 19, 21, 22) and continues throughout the Old Testament. Later, *Adon* ("Lord") replaces *Elohim* (e.g. Exod 23:17; 34:23; Deut 3:24).

Gabriel's Response (1:35–37)

[35] And answering, the angel said to her, "(The) Holy Spirit will come upon you, and (the) Power of the Most High will overshadow you. So also the (baby) who is to be born[236] *will be called holy*, Son of God. [Isa 4:3] [36] Now pay attention: Elizabeth, your relative, has herself become pregnant (with) a son in her old age. And this is the sixth month with her who is called barren. [37] For every word from God will not become powerless."

P: The subunit has two parts: a partial explanation (35) and implied directive (vv. 36–37) and is delimited by *power* and *powerless*. The *Holy Spirit* will circumvent the normal path to pregnancy, so that Jesus will be *the Son of God* in a unique sense. The creative moment, however, is hidden or *overshadowed*, as will be the case at the resurrection.

The *synkrisis* with John continues: Jesus is not simply "filled with" but conceived by *the Holy Spirit* (see 1:15).

R: In Scripture God's presence is depicted as a light hidden in a cloud that *overshadows* people for their protection (Exod 16:10; 24:15–18; 40:34–35).

Will be called holy evokes the messianic "branch" in Isaiah: "In that day the branch of the Lord shall be beautiful and glorious, and the fruit of the land shall be pride and honor of the survivors of Israel. And he who is left in Zion and remains in Jerusalem *will be called holy*, everyone who has been recorded for life in Jerusalem" (4:2–3 ESV, emphasis added). As with the allusion to Psalm 82, the communal thrust of the prophecy is fulfilled in our union with Christ, the *holy* one.

D: *Every word from God will not become powerless.* What if a single *word*, even the breath of a vowel, lodged under our brokenness and shame?

S: The revelation blossoms into full inclusive Trinitarianism: Jesus is *the Son of the Most High; (the) Holy Spirit, (the) Power of the Most High.* Both draw us into the Trinitarian life of God. The created body of Christ shares the holiness of the Spirit, anticipating Pentecost where Mary will also be present.[237]

236. Or "generated."

237. Matthew and Luke emphasize the holiness of Jesus: γεννηθὲν ἐκ πνεύματός ἐστιν ἁγίου (Matt 1:20); τὸ γεννώμενον ἅγιον (Luke 1:35). The Greek in Matthew is usually translated like "what is begotten is by the Holy Spirit," although *hagiou* (ἁγίου), which is rendered "holy" or "Holy," is in an unusual place. An alternative translation is "what is begotten by the Spirit *is holy*," which is closer to Luke: *will be called holy*.

Mary's Submission (1:38)

[38] Now Mary said, "Watch: the servant of the Lord. Let it be to me according to your word." And the angel departed from her.

D: *Mary's* response is sublime. May we all say to God's invitations: "*Let it be to* us *according to your word.*"

9: Mary Visits Elizabeth (Luke 1:39–45)

[39] Now in those days, Mary quickly got up and went to the hill country—to a city of Judah.[238] [40] And she went into the house of Zechariah and greeted Elizabeth. [41] And this happened: when Elizabeth heard Mary's greeting, the baby *leaped* in her womb. [Mal 4:2] And Elizabeth was filled with the Holy Spirit [42] and cried out with a *great* cry, saying: [Mal 4:5] "Blessed are you among women, and blessed is the fruit of your womb! [43] And why (has) this (been granted) to me—that the mother of *my Lord* might come to me? [44] For look: when the voice of your greeting came into my ears, the baby in my womb leaped with joy. [45] And blessed is she who believed! For there will be a fulfillment of the things that were spoken to her by *the Lord.*"

P: This unit is the heart of Luke's birth story, the center of the chiasm, bridging the stories of John and Jesus according Gabriel's direction. The evangelist focuses the unit with repetition, moving from third to first person: *when Elizabeth heard Mary's greeting, the baby leaped in her womb . . . "when the voice of your greeting came into my ears, the baby in my womb leaped with joy."* The *voice* went *into* Elizabeth's *ears* so that the *baby* could hear, a supernatural movement fulfilling the angelic announcement (1:15) and anticipating John's role as forerunner (1:15).

R: *Leaping* (*skirtaō*, σκιρτάω) fulfills Malachi's prophecy of Elijah's return: "for you who fear my name, the sun of righteousness shall rise with healing in its wings. You shall go out leaping (*skirtaō*) like calves from the stall" (4:2 [3:20 LXX] ESV). Luke deepens the connection with the adjective *great* (*megas*, μέγας): "Behold, I will send you Elijah the prophet before the great (*megas*) and awesome day of the Lord comes" (4:5 [3:22 LXX] ESV).

D: Christians have found a ground against abortion in this observation: *the baby leaped in* Elizabeth's *womb*. Jews took a low view of abortion,

238. Nazareth was near the border of Galilee and Samaria. Luke does not relate the name of the *city*, but since antiquity pilgrims have visited Ein Karem, a small village outside of Jerusalem as the place of John's birth. Priests normally lived near Jerusalem. The narrative does not relate if Mary traveled alone, but such an action would be rare.

whereas the common assumption in the Greco-Roman world, attributed to the "science" of the Stoics, was that a fetus is like a plant and becomes an animal only at birth when it begins to breathe.[239]

S: Elizabeth's response is Trinitarian: *Lord* is applied to the Father (v. 45) and Son (v. 43), as she is filled with *the Holy Spirit* (v. 41). The language echoes an ambiguity in the Psalter that Jesus will exploit: "The LORD says to my Lord" (Ps 110:1; see Luke 20:41–44). A ministry of *the Spirit* is to impart *joy*, which is expressed by, among other things, *leaping* or dancing and *crying out*.

10: Magnificat (Luke 1:46–55)

[46] And Mary said: "My *psuchē* magnifies the Lord, [1 Sam 2:1] [47] and my spirit rejoiced over God my savior [48] because he looked upon the humility of his servant. [1 Sam 1:11] For look: from now on all the generations will call me blessed.[240] [49] For the Powerful One did great things for me, and holy is his name. [50] And his mercy, from generation to generation, is upon those who fear him. [Ps 103:13, 17; Prov 1:7] [51] He did a mighty deed with his arm:[241] He scattered the arrogant by the intention of their hearts. [52] He pulled down the powerful from thrones and exalted the humble. [Job 5:11; 12:19] [53] He filled those who hunger with good things, and those who are wealthy he sent away empty-handed.[242] [54] He helped Israel, his servant, by remembering mercy [Isa 41:8] [55] as he spoke to our fathers—to Abraham and to *his seed* forever." [Gen 15:5]

P: The Magnificat, from the Latin "(My soul) magnifies," is a praise psalm in which a leader—in this case, Elizabeth—calls for praise and explains why it is appropriate (vv. 42–45).[243] Mary responds. Both confess Mary—and, by extension, God's people—as *blessed*, the recipient of God's favor (vv. 42, 45, 48). The psalm is delimited by the shared identity of Mary and *Israel* as God's *servant* (vv. 48 [*doulē*, δούλη], 54 [*paidos*, παιδός]).[244]

239. Hornblower and Spawforth, *Oxford Companion to Classical Civilization*, 1.

240. This claim is similar to the one Jesus makes about another Mary, who anoints his feet for burial (John 12:1–8; Mark 14:3–9; Matt 26:6–13), a tradition Luke omits (but see Luke 7:36–50).

241. Ps 89:10, 13; 2 Sam 22:8 Exod 6:6; Acts 13:17.

242. 1 Sam 2:5; Ps 107:9.

243. Bock, *Jesus according to Scripture*, 61.

244. For the form, which is also called a "hymn," see Pharis, *Hymns of Luke's Infancy Narrative*, 14–86; Tannehill, "Magnificat as Poem," 263–75.

Mary celebrates a divine reversal: the humble Son (Matt 5:5; 11:28–30) of this humble mother will bless all the humble servants of the Lord.[245]

R: Mary echoes Hannah's praise psalm, which is consistent with Luke presenting Elizabeth as her antitype. Overlapping and similar words are italicized:

> My heart *exults in the Lord*; my horn is exalted in the LORD. My mouth derides my enemies, because I *rejoice* in your salvation. There is none *holy* like the LORD: for there is none besides you; there is no rock like our God. Talk no more so very proudly, let not *arrogance* come from your mouth; for the LORD is a God of knowledge, and by him actions are weighed. The bows of *the mighty* are broken, but the feeble bind on strength.
>
> *Those who were full* have hired themselves out for bread, but *those who were hungry have ceased to hunger*. The barren has borne seven, but she who has many children is forlorn. The LORD kills and brings to life; he brings down to Sheol and raises up. The LORD makes poor and makes rich; *he brings low and he exalts*. He raises up the poor from the dust; he lifts the needy from the ash heap to make them sit with princes and inherit a seat of honor. For the pillars of the earth are the LORD's, and on them he has set the world. He will guard the feet of his faithful ones, but the wicked shall be cut off in darkness, for *not by might* shall a man prevail. The adversaries of the LORD shall be broken to pieces; against them he will thunder in heaven. The LORD will judge the ends of the earth; he will give strength to his king and exalt the horn of his anointed. (1 Sam 2:1–10 ESV).[246]

This psalm is delimited by the repetition of *horn*, a symbol of power and authority. Zechariah will refer to Christ as "a horn of salvation" (1:69). The final line, God "will exalt the horn of his anointed" or "Christ," is the first explicit reference to the messiah in the Old Testament, imbuing it with the authority of precedent.[247] The first praise psalm, then, is prophetically fulfilled in the second.

We also find intimations of resurrection and glory: "The LORD kills *and brings to life*; he brings down to Sheol *and raises up*." The implicit logic is that one cannot occur without the other: one must die to be brought to

245. Matthew's Presentation does not relate this tradition. Mary is "found" to be pregnant (1:18), suggesting she had been out of sight for some time.

246. For discussion, see Bauckham, *Gospel Women*, 60–61.

247. ὑψώσει κέρας χριστοῦ αὐτοῦ = וְיָרֵם קֶרֶן מְשִׁיחוֹ (1Sam 2:10 OG, MT). This is a canonical authority and is not intended to be a historical claim about the origins of messianism.

life; be found humble before one is glorified. Paul develops this in his letters: "That which you sow does not come to life unless it dies," he assures the Corinthians (1 Cor 15:36), and offers this interpretation of Psalm 68:18:

> Now to each one of us was given [the] grace according to the measure of the gift from Christ. So it says: *After ascending on high, he captured a host of captives. He gave gifts to human beings.* Now the [expression] *he ascended*—what is [its meaning] except that he also descended into the lower [parts] of the earth? The one who descended—*he* is also *the one who ascended* far above all the heavens, that he might fulfill all things. (Eph 4:7–10)

All this is consistent with Luke's emphasis on order—what rhetoricians call *taxis*.

D: The song may predate Luke's Gospel, so that the evangelist is incorporating liturgy.[248] If Mary is the ultimate author, the song is the chronological beginning of the New Testament.[249] We see this transition in the *Book of Odes*, where the Magnificat occurs immediately after prayers from the Hebrew Bible.[250] Luke implies a filling of the Spirit, which reoccurs at Pentecost.[251]

Literary borrowing is not a good reason to reject this scenario, as James Mays explains: "In the intellectual world of Judaism, one of the most important ways of understanding the meaning of present experience was to make sense of the contemporary by perceiving and describing it in terms of an established tradition."[252] Mary would have been familiar with Hannah's

248. See Knust and Wasserman, "Biblical Odes," 341–65. They note that "liturgical singing could sometimes preserve text" (342).

249. Scripture does not convey Mary's age, but she may have been twelve or thirteen. In a Greco-Roman context, the earliest age for a legally valid marriage was twelve, but most girls were married by sixteen (see Xenophon of Ephesus, *Ephesian Tale of Anthia and Habrocomes* 1.2, which speaks of a fourteen-year-old bride (see *Xenophon of Ephesus, Ephesian Tale of Anthia and Habrocomes* 1.2, which speaks of a fourteen-year-old bride). The text is cited in Kraemer, *Women's Religions*, 131. Gregory of Nyssa describes his sister's twelfth year as "the age when the bloom of adolescence begins to appear" (*Life of Macrina* 964 A).

250. There are also additions to Daniel found in Greek translations of the Hebrew Bible. In the Book of Odes, the song is titled "(The) Prayer of Mary, God-bearer" (Θεοτόκος), an epithet adopted at the Ecumenical Council of Ephesus in AD 431. Cyril of Alexandria was a great defender of this title against Nestorius.

251. Luke may withhold this detail in anticipation of Pentecost, but Gabriel's promise of the coming Holy Spirit need not only refer to the virginal conception, as noted by Gaventa (*Mary*, 58).

252. Mays, *Psalms*, 105. We find the same patterning in Judith (16:1–17).

plight from readings in the synagogue and would naturally find her place in God's story of redemption.

All the generations will call me blessed predicts a perpetual role for the psalm in the church's worship. The Magnificat is traditionally sung at *orthros* (ὄρθρος, "daybreak"), the last of the night offices, and continues as part of the Sunday liturgy in the Orthodox Church. In the West, it climaxes the *Liturgy of the Hours*, Vespers or Evensong at sunset.

Mary calls for "a radical shift in values."[253] Only the *humble* have space *to magnify the Lord*. John of Lycopolis (d. c. 395) describes humility as "the essential foundation of all virtues," an emphasis we find throughout the Christian tradition.[254] Humility is fear of the Lord who determines the ending of everything. We sin because we do not fear or fear something more than the Lord—wealth, power, or our own reasoning. Some reject humility and its fruit gentleness as weak and ineffective. There was a long season when, as a man, I feared gentleness. But God did more for the salvation of the world through a humble woman than all the sweat and violence of arrogant men. According to Luke's *taxis*, only the humble can be glorified.

S: *The Powerful One* tears down *the powerful*.

11: John's Birth (Luke 1:56–63)

[56] Now Mary remained with her for about three months and returned to her house. [57] Now concerning Elizabeth, the time for her to give birth was filled, and *she gave birth to a son*.[255] [Exod 2:22] [58] And the neighbors and her relatives heard about her—that the Lord enlarged his mercy with her—and they were rejoicing with her.

P: The scene fulfills Elizabeth's declaration: "So the Lord has done to me in the days that he concerned himself to take away my shame among people" (1:25). The verb translated *enlarged* (*megalunō*, μεγαλύνω) may bring the effect of greater esteem, the acquisition of honor in a community.[256]

R: Births often advance stories in Scripture; we find the same phrase after Moses marries Zipporah: "She gave birth to a son, and he called his name Gershom, for he said, 'I have been a sojourner in a foreign land'" (Exod 2:22).

253. Miller, *Rumors of Resistance*, 132.

254. Ward, *Lives of the Desert Fathers*, 59.

255. The two adversative conjunctions, here and in the next verse, mark transitions that suggest *Mary* did not assist with John's birth, although it is possible that Luke is not emphasizing chronology but simply moving her offstage to refocus on the Baptist.

256. BDAG, 623.

D: *Rejoicing* marks the reversal of shame and involves community (Luke 15:24, 29, 32; Heb 12:2), an integral ministry of the church. *When the Lord enlarges his mercy,* we may recognize this work and *rejoice*, dispelling any lingering, isolating shame for the member.

S: *Lord, you are tender and kind, if not prompt. We accept, even celebrate, your timing. It is enough to wait in faith, to hold one another in love, and to rejoice in expectation. Amen.*

[59] Now this happened on the eighth day: they came to circumcise the child and were calling him by the name of his father, Zechariah. [60] But his mother replied and said, "No, instead he will be called John." [61] And they said to her, "There is no one from your relatives called by this name." [62] And they were making signs to his father about what he would want to call him. [63] And motioning for a little writing tablet, he wrote, saying, "His name is John." And they all marveled.

P: In Luke, the mothers—Elizabeth and Mary (v. 31)—have a role in naming children (compare with Matt 1:21, 25), although the final decision rests with *Zechariah*, who, we learn, is mute *and deaf*. Whereas Elizabeth enjoys restored honor, there is a potential slight to the priest whose name will not pass to the next generation. The community, sensitive to this dynamic that is couched in tradition, nevertheless provides an opportunity for obedience to complete the fulfillment of the angel's prophecy: "Your wife, Elizabeth, *will give birth to a son [for you], and you shall name him* John. And there will be joy and gladness for you, and many will rejoice at his birth" (1:13–14). Luke heals this dishonor by remembering Zechariah's name in his Gospel.[257]

The people also *marveled* after *Zechariah* was delayed in the temple (1:21).

Naming at circumcision is customary and includes withholding discussion until the ceremony (Heb. *brit*), which may explain the confusion in this passage. Names were also considered to be prophetic (*nomen omen*): *John* means "Yahweh is gracious."

R: The Pentateuch requires male infants to be circumcised *on the eighth day* (Gen 17:12; Lev 12:3; see Acts 7:8; Phil 3:5).

D: According to Luke, writing is a way of speaking. He may well have used a *little writing tablet* (*pinakidion,* πινακίδιον) himself to compose his Gospel, making field notes.[258] Such *tablets* had a wax surface to be marked with a stylus.

257. Contrast with the Rich Man and Lazarus (Luke 16:19–31) or withholding Pharaoh's name in the exodus story.

258. The Greek is the diminutive form of *pinax* (πίναξ), a large dish (Luke 11:39).

12: Benedictus (Luke 1:64–79)

[64] Now his mouth was immediately opened and his tongue, and he was speaking, praising God. [65] And fear came upon all those who dwelled around them. And all these events were being discussed in all the hill country of Judea. [66] And all who heard placed (them) in their heart, saying, "What, then, will this child be?" For *the hand of the Lord* was also with him. [Exod 7:5]

P: With Mary's departure, Luke discloses village (communal) memory as his source. The people witness the reversal of Zechariah's discipline—"You shall be silent and not be able to speak until these days come to pass because you did not believe in my words that will be fulfilled in their season" (1:20)—and naturally experience *fear*.

R: *The hand of the Lord* evokes the Exodus: "The Egyptians shall know that I am the LORD, when I stretch out my hand against Egypt and bring out the people of Israel from among them" (Exod 7:5). This symbol of power becomes a motif (Exod 9:3; 13:3, 9, 14, 16; 16:3).

D: The church also experiences this enveloping *fear* in response to God's redemptive presence (Acts 5:5, 11).

S: *His mouth was immediately opened* is a divine passive: *the Lord opened* Zechariah's *mouth*, enabling him *to speak* and *to praise*, which should have been his original response. *Lord, may we discern your presence among and through us and live in appropriate fear. Amen.*

[67] And Zechariah, his father, was filled with the Holy Spirit and prophesied, saying:

To the People (1:68–75)

[68] "Blessed is[259] the Lord, the God of Israel! [Ps 41:13][260] For he visited and provided *redemption for his people.* [Ps 111:9] [69] And he raised up a *horn* of salvation for us in the house of *David*, his child, [Ps 132:17; 1 Sam 2:10; Ps 2] [70] just as he spoke through the mouth of the holy ones from the season of his prophets—[71] salvation from our enemies and from the hand of all who hate us—[72] to practice mercy with our fathers and to remember his holy covenant, [73] the oath that he swore to Abraham, our father, to give us, [Gen 12; 15] [74] redeeming (us) from the hands of enemies to serve him without fear [75] in holiness and righteousness before him all of our days."

259. Or "be." The verb is implied.

260. See Odes 9.68.

To the Child (1:76–79)

[76] "Now even you, child, will be called prophet of the Most High. For you will *go before the Lord to prepare his way,* [Isa 40:3] [77] to give knowledge of salvation to his people by the forgiveness of their sins, [78] through the compassionate mercies of our God in which *the dawn* will visit us from on high [Num 24:17] [79] *to shine* upon *those who sit in darkness* and *shadow of death,* to guide our feet to the way of peace." [Isa 9:1; Ps 107:10]

P: Zechariah finally joins in the responsive *praise* of Elizabeth and Mary. The Benedictus is a praise psalm with two stanzas.[261] The first (vv. 68–75) is delimited by *redemption* (*lutrōsis*, λύτρωσις [v. 68]) and *redeeming* (*lutroō*, λυτρόω [v. 74]), and is directed towards God's people. The opening is similar to a rabbinic prayer, the Fifteenth Benediction of the *Shemoneh Esreh*:

> Let the shoot of David (Your servant) speedily spring up and raise his horn in Your salvation . . . May you be blessed, O Lord, who lets the horn of salvation flourish.[262]

There was some form of this prayer in the first century (Matt 6:5–6), and Zechariah is able to celebrate its imminent fulfillment. The second stanza (vv. 76–79) focuses on the *child's* preparatory role. The whole unit is delimited by God's *visiting* (*episkeptomai*, ἐπισκέπτομαι, vv. 68, 78), a verb that may also be translated "care for" or "be concerned about" and can describe the official reception of a ruler (1 Thess 1:15–17).

The passage complements Matthew's presentation. The magi were moved by the dawn star of Balaam's oracle (Matt 2:2, alluding to Num 24:17), which also enlightened those sitting in the darkness (4:16).[263] For this denouement, Matthew links Isaiah (9:2) with Psalm 107 (v. 10), a *gezerah sheva*, the gist of which occurs in the Benedictus. The parallelism may be accidental. If the prayer is pre-Lukan, it may have influenced Matthew. But Luke may also be paying homage to the earlier evangelist. In any case, we have a significant thematic link in the two birth stories.

R: The first stanza's opening is a mosaic of the Psalter, anticipating a new exodus (*redeemed*), and echoes the finale of Hannah's prayer, which influenced the Magnificat: The Lord "will give strength to his king and

261. The traditional title is taken from the first word in the Vulgate: *Benedictus Dominus Deus Israel*, "Blessed be the Lord God of Israel."

262. Cited in Farris, "Canticles of Luke's Infancy Narrative," 100.

263. Robert Shedinger has shown convincingly that Matthew employs *gezerah sheva*, combining Isa 9:1 with Ps 107 [106 OG]:10, καθημένους ἐν σκότει καὶ σκιᾷ θανάτου, "sitting in darkness and shadow of death" ("Must the Greek Text Always Be Preferred?" 449–66).

exalt the *horn* of his anointed" or Messiah (1 Sam 2:11). The second stanza appropriates the *locus classicus* for the forerunner's ministry, "A voice cries: In the wilderness prepare the way of the Lord; make straight in the desert a highway for our God" (Isa 40:3 ESV), which will be cited more fully (Luke 3:4–6).

D: The Benedictus is traditionally recited in the morning—Lauds (Roman Catholicism) or Matins (Anglican): *Dawn will visit us from on High.* The prayer is helpful for one's daily intention, rehearsing the basic covenant obligations for God's people: (1) practicing mercy toward others, (2) remembering biblical promises, and (3) serving God. Jesus guides *our feet to the way of peace,* so that we, *the Way,* as Luke describes the church, may offer an alternative path.[264]

S: The Benedictus is Trinitarian. Zechariah is *filled with the Holy Spirit.* There is a delightful ambiguity: God *raised up a horn of salvation for us in the house of David, his child.*[265] On the one hand, *child* naturally refers to *David.* On the other, it may also refer to God's own *child.* Contextually, Luke holds together both senses (as we find in Ps 2), which allows prayer in God the Father, Son, and Holy Spirit.

Jesus is a *horn,* representing power.[266] As we shall learn with Theophilus, power is not the same reality as force. Christ will not reign by coercion, but example, unifying all people by invoking their nobility as image bearers of God. Jesus is the *dawn,* the moment before diffused sunlight becomes direct (see 2 Pet 1:19), a sacred passage around the world.

13: John's Maturation (Luke 1:80)

[80] Now the child was growing and being strengthened in spirit and was in *the wild areas* until the day of his commissioning to Israel. [Isa 40:3]

P: Luke conflates nearly thirty years, between the Baptist's adolescence and *commissioning* (*anadeixis,* ἀνάδειξις), a technical term for the public recognition of an official.[267]

R: *Spirit* (*pneuma,* πνεῦμα) refers to "the spirit of Elijah" (1:17). After predicting a drought, the prophet hides himself in the wilderness—the Wadi

264. See Acts 9:2; 19:9, 23; 24:14, 22; Belousek, *Good News,* 4–10.

265. *Child* may also be translated "servant." But the same root occurs at v. 76, which contextually refers to Zechariah's son, John.

266. See Ps 18:2; 89:17; 132:17; 148:14; Dan 7:7—8:24; 1 En. 90:6–12, 37; Test. Jos. 19.

267. BDAG, 62. Presumably, the Baptist did not go into the wilderness as a small child.

Cherith, east of the Jordan (1 Kgs 17:3). *The wild areas* fulfills the fulfillment of Isaiah's prophecy (40:3) in the Benedictus (1:76).

D: Luke offers a paradigm of spiritual formation. The word translated *child* (*paidion*, παιδίον) may refer to a prepubescent, but also anyone "open to instruction,"[268] and is closely related to *paideia* (παιδεία), training for a successful life. *Growing* (*auxanō*, αὐξάνω) refers to John's whole person, including his body.

S: *Being strengthened* (*krataioō*, κραταιόω) is in the passive voice, probably referring to the Holy Spirit's ministry. We will see the same pattern of being led by the Spirit into the wilderness with Christ (4:1). Most translations prefer the lower-case "spirit," referring to a constituent of John's person, which is appropriate and has a precedent in the Magnificat: "my spirit rejoices in God my savior" (1:47). But we should avoid a false dichotomy: the human "spirit" shares in the Holy Spirit whose ministry is to unite different persons—in this case, Elijah and John.[269] The same Spirit moves both prophets.

14: Jesus's Birth (Luke 2:1–7)

[2:1] Now it came about in those days a decree went out from Caesar Augustus—that the entire (civilized) world should be registered. [2] This registration became prominent when Quirinius was legate of Syria.

P: *Now* (*de*, δέ) transitions from the end of the Baptist's birth story. The additional *it came about in those days* allows for the temporal jump in the previous verse to his adulthood (1:80). Luke goes back in time to offer his version of the Incarnation that will also culminate in Christ's maturation (2:52). Referencing rulers was a common vehicle for marking time, but Luke is also beginning a new *synkrisis*.[270] By his own insistence, *Caesar* (63 BC–AD 14) was given the name *Augustus* ("exalted") by the Roman Senate after defeating Marc Antony and Cleopatra. Founding the Temple of *Caesar*, he added the title *Divi Filius* ("son of God") to his name. The empire grew and enjoyed relative peace under his leadership, but this required taxation.

Luke mentions a *registration* (or census) from Rome, which is fitting because his sequel, Acts, ends with Paul preaching Christ as the true son

268. BDAG, 749 (see 1 Cor 14:20).

269. It is best not to equate the human spirit with the Holy Spirit, but to speak of a union of different persons.

270. Josephus identifies the birth of his sons according to the year of an emperor's reign (*Life*). Justin probably depends on Luke when he claims: "Christ was born one hundred and fifty years ago in the time of Quirinius" (*1 Apol.* 46 [*ANF* 1:178]).

of God in that city. For this historical detail, he probably depends on Josephus, who relates a subsequent rebellion to the temple's destruction. Both mention Judas the Galilean (Acts 5:37; *J.W.* 2.117–8; *Ant.* 18.1–8), Theudas (Acts 5:36; *Ant.* 20.97), and the Egyptian (Acts 21:38; *J.W.* 2.261–3; *Ant.* 20.171). There is no other surviving census record. However, if we accept the common translation, "This was the first registration when Quirinius was governor of Syria" (ESV), then there is a chronological tension: Josephus claims Quirinius took office in AD 6 or 7 (*J.W.* 7.253; *Ant.* 18.3), whereas Luke, with Matthew, insists that Jesus was born before Herod the Great died (c. 4 BC). There are two translational solutions.[271] First, as a footnote in the English Standard Version mentions, the participial phrase ἡγεμονεύοντος τῆς Συρίας Κυρηνίου may be translated "before Quirinius was governor."[272] The adverbs "when" and "before" are not explicit in the Greek, but interpretive. This solution is not entirely satisfactory because the participle is in the present tense, which, when functioning temporally, normally describes contemporaneous action in relationship to the modified verb. Second, and more plausible, the adjective *prōtos* (πρῶτος) may attribute prominence to something.[273] This fits Luke's own storytelling because, as we noted, he alludes to the rebellion after Herod's death (Acts 5:37). He mentions *Quirinius* because it was the *legate's* responsibility to deploy the Roman legions stationed in *Syria* to quell the uprising.[274]

R: We may read this *registration* neutrally, if we forget God's disapproval of David doing the same (c. 975 BC).[275] The *(civilized) world* (*oikoumenē*, οἰκουμένη) signifies a Roman presence and firm boundaries from the "barbarians." Chester Starr refers to it as "an egotistical term inherited by imperial authors from the Hellenistic world."[276]

S: Everything ultimately belongs to God.

[3] And all were going out to be registered—each to his own city. [4] Now Joseph also went up from Galilee—from the city of Nazareth to

271. It is also possible that Luke is correcting an error in Josephus. *Antiquities* claims Herod was only fifteen years old when he came to the throne (14.158), which contradicts Josephus's own report that Herod was nearly seventy when he died (*Ant.* 17.148). He also contradicts Philo's depiction of Pilate. For more discussion, see Schwartz, *Reading the First Century*.

272. Wright, *Who Was Jesus?*, 89.

273. See Culy et al., *Luke*, 64. They follow Stephen Carlson who suggests: "This registration became most prominent when Quirinius was governing Syria."

274. *Legate* or more generally "governor." Most of the frontier districts of the Roman Empire were "imperial" provinces assigned to the *proconsular imperium* of the ruler, who sent out legates of the senatorial class to serve as governors.

275. 2 Sam 24; 1 Chr 21; but see Exod 11:7–13.

276. Starr, *History of the Ancient World*, 581.

Judea—to the city of David that is called Bethlehem, because he is from the house and ancestry of David, [5] to be registered with Mary who has been betrothed to him, who is pregnant.

P: Luke may appropriate Matthew's presentation: *Mary* is *betrothed* (*mnēsteuō*, μνηστεύω) *to Joseph* (Matt 1:18; Luke 2:5), who is of Davidic ancestry (Matt 1:20; Luke 2:4) yet she is pregnant (Matt 1:18; Luke 2:5); Jesus will be born in *Bethlehem* in *Judea* (Matt 2:1; Luke 2:4). He also answers a question: if Jesus grew up in *Nazareth*, as Matthew claims (Matt 2:23), why was he born in *Bethlehem*? Some have challenged the historicity of the answer, but two papyri from the general area and period corroborate the claim that it was necessary to return to one's *own city* for a census.[277] *Mary*, who is prone to travel (1:39–45), accompanies *Joseph* because he has agreed to a liminal marriage—between the betrothal and consummation, taking responsibility for her well-being (Matt 1:24–25). Luke also wants to portray *Joseph* and *Mary* as obedient to the *decree*—so much so that she is willing to travel pregnant (see Luke 23:29).

[6] Now it came about while they are there (that) the days for her to give birth were completed. [7] And she gave birth to her first-born son. And she wrapped him in swaddling clothes and laid him in a manger[278] because there was a not a place for them in the room (of the house).[279]

P: This would have been a remarkable inconvenience. Roman women typically gave birth seated on a special chair, with the aid of midwives. For most of human history, men generally have not participated, but Joseph probably had to assist.[280] *Swaddling clothes* were cotton strips that protected a baby from self-harm and the body's deformation.[281] The striking, unusual details around Christ's birth are consistent with Luke's suggestion that that they originate from Mary herself.

Many English translations presume there was no place for the family in "the inn." But the Greek word *kataluma* (κατάλυμα) is better translated *room*, an observation that goes back at least to 1584 when Francisco

277. British Museum papyrus 904 (AD 104) and Oxyrhynchus papyrus 255 (AD 48).

278. Jerome claims this manger was still visible in his time and consisted of a rock groove with plain clay walls in a side cave some 3 x 3 meters in size. According to an established tradition, Hadrian (in c. AD 135) made the cave a sanctuary to Adonis to eliminate its veneration by Christians.

279. Or "inn."

280. Veyne, *History of Private Life*, 9. See Luke 2:22; Exod 1:15–19.

281. Luke uses a very specific verb (*sparganoō*, σπαργανόω), a NT *hapax legomenon*. See Veyne, *History of Private Life*, 16.

Sánchez de las Brozas was reported to the Spanish Inquisition for it.[282] The typical home had two rooms—a front stable and a family living area (see Matt 5:14–15). Animals were brought in at night to protect them from the cold and theft.[283] Joseph's family probably had a home in Bethlehem, the place of their ancestry.[284] Indeed, the aim of a census was not to record a man's birthplace, but his property for taxation.[285] Because of the census, it may have been full, so that the front room stable was the most private space available. Luke uses *kataluma* one other place, and the reference is clearly to a room (22:11). This translation makes sense if Luke is using Matthew as a source because the first Gospel depicts the family living in a house (*oikia*, οἰκία) in Bethlehem for a season (2:11).

R: Luke may allude to Solomon, the son of David, who is remembered describing his birth as a common human experience:

> I also am mortal, like everyone else, a descendant of the first-formed child of earth . . . when I was born, I began to breathe the common air, and fell upon the kindred air; my first sound was a cry, as is true of all. I was nursed with care in swaddling clothes. (Wis 7:1–4 NRSV)

D: Bonaventure exhorts, "Embrace that divine manger; press your lips upon and kiss the boy's feet."[286]

S: Mary wraps Christ's body in the Incarnation (Luke 2:7); another Joseph and Nicodemus, for his burial and resurrection (John 19:40; 20:6). We held his body, and now are held by it. Despite our violence to Christ's body, human beings ultimately cared for it in birth and death. We honored him. *Lord Jesus, you felt mortality like everyone else, breathed our air, and cried like everyone else. Amen.*

15: Shepherds and Mary (Luke 2:8–20)

This unit echoes the birth of John with the shepherds functioning as witnesses (vv. 57–66). It has four movements: they receive witness (vv. 8–14) and confirmation by finding Mary, Joseph, and the baby (vv. 15–16), and then offer witness themselves (vv. 17–18); Mary becomes an eyewitness tradition bearer (vv. 19–20). The unit is also Luke's complement

282. Carlson, "Accommodations of Joseph and Mary," 326–42.

283. Bailey, *Jesus through Middle Eastern Eyes*, 28–29 (see Luke 13:10–17).

284. Bailey, "Manger and the Inn," 98–106.

285. Keener, *IVP Bible Background Commentary*, 184.

286. Bonaventure, *Soul's Journey*, 129.

to Matthew's magi guided by the angelic star (2:2, 9). Both groups of witnesses are marginal in their own way. Matthew's *angel of the Lord* makes an appearance (see Matt 1:20; 2:13) when earlier Luke mentioned Gabriel (Luke 1:19, 26).

Receiving Witness (2:8–14)

[8] And shepherds were in the same region, living outside[287] and taking turns guarding their flock by night.[288] [9] And an angel of the Lord appeared to them, and the glory of the Lord shined around them; and they became greatly afraid. [10] And the angel said to them, "Do not be afraid! For look: *I am proclaiming good news* to you of great joy that will be for all people, [11] because for you was born today[289] in the city of David a savior, who is Christ the Lord. [Isa 52:7] [12] And this is a sign for you: you will find a baby wrapped (in swaddling clothes) and lying in a manger." [13] And suddenly there was with the angel a great heavenly army, praising God and saying, [14] "Glory to God in the highest, and peace on earth in people of (his) delight."[290]

P: *And* (*kai*, καί) with *same region* closely link this scene to Christ's birth, along with the invitation to see his body (2:1–7). The unit is delimited by *glory* (vv. 9, 14), the light and heaviness of God's presence, which is reinforced by angelic involvement.[291] The *shepherds* naturally *became greatly afraid*, the *mysterium tremendum*, but are given normal biblical reassurance: *Do not be afraid!*

Luke may have been inspired by John's Gospel for the language of *sign* (*sēmeion*, σημεῖον). With the fourth Gospel's prologue, Christ's body is the *sign* or *sacramentum* of God's salvation, the *res* or reality. The *flock* was probably destined for sacrifice in the nearby temple, a foreshadowing of the cross.

The *synkrisis* becomes explicit—between "Caesar's earthly pomp and Christ's heavenly glory."[292] Rome boasted about bringing *peace* to the world (*pax romana*). They used words like *good news* and *savior*. From AD 14 to

287. Shepherds would curl up under a cloak to sleep. They kept their possessions in a skin pouch (1 Sam 17:40).

288. The *night* was divided up into watches.

289. *Today* or "this day" often signifies the present in-breaking of salvation in Luke's presentation (4:21; 5:26; 13:32–33; 19:5, 9; 23:43).

290. Some mss read "good will among people."

291. See Exod 16:7, 10: 24:17; Isa 22:24; Nah 2:20.

292. Keener, *IVP Bible Background Commentary*, 184.

180 (the death of Marcus Aurelius), the Mediterranean, with Judea-Galilee being an intermittent exception, was generally peaceful.[293] Tacitus notes there was *quies* or "quiet stability" in Judea (*Annals* 5.9). But this "peace" was maintained through brutality and primarily benefited the elite. Jews had suffered because the religious establishment in Jerusalem embraced Caesar instead of waiting for the messiah.

R: Moses was shepherding when the angel of the Lord appeared to announce the salvation of Israel from enslavement in Egypt (Exod 3:2). King David was also a shepherd (1 Sam 17:15; Ps 78:70–71).[294] They foreshadow the "good shepherd" (John 10:11). Indeed, angels appropriately announce the birth of Israel's shepherd, the *messiah*, to *shepherds*.[295] They herald a true "Prince of *peace*" (Isa 9:6), who will reconcile families (Mal 4:6) and end war between nations (Zech 9:9–12).

D: This unit contains a short yet beloved canticle, the Gloria in Excelsis, which is often read in the Christmas season. An expanded form became part of the Catholic mass. Luke may intend for the angels to proclaim, *Glory to God in the highest* . . . and for the disciples to respond, "*Blessed* is the King, *who comes in the name of the Lord*—in heaven (there is) peace and glory in the highest heaven!" (19:38).[296]

At Christ's baptism, the Father will say, "In *you* I take delight" (*en soi eudokēsa*, ἐν σοὶ εὐδόκησα 3:21); here, the angels similarly announce *peace in people of (his) delight* (*en anthrōpois eudokias*, ἐν ἀνθρώποις εὐδοκίας) in the context of Christ's body.

The shepherds first experience *glory* (*doxa*, δόξα) as a *shining around* (*perilampō*, περιλάμπω), an uncreated light the *angels* attribute to God. Many have experienced *the Lord* this way in contemplation, entering the mystery of Transfiguration, which redirects our deepest passion towards that Beauty (Symeon the New Theologian, Gregory Palamas).

S: Only Luke uses the expression *Christ the Lord* (Luke 2:11, 26; Acts 2:36), which identifies Jesus with Yahweh. His *glory* is displayed with the angels, but hidden in the *sign* of incarnation.

Finding Mary, Joseph, and the Baby (2:15–16)

[15] And it came about when the angels departed from them into heaven, the shepherds were speaking to one another, "We must go, then, to Bethlehem

293. Starr, *History of the Ancient World*, 575.

294. His part in God's salvation history is evoked (v. 11).

295. Harris, *Davidic Shepherd King*.

296. Brown, *Christ in the Gospels of the Liturgical Year*, ch. 9.

and see this word that has taken place, which the Lord made known to us!" [16] And hurrying they went and found Mary and Joseph and the baby lying in the manger.

P: The shepherds relate the *word* (*rēma*, ῥῆμα) to the sign of its fulfillment, as if it were a Scripture (and indeed Luke and the discernment of the church made it so).

D: Let us *speak to one another* to follow the immediate obedience of *the shepherds*. Revelation demands a response.

Offering Witness (2:17–18)

[17] Now after seeing (them), they made known about the word that was spoken to them about this child. [18] And all who heard marveled about what was spoken by the shepherds to them.

P: *Now* (*de*, δέ) pivots the story: the shepherds become witnesses, just as Luke has done in perpetuity by including their role. Presumably, they spoke to Joseph and Mary, but *all who heard* suggests a broader witness in the area. Ironically, shepherds may not have had the best reputation. Rabbinic literature lists them with thieves and cheats (*b. San.* 25b). They could not be admitted to court as witnesses—like the women who are the first to see the empty tomb. *To marvel* (*thaumazō*, θαυμάζω) is a fitting although incomplete (Luke 4:22; Acts 13:41) response that anticipates Christ's public ministry (Luke 9:43; 11:14) as well as the church's (Acts 2:7; 3:12). The parents will *marvel* again after they find Jesus in the temple (2:33).

D: Luke intends *shepherds* (*poimēn*, ποιμήν) literally here, but the slightly metaphorical sense of pastor also occurs in the Gospels: Jesus "saw a great crowd and was moved with compassion for them because they were *like sheep without having a shepherd*" (Mark 6:34). These shepherds actually become the first pastors in the Gospels: they receive a witness, confirm it through their own experience, and then witness to others. Too often pastors and priests sidestep the middle in their preparation, so that their witness becomes shrill and unconvincing.

Mary, the Tradition Bearer (2:19–20)

[19] Now Mary was remembering all these words, considering them in her heart. [20] And the shepherds returned, glorifying and praising God for everything that they heard and saw, just as it had been spoken to them.

P: *Now* (*de*, δέ) marks another transition: Luke reveals his source for the story, the eye-witness memory of *Mary*.

The final verse, which could be its own subunit marked by *And* (*kai*, καί), concludes the entire story (vv. 8–20). *Glorifying* is a fitting response to the *glory* that delimits the opening subunit.

D: These shepherds play no further role. They come, go, and their names are lost to history. Such is the case for most, but God gave them the same vision of glory Moses saw in the burning bush. We do not have to be great to be graced.

16: Simeon and Anna (Luke 2:21–38)

The first subunit forms a chiasm:

A Piety of Parents (2:21–24)

B Simeon's Piety (2:25–28a)

B' Simeon's Song (2:28b–32)

A' Piety of Parents (2:33–35)

Luke frames the unit by emphasizing Mary and Joseph's piety, humility, and poverty. At the center, Simeon "takes up" (*dechomai*, δέχομαι) the body of Christ (2:28a)—a verb that can also describe receiving a gift (see Phil 4:18). At the Lord's Supper, "After taking up (*dechomai*) the cup and giving thanks," Jesus said: "Take this and divide it among yourselves" (Luke 22:17). In contrast to Luke's very short account, we find the following elaboration in the *Arabic Infancy Gospel*:

> And when the time of his circumcision was come, namely, the eighth day, on which the law commanded the child to be circumcised, they circumcised him in a cave. And the old Hebrew woman took the foreskin (others say she took the navel-string), and preserved it in an alabaster-box of old oil of spikenard. And she had a son who was a druggist, to whom she said, "Take heed thou sell not this alabaster box of spikenard-ointment, although thou shouldst be offered three hundred pence for it. Now this is that alabaster-box which Mary the sinner procured, and poured forth the ointment out of it upon the head and feet of our Lord Jesus Christ, and wiped it off with the hairs of her head."[297]

There is a mythical quality to the story; the pedigree of whatever tradition stands behind it is probably unrecoverable. However, it is true to Luke's intimations of the Passion in the scene.

297. Cited in Hone, *Lost Books of the Bible*, 23.

The subsequent subunit featuring Anna (2:36–38), the female finale, reinforces these themes, like Mary's role after the shepherds (Luke 2:19–20).

Piety of Parents (2:21–24)

[21] And when *eight days* were fulfilled for him to be circumcised, his name was also called Jesus, the name called by the angel before he was conceived in the womb. [Gen 17:12]

P: The transition echoes Matthew, "She will give birth to a son, and you will call his name Jesus" (1:21), although the baby is named by the mother (see Luke 1:31), a motif in Luke's presentation (1:59). However, like Zechariah, Joseph presumably plays an active yet silent role (see v. 63).

Whoever *circumcised* Jesus is historically significant but is not mentioned. Joseph may have performed the operation. According to later rabbinic literature, the parents may have asked for something like a *brit milah* (or *bris*). Someone held Jesus, a *sandek*, and prayer were recited while a *mohel* performed the operation. The baby is named at this time, as Luke narrates.

R: When God covenanted with Abraham, he commanded, "He who is eight days old among you shall be circumcised" (Gen 17:12). Circumcision is a sign of this covenant and marks the child's entrance into it. The patriarch was promised, "kings shall come from you" (v. 6). God goes on to promise the birth of Isaac (vv. 15–27), and then, paradoxically, commands his sacrifice, although the son is ultimately spared (ch. 22).

D: Luke memorializes this event, but in Acts sides with Paul, Peter, and the decision of the Jerusalem Council to free the Nations (Gentiles) of this obligation. All people enter the new covenant through union with Christ as evidenced by the manifestation of his Spirit. In Judaism, a wife is not circumcised but partakes of the covenant through the husband. So it is between the church, the bride of Christ, and the groom. Mysteriously, we were all circumcised at this moment in Christ. As the angel of the Lord said in Matthew, "you will call his name Jesus because he will save his people from their sins" (1:21).

According to tradition, *Jesus* was *circumcised* on January 1. The event came to be seen as the first drawing of Jesus's blood. Rarely depicted in the first millennium, the circumcision of Christ became a popular subject in the tenth century, Renaissance, and Protestant periods.

S: *Lord Jesus Christ, your circumcision, if not the trauma of your birth, marks the beginning of your suffering on our behalf, your willingness to be plunged into the human condition. There is nothing small in your precious,* *unique life. Like a passive newborn, may we receive the Spirit's sanctifying work. We also remember the necessary devotion of your earthly parents, Mary and Joseph, and the faithfulness of the Jewish community that nurtured you. Amen.*

[22] And *when the days were fulfilled for their purification*, according to the Law of Moses [Lev 12:6], they brought him up to Jerusalem to present *before the Lord*, [Lev 12:7] [23] as it stands written in the Law of the Lord: *every male who opens the womb will be called holy before the Lord* [Exod 13:2, 12, 15; 12:16] [24] and to offer a sacrifice according to what has been said in the Law of the Lord: *a pair of turtledoves or two young pigeons.* [Lev 12:8 LXX]

P: The subunit itself is chiastic:

A Purification of Parents (v. 22a)

B Presentation before the Lord (v. 22b)

B' Called holy before the Lord (v. 23)

A' Sacrifice of Parents (v. 24).

The shell focuses on the parents. Luke implies Joseph assisted with the birth, so that both parents required *purification*. (Babies did not require purification.) Mary would have put her hands on the *pigeons*. Then a priest took them to the southwest corner of the temple and wrung one's neck as a sin offering and burned the other whole as a burnt offering.[298]

Jesus is *called* or acknowledged to be *holy* (*hagios*, ἅγιος), that is, committed to the *Lord*.

R: As a whole, the scene echoes Hannah giving Samuel to the tabernacle, which evoked the prayer that inspired the Magnificat (1 Sam 1:21—2:10). However, the *Law* is foregrounded, being mentioned three times. Luke employs *gezerah sheva*, citing two different yet related commands. *Every male who opens the womb will be called holy before the Lord* (πᾶν ἄρσεν διανοῖγον μήτραν ἅγιον τῷ κυρίῳ κληθήσεται) is probably a mixed citation from the Greek translation of Exodus.[299] In context, the command evokes the exodus when God killed all the first-born males in Egypt, and now, recontextualized, anticipates God the Father sacrificing his only Son, as Simeon's prophecy will imply. However, the language also mystically anticipates our salvation: Jesus *opens the womb* of eternal life, with Mary representing the church. The split citation, forming *inclusio* around

298. Keener, *IVP Bible Background Commentary*, 186.

299. See Exod 13:2 (διανοῖγον πᾶσαν μήτραν), 12 (πᾶν διανοῖγον μήτραν . . . ἁγιάσεις τῷ κυρίῳ), 15 (πᾶν διανοῖγον μήτραν, τὰ ἀρσενικά); and 12:16 (κληθήσεται ἁγία).

the subunit, is from a section in Leviticus on purification after childbirth (12:1–8). The mother was ritually unclean for seven days (v. 2); after her son's circumcision, she "shall continue for thirty-three days in the blood of her purifying" (v. 4). Then she can approach the sanctuary, and would normally offer a one-year-old lamb for a burnt offering and a pigeon or a turtle dove for a sin offering (v. 6). But if the mother's family cannot afford a lamb, *a pair of turtledoves or two young pigeons* could be used (v. 8).[300] By fusing Exodus and Leviticus together, Luke sets the stage for seeing the cross as atonement for sin and new birth.

D: Later apocryphal gospels raise the social status of the family.[301] But Luke wants the reader to know that Jesus was born into a poor family, a condition that increases his solidarity with most human beings. Clare of Assisi encourages us to see "the Lord who was poor as he lay in the crib, poor as he lived in the world, who remained naked on the cross."[302] Jesus will bless the poor and warn the wealthy (Luke 6:20–26). At the end of his life, he will storm the temple and confront those who exploit the poor through these sacrifices (Mark 11:15).

S: In this case, *the Lord* refers to God the Father. Jesus was born into the hands of his earthly father, Joseph, who needed *purification* along with his mother, Mary, but ultimately fell into the hands of his heavenly Father, *the Lord*, who intends to catch many other sons and daughters after his firstborn Son.

Simeon's Piety (2:25–28a)

[25] And look: there was a man in Jerusalem whose name was Simeon. And this man was righteous and God-fearing, looking[303] for *the comforting* of Israel. [Isa 40:1] And the Holy Spirit was upon him. [26] And it was disclosed to him by the Holy Spirit [that] he would not see death before he should see the Christ of the Lord. [27] And he came in the Spirit into the temple. And when the parents of the child Jesus entered to do the things accustomed by the Law for him, [28] he himself also took him up into (his) arms.

P: *And look* (*Kai idou,* Καὶ ἰδοὺ) marks a transition. We focus on *Simeon* who functions like Zechariah for the Baptist (Luke 1:69–77). (It is

300. The Septuagint translates "two young pigeons" (δύο νεοσσοὺς περιστερῶν).

301. See, e.g., Proto-Gospel of James 1.

302. Clare of Assisi, *Complete Works,* 230.

303. *Looking for* or "waiting" (*prosdechomai,* προσδέχομαι). Luke uses this verb more than any other NT writer (Luke 2:25, 38; 12:36; 15:2; 23:51; Acts 23:21; 24:15). For a similar concept, see 1 Thess 1:10 and Phil 2:29, which use the same verb.

striking how small Joseph's role is in Luke's presentation.) *The Proto-Gospel of James* claims *Simeon* succeeds Zechariah as chief priest (24.4), but Luke relates only that he is a *righteous and God-fearing man.*[304] (*Simeon* was a very common name.)

The *Holy Spirit* gave *Simeon* a personal revelation. He is allowed to see *the child* as *the Christ* or Messiah. A similar enlightenment takes place for disciples at the Transfiguration and after the resurrection (Luke 24:16, 31).

R: *Simeon* yearns *for the comforting of Israel*, a motif in Isaiah.[305] The prophet looks forward to the end of exile and a Davidic messiah.

D: At least some Jews believed prophecy had ceased after Malachi, so that its renewal would excite (1 Macc 4:46). However, before jumping to an adult Baptist, the new prophet, Luke celebrates *Simeon* as a prefiguring of Pentecost when "old men shall dream dreams" (Acts 2:17). Although further along in salvation history, we still ache for *the comforting of God's people* and to see *the Christ* face to face, *to hold him* in our *arms*. This comforting is a final, global event, and one that requires patience for the full unfolding of God's will, and yet God offers, even now, *personally redemptive moments* in this fallen world. Hope is not eternally deferred.

If we place this scene in the context of grace, it can be said that Simeon's piety did not earn God's response, but readied him for the *Spirit's* work. He was undistracted and listening. God is responsive to Simeon's desire, but they were also unified in will. The old man was *looking for the comforting of Israel* (*paraklēsin tou Israēl*, παράκλησιν τοῦ Ἰσραήλ); the *Holy Spirit* is "the Paraclete" or "Comforter" (*paraklētos*, παράκλητος, John 14:16).

S: The scene is Trinitarian, but *the Holy Spirit* is foregrounded—mentioned explicitly three times in three ministries: *the Spirit* comes, discloses, and accompanies. The first action is repeated at *Christ's* baptism (Luke 3:22), which is shared with all believers, who then enjoy *the Spirit's* discernment and presence.

Nunc Dimittus (2:28b–32)

[28b] And he blessed God and said: [29] "Now you are releasing your servant, Master, according to your *word* in peace. [Isa 40:8] [30] For my eyes saw your salvation [31] that you prepared before (the face of) all the

304. *God-fearing* (*eulabēs*, εὐλαβής) is appropriated only by Luke in the New Testament (see Acts 2:5; 8:2; 22:12; but see Mic 7:7), and is probably an evaluation of a person's character vis-à-vis the Law. Simeon's righteousness also links him to Zechariah and Elizabeth.

305. See Isa 40:1; 49:13; 51:3; 52:9; 61:2; 66:13.

peoples, [32] a light for the revelation of the peoples and *glory* of your people Israel." [Isa 40:5][306]

P: The Nunc Dimittus is the last of the three Advent songs after the Magnificat (1:46–55) and the Benedictus (1:67–79). Simeon adapts the liturgy of the synagogue, as we find in the early church: "*Blessed* be the God and Father of our Lord Jesus Christ" (2 Cor 1:3; Eph 1:3; 1 Pet 1:3). The song takes the form of a benediction (*berakah* in Hebrew) with three couplets (or bicola).[307] The first couplet (v. 29) declares his manumission from slavery. He is released *in peace*, a link with the Benedictus (1:79) and angelic announcement (2:14). The second couplet (vv. 30–31) offers the reason for peace: *For my eyes saw your salvation*. Instead of saying, "I saw," Simeon uses pleonasm, *my eyes saw*, to emphasize the sensory experiences. To see something with one's *own eyes* is the strongest confirmation. (It is partly for this reason that Jesus will heal the blind.) Although Simeon expresses personal gratitude, he recognizes the universal importance of God's *salvation*. The third couplet describes this salvation: *the peoples* (Gentiles) will have an opportunity to know God, as Israel did, through a divine rescue. The preposition *for* (*eis*, εἰς) conveys purpose and leaves open the option of rejecting the gospel, as Luke will narrate in his sequel. God also provided a Messiah to *Israel* to exchange their shame for *glory*.

R: After the first announcement of *comfort* in Isaiah (40:1), the ministry of the Baptist is foretold (vv. 3–5), a passage that is cited in the next chapter (Luke 3:4–6), and then we find this meditation on life's brevity:

> All flesh is grass, and all its beauty is like the flower of the field. The grass withers, the flower fades when the breath of the Lord blows on it; surely the people are grass. The grass withers, the flower fades, but the word (*rēma*, ῥῆμα) of our God will stand forever. (Isa 40:6–8 ESV)

Simeon feels mortality in his bones, and yet can depart *in peace according to your word* (*rēma*). He echoes Israel after being reunited with his lost son Joseph, "Now let me die, since I have seen your face" (Gen 46:30 ESV; see also Tob 11:9).

D: Since the fifth century, the Nunc Dimittis ("Now as you dismiss") has been sung or recited in the evening before sleep, reflecting "the desired state of mind of every person approaching death, including the small death that is symbolized every time we close our eyes and fall asleep."[308] We

306. See Luke 3:6; 52:10.

307. DelHousaye, *Engaging Ephesians*, 14–15; 1 Macc 4:30–33.

308. Bulson, *Preach What You Believe*, 27. At least since the fourth century, the Nunc Dimittis was chanted at Cathedral Vespers in the East. We read in the *Life of*

hear an echo in, "*Now I* lay me down to sleep . . ." As Luke will emphasize, *discipleship is a daily preparation for death*, a kind of exposure therapy (Luke 9:23). Most people deal with the inevitability of death through avoidance, which gradually separates them from their hearts.[309] It is healthier to face our deepest fear, but in manageable doses.

Furthermore, Simeon faces death *in peace* because he is a *servant* or "slave" (*doulos*, δοῦλος) and God is *Master* (*despotēs*, δεσπότης). In Roman culture, slaves would report to their masters in the morning to hear their orders; obedience allowed them to retire peacefully in the evening. However, I avoided the translation "slave" because the English does not fully capture the signified of *doulos* here. God is not enslaving but *releasing* Simeon. Jesus uses the same verb (*apoluō*, ἀπολύω) to encourage a disabled "daughter of Abraham": "Woman you are released (*apoluō*)" (Luke 13:12). There were no slaves in the Garden, and, by the redemption wrought though the baby in his hands, Simeon is *released* to where we all ultimately belong.

Simeon takes up the body of Christ at the beginning of the Gospel; Joseph and Nicodemus will take it down at the end (John 19:38–39); and we take it up in Communion. It is therefore entirely fitting that many liturgies cite the Nunc Dimittis at this time.

Simeon's vision is a win-win—a gain for Israel and the rest of the world, which is also Luke's heart. The gospel is not a zero-sum game because there is no scarcity in God or in the Garden. As God's Word, it will come true (see Rom 9–11).

S: *Father, we are your servants and you, our Master. Lord Jesus, you are the light of the Gentiles and the glory of Israel. Come, Holy Spirit, keep us faithful until our release. Amen.*

Piety of Parents (2:33–35)

[33] And his father and mother were marveling over what was spoken about him. [34] And Simeon blessed them and said to Mary, his mother, "Look, this (child) is set for the fall and rise of many in Israel and for a sign opposed—[35] but also a sword will pierce through your own soul—so that the intentions of many hearts might be revealed."

Mary of Egypt (c. 344–c. 421): "And having received the life-giving sacraments, she raised her hands to heaven, sighed with tears in her eyes and cried aloud" the prayer (cited in Krueger, "Scripture and Liturgy," 131. The prayer is in Rites I and II in the *Book of Common Prayer*, and is a regular part of Compline in the Roman Catholic Church.

309. Menzies et al., *Curing the Dread of Death*, 171.

P: After blessing God, Simeon now *blesses* Mary and Joseph. Anticipating Acts, the Spirit enables *Simeon* to prophesy. In this case, he is given an *interpersonal revelation* or oracle, which anticipates human resistance and rejection in the story (see 5:22; 6:8; 7:39; 11:17). Luke finally allows foreboding into the narrative. With the shepherds, the *sign* proved God's favor; here, its *opposition*.

D: If we read Matthew and Luke together, Joseph's greatest test came at the beginning; Mary's would come later: *a sword will pierce through your own soul.* Mary was not a martyr, but she suffered greatly watching her son crucified, a motif Luke may have taken from John (19:25–27). Yet she had subordinated her *soul* to God's will (1:46).

Simeon is also worthy of emulation as a *vehicle of blessing*. Instead of competing with other disciples or trying to control circumstances, may we joyfully serve until our release.

S: Mary's soul is pierced with her Son's side at the cross (John 19:31–37).

Anna (2:36–38)

[36] And Anna was a prophet, daughter of Phanuel, from the tribe of Asher. She was advanced in many days, having lived with her husband seven years from her virginity, [37] and she (lived as) a widow until she was eighty-four—(concerning) which she did not depart from the temple, worshiping with fasts and prayers night and day. [38] And at that hour, having come up, she was giving thanks to God and speaking about him[310] to all who were looking for the redemption of Jerusalem.

P: *And* (*kai*, καί) marks a continuation in the story. Luke enjoys juxtaposing male and female characters.[311] He may also evoke the truthfulness of twofold testimony (Deut 19:15). *Anna* (or "Hannah" if we follow the rough breathing mark in the modern Greek text) is remarkable in several ways. Unlike Simeon as well as Mary and Elizabeth, who prophecy (1:42, 46–55), she is given a title, *prophet* (*prophētis*, προφῆτις), a kind of formality anticipating women prophets in the early church (Acts 2:17; 21:9–10).[312] Also, aged *widows* like herself have a unique role in the church (Acts 6:1; 9:41; 1 Tim 5:3–16). She is from *Asher*, one of the ten "lost" tribes of Israel.

310. The antecedent of *him* is presumably Jesus.

311. See, e.g., Luke 7:11–17; 8:40–56; 15:3–7; Acts 5:1–11.

312. The noun προφῆτις is feminine, but BDAG recommends the same gloss as the masculine προφήτης, *prophet*. It occurs once more in the NT referring to a certain "Jezebel" (Rev 2:20). For more discussion, see DelHousaye, "Who are the Women Prophets?," 17.

Anna's name is nearly the same spelling as "Annas" (or "Hannas"), who will be briefly mentioned (3:2). Although not a priest or a man, she does what Annas, the male high priest, should have done.[313]

R: *Anna's* father *Phanuel* ("face of God") was presumably named after the biblical site ("Penuel"), an ancient sanctuary at a crossing of the lower Jaboc where Jacob wrestled with God (Gen 32:24–32) and Jeroboam, the first king of the ten northern tribes of Israel, fortified his capital (1 Kgs 12:25). *The redemption of Jerusalem* or Israel (see 2:25; 23:51) signifies God's decisive act to save his people (Isa 40:9; 52:9; 63:4), the focus of 1 Maccabees, but what of their internal rebellion and divisions?

D: *Anna* echoes in many ways Judith, a heroine in the Apocrypha. Both women are widows who regularly fasted and prayed (Jdt 8:2, 6, 31). The message in both stories is that God often works in ways that transcend cultural expectations. Anna's "rule of life" is exemplary, as Cyprian of Carthage (c. 200–258) exhorts: "Let not us, then, who are in Christ—that is, always in the lights—cease from praying even during night. Thus the widow Anna, without intermission praying and watching, persevered in deserving well of God, as it is written in the Gospel: 'She departed not,' it says, 'from the temple, serving with fastings and prayers night and day'" (*Dom. or.* 36).[314]

S: *Lord, we fast and pray day and night for the completion of our redemption. Protect our hearts from laziness and cynicism. Amen.*

17: Nazareth (Luke 2:39)

[39] And when they completed *all* the things *according to the Law* of the Lord, they returned to Galilee, to their own city, Nazareth. [Josh 1:7]

P: Luke comes full circle—back to *Nazareth* (1:26). Despite the different emphases, particularly the links Matthew makes between Jesus and Moses, the two evangelists end their birth narratives in the same way (Matt 2:23).[315]

The summation, *when they completed* (*teleō*, τελέω) *all the things according to the Law*, a motif in Luke's presentation (2:23, 24), emphasizes Mary and Joseph's piety. Jesus will cry out the same verb on the cross: "It has been completed (*teleō*, τελέω)!" (John 19:30). Total obedience—*all the things*—to *the Law* characterizes the passive beginning and active ending of Christ's life. This emphasis may have served apologetics, refuting criticisms

313. Although not stated, she may have been supported by the temple for her prayers—a practice taken up by the church (Acts 6:1–7).

314. Cited in Johnson, *Sacraments and Worship*, 349.

315. D adds Matthew's mysterious citation here.

of Christ's pedigree, but we find collaboration in Paul's early (c. AD 50) witness: "when the fullness of the time came, God sent out set his Son, after being born from a woman, after being born under (the authority of) *the Law*, that he might redeem those who are under the (curse of the) *Law*, that we may receive adoption as sons" (Gal 4:4–5).

R: Perhaps surprisingly, the phrase *according to the Law* occurs for the first time in Scripture at the beginning of Joshua, after the Pentateuch, when *the Lord* says to the new leader: "Only be strong and very courageous, being careful to do *according to all the law* that Moses my servant commanded you" (1:7).[316] The successful settlement of the Promised Land required total obedience, which, as the story progresses, sadly did not happen—until it was repeated and completed by Christ.

D: In Christ, *the Lord*, we are invited *to complete all things according to the Law*: "For the whole Law has been fulfilled by one commandment, in *You shall love your neighbor as yourself*" (Gal 5:14, citing Lev 19:18; see John 13:1).

S: *Lord, we cherish the Law because it belongs to you, to be used according to your will. May we never exploit the power of your word for selfish gain but live humbly by its truths. May every Nation and every citizen come into a loving relationship with you and one another. Amen.*

18: My Father's House (Luke 2:40–52)

[40] Now the child was growing and becoming strong, being filled with wisdom. And God's grace was upon him.

P: The summation echoes the final word on the Baptist before his public ministry, "Now the child was growing and becoming strong in Spirit and was in the wild areas until the day of his manifestation to Israel" (1:80); Luke may withhold mentioning the Spirit until Christ's baptism (Luke 3:22), although *God's grace was upon him* is probably synonymous.

[41] And his parents[317] would journey[318] every year to Jerusalem for the feast of Passover. [42] And when he became twelve years, they were going up according to the custom of the feast. [43] And when the days

316. Rahlfs text reads "practice according to (what) Moses commanded you" (ποιεῖν καθότι ἐνετείλατό σοι Μωυσῆς). The Greek is probably a relatively free translation of the Hebrew. The MT explicitly reads "all the Law" (כְּכָל־הַתּוֹרָה).

317. A few mss read "Both Joseph and Mary."

318. *Would journey*: The imperfect tense form may function iteratively, conveying a repetitive action.

were completed,[319] while they were returning, the boy Jesus remained in Jerusalem. And his parents did not know it. [44] But having thought he was among the company, they went a day's journey. And they were searching for him among the relatives and the acquaintances. [45] And not finding (him), they returned to Jerusalem, seeking him.[320] [46] And it came about that after three days they found him in the temple, sitting in the middle of the teachers and listening to them and questioning them. [47] Now all who were listening to him were amazed by his understanding and his answers. [48] And having seen him, they were dumfounded. And his mother said to him, "Child, why did you treat us this way? Look, your father and I, being greatly distressed, were seeking you." [49] And he said to them: "How is it that you were seeking me? Did you not know that it is necessary for me to be in the (rooms) of my Father?" [50] And *they* did not understand the word that he spoke to them. [51] And he went down with them and came to Nazareth and was submitting to them. And his mother was remembering all these words in her heart.

P: Mary provides this tradition—*remembering all these words in her heart*. Like the rest of the birth narrative, it is told from her perspective. The ordeal would have been strikingly memorable. The family was separated for a total of five *days*. If the *company* passed through Samaria, the journey between Galilee and *Jerusalem* took three days. Including *Passover* and week-long feast of Unleavened Bread, Joseph lost half a month of livelihood. There would also be the stress of traveling alone in a dangerous region.

This story marks the transition between the passive and active participation of Jesus. The "child Jesus" (*paidion*, παιδίον), at an earlier stage in development (2:27), has become the *boy Jesus* (*pais*, παῖς). Mary speaks, but he also speaks; he acts independently and *submits*. *Passover* will not be mentioned again until Passion Week (22:1, 7, 8, 11, 13, 15).[321] The end shadowing the beginning, the informed reader sees a soon-to-be-slaughtered child (see Luke 2:35). At this stage, he is welcome *in the temple* because he is not fully matured into God's call to repentance.

Jews felt especially close to the one true God in the temple and were sensitive to idolatry. *The feast of Passover*, the celebration of Israel's redemption from slavery in Egypt, was especially volatile when the city was overrun by pilgrims. Around the time of Herod's death, two famous teachers, Judas and Matthias, attracted young disciples and encouraged them to tear down

319. The week-long Feast of Unleavened Bread immediately followed the observance of Passover (Luke 22:1).

320. Presumably, the clan moved on, putting Jesus's family in a precarious situation.

321. *Three days* mirrors the separation of death between Jesus and his spiritual family (see Luke 8:21; Matt 12:40).

a golden eagle the king had erected in the temple, promising eternal life for their martyrdom (Josephus, *J.W.* 1.648). Herod burned them alive (654). Pilate will attack Galilean pilgrims (Luke 13:1). Although we cannot know, Jesus may have sat at Hillel's feet (d. c. 10 AD), the father of rabbinic Judaism. Luke explicitly mentions the name of Paul's rabbi, Gamaliel, who was Hillel's son or grandson (Acts 5:34–40; 22:3). Simeon ben Gamaliel, his son, will become a leader in the rebellion against Rome.[322] Hillel is most famously remembered for his summation of the Law: "What is hateful to you, do not to your neighbor: that is the whole Torah, while the rest is commentary thereof; go and learn it" (*b. Šabb.* 31a). As an adult, Jesus accepts this reading but goes further, encouraging the initiation of love even for enemies (Luke 10:25–37; Matt 7:12). The *boy Jesus listens and questions*. Josephus makes a similar claim about himself:

> While still a mere boy, about fourteen years old, I won universal applause for my love of letters; insomuch that the chief priests and the leading men of the city used constantly to come to me for precise information on some particular in our ordinances.[323]

Luke's anecdote may have been partially inspired by the historian. The matter of historicity may be approached two ways: the motif of a child prodigy may be fictitious in both accounts or, granting hyperbole to Josephus ("I won universal applause"), it was nevertheless common for older teachers to train younger men in Jerusalem. The accounts resemble what will become the Bar Mitzvah (Aramaic "son of the Law"), a rite of passage for Jewish males who have turned thirteen and must now bear their own responsibility for covenant faithfulness before God.[324] The relational dynamic between *Jesus* and *his parents* has this feel, although they are unprepared for the shift.

R: As expected, Luke continues to recapitulate Samuel and his family. Elkanah's household went every year to offer sacrifice, which could refer to *Passover* (1 Sam 1:21).[325] The typology works at the level of dramatic irony: like Hannah, Mary will leave her son in God's house but unwittingly (1 Sam 1:22).

D: This is the only reliable tradition we have about Jesus's adolescence. (Luke offers nothing of John's.) The apocryphal gospels offer several

322. Josephus, *J.W.* 6.114; *Life*, 191–192.

323. Josephus, *Life* 9 (Thackeray, LCL).

324. Evidence is lacking for the ritual in the first century, which takes on clearer definition in the Middle Ages, but there may have been something akin to it at the time of Christ.

325. The text is not specific and may refer to the feast of Tabernacles.

stories.[326] The eighteen years between this event and his baptism have been called the "lost," "silent," or "missing years." Some claim he visited India to study Buddhism. There are many superficial analogies between the two approaches to reality but some massive differences. Arthurian legend has him in Britain. The evidence for these scenarios, while theoretically possible, is weak. Jesus presumably grew up in *Nazareth*, working alongside his father and brothers, until his full maturation (see 1:80).

The story is morally complex. On the one hand, Jesus *submits* to *his parents*. He is surprised by their consternation. He appears humbler than Josephus.[327] *The Infancy Gospel of Thomas*, which re-presents this story (19), has Jesus belittle and even harm other teachers (6–8, 14–15). On the other, parents of adolescents can relate to Mary's frustration: *"Child, why did you treat us this way? Look, your father and I, being greatly distressed, were seeking you."* His behavior could be seen as insensitive, if not disrespectful. How could *My Father* not sting Joseph? As an adult, Jesus will require hatred for parents as a condition for becoming his disciple (Luke 14:26). If we allow complexity, the *yin* of the passage is that Jesus works the edges of his social world but short of anarchy: he *listens* and *submits*. The *yang* anticipates a Messiah who will flip the script, who cannot be controlled because of his supreme devotion to the Father's will: he *questions* and *distresses*.

The unit's finale may be taught as exemplary to young people. Jesus shows wisdom and maturity by listening before speaking and submitting to the authority of his parents (James 1:19). We find the paradigm in Antony of Egypt's development:

> Of course he accompanied his parents to the Lord's house, and as a child he was not frivolous, nor as a youth did he grow contemptuous; rather, he was obedient to his mother and father, and paying attention to the readings, he carefully took to heart what was profitable in them.[328]

But parents of Christian children must also surrender that responsibility for control to God's calling in their life, which may not parallel their will. It was extremely difficult for Thomas Aquinas's privileged family to accept

326. Irenaeus claims gnostics found significance in this unit: "The production, again, of the Duodecad of the Eons is indicated by the fact that the Lord was twelve years of age when he disputed with the teachers of the Law" (*Haer.* 3.2 [*ANF* 1:415]). A form of this story also occurs in the Infancy Gospel of Thomas 19.

327. In partial defense of Josephus, boasting was accepted and expected in ancient rhetoric. The historian is also defending himself from opponents.

328. Athanasius, *Life of Antony*, 30.

his call to the Dominican order. Francis of Assisi did not match the expectations of his father and famously walked out naked.

S: Readers enjoy the dramatic irony of Jesus already knowing more than the religious leaders because of his special relationship with the *Father*. "The fear of the LORD is the beginning of knowledge" (Prov 1:7 ESV). Jesus is not impressed by the power and beauty of the temple (see Mark 13:2). The story anticipates his adult penchant for *anachōrēsis*, departure to be alone with God. Time stood still for Jesus in the temple, seemingly oblivious to the passing *days*. This is the Triune gift to everyone in Christ—to know God as loving *Father* and gracious *Spirit*.

19: Jesus's Maturation (Luke 2:52)

[52] And Jesus was advancing [in this][329] wisdom and in stature and in grace with God and before people.

P: This summation completes an *inclusio*, "the child was growing and becoming strong, being filled with wisdom. And God's grace was upon him" (2:40), but also moves the story forward with the opening conjunction *And* (*kai*, καί) and accounts for nearly eighteen years of Christ's life—from twelve to around thirty (3:23). Unlike the story about the adolescent Jesus in the temple (2:41–51), either nothing was available to Luke or viewed as significant enough to include.

The verb translated *advancing* (*prokoptō*, προκόπτω) signifies "moving forward to an improved state."[330] Paul uses *prokoptō* to describe his Pharisaic training (Gal 1:14), but Luke emphasizes that Jesus was not formally educated in Jerusalem (see John 7:15; Acts 4:13); his knowledge of *God* as Father was personal, the highest form of *wisdom* (*sophia*, σοφία). By contrast, Luke describes Zacchaeus, a tax collector, as "small in *stature*" (τῇ ἡλικίᾳ μικρὸς), which may refer both to his physical height and reputation in the community. With the opening of the *inclusio*, *grace* signifies "favor" (so ESV).

R: This last of three maturity summations (1:80; 2:40) is the closest to the biblical archetype: "Now the boy Samuel continued to grow both in stature and in favor with the Lord and also with man" (1 Sam 2:26 ESV). In context, the author presents Samuel as God's alternative to Eli's immoral, blasphemous sons, which anticipates "the high priesthood of Annas and

329. If we follow ℵ, *wisdom* (σοφία) is arthrous and probably refers to the first occurrence of the substantive in Luke—at the beginning of the unit (2:40).

330. BDAG, 871.

Caiaphas" in the next unit (3:2). Luke has appropriated the Samuel origin story throughout the birth narrative.

Earlier leaders of God's people failed because of lapses in *wisdom*. Moses acted foolishly—just for a moment!—and was refused entrance into the Promised Land (Num 20:9–13; Deut 1:37; 3:25–26; 4:21). David became idle; his kingdom was never the same.

D: Paul warns against appointing elders who are new believers (1 Tim 3:6). If Jesus underwent this season of preparation, which happened to coincide with his physical maturation, so should disciples. *Wisdom* is time's effect on a yielding soul. There may be a long season of learning ahead of us.

Those in Christ are "acceptable to God and approved by people" (Rom 14:18).

S: *Father, in Christ, may we grow in wisdom, stature, and favor before you and our communities. Amen.*

Summation

We have taken a close look at the two canonical birth stories, noting similarities and differences. Luke focuses on Mary who may be his primary witness; Matthew, Joseph. Luke provides three prayers, whereas Matthew offers biblical citations. Luke features shepherds; Matthew, magi.

Despite differences, both accounts share common themes. Luke ties Jesus to John the Baptist, who is related maternally (1:36), the most unique element of his presentation. Like Mark, Matthew withholds discussing John until Christ's baptism and introduces conflict almost immediately. Herod the Great is pure villain—killing innocent babies. The most unique element of his presentation, the tragedy establishes Jesus as the antitype of Moses. Luke has no interest in telling this story; his conflict is more mundane: a righteous yet infertile couple. But if we look carefully, *both crises express the suffering of God's people.* Zechariah, Elizabeth, and Joseph are "righteous" (Matt 1:16; Luke 1:6). In both, there is a foreshadowing of the Passion. Herod kills children, and Zechariah is finally given a son who will tragically die (Luke 1:80; 3:19–20; Matt 14:3–12 par.). Both end with the family in Nazareth, the only place where the birth narratives overlap (Matt 2:22–23; Luke 2:39–40).

Matthew and Luke celebrate the fulfillment of God's promises in Jesus Christ, emphasizing his relationship to David (Matt 1:1, 20; Luke 1:32–33, 69). Anticipating new creation, they presume the virginal conception (Matt 1:18, 23; Luke 1:34–35). The *adoration of the infant Jesus* by the magi and shepherds is similar yet different (Matt 2:1–12; Luke

2:8–20). We are also struck by the supremacy of Christ. Moses and John are faithful, but Jesus is supreme.

Christians have been retelling these stories for over 2,000 years—in the west, usually during Advent ("coming"). The church united, paraphrased, and expanded the contributions of Matthew and Luke into the "Christmas story" or "Nativity."[331] The *res gestae*, the things that had taken place, became *res liturgicae*, the things enacted in the liturgy. Leo the Great (c. 400–461) writes:

> Today's festival renews for us the holy childhood of Jesus born of the Virgin Mary, and in adoring the birth of our Savior, we find that we are celebrating the commencement of our own life. For the birth of Christ is the source of life for the Christian people, and the birthday of the head is the birthday of the body.[332]

Christmas celebrates the incarnation or the beginning of our salvation in Christ. The great mystery of the Incarnation allowed the Son to identify completely with humanity without losing his deity, the hypostatic union. Matthew emphasizes his identification with an exiled people; Luke, the poor and oppressed. Francis of Assisi, who gave Christendom the nativity scene, invites our identification with him. Union with Christ, the central mystery of our faith, allows us to lead a fully human and spiritual life. We identify with one another's fragility and the ultimate goodness and power of God's will.

Jews similarly recite the *Haggadah*, a retelling of the exodus from Egypt at each Passover (Seder service). Matthew relates this practice to the exodus of the infant Jesus—"*Out of Egypt, I called my son.*"—foreshadowing the redemption of the cross, refreshing Passover. Meditating on this truth, we may elevate our hearts, minds, and actions. We step outside the everyday. Our Fathers wisely had us focus on Christ's birth in a season of death (winter) and his death in a season of life (spring). Disciples are always living and dying with Jesus.

Before moving on, we might pause and visualize the single cell that would become Christ's body. The Spirit comes upon Mary's egg, creatively acting on matter.[333] Among trillions of eggs, too small to see, one opens new creation. All that is mortally fragile may, in Christ, find life.

331. The Vulgate supplies the title *De nativitate Iesu* from which the Anglicized "Nativity of Jesus" is derived.

332. *Sermon* 26.2 (cited in Wilken, *Spirit of Early Christian Thought*, 44).

333. Barrett, *Holy Spirit*, 15.

4

Baptism

In chapter three, we learned some of the circumstances of Jesus's birth and its significance. Luke offers one incident from his youth—staying back at the temple (2:41–52). Otherwise, the Gospels relate nothing more until Jesus is about thirty, the age of maturation (Luke 3:23). They all begin his public ministry with the Baptist. John anticipated this transition in his opening (1:6–8, 15–18), and Luke develops the comparison: The Baptist is to Jesus as Samuel is to David. Matthew has John and Jesus make the same proclamation: "Repent! For the kingdom of the heavens has come near" (3:2; 4:17).

John the Baptist

Within the context of Second Temple Judaism, an academic designation for Jewish faith and practice between the return from exile and the destruction of Herod's temple (AD 70), the Baptist may be viewed as an independent reformer and "holy man devoted to God alone."[1]

As a young man, Josephus claims he left the Sadducees, Pharisees, and Essenes in Jerusalem to study with a certain Bannus, who lived in the wilderness, wore clothing made from trees, ate whatever "grew of themselves," and immersed regularly (*Life* 11).[2] The Baptist followed a similar way of life (Matt 9:14; John 1:35) and attracted disciples, although there is no evidence that Bannus baptized others or had a prophetic message for the people.

1. See Lupieri, "'Law and the Prophets were until John,'" 49–56. The quotation is from Keener, *Spirit in the Gospels and Acts*, 52.

2. Steve Mason finds Josephus's description stereotypical (*Josephus and the New Testament*, 39–41, 195, 204). Joan Taylor claims Bannus offers the closest parallel to John's way of life (*The Immerser*, 34).

To our knowledge John is the only prophet who physically immersed other people.[3] Josephus uses this unique practice to distinguish him from others with the same common name. The Synoptics also refer to John as "the Baptist" (*ho baptistēs*, ὁ βαπτιστὴς).[4] Yet the practice of self-immersion was common.

Immersion

Immersion or "baptism" before Christianity primarily signified the use of water for ritual purification (John 3:25).[5] It is grounded in the premise that a state of purity (*tohorah*) leads to holiness, a direct encounter with God, whereas impurity (*tum'ah*) threatens that union.[6] In Hebrew Scripture, the priesthood is tasked with the maintenance of purity: "They shall teach my people the difference between the holy and the common, and show them how to distinguish between the unclean and the clean" (Ezek 44:23 ESV).

The priests and their immediate families immersed daily to partake of the holy food tithed to the temple. The more zealous religious groups—the Essenes and probably the Pharisees—also immersed daily to offer holy prayers. Perhaps the average Judean-Galilean Jew immersed three or four times a month, based on sexual habits, menstruation cycles, and interaction with unclean liquids and people.

There were degrees of impurity. The greatest was sin—a violation of God's law and therefore a rupture or wound in nature—which required repentance and sacrifice.[7] But other manifestations, like sexual discharges and menstruation, followed the course of nature and were not inherently sinful.[8] Bodily purification was sufficient.

3. Robert Webb notes: "All evidence in Second Temple Judaism points to Jewish ritual bathing practices being self-administered" (Webb, "John the Baptist," 189). Elisha commands Naaman to immerse himself (2 Kgs 5:10).

4. Matt 3:1; 11:11; Mark 6:25; 8:28; Luke 7:20, 33.

5. Baptism can also function as a water-rite for the purpose of establishing a relationship with God. In the cult of Isis, membership was secured by individual baptism, which removed one's sins (Starr, *History of the Ancient World*, 605).

6. Purity is "a status, achieved by both moral integrity and ritual purification, which is required of Israel in order for God's holiness to reside among and protect them" (Harrington, *Purity Texts*, 8). David deSilva observes: "Pollution is dangerous in the presence of a holy God. It disqualifies the person from entering that presence and fellowship and, should he or she be foolish enough to stand before the holy God in an unclean state, threatens obliteration. It entails the loss of privilege (or absence of privilege) and hence is a dishonorable condition" (*Honor, Patronage, Kinship and Purity*, 248).

7. Harrington, *Purity Texts*, 10.

8. See Klawans, "Moral and Ritual Purity," 266–84.

Ritual purification, which has been analyzed across diverse cultures, involves three phases. First, the unclean person is *separated* from the population in a symbolic or physical way. Second, they enter a phase of *liminality*—"an in-between state in which they neither belong to their former status nor have yet entered into their new status." Finally, the person enters into a *clean* condition, often marked by some *rite of aggregation*, such as immersion.[9] The member is reunified with the community.

Miqveh

Jews often used a *miqveh*, a hewn pool with steps like a baptismal, for this rite when running or "living" water was otherwise inaccessible.[10] They were filled directly by rain or its collection from a cistern. The average *miqveh* was seven feet deep allowing full immersion, after which the worshiper could engage in private prayer at home (see Mark 7:3–4) or enter a sacred space (synagogue, temple) to reconnect with the holy.[11]

At first, John baptized in the Jordan River and then, after Jesus began his public ministry, at Aenon near Salim because of water accessibility.[12] A river was a natural alternative to a *miqveh.*

Luke traces John to a priestly family, but unlike his father he is not serving in the temple. Indeed, the Gospels remember friction between John and the temple authorities (Mark 11:27–33; Matt 3:7–10; John 1:19–34). Instead of funneling repentant sinners to the temple, he proclaimed the imminence of God's Kingdom.

Josephus claims John's work was not intended to effect forgiveness.[13] His Roman readers would have presumed, along with Jews, that remission from the debt of sin required sacrifice. Rather, his baptism was a cleansing right in anticipation of the Day of the Lord when the God of Israel would

9. deSilva, *Honor, Patronage, Kinship and Purity*, 265.

10. Archeologists have not found *miqva'ot* (pl. of the Hebrew) in Capernaum presumably because of the accessibility of the Lake of Galilee. The earliest occurrence of the word *miqveh* is in rabbinic literature. For a careful study that avoids anachronism but is not overly pessimistic, see Miller, *At the Intersection of Texts and Material Finds.*

11. According to the Sadducees and the Qumran community, in some cases the person had to wait until dusk. Archeologists have discovered *miqva'ot* beside local synagogues and adjacent to the temple.

12. The Synoptics place his ministry around the River. John specifically mentions "Bethany across the Jordan" (1:28) and uniquely Aenon (3:23). By the Byzantine period, they were uncertain of the place. Today, pilgrims visit three different sites: Yardenit, Qasr al-Yahud, and Wadi Kharrar (Hoppe, "Where Was Jesus Baptized?," 315–20).

13. This is reiterated by Bede and Theophylact of Ohrid (*CA* Mark 1). See Taylor, *Immerser*, 94.

either forgive or judge his people. The unclean people needed to repent and be purified because God was coming. All that is unclean is annihilated in the presence of the Holy.

Dress

John does not wear priestly linen, but according to Mark (1:6) and Matthew (3:2), a garment of camel's hair.[14] According to Jewish Law, the camel was unclean to eat (Lev 11:4; Deut 14:7), but wearing its hair was permissible as long as it fell naturally and was not be combined with other fabrics.[15]

Mark and Matthew complement the camel-hair garment with a leather belt, which evokes Elijah (1 Kg 1:8).[16] Mark ensures the connection by citing Malachi (3:1) in context (1:2). Both Gospels have Jesus identify John as Elijah (Mark 9:13; Matt 11:14).[17] Through Malachi God threatens to "come and strike the land with a decree of utter destruction" if the people do not repent before Elijah (4:5–6). Elijah did not die, but ascended into heaven: "Elijah because of great zeal for the law was taken up into heaven" (1 Macc 2:58). Some rabbis claimed Elijah would usher in the general resurrection—a view Jesus appeared to share.[18] There was a tradition that located Elijah's ascension in the area he was baptizing (2 Kgs 2:5–14).

Diet

John neither grew his own food nor was dependent on society for sustenance (see 1 Kings 17:4, 9). Locusts and honey (Judg 14:8–9) were near at hand in the wilderness.[19] The diet was also *kosher* and not subject to

14. The nearby Essenes wore only linen like priests serving in the temple (Josephus, *J.W.* 2.123). Egyptian priests and adherents of Isis, an Egyptian deity, also wore linen. Neo-Pythagoreans avoided wearing anything derived from animals. The *camel's hair* may evoke Zechariah: ". . . they [the prophets] will not put on a hairy robe in order to deceive" (13:4).

15. Ibba, "John the Baptist," 435–44. The hair was woven into strings and threads and knotted together to make fabrics.

16. Perhaps following John, who deemphasizes the Elijah connection, Luke omits the physical description of the Baptist.

17. Again, possibly in light of John, Luke omits the saying yet retains a softer identification in the birth narrative: John will come "in the spirit and power of Elijah" (1:17).

18. The Mishnah claims: "the resurrection of the dead comes through Elijah blessed be his memory" (*Sotah* 9:15 [Neusner]). Jesus identifies John as Elijah after predicting his death and resurrection, following the Transfiguration (metamorphosis).

19. Rabbinic literature claims there are 800 species of kosher locusts (Taylor,

tithing (*m. Ber.* 6:3). He could eat to survive (not for pleasure) without supporting the corrupted temple in Jerusalem.[20] The diet may have been intended as an expression of mourning, a fast in response to the sins of the nation (see 2:18).[21]

Later monks followed his example. John of Lycopolis "never ate bread or anything that needed to be cooked"; only "fruit."[22] The same was said about Apollo.[23] Abba Or "ate herbs and certain sweet roots."[24] However, his diet of locusts was more controversial. As we noted, the vegetarian Jewish believers who produced *The Gospel of the Ebionites* altered this detail; others interpreted it metaphorically.

In sum, the Baptist exemplifies a fundamental religious problem: *The ascetic exemplar adopts a way of life that cannot (or simply will not) be imitated by the majority*. Indeed, if this were the case, the infrastructure of society—a necessary condition for creating neighbors and sufficient exchange of goods and services among them for the common good—would fail. It would also adversely impact the family, God's means of populating each generation of his people. *We cannot all leave the city*. John had many admirers, but few followers. The gospel is an invitation for all people to be reconciled with God, providing a noble, spiritual way of life for many. Jesus will die in our place, opening a way to God by grace.

But perhaps we may avoid the opposite judgment: *monachatus non est pietas* ("monasticism is not true piety"). The Christian mission has been vastly enriched by men and women who were able to give all their time and energy to the gospel. Of course, there have been a lot of naughty monks and nuns as well. It is a matter of calling and mutual respect.

John is venerated as the transitional figure between the old and new covenants. He is featured prominently in *The Gospel of the Nazarenes and of the Ebionites*.

Christian monks, beginning with the Desert Fathers, adopted his dress.[25] They influenced the *Sufis* (from the Arabic word *suf* "wool"), who similarly reacted against the wealth and ease people were enjoying in the

Immerser, 34).

20. Lupieri, "'Law and the Prophets were until John,'" 49–56.

21. But the diet is not vegetarian, which distinguishes John from the Neo-Pythagoreans.

22. Ward, *Lives of the Desert Fathers*, 54.

23. Ward, *Lives of the Desert Fathers*, 71.

24. Ward, *Lives of the Desert Fathers*, 63.

25. Antony, as a young man, found "there was an old man who practiced from his youth the solitary life" (Athanasius, *Life of Antony*, 3).

cities.[26] The *Qur'an* develops Luke's presentation, depicting Zechariah praying for a son (*s.* 19.7). He is given wisdom for his chastity, kindness, and humility. The Mandaeans view John as the Messiah, not Jesus.

20: Political Context (Luke 3:1–2)

[3:1] Now in the fifteenth year of the governing of Tiberius Caesar—Pontius Pilate being governor over Judea, and Herod being tetrarch over Galilee, but Philip, his brother, being tetrarch over the region of Ituraea and Trachonitis, and Lysanius being tetrarch over Abilene, [2] *upon* the high priesthood of Annas and Caiaphas—*the word of God came upon* John, the son of Zechariah, *in the wilderness.* [Jer 1:1 OG; Isa 40:3]

P: For a third time, Luke anchors the gospel in history by relating it to the reigns of earthly authorities (see 1:5; 2:1), but this unit is the most elaborate.[27] He includes *Philip*, who plays no immediate role in the story except for his brother *Herod* Antipas stealing his wife, and *Lysanius*, who is even further removed. A *tetrarch* was a "ruler of a fourth part." The diversification of authority resulted from Roman intervention after Archelaus's disastrous management of Herod the Great's kingdom (see Matt 2:22). *Caesar* appointed a *governor over Judea* and carved up the rest of the land. The *high priest* headed up the Sanhedrin, which functioned as a supreme court. Although *Caiaphas* was officially *high priest*, his father-in-law, *Annas*, retained de facto prestige from serving in that role (from 6–15), especially since he was the first to be appointed by the Roman Legate Quirinius after Archelaus was deposed.

An informed, enfranchised first-century reader (like Theophilus?) might be impressed by the stability of the Julio-Claudian dynasty, especially after its demise in Nero's suicide (AD 68), and yet this list of names anticipates conflict: *Pontius Pilate, Herod, Annas, Caiaphas*—all will oppose Jesus.[28]

Luke takes the opportunity to clarify elements in Mark and John, exemplifying the careful research promised in the preface. Josephus may have provided specific information. The title *tetrarch* and name *Philip* focus Mark's presentation, which refers to Herod Antipas generally as a "king" and

26. They appear to have avoided linen, perhaps because of its associations with Egyptian paganism (Earhart, *Religious Traditions*, 659). There are many commentaries on the *Qur'an*'s presentation of John and Jesus in Sufism.

27. Marcion apparently began his version of Luke here.

28. Only Luke uses the epithet *Pontius* (Πόντιος) in the Gospels (see Acts 4:27; 1 Tim 6:13).

his brother from whom he takes Herodias as "Herod."[29] (Apparently, both brothers adopted their father's name.) After distinguishing *Annas* from the current high priest, *Caiaphas*, John nevertheless refers to him as *high priest* (18:13, 19).[30] The name *Annas* does not occur in Mark or Matthew.

John is finally called *in the wilderness* (1:80). *Herod* Antipas technically ruled this area, which was called Perea, but the language is intended to place the prophet on the margin of Roman administration. *Tiberius*, the adopted son of Augustus, began his sole reign in AD 14, which suggests *the word of God came* around AD 29. Repeating the preposition *upon* (*epi*, ἐπί), Luke may emphasize that God passed over the corrupt high priesthood.

R: Luke appropriates Jeremiah's opening superscription, "The word of God that came upon (τὸ ῥῆμα τοῦ θεοῦ ὃ ἐγένετο ἐπὶ) Jeremiah, the son of Chelcias, from (among) the priests, who was dwelling in Anathoth, in the land of Benjamin" (1:1 OG), which invites *synkrisis*: both prophets were sons of priests from the same region, called through a divine voice to provoke repentance in light of God's imminent judgment, and were imprisoned (see Matt 16:14; Jer 1:4–5; 37:18; 38:28). *In the wilderness* anticipates the citation from Isaiah in the next unit (3:3–6), creating a kind of *gezerah sheva*. Luke may follow Matthew who explicitly cites Jeremiah and then links Rachel to the same fulfillment in Isaiah (Matt 2:17; 3:1–6). As we noted, the passage is highly allusive. This *word* also came upon Elijah *in the wilderness* to mark the transition of political and prophetic power in the region (1 Kgs 19:4, 9–21). The angel announced to *Zechariah* that *John* would go "in the spirit and power of Elijah" (1:17), just as the company of prophets announced over Elisha, "The spirit of Elijah rests on Elisha" (2 Kgs 2:15). The types are uniting into one antitype.

D: Luke is not simply dating the gospel, but implying that every earthly authority, including *Caesar*, is accountable to *the word of God*.

S: *Heavenly Father, may your word be heard by all who have the power and authority to do good, to foster peace and mutual honor between nations and communities. May they taste the kindness of your Son and sweetness of the Holy Spirit. Amen.*

21A: The Baptist (Mark 1:2–6)

[2] As it stands written in [Isaiah, the prophet][31]: "*Look: I am sending my messenger before your face who will prepare your way,*" [Mal 3:1; Exod

29. Matthew also uses tetrarch (14:1).

30. Luke also associates them in Acts (4:6).

31. Codex Alexandrinus and later Byzantine mss read "in the Prophets," perhaps as

23:20] [3] *a voice crying in the wilderness: 'Prepare the way of the Lord, make his paths straight!'"* [Isa 40:3] [4] John came baptizing *in the wilderness* and proclaiming a baptism of repentance for the forgiveness of sins.[32] [5] And the whole region of Judea and all the Jerusalemites were going to him and were being baptized by him in the Jordan River, confessing[33] their sins. [6] And John would dress himself (with a cloak made from) camel's *hair* and a *leather belt* around his waist and was eating locusts and wild honey. [Mal 4:5–6; 2 Kgs 1:8]

P: This unit has two parts: a *florilegium* (vv. 2–3) and a summation of John's ministry delimited by his activity (v. 4) and lifestyle (v. 6). The center of the subunit describes the popular response to his ministry (v. 5). The whole unit is delimited by Malachi's eschatological vision (vv. 2, 6).

Mark immediately anchors the gospel in *Judea*, which is generally equivalent to the district called *Yehud* in the Persian Empire and related to Judah, one of two ancient Israelite tribes that remained loyal to the Davidic line until the Babylonian Captivity. The designation "Jew" or "Judean" (*Ioudaios*, Ἰουδαῖος) is derived from this region.

Jerusalem, not only the principle city of the region but also for many more Jews living in the diaspora, was a tightly interlocking political, economic structure resting on a common cultural and religious outlook. Like Athens for many Greeks, the city gathered together Jewish values and identity and those wanting to shape it. The Sadducees, Pharisees, Essenes—all had a presence within her walls. Pilgrims came from around the Mediterranean to worship and to pay the temple tax. Some placed Jerusalem at "the center of the earth" and therefore God's unfolding salvation (1 En. 26:1). Jesus will be crucified there. The "city of David" was partially restored after the exile, but not to her formal glory in the days of Solomon, until she became a focal point of Herod's ambition.[34] The king built citadels and palaces, a theatre and amphitheater, bridges and other monuments—all to raise the city's profile in the Roman Empire. John does not work from this center, but at the margins.[35] The center *goes* out to him. Mark allows a humorous image of pilgrims, after a long, arduous journey, walking into a ghost town; everyone

a corrective to the mixed citation. This is one of Bede's options, although he is aware of the variant (*C.A.* Mark 1), and it makes its way into the King James Version.

32. Some manuscripts add an article creating an epithet, "John the one who baptizes," perhaps under the influence of other passages (e.g., Mark 6:25; 8:28). The shorter, more natural reading is preferred.

33. Or "acknowledging."

34. Practically a character in the Gospel, I will adopt the feminine pronoun to describe Jerusalem.

35. A great amount of the literature from the period is by the disenfranchised.

has gone into *the wilderness*! *All the Jerusalemites* may be hyperbolic—there were probably between 30,000 and 50,000 Jews living in the city—but the Baptist must have captured the city's attention. They would have descended along the narrow, dangerous *path* to Jericho, the same *way* Jesus will ascend to the cross (see Luke 10:25–37).

The Jordan River cuts the region in half, flowing from the Sea of Galilee and emptying into the Dead Sea, the lowest point on earth.[36] (Today, the *river* marks the border between Israel and the Kingdom of Jordan.) The water depth typically varies from two to ten feet (maximum seventeen in places). There are salvific associations in the Gospels: Jesus will cross *the Jordan* (Mark 10:1; Matt 19:1) for safety (John 10:39–40), and people will cross to hear him preach and be healed (Mark 3:7–8; Matt 4:25). Genesis compares *the river* to those that watered Eden (13:10; see 2:10–14).

R: God parted *the Jordan River* for the people to enter the Promised Land, bookending the exodus (Josh 3:15–17; see Exod 14). The miracle repeated when Elijah struck the water with his cloak and again when Elisha took his place (2 Kgs 2:8, 14).[37] At least some in the first century were looking for a repeat of these stories. Josephus mentions a certain Theudas who declared himself a prophet and led a large group of Jews to *the river*, which he promised to part, but was executed by the Romans around AD 44 (*Ant.* 20.97–99).

This is the only place where Mark (or the narrator) cites Scripture, instead of characters in the story. The placement and peculiarity suggest emphasis.

Jerome (d. 420) notes that Mark actually cites Malachi before *Isaiah*.[38] The evangelist employs a *florilegium* or "gathering" of Scripture. The form may have originated in the century before Christ, perhaps from preaching in the synagogue, and occurs elsewhere in the New Testament (Rom 3:10–18; Heb 5:1–2).[39] A rule attributed to Hillel, *gezerah sheva* ("comparison with the equal"), explains the logic: two Scriptures that share a word or phrase or are analogous in some other way may be joined.[40] The citations from Mala-

36. The river actually begins a little north of the Sea of Galilee and travels roughly north to south over a course of 156 miles (251 kilometers).

37. God performed two other miracles through Elisha at the Jordan: healing Naaman's leprosy (2 Kgs 5:14) and making an axe head float (2 Kgs 6:6).

38. *C.A.* Mark 1.

39. We find similar exegesis in the Dead Sea Scrolls. Of particular significance is 4QFlor, which also cites from Psalm 2 and 2 Sam 7 (1 I, 21). We find the expression "in the last days" (Martiínez and Tigchelaar). But the fragment is more like a *pesher* commentary, lacking *dramatis personae*.

40. In the context of Torah, Susan Handelman defines the exegetical strategy as

chi and Isaiah share the substantive *way* (*hodos*, ὁδός), synonymous verbs meaning "to prepare," and, as we shall see, a new exodus theme. Mark mentions *Isaiah* because his long scroll is cited more than any other Scripture in his Gospel—indeed, along with Psalms and Deuteronomy, the prophet is the most popular conversation partner in Jewish literature of the period—and actually plays a role in the story (Mark 7:6).[41] The opening *As* (*Kathōs*, Καθὼς) subordinates this unit to the preceding title, "(The) beginning of the gospel of Jesus Christ, son of God" (Mark 1:1), which, as we noted earlier in our discussion of the Gospels' genre, may be dependent on Isaiah's language (40:9). In contrast, Malachi, which may not be a proper name at all—the Old Greek simply translates "my messenger"—is not mentioned in the New Testament and only once in the Old Testament.

Malachi found its canonical place as the final contributor to the Book of the Twelve, and can be read as a prophetic commentary on Exodus. Mark is actually citing Malachi's allusion to the second book of the Pentateuch:

> ἰδοὺ ἐγὼ ἀποστέλλω τὸν ἄγγελόν μου πρὸ προςώπου σου (Exod 23:20 LXX)
>
> Behold, I am sending my messenger before your face.

In context, Yahweh promises the conquest of Canaan to the exodus generation. But after Israel's rebellion to the covenant leading to exile, the prophets looked forward to a new exodus into *the wilderness*.[42] Just as there was an angel or "messenger" to guide Moses and the exodus generation in the wilderness (Exod 23:20–26), so Yahweh promises to return Elijah (Mal 3:23; 9:11). Jesus will allude to this prophecy, "It is necessary for Elijah to come first," identifying him as John the Baptist (Mark 9:12), which is anticipated here by their common dress, a *leather belt* (2 Kings 1:8). Elijah's return was to foster *repentance* among God's people.[43]

The citation from Isaiah, "*a voice crying in the wilderness: 'Prepare the way of the Lord, make his paths straight*'" (Isa 40:3), is part of a new exodus motif in which Yahweh "has made glorious the way of the sea, the land beyond the Jordan" (9:1).

---

finding an "analogy between two laws based on identical expressions in the Biblical text" (*Slayers of Moses*, 57). Rabbinic literature attributes the practice to Hillel from the generation before Jesus. For other examples in Mark, see 11:17 and 14:27. Mixed citations are common in the Dead Sea Scrolls.

41. See Mark 4:12; 7:6–7; 9:48; 11:17; 13:24–25. We find contemporary appeals to its fulfillment in the Dead Sea Scrolls (1QS VIII, 12–16). Eugene Boring claims Mark's presentation may be heard as "The Gospel According to Isaiah" (*Mark*, 406).

42. We also saw this theme in Matthew's birth story (see especially 2:15).

43. Wink, *John the Baptist*, 3.

D: Mark's Gospel may be described as a travelogue, the *way of the Lord*, Jesus Christ, which moves from persecution and suffering to resurrection and a day of reckoning.[44] This is also the way of the disciple: there is no glory before the cross. "Let us, therefore, without hesitation, renounce every earthly thing as an object of glorying."[45]

For Jews, Christians, and Muslims, Jerusalem elicits both a strong attraction and sadness. It is where God became uniquely present in the holy of holies but also left leading to desolation and exile: "How lonely sits the city" (Lam 1:1). Three religions fill, share, and contend for space. I have prayed in the Church of the Holy Sepulcher, the "holiest site in Christendom," and felt the weight of the place.[46] And yet our story does not begin here, but at the margins, which is usually where the ideals of any cultural identity are found.[47] Pilgrims often succumb to what is called "Jerusalem Syndrome," the delusion that they become an important character of Scripture, upon entering the city.[48] They are lost in the attraction, the beauty, instead of surrendering to God's formation in the wilderness.

S: *Florilegia* are a kind of biblical theology: oracles are gathered together according to topic and presume that God, the ultimate author of Scripture, continues to speak through them.[49] In Mark, the oracles are dialogical: the Lord speaks to the Lord, and the Holy Spirit enables the prophet to hear the conversation (12:35–37).[50] In this case, the citation from Malachi differs from the extant Hebrew and Greek texts:

> הִנְנִי שֹׁלֵחַ מַלְאָכִי וּפִנָּה־דֶרֶךְ לְפָנָי, Behold, I am sending my messenger, and he will prepare (the) way before me.
>
> ἰδοὺ ἐγὼ ἐξαποστέλλω τὸν ἄγγελόν μου καὶ ἐπιβλέψεται ὁδὸν πρὸ προςώπου μου, Behold, I am sending out my messenger and he will survey (the) way before my face.

44. See 8:27; 9:33–34; 10:17, 32, 46.

45. Marshall, *Cross of Christ*, 21.

46. Jacobs, *Jerusalem*, viii.

47. For a contemporary application of this typos, see Okihiro, *Margins and Mainstreams*, ix.

48. Jacobs, *Jerusalem*, x. The archetypes are so thick that a devout almost inevitably loses a sense of individuality.

49. The term "Biblical Theology" originated in the seventeenth century and vacillated between descriptive and constructive emphases (Childs, *Biblical Theology*, 4).

50. Johannes Schreiber offers essentially the same interpretation, except that he wrongly attributes the hermeneutic to a gnostic redeemer myth in line with Rudolf Bultmann ("Die Christologie des Markusevangeliums," 154–83; *Die Markuspassion*, 240–50. For more discussion, see Gathercole, *Preexistent Son*, 12–13; Guelich, "'Beginning of the Gospel,'" 6.

Mark's wording switches to the second person, allowing interpersonal communication:

> ἰδοὺ ἀποστέλλω τὸν ἄγγελόν μου πρὸ προςώπου σου, ὃς κατασκευάσει τὴν ὁδόν σου, Behold, I am sending my messenger before your face, who will prepare your way.

The antecedent of the first person pronoun is Yahweh, who emerges as the Father (Mark 1:11); the second person, the Son, who is also *the Lord* (1:1, 11).[51] Although *Jesus* might have heard this commission shortly before his baptism, the Scripture may assume his preexistence, as we find in John's prologue. The most natural context for the announcement is God's throne room. The next time the Father speaks, it is from heaven. Jesus also affirms that John's baptism is "from heaven" (11:30). Little is known about Malachi, but *Isaiah*, who is mentioned by name, was granted access to the divine throne room, and heard Yahweh say, "Whom shall I send, and who will go for us?" (Isa 6:8).

God the Father is the first actor in the narrative.[52] The Gospel begins with a conversation between the Father and Son.

21B: The Baptist (Matt 3:1–6)

[3:1] Now in those days John the Baptist appears, proclaiming *in the wilderness* of Judea [and][53] [2] saying, "Repent! For the kingdom of the heavens has come near." [3] For this is what was said through Isaiah the prophet, who says, *A voice crying in the wilderness: "Prepare the way of the Lord, make his paths straight!"* [Isa 40:3 OG] [4] Now John would dress himself with his outer garment from the *hairs* of a camel and a *leather belt* around his waist, and his diet was locusts and wild honey. [2 Kings 1:8] [5] Then Jerusalem and all of Judea and the whole region around the Jordan were going out to him, [6] and were being baptized by him in the Jordan [River],[54] confessing their sins.

P: The chiastic unit is delimited by *John's* (A) invitation to *repent* and (A') the crowd's response—*confessing their sins.* Location is also foregrounded: he

51. Jerome notes, "the voice of the Holy Spirit resounds to the Father concerning the Son" (*CA* on Mark 1).

52. God is "erster Figur der erzählten Welt" ("the first figure in the narrated world" (Blumenthal, *Gott im Markusevangelium*, 1).

53. Vat and א omit the conjunction, but it has broad representation in later mss.

54. Many later mss omit *potamō* (ποταμῷ) translated *River*. The shorter reading is usually preferred, although the absolute *Jordan* in the previous verse may have influenced the decision.

appears in the wilderness, and they *go out to him*. At the center is a (B) citation from Isaiah and (B') description of *John's* prophetic dress and diet.

Matthew retells Mark's opening just after Christ's birth narrative (1:18—2:23), rearranging the material for his emphasis on repentance and dropping the citation from Malachi, which he may have recognized as confusing. However, he (Matt 3:3) and Luke (3:4) will have Jesus cite the prophet's words in a different context. Like Mark, he emphasizes *John's* popularity, although the crowd will be dwarfed by those hearing Jesus (Matt 4:23–25). The announcement—*"Repent! For the kingdom of the heavens has come near"*—is unique to Matthew, who has Jesus say the same, forming bookends around the section (4:17). The précis is probably his version of Mark's, "The season has been fulfilled, and the kingdom of God has drawn near: repent and believe in the gospel!" (1:15). Instead of "kingdom of God," Matthew prefers "kingdom of the heavens," the first of possibly thirty-four instances in his Gospel.[55] It is "the central theme" of his Gospel.[56] Unlike Greek, there is no singular form for "heaven" in Hebrew or Aramaic. So we may have a Semitism.[57] Most treat the two expressions as referring to the same reality. Matthew, it is claimed, used *heavens* as a circumlocution to discourage voicing the Tetragrammaton (יהוה),[58] but "kingdom of God" occurs four times in his Gospel (12:28; 19:24; 21:31, 43).[59] Matthew and Mark probably refer to the same reality, God's reign, but "heavens" more specifically evokes the central symbol of that reign, God's throne, a metonymy that Jesus took from Isaiah:

> Heaven is my throne, and the earth is my footstool. (Isa 66:1)
>
> But *I* say to you not to swear at all! Either by heaven because it is the throne of God or by the earth because it is the footstool of his feet. (Matt 5:34–35)

The language contrasts with the kingdoms of the earth, "God's footstool," and anticipates the Lord's Prayer: "Our Father who art in heaven [lit. "heavens"] . . . Thy will be done on earth as it is in heaven" (Matt 6:9–10).

55. Matt 3:2; 4:17; 5:3, 10, 19 (x2), 20; 7:21; 8:11; 10:7; 11:11, 12; 13:11, 24, 31, 33, 44, 45, 47, 52; 16:19; 18:1, 3, 4, 23; 19:12, 14, 23; 20:1; 22:2; 23:14. There are variants in these references: 7:21; 19:24.

56. Ramsdell, "Kingdom of Heaven," 124–33.

57. While only Matthew uses the expression in the New Testament, it occurs in rabbinic literature (e.g., *m. Ber.* 2:2) and the LXX (e.g., Ps 2:4).

58. Nicholls, *Christian Antisemitism*, 67.

59. These references occur later and may reflect editorial exhaustion, but Matthew writes "God" (*theos*, θεός) throughout his presentation.

Matthew, then, may be offering a literal translation of what Jesus actually said (*ipsissima verba*).[60]

The language emphasizes space over time. The verb translated *has come near* (*ēngiken*, ἤγγικεν) is a perfect tense form, which usually presents the action to the mind's eye as happening in the past but with a dynamic, enduring effect on the present. The *heavens*—that is, God's throne—is perched over Mount Zion, a common Jewish presupposition at the time, so that salvation and judgment are very near.

R: Matthew presents the prophecy as God's response to Rachel's cry, the climax of his birth narrative (2:18).[61] God is coming. His throne has wheels, as Ezekiel saw (1:4–26), the *Ma'aseh Merkavah* ("Account of the Chariot"), which explains the specific instructions: *Prepare the way of the Lord! Make straight his paths!* The *Baptist* probably describes what he sees (see John 1:32).

D: Repentance begins by acknowledging that God alone is sovereign. Jesus would have us look at the sky, with *the Baptist*, and see the Father's throne, so that everything is under this context. The Jesuits express this with the motto, "Finding God in all things."

S: *Lord, you are coming! You are always coming!*

21C: The Baptist (Luke 3:3–6)

[3] And he went into the whole surrounding region of the Jordan, proclaiming a baptism of repentance for the forgiveness of sins, [4] as it stands written in the scroll of the words of Isaiah the prophet: *A voice crying in the wilderness: "Prepare the way of the Lord, make his paths straight!"* [5] *Every valley will be filled, and every mountain and hill will be brought low; and the crooked things will be made straight, and the rough ways (will be made) into smooth paths;* [6] *and all flesh will see God's salvation.* [Isa 40:3–5 OG]

P: Luke may have been influenced by the other evangelists. He appropriates Mark's citation formula, *as it stands written*, but, with Matthew, drops the Malachi citation. Like the fourth Gospel, he omits the description of John's dress and diet and emphasizes instead his itinerant ministry (John

60. John Caputo claims the reverse—that "kingdom of God" is *ipsissima verba*—but with little argument ("Instants, Secrets, and Singularities," 81).

61. *Gezerah sheva*: unlike the previous fulfillment citations, but in both cases here, Matthew gives the name of the prophet: Jeremiah and Isaiah, respectively. There is the repetition of the substantive "voice" (2:18; 3:3). "Ramah" and John are in the Judean wilderness.

1:28; 3:23; 10:40).[62] Unlike Matthew's *inclusio*, which focused on repentance and confession, Luke's emphasizes *forgiveness* and *salvation*.[63]

R: Luke treats his readers to the fullest citation from *Isaiah* (40:3–5; contrast with Mark 1:2–4; Matt 3:3). We get more description of God's highway, leading to Jerusalem. The earlier prophet envisions a massive project—filling *valleys* and levelling *mountains*. The description is ironic because the Romans excelled at highway construction.[64] They will have a role, but will not be the primary agents. Luke will return to this *way* in the parable of the Good Samaritan (10:30) and again before the Passion (19:1) to mark Jerusalem's rejection of the prophet's *crying*. The longer citation also anticipates Jesus extensively reading from the same *scroll* in Nazareth to inaugurate his ministry (4:17).

D: *All flesh* anticipates the global mission inaugurated in Luke's sequel. Peter, Paul, other apostles, deacons, Luke himself to Theophilus—all will re-present the death and resurrection of Christ as the fulfillment of Scripture, so that everyone will have an opportunity to *see God's salvation*. We are part of this massive project, following John's example. It will become clear that the Holy Spirit *straightens, fills, lowers*, and *smooths* our way of evangelism, but this includes barriers and suffering (Acts 14:19–23; 16:6).

S: There is space for a Trinitarian meditation here in *the way of the Lord* Jesus, the work of the Spirit, and God the Father's *salvation*. The Holy Spirit enables *all flesh* to see Christ on cross, the instrument of our redemption.

21D: The Baptist (John 1:19–24)

[19] And this is the witness of John[65] when the Jews from Jerusalem sent [to him][66] priests and Levites to ask him, "Who are you?" [20] And he confessed and did not deny—that is, he confessed, "*I* am not the Christ." [21] And they asked him, "Then, who? Are you Elijah?" [Mal 4:5] And he says, "I am not." "Are you the Prophet?" [Deut 18:15, 18] And he answered, "No." [22] So they said to him, "Who are you? (Tell us) that we might give

62. Anderson, *Fourth Gospel*, 113.

63. These contrastive emphases are not contradictory because what is not emphasized remains an integral part of the discourse (yin and yang). At this point, after incorporating the birth narratives of Luke and Matthew, Tatian returns to John's prologue to contextualize the Baptist (3.46–56 = John 1:7–17).

64. See, e.g., the Roman road from Cazanes near the Iron Gates.

65. And this is the witness of John echoes the opening (1:7), serving almost as a superscription. John witnesses three times (1:19–28, 29–34; 3:22–36).

66. Vat may preserve this phrase, which was perhaps seen as redundant. The majority of our witnesses contain the shorter reading. The sense is little affected.

an answer to those who sent us. What are you claiming about yourself?" [23] He said, "I am *a voice crying out in the wilderness: 'Straighten the way of the Lord!,'* as Isaiah the prophet spoke." [Isa 40:3 OG] [24] And they were sent from the Pharisees.[67]

P: The unit is delimited by repeating *sent* (*apostellō*, ἀποστέλλω vv. 19, 24) and terminates with the disclosure that *the Pharisees* are the interested party, which anticipates Nicodemus coming to Jesus, an escalation (3:1). Opening the narrative proper, these questions unpack *the witness of John* in the prologue (1:6–8, 15–18), which is subdivided into a negative (apophatic) and positive (kataphatic) expression:[68]

Vv. 20–21—John is *not* the Christ, Elijah, or the Prophet

Vv. 22–23—He is *a voice crying out in the wilderness.*

This is the only mention of *priests and Levites* as a group in the New Testament, although a "priest" and "Levite" occur in the parable of the Good Samaritan (Luke 10:31–32). The *Levites* were descendants of Levi, one of the twelve sons of Jacob (Israel); they were distinguished from the other tribes to serve as *priests* on their behalf.[69] By the first century, the term *Levite* could describe a more specific group—those who sang psalms, the temple liturgy, while *priests* offered the daily sacrifice.[70] (In some expressions of Judaism today, the cantor is ordained for this role like a rabbi.) Collectively, they served as mediators between Israel and God. The priests also had the responsibility of preserving and interpreting Scripture, which explains their curiosity, if not suspicion, about the Baptist.[71]

67. The NIV strangely translates as Καὶ ἀπεσταλμένοι ἦσαν ἐκ τῶν Φαρισαίων as "Now the Pharisees who had been sent," turning the object of the preposition into the subject. See the ESV for a better rendering.

68. The evangelist uses an article before *John* at v. 29, which is probably referring back to the anarthrous occurrences in the prologue (1:6, 15).

69. The Old Testament does not claim that Levi himself was a priest, but identified his descendant Aaron taking that role. But *Aramaic Levi*, a later Jewish retelling of Scripture, presumes Jacob's son functioned as priest (Werman, "Levi and Levites," 211–25).

70. See 1 Chr 16; 2 Chr 29:30; Sir 50:16–17; 1 Macc 4:54; Philo, *Moses* 1.159–173; 11QPsa XXVII 2–11; m. Tamid 7:4; Beckwith, "Courses of the Levites," 499–524; Jeffrey, "Philo's Impact on Christian Psalmody," 152. Several psalms have specific recitation days according to the Old Greek: Ps 24, Sunday; Ps 48, Monday; Ps 94, Wednesday; Psalm 93, Friday; Psalm 92, Sabbath (= MT). We find the role of "psalm-singer" in some contexts (Penner, *Patterns of Second Temple Prayer*, 58–59).

71. Mason, "Priesthood in Josephus," 657–61. The priestly class relied upon the expertise of scribes for the preservation of Scripture and possibly, depending on the relationship, the exegetical skill of the Pharisees.

In light of Luke's presentation, the encounter is ironic because *John* himself is the son of a priest (1:5)! The Baptist is performing his duty, *crying out*, but at the margins (*in the wilderness*). The *Levites*, who should be singing in the temple, are coming out to interrogate him!

Also surprising is the implication that *the Pharisees* controlled the *priests and Levites*, which may reflect the social world when the Gospel was published after the temple's destruction in AD 70, although the Dead Sea Scrolls evidence Pharisaic influence in the temple before Christ.[72] Some of the priests probably identified as Pharisees.[73]

With each question, *John* shortens his response, which anticipates his self-erasure (3:27–30). The interlocutors do not ask if he is *the Christ* (*ho Christos*, ὁ Χριστός), but he makes the denial anyway. The title functions at two levels: in the immediate context, the article *the* (*ho*, ὁ) before *Christ* determines that *the* Messiah is under discussion; it also points back to the prologue that mentions "Jesus Christ" (1:17).[74] At the story level, then, the Baptist is indirectly witnessing to Jesus as the Messiah.

R: The second denial, that he is not *Eljiah*, is surprising in light of the presentations of the other Gospels, especially Mark's appropriation of Malachi (1:2, 6).[75] D. A. Carson suggests the Baptist is ignorant of his full role in the dawning of God's Kingdom,[76] which, I would add, matches his confusion about Jesus (Matt 11:3; Luke 7:19). In the other Gospels, he never claims to be Elijah, despite the symbolism of his dress.[77] The fourth Gospel plays with this dramatic irony by placing Malachi's prophecy in the prologue (v. 6). Indeed, the very question, *Are you Elijah?*, suggests outsiders recognized the parallels. We find a motif that only Jesus knows our true identity and names us accordingly (1:42; 10:3). John allows Jesus to reveal his identity (see 5:31–47). Nevertheless, after reading through the other Gospels, Luke may have recognized the tension and offered a clarification: the Baptist comes "in the spirit and power of Elijah" (1:17).

72. Josephus's treatment of the Pharisees changes between *War* and *Antiquities* in a way that suggests that the religious group became more powerful after the largely priestly group, the Sadducees, ended with the temple.

73. For discussion, see von Wahlde, "Relationship between Pharisees and Chief Priests," 506–22.

74. This is called the anaphoric use of the article.

75. See the parallel passages above, Mark 9:13, and Matt 17:11–13. This seems to have been recognized by Tatian, who, when juxtaposing the introductions of the Baptist in John and Matthew, drops the reference to the leather belt.

76. See Carson, *John*, 143.

77. We should note that the "leather belt" is a subtle allusion that would have become significant after Jesus linked John to Elijah.

The question, *Are you the Prophet?*, alludes to the prophecy in Deuteronomy (see John 4:44; 5:46; Acts 3:22; 7:37):

> The LORD your God will raise up for you a prophet like me from among you, from your brothers—it is to him you shall listen . . . "I will raise up for them a prophet like you from among their brothers. And I will put my words in his mouth, and he shall speak to them all that I command him." (18:15, 18 ESV)

The Baptist just contrasted Jesus with Moses in the prologue: "the Law was given through Moses; Grace and Truth came (to be) through Jesus Christ" (1:17).

Even John's citation of Isaiah is shortened! Instead of *etoimasete* (ἑτοιμάσατε "prepare"), he says, *euthanate* (εὐθύνατε "make straight"), a conflation of the remaining line, "Make his paths straight" (εὐθείας ποιεῖτε τὰς τρίβους αὐτοῦ). The fourth Gospel uniquely places the verse from Isaiah on John's lips, although Mark's dialogical opening could he heard as including a command to the Baptist: *"Prepare the way of the Lord, make his paths straight!"* (Mark 1:3; see also Luke 3:2).

D: Public confession was important in John's community: "Who is the liar, but the one who denies (*ho arnoumenos,* ὁ ἀρνούμενος) that Jesus is *the Christ*" (1 John 2:22). John, then, is exemplary. We too are called to be a voice in the wilderness, in the city, at the margins, in the center—wherever God summons us. John *prepared the way of the Lord's* first coming; we, his second.

We are struck by the dramatic irony that John does not know who he *ultimately* is. "Beloved, we are already children of God," writes the same author of the fourth Gospel, "but it has not yet been revealed what we will be" (1 John 3:2). Who we are is finally up to God: "*What is molded will not say to the molder, "Why did you make me this way?*" (Rom 9:20, citing Isa 29:16). John Calvin (1509–1564) opens his *Institutes* by claiming people cannot understand themselves apart from God because "the talents which we possess are not from ourselves and that our very existence is nothing but a subsistence in God alone."[78] Our *Lord* Jesus comes to tell us who we are: "I will know, as also I have been known" (1 Cor 13:12).

My father sat under a brilliant Hebrew professor, who, as a Jewish boy, trusted Jesus as Messiah. Towards the end of this life, suffering from Alzheimer's, he forgot this commitment and rejected the gospel. But his memories are held by Christ, so that his soul will be reunited to a transformed

78. The translation is by John Allen in Calvin, *Institutes,* 1:47.

body at the resurrection: "God is not unjust to forget your work and the love that you showed for his name" (Heb 6:10).

S: *Lord, we surrender our idolatrous and self-limiting identities and wait, like creatures in the Garden, for you, our last Adam, to tell us who we are—rock or thunder, dust or silence. Amen.*

21E: The Baptist (John 5:31–47)

[31] "If I witness about myself, my witness is not true. [32] There is another who witnesses about me, and I know that the witness that he witnesses about me is true. [33] *You* have sent to John, and he has witnessed to the truth. [34] Now *I* am not receiving this witness from a human, but I say these things that you might be saved. [35] *That one* was the brightly burning *lamp*;[79] *you* were willing to rejoice for an hour in his light. [Ps 132:17] [36] But *I* have a witness greater than John. For the works that the Father has given to me (he gave), that I might complete them. [37] And the Father who sent me—he has witnessed about me. His voice you have never heard, nor have you seen his *form*. [Ezek 1:26] [38] And you do not have his word (*logos*) remaining in you because *you* do not believe him whom he sent. [39] You search the Scriptures because *you* think by means of them you have eternal life, and they are the ones witnessing about me! [40] And you do not want to come to me that you may have life. [41] I do not receive *glory* from human beings, [42] but I have known you—that you do not have the love of God in yourselves. [43] *I* have come in the name of my Father, and you did not receive me. If another comes in his own name, him you will receive. [44] How are you able to believe while receiving *glory* from one another[80] and are not seeking the *glory* from the only God? [Ezek 1:28]

P: This unit is highly allusive to earlier parts of the story, especially the prologue. Recognizing that he is already on trial, Jesus calls four *witnesses*, the Baptist (vv. 32–35), the *works* or signs (v. 36), *the Father* (vv. 37–38), and *Scripture* (v. 39). The unit is delimited by a contrast between a messiah who is reticent *to witness* (v. 31) and an imposter who *comes in his own name* (v. 43). In the years leading up to the destruction of the temple (AD 70), many were deceived by false messiahs.[81]

79. ὁ λύχνος ὁ καιόμενος καὶ φαίνων is probably hendiadys because of the anarthrous φαίνων.

80. The religious leaders were distracted by self-love, a desire to be honored by others.

81. See Mark 13:6, "Many will come in my name"; Josephus, *J.W.* 2.258–265.

While no longer participating in the story, Jesus draws on his forerunner, the Baptist. *The witness that he witnesses about me:* we find a similar redundancy for emphasis before John's testimony, "he confessed and did not deny—that is, he confessed" (1:20). *You have sent to John* evokes the earlier disclosure: "they were sent from the Pharisees" (1:24), who are now focused on Jesus. *I am not receiving this witness from a human* goes back to the prologue: "There was a human *who has been sent from God* (1:6), which alludes to Malachi's prophecy of Elijah's return (4:5). John describes himself as "*a voice*" (1:23), but Jesus claims he is *the brightly burning lamp* (*ho luchnos ho kaiomenos kai phainōn,* ὁ λύχνος ὁ καιόμενος καὶ φαίνων). This would create tension with the prologue—"That one [John] was not the light (*to pfōs,* τὸ φῶς), but (he came) that he might witness about the light" (1:8)—were it not for the escalation: a *lamp* (*luchnos*) is vastly smaller and ephemeral compared to the primordial "light" (*pfōs*) of creation that is always shining.[82] The lesser light served the greater. *Brightly burning* describes the short intensity of John's ministry. The interlocutors willingly entered into his *joy*, but only *for an hour*: when the "true light" came (1:9), the focus of his witness, they demurred.

Of greater significance are *the works that the Father has given to me*—seven of which frame a large portion of the fourth Gospel. John did not perform these signs, which are superior because they are part of the reality that prophets foretold. The verb translated *I might complete* (*teleioō,* τελειόω) anticipates the summative accomplishment of the cross: "It has been completed (*teleioō*)!" (19:30).

The Father who sent me—he has witnessed about me evokes the locution the Baptist heard at Christ's baptism:

> I have seen *the Spirit* descending like a dove from heaven, and it remained *upon* him. And I did not know him, but the one who sent me to be baptizing with water—that one said to me: "*Upon* whom you see the Spirit descending and remaining *upon* him—this is the one who is baptizing with (the) Holy Spirit." (1:32–33)

His voice you have never heard, nor have you seen his form is intended as a contrast to the Baptist and extends the sense of the prologue: "No one has ever seen God; the only God, the one who is at the chest of the Father—that one explained him" (1:18).[83] This intertextuality suggests God

82. In his farewell speech, John compared his role to the waxing and waning of the sun or moon: "he must increase, but I must decrease" (3:30).

83. Although the religious leaders might acknowledge that they had neither seen the *form* of God nor heard his audible voice, they might claim to have been a part of a people who *heard* God's *voice* when he gave the Law at Mount Sinai (Exod 19:16–25;

can be seen as *the Spirit* descending in the *form* (*eidos*, εἶδος) of a dove and in the incarnation of the Son, so that Jesus uses *word* (*logos*, λόγος) as a disguised self-reference. The verb translated *remains* (*menō*, μένω) may also be rendered "abide" and refers to the special, unitive relationship between God and the disciple (14:10; 15:4). *You did not receive me* recalls the invitation in the prologue: "whoever received him, he gave them the right to become God's children" (1:12).

Instead of these *witnesses*—the Baptist, the signs, and perichoretic revelation of the Father through the Spirit and Logos—the Pharisees *search the Scriptures*.[84] The rabbis placed the study of *torah*, both Scripture and oral tradition, above all other acts of piety. Hillel claims: "Lots of Torah, lots of life."[85] Despite their reputation for being skilled teachers, the Pharisees lack the interpretive key to discover *eternal life*, which ironically was staring them in the face!

I have known you—that you do not have love for God in yourselves echoes the disclosure before Nicodemus, a Pharisaic teacher, who interrogates Jesus, who "was aware of what was in the human" (2:25), which is now identified as lacking *the love of God* (*hē agape tou theou*, ἡ ἀγάπη τοῦ θεοῦ). The genitive case is ambiguous, allowing the sense to be a human's love for God or God's love for the human or both.[86] In any case, the context suggests that Jesus looked into the hearts of his judges and saw that their motivation was not *love* but self-glorification.

R: Jesus presupposes the biblical mandate that truth is determined by multiple, harmonious witnesses (Deut 17:6; 19:15), a method that will be withheld at his trial.[87] To explain John's role, he appropriates Psalm 132: "I

Deut 4:11–12, 33). Nevertheless, when God finally speaks, they only hear thunder or the voice of an angel (12:28–29).

84. The verb translated *search* (*eraunaō*, ἐραυνάω) describes making a careful or thorough effort to learn something (BDAG, 389). The verb reoccurs at 7:52 where the Pharisees challenge others to search the Scriptures and see that no prophet comes from Galilee. While the verb could be an imperative, the indicative best fits the context (Pate, *Writings of John*, 87n8).

85. M. Avot 2:7 (Neusner).

86. We encounter the same ambiguity in Romans (5:5). Rudolf Bultmann argues that an objective genitive is intended (*Gospel of John*, 269n2). The phrase, then, refers "to the exclusion of God from their life; they have no interest in him." God's love for sinners is emphasized in the conversation with Nicodemus (3:16). Scholars are moving towards a both/and, the so-called "plenary genitive." The case is ideally suited for holding the ambiguity.

87. Later rabbis were especially scrupulous about this: "a person is not believed to testify in his own behalf" (m. Ketub. 2:9 [Neusner]).

prepared a *lamp* for my Messiah" (v. 17).[88] In the psalm, God claims Zion as his eternal resting place where a descendant of David will reign forever. By rejecting the lamp and Messiah, the Pharisees place themselves in the role of villain: "His enemies," God says, "I will clothe with shame, but on him his crown will shine" (v. 18 ESV). When the heaven opened, Ezekiel saw God's throne and one seated "as the *form* (*eidos,* εἶδος) of man" (1:26). He is the climax of the prophet's vision, who, overwhelmed by "the glory of the LORD," fell on his face (1:28 ESV). After alluding to the passage, Jesus uses *glory* (*doxa,* δόξα) three times presumably self-referentially: "we perceived his *glory—glory* as the only one from the Father" (1:14). James speaks of our glorious Lord Jesus" (2:1). The Pharisees see a human body in front of them, the effect of the Incarnation, but they do not perceive his *glory.*

D: The emphasis falls on human responsibility in this passage—*you were willing . . . you do not believe . . . you do not want to come to me . . . you did not receive me.* But God is not stingy: the religious leaders would not reject God from a lack of evidence. "They are without excuse," Paul claims (Rom 1:20). Furthermore, despite their hostility, Jesus desires their salvation: *I say these things that you might be saved.* With the Pharisees, we, the Gospel's intended readers (20:30–31), are personally responsible for how we respond to God's witnesses.

What keeps the Pharisees from *eternal life*? Jesus highlights two pathologies: pride and provincialism. In line with the doctrine of the two books—"creation" (*liber naturae*) and "Scripture" (*liber scripturae*)—Jesus points out the danger of interpreting the Bible apart from other revelation. The Logos is the quintessence of revelation. We must therefore avoid the error of the Pharisees and read Scripture *with Jesus.* If we read this scene with the religious leaders, there is only the outing of a heretic, Jesus. But if instead we read with Jesus, the loving work of the Trinity emerges. As the evangelist makes clear, this is the illuminative work of the Holy Spirit. A symptom of *loving God* is a desire *to glorify* his *name,* not ourselves. We are invited to follow John and Jesus in the only path to God—humility.

This teaching also leads to an interpretive principle: *our knowledge of authors, or lack thereof, shapes our understanding of their communication.* The Pharisees did not know the Triune God, the ultimate author of Scripture, and therefore read it slant. They clearly were not receiving the words before God's throne like Jesus, Ezekiel, and the other prophets. A US citizen would read a letter from the Internal Revenue Service differently than an anonymous flyer.

88. Köstenberger, *John,* 191. The Old Greek is ἡτοίμασα λύχνον τῷ χριστῷ μου (131:17).

In short, like many today, they did not hear the thunder or see the lightening or feel the hair rise on the back of their necks.

S: The finale of the unit, *the glory from the only God*, complements the prologue: "No one has ever seen God; the only God, the one who is at the chest of the Father—that one explained him" (1:18). Both the Father and the Son are *the only God*, a paradox of unity and diversity that opens the fourth Gospel (1:1–2). The allusion to the Father's announcement about the Holy Spirit puts this unit into a Trinitarian context. Unlike the Pharisees, the Logos was motivated to take on flesh and die on the cross because of his *love* for *the Father*, which probably includes the Spirit and *Father's love* for him, and a desire *to glorify* him, which may include *the Father* and Spirit's desire *to glorify* him.

A unique role of the Son is to be "the radiance" of God's "glory and the representation of his being" (Heb 1:3; see John 14:9).

21F: The Baptist (John 10:39–42)

[39] [So][89] they were seeking again to arrest him, and he escaped from their hand. [40] And he went [again][90] beyond the Jordan to the place where John was first baptizing. And he remained there. [41] And many came to him and were saying, "John did no sign, but everything that John said about him was true." [Deut 13:1–5] [42] And many believed into him there.

P: This unit, the final mention of *John* in the fourth Gospel and a confirmation of his witness, is delimited by an emphasis on location—*place* (*topos*, τόπος) and *there* (*ekei*, ἐκεῖ). Jesus returns to where he was baptized—*beyond* (that is, east of) *the Jordan* River in Bethany or Bethabara (1:28, 36). The Promised Land has proven hostile; Jesus is about to complete his mission on the cross, but *escapes* at this point.

The *synkrisis* between the two men remains to the end: *John* did not perform *signs* (see 5:36), but his witness of Jesus has proven *true*, which leads to a partial fulfillment of the prologue: ". . . that all might *believe* through him" John (1:7).[91] Mentioning *sign* here anticipates the seventh, climactic

89. There are four different starts to this unit in the witnesses. D reads *kai* (καί) "and," perhaps stressing continuity with the preceding unit. Papyrus 45 has *de* (δέ) "but," stressing discontinuity. P66 and ℵ offer *oun* (οὖν), which is adopted by the Nestle-Aland editors. Still other witnesses lack any transitionary particle. The ESV opts for the translation "again," which is not the most immediate option for any of these readings.

90. *Again* (*palin*, πάλιν) is absent in Papyrus 66 and a few other witnesses. The adverb could be read as editorial aid.

91. The contrast is emphasized by the *men/de* construction in Greek.

raising of Lazarus, which immediately follows in a different Bethany near Jerusalem (11:1, 18) where another mixed reaction occurs (vv. 45–46).[92]

R: A false prophet encourages idolatry (Deut 13:1–5); in the preceding unit, Jesus is nearly stoned for presenting himself as God (John 10:33). The Baptist pointed the people to someone who normally would seem to be a blasphemer, and yet *everything* he *said about him was true*.

D: This unit, which Dale Bruner labels "The Good Ending," marks the ultimate success of the Baptist's life. His witness proved to be *true* and many *believed* in Jesus. Bruner notes, "To be completely truthful about Jesus is the goal of every witness to Jesus."[93]

We cannot be snatched from Christ's *hand* (10:28–29), but God can snatch Christ and his people from the enemy's *hand*.[94] There is ultimate safety in our baptism: we are in Christ *beyond the Jordan*. In the meantime, we must *believe into* (*pisteuō eis auton*, πιστεύω εἰς αὐτὸν) Christ and *remain* (*menō*, μένω) in him.[95] John Chrysostom picks up the departure motif: "He urges them to flee noisy crowds and to pray in solitude."[96] In the centuries that followed, monks followed Jesus *there* and took up prayer in caves.

S: *Lord, you are our safety, our haven. We trust the signs and wait in faith. Save us, Lord Jesus!*

22A: Rebuke (Matt 3:7–10)

[7] But after seeing many of the Pharisees and Sadducees coming towards[97] [his][98] baptism, he said to them: "Brood of vipers![99] Who warned[100] you to be fleeing from the coming wrath? [8] So bear fruit worthy of repentance,

92. Although subtle, John wants the reader to make the connection by claiming this was where *John was first baptizing* to distinguish the location from Aenon near Salim (3:23). Bonaventure misses this cue (*John*, 579).

93. Bruner, *Gospel of John*, 649.

94. Bruner, *Gospel of John*, 648.

95. Bruner, *Gospel of John*, 649.

96. Cited by Bonaventure, *John*, 579.

97. Or "against." The preposition *epi* (ἐπί) with the accusative can convey either sense.

98. The possessive pronoun is absent in our earliest witnesses, the original hand of ℵ and Vat, as well as Origen's text.

99. Or "offspring of snakes."

100. Warned or "revealed to" (*hypdeiknumi*, ὑποδείκνυμι): The verb may signify directing one's attention, often in a didactic, moral sense. There is also a revelatory meaning in later Christian writings—visions granted to martyrs for whom the Lord has shown the eternal blessings that no earthly eye can behold.

[9] and do not presume to be saying with each other, 'We have father Abraham.' For I say to you, God is able from these stones to raise up children to Abraham. [10] Instead, the ax is already resting against the root of the trees. So any tree that does not bear good fruit is chopped down and cast into fire."[101]

P: Jerusalem served as metonymy for "the priests and scribes of the people" colluding with Herod (2:3); *the Pharisees and Sadducees* now fill the role of villain. The pairing is surprising because the two groups opposed one another, but the enemy of an enemy is a friend.[102] They had to work together in the Sanhedrin, the supreme religious body of the land, to preserve the status quo from the Kingdom (3:2). Matthew will bring them together to oppose Jesus.[103] The text may be read that they came to be baptized or, as the overall context suggests, *towards [his] baptism*—that is, to evaluate critically.[104] John is blunt: *"Brood of vipers!"* (*gennēmata echidnōn*, γεννήματα ἐχιδνῶν). Forced out of their protective hole, they are fleeing a wildfire.[105] The language is apocalyptic, but a universal conflagration is probably not the focus, but the temple's imminent destruction, a prophecy that Jesus will also take up (Matt 24). The *Sadducees* perished in this event, and the *Pharisees* were transformed.[106] However, Jesus takes up the same epithet but with escalation: "Brood of vipers, how will you flee from the judgment of Gehenna?" (Matt 23:33; see also 12:34).

The Baptist makes a clever and memorable pun lost in translation: *children* in Hebrew (*banim*) or Aramaic (*benaya*) is similar to that for *stones* (*abanim, abenaya* respectively), a subtle reminder that Matthew may be preserving a very early tradition. It is easy to see why Gentile

101. For similar language, see 1QapGen ar: "the man coming from the South of the land, with a sickle in his and fire with him" (XV, 10 [Martiínez and Tigchelaar]). *Fire* links this and the following two sayings (vv. 10, 11).

102. Paul attempts to divide them (Acts 23:7). Matthew employs a pattern where *Pharisees* is modified by an article and *Sadducees* is anarthrous and joined by the conjunction *kai* (καί), so that the unity of the grouping is emphasized.

103. Jesus (apparently without his disciples—see 16:5) takes a boat to the region of Magadan (15:39) where they request a sign from heaven (16:1; see also vv. 6, 11, 12).

104. Bock, *Jesus according to Scripture*, 81. Matthew employs an adversative conjunction *de* (δέ), translated *But*, to demarcate the religious leaders from the rest of the audience. John preserves a similar tradition (John 1:19–28), except that "the Jews," which he equates with the Pharisees (John 1:24), send priests and Levites to enquire about the Baptist's authority.

105. Bock, *Jesus according to Scripture*, 82. Craig Keener notes that, according to ancient Mediterranean tradition, vipers killed their mothers during birth, and so represented patricide, the worst of sins ("Brood of Vipers," 3–11).

106. See Stemberger, *Jewish Contemporaries of Jesus*; Wellhausen, *Pharisees and the Sadducees*.

Christians might have treasured this saying, but even the *Pharisees* rejected the premise that merely being a relative of *Abraham* was salvific. Jewish tax collectors, prostitutes, and other "sinners" were not part of the covenant community. As Jesus will do, the Baptist uses their own teaching to unmask the hypocrisy of the religious leaders.

R: The rebuke echoes the salvation of Lot and his family from Sodom, except for the ironic twist that the religious leaders were oblivious to the imminent destruction by *fire* (Gen 19). They play the role of the Sodomites, for whom *Abraham* interceded but was unable to save because there were not ten righteous in the city (Gen 18:22–33). *Brood of vipers* alludes to the Protoevangelium, the progeny of the Satanic Serpent in the Garden, who will be thrown into the lake of *fire* (Gen 3:15; Rev 20:7–10). Jesus is the true "son of Abraham," the fulfillment of God's promise (Matt 1:1).

D: John juxtaposes God's free sovereignty with the responsibility for God's people to bear fruit, a yin and yang we find throughout Scripture. The human response is unpacked in the following unit (3:10–14). Here, the Baptist rebukes the abuse of privilege, an unearned advantage, anticipating a perennial debate in the church: if we embrace *sola gratia*, that we are saved from God's judgment by grace alone, how do we escape antinomianism? The binary opposition between Augustine and Pelagius was partially resolved at the Council of Orange (529)—the latter was rejected; the former, softened by the influence of John Cassian—but erupted again in the Reformation. Lutheran (1999) and Methodist (2006) churches have now joined the Catholic Church to affirm, "By grace alone [*sola gratia*], in faith in Christ's saving work and not because of any merit on our part, we are accepted by God and receive the Holy Spirit, who renews our hearts while equipping us and calling us to good works," but the issue continues to divide.[107] Assurance of salvation, centered in God's underserved grace and received with obedient humility, is a great consolation for insecure believers, but, coupled to indolent privilege, diseases the soul.[108]

Evagrius of Pontus (346–399) isolated *akēdia* (ἀκηδία), "not caring," as one of the eight great temptations, which also made Gregory the Great's list of seven deadly sins. The word is variously translated—"apathy," "indifference," "restlessness," "boredom," "sloth"—but John Cassian, who fostered awareness of the vice in the west, respects its complexity by transliterating the Greek into Latin (*acedia*). In *Praktikos*, Evagrius describes *acedia* as the noon day devil—when "the sun barely moves, if at all, and

107. For the quotation and more discussion, see Oden, *Justification Reader*, 115.

108. The pathologies of privilege are observed in affluent youth (Levine, *Price of Privilege*).

that the day is fifty hours long"—and the monk feels trapped in his daily prayers and labor. It plays with the existential dilemma of life's seemingly meaningless repetition. In community, *acedia* manifests as desiring to be free from the suffering of care.[109]

European Christians recognize *acedia* in the malaise of their communal piety; the demon attacks what is most established like the fire that nearly consumed Notre Dame,[110] but is also manifest in the youthful fear of missing out, the impatience of a new employee for recognition or a midlife crisis.[111] The Baptist suggests a disciplined repentance as a remedy for privilege and *acedia*—what came to be called a "rule of life." The Benedictines focused on the most repetitive and therefore vulnerable parts of the day—*ora et labora* (prayer and labor). We may also attend to diet and exercise.

S: To say that *God is able from these stones to raise up children to Abraham* is to claim that God is a free and omnipotent creator, who determines the benefactors of Abraham's covenant. *Stones* are even more barren than elderly Sarah, but all things are possible with God.

22B: Rebuke (Luke 3:7–9)

[7] So he was saying to the crowds who were coming out to be baptized by him, "Brood of vipers! Who warned you to be fleeing from the coming wrath? [8] So bear fruits worthy of repentance, and do not begin to say among yourselves, 'We have father Abraham.' For I say to you that God is able to raise from these stones children to Abraham. [9] And the ax is already resting against the root of the trees. So every tree that does not bear good fruit is chopped down and cast into the fire."

P: Luke appropriates nearly every word of Matthew's presentation, except his villains, "the Pharisees and Sadducees," the long description of *the crowds*—"Jerusalem and all of Judea and the whole region around the Jordan" (Matt 3:5)—and their response.[112] Luke may have recognized the odd coupling of the religious leaders (see Acts 23:1–10) or wanted to foreshadow the challenge of Jews accepting Gentiles into Abraham's family, the focus of his sequel. In any case, he is not misrepresenting Matthew, who has John call *everyone* to repent (3:2). Dropping *the crowds'* response, "confessing their

109. Norris, *Acedia and Me*, 3.

110. See Nault, *Noonday Devil.*

111. A surprising manifestation is health anxiety, a preoccupation with our physical well-being (Evagrius of Pontus, *Antirrhētikos* 6.32).

112. Sixty of sixty-four words overlap in Greek (Bock, *Jesus according to Scripture,* 81).

sins" (Matt 3:6), Luke simply goes back a little in narrative time, inferring that John gave them the same warning as the Pharisees and Sadducees. The generalization also allowed a chiasm to bring order to his integration of various sources, a phenomenon we also saw in his retelling of Matthew's birth story:

A Crowds (3:7–11)

B Tax Collectors (3:12–13)

B' Soldiers (3:14)

A' Crowds (3:15–18).

The tax collectors and soldiers fill the slot of Matthew's Pharisees and Sadducees; like them, invitations are given but their response is left out of the story.

R: True children of *Abraham* act like the patriarch, the exemplar of faithfulness (John 8:39; Rom 4:16).

D: Although Christian baptism differs from John's, this principle remains: Baptism without reformation of character, the purifying of the heart (soul), is insufficient (Matt 28:19–20). Those who proclaim this will always be hated by those who, like *vipers*, find a comfortable hole to play out their religious fiction (Matt 5:11). We must live simply and humbly before God.

S: *Lord, you graciously made us who were not your people your people. May this privilege bless all creation. Amen.*

23: Teaching (Luke 3:10–14)

[10] And the crowds were asking him, saying: "What, then, should we do?"[113] [11] Now answering, he was saying[114] to them: "The one who has two tunics, he must share with him who has none. And the one who has food must do the same thing." [12] Now tax collectors[115] also came to be baptized, and said to him, "Teacher, what should we do?"[116] [13] Now he said to them, "Collect no more (than) what has been arranged for you." [14]

113. D reads: "What should we do in order to be saved?" A few other witnesses read "that we might live."

114. A few witnesses read "he says."

115. Or "toll collectors."

116. D reads: "What should we do in order to be saved?"

Now soldiers[117] were also asking him, saying, "And what should *we* do?"[118] And he said to them, "Rob no one by force nor through extortion and be content with your wages."

P: This unit, which forms the center of the chiasm discussed in the previous unit, is unique to Luke and anticipates Acts. What John commands *the crowds* to do the Spirit does in the church: "They were selling their possessions and properties, and were sharing them with all according to whoever was having a need" (Acts 2:45). As the chiasm suggests, obeying these commands requires the Holy Spirit's intervention (Luke 3:15–18).

The call to repentance naturally leads to the question, *What then should we do?* (Luke 3:3, 8, 10), a motif in the Gospel and Acts for the human response to the invitation to salvation. A Jewish *teacher* basically taught in two forms—*haggadah* or "narrative" and *halakah*, which concretizes normative truth into specific laws. The Hebrew word is derived from the verb *halaq* ("the way to go").[119] These directives are intended to draw Israel closer to one another on their journey back to God.

The soldiers' question is especially emphatic in Greek: "*what should <u>we</u> do?*"[120] Although some claim they are Jewish police accompanying the *tax collectors* or Herodian mercenaries, the group is probably light auxiliary non-Jewish troops recruited by Rome in Syria.[121] The scene, therefore, anticipates the inclusion of the Gentiles into God's people, a core emphasis in Luke's story. The Baptist has just criticized Israelites for relying on their descendant Abraham: "God is able to raise from these stones children to Abraham" (3:8). For this implication, Luke probably drew upon the eyewitness accounts of Matthew (3:9) and John (1:29).

R: Ancient Israelite Scripture blends *haggadah* and *halakah*. The story of God's initial creation led to several commands (Gen 1:28–29; 2:16–17, 24), a pattern that is repeated after the flood and exodus. The eventual empowerment of the Spirit, the hope of John's baptism, distinguishes and escalates this moment in God's salvation history. Josephus claims the Baptist required people to express repentance through acts of "justice" (*dikaiosunē*, δικαιοσύνη) toward one another" (*Ant.* 18.117). But these commands go further than the Law and Prophets. John is most

117. In Egypt the military or police occasionally would accompany the tax collector. Such "hired guns" had a reputation for theft and banditry.

118. D reads: "What should we do in order to be saved?"

119. The Hebrew word is spelled variously (e.g., *halachah*).

120. Only their response has an unnecessary pronoun for the subject in the unit (τί ποιήσωμεν καὶ ἡμεῖς).

121. Keener, *IVP Bible Background Commentary*, 188.

similar to the Essenes, except that they required converts to give everything to the leaders of the community.[122]

D: *The crowds, tax collectors, soldiers*—all were part of a system that responded to scarcity with competition. Competition is so much a part of daily life that we are seldom aware of its power. Is it natural? Competition between children appears to be a learned social behavior, not an innate characteristic, and does not appear, even in embryonic form, until about four to six years of age.[123] How is competition just when not everyone has been given equal power or access to resources? How did it come about that someone in the audience had *two tunics* while another in the community had none? Jesus will tell a parable about an unrighteous man who had too much and Lazarus, who was righteous and had nothing (Luke 16:19–20). Of course, this is not always the case: in Acts, wealthier Christians, like Barnabas, cheerfully shared their wealth with others. Yet competition should have no place in the church (1 Cor 3:1–21). We find the impact of this truth in the early church where need, not virtue, was the primary criterion for care.[124] Martin of Tours (316–397) is lovingly remembered for his compassion:

> So it came about that one day when he had nothing on him but his weapons and his uniform, in the middle of a winter that had been fearfully hard beyond the ordinary, so that many were dying from the extreme cold, he met at the city gate of Amiens a coatless beggar, who had been asking passers-by to have compassion for him, but all had gone past the unfortunate creature. Then the God-filled man understood, from the fact that no one else had had compassion, that this beggar had been reserved for him. *But what should he do?* [Luke 3:14] He had nothing with him but the cloak he had on, for he had already parted with the rest of his clothing for similar purposes. So he took the sword he was wearing and cut the cloak in two, and gave half to the beggar, putting on the rest himself again.[125]

The example of Martin and John's teaching differ from the Essenes in another way: the sectarian group only cared for one another, whereas the invitation here seems to be caring for anyone God brings to our excess

122. Josephus, *J.W.* 2.122–123; Philo, *Hypothetica* 11.10.

123. Newman, *Competition in Religious Life*, 24.

124. Richardson, *Early Christian Care for the Poor.*

125. I slightly modified the translation by F. R. Hoare in Noble and Head, *Soldiers of Christ*, 7.

(see Luke 10:25–37). What is impossible for human beings is possible with God.[126]

The Baptist does not reject de jure authority but de facto corruption. The *toll collectors* and *soldiers* are not required to resign or to betray their human authorities: "Render to Caesar" (Luke 3:1–2; 20:24).

24A: The Stronger One (Mark 1:7–8)

[7] And he proclaimed, saying, "The one who is stronger than me is coming after me—of whom I am not qualified to bow before and loosen the strap of his sandals. [8] *I* baptized you with water, but *he* will baptize you in[127] (the) Holy Spirit." [Isa 11:1][128]

P: This unit is comprised of a saying in which John predicts the coming one will have more authority and power than himself, mirroring the language of the opening *gezerah sheva*: the messenger was to go before the Son's "face" to prepare the way of salvation by calling the people to repentance in the wilderness (1:1–3). We now see the thematic, chiastic structure of Mark's opening:

A Isaiah's Servant (1:1)

B Malachi's Elijah (1:2)

C Elijah preaches Isaiah's gospel (1:3)

B' John is Elijah (1:4–6)

A' Jesus is Isaiah's Servant (1:7–8).

But unlike Elijah, John is not remembered for performing miracles. Although filled with the Spirit—the necessary condition for prophecy—he could not share this empowerment with others, but only prepare the way.

126. I share the skepticism of Reinhold Neibuhr concerning the human capacity to sacrificial love, especially in large groups, but God can miraculously expand the heart.

127. Or "with" (NIV, ESV). But if one follows א and the editors of the Nestle-Aland text, the earliest text available to us reads ὕδατι . . . ἐν πνεύματι ἁγίῳ. Matthew's wording (see below) contaminated Mark. The word translated *water* is in the dative case, conveying the means or modality of the action. The role of the *Holy Spirit* is conveyed differently—with a preposition phrase that regularly describes the context of an action. *Holy Spirit* is written as a nomen sacrum, an abbreviation for divine names, in the earliest witnesses (Comfort, *Commentary*, 178).

128. There is no article before *Holy Spirit* in Greek, as we find in the allusion to Isa 11:1 in the Hebrew MT and OG.

R: Some Jews looked forward to a *spiritually* anointed messiah in Isaiah: "(the) Spirit of the Lord is upon (*epi,* ἐπί) me" (see 11:1–16).[129] The Baptist emphasizes the gift of "strength" (*ischuos,* ἰσχύος [v. 2]). Mark uses the adjectival form of the noun.[130] In context, this empowerment will overcome conflict: "he shall strike the earth with the rod of his mouth, and with the breath of his lips he shall kill the wicked" (Isa 11:4 ESV). With other prophets, Isaiah also looked forward to the *Spirit's* outpouring on the righteous in God's Kingdom: "I will pour my Spirit upon your offspring and my blessing on your descendants" (Isa 44:3 ESV; see Ezek 39:29; Joel 2:28).

D: Even granting hyperbole, John expresses remarkable humility: normally, only a slave or woman removed the *sandals* and washed the guest's feet upon entering a home.[131] Furthermore, he predicts the benefit of others, not himself: *he will baptize you.* The Baptist knew, like Elijah, that the prophetic mantle was to be given to another. There is also escalation: Jesus, the antitype of Elisha, will share the *Spirit* with others. This saying anticipates our empowerment.

The successful evangelism of the first Christians led to the greatest transformation the West has ever seen. By the end of the fourth century, half the Roman Empire, around thirty million people, were Christians. A century later Paganism was nearly extinguished. Like so many, Augustine was not first drawn to Christ because of reason, but power over his sin. In a treatise *Against the Academics,* he resolves "never to depart from the authority of Christ, for I find none that is stronger."[132] He had been deceived by the Manichaeans who claimed that reason alone was sufficient for wisdom. Something had to shift in his heart, a reordering of passion, that a merely human determination could not effect. The successful re-evangelism of the West will be no different: *Come, Holy Spirit, fill the hearts of your faithful and kindle in us the fire of your love.*

S: John prophesies the dual movement of God for salvation, the coming of *the stronger one* and the baptism of *the Spirit*, anticipating the formal introduction of the Triune God at the Baptism. If our Greek text is correct

129. See, e.g., 1 En. 49:3; PsSol. 17.37; 18.7.

130. ἰσχυρότερός is the comparative form of the adjective ἰσχυρός.

131. According to Patrick Fass, "foot washing was symbolic: in removing one's shoes, one was shaking off earthly bonds. One could no longer run into the street but had entered the spiritual sphere of the triclinium" (*Around the Roman Table,* 53). The slave used warm water in winter and cold in summer. Untying the thong of a sandal is considered by Rabbi Joshua ben Levi in the Babylonian Talmud to be below Jewish slaves (Ketub. 96a). Students of rabbis were to serve their teachers like a slave, but not to the point of taking off their sandals (Carson, *John,* 146).

132. Cited in Stumpf, *Socrates to Sartres,* 143.

(see note), Mark probably intends a distinction between a baptism *with* water—a mere instrument—and a baptism *in (the) Holy Spirit*, who is presented in his Gospel as a person, not a mere force (1:12; 3:22–30; 13:9–13). The "Spirit of the Lord," according to Isaiah, "shall rest upon" the messiah. To be in Christ is to be *in the Holy Spirit*: *All your breakers and your waves have gone over me* (Ps 42:7).

24B: The Stronger One (Matt 3:11–12)

[11] "*I* baptize you in water for repentance, but the one coming after me is stronger than me—concerning whom, I am not qualified to carry his[133] sandals. *He* will baptize you in (the) Holy Spirit and fire—[12] concerning whom, the thresher is in his hand;[134] and he will clean out his threshing floor and gather his grain[135] into the barn, but will torch the chaff with unquenchable fire!"

P: The saying is more threatening in Matthew, which fits the polemical moment after Pharisees and Sadducees invade the scene (3:7). The *thresher* (*ptuon,* πτύον), a forklike shovel, was used to toss the harvested grass into the wind. The heavier grain fell on the ground, *the threshing floor*, while the *chaff* blew away and gathered in piles for kindling.

The role of *fire* (*pur,* πῦρ) is ambiguous. The image may be positive, purification for the joy of God's presence. But, as *inclusio* around the saying, the emphasis is *unquenchable* judgment.

R: Isaiah closes with a vision of judgment: "For behold, the LORD will come in fire, and his chariots like the whirlwind, to render his anger in fury, and his rebuke with flames of fire. For by fire will the LORD enter into judgment, and by his sword, with all flesh; and those slain by the LORD shall be many" (66:15–16 ESV; see also 26:11; 65:15).

D: John's threat shocks ancient and modern sensibilities. The Greeks believed only gross sinners, like Tantalus and Sisyphus, received retributive punishment.[136] The later rabbis—more interested in unity than internecine conflict—take a generous view of salvation: "All Israelites have a share in the world to come."[137] But we find similar warnings in the Dead Sea Scrolls that were discovered near the Baptist's ministry.

133. There is no possessive pronoun in the Greek, but an article that may convey this syntax.

134. Metonymy for a manifestation of God's power (e.g., Exod 9:3; Deut 2:15).

135. This grain signifies the true sons of God, who are not necessarily Jews.

136. Hornblower and Spawforth, *Companion to Classical Civilization*, 210.

137. M. Sanh. 10:1 (Neusner).

John presumes all Israel is culpable before God; with Isaiah ("all flesh"), Paul will indict all humanity (Rom 1—3). In context, the necessary human response is *repentance* in thought and behavior (Matt 3:1–10). Although Jesus announces good news and offers love and healing, he does not reverse John's warning. The apocalyptic motif of burning the wicked resurfaces in his parables (Matt 13:30, 42). He comes to suffer and die on behalf of his people but also to extend the prophetic warning to the ends of the earth, to be realized upon his return as the glorified son of man (Matt 28:16–20).

S: John puns the dual sense of the Greek word *pneuma* (πνεῦμα), which can be translated *Spirit* or "wind" (see also John 3:8). The *Spirit* blows *the chaff* from the *threshing floor*, revealing the grain.

24C: The Stronger One (John 1:25–31)

[25] And they asked him and said to him, "Why, then, are you baptizing
if you are not the Christ nor Elijah nor the Prophet?" [26] John answered
them, saying: "*I* baptize in water. Among you has stood one you do not
know—[27] the one who is coming after me, of whom I am not worthy to
loosen the strap of his sandal." [28] (These things happened in Bethany [or
Bethabara] beyond the Jordan where John was baptizing.) [29] On the next
day, he sees Jesus coming to him and says, "Look, the lamb of God who lifts
up[138] the sin of the world! [30] This is he for whom I spoke: 'A man[139] is
coming after me who has been before my (face) because he was before me.'
[31] And I did not know him. But rather so that he might be revealed to
Israel—for this reason, I came baptizing in water."

P: This unit, cleaved by a geographical observation (v. 28) and wrapped by an *inclusio* of water baptism (vv. 26, 31), reinforces what was claimed in the prologue (1:1–18): *Christ* is superior to John because of his pre-creation relationship with the Father. The *Lamb of God*, whose blood (life) "purifies us from all sin" (1 John 1:7), clarifies "the Law was given through Moses; Grace and Truth came to be through Jesus Christ" (1:17). The Baptist foreshadows the cross, *who lifts up* (*airō*, αἴρω) *the sin of the world*, although he may not have understood the full implication of his words (2 Pet 1:20). Later, in the Synoptic portrait, he appears confused by Christ's ministry (Matt 11:3; Luke 7:19). John elaborates upon the saying in Mark (1:7–8), but infuses the Baptist's confession with irony to convey a *sensus plenior* ("fuller sense").

138. Or "takes away" (*airō*, αἴρω).

139. Or "husband" (*anēr*, ἀνήρ).

Luke claims Jesus and the Baptist were relatives (Luke 1:36), which seems to jar with *I did not know him*. But Luke does not join them together in the same scene, except in utero, before their public ministries: John "was in the wild areas until the day of his commissioning to Israel" (1:80). The claim, as D. A. Carson notes, "does not mean that John did not know him at all, but only that he did not know him as the Coming One."[140] This paradigm shift occurred at Christ's baptism, which is addressed in the next unit (John 1:32–34). He may have known Jesus as a relative, but not as the Father's unique Son filled with the Holy Spirit.

This unit is historically important because it potentially locates Jesus's baptism, which would be significant for pilgrimage, although there is a textual variant. *Bethany* (*Bēthania*, Βηθανία) may be an alternative spelling for Batanea, which is Old Testament Bashan, a region north-east of the Jordan.[141] If so, the reference is too general for a specific location. But several manuscripts read "Bethabara" (Βηθαβαρά), which may signify "place of crossing," and probably refers to Al-Maghtas ("the baptism") in Jordan. The name occurs on the Madaba Map and in the Talmud (בית עברה).[142] Although these witnesses are not the earliest, they offer the more difficult reading, which is a criterion for isolating the most original wording.[143] Origen found this reading in a few manuscripts that were available to him and preferred, and is followed by John Chrysostom.[144] Against this, however, is John's own seeming clarification *beyond the Jordan* to distinguish this Bethany from a village near Jerusalem (John 11:1, 18). In any case, the two names do not contradict one another and may refer generally and specifically to the same location. At the end of the twentieth century, an ancient church was rediscovered at Al-Maghtas, just east of the Jordan and slightly north where the river empties into the Dead Sea. The early church embraced this site as the place where John baptized Jesus. Pilgrims were baptized in a cruciform pool, rested, and worshiped there; hermits prayed in caves.[145]

140. Carson, *John*, 151.

141. Carson, *John*, 146–47.

142. Lagrange, "JÉRUSALEM D'APRÈS LA MOSAÏQUE DE MADABA," 450–58. The Greek description for the location is clear and easily translated: "Bethabara, the (place) of Saint John's baptizing." There are multiple images available on the internet.

143. Βηθαβαρά is a New Testament *hapax legomenon*. It is easier to imagine this more obscure reading giving way to Βηθανία than the reverse, contrary to Metzger's claim: "if Βηθαβαρᾷ were original, there is no adequate reason why it should have been altered to Βηθανίᾳ" (*Textual Commentary*, 200).

144. See Metzger, *Textual Commentary*, 199–200.

145. Waheeb, "Discovery of Bethany Beyond the Jordan River," 115–26.

R: *Beyond the Jordan*, a biblical expression, refers to a wilderness in the land of Moab where Moses recapitulated the Law before before the next generation entered (Deut 1:1, 5). Jesus was probably baptized where the first "Jesus," Joshua (the names are spelled the same in Greek), led God's people through the Jordan River that God miraculously parted, an echo of the Red Sea at the beginning of the journey (Josh 3), and where Elijah ascended to God in a cloud chariot (2 Kgs 2:9, 11).

The lamb of God (*Ho amnon tou Theou,* ὁ ἀμνὸς τοῦ θεοῦ) functions as the antitype to the lambs sacrificed in place of the firstborn sons in Egypt. "Male," "without blemish," they were killed by the people (Exod 12:5, 6); their blood, a "sign," was, in a sense, *lifted up* "on the two door posts and the lintel of the houses" (vv. 7, 13). "When I see the blood," God says, "I will pass over you, and no plague will befall you to destroy you, when I strike the land of Egypt" (v. 13). The Paschal *lamb* is technically not a sin offering, but the Suffering Servant in Isaiah embodies the type by going to slaughter as a *lamb* (42:1–9; 49:1–13; 50:4–11; 52:13–53). There is also escalation: whereas the lambs in the first Exodus only saved the sons of Israel, the *lamb of God* "is propitiation for our sins—not for ours only but also for the whole *world*" (1 John 2:2; see also John 3:16).

D: We all get to cross the Jordan in Christ. To abide in Christ is to be in his home, to enjoy his protective blood on the door posts and lintel.

S: Many traditions offer this prayer, *Agnus Dei,* in the breaking of the bread:

> *Agnus Dei, qui tollis peccata mundi, miserere nobis.*
>
> *Agnus Dei, qui tollis peccata mundi, miserere nobis.*
>
> *Agnus Dei, qui tollis peccata mundi, dona nobis pacem.*
>
> Lamb of God, who takes away the sins of the world, have mercy upon us.
>
> Lamb of God, who takes away the sins of the world, have mercy upon us.
>
> Lamb of God, who takes away the sins of the world, grant us peace.

24D: The Stronger One (Luke 3:15–18)

[15] Now while the people were waiting expectantly and all were questioning in their hearts about John, if *he* could be the Christ, [16] John answered, saying to all, "I baptize you with water, but the one who is stronger than me

is coming. Concerning whom, I am not qualified to loosen the straps of his sandals. *He* will baptize you in (the) Holy Spirit and fire.[146] [17] Concerning whom, the thresher is in his hand to clean out his threshing floor and to gather the grain into his barn. But he will torch the chaff with unquenchable fire!" [18] So also with many other exhortations he was proclaiming the good news to the people.

P: This unit completes the chiasm of the episode, mirroring John's rebuke (see Luke 3:7–9). As usual, Mark is Luke's point of departure for retelling the story, employing the Gospel's "*with* water" (Matthew and John read "in water.") and the image of *loosening sandal straps* (Matthew has "carry"). Luke tends to generalize the particular interlocutors in other traditions, as we see in the immediate context when Matthew depicts John rebuking "the Pharisees and Sadducees" (3:7) but Luke reads "the crowds" (3:7). He does the same here: John's delegation from the Pharisees (John 1:24) mirrors the concern of *the people*, who form *inclusio* around the unit.[147] The Baptist's response overlaps with John's presentation:

> ἀπεκρίθη αὐτοῖς ὁ Ἰωάννης λέγων· ἐγὼ βαπτίζω ἐν ὕδατι (John 1:26)
>
> John answered them, saying, "I baptize with water"

> ἀπεκρίνατο λέγων πᾶσιν ὁ Ἰωάννης· ἐγὼ μὲν ὕδατι βαπτίζω ὑμᾶς (Luke 3:16)[148]
>
> John answered, saying to all, "I Baptist you with water"

In Mark and Matthew, the saying is unsolicited. In John, the Baptist responds to his interlocutors by denying that he is *ho Christos* (ὁ χριστός, *the Christ*, 1:20). According to Luke, the people wonder if he is *the Christ* (ὁ χριστός, 3:15); the actual denial in John resurfaces in Acts:

> οὗ οὐκ εἰμὶ [ἐγὼ] ἄξιος ἵνα λύσω αὐτοῦ τὸν ἱμάντα τοῦ ὑποδήματος (John 1:27)
>
> "of whom I am not worthy to loosen the straps of his sandals"

> οὐκ εἰμὶ ἐγώ· ἀλλ᾽ ἰδοὺ ἔρχεται μετ᾽ ἐμὲ οὗ οὐκ εἰμὶ ἄξιος τὸ ὑπόδημα τῶν ποδῶν λῦσαι (Acts 13:25)

146. Or "the holy and fiery spirit."

147. Shellard, *New Light on Luke*, 217; Anderson, *Fourth Gospel and the Quest for Jesus*, 113.

148. Cribbs, "St. Luke," 432.

> "I am not he. But, behold, after me one is coming of who I am not worthy to loosen the sandals of his feet."[149]

Luke also appropriates the Baptist's apocalyptic warning *of unquenchable fire* in Matthew. All four Gospels are represented![150] But whereas Matthew appears to interpret *fire* only negatively, Luke finds a positive connotation for *He will baptize you in (the) Holy Spirit and fire.* "Tongues as of fire" accompany the filling of the Spirit at Pentecost, the fulfillment of the Baptist's prophecy (Acts 2:3). Origen completes this trajectory, seeing both senses—a blessing for the righteous and a judgment for the wicked.[151] This dual meaning is suggested by the chiastic structure of the unit; in the parallel unit, John says, "every tree that does not bear good fruit is chopped down and cast into the fire" (3:9).

D: The Holy Spirit changes things. The heat of a fire causes wood, with the potential to be hot, to become hot, effecting a change in the wood (Aquinas *S.T.* 3). Change is often marked by coming into being and passing away, but the pattern is disrupted in the burning bush and then again at the Transfiguration. Symeon the New Theologian (949–1032) describes union with Christ in the Eucharist: "I, who am but straw, receive the Fire, and—unheard of wonder!—am inflamed without being consumed, as of old the burning bush of Moses."[152] The following is a story about two desert fathers in the fourth century:

> Abba Joseph said to Abba Lot, "You cannot be a monk unless you become like a consuming fire." Abba Lot went to see Abba Joseph and said to him: "Abba, as far as I can say my little office, I fast a little, I pray and meditate, I live in peace and as far as I can, I purify my thoughts. What else can I do?" Then the old man stood up and stretched his hands toward heaven. His fingers became like ten lamps of fire, and he said to him: "If you will, you can become all flame."[153]

By the Spirit, we change—becoming all flame—while remaining who we are. This change is felt passively in the passing away of worldly desire and birth of love and actively through the pain of a fiery trial for the testing of our faith (Mark 10:38; Jas 1:2–4; 1 Pet 1:7; 4:12).

149. Shellard, *New Light on Luke*, 217.

150. The integration finds its completion in Justin who blends Matthew and Luke together (*Dial.* 48).

151. See Dunn, "Spirit-and-Fire Baptism," 81–92.

152. Cited in Harpur, *Love Burning in the Soul*, 112.

153. Ward, *Sayings of the Desert Fathers*, 103 (slightly revised).

S: *Holy Spirit, we wait expectantly, holding our questions and faith in Christ, yearning to become all flame. Enlighten us. Amen.*

25A: Christ's Baptism (Mark 1:9–11)

[9] And it came about in those days: Jesus came from Nazareth of Galilee and was baptized into the Jordan[154] by John. [10] And rising out of the water, suddenly[155] he saw[156] the heavens[157] tearing apart and the[158] Spirit descending like a dove into him.[159] [11] And there was a voice from the heavens: "You are my beloved Son. In you I take delight." [Gen 22:12; Ps 2:7]

P: *And it came about* (*Kai egeneto*, Καὶ ἐγένετο), a common transition, allows time between John's prophecy (v. 8) and its otherwise swift fulfillment (*in those days*). Unworthy to wash his feet, John still baptizes Jesus, who is then filled with *the* promised *Spirit*. The transition also foreshadows conflict: *Jesus* travels from the northern province of *Galilee*, the jurisdiction of Herod Antipas, who kills the Baptist (see 6:14–29), from *Nazareth*, a place of familial rejection (6:1–6a), to the southern province of Judea, which was under the de jure authority of Pontius Pilate (15:1–15) and the de facto influence of the high priest (14:53–65), who kill him. The finale of the unit, *I take delight*, may form *inclusio*, suggesting the divine point of view on the action. In Greek translations of Scripture, the verb *eudokeō* (εὐδοκέω) describes God's acceptance of sacrifice.[160] What the earthly authorities intended for evil, God purposed for good.

Rabbis claimed God stopped speaking directly to human beings after Malachi but might communicate to those worthy of the divine presence

154. Mark has given the fuller expression "Jordan River" at v. 5.

155. Or "suddenly" (*euthus*, εὐθύς) is one of Mark's favorite rhetorical devices, occurring forty-one times. (The adverb occurs only five times in Matthew, once in Luke, and three times in John.) The word often expresses a surprising action or an effect from a mysterious cause.

156. Mark appears to emphasize that Jesus had a private experience (Bock, *Jesus according to Scripture*, 86).

157. Mark may evoke the opening line of Scripture (Gen 1:1). After this unit, he generally reverts back to the singular form in keeping with standard Greek (4:32; 6:41; 7:34; 8:11; 10:21; 11:30, 31; 13:27, 31, 32; 14:62; but see 11:25, 26; 12:25; 13:25).

158. *The* may allude back to the first occurrence of Holy Spirit, which lacks an article (1:8).

159. For this reading, see Dixon, "Descending Spirit and Descending Gods," 759–80.

160. See, e.g., Lev 7:18; Sir 31:23.

(*shekinah*) through a *bat kol* ("daughter of a voice") or "coo of a *dove*."[161] The Babylonian Talmud opens with a response from Rabbi Jose ben Halafta, who was asked by Elijah if he heard anything while praying in the ruins of Jerusalem:

> I heard a divine voice [*bat kol*], cooing like a dove and saying: "Woe to the children, on account of whose sins I destroyed My house and burnt My temple and exiled them among the nations of the world! (b. Ber. 3a)[162]

The *dove's* call sounds like a lament (Isa 38:14, "mourning dove")—a fitting simile within a simile. God is not merely offering commentary on the lingering devastation of the Exile, but sadness over the ruptured relationship (Gen 3:9). A *bat kol* often attended *halakik* decisions—contextualized rules and rhythms for covenant between God and people—as a kind of backing, like the more direct relationship between the Law and Prophets, but some rabbis were concerned about its subjectivity (b. Eruv. 13b).[163]

The mystery of the *Son's* experience may be partially illumined by this background.[164] The rabbinic discussion comes from a later period, but is rooted in postexilic reflection on God's distancing reaction to the many violations of the covenant. Unlike the rest of the people, Mark does not present Jesus confessing sin (1:5). He identifies with a sinful Israel through baptism, yet is innocent.[165] The Father's voiced pleasure and *the Spirit's* movement toward *the beloved son* mark the end of exile.

R: The *Akeda* or "Binding of Isaac," one of the most horrific, inexplicable moments in salvation history, is repeated and completed with God's own Son. The Father echoes the angel's assurance to Abraham, having been required to sacrifice Isaac: "I know that you fear God: you did not spare your beloved son because of me" (Gen 22:12 LXX).[166]

The *bat kol* also echoes the second psalm where the king of Israel is declared God's son and vice-regent on earth (v. 7):[167]

161. Keener, *Spirit in the Gospels and Acts*, 54.

162. Epstein, *Babylonian Talmud*, 3a (Simon).

163. Eisenberg, *What the Rabbis Said*, 7.

164. Dalman and Lightfoot, *Jesus Christ in the Talmud*, 20. Cranfield claims Mark and Jesus were conscious of this form (*Mark*, 54).

165. Campbell, "Jesus and His Baptism," 191–214.

166. The Greek overlaps: τοῦ υἱοῦ σου τοῦ ἀγαπητοῦ—ὁ υἱός μου ὁ ἀγαπητός (Mark 1:11). See Keener, *Spirit in the Gospels and Acts*, 55; Huizenga, *New Isaac*; Rindge, "Reconfiguring the Akedah and Recasting God," 755–74.

167. Stanton, *Jesus and Gospel*, 43; Keener, *Spirit in the Gospels and Acts*, 56; Davies and Allison conclude: "The first line of our text is from or has been influenced by Ps.

> As for me, I have set my King on Zion, my holy hill. I will tell of the decree: The LORD said to me, "You are my Son; today I have begotten you. Ask of me, and I will make the nations your heritage, and the ends of the earth your possession. You shall break them with a rod of iron and dash them in pieces like a potter's vessel." (Ps 2:6–9 ESV)

This royal psalm may have originated as part of the liturgy celebrating the accession to the throne of a king in pre-exilic Jerusalem.[168] The language presupposes a covenant that God made with David, which is grounded in a promise that God made to Abraham (Gen 12:1–3):

> When your days are fulfilled and you lie down with your fathers, I will raise up your offspring after you, who shall come from your body, and I will establish his kingdom. He shall build a house for my name, and I will establish the throne of his kingdom forever. I will be to him a father, and he shall be to me a son. When he commits iniquity, I will discipline him with the rod of men, with the stripes of the sons of men, but my steadfast love will not depart from him, as I took it from Saul, whom I put away from before you. And your house and your kingdom shall be made sure forever before me. Your throne shall be established forever. (2 Sam 7:12–16 ESV)

After the fall of the Davidic monarchy, the promise was interpreted prophetically.[169]

I suggest God the Father adopted these passages in the affirmation over his Son, but with escalation. God complicates his promise to Abraham by commanding him to sacrifice his beloved son Isaac, the very means of the fulfillment of his words. And yet God relents at the last moment. Why? Because Isaac is a type or shadow of God's Son. Whereas Abraham was spared the horror of taking Isaac's life, God the Father keeps his promise to reverse the effect of the Fall by sacrificing his own *beloved Son*. David's son is also a type. But unlike Solomon and other descendants Jesus is not adopted by God at his coronation. The Father does not say, "today I have begotten you," but "You *are* my beloved Son," or, as Ludolph paraphrases, "he is my Son by nature, not

---

2:7 (LXX?) while the next two lines are derived from a non-LXX version of Isa. 42:1" (*Matthew*, 1:338).

168. On this point, see the seminal work of Sigmund Mowinckel (1884–1965). The divine utterance is reminiscent of ancient Near East coronation liturgies. The announcement is cited in Hebrews (1:5; 5:5). Paul also applies the language to Jesus's resurrection (Acts 13:32, 33; see Rom 1:3–4). Luke portrays Jesus's departure as a coronation.

169. DelHousaye, "Across the Kidron," 117–32.

simply by adoption."[170] "The begetting of the Son," sings Ephrem the Syrian (c. 306–373), "is exalted above the questioning of humanity."[171] Furthermore, Jesus is not disobedient and therefore deserving of the "rod" and "stripes," but is sinless: "He did not need to be cleansed but became the source of cleansing for us."[172] For this reason, Jesus distances himself from Davidic messianic expectation in the second Gospel (Mark 12:35–37).

D: This disclosure contributes to the dramatic irony of Mark's opening, placing a demand on the reader.[173] We know who Jesus is, at least superficially, but no one, except for the demons (3:11; 5:7), identifies him as such until the end of the story, and it is the centurion charged with his execution (15:39)! But perhaps we might turn this irony on ourselves: How well do we know Jesus? We are taking this meditative journey to know him as the Father does, so that he is ever more beloved to us.[174] We may even begin to love our enemies by seeing them through the eyes of a loving parent, let alone our fellow disciples.

Jesus models a loving and brotherly presence among God's people, identifying with them and ministering to their needs, a path taken by Charles de Foucauld (1858–1916). Pope Benedict XVI, who beatified the hermit to the Berbers, offers this gloss:

> Thus, to go down into the river and be washed was a gesture of humility, a humble prayer for pardon and grace. In other words, that descending is a symbolic dying of the old life to obtain the grace of a new life. If Jesus, the Lamb without sin, joins the file of sinners lining up for the confessional, so to speak, if with that public gesture he makes himself one with sinners, receiving the sacrament of sinners, at that moment begins his hour, the hour of the Cross.[175]

170. Ludolph of Saxony, *Life of Christ*, 1:435. Contrast with the Ebionite gospel that puts the begetting language into the mouth of the Father.

171. Ephrem the Syrian, *Hymns on Faith*, 58 (1:3).

172. Ludolph of Saxony, *Life of Christ*, 1:421.

173. Camery-Hoggatt, *Irony in Mark's Gospel*, x.

174. Some rabbis saw the bird as symbolic of Israel (Harpur, *Love Burning*, 16). Hugh of St. Victor saw the church in the *dove*: one wing represented the active life; the other, the contemplative; the blue sheen of the wings, thoughts of heaven; yellow eyes, wisdom for the future; red feet, the blood of the martyrs.

175. Ratzinger, *Journey to Easter*, 15.

S: *The heavens tearing apart* mark God's intervening presence.[176] In Hellenistic literature, a *dove* represents the arrival of a god.[177] Jesus presents *doves* as pure—a fitting image for the *Holy* Spirit (Matt 10:16). The gentle bird is "preeminent among animals as a cultivator of charity."[178]

God the Father calls Jesus to serve Israel and ultimately the world as Prophet, Priest, and King.[179] As priest, the Messiah represents Israel before God. But unlike high priests before him, he becomes the sacrifice (Mark 10:45).

25B: Christ's Baptism (Matt 3:13–17)

[13] Then Jesus appears[180] from the Galilee at the Jordan beside John to be baptized by him. [14] But John[181] was attempting to prevent[182] him, saying, "I myself need to be baptized by you, and you come to me!" [15] But answering, Jesus said to him: "Permit it now. For it is very appropriate for us to fulfill all righteousness." Then he permitted him. [16] Now after being baptized, Jesus immediately came up from *the water*. And look: the heavens were opened [to him],[183] and he saw [the][184] *Spirit of God* descending like a dove [and][185] coming *upon* him. [Gen 1:2; Isa 61:1] [17] And look: a voice from the heavens was saying: "This is my beloved Son in whom I take delight." [Gen 22:12; Ps 2:7]

P: Matthew follows Mark's presentation, but depicts *John* as reticent, which anticipates a later struggle (11:2). On the one hand, John expresses humility, which is often emphasized in patristic interpretation: *I need to be baptized by you*. On the other, he initially resists God's will, not because of disobedience but the mysterious turn in God's work of salvation that was hidden from everyone (Matt 13:11; Eph 3:7–13). Matthew also switches the Father's response to the third person—"*This is*"—to anticipate the parallel

176. See, e.g., Isa 64:1; Ezek 1:1; John 1:51; Acts 7:56; Rev 4:1.

177. Dixon, "Descending Spirit and Descending Gods," 760.

178. Ludolph of Saxony, *Life of Christ*, 1:432.

179. The three epithets are mentioned by Pseudo-Jerome (*CA* on Mark 1). See Otto, "Baptism and the *Munus Triplex*," 217–25.

180. The same verb introduces John and Jesus into the narrative (3:1).

181. Or "he." Several mss omit the proper name. The sense is little affected.

182. Or "was preventing" *diekōluen* (διεκώλυεν). The imperfect tense allows a special syntax in which an action is attempted but not accomplished ("conative imperfect").

183. Our earliest mss omit the pronoun.

184. Our earliest mss omit the article.

185. Our earliest mss omit the article.

locution to Peter, James, and John at the Transfiguration (17:5), so that the tradition becomes more didactic.[186]

R: Matthew expands Mark's "the Spirit" to "Spirit of God" (*pneuma theou*, πνεῦμα θεοῦ), an allusion to the first day of creation: "(The) Spirit of God (*pneuma theou*, πνεῦμα θεοῦ) was being carried over the water, and God said, 'Let there be light'" (Gen 1:2–3 LXX). At Christ's baptism, the *Spirit* moves over *the water* and then the Father speaks (see John 1:4–5, 9). The Scriptures interpenetrate: baptism illumines a shadow in the creation story: the Hebrew verb behind "being carried over" (*rachaph*, רָחַף) occurs in the piel stem only once elsewhere in Scripture—when Moses reminds his readers of their "Creator, who made you and formed you" (v. 6) "like an eagle that stirs up its nest, that flutters (*rachaph*, רָחַף) over its young, spreading out its wings, catching them, bearing them on its pinions" (Deut 32:6, 11 ESV).

Matthew has explicitly presented Christ's birth and maturation as the fulfillment of prophecy.[187] Hearing an echo of Isaiah—"Out of the anguish of his soul he shall see and be satisfied; by his knowledge shall the righteous one, my servant, make many to be accounted righteous, and he shall bear their iniquities" (53:11 ESV), Oscar Cullmann (1902–1999) claims the baptism prefigures the cross by which *righteousness* is accomplished.[188] So the evangelist amplifies the appeasement element in Mark's presentation. *Righteousness* (*dikaiosunē*, δικαιοσύνη) refers to God's expectation for covenant relationship through normative behavior, which Jesus will clarify as the imitation of the Father's love, even for one's enemy (3:15; 5:6, 10, 20; 6:1, 33; 21:32).[189] It is "the perfection of all virtues."[190] But Christ must first deal with the problem of sin, the separation between the people and their God.

Matthew makes another allusion to Isaiah by subtly rephrasing Mark's "he saw . . . the Spirit descending like a dove into him" to *he saw [the] Spirit of God descending like a dove [and] coming upon* (*epi*, ἐπί) *him* to match, "(the) Spirit of the Lord is upon (*epi*, ἐπί) me because he anointed me to proclaim good news to the destitute" (Isa 61:1 OG).[191] Matthew infuses this

186. For the assumption that God is addressing the crowds, see, e.g., Harpur, *Love Burning*, 16. But the locution it is more likely directed to John, affirming his submission to Jesus's request, which correlates with John (1:32–34) and 2 Peter (2:17).

187. Davies and Allison, *Matthew*, 1:326–27; Turner, *Matthew*, 118. According to Jerome, the non-canonical Gospel of the Nazarenes claims Jesus's mother and brothers urged Jesus to be baptized by John and that he was originally opposed to it (*Pelag.* 3.2).

188. Cullmann, *Baptism in the New Testament*, 18–19.

189. See Przybylski, *Righteousness in Matthew*, 105.

190. Ludolph of Saxony, *Life of Christ*, 1:424.

191. Πνεῦμα κυρίου ἐπ᾽ ἐμέ, οὗ εἵνεκεν ἔχρισέν με· εὐαγγελίσασθαι πτωχοῖς

line into another scene (11:1). We shall often return to this prophecy; here it is only necessary to note that Isaiah anticipates both the empowerment and sacrificial appeasement of the scene.

D: An early West Syriac baptismal service contrasts baptism with Eve's womb:

> Instead of the womb of Eve which produced children who are mortal and corruptible may this womb of water produce children who are heavenly, spiritual, and immortal.[192]

The Syrian theologian and poet Jacob of Serugh notes:

> Christ came to baptism, he went down and placed in the baptismal water the robe of glory, to be there for Adam, who had lost it.[193]

The scene is similar to when Jesus washes the feet of his disciples, but Peter initially refuses (John 13:1–11). The Kenosis (emptying) of Christ's ministry is incarnated in acts that normally would be unbecoming between superiors and subordinates, but that is the topsy-turvy world of the kingdom. The humility of the Son weds to that of John and together they fulfill righteousness. *May we recognize and join ourselves to the shockingly unpresuming work of our Lord. Amen.*

S: Matthew invites us to see the Triune God. The scene opens with a dramatic present (*appears*) and the pleonasm of two prepositional phrases (*at the Jordan beside John*). After our eyes are fixed on Jesus, twice we are prompted *And look* (*kai idou,* καὶ ἰδού)—first, in reference to the descent of *the Spirit* and then the affirmation of the Father. At the end of the Gospel, Jesus tells the disciples to baptize "in the name of the Father and of the Son and of the Holy Spirit" (28:19).

Jesus is our prophet, priest, and king. As prophet, Jesus is filled with the Holy Spirit, placing his teaching into the category of Scripture. It is probably not accidental that Matthew has Jesus "open his mouth" after this event, offering the Sermon on the Mount (5:2).

25C: Christ's Baptism (John 1:32–34)

[32] And John witnessed, saying: "I have seen *the Spirit* descending like a dove from heaven, and it remained *upon* him. [Isa 61:1] [33] And I did not

---

ἀπέσταλκέν με.

192. Brock, *Spirituality in the Syriac Tradition*, 62.

193. Brock, *Spirituality in the Syriac Tradition*, 64.

know him, but the one who sent me to be baptizing with water—that one said to me: '*Upon* whom you see the Spirit descending and remaining *upon* him—this is the one who is baptizing with (the) Holy Spirit.' [34] And I have seen and have witnessed that this is the [elect][194] of God."

P: Matthew's reorientation of Mark, focusing on the didactic experience of others, is completed in John, who portrays the Baptist seeing *the Spirit* and hearing the Father.[195]

R: With Matthew, John also emphasizes the fulfillment of Isaiah's vision, "(The) Spirit of the Lord is upon me" (61:1 OG), using the preposition *upon* (*epi,* ἐπί) three times.[196] The prophet adds that God sent this anointed figure "to heal the broken in heart" like Martha and Mary over their brother's death (11:1–44) and "to recover sight to the blind" like the man in Jerusalem (9:1–41).[197] The Baptist sees the cause of the effect—the seven signs that occupy a large part of John's presentation.

God's *Spirit* would come upon those in the old covenant but not necessarily *remain* (1 Sam 16:14; Ps 51:11; see Judg 16:20).

D: John makes the baptism of God's *elect* semi-public. The tradition is not merely predicated on the subjective experience of Jesus in the water, but another eyewitness—a prominent theme in the fourth Gospel (John 5:30–47). The perception of the Baptist will be juxtaposed with the confusion of people towards the end of the story (12:27–36).

Lord and Father, may we see your Spirit at work and play. Wash our eyes and quiet our hearts. Amen.

S: If we have the right wording (see note), the Baptist presents Jesus as *the elect of God* (*ho eklektos tou theou,* ὁ ἐκλεκτός τοῦ θεοῦ).[198] The language normally refers to Israel, the recipient of God's promises and covenant.[199] Jesus Christ, the Messiah, represents (embodies) them, along with the rest of humanity, before God (see Matt 2:15). We who are not part of ethnic Israel are *elect* or "chosen" in him, an inclusion anticipated by John

194. Or "son of God." Both wordings are early and have diverse attestation. It is easier for the more unusual reading to give way to the more general (see Comfort, *Commentary*, 249; Skinner, "'Son of God' or 'God's Chosen One,'" 341–57).

195. In rabbinic thought, the Holy Spirit (*ruach ha-kodesh*) only remains with the righteous (Eisenberg, *What the Rabbis Said*, 8).

196. πνεῦμα κυρίου ἐπ' ἐμέ οὗ εἵνεκεν ἔχρισέν με εὐαγγελίσασθαι πτωχοῖς ἀπέσταλκέν με ἰάσασθαι τοὺς συντετριμμένους τῇ καρδίᾳ κηρύξαι αἰχμαλώτοις ἄφεσιν καὶ τυφλοῖς ἀνάβλεψιν.

197. The reference to healing the blind is in the Old Greek translation of the Hebrew.

198. We are not entirely dependent on the wording of this passage for this discussion because the same title occurs at Luke 23:35.

199. See, e.g., the Greek translations of 1 Chr 16:13; Ps 104 [MT 105]: 6, 43; Isa 42:1; 43:20; 65:9.

(12:20–26) and unpacked by Paul and Peter.[200] Karl Barth (1886–1968) focused double predestination on Christ alone: "He is the election of God before which and without which and beside which God cannot make any other choices . . . apart from Him there is no election,"[201] so that Christ, the God-man, is both the chosen and rejected one; in Christ, there are no longer two distinct groups of elect and reprobate. Christ, "the image of the invisible God," is called to reconcile God and humanity; our election is participation in this mission.[202]

John introduces an important word. Jesus will invite disciples to *remain* (*menō*, μένω) or "abide" with him and the Father through the mutual indwelling of the Holy Spirit (14:10; 15:4). The verb signifies remaining with someone.[203]

25D: Christ's Baptism (Luke 3:21–22)

[21] Now it came about when all the people had been baptized and Jesus had been baptized and was praying, the heaven was opened; [22] and the Holy Spirit descended in bodily form as a dove *upon* him, and a voice came from heaven: "You are my beloved Son. In you I take delight." [Isa 61:1]

P: Only Luke mentions that Jesus was *praying*, a major emphasis in his presentation.[204] Otherwise, he is more concise than the other evangelists while appropriating some of their additions to Mark's template. Instead of "into him" (*eis auton*, εἰς αὐτόν), Luke follows Matthew's "upon him" (*ep'auton*, ἐπ' αὐτόν), which clarifies the fulfillment of Isaiah's vision (61:1). Neither John nor Luke depicts John *baptizing* Jesus to emphasize the unique immersion of *the Holy Spirit*.[205] Luke employs ambiguity with the passive voice (*Jesus had been baptized*) and describes John's arrest before the baptism! At each redaction—Matthew's appropriation of Mark, John's appropriation of Mark and John, and Luke's appropriation of Matthew and John—the Baptist moves farther from the stage until he disappears. The provenance of the fourth Gospel is traditionally Ephesus; Paul encounters disciples of John there in Luke's sequel (Acts 19:1–10). Unlike Christians, they had yet to receive *the Holy Spirit*. Presumably, the later evangelists

200. See 1 Thess 1:4–5; Rom 8:33; Eph 1:3–14; 1 Pet 1:1, 20.

201. Barth, *CD* 2/2:94–65. He grounds the claim in exegesis from John's Gospel (95–99).

202. McDonald, *Reimaging Election*; Newbigin, *Gospel in a Pluralist Society*, 83–87.

203. See John 1:38; 2:12; 4:4; 7:9; 8:31, 35; 11:6; 12:46; 15:9; 19:31.

204. See Luke 5:16; 6:12–16; 9:18–22, 28–29; 11:1–8; 18:1–8; 22:31–34; 23:34.

205. Cribbs, "St. Luke," 429; Shellard, *New Light on Luke*, 216; Luke 1:17, 76; 7:27.

adjusted their presentations to account for the popularity of the Baptist in that region. The scene will be recapitulated at Pentecost: everyone is together *praying* before the *Holy Spirit* descends (Acts 2:15–26).[206]

Instead of emphasizing the union of the Spirit between Jesus and the Baptist at this stage, Luke anticipates the moment by having John leap with joy in the womb of his mother (Luke 1:41, 44).

R: The allusion to Isaiah (61:1) will be explicitly cited as fulfilled when Jesus preaches in Nazareth (Luke 4:18–19). We learn that the Spirit's role was to "anoint" him, the meaning of Christ (messiah), for a public ministry of justice, healing, freedom, and rest. The *opening of heaven* is God's response to an ancient prayer from an exiled people: "Look down from heaven and see, from your holy and beautiful habitation . . . For you are our Father . . . Oh that you would rend the heavens and come down" (Isa 63:15–16; 64:1 ESV).[207]

Presumably, Jesus *was praying* as representative of God's people. Like the exodus, God had heard the cries of his people and is full of compassion for them (Exod 3).

D: "Christ prayed at this moment," notes Ludolph, "to instruct us how we should pray after we have been baptized."[208] We are no longer exiled and alienated from God, but pray against the temptations of the devil, which are sure to follow, and for insight into the mystery of our union with Christ. Baptism came to represent a gate between the purgative and illuminative stages of the journey back to God.

S: Luke claims an otherwise invisible *Spirit* took a *bodily form* (*sōmatikos*, σωματικός). The language is similar to the Incarnation (John 1:14) and may be inspired by the links between the Son and Spirit in the Upper Room Discourse (John 14:15–31). Paul uses the same adjective to describe the Son: "in him dwells bodily (*sōmatikos*) all the fullness of deity" (Col 2:9). These two embodiments of the divine are united in the church, the body of Christ. The Holy Spirit recreates us into the resurrected body of the Son, the beginning of new creation. We are also therefore proleptically present here in Christ's baptism. Luke shows this by having the Holy Spirit hover over the church at Pentecost.

In ancient Israel, a would-be king underwent a three-part accession to the throne: *designation*, which might be said to happen at Jesus's baptism; *demonstration*, which occurs from this point forward in various attacks

206. Shellard, *New Light on Luke*, 215–16.

207. Stanton, *Jesus and Gospel*, 42. In other translations, the final verse is numbered 63:19 following the MT.

208. Ludolph of Saxony, *Life of Christ*, 1:432.

against Satan; and *coronation*, which Luke will narrate at the end of his presentation.[209] David receives the Spirit of YHWH in anticipation of his reign (1 Sam 16:13). Jesus is similarly anointed for these tasks by the Holy Spirit, a vehicle of purification, restoration (forgiveness), and power.

History, Revelation, and Sacrament

Historians are confident that Jesus was baptized by John the Baptist.[210] They employ the criterion of embarrassment: why would the early church make up a story that implies the superiority of a founder of one of their rival groups? We see the diminishment of the Baptist's role in each retelling of the story, but never fully excised. All four evangelists relate the event, with some diversity, meeting the criterion of multiple attestation.[211] Now we may attend to the meaning of the event.

The feast of Epiphany, particularly in the East, celebrates the reintroduction of the Triune God (*theos*, θεός) to creation at Christ's baptism. Jacob of Serugh (c. 451–521) observes: "At the time of the Epiphany of Christ, the Trinity appeared at the Jordan."[212] The heavens open, God floods the scene. The Spirit is "of" or "from God" (Matt 3:16), as is the Son by virtue of their relationship. The three personal agents in the scene—Son, Spirit, and Father—are united in love.[213] "There are three," Augustine notes, "the lover, the beloved, and the love."[214] God the Father, the lover, is revealed as such in the Son, who is *beloved*, the representative of God's people, and the Spirit conveys this love. The eastern fathers describe the Triune God as a "Great Round Dance in which Love flames forth from one Person to the Other in a flow that never ceases."[215] The threefold disclosure of God finds a communal response in the troparion of the feast:

209. Shelton, "Ancient Israelite Pattern of Kingly Accession," 61–73.

210. E. P. Sanders accepts the baptism as a nearly indisputable fact (*Jesus and Judaism*, 326–27).

211. The distinctives require Tatian to blend the presentations of Matthew, Luke, and John (4.28–40).

212. Jacob of Serugh, *Homily on Epiphany* 33 (PO 43:565); cited in Wilken, *Spirit of Early Christian Thought*, 326. Bede notes: "The mystery of the Trinity also is shown forth in the baptism" (*CA* on Mark 1).

213. In later passages, Jesus relates to the Spirit as a person, who is about to cast Jesus into the wilderness (1:12).

214. *Ecce tria sunt, amans et quod amatur et amor* (Augustine, *Trin.* 8.10).

215. Griffin, *Wonderful and Dark Is This Road*, 151. The eastern fathers generally began their meditation with the Father, Son, and Holy Spirit and then proceeded to their unity, whereas the Augustinian tradition begins with *De Deo Uno* and moves to

When Thou, O Lord, was baptized in the Jordan,
The worship of the Trinity was made manifest.
For the voice of the Father bore witness unto Thee,
Calling Thee the beloved Son,
And the Spirit in the form of a dove
Confirmed His word as sure and steadfast.
O Christ our God, Who hast appeared and enlightened the world,
Glory to Thee.[216]

We find the same interpretation in the West. Christ, Ludolph notes, "was baptized to reveal the mystery of the Trinity."[217] However, the Triune God is primarily celebrated on the Sunday after Pentecost.

Aquinas advises restraint in discussing this mystery (*S.T.* 31.2). Although it is not necessarily inappropriate to seek analogies of the Trinity in creation, as Augustine did with memory, reason, and will, we should mind the gaps in our understanding. John of Damascus observes, "it is quite impossible to find in creation an image that will illustrate in itself exactly in all details the nature of the Holy Trinity."[218] God reveals and conceals. The full reality of the scene may only have been available to Jesus and the Baptist: the "pure in heart" will see God (Matt 5:8). Onlookers may have seen an otherwise normal immersion of a human being. The Father speaks to the Son and prophet outside the scene; "The voice and the dove were only symbolic manifestations of the Father and the Spirit."[219]

Father, Son, and Holy Spirit, you are like a still, dark sea, a dance of three kissing fires. Drown our flesh and enflame our hearts. Amen.

The sacrament of baptism was instituted when Christ was baptized, although our participation in this mystery was not secured until his death and resurrection, which paid the penalty for our sin (Aquinas *S.T.* 3, q. 66, a. 2). To understand a little of this mystery, we may employ Augustine's distinction between *sacramentum* and *res*. A sacrament, to use the English transliteration, is "a visible sign of invisible grace," the *res* or "reality."[220] Similarly, there is a difference between a word (signifier) and what it

---

De Deo Trino (Augustine, *Trin.* 14).

216. Cited in Coniaris, *Introducing the Orthodox Church*, 23. A *troparion* (τροπάριον) is a short hymn of one stanza.

217. Ludolph of Saxony, *Life of Christ*, 1:421.

218. John of Damascus, *Orthodox Faith* 1.8 (*Writings*, 183 [Chase]).

219. Ludolph of Saxony, *Life of Christ*, 1:437.

220. Ludolph of Saxony, *Life of Christ*, 1:442.

represents (signified). The church teaches that Jesus and John describe what would otherwise be invisible at our baptism.[221]

The difference between *sacramentum* and *res* goes a long way in explaining conflict over the rite in church history. Few would disagree that union with Christ is necessary for salvation, the *res*, but what about the specifics and timing of the sacramental rite? We find diversity in the early church. The Didache, a first-century work, exhorts:

> Baptize in the name of the Father of the Son and of the Holy Spirit in running water. But if you have no running water, then baptize in some other water; and if you are not able to baptize in cold water, then do so in warm. But if you have neither, then pour water on the head three times in the name of Father and Son and Holy Spirit. (7:1–3)[222]

In the Syriac church, adult baptism was predominate through the first four centuries, and then transitioned to infant baptism as "the potential entry into a new mode of existence."[223] Today, a majority of Christians baptize their infants, but a sizable group waits until after a profession of faith.[224]

What, then, is the *res* of baptism? In short, it is union with Christ—in whom the story of God's redemption of a people, Israel, is repeated and completed. Jesus "opened the gates to the kingdom of heaven at the spot where the children of Israel had entered the Promised Land."[225] John Chrysostom notes, "Here, Jewish baptism ceases and is abolished, and Christian baptism begins."[226] As the Baptist predicted and Paul teaches, we are baptized into the death and life of Christ (Rom 6). The Spirit who rested upon him finds a place in us, so that we are united with the Son who is one with the Father.[227] In Christ, we join new creation: "the Spirit

221. Ludolph of Saxony, *Life of Christ*, 1:431. Theophan the Recluse (1815–1894) notes: "In the sacraments of baptism and confession the Lord enters into man by His grace," leading to a threefold communion: "a first in thought and intention, which happens at the time of conversion; and two others which are actual, of which one is hidden, invisible to others and unknown to oneself, and the other is evident both to oneself and to others" (cited in Groeschal, *Journey*, 18).

222. Holmes, *Apostolic Fathers*, 355.

223. Brock, *Spirituality in the Syriac Tradition*, 73.

224. The ambiguity can be seen in the otherwise unity between Presbyterians and Reformed Baptists. Mystery is messy. Karl Barth registers inconsistencies in Calvin's *Institutes* (*Teaching*, 49).

225. Ludolph of Saxony, *Life of Christ*, 1:430.

226. Cited in Ludolph of Saxony, *Life of Christ*, 1:428.

227. This reading goes back to the earliest commentary on Mark (Cahill, *First Commentary on Mark*, 34). See also Brock, *Spirituality in the Syriac Tradition*, 62.

of God was hovering over the face of the waters . . . Then God said, 'Let us make man in our image, after our likeness'" (Gen 1:2, 26 ESV). Through adoption, we come to know the Father as lover, the Son as beloved, and the Holy Spirit as the love that binds: "the Son of God received baptism so that all those born again in baptism might become, and appear to be, sons and daughters of God, and brothers and sisters to him."[228] We become a member of Christ's body, the church (1 Cor 12:13). We enter the fold of the Good Shepherd (John 10).[229] Baptism, then, marks the beginning of a new identity and mode of existence. For this reason, all four evangelists place the event at the beginning of Jesus's public ministry.

There is also the subjective appropriation of this reality. For this reason, some traditions describe baptism as a "betrothal."[230] "The mystics of the Church," Catherine De Hueck Doherty (1896–1985) notes, "call us to experience God by being in love with him; he is already in love with us."[231] I remember looking down at a ring on my finger, the day after I was married, and the sign felt foreign to me. Over time, however, the ring and reality came together. "In this core experience," notes Henri Nouwen (1932–1996), "Jesus is reminded in a deep, deep way of who he really is."[232] Kurt Thompson, another Christian well-informed by psychology, puts it this way: "He did not simply grow in what he knew *about* God, but in his *felt awareness of God's pleasure with him.*"[233] We get to re-live what cannot be remembered—our first experience after birth, staring into the face of our loving mothers (The mind and body of Christ were integrated, as will be shown in the temptations in the wilderness.) The Holy Spirit, the Spirit of Christ, ministers to our spirit. We know we are the beloved in Christ when the Spirit pours God's love into our hearts and leads us to pray "Abba" before the loving Father.

The Son and Spirit are foregrounded in the scene, and the transcendence and mystery of the Father are preserved, as we find elsewhere in the New Testament. However, the Father is not outside the scene, because

228. Ludolph of Saxony, *Life of Christ*, 1:422.

229. Brock, *Spirituality in the Syriac Tradition*, 69; Ludolph of Saxony, *Life of Christ*, 1:432.

230. Brock, *Spirituality in the Syriac Tradition*, 64; Ludolph of Saxony, *Life of Christ*, 1:428.

231. From the preface of Catherine of Genoa, *Purgation and Purgatory*, xiv.

232. Nouwen et al., *Spiritual Direction*, 28. By this, I do not believe Nouwen meant to imply that Christ was ignorant of his identity, but Mark, the earliest tradition-bearer, suggests the Father's affirmation was meaningful to Jesus, an encouragement to carry out his mission.

233. Thompson, *Anatomy of the Soul*, 144.

there is only one God and therefore the Father cannot be separated from the Son and Spirit.

Ludolph describes baptism as "the foundation of virtues."[234] The awakening of love is the first sign of the Spirit, which leads to other fruit (Gal 5:22–23).[235] This quiet work is the bridge to God, and is freely given to all believers, that we might join in the being and work of God for all creation. To focus on this ministry of the Holy Spirit, the early church would also anoint the baptized with oil. This "mark" (Syriac *rushma*), the replacement of circumcision in Judaism, signifies sonship, ownership, cleansing, healing, and protection.[236] John Wesley (1703–1791) uses the expression "second blessing" to describe a believer's deliverance from inward and actual sin, which was appropriated in the Pentecostal tradition to describe what might be called the loud work of the Spirit we find in the book of Acts—speaking in different languages, healing, and casting out demons. Sadly, this also has caused division in the church. In my opinion, the apostle Paul prioritizes love for all believers while emphasizing the unique ways the Spirit manifests in each member for the edification of the whole body, including drawing new believers into the fold (1 Cor 12–14). The Holy Spirit is free to be quiet or loud in the life of any believer. Jesus will not accept someone who performs miracles in his name but failed to obey the Spirit's prompt to love God and neighbor (Matt 7:13–23). We also must not "quench the Spirit" (1 Thess 5:19–22).

If the effect of the *sacramentum* and *res* of baptism is to be filled with the Holy Spirit, then we are free to receive whatever is given for the journey and to follow however we are led. As the Father spoke to the Son through the Spirit, God may speak to other sons and daughters. These locutions may take place in the mind's ear or mediated through external sounds in creation. As with the *bat kol* over Jesus, the voice may be discerned as God's through a congruency with Scripture. Augustine offers a famous example from his conversion:

> Suddenly I heard a voice from some nearby house, a boy's voice or a girl's voice, I do not know: but it was a sort of sing-song repeated again and again, "Take and read, take and read." (*tolle, lege, tolle, lege*) [. . .] Damming back the flood of my tears, I arose, interpreting the incident as quite certainly a divine

234. Ludolph of Saxony, *Life of Christ*, 1:422.

235. Brock, *Spirituality in the Syriac Tradition*, 75.

236. Brock, *Spirituality in the Syriac Tradition*, 68.

> command to open my book of Scripture and read the passage at which I should open.[237]

A brother told me about his experience. He was raised in a Pentecostal church, but had not spoken in tongues. This troubled him, and he would often confess any sin that came to mind. One day, he heard the sound of many waters and a voice from outside and within, "Danny, I love you."

So far, we have read this tradition through two elements of the soul—will and reason. The Holy Spirit transforms our will though love; we discern the ministry of the Spirit through the right interpretation of Scripture. Only memory, which is the most constitutive of our identity in Christ and experience of God, has yet to be addressed. I was baptized when I was six years old. My historical memories are few: it was evening; I was the first to go down into the baptismal and was dunked by my father, the pastor of the church. I wore brown corduroy pants. After meditating on Paul's understanding of baptism, I came to the realization that it was important to re-actualize that reality, union with Christ, on a daily basis. As often as we enter, the more we change. Since then, I often return to the water of that baptismal in my memory, to relive the transition. The following is an exercise that I share with others:[238]

> Offer a few deep, slow breaths and walk into the Jordan River. Feel the cool water rise to your chest. You hear David say, "*Deep calls to deep. At the roar of your waterfalls, all your breakers and your waves have gone over me.*" Allow yourself to be immersed fully into the water. Spend time in the darkness. Allow yourself to feel God's presence there. You hear Paul say, "*So we (are) buried together with him through this baptism into death, so that as Christ was raised from those who are dead through the glory of the Father, in the same way also we might walk in newness of life.*" Imagine breathing out your last breath. What is your final thought and feeling? You gently surface and open your eyes and see *the heavens tearing apart and the* Holy *Spirit descending like a dove into you.* Again, you hear Paul: "*The love of God is poured out in our hearts through the Holy Spirit, who was given to us*" (Rom 5:5). You hear *a voice from the heavens*: "You are my beloved.[239] I delight in you. I created you to love and to be loved forever."

237. Augustine, *Confessions*, 178 (book 8).

238. According to Kurt Thompson, engaging in exercises like this for six weeks changes the neural networks of our brain (*Anatomy of the Soul*, 143).

239. Benjamin Bacon recommends the translation "my son, the Beloved" ("Supplementary Note," 28–30).

This is who and where we are. Here, we can begin to work on all our deepest, most gripping questions—by the Spirit in the Son before the Father. Before the Father, we are safe. Before the Father, we find rest. Before the Father, we are happy. There is an interruption in this pattern with Jesus, who had to bear the sins of the world after his baptism, but not us. Jesus died in our place to offer us this space. In this life, Jesus warns there will still be trouble (John 16:33), but before the Father we are *ultimately* safe, at rest, and happy. The Holy Spirit allows us to experience some of these blessings today as grace. Fear, anxiety, restlessness, and unhappiness are a part of this life, but they can now be framed as invitations to pray in this awareness, to trust in God's providential care. Baptism begins what can be a long journey towards the center of the heart.

As soon as we fell out of the womb, we reached for love. This was our first response to the world; we needed a caregiver. Reborn, God is there to catch us. God touches us through the Holy Spirit. Loved, we begin to grow and hear God speak.

Centering Prayer

The Christian tradition offers two prayers that encourage assimilation into the mystery of baptism.[240] What came to be called "Centering Prayer" is rooted in the early monastic tradition, particularly in the *Conferences* of John Cassian, who describes contemplation as the laying aside of "roving thoughts" to focus on God.[241] To return from distraction, he recommends saying, "O Lord make haste to help me." This way of praying is developed in *The Cloud of Unknowing*. The cloud represents the boundary between our finiteness and God's infinite "being" or essence, which cannot be crossed through rumination: "Everything you think about, all the time you think about it, is 'above' you, between you and God. And you are that much farther from God if anything but God is in your mind"; "If you look carefully you will find your mind not occupied with this darkness at all, but definitely engaged with something less than God."[242] This cloud of mystery can only be pierced by our loving attention: "Love may reach up to God himself even in this life—but not knowledge."[243] To encourage this focus, the writer encourages using a sacred word: "Take just a little word, of one syllable rather than of two. With this word strike down every kind of thought under the cloud of forgetting."

240. They manifest the apophatic and kataphatic sides of the tradition respectively.

241. 9.3 (*NPNF2* 11:388).

242. *Cloud*, 67, 73.

243. Cassian, *Cloud*, 73.

Basel Pennington, William Meninger, and Thomas Keating popularized this prayer towards the end of the twentieth century.[244]

The goal of Centering Prayer is not emptying the mind, as is common in non-Christian forms of meditation, but, as John of the Cross (1542–1591) puts it, learning "to abide in that quietude with a loving attentiveness to God," who is already focused and working on us.[245] The prayer marks a transition between active meditation and an openness to the fruit of passive contemplation.

Keating recommends twenty-minute periods twice a day. The guidelines for Centering Prayer are:

1. Choose a sacred word to represent your intention to consent to God's presence and action within. (I recommend Christ's own word *Abba*, "dad" in Aramaic.)

2. Find a comfortable position, close your eyes, and silently introduce the sacred word as your consent to God's presence and action within.

3. When distracted, gently return to the sacred word.

4. At the end of the prayer period, remain in silence for a few minutes and then conclude with a prayer.[246]

Prayer of Examen

The goal of illumination is increased awareness of God's presence, character, and will. For this, Ignatius of Loyola (1491–1556) recommends the Prayer of Examen, a way of "reviewing your day in the presence of God,"[247] with a balance of grace and correction. We begin to see more of God each day, but also our behavior in that light.[248] Ignatius allowed Jesuits to forgo other disciplines because of constraints, but not the Examen, which is traditionally offered twice a day—at noon (or in the morning) and before sleep.

1. Sit with Jesus before the Father, and invite the Holy Spirit to review your day.

244. Pennington, *Centering Prayer*.

245. Kavanaugh, *John of the Cross*, 116 (*Ascent of Mount Carmel*, ch. 12). See Benner, *Sacred Companions*, 102, 116.

246. This is a slight adaption from Thomas Keating's guidelines.

247. There are many introductions to the Examen. See, e.g., Hamm, "Rummaging for God," 104–10; Manney, *Prayer That Changes Everything*, 55–57.

248. Manney, *Prayer That Changes Everything*, 3.

2. Review the day (or period). Look for the "hidden Christ,"[249] manifestations of the Spirit (seven gifts, fruit), and when you felt especially close to God—the "spirit of consolation." Thank God for these graces. (Ignatius believed remembering grace imparted even more grace.[250]) Also look for missed opportunities, sin, and when you felt distant from God—the "spirit of desolation." Confess this resistance or insensitivity to the Lord's teaching and leading of the Holy Spirit.

3. Review the feelings that surface in the replay of the day. Choose one of those feelings, especially if one is dominate, and pray from it.

4. Look towards tomorrow (or the next portion of the day) with hope.[251] Thanksgiving moves to request. Many like to end the *Examen* with the Lord's Prayer (*Pater Noster*), which addresses the daily needs of provision, forgiveness, and protection.

Feelings are the spontaneous, interpretive responses we give to events. They reveal "what we *really* think about events and relationships," although they may be based on false beliefs.[252] Culture and the frenetic pace of life discourage attending to feelings, but ignoring them may lead to, among other pathologies, chronic anxiety and depression. We find various lists of feelings. The Christian tradition has emphasized four natural passions: joy, hope, fear, and sorrow.[253] Paul Eckman finds six universal emotions that can be identified from facial expressions: anger, disgust, fear, happiness, sadness, and surprise.[254] Chip Dodd focuses on eight feelings: hurt, loneliness, sadness, anger, fear, shame, guilt, and gladness.[255] The diversity reveals the complexity of emotional life. Despite the negative connotations we attach to most of them, feeling are a gift from God, an invitation to cast out a false belief or to surrender a place where truth has yet to penetrate our heart.[256]

249. Benner, *Sacred Companions*, 114.

250. Egan, *Ignatius Loyola*, 70.

251. Hamm, "Rummaging for God," 107–8.

252. Fryling, *Seeking God Together*, 57 (emphasis hers).

253. Kavanaugh, *John of the Cross*, 77.

254. Eckman, *Emotions Revealed*.

255. Dodd, *Voice of the Heart*.

256. Fryling, *Seeking God Together*, 60.

26A: Temptation (Mark 1:12–13)

[12] And suddenly the Spirit casts him into the wilderness. [13] And he was in the wilderness forty days to be tempted by the Satan, and he was among the wild animals; and the angels[257] were serving him.

P. *And* (*kai*, καί) transitions from Christ's baptism when *the Spirit* "descended into (*eis*, εἰς) him" (v. 10) and now *casts him into* (*eis*, εἰς) *the wilderness* (*erēmos*, ἔρημος), an adjective that may be translated like a noun—"the wild, lonely, or deserted (place)."[258]

The Spirit casting (*ekballō*, ἐκβάλλω) Jesus is almost a violent image: shortly, Mark will employ the verb to describe exorcism (1:34, 39). Indeed, Jesus will *cast* out demons by the Spirit,[259] but yields here to the same power (see 3:22–30) to engage in spiritual warfare.[260] The infinitive *to be tempted* presumes *the Spirit*, in concert with the Father, intended the contest. We find a similar concept of two opposing spirits in Rule of the Community.[261] In The Testament of the Twelve Patriarchs, we find a persistent hope that God will raise up a savior to destroy the power of Beliar and his spirits.[262]

The Satan (*Satanas*, Σατανᾶς), a transliteration of the Hebrew שָׂטָן, signifies "enemy." He will return to pluck the gospel out of human hearts (4:15) and, once again, *to tempt* Jesus away from the cross (8:33).

Mark uniquely includes *wild animals* (*thērion*, θηρίον), which emphasizes the danger of the region (Deut 8:15; Isa 13:21; 34:14) but perhaps also Christ's authority and divine protection (Ezek 34:25; Dan 6:22).[263]

The *angels* assist Christ's submission to this direction by *serving* (*diakoneō*, διακονέω) *him*, a verb that soon will describe the hospitality of Peter's mother-in-law, which included serving a meal (1:31).

257. Or messengers (see 1:2), which emphasizes the angelic beings' role.

258. The adjective is technically a "substantive."

259. See 1:34, 39; 3:15, 22, 23; 6:13; 7:26; 9:18, 28, 38.

260. Joel Marcus notes, "It is as though the Spirit, having finally found the human instrument through whom it can accomplish its ends, is now spoiling for a fight with the Adversary" (*Mark*, 1:168).

261. God "created man to rule the world and placed within him two spirits so that he walk with them until the moment of his visitation: they are the spirits of truth and deceit" (1QS III, 17–19 [Martínez and Tigchelaar]).

262. See T. Levi 18:12; T. Jud. 25:3; T. Zeb. 9:8; T. Dan 5:10–11.

263. Tatian's harmony retains this detail (4.44). For the motif of danger, see Heil, "Jesus with the Wild Animals," 63–78. We find several references to the dangers of wild animals (T. Sol. 10:3 C; PsSol. 13.3–4; 1 Clem. 56:12). Habakkuk mentions "panthers" and "wolves at night" (1:8; cited in 1QpHab III, 6–7). Luke records a related saying: "I have given you authority to tread upon serpents and scorpions and over all the power of the Enemy" (10:19).

R: The scene recapitulates the fall of the first human beings (Gen 1–3) and the exodus generation, but also the partial reversals with Job and Elijah. Linking *Satan* with *wild animals* in the context of *temptation* evokes the serpent in the Garden of Eden (Gen 3). Those who were redeemed from Egypt through Moses nevertheless succumb and languish for *forty* years in *the wilderness*. In the heavenly throne room, which opens Mark's Gospel (1:2–3), God praises Job as the Father does with the Son at his baptism (v. 11), but Satan challenges his evaluation (1:8–11).[264] Elijah, who was just compared to the Baptist (1:6), *was served by angels* (1 Kings 19:4–8) before he is replaced by Elisha. With Eve and Job, *Satan* explicitly challenges God's word, but he can also be implicated for the discouragement of the exodus generation, Job, and Elijah, so that the effects of the fall are not entirely reversed. These allusions clarify the "way" opened by the Baptist and Jesus—not just through the Jordan River to the Promised Land, but a return to Eden.

In this context, Jesus among the *wild beasts* may foreshadow the renewal of creation.[265] "God made the wild animals (*to thēria*, τὰ θηρία) of the earth . . . and God saw that it was good" (Gen 1:25). The wild beasts grow mild "at his sight" (Milton, *Paradise Regained* 1.310–312). Unlike the Baptist (1:6), he neither kills nor takes from animals for sustenance but depends on angelic nourishment.[266] Isaiah, who was just cited (1:2–3), anticipated the end of violence between predator and prey (Isa 11:6–9; 65:25).[267]

D: During the Neronian Persecution (64), Christians "were clad in the hides of beasts and torn to death by dogs" (Tacitus, *Annals* 15.44). A generation later Ignatius of Antioch[268] was probably fed to lions in the Coliseum. The *Historia Monachorum in Aegypto* describes monks slaying wild beasts.[269]

264. Many have seen Job as a type of Christ, who, like his predecessor, purifies (*katharizō*, καθαρίζω) his family before God through sacrifice, but with the escalation of the righteous sufferer becoming the offering. In Jubilees, Mastema (Satan) encourages God to test Abraham's faith through Isaac's sacrifice (17:16).

265. We find this reading in Christian literature, like the Acts of Philip. The rabbis speak of *tikkun olam* ("the healing of the world"), leading to ecological flourishing.

266. See 4:19, 38; 9:17; 12:12. The Greek may be translated: "And he was with the animals, *but* the angels were serving him [meals]."

267. In Jubilees, the animals spoke a common language before the Fall (3:28).

268. Some would date his birth to around 35.

269. Ward, *Lives of the Desert Fathers*, 50.

The devil complains to Antony about the crowds of monks invading his domain.[270] "Why do you persecute me?," he complains to Benedict.[271]

Yet the gospel can also bring peace to the human-creature relationship. When the *wild beasts* were brought to devour Alexander of Jerusalem (d. 251), some, according to his *Vita*, licked his feet. Jerome notes that when Paulus, the "founder of the monastic life," died, two lions "came straight to the corpse of the blessed old man and there stopped, fawned upon it and lay down at its feet, roaring aloud as if to make it known that they were mourning in the only way possible to them."[272] Before that, a raven had fed him bread. Amoun "summoned two large serpents" and "ordered them to remain in front of the hermitage and guard the door" of his home against thieves.[273] Abba Bes calmed a hippopotamus.[274] Theon kept "company with wild beasts" and shared his water with them.[275] Anthony of Pedua preached to fish; Francis, to birds as brothers and sisters.

Angelic provision apparently continued: "every three days an angel used to bring [Abba Or] heavenly food and put it in his mouth."[276]

The two interpretations of the wilderness are not mutually exclusive. Monks invaded the wilderness to exorcise demons from Eden, or as Milton's famous works are titled, *Paradise Lost* and *Regained.* After spiritual conflict, the monk enjoys peace.

Yet the fulfillment of the vision requires a physiological transformation of predators and other flesh-eaters, which has yet to happen. Animals still eat animals, and, more importantly, some animals *must eat* animals to thrive—obligate carnivores, such as lions.

S: The Father is not an explicitly mentioned in this unit. But the one who sent the Baptist as an *angelos* (ἄγγελος), translated "messenger," to aid his Son (1:2) presumably also sent these *angels* (*aggeloi,* ἄγγελοι) for his care.[277] The Father loves the Son and will not ultimately abandon him, a precursor to the cross (15:34). Nevertheless, this and the preceding unit featuring Christ's baptism invite a juxtaposition of the Father's immanence and transcendence. Angels mediating between human beings and a more transcendent God is a

270. Athanasius, *Life of Antony*, 62.

271. Gregory, *Dial.* 2.8.

272. Jerome, *Life of Paul* (*NPNF*2 6:302).

273. Ward, *Lives of the Desert Fathers*, 80.

274. Ward, *Lives of the Desert Fathers*, 66.

275. Ward, *Lives of the Desert Fathers*, 68.

276. Ward, *Lives of the Desert Fathers*, 64.

277. Although the Greek noun *angelos* (ἄγγελος) may be translated "angel," referring to a supernatural being if warranted by the context, the primary signification of the word is "being sent." An ambiguity occurs at Mark 13:27.

motif in contemporary Jewish literature. The Father remains present to the Son, but not in the same way as his baptism. Indeed, the Father is the final agency behind *Satan's* temptation. *Heavenly Father, this is very difficult! How do I receive love from someone who allows harm into my life?*

In Greco-Roman mythology, gods have a double aspect: "Apollo in his daimonic aspect brings plague on the Greek army, though in his beneficent aspect he embodies the light-bringing power of the rising sun."[278] Zoroaster (c. 628–c. 551) apparently reduced the Iranian pantheon to two opposing forces, the Progressive mentality (*Spenta Mainyu*) and the Destructive Mentality (*Angra Mainyu*), but under one God (*Ahura Mazda*). Isaiah, who was cited as an authority at the beginning of the Gospel (1:2), also has God say: "I form the light, and create darkness: I make peace, and create evil (*ra*, רע): I the LORD do all these *things*" (45:7 KJV). In context, Yahweh is asserting his universal sovereignty—there is no force outside his control. Yet God condemns evil through the same prophet, as if it were external to himself, which is consistent with the majority witness of Scripture.[279] God does not self-identify as evil but good (Exod 33:19; Ps 34:8; 107:1; 145:9). In this Gospel, Jesus presents God as good (Mark 10:18).

Martin Luther distinguishes between God's alien work (*opus alienum Dei*), which may include the maintenance of justice through violence, and God's proper work (*opus proprium Dei*) of forgiving and saving.[280] He refers to these works as God's left and right hand, respectively. The Father holds the Son with both of these hands: the beloved is nevertheless tested. After losing his property and children,

> Job arose, and rent his mantle, and shaved his head, and fell down upon the ground, and worshipped, And said, Naked came I out of my mother's womb, and naked shall I return thither: the LORD gave, and the LORD hath taken away; blessed be the name of the LORD. In all this Job sinned not, nor charged God foolishly. (Job 1:20–22 KJV)

Spiritual adulthood is making peace with these hands.

This complicates *Satan's* role in the divine economy. In the majority of Old Testament references, he "is a sort of angelic prosecuting attorney to whom God has delegated the task of accusing human beings," but, as Joel Marcus also notes, Satan is portrayed as an evil enticer of Israel (1 Chr 21:1).[281] He is accountable to God but hostile to God's people. We find a

278. Ward, *God*, 27.

279. E.g., 1:16; 5:20; 7:15–16; 13:11.

280. Kärkkäinen, *Doctrine of God*, 102–3.

281. Marcus, *Mark*, 1:167n13.

similar ambiguity in Paul's discussion of his thorn in the flesh: God allows Satan, an enemy of the gospel, to impale an apostle for that same gospel (2 Cor 12:1–10; see 2:11; 11:14; 6:14—7:1). Despite this accountability, Satan exercises some autonomy of will and power.

The verb *peirazō* (πειράζω), which is translated *tempted*, may also signify discovering the character of someone through testing, the purpose of Greco-Roman biography, a genre appropriated by the evangelists. The action may be interpreted from two different viewpoints and agencies: Satan, the immediate agent, acted in way for Jesus to fail, the meaning of temptation; but God, who does not "tempt" (Jas 1:13) acted for his victory, the point of testing.[282] When God tested (*peirazō*) Abraham, which was alluded to in Christ's baptism, it was to demonstrate his faithfulness (Jas 2:21–23; see 1:3; Heb 11:8–12). God redeems evil for higher purposes (Gen 45:5; 50:20). *Come, Holy Spirit! You came into Jesus, and then cast him into the wilderness. And so you come to us. Amen.*

26B: Temptation (Matt 4:1–11)

[4:1] Then Jesus *was taken up* into the wilderness by the Spirit to be tempted by the devil. [Deut 9:9] [2] And having fasted forty days and forty nights, he later became hungry.

P: *Then* (*Tote*, Τότε) has this scene immediately follow the baptism and indwelling *Spirit* (4:13–17). That *Jesus became hungry* makes the first temptation significant.[283]

Matthew retells and expands Mark's story. Jeffrey Gibson notes, "Critical scholarship has demonstrated that the Markan version of this tradition is not only more primitive than that of both Matthew and Luke, but is to some extent their literary source.[284] He uses the Septuagint's translation of Satan—*devil* (*diabolos*, διάβολος), which means "one who engages in slander," a false claim that damages another's reputation.[285] (We find several names for this malevolent yet divinely constrained being in Jewish literature, and it was common to use different names in the same work.) Instead of emphasizing Mark's emphasis on the battle between the Holy Spirit and Satan, Matthew and Luke expand on the Son's participation.

282. Gerhardsson, *Testing of God's Son*, 27–28.

283. The aorist tense of the verb (*epeinasen*, ἐπείνασεν) may convey an ingressive sense, emphasizing the beginning of an action.

284. Gibson, *Temptations of Jesus*, 25.

285. BDAG, 226–27.

R: *Was taken up* (*anoigō*, ἀνοίγω), softer than Mark's casting language (1:12), evokes Moses's ascent:

> When *I went up* the mountain to receive the stone tablets, the tablets of the covenant the LORD made with you, I stayed on the mountain *forty days and forty nights.* I did not eat food or drink water." (Deut 9:9 ESV emphasis added; see also Exod 34:28)[286]

Meanwhile, the people made the golden calf (Deut 9:13–29). And then Moses fasts for the same period again—interceding on behalf of their sin (v. 18). The Lord accepts his intercession. Jesus, the Messiah (1:16), similarly "will save his people from their sins" (1:21; 2:15). As one might imagine, this rather obvious typology was a common patristic interpretation.[287]

Elijah fasted for the same period in the wilderness on a journey back to Mount Horeb where he experienced God's presence in a "thin silence" (1 Kgs 19:12). These complementary traditions will culminate in the Transfiguration where Moses and Elijah are presented in Christ's company on a mountain (Matt 17:1–13).

D: The allusion to Moses may suggest that Jesus also abstained from water, although he is not tempted to drink and the text only says *he became hungry.* But if so, he and Moses were supernaturally sustained; otherwise, a human being cannot survive. If one hears an invitation to fast completely from food for forty days and nights, it may be possible but wise to consult with a physician.

S: The Holy Spirit led the Son into Mary's womb, a place of safety, and now into the dangerous wilderness: *fear not, for I am with you.* Like a fire and cloud, the Spirit leads us to the Promised Land.

First Temptation (4:3–4)

[3] And having come, the tempter said to him, "If you are (the) son of God,[288] speak that these stones become loaves of bread." [4] But he answered and said:[289] "It stands written: *Not on bread alone will the human being live, but on every word coming through God's mouth.* [Deut 8:3 LXX]

286. See the earlier Mosaic typology at Matt 2:1–18. Deuteronomy recasts Exodus (24:18), a story that invited commentary (Jub. 1:1–4). Some rabbis claim Moses was made to wait six days (see Mark 9:2) before the Word came to rest on him, so that "he might be purged of all food and drink in his bowels, before he was sanctified and became like the ministering angels" ('Abot R. Nat. A 1).

287. Allison, *Studies in Matthew*, 123–25.

288. The devil reiterates the Father's own affirmation of the Son (3:17).

289. The attendant circumstance participle ἀποκριθείς essentially piggybacks on

P: The *devil* approaches Jesus as the *tempter* (substantive participle of *peirazō*, πειράζω)—that is, the primary agency of temptation (and intermediate agent of divine testing). He begins by challenging the Father's affirmation at Christ's baptism: *if you are the son of God* (see 3:17).[290]

R: Jesus cites Scripture for the first time in Matthew—from the Torah or Pentateuch (nearly two out of three of his citations are taken from this section of the Hebrew Bible or Old Testament). Moses is explaining the forty-year sojourn in the wilderness:

> That he might humble you, testing you to know what was in your heart, whether you would keep his commandments or not. And he humbled you and let you hunger and fed you with manna, which you did not know, nor did your fathers know, that he might make you know that man does not live by bread alone, but man lives by every word that comes from the mouth of the LORD. (Deut 8:2–3 ESV)[291]

Matthew has equipped us twice to understand this allusion. First, he already evoked Deuteronomy in the setting, presenting Jesus as a new Moses, as he did in the birth narrative. But Moses struck a stone for water in the wilderness when God told him only to speak to it (Num 20:8) and disqualified himself from entering the Promised Land:

> Then Moses and Aaron gathered the assembly together before the rock, and he said to them, "Hear now, you rebels: shall we bring water for you out of this rock?" And Moses lifted up his hand and struck the rock with his staff twice, and water came out abundantly, and the congregation drank, and their livestock. And the LORD said to Moses and Aaron, "Because you did not believe in me, to uphold me as holy in the eyes of the people of Israel, therefore you shall not bring this assembly into the land that I have given them." These are the waters of Meribah, where the people of Israel quarreled with the LORD, and through them he showed himself holy. (Num 20:10–13 ESV)

---

the conjugated verb εἶπεν, adopting its tense. It is an economic way to coordinate two actions. This construction is common in Matthew.

290. Turner, *Matthew*, 118. The protasis in Greek (εἰ υἱὸς εἶ τοῦ θεοῦ) may be classified as a first class conditional, which is an assumed truth for the sake of argument (Wallace, *Greek Grammar*, 679–712). Perhaps the tempter (must) accept Christ's sonship at one level, but nevertheless seeks to dethrone him. Theodore of Mopsuestia, part of the Antiochene school, claims Jesus needed to prove to himself that he was God's son (*On the Incarnation* 13). I struggle to find justification for this in the context.

291. Interestingly, Matthew himself does not cite the Torah, perhaps implying that Jesus is the only interpreter of God's laws (Powery, *Jesus Reads Scripture*, 250).

It is probably significant that God still worked through Moses, offering water to the people, but held him personally accountable.

Second, Matthew earlier cited Hosea in reference to Christ: "Out of Egypt, I called my Son" (2:15, citing Hos 11:1). But God did not call Moses, but a people as the Old Greek translation of the prophet emphasizes ("his children"). Jesus is like Moses interceding for a people, but he is greater than the Lawgiver because he *embodies* that people before God, an implication of his willingness to be baptized with sinners (see Heb 3:1–6), while also, as Immanuel, bringing God to the people.[292] Jesus, then, remains in the wilderness for forty days as Israel learned obedience there for forty years and, unlike Moses, will not be prevented from taking the land like Joshua (spelled "Jesus" in Greek).[293]

Matthew enhances our understanding of the Old Testament: although not mentioned, we now know that the devil tempted the exodus generation and Moses in the wilderness as the serpent did in the garden. An invisible, malevolent agency contributes to the mystery of sin. We are invited to read Satan into many passages.[294]

Embodying trust and obedience, Jesus is willing to wait on God's promise in a parched land:

> The LORD your God is bringing you into a good land, a land of brooks of water, of fountains and springs, flowing out in the valleys and hills, a land of wheat and barley, of vines and fig trees and pomegranates, a land of olive trees and honey, a land in which *you will eat bread without scarcity*, in which you will lack nothing. (8:7–9 ESV)

We have been reading Matthew's presentation of the Temptation in stereo—between the Law (Moses) and Prophets (Elijah). Jeremiah claims: "When your words were offered, I devoured them" (15:16); God commands Ezekiel: "eat this scroll" (3:1; see also Rev 10:8–11). Perhaps punning on the Baptist's diet (Matt 3:4), the Law is described as being sweeter than honey (Ps 19:9–10; Prov 24:13–14).

D: Like other characters in the Gospel, *the devil* is not given any physical description. Does Jesus see this slanderer, or is he hearing an

292. Michael Theophilos notes, "Matthew seems to have overlaid or combined the existing Israel typology . . . with specific Mosaic/Exodus elements" (*Abomination of Desolation*, 27n25).

293. For the Deuteronomic background, see Dupont, "L'arrière-fond biblique," 287–88. Richard Ounsworth explores Joshua typology in Matthew (*Joshua Typology*, 1–5).

294. We saw a similar interpretive activity with Wisdom being read back into the creation story.

internal voice like many of us experience temptation (see Heb 4:15)? In any case, *the devil* approaches Jesus like an anxious thought, exploiting the human survival instinct. Unlike Moses, who lapsed along with the people in mistrust and disobedience, we are invited to hold our deepest fears before God in faith. *The devil* wants us to believe that, *if led into the wilderness, we will not have enough.*

Fasting may function as a means of grace to weaken this temptation because we have already volunteered to withhold consumption. With the Spirit, Jesus spent forty days and nights preparing himself for this temptation, a kind of exposure therapy.[295] However, the very slow consumption of each word of Scripture is another means of grace (*Lectio Divina).* Indeed, Matthew implies that Jesus was sated by God's Word before *he became hungry.* The King James Version of the Bible has 783,137 words—quite a banquet for English readers![296] But in this case, the life-giving *word coming through God's mouth* was, "You are my beloved son" (Matt 3:17), the very truth the devil attacked. His tactic has always been to challenge God's word.

Many fear going to bed hungry.[297]

S: Jesus does not exploit his position with God, as the devil would have him do—*If you are the son of God*—but expresses solidarity with us—*Not by bread alone shall the human being live, but on every word coming through God's mouth.* The Son is more than us, but still one of us.

Second Temptation (4:5–7)

[5] Then the devil takes him into the holy city. And he set him upon the pinnacle of the temple [6] and says to him, "If you are the son of God, throw yourself down. For it stands written: *He will command his angels about you,* and *upon (their) hands they will lift you up, lest you strike your foot against a stone.*" [Ps 91:11–12][298] [7] Jesus said to him: "On the other hand, it stands written: *You will not test the Lord your God.*" [Deut 6:16 LXX]

295. See Abramowitz et al., *Exposure Therapy for Anxiety*, 173–200.

296. The New Testament, of course, was not written at the time of Christ and there were discussions among teachers about what constituted Scripture, but that is not a concern here.

297. Approximately a billion people face this reality.

298. The citation mirrors the Old Greek as we have it with some wording omitted in the middle: ὅτι τοῖς ἀγγέλοις αὐτοῦ ἐντελεῖται περὶ σοῦ τοῦ διαφυλάξαι σε ἐν πάσαις ταῖς ὁδοῖς σου ἐπὶ χειρῶν ἀροῦσίν σε μήποτε προσκόψῃς πρὸς λίθον τὸν πόδα σου (Ps 90:11–12); ὅτι τοῖς ἀγγέλοις αὐτοῦ ἐντελεῖται περὶ σοῦ καὶ ἐπὶ χειρῶν ἀροῦσίν σε, μήποτε προσκόψῃς πρὸς λίθον τὸν πόδα σου (Matt 4:6).

P: The first and second temptations are linked by repeating *son of God* and *stone* (see 4:3). But now *the devil* removes Jesus from the wilderness and brings him into the very heart of the Jewish community—Jerusalem, *the holy city* (Luke 4:9). The *temple's pinnacle* (*pterugion*, πτερύγιον) or "tip" was understood to be directly below God's throne that was surrounded by *angels*.[299] This location would capture God's attention in heaven and worshipers below and may explain why Jesus would even desire *to throw* himself *down*. By forcing God's *hand* in this public, sacred space, he might avoid the indignity and suffering of the cross. The people would receive him as Messiah. When Jesus finally enters Jerusalem, he is "humble, and mounted on a donkey" (Matt 21:5).

As with the first temptation, the issue is timing and trust. God provided angelic protection for Jesus and his family throughout their time between Egypt and Israel (2:13, 19) and will ultimately rescue *the Son* from death, as announced by the angel of the Lord after rolling back the *stone* (28:2); according to the Jewish map of the universe, God will raise and seat Jesus directly above the temple. But all this is God's response to the Son's faithfulness.

R: The exodus generation *tested* (*ekpeirazō*, ἐκπειράζω) God:

> Yet they sinned still more against him, rebelling against the Most High in the desert. They tested God in their heart by demanding the food they craved. They spoke against God, saying, "Can God spread a table in the wilderness? He struck the rock so that water gushed out and streams overflowed. Can he also give bread or provide meat for his people?" (Ps 78:17–20 ESV)[300]

The line *lest you strike your foot against a stone* may echo Moses disobediently striking the rock with his staff.

Psalm 91, a meditation on God's presence and protection, was read by contemporary Jews to cast out demons and remains part of the Catholic Church's rite of exorcism and yet *the devil* cites it![301] Employing a literal interpretation, it can be shown that the words are taken out of context. The psalmist requires trust, the opposite of the devil's application (vv. 2, 4), and God says, "Because he holds fast to me in love, I will deliver him" (v. 14).[302]

299. Scholars are uncertain about the precise location. I am inclined to identify the *pinnacle* with the southwest corner, a major junction of a north-south street running through Jerusalem.

300. See also Exod 17:2; Num 14:22; Deut 6:16; 8:16.

301. Embry et al., *Early Jewish Literature*, 1:153.

302. The verb חשק (Qal with *bet* preposition) regularly describes sexual desire leading to marriage (Gen 34:8; Deut 21:11).

Although Jesus is not necessarily committed to a literal hermeneutic, he rebuts the reading by employing a different Scripture but again from Deuteronomy (6:16). Moses promises that Israel will cast out all their enemies from the land *by their faithfulness* (v. 19). Apart from such cleaving, the words of the psalmist on the lips of the devil become false comfort.

D: In *The Brothers Karamazov*, Fyodor Dostoyevsky (1821–1881) relates a parable about Jesus, who quietly returns to Seville when heretics were burned at the stake (1481). He is promptly arrested by "the Grand Inquisitor" after raising a child from the dead. The gloomy old man tells Christ the church no longer needs him: his return would only interfere with their desire to save humanity from their freedom. Admitting allegiance to Satan, the inquisitor tells Jesus he should have capitulated to the temptations because people always follow the powerful one who fills their bellies. By throwing himself down, Jesus would solidify his mythical power over the people. And, then, taking over the empire, he could actually save them, like Caesar. The parable resolves ambiguously with Jesus kissing the inquisitor and disappearing into "the dark alleys of the city."

The verb translated *test* is a slight variant of *peirazō* (πειράζω), which describes what God is allowing the devil to do to Jesus (see 4:1)! This asymmetry in the divine-human relationship may be difficult to accept without a robust, introspective understanding of our ignorance and sin.

Hegesippus (c. 110–180) claims the temple authorities placed Jacob, the brother of Jesus, on the *pinnacle of the temple*; after confessing Christ, *they threw him down*. He miraculously survived, but was subsequently stoned and clubbed to death (cited in Eusebius, *Hist. eccl.* 2.23.4–18). Fear of falling is an archetypal nightmare.[303]

We read Scripture like the devil by offering false comfort to the unfaithful. Vincent of Lérins (d. c. 445) claims *the devil* speaks behind heretical interpretations of the Bible. The temple has become the church, so that Jesus is encouraged to throw himself down from her tradition and teaching.[304]

There is an important distinction between request and demand. The first is a powerful prayer; the second, a vain usurpation.

For those suffering with suicidal ideation or a seemingly impossible future, there is an invitation to keep walking with Jesus (or begin to do so).[305]

303. It is one of the big three nightmares, including being chased and drowning. In one study of college students, falling was the most common nightmare (Stevens, *Archetype Revisited*, 311).

304. McCracken, *Early Medieval Theology*, 77.

305. Apart from divine intervention, *the devil* would be inviting Jesus to suicide, who has just been summoned to suffer and die. The emotional breakdown in Gethsemane shows that this weighed on Jesus, who, like a patient diagnosed with a painful

Christian suicides may seem like a paradox but they were so common that the early church had to classify this supreme self-harm as a mortal sin.[306] Approximately a million people take their life each year.

S: God cannot be *tested* because there is no person or principle through whom such a judgment can be made. What keeps this from becoming impersonal fate is God's personhood. Jesus is not consigning himself to chance or fate, but the inscrutable yet loving Father and Holy Spirit.

Third Temptation (4:8–11)

[8] Again, the devil takes him to an exceedingly high mountain and shows him all the world's kingdoms and their glory. [9] And he said to him, "All these things I will give you, if you fall down and worship me." [10] Then Jesus says to him: "Go, Satan! For it stands written: *You will worship the Lord your God and him alone will you serve.*" [Deut 6:13 LXX]

P: *Again, the devil takes* Jesus somewhere. Matthew has a special interest in *mountains* that are contrastive to Mount Zion and the temple (5:1; 17:1; 28:16). We have moved out of Judaism into the global implications of God's anointed Son (see Ps 2). The invitation to *fall down* matches "throw yourself down" in the previous temptation (v. 6), but before a different master. *The devil* desires the obeisance the magi showed the infant Jesus: "And falling (to their knees), they worshiped him" (2:11). Instead, Jesus expresses monotheistic piety, like what we find on the lips of Daniel in Bel and the Dragon: "I bow down only before the Lord my God, because he is the living God" (25 Theodotion).[307] Jesus may voice *Satan*, the *devil's* more direct name, to take control of the situation like an exorcism (see Mark 5:9). *Go* is more forceful than all of *the devil's* conditional ("If") commands.

Once again, the challenge of the temptation is timing and trust. As with bread and protection, the Father's will is to glorify the Son, but there can be no glory before the cross.

Did *Satan* actually have the authority to *give* Jesus *all the world's kingdoms and their glory?* In another Gospel, Jesus calls him "a liar and the father of lies" (John 8:44). Nevertheless, it was common to attribute political oppression to Satanic influence. The Dead Sea Scrolls refer critically to "the kingdom of the Kittim," a code word for the Romans (1QpHab II, 13–14), but behind their power is "the dominion of Belial," an equivalent to *the devil* (1QS I, 18). 1 John claims "the whole world lies in the power of the evil one" (5:19).

---

and terminal disease, might opt out of that path as a final expression of freedom.

306. Colt, *November of the Soul*, 1.

307. Translation is by Peter Flint in Embry et al., *Early Jewish Literature*, 1:90.

Paul even describes Satan as "the god of this age" (2 Cor 4:4). The subsequent exorcisms and crucifixion in Matthew's Gospel attest to the pervasive authority of Satan. But after the resurrection Jesus claims, "All authority in heaven and on the earth is given to me" (28:18).

R: Although several Scriptures are alluded to or cited in the story, Jesus persistently appropriates Deuteronomy (8:3; 6:16, 13). With each temptation, he moves closer to the *Shema*—what by the first century had become the foundational prayer of Jewish piety:

> Hear, O Israel: The LORD our God, the LORD is one. You shall love the LORD your God with all your heart and with all your soul and with all your might. And these words that I command you today shall be on your heart. (Deut 6:4–6 ESV)[308]

Jesus describes this prayer as the "first commandment" (Mark 12:29). The Father has just voiced his love for the Son (3:17), and the Son is reciprocating in faithful covenant relationship. The *Shema,* when internalized, is the primary defense against temptation. The actual citation in this passage, *You will worship the Lord your God and serve him alone*, embodies the *Shema* that immediately precedes it.[309]

D: We demonstrate our love for God by *worshiping* and *serving* him. *To worship* (*proskuneō*, προσκυνέω) is to prostrate oneself and kiss the master's feet or the hem of his garment.[310] The verb rendered *to serve* (*latreuō,* λατρεύω) only describes religious duties in the New Testament and may also be translated "worship." Ignatius of Loyola appropriates this passage for the opening of his *Spiritual Exercises*:

> Man has been created to this end: to praise the Lord his God, and revere Him, and by serving Him be finally saved. All other things on earth, then, have been created because of man himself, in order to help him reach the end of his creation. It follows, therefore, that man may use them, or abstain from them, only so far as they contribute to the achievement of that end or hinder it.[311] Consequently, we must harbor no difference among all created things (as far as they are subject to our free will, and not forbidden). Therefore, as far as it belongs to us, we should not look for health more than for sickness, nor should we prefer wealth to poverty, honor to contempt, a long life to a short one.

308. In the rabbinic form, the *Shema* includes three Scriptures (Deut 6:4–9; 11:13–21; and Num 15:37–41).

309. Note specifically the repetition of "your God."

310. The related verb *kuneō* (κυνέω) means "to kiss."

311. The utilitarian view of creation differs from Franciscan spirituality.

> But, from all these things, it is convenient to choose and desire those that contribute to the achievement of the end.[312]

Prodding for a weakness in God's Son, *Satan* exposes his own Achilles' heel—the desire to be *worshiped* as God. In a passage traditionally applied to Satan's fall, Ezekiel describes the root sin: "Your heart was proud because of your beauty" (Ezek 28:17 ESV).[313] The Hebrew *gavah libo* (גָּבַהּ לִבּוֹ) describes self-elevation—a desire to usurp God's throne. But *Satan* was cast from God's mountain (v. 16).

There is an obvious political dimension to this temptation: if Jesus received all earthly authority this way, the status quo would be maintained instead of inaugurating God's Kingdom. He would just be another politician.

After survival needs are met, many fear failure or not realizing one's potential for greatness, a concept popularized by Abraham Maslow (1908–1970) with antecedent in Aristotelian philosophy.

S: Ironically, Jesus, who is Immanuel ("God with us"), not only reverses the sin of the exodus generation and first human beings, but *the* original rebellion of Satan "in Eden, the garden of God" by surrendering to the will of the Father (Ezek 28:13 ESV).

[11] Then the devil left him and look: angels came and were serving him.

P: This clause forms *inclusio* with vv. 1–2, completing Matthew's appropriation of Mark. The *angels*, mentioned by *the devil*, finally come to God's Son.

R: The citations from Deuteronomy evoke God's provision of manna, "daily bread" (Matt 6:11), in the wilderness: God "let you hunger *and fed you with manna*" (Deut 8:3).[314]

D: The Father rewards the Son's patience and trust by removing what agitates and providing the need. This may happen relatively quickly or, in Paul's case, relief may tarry as an opening for grace (2 Cor 12:1–10).

312. Wolff, *Spiritual Exercises*, 11.

313. Matthew may echo in this passage Ezekiel's vision of the temple's restoration: "In visions of God he brought me to the land of Israel, and set me down on a very high mountain" (ἐπ' ὄρους ὑψηλοῦ σφόδρα).

314. The psalmist ties God's provision to the Exodus: "I am the LORD your God, who brought you up out of the land of Egypt. Open your mouth wide, and I will fill it" (Ps 81:10 ESV).

26C: Temptation (Luke 4:1–13)

[4:1] Now Jesus, full of (the) Holy Spirit, returned from the Jordan and was being led by the Spirit in the wilderness[315] [2] forty days, being tempted by the devil.[316] And he did not eat anything in those days; and when they were completed, he became hungry.

P: *Now* (*de*, δέ) transitions from the genealogy that terminated with Adam, "the (son) of God" (3:38). Luke delimits the unit with an *inclusio* of *the devil's* temptation (4:2, 13). The *Jordan* evokes the descent of *the Spirit* at Christ's baptism (3:3, 21–22). The imperfect tense *was being led* (*ēgeto*, ἤγετο) emphasizes the ongoing relationship between the Son and *Spirit* in which the former follows the latter.

Inspired by Matthew's genealogy (1:2–17), Luke also appropriates the first Gospel's expansion of the temptation story (4:1–11) but in his own way. The phrase *full of (the) Holy Spirit*, which is not present in Matthew's version, occurs elsewhere in the New Testament only in Acts (7:55; 11:24; see also 6:5), which suggests Luke is offering his own interpretation of the tradition. Matthew retains a place for fasting in the church (6:16–18), but does not develop the significance of the discipline (perhaps because of an overemphasis by the Pharisees). Luke suggests a modest dualism: *an empty stomach offers space to be filled with the Spirit* (see Acts 9:9, 18; 13:1–4; 14:23). Jesus, he uniquely emphasizes, *did not eat anything in those days*. Matthew attributes the supernatural provision to consuming God's Word.

R: After David's anointing, "the Spirit of the Lord rushed upon" him "from that day forward" (1 Sam 16:13), as with Joshua (Num 27:18).

D: As Luke notes, Jesus "was led by the Spirit" (*ēgeto en tō pneumati*, ἤγετο ἐν τῷ πνεύματι). His traveling companion, the apostle Paul, uses the same language with the Galatians:

> By the Spirit walk, and fleshly yearning [temptation] you will never complete. For the flesh yearns against the Spirit, and the Spirit against the flesh. For these oppose one another, that you might not practice the things you want. But if by the Spirit you are being led [*pneumati agesthe*, πνεύματι ἄγεσθε], you are not under Law. (Gal 5:16–18)

We often meditate on Christ submitting to the will of the Father, a central truth in the Gospels, but Jesus also allows the Holy Spirit to lead (*agō*, ἄγω) his ministry. The verb signifies directing the movement of someone

315. Later manuscripts read "into the wilderness" (= Matt 4:1).

316. D reads "Satan."

from one place to another.[317] The Holy Spirit, then, is responsible for the twists and turns of the Jesus story in the Gospels and is therefore able to recapitulate that story in the life of every disciple, leading us through the wilderness into the Kingdom of God.

We see this in Paul's letter to the Galatians. The Holy Spirit *led* Jesus to eat with tax collectors and sinners and then Peter to have table fellowship with Gentiles in Antioch. But Peter became intimidated and momentarily stepped out of this leading, so that Paul had to confront him (Gal 2:11–14). Likewise, the Galatians had received the Holy Spirit (3:1), but were intimidated by the Pharisees, the same religious group that opposed Jesus for reinterpreting the Mosaic Law. Luke notes that some Pharisees became Christians and opposed Paul's inclusion of Gentiles into the new covenant without circumcision (Acts 15:5). If disciples are led by the Spirit, they are following the author of the Law (see Heb 3:7) and therefore cannot transgress it.

In this context, our response to temptation enables us to discern the leading of the Spirit in our lives. Paul continues:

> Now the works of the flesh are obvious, which are [adultery[318]], sexual immorality, uncleanness, lack of self-control, idolatry, sorcery, hostilities, division, jealousy, tantrums, sects, [murders[319]], envies, drinking parties, gluttonous meals, and things like these, (concerning) which I forewarn you, just as I forewarned, that those who practice such things will not inherit the kingdom of God. (Gal 5:19–21)

The apostle contrasts Spirit with "flesh," which, in context, is living out of step with the Holy Spirit. The "fruit" or harvest of walking by the Spirit is

> Love, joy, peace, patience, kindness, goodness, faithfulness, gentleness, self-control. (Gal 2:22–23)

The final fruit, "self-control" (*egkrateia*, ἐγκράτεια), is especially helpful for temptation. Paul appropriates Isaiah, who promised abundant fertility in the coming new age—what came to be called the seven gifts of the Spirit:

> And a staff from the root of Jesse shall come, and a flower from the root shall rise. And the Spirit of God will rest upon him—a Spirit of wisdom and understanding, a Spirit of counsel and strength, a Spirit of knowledge and godliness. The Spirit of the

317. BDAG, 16–17.

318. We find this reading in a few mss.

319. We find this reading in later codices.

> fear of God shall fill him—he shall not judge according to appearance nor decide according to report. (11:1–3 OG)[320]

The prophet anticipates the Davidic ancestry of Jesus ("the root of Jesse") and his baptism ("the Spirit of God will rest upon him"). Luke (4:1) explicitly alludes to this passage ("full of the Holy Spirit"). The same Spirit who empowered Jesus in the wilderness against the devil helps us. Paul encourages the Corinthians:

> No temptation has seized you except (what is common to) humanity. But God is faithful, who will not permit you to be tempted beyond what you are able (to endure). Instead, he will make with the temptation also the way out, so that you are able to endure. (1 Cor 10:12–13).

Ignatius of Loyola calls this process the discernment (*discretio*) of spirits. The maturing disciple reviews each day to recall thoughts and actions that led to a feeling of consolation or desolation, of drawing closer to God or the spirit of the age. The author of Hebrews observes: "Solid food is for the mature, who because of use have trained (their) powers of discernment, possessing the ability to discriminate between good and evil" (5:14).

The human response or responsibility to such leading is surrender.[321] The definitive expression is modelled by Jesus in Gethsemane near the end of the story ("not my will but your will be done"), but he offers a preparatory model in the wilderness at the beginning. German Christians called this surrender leading to peace *Gelassenheit* ("composed releasement," a "letting-be").[322] Johannes Tauler (c. 1300–1361) uses the expression to describe the emptying of the "creaturely" or flesh to be filled with God's grace, which Martin Luther relates to faith.[323]

S: Although not unique to Luke's presentation, Acts, the sequel, shows that the *Holy Spirit* leads the body of Christ, the church, just as he does here. C. K. Barrett notes, "It is clear that the author of Acts thought of the history of the church, at least in its early days, as governed, from first to last, by the Spirit of God."[324]

320. Beale, "Old Testament Background," 1–38.

321. See, e.g., Teresa of Ávila, *Interior Castle*, 29–30, 61, 73, 87, 133, 137.

322. Davis, *Heidegger and the Will*, xxv.

323. Davis, *Heidegger and the Will*, xxv. Meister Eckhart (c. 1260–c. 1328) similarly recommends "detachment" (*Abgescheidenheit*).

324. Barrett, *Holy Spirit and the Gospel Tradition*, 1.

First Temptation (4:3–4)

[3] Now the devil said to him, "If you are (the) son of God, speak to this stone, so that it becomes *bread*." [4] And Jesus responded to him: "It stands written: *not by bread alone will the human being live*." [Deut 8:3]

P: In Luke's version, Jesus uses *the devil's* exact word *bread* as a springboard into the biblical rebuttal.[325]

R: Luke makes a special contribution to the tradition by linking the title *son of God* to Adam at the end of the genealogy (3:38), whereas Matthew emphasizes Israel's sojourn in the wilderness. However, the fall of Adam and Eve and Israel's failure are typologically related.[326] The evangelist exploits Jewish tradition about the first human being. In Jubilees Adam, after being created, does not enter the Garden of Eden for forty days (3.9); and, after the Fall, according to the first-century Jewish work Life of Adam and Eve, he fasts for forty days in repentance.[327]

The New Testament links Satan with the Serpent in the Garden of Eden, but does not explain his motivation to tempt Eve.[328] Tradition points to envy: "Adam was reclining in the Garden of Eden and the ministering angels stood before him, roasting meat for him and cooling wine for him. Along came the serpent and saw him, beheld his glory, and grew jealous of him."[329] Angels apparently were not created in God's image. Paul presents Jesus as "*the* image of the invisible God" (Col 1:15). He writes:

> For this (reason), just as through one person [Adam] sin entered into the world, and through sin death, in the same way death also came to all people for everyone sinned. For until the Law sin was in the world, but sin is not imputed when there is no Law. But death reigned from Adam until Moses—even over the ones who did not sin in the likeness of the overstepping of Adam, who is a type of the one to come. (Rom 5:12–14)

325. Matthew uses the plural—"stones" and "loaves of bread."

326. Seth Postell claims Adam's fall "intentionally foreshadows Israel's failure to keep the Sinai Covenant as well as their exile from the Promised Land in order to point the reader to a future work of God in the 'last days'" (*Adam as Israel*, 3). For Christ as antitype, see Crowe, *Last Adam*; Lee, *Son of Man as the Last Adam*.

327. Charlesworth, *Pseudepigraha*, 2:258 (6 Latin).

328. Rom 16:20; Rev 12:9.

329. Goldin, *Fathers According to Rabbi Nathan*, 11 (A1). The Wisdom of Solomon presumes Satan attacked out of envy (2:24). Athanasius, commenting on the devil's pursuit of Antony, claims the devil "despises and envies good" (*Vit. Ant.* 5). Antony also attributes this motive to demons (21).

A type (*typos*, τύπος) is a shadow, a prophecy; antitype (*antitypos*, ἀντίτυπος), what is foreshadowed, a fulfillment. A type and its antitype are never identical but analogous.[330] The latter is greater than the former. If the Satanic serpent attempted to dethrone Adam and Eve, all the more *God's Son*.

Irenaeus developed these biblical cues into a theology of recapitulation:

> When He [Jesus] became incarnate, and was made man, he commenced afresh [or recapitulated] the long line of human beings, and furnished us, in a brief, comprehensive manner, with salvation; so that what we had lost in Adam—namely, to be according to the image and likeness of God—that we might recover in Christ Jesus.[331]

This typology with escalation helped the church unite the Old and New Testaments and remains helpful as an explanation for the gospel, as Rowan Williams, the former archbishop of Canterbury, notes: "The event of Jesus remakes humanity, by its enactment of archetypal human situations in such a way as to direct them Godward."[332] Jesus recapitulates the temptation scene in the Garden of Eden and forces a different ending. Salvation now becomes a matter of union with him through the Holy Spirit.

D: Stephen Wright conveys the remarkable significance of this typology: "Jesus is the new representative of the race. He has set it on a new trajectory."[333] This is the mysteriously beautiful, joyful yet difficult life in the Spirit.

Second Temptation (4:5–8)

[5] And after leading him up, he showed him all the kingdoms of the inhabited earth in a moment of time.[334] [Psalm 2] [6] And the devil said to him, "I will give you all this authority and their glory because it has been

330. 1 Peter (3:21) uses this language to describe the relationship between the flood (type) and baptism (antitype).

331. Irenaeus of Lyon, *Haer.* 3.18 (*ANF* 1:446); see also 21.1.

332. Williams, *Wound of Knowledge*, 39. He notes the Pauline connection. See also Beale, *New Testament Biblical Theology*. The creation story presents Adam as king and priest in the temple-like Eden, who is given the task to extend this to the whole of the earth but fails the covenant obligation (45). Yet "Christ has come as the end-time Adam to do what the first Adam should have done and to reflect his Father's image perfectly and to enable his people to have that image restored in them. In doing so, Christ is restarting history, which is a new-creational age to be successfully consummated at his final coming" (465).

333. Stevenson and Wright, *Preaching the Incarnation*, 157.

334. A reference to at least the Roman Empire (Luke 2:1).

delivered over to me, and to whomever I wish to give it. [7] So if you worship before me, everything will be yours." [8] And answering, Jesus said to him: "It stands written: *You will worship the Lord your God, and him alone will you serve.*" [Deut 6:13 LXX]

P: Luke places Matthew's third temptation in the middle, which turns the two protases ("if-clauses") *If you are the son of God* into *inclusio* (vv. 3, 9), highlighting the allusion to Adam. While shortening the first temptation, Luke allows the devil to speak at greater length (contrast with Matt 4:9). Perhaps Luke saw this unit as especially significant because of the Ascension, which he alone narrates (Luke (24:50–53; Acts 1:6–11), when the Father takes the *authority* from the devil and *glorifies* the Son.

Third Temptation (4:9–12)

[9] Now he led him to Jerusalem, and set him on the pinnacle of the temple. And he said to him, "If you are the son of God, throw yourself down from here. [10] For it stands written: *He will command his angels about you to guard you* [Ps 91:11] and [11] *upon (their) hands they will deliver you, lest you strike your foot against a stone.* [Ps 91:12] [12] And Jesus answered and said to him: "It has been said:[335] *You will not test the Lord your God.*" [Deut 6:16 LXX] [13] And after completing every temptation, the devil departed from him until (another) season.

P: It is fitting for the temptations to climax at *Jerusalem*, which functions as the hinge for the Gospel and Acts.[336] Jesus must suffer there and die (see Luke 9:51).

The most distinctive element of Luke's presentation, besides the arrangement, is a resolution that is naturally absent in Matthew's penultimate presentation: *And after completing every temptation, the devil departed from him until (another) season.*[337] The evangelist divides the life of Christ into three *seasons* (*kairos*, καιρός) marked by two transitions. The first season moves from infancy to maturity (2:52; 3:23) and is delimited by the temptation story, a rite of passage. The second season is Christ's public ministry, which culminates in Gethsemane with a great contest (22:39–46), leading to the shorter yet very intense *season* of his death, resurrection, and ascension.

335. D and W read γέγραπται. The more difficult reading is preferred.

336. He replaces Matthew's "holy city" with *Jerusalem*.

337. Tatian blends all three Synoptic presentations, although he follows Matthew's order (4.42—5.3). Yet he includes Luke's distinctive *until (another) season* (5.3 = Luke 4:3).

D: John of the Cross (1542–1591) posits two "dark nights" in the Christian journey back to God—that of the "senses" and of the "spirit."[338] The first often follows baptism and the initial maturation of the believer; it is rite of passage in which the ordinary pleasures of fellowship with God are stripped away leading to surrender into one's specific calling, a season of ministry and deeper knowledge of God. This liminal season is common and more soul work is required. The second, which is rarer, marks the transition into full union with God. Here, with an even more intense sense of abandonment, all that is fleshly is stripped away.

Wilderness

The Spirit led the Son into the wilderness, a lonely, parched expanse off the Jordan River, a land for grazing, not cultivation, a place for ascetics to escape idolatry.[339] It is what must be endured before crossing the Jordan River into the Promised Land (Isa 40:3; 1QS VIII, 12–16; IX, 19–20). Demons finally introduce themselves there; the canyons echo strange sounds (Deut 32:10).

On a map, the wilderness might easily be ignored as merely space between cities and political divisions.[340] It surrounds gardens. The occasional oasis pushed people very close together; except for hermits and nomads, the wilderness became home only for those who had no other place to go.[341] The mad went into the wilderness (Luke 8:29). God punishes by uncreating cities into wilderness.[342]

The wilderness is not immediately conducive to the body. Life often ends in the desperate search for water. Our skin burns. But like a sprout breaking through clay our soul grows best when the flesh is vulnerable. Time in the wilderness shrinks the ego, a necessary uncreation for union with Christ.

338. For more discussion, see Doohan, *Contemporary Challenge of John*.

339. The Hebrew word translated "wilderness" (*midbar*, מִדְבָּר) originally meant "place of herding." For some of the themes and references in this section, I am indebted to William Propp's article "Wilderness" in Metzger and Coogan, *Oxford Companion to the Bible*, 798–99.

340. Mark distinguishes the wilderness from the region of Judea and Jerusalem under the authority of Pilate (1:5) and Galilee and Nazareth under Herod Antipas (1:14). Jesus may have departed into Nabatea, a client kingdom at the time. The maps in my Bibles did not notice the wilderness.

341. See Gen 16:6–14; Exod 2:15; 1 Sam 22:2; 1 Kgs 19; Jer 9:1; 48:6; Ps 55:7–8.

342. See Isa 6:11–12; 14:17; Jer 9:11; 22:6; 50:39–40; 51:43; Ezek 6:6; Hos 2:3, 6; Joel 2:3; Zeph 2:13; Ps 107:33–34.

The wilderness, untouched by human hands, is also beauty in the raw—sounds and patterns go back to God. At dusk, the landscape may iconize primordial creation (Jer 2:6, 31; Deut 32:10). Hagar (Gen 16:7; 21:19), Moses (Exod 3:1—4:17), Elijah (1 Kgs 19)—all flee there to meet God. The exodus generation had the opportunity, but preferred idols (Deut 32:10; Hos 9:10). It is the place for covenant (Exod 19:1—Num 10:10) and crucible where God's power meets our surrender.

Entrance

We saw the Father's love pour into the Son through the Spirit. We can therefore see our Lord's obedience—indeed, the entire journey—as a response to love, which is a greater motivation than fear or shame (1 John 4:18).

The same Holy Spirit leads us into the wilderness, a place for intimacy with God and spiritual warfare, for our formation. Peter writes "to the chosen nomads of the *Diaspora*" (1 Pet 1:1). But we go as the Father's "beloved" with the Spirit in the Son. We are not alone, but companioned by God and one another. John Chrysostom prays that "every baptized person might patiently sustain greater temptations after his baptism, nor be troubled, as if this which happened to him was contrary to his expectation, but might bear up against all things, and come off conqueror."[343] Bede (c. 672–735) notes:

> We give thanks that the hostile Egyptians drowned when we passed through the Red Sea [in baptism], but there are other foes to be fought as we journey through the desert of daily life. Christ's grace leads the way, but still we can only vanquish these enemies with great effort as we make our way to the Promised Land.[344]

At least since Tertullian, Jesus has been understood as repeating Israel's history in the wilderness: Where Adam and God's people fail, he succeeds (*De bapt.* 20). The author of Hebrews claims,

> So having a great high priest, who went into the heavens, Jesus, the Son of God, we must hold fast the confession. For we do not have a high priest who cannot sympathize with our weaknesses, but one who has been tempted in every way as (we are, but) without sin. (Heb 4:14–15)

Jesus repeats and completes their story. The problem resolves in his flesh; those in Christ are therefore free to let go of Adam. We "unself" to our past,

343. Aquinas, *CA* on Mark 1.

344. Cited in Ludolph of Saxony, *Life of Christ*, 1:432.

and grow into our future. We are summoned to the wilderness *as* victors in Christ. Yes, our faith is being tested, but we go in the Father's confidence that *we shall overcome*. Jesus offers three lessons: Depend on God, Do not test God, and serve God. We are God's children, and the devil has no ultimate power over us: "You are from God, little children . . . greater is he who is in you than he who is in the world" (1 John 4:4). James opens: "Consider it pure joy, my brothers, whenever you encounter various temptations (or trials), because you know that the testing of your faith produces steadfastness. Now let endurance have its perfecting work, so that you may be perfect and complete, lacking in nothing" (1:2–4).

Distraction

There is an archetypal quality to the three temptations. In the Buddhist tradition, the demon Māra sends three daughters, Discontent, Delight, and Desire, to distract the young Siddhattha Gotama from enlightenment.[345] Jewish and Greco-Roman writers divided temptation into three great vices—pleasure, power, and possessions.[346] And there is the tripartite temptation in the Garden of Eden:

> When the woman saw that the tree was good for food, and that it was a delight to the eyes, and that the tree was to be desired to make one wise, she took of its fruit and ate. (Gen 3:6 ESV; see 1 John 2:16)

The number three appears to function as a merism, referring to the totality of temptation. The author of Hebrews claims Jesus was tempted "in every way" (4:15). So we do not have to be overly concerned about identifying the precise significance of each temptation, which is fortunate because there are several interpretations—many of which may contain some complementary truth. The author mentions the first Jesus, translated Joshua (the two names are spelled the same in Greek), who was instructed to drive out seven idolatrous people groups (Josh 3:10; see Heb 4:8), which were seen as a type for the seven deadly sins.

The echoes of the fall story in Luke suggest the temptations prey on the human frustration of limits. Will Jesus accept God's will for his life,

345. Wallis, *Dhammapada*, 107.

346. Blomberg, *Neither Poverty Nor Riches*, 127. Gibson rejects this reading for being anachronistic, but the triad is a motif in contemporary literature and is a standard patristic interpretation (*Temptations of Jesus*, 96). Later Christian teachers taught that Satan enslaved people through meat and drink, gold, war, and woman—all of which were renounced by monks (Duby, *Age of the Cathedrals*, 57).

as confirmed at his baptism, or seek to redefine it?[347] There is also escalation: Adam and Eve did not have any needs in Paradise, whereas Jesus faces starvation and has been called to suffering and death. Even the offer of all the kingdoms, which may appear as a want, was probably another shortcut to glory apart from the cross. John Howard Yoder (1927–1997), a pacifist, claims Jesus was tempted by a crusade mentality—to accomplish his ministry through coercion and violence instead of martyrdom.[348] That matches contemporary hopes in a Davidic messiah. However, the Son does not attempt a counterplot, but surrenders to the Father's story. He models the more difficult path of trusting God with unmet needs, including survival. He would not be given his seventy years (Ps 90:10) or most of the comforts that make a difficult life and ministry bearable. He is not being tempted in Paradise, but the wilderness.

Yet this story is not merely about deprivation. The devil wants to lure Jesus away from the Father's affirmation, "You are my beloved son," which the monk Basil Pennington (1931–2005) identifies as Christ's "true self."[349] Satan, the father of lies, can only produce a "false self"—an identity based on possessions, reputation, and action (work, career). This battle is also archetypal. The Buddhist training manual, *Dhammapada*, claims "the greatest of victories is the victory over oneself."[350] Muhammad (c. 570–632) offers a similar judgment: "The most excellent *jihad* is that for the conquest of self"—"Every human being has two inclinations—one prompting him to good and impelling him thereto, and the other prompting him to evil and thereto impelling him."[351] Philosophers call this battle *akrasia* (ἀκρασία), the state of acting against our better judgment. The Father communicates his love before the Son does anything. This is the new piece to the old archetype. Paul similarly describes God's love toward us, and encourages believers to take off their old identity in Adam (Rom 5:8; Eph 4:22–24). We find ourselves and the satisfaction of our greatest need in God's love.

347. Gibson, *Temptations of Jesus*, 96. Peter Scazzero notes, "The essence of the temptation was to transgress or cross over the limits God has placed around him" (*Emotionally Healthy Church*, 144). Alice Fryling glosses the fall story: "Adam and Eve could not have it all. When they reached out to eat from that tree, they were saying to God that they would not accept the limitations God put in their lives" (*Seeking God Together*, 81).

348. Yoder, *Politics of Jesus*, 98. This view is furthered by Gibson, *Temptations of Jesus*, 96–97.

349. Pennington, *True Self/False Self*.

350. Translation is by Juan Mascaró in Wallis, *Dhammapada*, 50.

351. He adds, "but divine assistance is near, and he who asks for the help of God in contending with the evil promptings of his own heart obtains it" (Al-Suhrawardy, *Sayings of Muhammad*, 49, 93).

Temptation is often described as the desire to do something for immediate pleasure that we come to regret. The philosopher David Hume (1711–1776) found the human preference for short-term rewards over long-term goals to be pandemic. We do find this sense in James:

> No one, because one is tempted, should say, "I am being tempted by God." For God is untemptable by evil things. Rather, he himself does not tempt anyone. Instead, each is tempted by one's own desire, being drawn out through baiting. Then this desire, after conceiving, delivers sin. But this sin, which has run its course, births (only) death. (1:13–15)

The author appropriates the Jewish concept of the "evil inclination" (*yetser ha-ra*). 4 Ezra claims Adam sinned because he had an evil heart (*cor malignum*, 3:20) in which a grain of evil seed (*granum seminis mali*) had been sown, contributing to its growth (4:30). All of Adam and Eve's descendants have the same soil (3:22, 26; see also Sir 37:3).

There is no evidence, however, that Jesus had an evil heart. He does not repent like the rest of the people coming to John for baptism. The author of Hebrews attributes the words of the psalmist to the Son at his incarnation, "*I have come to do your will, O God*" (10:7; Ps 40:7–8). The wills of Jesus and the Father are distinguishable yet united. Instead, the Son undergoes the temptations that believers face after the purification of their baptism, after picking up their cross to follow him. We are still vulnerable to temptation, but in the way Jesus was before his resurrection and glorification: to betray our calling and sharing in the sufferings of Christ.

This passage invites believers to disassociate from the temptation, which is essentially the voice of Satan, an appeal to fall back into their false self, to reject God's love. This disassociation does not remove personal responsibility for our behavior, but temptations are not who we are in Christ. This is evident to any maturing Christian facing temptation who asks two questions:

> What am I about to do?
>
> What do I want to do?

Satan no longer dictates the deepest desires of our heart; there, we are safe to commune with God and find grace to overcome. Without being prideful, many disciples have confided to me that, after turning inward, they found that the deepest desire of their heart was to love and be loved.[352]

352. From a female perspective, see Shepherd, *Your Heart's Desire*; from a male, Muldoon, *Longing to Love*.

Nevertheless, it would be irresponsible (and hypocritical) not to acknowledge a difference between Jesus and his followers: unlike a sinless Christ, our minds and bodies *remember* unwholesome patterns of thought and behavior that make overcoming the sinful impulse difficult. Jesus says: "The spirit is willing, but the flesh is weak." For this reason, Paul exhorts,

> *You* (were taught) to take off (the clothes) with reference to (your) former way of life, the old human being, who is being seduced according to deceitful lusts. But (you were taught) to be (continually) renewed in the spirit, that is, the mind. And (you were taught) to put on the (clothes of) the new person, who was created according to God in righteousness and holiness of the truth. (Eph 4:22–24)

Satan often comes when we are exhausted and lonely or especially busy when there is little time to process between those two questions. Sometimes, we are strong and the temptations pass over like migrating birds. But in moments of weakness, they swoop down and tear our flesh. Matthew's emphasis on the recapitulation of the Exodus story offers wisdom. The body of Christ, the church, is somewhere between Egypt and the Promised Land. Like the exodus generation, the comforts of idolatry attract the heart.[353]

How, then, is temptation overcome in our life? The simple answer is God through us. Self-control is the final fruit of the Spirit (Gal 5:23). The nexus between divine sovereignty and human responsibility is mysterious, but the spiritual theologian Evan Howard notes:

> There is virtually no Christian community that emphasizes the work of God to the complete denial of human activity in the sanctifying life of the believer. And, conversely, there is no Christian community that emphasizes the work of the human to the denial of God's gracious initiation in some form.[354]

We see this divine and human work in Antony's defeat of Satan in the wilderness of Egypt:

> The devil, who despises and envies good, could not bear seeing such purpose in a youth, but the sort of things he had busied himself in doing in the past, he set to work to do against this person as well. First, he attempted to lure him away from the discipline, whispering to him the remembrance of his wealth, care for his sister, the bonds of kinship, love of money, love of glory, the various pleasures of food and the other relaxations

353. Garrett, *Temptations of Jesus*, 22.

354. Howard, *Brazos Introduction to Christian Spirituality*, 233.

> of life, and at last the difficulty of virtue and the labor of it; he suggested also the infirmity of the body and the length of time involved (for training). In a word he raised in his mind a great dust cloud of considerations, wishing to debar him from his settled purpose. But when the enemy saw himself to be too weak for Antony's determination, and that he rather was conquered by the other's firmness, overthrown by his great faith and falling through his constant prayers, then at length putting his trust in the weapons that are "in the navel of his belly" and boasting in them—for they are his first snare for the young—he attacked the young man, disturbing him by night and harassing him by day, so that even the onlookers saw the struggle that was going on between them. The one would suggest foul thoughts and the other counter them with prayers: the one fire him with lust the other, as one who seemed to blush, fortify his body with faith, prayers, and fasting. And the beleaguered devil one night even took upon him the shape of a woman and imitated all her acts simply to beguile Antony. But he, his mind filled with Christ and the nobility inspired by him, and considering the spirituality of the soul, quenched the coal of the other's deceit. Again, the enemy suggested the ease of pleasure. But he, like a man filled with rage and grief, turned his thoughts to the threatened fire and the gnawing worm; and setting these in array against his adversary, passed through the temptation unscathed. All this was a source of shame to his foe. For he, deeming himself like God, was now mocked by a young man; and he who boasted himself against flesh and blood was being put to flight by a man in the flesh. For the Lord was working with Antony—the Lord who for our sake took flesh and gave the body victory over the devil, so that all who truly fight can say, "not I but the grace of God that was with me." [1 Cor 15:10] (1.5)[355]

The story is patterned after the Gospels, and is an early expression of a tradition that posits a space between temptation and sin.[356] The *Imitation of Christ* describes the progression from an external stimulus to the exercise of free will: "first there comes in the mind an evil thought: next, a vivid picture: then delight, and urge to evil, and finally consent."[357] We only sin by consenting to what we could reject, although the temptation grows more powerful at each stage.

355. I have slightly altered Robert Cregg's translation in Athanasius, *Life of Antony*, 33–34.

356. Athanasius, *Life of Antony*, 4.

357. À Kempis, *Imitation of Christ*, 41.

When tempted, Antony "turned his thoughts" towards God. The Christian psychologist Scott Symington recommends the analogy of a front and side screen in the mind's eye. The front screen "represents the present moment and life-giving internal activity—all the thoughts, feelings, and images that translate into well-being and a life well lived."[358] The side screen is "the place where the fears, worries, unhealthy urges, and destructive moods show up."[359] We aim to focus on the front screen. When the side screen threatens our attention, we acknowledge its presence without over-reacting and then re-focus on the front screen. This two-step process gradually weakens the power of the temptation.

Antony also imitates Jesus by departing from his community and fasting, which contribute the weakening of the side screen, as well as meditating on Scripture to fortify the front screen.[360]

Departure

Jesus is led by the Spirit into a solitary place—what came to be called *anachōrēsis* (ἀναχώρησις, "departure").[361] The pattern is repeated throughout his ministry and finally at Gethsemane, but now with an exhortation to the disciples to depart for watchfulness and prayer in order to attack the weakness of the flesh in tests with Satan. After encountering the resurrected Christ, Paul departed into Arabia (Gal 1:17). Antony fled into the Egyptian wilderness; at age twelve, Martin of Tours "longed for the desert."[362] Benedict spent three years alone in a cave outside of Rome before surfacing with his rule;[363] Francis of Assisi "began to seek out solitary places" before fully surrendering to God.[364] Catherine of Siena was very active in her short adult life, but, at eighteen, she began to live in solitude, leaving her room only for Mass.[365]

This invitation may feel unattractive to lonely people. We should not celebrate social isolation.[366] But sometimes God pushes everyone else away

358. Symington, *Freedom From Anxious Thoughts*, 4.

359. Symington, *Freedom From Anxious Thoughts*, 4.

360. Symington goes in a different yet complementary direction, recommending the "anchors" of mindfulness, healthy distractions and activities, and loving action.

361. Amélineau, "Voyage d'un moine égyptien dans le desert," 166–94.

362. Noble and Head, *Soldiers of Christ*, 6 (*Life* 2).

363. Gregory the Great, *Dialogues*, book 2.

364. Armstrong et al., *Francis of Assisi*, 2:534.

365. Catherine of Siena, *Dialogue*, 4.

366. Holt-Lunstad, "Potential Public Health Relevance," 127–30.

so that we can be alone with him, a pattern that goes back to Jeremiah, who was commanded to remain single, although there was no word for "bachelor" at the time (Jer 16:2), and to refrain from social events, like weddings and funerals (16:5–9).[367] God also called him to deliver an unpopular message of imminent exile, but says:

> "Then you will call upon me and come and pray to me, and I will hear you. You will seek me and find me, when you seek me with all your heart. I will be found by you," declares the LORD. (29:12–14a ESV)

Neuroscience shows that merely changing our physical position—like moving from one room to another—begins to shift our mind-set.[368]

The humblest of all beings, God is in every room but rarely acknowledged. We have to be alone to discover that we are never alone.

Intimacy with God leads to transformation: if our false self is largely formed through interaction with others, departure first uncreates and then recapitulates this socialization but now with the Triune God. Some of us find identity in work, but we are more than jobs; some in parenting, but we are more than parents; some in culture, but we are more than culture. These self-limitations disappear before God.

Faith is healthiest between the poles of aloneness with God, the original meaning of "monk," and God in community. The disciple is individually and corporately one with Christ: "Together one, in the one Christ, on the way to the one Father."[369] Jesus presents aloneness with God as a means of refreshment and empowerment for serving others, although this balance has not always been maintained. Basil (c. 329–379) chides the solitary monk, "Whose feet will he wash?"[370] The bishop emphasized the communal dimension of faith, centered on the Eucharist, so that life became shared thanksgiving. The Dominicans reacted against the isolationism of the Cistercians, taking the gospel to the people. Desiderius Erasmus (1466–1536) and the Reformers were quite hostile: *monachatus non est pietas* ("monasticism is not true piety"). However, the spirituality of non-monastic Christians has suffered from a false dichotomy. The Eucharist is a beautiful gift from Jesus to all Christians, but he also invites us into closets to be alone with God.

367. Hoffeditz, *They Were Single Too*, 55–66.

368. Thompson, *Anatomy of the Soul*, 165.

369. *Sermon on Psalm 147*, 28; cited inAugustine, *Rule of Saint Augustine*, 45.

370. Morison, *Basil and His Rule*, 43.

Although some may be called to a permanent *anachōrēsis*, like Carthusian monks praying on our behalf, the dominant pattern, beginning with Jesus, is for a temporary season of departure for training before a public ministry and then as part of a sustainable rhythm to complete the work.[371] "To leave God for others is to find him," writes Albert Peyriguère (1883–959) to a nun seeking spiritual direction.[372] The littlest of people have gone into the wilderness only to return as giants.

Fasting

Scripture does not denigrate the body—being fearfully and wonderfully made—but elevates the soul. "Is not life more than food?" (Matt 6:25). And yet we live in a world that stuffs the body and starves the soul. Paul criticizes those who make their stomachs god (Phil 3:19). The body is more real for most of us than the soul, so it demands our attention. Like God, the soul may be known by its effects but cannot be seen. The aim of the disciple is not to abuse or devalue the body, which is part of creation and will be transfigured at the resurrection, but to be mindful firstly of God and the soul, so that what is invisible may capture our focus. Many have confided with me that fasting, as a way of intensifying prayer, increases spiritual awareness. Sometimes, we need to fast the body to feed the soul.[373]

Fasting may also reveal how we use comfort to avoid processing the challenges of life.[374] Overconsumption often results from the negative associations we have with memories and emotions.[375] Removing coping mechanisms allows space to confront our demons.

The forty-day fast became paradigmatic for pious Jews and Christians.[376] Francis of Assisi fasted for forty days, but partially broke it on the thirty-ninth, eating half a loaf of bread, to attack pride. Orthodox, Catholic, and Protestant Christians participate in Lent, a forty-day (approximately six-week) period of fasting and repentance before Easter.[377] The discipline is

371. There is a pattern of retiring from public life, a permanent hermitage, after being released by Jesus. This was exemplified by Pope Benedict XVI who shocked the world by retiring for prayer.

372. Peyriguère, *Voice from the Desert*, 21.

373. See John 4:34; see also Proto-Gospel of James 1.4.

374. Thompson, *Anatomy of the Soul*, 177.

375. Cargill, *Psychology of Overeating*.

376. Seeking illumination from God, Baruch prays for forty days (3 Bar 4:14). Joachim, the father of Mary, does the same (Proto-Gospel of James 1.4).

377. "Lent" is from the Anglo-Saxon word *lencten*, meaning "spring," but is

usually less rigorous than complete abstention from food. Ash Wednesday begins the season. The most distinctive element of the service is the imposition of ashes. The priest marks a cross on the forehead of the worshiper with ash, a sign of mortality and penance, and says, "Remember that you are dust, and to dust you shall return."[378] The ash is made by burning the palm branches from the previous year's Palm Sunday—a reminder that we are saved by the death and resurrection of Christ but still need to confess and address our sin (Jas 5:16; 1 John 1:9).

Talking Back

Overreaction empowers temptation. But if a feeling is attached to a falsehood, like the devil's distortion of Scripture, it is important to follow Jesus in what the monks call *antirrhētikos* "talking back." In a book with that title, Evagrius of Pontus writes, "In the moment of struggle, when the demons attack us and prick us with darts, we must answer them with a verse from Holy Scripture, so that filthy thoughts do not persist in us."[379]

Remembering

In Matthew's account, Jesus receives God's Word (*rēma*, ῥῆμα) as food. Bread sustains life; wine may sweeten it, but only God's Word feeds and protects the soul. As we noted, Christ's fixation on Scripture reflects his Jewish heritage but also grounded the Christian tradition. The *Imitation of Christ* encourages us to "seek food for our souls rather than subtleties of speech"—merely entertaining sermons.[380] Disciples can become fixated on non-biblical writings, especially a charismatic teacher or theological system, but Jerome set the precedent against this after sharing a nightmare where he was accused before God's judgment seat of being a Ciceronian rather than a Christian. (Cicero shaped Latin to the point that his handiwork may

ultimately derived from the Greek *Tessarakostē*, referring to the "fortieth" before Easter. In the Roman Catholic Church, Lent begins on Ash Wednesday and ends on Holy Thursday. For most Protestant churches, it begins the same time but ends on Holy Saturday. Sundays are not included. The practice differs from the Muslim pillar of Ramadan, which requires abstinence from food and drink during the light hours of a lunar month.

378. For the use of ash in repentance, see Job 42:6; Jer 6:26; Ezek 9:4; Dan 9:3; Matt 11:21; Luke 10:13.

379. The translation from the Syriac is by Michael O'Laughlin in Wimbush, *Ascetic Behavior In Greco-Roman Antiquity*, 246.

380. À Kempis, *Imitation of Christ*, 33.

be seen throughout the Vulgate.) The Massachusetts Bay Colony, a reflection of Puritan values, legalized the "Old Deluder Satan Act" (1647), which mandated the establishment of grammar schools for the study of Scripture to make people less gullible to Satanic temptation.[381]

Jesus probably did not go into the wilderness with biblical scrolls, but was armed by what he could recall. Antony "paid such close attention to what was read that nothing from Scripture did he fail to take in—rather he grasped everything, and in him memory took the place of books."[382]

Scripture is precious because reality is not entirely cyclical: some important things happen only once; if forgotten, they are lost.[383] The salvation of the exodus and the testing of the wilderness happened once. Jesus died on the cross once and for all. We remember in Passover and Eucharist. Moses says: "And you shall remember the whole way that the LORD your God has led you these forty years in the wilderness" (Deut 8:2 ESV). That season was about to end—it would no longer be anywhere but in their collective memory. God's people, who are, until the end, always on the verge of entering the Promised Land, must remember the ancient journey. Moses addresses those who watched their parents die in the wilderness. Those of us who survived the twentieth century look back on unspeakable horrors—world wars, genocides, AIDS, a Great Depression. Our children have not seen these things and will not unless they hear the story.

Implicit (Emotional) Memory

As we noted, memory is traditionally understood as a constituent of the soul (along with reason and will). Neuroscientists classify memory two ways. *Implicit memories* do not require conscious deliberation, but allow us to walk, ride a bike, and so on. Since much of life is repetitive, little is deliberative. Nevertheless, our emotional responses to life's challenges are largely dictated by implicit memory.[384] Walter Benjamin (1892–1940) de-

381. Stephen Greenspan notes, "It is interesting to discover that public education in North America began not (as generally believed) to prepare young people for work or other aspects of adult life, but rather to make them less gullible and vulnerable to exploitation" (*Annals of Gullibility*, 36).

382. Athanasius, *Life of Antony*, 32.

383. Events interpenetrate one another to the point that everything is connected. Yet unless singular events are remembered they are very difficult to extract from the soup of reality. God's singular activities are a basic ingredient to reality, but can only be isolated by those who remember what God has done (Rom 1).

384. Approximately 80 percent of emotional conflict between couples in marriage is rooted in memories before their relationship began (Thompson, *Anatomy of the*

scribes memory as "the medium of our past experience, just as the earth is the medium in which dead cities lie buried."[385] We naturally try to forget what displeases us. Trauma victims may avoid processing their abuse because remembering is reliving, which overwhelms.[386] But God is with us and *has been* with us, although his past presence is like a buried treasure. A while ago, I was driving my family across the desert to San Diego, California. They noticed sand dunes and asked to pull over. After the kids played for a while, we got back into the car to pull out, but the tires had sunk into the sand. We were completely alone. I was filled with dread. (In retrospect, we could have called for a tow, but anxiety often clouds reason.) There was a trailer in the distance. I walked over and knocked on the door. A man named Homer answered. Telling him what happened, he looked annoyed but found a chain, drove his truck over, and pulled us out of the sand. After the trip, my mind remembered Homer; but my body, the dread, which created a phobia that triggered whenever my wife asked to take a road trip. But I eventually felt God's presence in Homer.

A few years earlier, I rushed to the hospital after hearing that my six-year old nephew, Austin Moore, was being treated for a brain tumor, which had taken everyone by surprise. The day before he complained of a headache and then became delirious. We watched Austin die in his mother's arms. For a long time, I struggled to admit my anger towards the Lord. When I got to the hospital, I asked two other pastors to pray with me for Austin's healing. "If there was ever a good time for God to intervene," I thought to myself, "it was now." When Julie, the mother, was holding Austin, I saw something that I did not think was relevant and had excluded it from this traumatic narrative for several years: I saw Michelangelo's *Pietà*, which I had seen when visiting St. Peter's Basilica during my honeymoon, superimposed over Julie and Austin. Several years later, I was remembering Austin with an uncle, who had been with us at the hospital, but did not mention what I saw. He shared that he saw the same statue. Shocked, I suddenly felt God enter that sad chapter in our story.

After teaching this, a woman shared with me how she walked away from the Lord after her husband, a worship pastor, committed adultery against her with her friend from church. She spent several years going from club to club until God warned her in a dream that death would come soon if she did not repent. After confessing her sin, she also came to see that

---

Soul, 68–72).

385. Benjamin, *Berlin Childhood around 1900*, xii.

386. Hebrew Scripture is remarkable in this regard. National memories are often self-serving where God's prophets are almost merciless in their rebukes of Israel. Sadly, this introspective truth has been misappropriated for anti-Semitic purposes.

God was lovingly holding her through the whole season. Through the Spirit, Jesus, Immanuel, reveals God's often mysterious presence in our stories. But we must be willing to come into the light, to remember, and to tell our bodies a redemptive narrative.

Explicit (Episodic) Memory

There are also explicit memories, which are factual and autobiographical. Like recalling a date, this memory requires attention and rehearsal.[387] A more specific form of explicit memory is episodic, which is how events and experiences are integrated into our story. Jesus weds the story of God's people, which was rehearsed every week in the synagogue at Nazareth, to his own (see Luke 4:16–30).

Jesus heard what was written to remember why we all are living. He remembers what Moses and the exodus generation heard, in a different place and time. What they heard and remembered and wrote is clarifying what would otherwise be an ambiguous, lonely, terrifying experience. He remembers God's Word, the disobedience of his people, and broke the unwholesome cycle by acting differently, so that temptation never became sin.

Memory is becoming a lost art. In classical education, children memorized thousands of poetic lines. According to a recent study, the Psalms "were intended to be memorized with a view to being publicly recited for the purpose of inculcating the nation's values."[388] The invitation here is to memorize Scripture within the context of God's great redemptive story and ask the Holy Spirit for illumination.

27: Friend of the Bridegroom (John 3:22–30)

[22] After these things Jesus and his disciples went into the Judean land, and there he was staying with them and was baptizing.

P: *After these things* (*Meta tauta*, Μετὰ ταῦτα): English translations sometimes obscure the plural in Greek (e.g., ESV "After this"). The transition at least includes the encounter with Nicodemus (3:1–15) but perhaps also the wedding at Cana, the first sign (2:1–12).[389] The reader will learn

387. It requires the integration of the hippocampus (Thompson, *Anatomy of the Soul*, 74).

388. Wenham, *Psalms as Torah*, 46.

389. Bonaventure notes: "The Lord had manifested himself to the Jews by a sign of power [Wedding in Cana] and a word of instruction [in Temple and with Nicodemus" (*John*, 199).

that Jesus, in fact, *was* not *baptizing* but his disciples (4:2). Apparently, he oversaw their continuation of John's ministry.

[23] But John was also baptizing in Aenon near Salim because there was much water there. And they were coming and being baptized [24] because John has not yet been thrown into prison. [25] So an argument broke out between the disciples of John and a Judean[390] over purification. [26] And they come to John and say to him, "Rabbi, (the one) who was with you beyond the Jordan, for whom you have witnessed, look—this one is baptizing and everyone is going to him!"

P: *But* (*de*, δέ) is often left untranslated (e.g., ESV), although it marks conflict.[391] The Baptist has moved from *beyond the Jordan* (1:28), allowing space for Christ's baptism that was predicted (v. 33). *Aenon* (*Ainōn*, Αἰνών), a toponym, is derived from a Hebrew word meaning "spring," a natural fountain, which supports the observation that *there was much water there*. The place is otherwise unmentioned and, at this time, cannot be located with certainty.[392]

The evangelist knows Mark claims that Jesus began his Galilean ministry after the Baptist's arrest (1:14). This is the lesser significance to *because John has not yet been thrown into prison* (see below). Whereas the second Gospel has no interest in their overlapping ministries, the fourth emphasizes the *synkrisis*. The word translated *argument* (*zētēsis*, ζήτησις) may describe divisive controversy (1 Tim 6:4; Titus 3:9). As we noted, *purification* (*katharismos*, καθαρισμός) is the effect of baptism, that is, immersion in water. Just as the Baptist was questioned for his own idiosyncratic baptismal rite in that region (1:25–28), Jesus and his disciples are coming under scrutiny for it. Yet the Baptist also hinted—the Synoptic Gospels are explicit—that the modality will change: "I baptize with water" (1:26). The reference to *much water* anticipates the superiority of Christ's baptism in the Spirit (1:26; 3:5; see 4:13–14).[393] John's baptism ceases with his passing, but the Holy Spirit will come after Christ's resurrection (14:15–31; 16:4–15; 20:22). The antecedent

390. The reading "Judeans" (P75) is probably not original. A *Judean* has slightly better textual support (P66, A, B), is the harder reading, and conforms to John's style (Köstenberger, *John*, 140; Lincoln, *John*, 157).

391. The KJV wrongly translates the adversative conjunction as "And."

392. See, however, the Madaba Map for a sixth-century identification that is directly across the Jordan River from Bethebara, the original location of the Baptist's ministry near Jericho. The Greek reads Αἰνών ἔνθα νύν ὁ Σαπσαφάς: "Ænon, where now is Sapsaphas"; Βέθαβαρά το τού ἁγίου Ιωάννου τού βαπτίσματος: "Bethabara, the place of baptism of St. John." Bonaventure incorrectly identifies *Salim* with Salem (see Heb 7:1; *John*, 200).

393. Bonaventure, *John*, 200.

of *they come* may include *the Judean*, but is primarily *John's disciples*, who seem to be jealous: *everyone is going to him!*

R: The conflict echoes the friction between Abraham and Lot's herdsmen in the same region (Gen 13). Lot chose the well-watered Jordan Valley and settled near Sodom.

D: The Baptist models what he is about to preach by making space for the Son's ministry. I often try to save or reform people when the only course is God's mysterious work. Who—the temple authorities, the Baptist, or Christ and the Holy Spirit—offers true purification to remain in God's presence? And what is the relationship of this purification, if any, with the inevitable suffering that comes after following Jesus (15:18—16:4; 21:18–19)?

S: *This little story intensifies our yearning for you, Holy Spirit! Come, giver of love and wisdom, fill our hearts with the Father and Son. We ache for your ever fuller presence, Triune God. Amen.*

[27] John answered and said, "A human being cannot receive anything except what has been given to him from Heaven.[394] [28] *You* must witness [for me][395]—that I said, '*I* am not the Christ, but I am sent before that one.'"

P: Although *John* is mentioned twice more (5:33–36 and 10:40–41), this is his final appearance, bookending the first interrogation (1:19–42). He echoes the prologue, "a *human being sent* . . ." (1:6), and his first response (1:20, 27), except that he now commands his disciples to offer the same *witness*—perhaps even to follow Andrew, Peter, and John into Jesus's discipleship circle.

R: Scripture often speaks of a person's "portion" from God.[396] The divine passive *has been given* may extend back to the creation story—when God gives Adam, the first *human being*, every tree in the garden, but not "the tree of the knowledge of good and evil" (Gen 2:17).

[29] The one who has the bride is the bridegroom.[397] But the friend of the bridegroom, who stands and listens for him, rejoices greatly because of the voice of the bridegroom. So this joy of mine has been fulfilled. [30] That one must be increasing, but I am decreasing myself.[398]

P: John responds with an allegorical parable: Jesus is *the bridegroom*, and those who are going to him and John for baptism are *the bride*. As *friend*

394. The article (τοῦ οὐρανοῦ) may particularize this noun as a circumlocution for God.

395. The pronoun *for me* (*moi*, μοι) is absent in P75 and ℵ.

396. See, e.g., Josh 15:13; 18:10; Job 20:29; 27:13; 31:1; Eccl 9:9; Jer 13:25.

397. The translation *bridegroom* for *numphios* (νυμφίος) is intended to draw out the similar spelling in Greek with bride (*numphē*, νύμφη).

398. The infinitive ἐλαττοῦσθαι is in the middle voice, which allows the Baptist to emphasize his role in the activity (*decreasing myself*).

of the bridegroom, John leads the bride to *the bridegroom* and waits for him to announce the consummation of the marriage.[399]

The response also reveals the significance of the first sign, the Wedding at Cana (2:1–12). The evangelist may have wanted to expand on Jesus's more subtle self-identification as groom for repentant sinners in Mark (2:18–22).[400] This motif was significant for Christians in and around Ephesus in the first century. Paul uses the tradition to exhort husbands to love their wives as Christ loved the church but is primarily interested in the mystery of union with Christ (Eph 5:25–27). The Marriage Supper of the Lamb is described in Revelation (19:6–10; 21:9–10), which was addressed, in part, to the church in Ephesus (2:1–7).

This is the first occurrence of *friend* (*philos*, φίλος) in the Gospel and is in the background when Jesus declares, "No one has greater love than this, except that someone lay down his life for his friends" (15:13). This is the greater significance of *because John has not yet been thrown into prison*—that the Baptist ultimately died for the union of the *bride* and his *friend*, the *bridegroom*.

D: In this passage, John pays homage to his first teacher, who testifies to the deepest mystery of the Christian tradition—union and friendship with Christ and one another in the Triune God. This is the final solution to the human condition, the only real healing for humanity, but entering this mystery requires un-selfing: "He must increase, but I must decrease" (3:30 KJV). In context, the Baptist is not so much making an existential statement as acknowledging the right focal point of the occasion, a wedding. True ministers remain focused on the groom and bride.

The Baptist sounds like Democritus (c. 460–c.370 BC), who encouraged the acceptance of limits, the unique set of boundaries everyone faces in a broken world of scarcity, but also valued the *joy* that comes from celebration. Paul wanted to go to Bithynia, "but the Spirit of Jesus did not allow" this (Acts 16:7). Instead, he was led to establish a church in Philippi that gave him *joy* in prison (see Philippians). The Baptist's *joy* (*chara*, χαρά) may be surprising—elsewhere he refuses to celebrate with his generation—but this "experience of gladness" is the appropriate emotional response to a wedding.[401]

Origen adopted the Greco-Roman *paideia* model to educate new Christians—the moral, natural, and inspective (contemplative)—which

399. Lincoln, *John*, 161.

400. The prophetic metaphor of Yahweh as bridegroom and Israel his bride (e.g., Isa 62:5; Jer 2:2; Hos 2:14–20) is discussed there.

401. BDAG, 1077.

became a standard progression of Bible study through Proverbs, Ecclesiastes, and Song of Songs.[402] When entering a monastery, the abbot would assign Proverbs to a young monk who needed to learn focus and self-discipline. In middle age, he turned to Ecclesiastes to learn how to give up most of what he acquired in youth. Old age afforded the opportunity to meditate on Song of Songs to prepare for facing the Beloved and fully entering into the marriage supper of the lamb.

S: *Father of Heaven, we open our palms to your gifts, even those that feel more like losses, and seek rest in your plan. We surrender to your Spirit. Amen.*

28A: Doubt and Praise (Matt 11:1–19)

[11:1] And it came about when Jesus finished giving detailed instructions[403] to his twelve disciples, he departed from there in order to teach and *to proclaim*[404] in their cities.[405] [Isa 61:1]

P: After a transition from the missionary discourse (ch. 10), Matthew refocuses on the Baptist's ministry. The long unit is delimited by *inclusio*—"the works of the Christ" (v. 2) and "wisdom is justified by her works" (v. 19), and is comprised of four subunits: 11:1–6, 7–11, 12–15, and 16–19. Jesus vacillates between challenge and praise.

The Question (11:2–6)

[2] But John, after hearing in prison the works of the Christ,[406] having sent through his disciples, [3] said to him, "Are you the one who is coming, or should we wait for another?" [4] And Jesus answered and said to them: "Go and announce to John what you are hearing and seeing: [5] *blind are seeing and lame are walking*—lepers are being cleansed—and *deaf are hearing* and *dead are being raised* and *destitute are receiving good news.* [Isa 29:18–19; 35:5; 42:7, 18; 35:6; 26:19; 61:1] [6] And blessed is whoever is not offended by me."

402. McGinn, *Essential Writings of Christian Mysticism*, 150.

403. This is the sense BDAG attributes to *diatassō* (διατάσσω) in this context (237–38). The verb looks back to the entire missionary discourse in chapter 10.

404. The presumed object is "the gospel of the kingdom" (4:23).

405. The pronoun *their* may evidence a schism between Matthew's first readers and the larger Jewish community. The issue is debated.

406. A few witnesses read "Jesus," which makes sense if John is questioning Jesus's messianic identity.

P: The Baptist may have depended on his *disciples* for survival.[407]

Matthew already suggested a tension between the two groups of *disciples* over fasting (9:14–17). The Baptist's ministry was ascetic; Jesus's, celebratory. A certainty John embraced about the *one who is coming* is that he would judge the sinner (3:7).[408] But since echoing his proclamation, "Repent, for the kingdom of the heavens has drawn near" (3:2; 4:17), Jesus has been forgiving, healing, and sharing tables with sinners. Yet the question may evidence confusion more than rejection.[409] How does such behavior "fulfill all righteousness" (3:15)?

Christ points to literal fulfillments from the most popular prophet of the day, Isaiah (see **R** below), but also presumes his ministry is *offensive*.[410] This suggests continuity and discontinuity with contemporary messianic expectation.

R: As the antitype of Elijah, the Baptist's doubt should not be surprising. The earlier prophet became discouraged from isolation and the evil of Ahab and Jezebel, leading to his retirement (1 Kgs 19).

Jesus cites from eschatological sections of Isaiah, a florilegium that describe the era of salvation (Isa 29:18–19 "the eyes of the blind shall see"; 35:5 "the eyes of the blind shall be opened"; 42:7 "To open the eyes that are blind"; 42:18 "you that are blind, look up and see"; 35:6 "Then the lame shall leap like a deer"; 26:19 "Your dead shall live"; 61:1 "He has sent me to bring good news to the poor"). Isaiah does not mention *lepers*, but the reference evokes the first cleansing (healing) after the Sermon on the Mount (8:1–4).[411]

Appropriating Isaiah creates a tension: amidst this healing, the prophet also announces freedom for prisoners (42:7), but John languishes in *prison*.

D: Jesus, who goes ahead of us, often departs from the script. As God's prophet, John was not responsible for understanding or interpreting the message, but to proclaim God's oracles (2 Pet 1:20). He surprises John and us, and invites everyone to follow into the mystery. He calls the Baptist to

407. See also Josephus, *J.W.* 1.161; *Ant.* 14.83; 18.111. John Meier observes: "Often prisoners were dependent on family and friends for food and other supplies, which the imprisoning officials sometimes did not provide. While strict confinement without any visitors was known, the presumption of almost all the NT texts that deal with the topic is that access to the imprisoned is possible (e.g., Heb 13:3; Acts 23:16)" (*Marginal Jew*, 2:198–99.

408. Dunn, *Jesus Remembered*, 447.

409. Brian Dennert notes, "Matthew shows that John's understanding is incomplete but that he is teachable" (*John the Baptist*, 227).

410. The verb (*skandalizō*, σκανδαλίζω) may also describe "stumbling."

411. That is the case in both the Hebrew and Greek.

a faith beyond understanding, to rest in Christ's reading of Scripture. The Baptist suffers from a foundationalist ideology—namely, unless everything makes sense, nothing does. He fixates on the injustice of his own situation and how Jesus departs from his expectations and becomes blind to God's *works*. Jesus invites his beloved forerunner into a faith that leads to understanding. Similarly, we are asked to believe to understand.

S: *Lord, how often I have fixated on my expectations for life and you, and become blind to your ways. I ask for a faith that sees more of you. Amen.*

Greatest and Least (11:7–11)

[7] Now while they were departing, Jesus began to speak to the crowds about John: "What did you go out into the wilderness to behold: A reed being shaken by wind?[412] [1 Kgs 14:15] [8] But what did you go out to see: A human being dressed in soft clothing? Look: those who wear soft clothing are in the houses of kings. [9] But what did you go out to see? A prophet? Yes, I say to you—even more than a prophet. [10] This is (the one) concerning whom it has been written: *Look, I am sending my messenger before your face, who will prepare your way before you.* [Mal 3:1] [11] Amen, I say to you: among those born by women, there has risen no one greater than John the Baptist. But the one who is least in the kingdom of the heavens is greater than he.

P: *John* and *Jesus* share the same *crowds*: those who *beheld* the Baptist are listening to the Christ. After the Sermon on the Mount (4:25—5:1; 7:8), the collective response of this group has been ambivalent—from praising God in response to healings (9:8) and expressing wonder over exorcisms (9:33) to laughing at Jesus (9:23–24).

For emphasis, Jesus repeats the same question three times, the first and fullest expression of which is *What did you go out into the wilderness to behold?*[413] It is a question about the Baptist's identity but also the stirring of their own heart: *What* compelled them to leave the comfort and security of the city?

The verb translated *behold* (*theaomai,* θεάομαι) implies the *crowds* were impressed by the Baptist. Jesus praises his asceticism, an appealing alternative to the powers that be. They will be *shaken* (24:29), but John is sturdy.

412. A *reed* could be hollowed out and played as a "flute." See v. 17 where the Baptist refuses to dance along with flute music. (The potential pun only makes sense in Hebrew/Aramaic.)

413. The slight shortening of repeated statements and questions is a standard solution to the constraint of space and attention span (see, e.g., John 1:19–21).

Soft clothing suggests an effeminent, gluttonous lifestyle.[414] His description would appeal to Romans, who, suspicious of elegance (*luxuria*), built their empire on hardened manliness (*firmitas*). In his own strange way, the Baptist embodies the cardinal virtues of "wisdom" (*phronēsis* [φρόνησις] or *sophia* [σοφία]), "justice" (*dikaisunē*, δικαιοσύνη), and "courage" (*andreia*, ἀνδρεία), and therefore is more fit to rule than Herod Antipas or Pilate.

Jesus elevates John over earlier *prophets*, who he is citing as authoritative (Isaiah, Malachi), because he himself is partly the fulfillment of their words. Indeed, *among those born by women, there has risen no one greater than John the Baptist.*

But this genuine praise leads to a shocking reversal: *the one who is least in the kingdom of the heavens is greater than he. Born by a woman*, a euphemism for humankind, often emphasizes frailty and mortality (see also Job 14:1; 15:14; 25:4). Jesus elevates someone who has taken on a new existence—"born again" or "regenerated" (see Matt 19:28 and the development of this motif in John 3). The contrast is not meant to disparage the Baptist because his role was to prepare the people for this work of the Spirit (3:11–12).

R: Jesus may just as well be asking the exodus generation why they were willing to leave Egypt and follow Moses into the *wilderness*.

Although Matthew dropped the Malachi citation earlier from Mark's opening (contrast Mark 1:2 with Matt 3:3), he includes it here and on the lips of Jesus. It presents the Baptist as the guiding cloud of the Exodus story.[415]

In contrast, Jesus alludes to the prophecy Ahijah *the prophet* said to the wife of Jeroboam over the imminent death of their son and exile of their people:

> At that time Abijah the son of Jeroboam fell sick. And Jeroboam said to his wife, "Arise, and disguise yourself, that it not be known that you are the wife of Jeroboam, and go to Shiloh. Behold, Ahijah the prophet is there, who said of me that I should be king over this people. Take with you ten loaves, some cakes, and a jar of honey, and go to him. He will tell you what shall happen to the child." Jeroboam's wife did so. She arose and went to Shiloh and came to the house of Ahijah. Now Ahijah could not see, for his eyes were dim because of his age. And the LORD said to Ahijah, "Behold, the wife of Jeroboam is coming to inquire of you concerning her son, for he is sick. Thus and

414. See Luke 16:19–31; Josephus, *J.W.* 6.211; 7.338.

415. Darrell Bock observes, "John is a commissioned, end-time messenger. He is sent to guide the people as Yahweh's cloud had done in the wilderness. The way to follow God was revealed by him" (*Jesus according to Scripture*, 179).

> thus shall you say to her." When she came, she pretended to be another woman. But when Ahijah heard the sound of her feet, as she came in at the door, he said, "Come in, wife of Jeroboam. Why do you pretend to be another? For I am charged with unbearable news for you. Go, tell Jeroboam, 'Thus says the LORD, the God of Israel: "Because I exalted you from among the people and made you leader over my people Israel and tore the kingdom away from the house of David and gave it to you, and yet *you have not been like my servant David, who kept my commandments and followed me with all his heart, doing only that which was right in my eyes*, but you have done evil above all who were before you and have gone and made for yourself other gods and metal images, provoking me to anger, and have cast me behind your back, therefore behold, I will bring harm upon the house of Jeroboam and will cut off from Jeroboam every male, both bond and free in Israel, and will burn up the house of Jeroboam, as a man burns up dung until it is all gone. Anyone belonging to Jeroboam who dies in the city the dogs shall eat, and anyone who dies in the open country the birds of the heavens shall eat, for the LORD has spoken it."' Arise therefore, go to your house. When your feet enter the city, the child shall die. And all Israel shall mourn for him and bury him, for he only of Jeroboam shall come to the grave, because in him there is found something pleasing to the LORD, the God of Israel, in the house of Jeroboam. Moreover, *the LORD will raise up for himself a king over Israel who shall cut off the house of Jeroboam today. And henceforth, the LORD will strike Israel as a reed is shaken in the water, and root up Israel out of this good land that he gave to their fathers and scatter them beyond the Euphrates, because they have made their Asherim, provoking the LORD to anger*. And he will give Israel up because of the sins of Jeroboam, which he sinned and made Israel to sin." Then Jeroboam's wife arose and departed and came to Tirzah. And as she came to the threshold of the house, the child died. And all Israel buried him and mourned for him, according to the word of the LORD, which he spoke by his servant Ahijah the prophet. (1 Kgs 14:1–18 ESV)

Perhaps we are not going too far to see a preference for a Davidic messiah in this passage, the first italics, and God's judgment upon those who identify with the sinful powers that be, the second italics.

D: People will be drawn to the effect of God's presence in his disciples—in this case, self-discipline. It is unnecessary to look like their previous paradigms of success—their kings, athletes, actors, and politicians.[416] They are drawn to our freedom, the dream that led the exodus generation into the *wilderness*, and to Immanuel, God with us. But such attraction emanates from our citizenship in the *Kingdom*, God's authority over our lives, not ourselves.

Jesus also reminds us about the importance of context. We take on the strengths and weaknesses of our intimate associations. Too much time with *kings* leads to a softness that cannot survive in the *wilderness*.

S: This and the previous unit further unpack the opening of Mark's Gospel where the Father addresses the Son about the Baptist. The people were drawn to John's self-discipline, which came from his unique relationship with God as one even greater than a prophet. Despite his own confusion, John came to bring people to God's Son. So we are left with an irony: *What did* they *go out into the wilderness to behold?* The person standing before them!

Elijah and the End of Prophecy (11:12–15)

[12] But from the days of John the Baptist until now the kingdom of the heavens is forcefully advancing (*biazetai*), and forceful men (*biastēs*) are seizing (*harpazō*) it. [13] For all the Prophets and the Law prophesied until John. [14] And if you are willing to receive, he himself is Elijah, who is about to come.[417] [15] Whoever has ears, hear!

P: The verb *biazetai* (βιάζεται) may be in the passive or middle voice.[418] The NIV adopted the middle voice: "the kingdom of heaven has been forcefully advancing, and forceful men lay hold of it," which aptly describes the healings and exorcisms of Jesus's public ministry *and* the complication of John's imprisonment.[419] The KJV chose the passive: "the kingdom of heaven suffereth violence, and the violent take it by force" (followed by NAS and ESV), which emphasizes the plight of the Baptist. But John does not embody the *Kingdom*, as the previous unit clarifies, although he is the "tip of the spear." Furthermore, Luke appears to treat the verb as a middle (16:16). The substantive adjective *biastēs* (βιαστής) is a cognate of the verb *biazetai*. With the verb translated *are seizing* (*harpazō*, ἁρπάζω), Jesus is describing

416. Sometimes, I feel that many leaders in my evangelical tradition try too hard to look like successful people in the world.

417. The Greek is a first class conditional, which presumes the truth of the protasis (*if you are willing to receive*). Josephus and the Gospels presume the crowds revered the Baptist.

418. BDAG, 175–76. The ambiguity persists in the earliest citation because Justin does not offer comment (*Dial.* 51).

419. Nolland, *Gospel of Matthew*, 458.

the opposition to the *Kingdom* who arrested *John*—Herod Antipas, Herodias, and their people, the Herodians—but there is also a spiritual dimension as the exorcisms demonstrate.

R: *All the Prophets and the Law prophesied until John:* The reference to *Elijah* presumes the Malachi citation above. The prophetic book, traditionally seen as the last of its kind, ends with a promise, "I will send you Elijah" (4:5), and a warning to repent. Jesus's ministry, extending to the present, is "the great and awesome day of the Lord."[420] Jesus also wields these Scriptures in the Sermon on the Mount to resist the devil.

The language presumes a fulfillment of Scripture, one of Matthew's interests, but perhaps also a *definitive* fulfillment—a real break between BC and AD. If so, this clarifies the earlier claim in the Sermon on the Mount (5:17–19). This earlier Scripture will remain God's Word, contrary to Marcion, but it will be read backwards—from the Christ event back into earlier interpretations, as Matthew has demonstrated. (Jesus may invite this by mentioning the *Prophets* before the *Law*.) Jesus treats Scripture as a unified prophetic word.

D: The powers that be face in the gospel a different seemingly weaker power that in their heart they know will someday overpower them.

S: *Lord, we have ears. May we hear and receive your truth. Amen.*

Children in the Market (11:16–19)

[16] "But to what will I compare this generation? It is like children sitting in the markets, who are calling to the others. [17] They say, 'We played the flute for you, and you did not dance. We sang a dirge, and you did not beat (your breast).' [18] For John came neither eating nor drinking, and they say, 'He has a demon.' [19] The son of man came eating and drinking, and they say, 'Look, (this) man is a glutton and a drunk, a friend of tax collectors and sinners.' But Wisdom is justified by her works."

P: Jesus uses the everyday sight of *children* playing in *the market*, the center of communal life outside the synagogue in Israel, to illustrate how he and the Baptist were marginalized by their opponents. *John* plays the role of the ascetic; Jesus, the *glutton*. (We find similar contrasts of personality in the Gospels between Peter and John and Mary and Martha.) The response is chiastic, ironic, and perhaps humorous: (A) a group of children pretend to be in a wedding (*We played the flute*), but (A') John refuses to participate, as if he were at a funeral; (B) they later pretend to be

420. Subsequent Christian writers describe the present as "these last days" (Heb 1:2; see also 2 Tim 3:1) and "later times" (1 Tim 4:1).

in a funeral (*We sang a dirge*), but (B') Jesus is celebrating a wedding—the reconciliation of *sinners* with God. In either case, the contrastive behavior of John and Jesus elicits slander. To John: *He has a demon*; to Jesus: *[this] man is a glutton and a drunk.*

R: *This generation*, a pejorative Jesus uses to describe those who reject the gospel, highlights the community's responsibility to the fulfillment of Scripture.

D: In general, people ignore *Wisdom* until it is too late.

S: Shortly, Jesus will present himself as *Wisdom* (11:28–30; Sir 24:19–20).[421] He employs typology to contextualize John, but is more coy about himself as the antitype of Solomon, the son of David (Matt 1:1). Jesus has been acting like the ancient gluttonous king, except that his motivation is righteous, and is the wisest of men (1 Kgs 3:28; 4:29–30).

28B: Doubt and Praise (Luke 7:18–35; 16:16–17)

The Question (7:18–23)

[18] And his disciples reported to John concerning all these things. And having called two of his disciples, John [19] sent (them) to the Lord, saying, "Are you the one who is coming, or should we look for another?" [20] Now coming to him, the men said, "John the Baptist sent us to you, saying: 'Are you the one who is coming, or should we looking for another?'" [21] In that hour, he healed many from illnesses and diseases and evil spirits; and many blind people he showed favor to see. [22] And he answered and said to them: "Go and report to John what you saw and heard: *blind are seeing, lame are walking*—lepers are being cleansed—(and)[422] *deaf are hearing, dead are being raised, destitute are receiving good news* [Isa 29:18–19; 35:5; 42:7, 18; 35:6; 26:19; 61:1] [23] And blessed is the one who is not offended by me."

P: Matthew is comfortable having a person speak through an intermediary (1:22; 3:3; 8:5–13); Luke, less so (7:1–10), which leads to a redundancy that rhetorically emphasizes the question: *Are you the one who is coming, or should we look for another?* He also clarifies how *John* heard about "the works of Christ" (Matt 11:2) and makes explicit that *the two men*, the legal requirement for eyewitness testimony, see healings take

421. For more discussion of Jesus as Wisdom, see Witherington, *Jesus, the Sage*. John Meier suggests wisdom refers "to God's wise, well-ordered plan of salvation, which is now reaching its climax" (*Marginal Jew*, 2:152). It is interesting that Jesus retains the femininity of personified Wisdom in the Hebrew Bible.

422. The conjunction may not be original, although it does occur in our earliest witnesses.

place. (Matthew does not relate how many of John's disciples question Jesus, allowing for a crowded scene.) The ensuing discussion does not follow a long missionary discourse (cf. Matt 10:1–42), but Jesus raising a widow's son from the dead (7:11–17), which foregrounds the claim *dead are being raised*. This is also the second time Jesus has cited the line *destitute are receiving good news*; the first occurs in the Nazareth Manifesto (Luke 4:18; see also 6:20), establishing it as a motif.

D: From Luke's emphases, we see ideal disciples who obediently and faithfully transmit the message of their teacher. If they were this careful with the Baptist, all the more disciples who saw Jesus as their *Lord* would protect the truth.

Luke uniquely claims Jesus *showed favor* (*charizomai*, χαρίζομαι). The verb is related to the noun "grace" or "favor" (*charis*, χάρις). He rightly presents the *Lord* as a benefactor or patron, who bestows favor on his clients, a role that Theophilus may have played in a smaller way.[423] In these cases, the culturally appropriate response is gratitude (see Luke 17:11–19).

S: *Lord, we give thanks for your favor in our lives, for turning to us and saving us from the death and decay of this world, for healing our brokenness, and for sharing the gospel with us. Amen.*

Greatest and Least (7:24–30)

[24] And after the messengers of John left, he began to speak to the crowds about John: "What did you go out into the wilderness to watch? A reed being shaken by the wind? [25] But what did you go out to see? A man dressed in soft clothing? Behold, those (who are) in glorious clothing and are living in luxury are in palaces. [26] But what did you go out to see? A prophet? Yes, I say to you, indeed, more than a prophet. [27] This is about whom it has been written: *Behold, I am sending my messenger before your face, who will prepare your way before you*. [Mal 3:1] [28] I say to you: among those born of women no one is greater than John. But the least in the Kingdom of God is greater than he." [29] And the whole crowd and the tax collectors,[424] hearing this, justified God, having been baptized by the baptism of John. [30] But the Pharisees and the scribes rejected God's plan for them, having not been baptized by John.

P: Luke follows Matthew closely, but adds reaction to the teaching, evoking John's exhortations to the *crowds* and *tax collectors* (3:7–14).

423. See, e.g., Oropeza, "Expectation of Grace," 207–26.

424. Or toll collectors.

Children in the Market (7:31–35)

[31] "Therefore, to what will I compare the people of this generation, and to what are they like? [32] They are like children in the market, sitting and calling to one another. They say, 'We played the flute for you, and you did not dance; we sang a dirge, and you did not weep.' [33] For John the Baptist came not eating bread or drinking wine, and you say, 'he has a demon.' [34] The son of man came eating and drinking, and you say, 'Look: a glutton and a drunkard, a friend of tax collectors and sinners.' [35] And yet wisdom is justified by all of her children.'"

P: As we noted, Matthew creates *inclusio* with "the works of the Christ" at the head of his unit (11:2). Luke's reading creates a nearer *inclusio* by repeating *children* (vv. 32, 35). Otherwise, with some minor stylistic variation, the accounts are nearly identical.

Forcefully Advancing (16:16–17)

[16] The Law and the Prophets were until John; from then the good news of the Kingdom of God is proclaimed, and everyone forcefully advances himself (*biazetai*) into it. [Matt 11:12] [17] But it is easier for the heaven and the earth to pass away than for one *vav* of the Law to become void. [Matt 5:18]

P: Luke has united two sayings from Matthew's presentation (*gezerah sheva*). The linking word is *Law* (*nomos*).[425] Together, they maintain continuity and discontinuity with Israel's salvation history. The unit introduces The Rich Man and Lazarus (16:19–31), which presupposes the enduring value of "Moses and the Prophets" for repentance (16:29).[426] In context, the Pharisees are Law-breakers because of their idolatrous love for money (16:14).[427] But, as the influential Protestant scholar Hans Conzelmann (1915–1989) saw, the unit divides time into two epochs of salvation, which is consistent with the original context in Matthew.[428]

But Luke slightly ambiguates the saying by switching Matthew's description of *John's* arrest—"forceful men are seizing" (Matt 11:12) to *everyone*

425. He inverts the original order of the first saying. He does not include the reference to the Baptist in Matthew's presentation because it is not apropos to the context.

426. Luomanen, *Entering the Kingdom*, 76. I do not share his presupposition of Q theory.

427. Emmrich, *At the Heart of Luke*, 89.

428. Conzelmann, *Theology of St. Luke*, 21. The original German title is *Die Mitte der Zeit* ("the middle of time"). For critique, see Wink, *John the Baptist*, 51–52.

forcefully advances himself (biazetai) into the Kingdom.[429] The Baptist is no longer the focus at this point in the narrative. Instead, he is more interested in the popular response to the gospel. The saying unpacks his earlier addition to Matthew in the unit: "And *the whole crowd* and the tax collectors, hearing this, justified God, having been baptized by the baptism of John. But the Pharisees and the scribes rejected God's plan for them, having not been baptized by John" (7:29–30).

The final line, which is taken from the Sermon on the Mount, is illustrated by a teaching on divorce that is also derived from that discourse: "Anyone who divorces his wife and marries another commits adultery. And the one who marries a woman who has divorced herself from a husband commits adultery" (Luke 16:18; see Matt 5:31–32). Far from the *Law* becoming *void*, the gospel is even more stringent. One cannot hide a lust for adultery or wealth behind sophistic interpretations of Scripture. Sinners and tax collectors knew they were sinners and seized the opportunity *to forcefully advance into the Kingdom*. The Pharisees and scribes refused to repent.

D: Martin Luther emphasized a distinction between law and gospel, whereas his followers, along with John Calvin, sought a more positive relationship. Luke maintains a creative tension between human responsibility and divine sovereignty. As can be seen in his sequel, Acts, God is merciful towards those who acknowledge their sin and are united to Christ, and the Holy Spirit empowers them to obey even more stringent obligations in the new covenant.

S: *Come, Holy Spirit, empower our love for one another. Amen.*

29A: Arrest and Murder (Mark 6:14–29)

This unit allows time for the mission of the Twelve apostles (6:7–13). The grotesque banquet scene will be juxtaposed with the feeding of the five thousand (6:30–44).

Herod's Misidentification (6:14–16)

[14] And King Herod heard. For his name became known, and he was saying, "John, the one who baptizes, has been raised from those who are dead!

429. The original hand of א may have omitted the line for this reason. If original, perhaps Luke intends the passive voice: "everyone is forcefully urged into it." For the sense of "urge," see Luke 24:29 and Acts 16:15. However, the verb is clearly in the middle voice in these places. It is more consistent to presume Luke read Matthew's wording as a middle.

And because of this the powers are working in him." [15] But others were saying, "He is Elijah." [Mal 4:5] Still others were saying, "a prophet like one of the prophets." [Deut 18:15, 18] [16] But hearing, Herod was saying, "John whom *I* beheaded—this one was raised!"

P: This subunit is framed by *Herod's hearing* and misidentification of Jesus as *John* redivivus.[430] Mark plays with the irony of the *name* of Jesus *becoming known*—who is not mentioned in the unit, a rarity in this Gospel—while he is being confused with others! The misidentification may have begun when the Pharisees went the Herodians, his entourage, to destroy Jesus after seeing him restore a hand on the Sabbath (3:1–6). These misidentifications will persist, even after the mission (8:28).

Herod Antipas was technically a "tetrarch" ("ruler of a fourth") of Galilee and Berea, but likely appropriated the title *King* in a de facto way (see 6:23; Josephus, *Ant.* 17.188). He suffers from confirmation bias, but is confronted with a double conundrum. Jesus *must* be *John*, but *John* is dead and was not remembered by Josephus or the New Testament for performing any miracles. This forces the tetrarch into the supernatural. People who died before their allotted span were believed to be barred from full entry into the underworld and therefore became ghosts (6:49).[431] Herod may also assume a form of reincarnation, which was popularized from the East through the writings of Plato, Neo-Pythagoreans, and Orphics.[432] In any case, he potentially blasphemes the Holy Spirit by attributing the supernatural works around the gospel to demonic *powers* (3:28–30; see Acts 10:38; Eph 1:21; 3:7, 16, 20). The misidentification also puts Jesus in danger: if *Herod beheaded John*, what will he do to remove the ghost of his sin?

R: The second popular misidentification identifies Jesus as *Elijah*, which evokes Malachi's prophecy (4:5), which has already been discussed.[433] Keeping with the opening of the Gospel (1:2–8), Jesus will relate *John* to *Elijah* (9:13). The third misidentification is probably an allusion to Deuteronomy, which has already been discussed in John's appropriation of this passage (1:21).

D: *Herod hears* but does not understand because of confirmation bias, the tendency to interpret experience in a way that confirms one's beliefs (see 4:9). As we noted, even disciples suffer from this hard-heartedness. It appears

430. The unit is chiastic: (A) Herod, (B) popular view, (B') popular view, (A') Herod. This delimitation of the subunit is often missed (see, e.g., ESV).

431. Bolt, *Jesus's Defeat of Death*, 160.

432. Burkert, *Greek Religion*, 299–300.

433. See commentary on John 1:6.

to be a universal human tendency.[434] The Enlightenment hoped to overcome this stumbling block to truth. Voltaire (1694–1778) notes, "The interest I have in believing in something is not a proof that something exists."[435]

Paradoxically, Mark describes faith as the opposite of confirmation bias. Is not faith, we might reasonably ask, a kind of confirmation bias? Are not the faithful supposed to believe contrary to evidence? That actually describes the Pharisees and scribes in Mark's presentation. What if faith is more radical than fundamentalism? What if faith, in part, is openness to reality as it confronts us?

S: *Holy Spirit, at work in Christ to oppose all that is Satanic and to renew the face of the earth, come and ignite our hearts. Amen.*

Story of the Baptist's Death (6:17–29)

[17] For Herod himself,[436] after sending (men), arrested John and bound him in prison because of Herodias, the wife of Philip, his brother, because he had married her. [18] For John was saying to Herod, "It is not lawful to have the wife of your brother." [Lev 18:16; 20:21; 2 Sam 12]

P: Mark obliquely referred to *John* being "handed over" at the beginning (1:14), which allowed space for Jesus's mission, and is now filling out the backstory. The imperfect tense form *elegen* (ἔλεγεν, *was saying*) suggests the Baptist was repeatedly rebuking *Herod*. Presumably, this was not face to face but through his public teaching, which is politically subversive. As part of a unit allowing time for the mission of the Twelve, Mark invites a contrast between Jesus and *Herod* (*synkrisis*). Both men send (*apostellō*, ἀποστέλλω) others to carry out their objectives (see 6:7), but their different priorities reveal opposing kingdoms. *John* affirms one and opposes the other.

R: *Herod* violates incest laws in the Mosaic Law:

> You shall not uncover the nakedness of your brother's wife; it is your brother's nakedness. (Lev 18:16)
>
> If a man takes his brother's wife, it is impurity. He has uncovered his brother's nakedness; they shall be childless. (20:21 ESV)

John alludes to these Scriptures by calling the marriage *not lawful* (*ouk exestin*, οὐκ ἔξεστίν). Since a husband and wife become one flesh, to "uncover the nakedness your brother's wife" is to uncover "your brother's

434. See, e.g., chapter 1, "If You Are Human, You Are Biased," in Ross, *Everyday Bias*, 1–16.

435. Cited in Coyne, *Faith Vs. Fact*, 29.

436. The Greek emphasizes *Herod's* responsibility in the action.

nakedness," which is a recapitulation of Ham's sin against his father Noah (Gen 9:22–23). Whereas Jesus is reversing the effects of the Fall, *Herod* is perpetuating them.

John expresses courage, a cardinal virtue, by speaking truth to power, a pattern we see in prophets before him. There is an echo of Nathan rebuking David for his adultery with Bathsheba (2 Sam 12).

D: To what degree should the Christian imitate the example of John speaking truth to power? The expression probably originates from a pamphlet, *Speak Truth to Power: a Quaker Search for an Alternative to Violence,* that was disseminated in 1955.[437] George Fox (1624–1691) founded Quakerism in reaction to what he perceived as the malaise of the Anglican Church. In my opinion, the Christian appropriation of John should not be direct but mediated through Christ. However, Jesus himself calls Herod a "fox" (Luke 13:32) and critiques his way of life (see Matt 11:1–6 par.). I believe the Church is moving into a season of diverse unity, a lens through which we are able to appreciate both the radical and centrist movements of the Spirit. The gospel, by definition, is a truth that must be spoken both to the weak and the powerful. Concerning the latter, the Gospels consistently presume a conflict of kingdoms. The prophetic office continues in the church and ecclesial authorities, like the bishops, would do well to listen.

S: Jesus is criticized for eating with tax collectors and sinners, which is actually a marriage between Yahweh and adulterous Israel (2:20) that will lead to the groom's self-sacrifice, but *Herod* marries for self-gratification.

[19] Now Herodias was nursing a grudge against him and wanted to kill him. And yet she was not able [20] because Herod was afraid of John, knowing him to be a righteous and holy man, and was protecting[438] him. [1 Kgs 19:2] And hearing him, he was perplexed and yet he heard him gladly.

P: *Herodias wants to kill* John, who threatened to delegitimize her authority, but *Herod* also fears the Baptist's character (*righteous*) and special relationship (*holy*) with God. John remains consistent, presumably preaching the same message of repentance and faith in public and prison.

The scene anticipates Jesus standing before Caiaphas, the high priest, and Pilate, the Roman prefect.

R: There are potentially two typologies in the passage: *Herod* may follow David's example with Nathan and repent (Psalm 51), or Ahab, who is influenced by his wife Jezebel (1 Kgs 16–22) like Adam was to Eve.[439] The

437. Muers, *Testimony*, 93–94. She discusses Noam Chomsky's appropriation of the language.

438. Or "defending."

439. For the latter typology, see Janes, "Why the Daughter of Herodias Must Dance," 443–67.

latter typology relates to John as Elijah redivivus, who asked, "How long will you waver between two opinions" (1 Kgs 18:21)?

D: The verb translated *perplexed* (*aporeō*, ἀπορέω) is related to the noun *aporia* (ἀπορία), which can be translated "perplexity" or "anxiety." In this context, this unsettled state is an invitation to repentance and surrender. Herod's initial sin, incest, has become the temptation for another sin, leading to destiny. It would seem, though, that the king could still break this pattern. There are many causes for anxiety; one is resistance to God's Word: "Today, if you hear his voice, do not harden your hearts" (Heb 4:7).

S: *Lord, help us to surrender any power, wealth, or comfort that hardens us to your Word. Amen.*

[21] And an opportune day came when Herod offered a banquet for his birthday for his administrators and colonels[440] and heads of Galilee.[441] [22] And when his[442] daughter by Herodias entered and danced, she gave pleasure to Herod and those who were reclining. The king said to the young girl, "Ask me whatever you want, and I will give (it) to you." [23] And he [solemnly][443] swore an oath to her: "Whatever you ask me, I will give to you—up to half of my kingdom." [24] And departing, she spoke to her mother: "What should I ask for?" Now she said, "The head of John who baptizes." [25] And going very quickly to the king, she asked, saying, "I want right away that you give me the head of John the Baptist on a platter." [26] And the king, who became very sad, because of the oaths and those who are reclining did not want to refuse her. [27] And immediately, after sending an executioner, the king commanded (him) to bring his head. And going, he beheaded him in the prison [28] and brought his head on a platter and gave it to the young girl. And the young girl gave it to her mother. [29] And hearing, his disciples came and took his corpse and buried it in a grave.

P: Privileged Romans celebrated birthdays with a lavish banquet (*convivium*) or more specifically the *cena*, which involved family and close associates. It was intended to be a feast for the senses—luxurious tableware, exotic food and drink, and diverse forms of entertainment. The *cena* took place in the dining room that was often replete with mosaics and statues. Host and guests *reclined* on couches. Women were allowed to participate in Roman culture, but the *symposium* of the Greeks only allowed females as entertainers and courtesans, which is consistent with *Herodias* being

440. For the translation, see Barnett, *Jesus and the Rise of Early Christianity*, 114.

441. Heads of Galilee were estate owners and civic leaders (Barnett, *Jesus and the Rise of Early Christianity*, 114).

442. Later manuscripts read "her daughter," a seeming correction. But Mark heightens the incestuous connotation.

443. Following D; πολλά may be in P45.

outside the scene and her daughter's role. Presumably, there was musical accompaniment to her *dancing*. The *platter* (*pinax*, πίναξ) is a grotesque appropriation of the scene.

The scene exposes *Herod* to be the opposite of the Baptist—someone given to foolish, impulsive decisions from a lack of self-control. *Herodias* exploits her own daughter's sexuality to manipulate her husband, drawing her into their sin.[444]

The conclusion sets up a *synkrisis* between the *disciples* of the Baptist and those of Jesus, who will abandon his *corpse* to be buried by others. Indeed, the scene anticipate Jesus's betrayal after the Passover meal.

R: The kings (Ahab, Herod) are ambivalent to God's prophet, Elijah and John (or Elijah in John), while the queens go for the kill (1 Kgs 19).

D: Herodias *wanted* to kill the Baptist (v. 19); Herod offers her daughter whatever *she wants* (v. 22), which requires him to do what he *did not want* (v. 26). One double bind leads to another.

29B: Arrest and Murder (Matt 14:1–12)

[14:1] In that season, Herod the tetrarch heard the rumor about Jesus [2] and said to his servants,[445] "This is John the Baptist! *He* was raised from the dead ones; and because of this, the powers are working in him." [3] For Herod, after seizing and binding John, put him in prison because of Herodias, the wife of Philip, his brother. [4] For John was saying to him, "It is not lawful for you to have her." [Lev 18:16; 20:21; 2 Sam 12] [5] And while desiring to kill him, he feared the crowd because they were holding him as a prophet. [6] But when the birthday of Herod came, the daughter of Herodias, the wife of Philip his brother, danced in the middle and pleasured Herod. [7] So with an oath he confessed to give to her whatever she might ask. [8] But after being persuaded by her mother, she said, "Give me here on a platter the head of John the Baptist." [9] And although he was saddened, the king, because of the oaths and those reclining, ordered (it) to be given. [10] And he sent (an executioner) and beheaded John in prison. [11] And his head was brought on a platter and was given to the young girl; and she brought (it) to her mother. [12] And having come, his disciple took the corpse and buried it; and having gone, they told Jesus.

444. Herodias's daughter is probably *Salome* as Josephus notes (see Hoehner, *Herod Antipas*, 151–54).

445. Or "children" or "child servants" (*pais*, παῖς). This is Matthew's preferred language (see 8:6).

P: *Jesus* may be the source of this story (v. 12). Matthew places it after his rejection at Nazareth (13:53–58) and before the feeding of the five thousand (14:13–21).

Matthew tends to use fewer words than Mark, passing over the alternative views of Jesus's identity and the lurid details of the banquet scene. He also changes the title "king" to the more historically precise *tetrarch*, perhaps to distinguish this *Herod* from his father, Herod the Great, who was declared a king by the Romans and had a prominent role in his birth narrative of Jesus. In addition to the demotion, his portrait of Antipas is less sympathetic, shifting the desire to kill the Baptist from *Herodias* to the *tetrarch*. Her role is lessened, but Matthew sets up a *synkrisis* between *Herodias* and Pilate's unnamed wife, who recommends doing nothing harmful to Jesus (27:19).

D: Jesus banned oaths (*orkos*, ὅρκος) in the Sermon on the Mount (5:33–37), and Herod foolishly exemplifies why. For this reason, Matthew may have retained Mark's note (6:26) about the tetrarch's *sadness*—not for the sake of John but the consequences of his foolish behavior.

S: *Lord Jesus, let our yes be yes and our no be no. Anything beyond this is evil. Amen.*

Josephus on the Baptist

We have been referencing the Jewish historian Josephus throughout our discussion of John because he probably provides an independent witness to the Baptist's ministry and death.[446] His summation offers a general corroboration for the Gospels, but also creates a few tensions:

> Now some of the Jews were thinking that Herod's army was destroyed by God—indeed quite justly—who avenged himself[447] according to what was required of John, who is called the Baptist (*baptistēs*, βαπτιστής). For indeed Herod killed him, who was a good man (*agathon andra*, ἀγαθὸν ἄνδρα) and called the Jews to the labor of virtue (*aretēn epaskousin*, ἀρετὴν ἐπασκοῦσιν)—both the matters concerning justice (*dikaiosunē*, δικαιοσύνη) toward one another and surrendering piety (*eusebeia*, εὐσέβεια) toward God—and (thereafter) to undergo baptism.[448] For indeed (God) recognizes this baptism as acceptable before him, not for

446. As we noted, he may be dependent on Luke, but, as we attempt to show here and elsewhere, the reverse is more likely.

447. Reading τινυμένου as a middle.

448. See Taylor, *Immerser*, 94.

> the dismissal of certain sins, but for the purification of the body (*hagneia tou sōmatos*, ἁγνεία τοῦ σώματος). Indeed, the soul had been purified beforehand by justice. (*Ant.* 18.116–117)[449]

The Christian reader may be surprised to learn that Josephus has more to say about John than Jesus, but this is consistent with the impression from the New Testament that the Baptist was immensely popular in the first century throughout major cities in the Mediterranean.[450]

Josephus notes that Antipas imprisoned John in Machaerus (Μαχαιροῦς), a palatial fortress east of the Dead Sea near or on "the mountains of Arabia" at the border of his territory (*Ant.* 18.119), a detail not recorded in the Gospels. It is sixteen miles (25 km) from the mouth of the Jordan River. The name is derived from *machaira* (μάχαιρα) "sword." Herod the Great rebuilt it in 30 BC to safeguard his territories.

The basic outline of events is corroborated by Josephus, who provides an interesting back story. To marry Herodias Antipas divorced his first wife, Phasaelis, the daughter of King Aretas IV Philopatris around AD 26. This was politically foolish because their union had reconciled the Nabateans and the Herodian dynasty. Enraged, Aretas attacked Herod (AD 36) inflicting a severe defeat (*Ant.* 18:116–117). The historian claims many Galileans believed this was God's judgment on Herod. Luke appears to know this larger context—*about all the evil things that Herod had done* (3:19). He departs from Mark and Matthew by omitting the name of Antipas' brother Philip. Although the omission may be accidental, we are left with a seeming harmonization of the two well-known accounts.

Josephus also confirms that Antipas unjustly executed the Baptist. However, as we have seen, corelating two independent witnesses to a complex historical series of events is often challenging. There are two tensions here. Raymond Brown, following Josephus, attributes an error to Mark: "Herodias was the wife not of Philip but of another brother named Herod."[451] But Josephus and Mark probably refer to the same person—Herod Philip.[452] Herod the Great's children often took his name (for example, Herod Antipas). If Mark knew the alternative name, he may be avoiding the ambiguity

449. Fortunately, textual criticism is unnecessary: this passage is in all extant witnesses and is cited by Origen. The translation is mine from the Loeb Classical Library (8:80).

450. For Ephesus in Asia Minor, see Acts 18:24–28; 19:1–7. The first passage suggests the Baptist was known in Alexandria. Josephus writes for a curious Roman audience.

451. Brown, *Introduction to the New Testament*, 135. See Josephus, *Ant.* 18.109–110.

452. Hoehner, *Herod Antipas*, 131–39. In Roman culture, a name was not static but often evolved. This ambiguity is a perennial challenge for Roman historians.

of two Herods in the same sentence. Relating the similar names *Herod* and *Herodias* emphasizes the incestuous relationship. Josephus similarly does not offer the man's full name. Brown seems to assume that Mark is referring to Philip the tetrarch, but he does not claim this. Luke, who does mention the tetrarch (3:1), simply identifies Herodias' first husband as Antipas' brother, which is consistent with Josephus (3:19). Josephus and Mark also emphasize different causes for the incarceration. The historian notes the concern Antipas had for the popularity of the Baptist; the evangelist, rebuke for his incest. Both explanations may be true, an instance of overdetermination. Drawing attention to the tetrarch's sin, especially in a pious Jewish context, would be seen as politically subversive.[453]

According to the standards of historiography, the minor tensions between Josephus and the Gospels suggest independent sources, which may allow more confidence for making historical claims.

29C: Arrest and Murder (Luke 3:19–20; 9:7–9)

[3:19] But Herod, the tetrarch, while being reproved by him about Herodias, the wife of his brother, and about all the evil things that Herod had done—[20] he also went beyond all of this [and][454] shut John up in prison.

[9:7] Now Herod, the tetrarch, heard about all the things taking place and was confused. For it was said by some, "John was raised from the dead ones." [8] But by some, "Elijah appeared." But by others, "a certain prophet of the ancients rose." [9] But Herod said: "John I beheaded. But who is this about whom I am hearing such things?" And he was seeking to see him.

P: Luke adopts Matthew's more precise title, *tetrarch* (Matt 14:1) and Mark's misidentifications (Mark 6:15). Both evangelists identify *Herod's brother* as Philip (Mark 6:17; Matt 14:3), but Luke may drop the name because of its tension with Josephus's account. He also sides with the historian in making *Herod's* treatment of the Baptist his greatest sin. Luke does not relate the specific sin, incest, or the Baptist's death, seeming to rely upon the accounts in Mark (6:17–29) and Matthew (14:3–12). With Matthew in contrast to Mark, Luke withholds complexity from *Herod*. He uniquely emphasizes the conflict between *John* and *Herod: and about all the evil things that Herod had done—he also went beyond all of this*. That *Herod was seeking to see* Jesus adds suspense and anticipates their encounter (23:6–12), which only occurs in Luke's presentation.

453. Keener, *IVP Bible Background Commentary*, 143.

454. The conjunction is absent in our earliest witnesses.

It is interesting how treatments of John's departure shorten with each retelling—from Mark to Matthew to Luke. John, who passes over the event, is aware of competition between disciples of John and Jesus (John 1:8; 3:26), as well as Luke (Acts 19:1–10). Perhaps after giving the Baptist half the attention in the birth narrative, Luke wanted to remove him from the story to focus entirely on Jesus.

D: Persecuting the righteous is an especially grave sin that leads to destruction.

Summation

In this chapter, we saw John prepare the way for Jesus by calling the people to "preemptive repentance," a turning to God before punishment.[455] His influence on the Jesus story is impressive. What surfaces is a *profound obedience to God and courageous defiance against those who reject God's Law.* But instead of coming in judgment, Jesus identifies with his sinful people in baptism as their Messiah, which confuses the Baptist who is removed from the story in prison and death. As the primary witness of Christ's ministry, John and Luke draw out implications in the Baptist's teaching that might have surprised him: Jesus is the final Passover lamb, not only for Israel but the Gentile world as well (John 1:29; Luke 3:14).

We learn a difficult yet possible application: God may remove faithful servants from ministry to deepen their understanding and make space for others along the journey.

The Holy Spirit enters Jesus, empowering him for ministry. Jesus reverses the temptation of the first Adam (Luke) and the Exodus generation (Matthew) in the wilderness. He is victorious, and we learn to be faithful too by yielding to the Spirit and following our Lord's example, united to him in baptism.

455. Gillman, *Way Into Encountering God*, 40. God's spokesperson reveals what *would* happen if the people do not repent. They are given two paths—one leading to life; another, death.

Bibliography

À Kempis, Thomas. *The Imitation of Christ*. Translated by Leo Sherley-Price. London: Penguin, 1952.

Abramowitz, Jonathan S., et al. *Exposure Therapy for Anxiety: Principles and Practice*. New York: Guilford, 2011.

Adams, Sean A. *The Genre of Acts and Collected Biography*. Society for New Testament Studies Monograph Series 156. Cambridge: Cambridge University Press, 2013.

Adkins, Lesley, and Roy A. Adkins. *Handbook to Life in Ancient Rome*. Oxford: Oxford University Press, 1994.

Aland, Barbara, et al., eds. *Novum Testamentum Graece*. 28th ed. Stuttgart: Deutsche Bibelgesellschaft, 2012.

Aletti, Jean-Noël. *The Birth of the Gospels as Biographies: With Analyses of Two Challenging Pericopae*. Analecta Biblica Studia 10. Translated by Peggy Manning Meyer. Rome: Pontifical Biblical Institute, 2017.

Alexander, Loveday. *The Preface to Luke's Gospel: Literary Convention and Social Context in Luke 1.1–4 and Acts 1.1*. Cambridge: Cambridge University Press, 1993.

Allen, Diogenes. *Philosophy for Understanding Theology*. Atlanta: John Knox, 1985.

Allison, Dale C. *Studies in Matthew*. Grand Rapids: Baker Academic, 2005.

Al-Suhrawardy, Abdullah Al-Mamum. *The Sayings of Muhammad*. Whitefish, MT: Kessinger: 2010.

Amélineau, Émile. "Voyage d'un moine égyptien dans le desert." *Recueil de travaux relatifs à la philologie et à l'archéologie égyptiennes et assyriennes* 6 (1885) 166–94.

Anderson, Paul. *The Fourth Gospel and the Quest for Jesus: Modern Foundations Reconsidered*. Library of New Testament Studies 321. London: T. & T. Clark, 2006.

Andreopoulos, Andreas. *Metamorphosis: The Transfiguration in Byzantine Theology and Iconography*. Crestwood, NY: St. Vladimir's Seminary Press, 2005.

Anselm. *Proslogion with the replied of Gaunilo and Anselm*. Translated by Thomas Williams. Indianapolis; Cambridge: Hackett, 2001.

Aquinas, Thomas. *On Evil*. Translated by Richard Reagan. Oxford: Oxford University Press, 2003.

———. *Summa Theologiae: A Concise Translation*. Translated by Timothy McDermott. Allen, TX: Christian Classics, 1991.

———. *Thomas Aquinas: Selected Writings*. Edited by Ralph McInerny. New York: Penguin, 1998.

Aristotle. *The Basic Works of Aristotle.* Edited by Richard McKeon. New York: Modern Library, 2001.

———. *Poetics.* Translated by Preston H. Epps. Chapel Hill, NC: The University of North Carolina Press, 1970.

Armstrong, Regis J., et al., eds. *Francis of Assisi.* 3 vols. New York: New City, 1999.

Ashmon, Scott. *Birth Annunciations in the Hebrew Bible and Ancient Near East: A Literary Analysis of the Forms and Functions of the Heavenly Foretelling of the Destiny of a Special Child.* Lewiston, NY: Mellen, 2012.

Athanasius. *Against the Arians.* Edited by Philip Schaff and Henry Wace. A Select Library of Nicene and Post-Nicene Fathers of the Christian Church Second Series volume 4. Reprint. Grand Rapids: Eerdmans, 1987.

———. *The Life of Antony and the Letter to Marcellinus.* Translated by Robert C. Gregg. New York: Paulist, 1980.

Augustine. *Confessions.* Translated by F. J. Sheed. New York: Sheed and Ward, 1943.

———. *The Rule of Saint Augustine.* Translated by Raymond Canning. Kalamazoo, MI: Cistercian, 1996.

———. *The Trinity.* Translated by Stephen McKenna. Washington, DC: Catholic University of America Press, 2002.

Aune, David. "The Gospels as Ancient Biography and the Growth of Jesus Literature." In *The New Testament in Its Literary Environment,* edited by David Aune, 46–76. Philadelphia: Westminster, 1987.

———. *Jesus, Gospel Tradition and Paul in the Context of Jewish and Greco-Roman Antiquity.* Wissenschaftliche Untersuchungen zum Neuen Testament 303. Tübingen: Mohr Siebeck, 2013.

Ausloos, Hans, and Bénédicte Lemmelijn. *The Book of Life: Biblical Answers to Existential Questions.* Louvain Theological and Pastoral Monographs 41. Leuven; Grand Rapids: Peeters; Eerdmans, 2010.

Bacon, Benjamin W. "The Five Books of Moses against the Jews." *Expositor* 15 (1918) 56–66.

———. "Supplementary Note on the Aorist εὐδόκησα, Mark i.11." *Journal of Biblical Literature* 20 (1901) 28–30.

Badcock, Gary D. *Light of Truth and Fire of Love: A Theology of the Holy Spirit.* Grand Rapids: Eerdmans, 1997.

Bailey, James, and Lyle B. Vander Broek. *Literary Forms in the New Testament: A Handbook.* Louisville, KY: Westminster John Knox, 1992.

Bailey, Kenneth E. "Informal Controlled Oral Tradition and the Synoptic Gospels." *Asia Journal of Theology* 5 (1991) 34–54.

———. *Jesus Through Middle Eastern Eyes.* Downers Grove, IL: InterVarsity, 2008.

———. "The Manger and the Inn: The Cultural Background of Luke 2:7." *Bible and Spade* 20 (2007) 98–106.

Bakhtin, Mikhail. "Forms of Time and of the Chronotope in the Novel: Notes towards a Historical Poetics." In *Narrative Dynamics: Essays on Time, Plot, Closure, and Frames,* edited by Brian Richardson, 15–24. Columbus, OH: The Ohio State University Press, 2002.

Bale, Alan J. *Genre and Narrative Coherence in the Acts of the Apostles.* London: T. & T. Clark, 2015.

Barclay, William. *The Gospel of John.* Louisville, KY: Westminster, 2001.

Barnett, Paul. *Jesus and the Rise of Early Christianity: A History of New Testament Times.* Downers Grove, IL: InterVarsity, 1999.

Barrett, C. K. *The Gospel According to St. John: An Introduction with Commentary and Notes on the Greek Text.* 2nd ed. Philadelphia: Westminster, 1978.

———. *The Holy Spirit and the Gospel Tradition.* London: SPCK, 1958.

Barth, Karl. *Church Dogmatics: The Doctrine of God.* Translated by G. W. Bromiley et al. Edinburgh: T. & T. Clark, 1957.

———. *The Teaching of the Church Regarding Baptism.* Translated by Ernest A. Payne. Eugene, OR: Wipf & Stock, 2006.

Barton, John. *Reading the Old Testament: Method in Biblical Study.* 2nd ed. Louisville, KY: Westminster, 1996.

Bauckham, Richard. *Gospel of Glory: Major Themes in Johannine Theology.* Grand Rapids: Baker Academic, 2015.

———. *Gospel Women: Studies of the Named Women in the Gospels.* Grand Rapids: Eerdmans, 2002.

———. *The Gospels for All Christians: Rethinking The Gospel Audiences.* Grand Rapids: Eerdmans, 1998.

———. *Jesus and the Eyewitnesses: The Gospels as Eyewitness Testimony.* Grand Rapids: Eerdmans, 2006.

———. *The Testimony of the Beloved Disciple.* Grand Rapids: Eerdmans, 2004.

Bauer, David R. *The Structure of Matthew's Gospel: A Study in Literary Design.* Sheffield: Sheffield Academic, 1996.

Bauer, Susan Wise. *The History of the Ancient World: From the Earliest Accounts to the Fall of Rome.* New York: Norton, 2007.

Baur, Walter, et al. *Greek-English Lexicon of the New Testament and Other Early Christian Literature.* 3rd ed. Chicago: University of Chicago Press, 2000.

Beale, Greg K. *New Testament Biblical Theology: The Unfolding of the Old Testament in the New.* Grand Rapids: Baker Academic, 2011.

———. "The Old Testament Background of Paul's Reference to 'the Fruit of the Spirit' in Galatians 5:22." *Bulletin for Biblical Research* 15 (2005) 1–38.

Beale, Greg K., and Mitchell Kim. *God Dwells Among Us: Expanding Eden to the Ends of the Earth.* Downers Grove, IL: InterVarsity, 2014.

Beare, Francis Wright. *The Gospel according to Matthew.* San Francisco: Harper & Row, 1981.

Becker, Eve-Marie. "The Reception of 'Mark' in the 1st and 2nd Centuries C.E. and Its Significance for Genre Studies." In *Mark and Matthew II, Comparative Readings: Reception History, Cultural Hermeneutics, and Theology*, edited by Eve-Marie Becker and A. Runesson, 15–36. Wissenschaftliche Untersuchungen zum Neuen Testament 304. Tübingen: Mohr Siebeck, 2013.

Beckwith, Roger T. "The Courses of the Levites and the Eccentric Psalms Scrolls from Qumran." *Revue de Qumrân* 11 (1984) 499–524.

Belousek, Darrin W. Snyder. *Good News: The Advent of Salvation in the Gospel of Luke.* Collegeville, MN: Liturgical, 2014.

Bendoraitis, Kristian A. *'Behold, the Angels Came and Served Him': A Compositional Analysis of Angels in Matthew.* Library of New Testament Studies 523. London: Bloomsbury, 2015.

Benjamin, Walter. *Berlin Childhood around 1900.* Translated by Howard Eiland. Cambridge, MA: Harvard University Press, 2006.

Benner, David G. *Sacred Companions: The Gift of Spiritual Friendship and Direction.* Downers Grove, IL: InterVarsity, 2002.

Benson, Herbert, and Miriam Z. Klipper. *The Relaxation Response.* 2nd ed. New York: HarperTorch, 2000.

Bernard of Clairvaux. *Selected Works.* Translated by G. R. Evans. New York; Mahwah, NJ: Paulist, 1987.

Bettenson, Henry, and Chris Maunder, eds. *Documents of the Christian Church.* 2nd ed. Oxford: Oxford University Press, 2011.

Bevans, Stephen B. *An Introduction to Theology in Global Perspective.* Maryknoll, NY: Orbis, 2009.

Bird, Michael F. *The Gospel of the Lord: How the Early Church Wrote the Story of Jesus.* Grand Rapids: Eerdmans, 2014.

Bird, Michael F., and Joel Willitts, eds. *Paul and the Gospels: Christologies, Conflicts and Convergences.* Library of New Testament Studies 411. New York: Bloomsbury T. & T. Clark, 2011.

Black, C. Clifton. "Mark as Historian of God's Kingdom." *Catholic Biblical Quarterly* 71 (2009) 64–83.

Black, Mark C. *Luke.* College Press NIV Commentary. Joplin, MO: College, 1996.

Black, Matthew. "The Use of Rhetorical Terminology in Papias on Mark and Matthew." *Journal for the Study of the New Testament* 37 (1989) 31–41.

Blackman, Philip. *Mishnayoth: Seder Nashim.* 6 vols. Brooklyn: Judaica, 2000.

Blanton, P. Gregg. *Contemplation and Counseling: An Integrative Model for Practitioners.* Downers Grove, IL: IVP Academic, 2019.

Blomberg, Craig L. *The Historical Reliability of John's Gospel: Issues and Commentary.* Downers Grove, IL: InterVarsity, 2001.

———. *Neither Poverty Nor Riches: A Biblical Theology of Material Possessions.* Grand Rapids; Cambridge: Eerdmans, 1999.

Blumenthal, Christian. *Gott im Markusevangelium: Wort und Gegenwart Gottes bei Markus.* Biblisch-Theologische Studien 144. Neukirchen-Vluyn: Neukirchener Verlag, 2014.

Bock, Darrell. *Jesus according to Scripture: Restoring the Portrait from the Gospels.* Grand Rapids: Baker Academic, 2002.

Bockmuehl, Markus. "Matthew 5.32; 19:9 in Light of Pre-Rabbinic Halakah." *New Testament Studies* 35 (1989) 291–95.

Bodhi, Bikkhu. *In the Buddha's Words: An Anthology of Discourses from the Pāli Canon.* Boston: Wisdom, 2005.

Boersma, Hans. *Scripture as Real Presence: Sacramental Exegesis in the Early Church.* Grand Rapids: Baker Academic, 2017.

Bolt, Peter G. *Jesus's Defeat of Death: Persuading Mark's early readers.* Society for New Testament Studies Monograph Series 125. Cambridge: Cambridge University Press, 2003.

Bonaventure. *Commentary on the Gospel of John.* Translated by Robert J. Karris. St. Bonsventure, NY: Fanciscan Institute, 2007.

———. *The Soul's Journey Into God, The Tree of Life, The Life of St. Francis.* Translated by Ewert Cousins. New York: Paulist, 1978.

———. *Works of St. Bonaventure: St. Bonaventure's Commentary on the Gospel of Luke: Chapters 1–8.* Edited by Robert J. Karris. Saint Bonaventure, NY: Franciscan Institute, 2001.

Bond, Helen K. *The Historical Jesus: A Guide for the Perplexed.* London: T. & T. Clark, 2012.

Boomershine, Thomas. *The Messiah of Peace: A Performance-Criticism Commentary on Mark's Passion-Resurrection Narrative.* Biblical Performance Criticism 12. Eugene, OR: Cascade, 2015.

Boring, M. Eugene. "Mark 1:1–15 and the Beginning of the Gospel." *Semeia* 52 (1990) 43–82.

———. *Mark: A Commentary.* Louisville, KY: Westminster John Knox, 2006.

Bovon, François. *Luke 1: A Commentary on the Gospel of Luke 1:1—9:50.* Hermeneia. Translated by C. M. Thomas. Minneapolis: Augsburg, 2002.

Braaten, Carl E., and Robert W. Jensen, eds. *Union with Christ: The New Finnish Interpretation of Luther.* Grand Rapids: Eerdmans, 1998.

Brant, Jo-Ann. *John.* Paideia. Grand Rapids: Baker Academic, 2011.

Breese, Burtis Burr. *Psychology.* New York: Charles Scribner's Sons, 1917.

Brock, Sebastian P. *Spirituality in the Syriac Tradition.* Kerala: St. Ephrem Ecumenical Research Institute, 2005.

Brown, Raymond. *The Birth of the Messiah: A Commentary on the Infancy Narratives in the Gospels of Matthew and Luke.* New York: Doubleday, 1999.

———. *Christ in the Gospels of the Liturgical Year.* Edited by Donald D. Witherup. Collegeville, MN: Liturgical Press, 2008.

———. *A Coming Christ in Advent: Essays on the Gospels Narratives Preparing for the Birth of Jesus (Matthew 1 and Luke 1).* Collegeville, MN: Liturgical, 1988.

———. *An Introduction to the New Testament.* New York: Doubleday, 1997.

———. *Mary in the New Testament.* Philadelphia; New York: Fortress; Paulist, 1978.

———. *The Virginal Conception and Bodily Resurrection of Jesus.* Mahweh, NJ: Paulist, 1973.

Bruner, Frederick Dale. *The Gospel of John: A Commentary.* Grand Rapids: Eerdmans, 2012.

Bruner, Jerome. "The Narrative Construction of Reality." *Critical Inquiry* 18 (1991) 1–20.

Brunner, Emil. *Our Faith.* Translated by John W. Rilling. New York: Charles Scribner's, n.d.

Bruns, J. Edgar. *The Christian Buddhism of St. John: New Insights Into the Fourth Gospel.* New York: Paulist, 1971.

Bryan, C. *A Preface to Mark: Notes on the Gospels in its Cultural and Literary Setting.* Cambridge: Cambridge University Press, 1993.

Bulson, Michael E. *Preach What You Believe: Timeless Homilies for Deacons.* New York: Paulist, 2005.

Bultmann, Rudolf. *The Gospel of John: A Commentary.* Translated by G. R. Beasley-Murray et al. Philadelphia: Westminster, 1971.

———. "History and Eschatology in the New Testament." *New Testament Studies* 1 (1954–1955) 5–16.

———. *The History of the Synoptic Tradition.* Translated by John Marsh. Oxford: Basil Blackwell, 1968.

Burkert, Walter. *Greek Religion.* Translated by John Raffan. Cambridge, MA: Harvard University Press, 1985.

Burkitt, F. Crawford. *The Gospel History and its Transmission.* 3rd ed. Edinburgh: T. & T. Clark, 1911.

Burridge, Richard A. "About People, by People, for People: Gospel Genre and Audiences." In *The Gospels for All Christians*, edited by Richard Bauckham, 113–46. Grand Rapids: Eerdmans, 1999.

———. *Four Gospels, One Jesus? A Symbolic Reading*. Grand Rapids: Eerdmans, 2005.

———. *What Are the Gospels? A Comparison with Greco-Roman Biography*. 2nd ed. Grand Rapids: Eerdmans, 2004.

Butler, J. Glentworth. *The Fourfold Gospel*. New York: Funk & Wagnalls, 1889.

Cadbury, Henry J. *The Making of Luke-Acts*. 2nd ed. London: SPCK, 1958.

Cahill, Michael, ed. *The First Commentary on Mark: An Annotated Translation*. Translated by Michael Cahill. Oxford: Oxford University Press, 1998.

———. "The First Markan Commentary." *Revue Biblique* 101 (1994) 258–68.

Calhoun, Adele Ahlberg. *Spiritual Disciplines Handbook*. Downers Grove, IL: InterVarsity, 2015.

Calvin, John. *Institutes of the Christian Religion*. 2 vols. Translated by John Allen. Philadelphia: Presbyterian Board of Christian Education, 1952.

Camery-Hoggatt, Jerry. *Irony in Mark's Gospel: Text and Subtext*. Society for New Testament Studies Monograph Series 72. Cambridge: Cambridge University Press, 1992.

Campbell, K. "Matthew's Hermeneutic of Psalm 22:1 and Jer 31:15." *Faith and Mission* 24 (2007) 46–58.

Campbell, R. A. "Jesus and His Baptism." *Tyndale Bulletin* 47 (1996) 191–214.

Caputo, John D. "Instants, Secrets, and Singularities: Dealing Death in Kierkegaard and Derrida." In *Søren Kierkegaard: Critical Assessments of Leading Philosophers*, edited by Daniel W. Conway and K. E. Gover, 3:64–86. New York: Routledge, 2002.

Card, Michael. *Luke: The Gospel of Amazement*. Downers Grove, IL: InterVarsity, 2011.

Cargill, Kim. *The Psychology of Overeating: Food and the Culture of Consumerism*. New York: Bloomsbury, 2015.

Carlson, Stephen C. "The Accommodations of Joseph and Mary in Bethlehem: Κατάλυμα in Luke 2.7." *New Testament Studies* 56 (2010) 326–42.

———. "The Davidic Key for Counting the Generations in Matthew 1:17." *Catholic Biblical Quarterly* 76 (2014) 665–83.

Carnes, Natalie. *Beauty: A Theological Engagement with Gregory of Nyssa*. Eugene, OR: Cascade, 2014.

Carroll, Patricia. "Moving Mysticism to the Center: Karl Rahner (1904–1984)." *The Way* 43 (2004) 41–52.

Carruthers, Mary. *The Craft of Thought: Meditation, Rhetoric, and the Making of Images, 400–1200*. Cambridge: Cambridge University Press, 1998.

Carson, D. A. *The Gospel According to John*. Pillar Commentary Series. Grand Rapids: Eerdmans, 1991.

Cassian, John. *The Conferences*. Edited by Philip Schaff and Henry Wace. A Select Library of Nicene and Post-Nicene Fathers of the Christian Church Second Series 11. Reprint. Grand Rapids: Eerdmans, 1986.

Casson, Lionel. *Travel in the Ancient World*. Baltimore, MD: John Hopkins University, 1994.

Catherine of Genoa. *Purgation and Purgatory, The Spiritual Dialogue*. Translated by Serge Hughes. Mahwah, NJ: Paulist, 1979.

Catherine of Siena. *The Dialogue*. Translated by Suzanne Noffke. Mahwah, NJ: Paulist, 1980.

Chan, Wing-Tsit, ed. *A Source Book in Chinese Philosophy.* Princeton: Princeton University Press, 1963.

Chancey, Mark. *The Myth of a Gentile Galilee.* Society for New Testament Studies Monograph Series 118. Cambridge: Cambridge University Press, 2002.

Charlesworth, James H. *Pseudepigrapha.* 2 vols. New York: Doubleday, 1983.

Chaze, Micheline. *L'Imitatio Dei Dans Le Targum Et La Aggada.* Paris: Peeters, 2005.

Cheney, Johnston M. *Life of Christ in Stereo: The Four Gospels Speak in Harmony.* New York: Doubleday, 1984.

Childs, Brevard. *Biblical Theology of the Old and New Testaments: Theological Reflection on the Christian Bible.* Minneapolis: Fortress, 1992.

Chilton, Bruce. *Rabbi Jesus: An Intimate Biography.* New York: Doubleday, 2002.

Chrysostom, John. *The Homilies of St. John Chrysostom, Archbishop of Constantinople, on the Gospel of St. Matthew.* Translated by George Prevost. Grand Rapids: Eerdmans, 1983.

———. *Saint John Chrysostom, Commentary on Saint John the Apostle and Evangelist, Homilies 1–47.* Translated by Sister Thomas Aquinas Goggin. Washington, DC: Catholic University of America Press, 1957.

Chryssavgis, John. *In the Heart of the Desert: The Spirituality of the Desert Fathers and Mothers.* 2nd ed. Bloomington, IN: World Wisdom, 2008.

Clare of Assisi. *The Complete Works.* Translated by Regis J. Armstrong and Ignatius C. Brady. Mahwah, NJ: Paulist, 1982.

Clement of Alexandria. *Clement of Alexandria.* Translated by G. W. Butterworth. LCL. Cambridge, MA: Harvard University Press, 1999.

Clements, E. Ann. *Mothers on the Margin? The Significance of the Women in Matthew's Genealogy.* Eugene, OR: Pickwick, 2014.

Clifford, Richard J. *Proverbs.* Louisville, KY: Westminster John Knox Press, 1999.

Clivaz, Claire, ed. *Infancy Gospels: Stories and Identities.* Wissenschaftliche Untersuchungen zum Neuen Testament 281. Tübingen: Mohr Siebeck, 2011.

The Cloud of Unknowing and Other Works. Translated by Clifton Wolters. London: Penguin, 1978.

Cohen, Jeremy. *Sanctifying the Name of God: Jewish Martyrs and Jewish Memories of the First Crusade.* Philadelphia: University of Pennsylvania Press, 2004.

Cohen, Shaye J. D. *The Beginnings of Jewishness: Boundaries, Varieties, Uncertainties.* Berkeley: University of California Press, 1999.

Cohen, Sheldon, et al. *Behavior, Health, and Environmental Stress.* New York: Springer, 1991.

Collins, Adela Yarbro. *Mark: A Commentary.* Hermeneia Commentary Series. Minneapolis: Fortress, 2007.

Colt, George Howe. *November of the Soul: The Enigma of Suicide.* New York: Scribner 2006.

Comfort, Philip Wesley. *A Commentary on T=the Manuscripts and the Text of the New Testament.* Grand Rapids: Kregel Academic, 2015.

———. *Encountering the Manuscripts: An Introduction to New Testament Paleography and Textual Criticism.* Nashville: Broadman and Holman, 2005.

Comfort, Philip Wesley, and David P. Barrett, eds. *The Text of the Earliest New Testament Greek Manuscripts: New and Complete Transcriptions with Photographs.* Wheaton, IL: Tyndale, 2001.

Coniaris, Anthony M. *Introducing the Orthodox Church: Its Faith and Life*. Minneapolis: Light and Life Publishing, n.d.

Conzelmann, Hans. *The Theology of St. Luke*. Translated by Geoffrey Buswell. New York: Harper, 1960.

Copan, Paul, and William Lane Craig. *Creation Out of Nothing*. Grand Rapids: Baker Academic, 2004.

Cousland, J. R. C. *Holy Terror: Jesus in the Infancy Gospel of Thomas*. New York: Bloomsbury T. & T. Clark, 2017.

Coyne, Jerry A. *Faith Vs. Fact: Why Science and Religion are Incompatible*. London: Penguin, 2015.

Cranfield, C. F. B. *The Gospel According to St. Mark*. Cambridge: Cambridge University Press, 1959.

Cranmer, Thomas. *Writings of the Rev. Dr. Thomas Cranmer*. London: The Religious Tract Society, 1831.

Crawford, Sidnie White. *Rewriting Scripture in Second Temple Times*. Grand Rapids: Eerdmans, 2008.

Crenshaw, James L. *Old Testament Wisdom: An Introduction*, 2nd ed. Louisville, KY: Westminster John Knox, 2010.

Cribbs, F. Lamar. "A Study of the Contacts That Exist Between St. Luke and St. John." In *Society of Biblical Literature: 1973 Seminary Papers. Vol. 2*, edited by George MacRae, 1–93. Cambridge, MA: Society of Biblical Literature, 1973.

———. "St. Luke and the Johannine Tradition." *Journal of Biblical Literature* 90 (1971) 422–50.

Crook, Zeba. *Reconceptualising Conversion: Patronage, Loyalty, and Conversion in the Religions of the Ancient Mediterranean*. Berlin: Walter de Gruyter, 2004.

Crossley, James G. *The Date of Mark's Gospel: Insight from the Law in Earliest Christianity*. Journal for the Study of the New Testament Supplement Series 266. London: T. & T. Clark, 2004.

Crowe, Brandon D. "The Chiastic Structure of Seven Signs in the Gospel of John: Revisiting a Neglected Proposal." *Bulletin for Biblical Research* 28 (2018) 65–81.

———. *The Last Adam: A Theology of the Obedient Life of Jesus in the Gospels*. Grand Rapids: Baker Academic, 2017.

Cullmann, Oscar. *Baptism in the New Testament*. Translated by J. K. S. Reid. London: SCM, 1950.

Culy, Martin, et al. *Luke: A Handbook on the Greek Text*. Waco, TX: Baylor University Press, 2010.

Dalman, Gustav, and John Lightfoot. *Jesus Christ in the Talmud and Commentary on the Gospels from the Talmud and Hebraica*. Edited by Randolph Parrish. Reprint. Eugene, OR: Wipf & Stock, 2002.

Damm, Alex. *Ancient Rhetoric and the Synoptic Problem: Clarifying Markan Priority*. Bibliotheca Ephemeridum Theologicarum Lovaniensium 252. Leuven: Peeters, 2013.

Dark, Ken. "Has Jesus' Nazareth house been found?" *Biblical Archeology Review* 41 (2015) 54–63.

Dauer, Anton. *Die Passiongeschichte im Johannesevangelium: Eine traditionsgeschichtliche und theologische Untersuchung zu Joh 18,1—19,30*. Munich: Kösel-Verlag, 1972.

———. *Johannes und Lukas: Untersuchungen zu den johanneisch-lukanischen Parallelperikopen Joh 4,46–54/Lk 7,1–10–Joh 12, 1–8/Lk 7,36–50; 10,38–42–Joh 20,19–29/Lk 24, 36–49*. Würzburg: Echter Verlag, 1972.

Davies, J. G. *The New Westminster Dictionary of Liturgy and Worship*. Philadelphia: Westminster, 1986.

Davies, W. D., and Dale Allison. *The Gospel According to Saint Matthew*. International Critical Commentary Series. 3 vols. London: T. & T. Clark, 1988, 1991, 1997.

Davis, Bret W. *Heidegger and the Will: On the Way to* Gelassenheit. Evanston, IL: Northwestern University Press, 2007.

Davis, John Jefferson. *Meditation and Communion With God: Contemplating Scripture in an Age of Distraction*. Downers Grove, IL: Intervarsity, 2012.

Dawson, Zachary K. "*Monogenēs* and the Social Trinity: A Test Case for Using Lexical Semantics in Systematic Theology." *McMaster Journal of Theology and Ministry* 18 (2016–2017) 32–66.

De Hueck Doherty, Catherine. *Essential Writings*. Edited by David Meconi. Maryknoll, NY: Orbis, 2009.

de Jáuregui, Miguel Herrero. *Orphism and Christianity in Late Antiquity*. Belin: De Gruyter, 2010.

de Lubac, Henri. *Medieval Exegesis*. 3 vols. Translated by Marc Sebanc and E. M. Macierowski. Grand Rapids; Edinburgh: Eerdmans; T. & T. Clark, 1998, 2000, 2009.

Dehaan, M. R. *The Chemistry of the Blood*. Grand Rapids: Zondervan, 1943.

Deines, Roland. "Did Matthew Know He Was Writing Scripture?" *European Journal of Theology* 22 (2013) 101–9.

Del Agua, A. "Die 'Erzählung des Evangeliums im Lichte der Derasch Methode." *Judaica* 47 (1991) 140–54.

DelHousaye, John. "Across the Kidron: Reading the Psalms with David and Jesus." In *How Firm a Foundation*, edited by John DelHousaye et al., 110–26. Wheaton, IL: Crossway, 2018.

———. *Engaging Ephesians: An Intermediate Reader and Exegetical Guide*. Wilmore, KY: GlossaHouse, 2018.

———. "Jesus and the Meaning of Marriage: A Close Reading of Mark 10:1–12." *The Journal for Biblical Manhood and Womanhood* 21 (2016) 80–89.

———. "Jewish Groups at the Time of Jesus." In *Understanding the Big Picture of the Bible: A Guide to Reading the Bible Well*, edited by Wayne Grudem et al., 100–106. Wheaton: Crossway, 2012.

———. "John's Baptist in Luke's Gospel." In *Christian Origins and the Establishment of the Early Jesus Movement*, edited by Stanley E. Porter and Andrew W. Pitts, 32–48. Leiden; Boston: Brill, 2018.

———. "Post-Structuralist Criticism." In *Literary Approaches to the Bible*, edited by Douglas Mangum and Douglas Estes, 257–73. Seattle: Lexham, 2017.

———. "Praying with *Kavanah*: Watching Christ from Death to Glory." *Journal of Spiritual Formation and Soul Care* 2 (2009) 87–100.

———. "Who are the Women Prophets in the Bible?" *Mutuality* 16 (2009) 17.

Dennert, Brian C. *John the Baptist and the Jewish Setting of Matthew*. Wissenschaftliche Untersuchungen zum Neuen Testament 2/403. Tübingen: Mohr Siebeck, 2015.

Dennison, J. T. "Micah's Bethlehem and Matthew's. Micah 5:2-5." *Kerux* 22 (2007) 4–11.

deSilva, David A. *4 Maccabees*. Sheffield: Sheffield Academic, 1998.

———. *Honor, Patronage, Kinship and Purity: Unlocking New Testament Culture.* Downers Grove, IL: InterVarsity, 2000.

Devitt, Amy J. *Writing Genres.* Carbondale, IL: Southern Illinois University Press, 2004.

Dhammapada. Translated by Juan Mascaró. London: Penguin, 1973.

Dibelius, Martin. *From Tradition to Gospel.* Translated by Bertram Lee Woolf. New York: Charles Scribners's Sons, 1934.

Dixon, Edward P. "Descending Spirit and Descending Gods: A 'Greek' Interpretation of the Spirit's 'Descent as a Dove' in Mark 1:10." *Journal of Biblical Literature* 128 (2009) 759–80.

Dodd, C. H. *Historical Tradition in the Fourth Gospel.* Cambridge: Cambridge University Press, 1962.

Dodd, Chip. *The Voice of the Heart: A Call to Full Living.* Nashville: Sage Hill Resources, 2014.

Doohan, Leonard. *The Contemporary Challenge of John of the Cross: An Introduction to His Life and Teaching.* Washington, DC: ICS, 1995.

Doole, J. Andrew. *What Was Mark for Matthew? An Examination of Matthew's Relationship and Attitude to His Primary Source.* Wissenschaftliche Untersuchungen zum Neuen Testament 2/344. Tübingen: Mohr Siebeck, 2013.

Dowling, Levi H. *The Aquarian Gospel of Jesus the Christ.* Camarillo, CA: DeVorss, 2003.

Drane, John. *Introducing the New Testament.* 3rd ed. Minneapolis: Fortress, 2011.

Drobner, Hubertus R. *The Fathers of the Church: A Comprehensive Introduction.* Translated by Siegfried S. Schatzmann. Peabody, MA: Hendrickson, 2007.

Duby, Georges. *The Age of the Cathedrals: Art and Society, 980–1420.* Translated by Eleanor Levieux and Barbara Thompson. Chicago: University of Chicago Press, 1981.

Duff, T. E. "Plutarchan synkrisis: comparisons and contradictions." In *Rhetorical theory and praxis in Plutarch*, edited by L. Van der Stockt, 141–61. Leuven: Peeters, 2000.

Duling, D. C. "Solomon, Exorcism, and the Son of David." *Harvard Theological Review* 68 (1975) 235–52.

Dunn, James D. G. *Jesus, Paul, and the Gospels.* Grand Rapids: Eerdmans, 2011.

———. *Jesus Remembered.* Grand Rapids; Cambridge: Eerdmans, 2003.

———. "Spirit-and-Fire Baptism." *Novum Testamentum* 14 (1972) 81–92.

Dupont, J. "L'arrière-fond biblique du récit des tentations de Jesus." *New Testament Studies* 3 (1956–1957) 287–88.

Earhart, Byron H. *Religious Traditions of the World.* New York: HarperCollins, 1993.

Eckman, Paul. *Emotions Revealed: Recognizing Faces and Feelings to Improve Communication and Emotional Life.* New York: Henry Holt and Company, 2003.

Edwards, James R. *The Gospel According to Luke.* Grand Rapids: Eerdmans, 2015.

———. *The Hebrew Gospel and the Development of the Synoptic Tradition.* Grand Rapids: Eerdmans, 2009.

Egan, Harvey D. *Ignatius Loyola, the Mystic.* Wilmington, DE: Michael Glazier, 1987.

Ehrman, Bart D., and Zlatko Pleše. *The Apocryphal Gospels: Texts and Translations.* Oxford: Oxford University Press, 2011.

Eisenberg, Ronald L. *What the Rabbis Said.* Westport, CT: Greenwood, 2010.

Eliade, Mircea. *History of Religious Ideas.* 3 vols. Translated by various. Chicago: University of Chicago Press, 1981–1988.

Elliott, James Keith. *New Testament Textual Criticism: The Application of Thoroughgoing Principles: Essays on Manuscripts and Textual Variation.* Leiden: Brill, 2010.

Embry, Brad, et al. *Early Jewish Literature: An Anthology.* 2 vols. Grand Rapids: Eerdmans, 2018.

Emmrich, Martin. *At the Heart of Luke: Wisdom and Reversal of Fortune.* Eugene, OR: Pickwick, 2013.

Ephrem the Syrian. *The Hymns on Faith.* Translated by Jeffrey T. Wickes. Washington, DC: The Catholic University of America Press, 2015.

Epstein, I., ed. *Hebrew-English Edition of the Babylonian Talmud. Berakoth.* Translated by Maurice Simon. London: Soncino, 1990.

Erbse, Hartmut. "Die Bedeutung der Synkrisis in der Parallelbiographien Plutarchs." *Hermes* 84 (1956) 389–424.

Estelle, Bryan D. *Echoes of Exodus: Tracing a Biblical Motif.* Downers Grove, IL: IVP Academic, 2018.

Eusebius of Caesarea. *Ecclesiastical History.* Translated by J. E. L. Oulton. 2 vols. LCL. Cambridge, MA: Harvard University Press, 2000.

Evans, Craig A. "Mark's Incipit and the Priene Calendar Inscription: From Jewish Gospel to Greco-Roman Gospel." *Journal of Greco-Roman Christianity and Judaism* 1 (2000) 67–81.

Faddiman, James, and Robert Frager, eds. *Essential Sufism.* Edison, NJ: Castle, 1997.

Fairbairn, Donald. *Life in the Trinity.* Downers Grove, IL: InterVarsity, 2009.

Farnell, David F. "How Views of Inspiration Have Impacted Synoptic Problem Discussions." *The Master's Seminary Journal* 13 (2002) 33–64.

Farmer, William R. *The Gospel of Jesus: The Pastoral Relevance of the Synoptic Problem.* Louisville, KY: Westminster John Knox Press, 1994.

———. *The Synoptic Problem.* New York: Macmillan, 1964.

Farrar, Frederic William. *The Life of Christ.* New York: Lovell, Coryell, and Co., 1887.

Farrer, Austin. "On Dispensing with Q." In *Studies in the Gospels: Essays in Memory of R. H. Lightfoot,* edited by D. E. Nineham, 55–88. Oxford: Blackwell, 1955.

Farris, Stephen. "The Canticles of Luke's Infancy Narrative." In *God's Presence: Prayer in the New Testament,* edited by Richard N. Longenecker, 91–112. Cambridge; Grand Rapids: Eerdmans, 2001.

Fass, Patrick. *Around the Roman Table.* New York: Palgrave Macmillan, 2003.

Fishbane, Michael. *Biblical Interpretation in Ancient Israel.* Oxford: Clarendon, 1985.

———. *The Garments of Torah: Essays in Biblical Hermeneutics.* Bloomington, IN: Indiana University Press, 1992.

Fitzmyer, Joseph A. *The Gospel According to Luke: Introduction, Translation, and Notes.* Anchor Bible Commentary Series. New York: Doubleday, 1985.

Fox, Matthew. *Breakthrough: Meister Eckhart's Creation Spirituality in New Translation.* New York: Image, 1980.

Francis de Sales. *Introduction to the Devout Life.* New York: Vintage, 2002.

Frey, John M. *Spolia in Fortifications and the Common Builder in Late Antiquity.* Leiden: Brill, 2015.

Freyne, Sean. *Jesus: A Jewish Galilean. A New Reading of the Jesus Story.* London: T. & T. Clark, 2006.

Friedländer, Renate. "Eine Zeichnung des Villard de Honnecourt und ihr Vorbild." *Wallraf-Richartz Jahrbuch* 34 (1972) 349–52.

Fryling, Alice. *Seeking God Together: An Introduction to Group Spiritual Direction*. Downers Grove, IL: InterVarsity, 2009.

Fusillo, Massimo. "From Petronius to Petrolio: *Satyricon* as a Model-Experimental Novel." In *The Ancient Novel and Beyond*, edited by Stelios Panayotakis et al., 413–24. Leiden: Brill, 2003.

Fuster, Joaquín M. *Memory in the Cerebral Cortex: An Empirical Approach to Neural Networks in the Human and Nonhuman Primate*. Cambridge, MA: MIT Press, 1999.

Gahan, J. J. "'Imitatio and Aemulatio' in Seneca's 'Phaedra.'" *Latomus* 46 (1987) 380–87.

Gallagher, Edmon L., and John D. Meade. *The Biblical Canon Lists from Early Christianity: Texts and Analyses*. Oxford: Oxford University Press, 2017.

Gambero, Luigi. *Mary and The Fathers of the Church: The Blessed Virgin Mary in Patristic Thought*. Translated by Thomas Buffer. San Francisco: Ignatius, 1999.

Garrett, Susan R. *The Temptations of Jesus in Mark's Gospel*. Grand Rapids: Eerdmans, 1998.

Garský, Zbyněk. *Das Wirken Jesu in Galiläa bei Johannes: Eine strukturale Analyse der Intertextualität des vierten Evangeliums mit den Synoptikern*. Wissenschaftliche Untersuchungen zum Neuen Testament 2/325. Tübingen: Mohr Siebeck, 2012.

Gathercole, Simon J. *The Preexistent Son: Recovering the Christologies of Matthew, Mark, and Luke*. Grand Rapids: Eerdmans, 2006.

Gaventa, Beverly Roberts. *Mary: Glimpses of the Mother of Jesus*. Minneapolis: Fortress, 1999.

Geldard, Richard. *Remembering Heraclitus: The Philosopher of Riddles*. Edinburgh: Floris, 2000.

Gentry, Peter. "The Atonement in Isaiah's Fourth Servant Song (Isaiah 52:13–53:12)." *The Southern Baptist Journal of Theology* 11 (2007) 20–47.

Gerhardsson, Birger. *The Testing of God's Son*. Lund: CWK Gleerup, 1966.

Gerson, Lloyd P. "Plato on Identity, Sameness, and Difference." *The Review of Metaphysics* 58 (2004) 305–32.

Gibson, Jeffrey B. *The Temptations of Jesus in Early Christianity*. New York: Bloomsbury T. & T. Clark, 2004.

Gillman, Neil. *The Way Into Encountering God in Judaism*. Woodstock, VT: Jewish Lights, 2000.

Girard, Marc. "La composition structurelle des sept 'signes' dans le quatrième évangile." *Sciences Religieuses* 9 (1980) 315–24.

Goldberg, G. J. "The Coincidences of the Emmaus Narrative of Luke and the Testimony of Josephus." *Journal for the Study of the Pseudepigrapha* 13 (1995) 59–77.

Goldin, Hyman. *Ethics of the Fathers*. New York: Hebrew, 1962.

Goldin, Judah. *The Fathers According to Rabbi Nathan*. New Haven, CT: Yale University Press, 1955.

González, Justo. *The Story Luke Tells: Luke's Unique Witness to the Gospel*. Grand Rapids: Eerdmans, 2015.

Goodacre, Mark. *The Synoptic Problem: A Way Through the Maze*. London: T. & T. Clark, 2001.

Goppelt, Leonhard. *Typos: The Typological Interpretation of the Old Testament in the New*. Translated by Donald H. Madvig. Grand Rapids: Eerdmans, 1982.

Gort, Jerald D. "Syncretism and Dialogue: Christian Historical and Earlier Ecumenical Perceptions." In *Dialogue and Syncretism: An Interdisciplinary Approach*, edited by Jerald D. Gort et al., 36–51. Grand Rapids: Eerdmans, 1989.

Goulder, Michael D. "Is Q a Juggernaut?" *Journal of Biblical Literature* 115 (1996) 667–81.

———. "Luke's Knowledge of Matthew." In *Minor Agreements Symposium Göttingen 1991*, edited by Georg Strecker, 143–62. Göttingen: Vandenhoeck & Ruprecht, 1993.

Grabbe, Lester L. *Wisdom of Solomon*. New York: T. & T. Clark, 2003.

Grafton, Anthony, and Megan Williams. *Christianity and the Transformation of the Book: Origen, Eusebius, and the Library of Caesarea*. Cambridge, MA: Harvard University Press, 2006.

Greenspan, Stephen. *Annals of Gullibility*. Westport, CT: Praeger, 2009.

Gregory, Andrew. *The Reception of Luke and Acts in the Period Before Irenaeus: Looking for Luke in the Second Century*. Tübingen: Mohr Siebeck, 2003.

———. "The Third Gospel? The Relationship of John and Luke Reconsidered." In *Challenging Perspectives on the Gospel of John*, edited by John Lierman, 109–34. Tübingen: Mohr Siebeck, 2006.

Gregory of Nyssa. *Life of Macrina*. Translated by W. K. Lowther Clarke. London: SPCK, 1916.

———. *Life of Moses*. Translated by Abraham J. Malherbe and Everett Ferguson. Mahwah, NJ: Paulist, 1978.

Griesbach, Jakob. *Synopsis Evangeliorum Matthei Marci et Lucae una cum iis Joannis pericopis: Quae historiam passionis et resurrectionis Jesu Christi complectuntu*. 2nd ed. Halle: J. J. Curtii Haeredes, 1797.

Griffin, Emilie. *Wonderful and Dark Is This Road: Discovering the Mystic Path*. Brewster, MA: Paraclete, 2004.

Groeschal, Benedict J. *The Journey of Faith: How to Deepen Your Faith in God, Christ, and the Church*. Huntington, IN: Our Sunday Visitor, 2010.

Grudem, Wayne. *Systematic Theology: An Introduction to Biblical Doctrine*. Grand Rapids: Zondervan, 1994.

Guelich, Robert A. "'The Beginning of the Gospel' Mark 1:1–15." *Biblical Research* 27 (1982) 5–15.

Gu, Ming Dong. *Chinese Theories of Fiction: A Non-Western Narrative System*. Albany, NY: State University of New York Press, 2006.

Guigo the Carthusian. *Guido II: Ladder of Monks and Twelve Meditations*. Kalamazoo, MI: Cistercian, 1979.

Gundry, Robert H. "How Soon a Book?" *Journal of Biblical Literature* 115 (1996) 321–25.

Gurtner, Daniel M. "Genealogies." In *Encyclopedia of the Historical Jesus*, edited by Craig A. Evans, 211–12. New York: Routledge, 2014.

Haami, Bradford. *Pūtea Whakairo: Māoli and the Written Word*. Wellington: Huia, 2004.

Hachlili, Rachel. *Ancient Synagogues—Archaeology and Art: New Discoveries and Current Research*. Handbook of Oriental Studies, Section 1: The Near and Middle East 105. Leiden: Brill, 2014.

Hadas, Moses. *Ancilla to Classical Reading. A Common Reader Edition*. New York: Akadine, 1999.

Hägg, Tomas. *The Art of Biography in Antiquity.* Cambridge: Cambridge University Press, 2012.

Hagner, Donald A. *The New Testament: A Historical and Theological Introduction.* Grand Rapids: Baker Academic, 2012.

Hamerton-Kelly, R. *Pre-Existence, Wisdom, and the Son of Man: A Study of the Idea of Pre-Existence in the New Testament.* Cambridge: Cambridge University Press, 2004.

Hamm, Dennis. "Rummaging for God: Praying Backwards Through Your Day." In *An Ignatian Spiritual Reader: Contemporary Writings on Saint Ignatius of Loyola, the Spiritual Exercises, Discernment, and More*, edited by George W. Traube, 104–10. Chicago: Loyola, 2008.

Handelman, Susan A. *The Slayers of Moses: The Emergence of Rabbinic Interpretation in Modern Literary Theory.* Albany, NY: State University of New York Press, 1982.

Hare, Douglas R. A. *The Theme of Jewish Persecution of Christians in the Gospel According to St. Matthew.* Society for New Testament Studies Monograph Series 6. Cambridge: Cambridge University Press, 1967.

Harpur, James. *Love Burning in the Soul.* Boston, MA: New Seeds, 2005.

Harrington, Hannah K. *The Purity Texts.* Companion to the Qumran Scroll 5. New York: Bloomsbury T. & T. Clark, 2004.

Harris, Murray J. *John.* Nashville: B&H, 2015.

Harris, Sarah. *The Davidic Shepherd King in the Lukan Narrative.* Library of New Testament Studies 558. New York: Bloomsbury, 2016.

Harrison, Eric. *The Foundations of Mindfulness: How to Cultivate Attention, Good Judgment, and Tranquility.* New York: The Experiment, 2017.

Head, Peter M. *Christology and the Synoptic Problem: An Argument for Markan Priority.* Society for New Testament Studies Monograph Series 94. Cambridge: Cambridge University Press, 1997.

———. "A Text-Critical Study of Mark 1.1: 'The Beginning of the Gospel of Jesus Christ.'" *NTS* 37 (1991) 621–29.

Heil, John Paul. "Jesus with the Wild Animals in Mark 1:13." *Catholic Biblical Quarterly* 68 (2006) 63–78.

Henderson, Ian H. *Jesus, Rhetoric and Law.* Leiden: Brill, 1996.

Hengel, Martin. *The Charismatic Leaders and His Followers.* Translated by James Greig. Eugene, OR: Wipf and Stock, 2005.

———. *Judaism and Hellenism: Studies in Their Encounter in Palestine During the Early Hellenistic Period.* Translated by John Bowden. Philadelphia: Fortress, 1974.

———. *Studies in the Gospel of Mark.* Minneapolis: Fortress, 1985.

Heschel, Abraham. *Who is Man?* Stanford: Stanford University Press, 1965.

Hezser, Catherine. *Jewish Literacy in Roman Palestine.* Tübingen: Mohr Siebeck, 2001.

Hill, Charles E. "'The Truth Above All Demonstration': Scripture in the Patristic Period to Augustine." In *The Enduring Authority of the Christian Scriptures,* edited by D. A. Carson, 43–88. Grand Rapids: Eerdmans, 2016.

Hoehner, Harold. *Herod Antipas: A Contemporary of Jesus Christ.* Society for New Testament Studies Monograph Series 17. Cambridge: Cambridge University Press, 1972.

Hoffeditz, David M. *They Were Single Too: 8 Biblical Role Models.* Grand Rapids: Kregel, 2005.

Holman, Susan R., ed. *Wealth and Poverty in Early Church and Society.* Grand Rapids: Baker Academic, 2008.

Holmes, Michael W. *The Apostolic Fathers: Greek Texts and English Translations.* Grand Rapids: Baker Academic, 2007.

Holt-Lunstad, Julianne. "The Potential Public Health Relevance of Social Isolation and Loneliness: Prevalence, Epidemiology, and Risk Factors." *Public Policy Aging Rep.* 27 (2018) 127–30.

Holtzmann, Heinrich Julius. *Die synoptischen Evangelien: Ihr Ursprung und geschichtlicher Charakter.* Leipzig: Engelmann, 1863.

———. *Lehrbuch der historisch-kritischen Einleitung in das Neue Testament.* Freiburg: Mohr, 1885.

Hone, William. *The Lost Books of the Bible.* New York: Chartwell, 2016.

Honigman, Sylvie. *Tales of High Priests and Taxes: The Books of the Maccabees and the Judean Rebellion against Antiochos IV.* Oakland: University of California Press, 2014.

Hoppe, L. J. "Where Was Jesus Baptized? Three Alternatives." *The Bible Today* 45 (2007) 315–20.

Hornblower, Simon, and Antony Spawforth, eds. *The Oxford Companion to Classical Civilization.* Oxford: Oxford University Press, 1998.

Horsley, Richard A. *In the Shadow of Empire: Reclaiming the Bible as a History of Faithful Resistance.* Louisville, KY: Westminster John Knox, 2008.

———. "Jesus und imperiale Herrsschaft—damals und heute. Ein Versuch, Jesu Botschaft von der Königsherrschaft Gottes von ihrer politischen Harmlosigkeit zu befreien." *Bibel und Kirche* 62 (2007) 89–93.

Howard, Evan B. *The Brazos Introduction to Christian Spirituality.* Grand Rapids: Brazos, 2008.

Howard, George. *Hebrew Gospel of Matthew.* Macon, GA: Mercer University Press, 1995.

Hughes, David. *The Star of Bethlehem: An Astronomer's Confirmation.* New York: Walker, 1979.

Huizenga, Leroy A. *The New Isaac: Tradition and Intertextuality in the Gospel of Matthew.* Supplements to Novum Testamentum 131. Leiden: Brill, 2009.

Humble, Susan Elizabeth. *A Divine Round Trip: The Literary and Christological Function of the Descent/Ascent Leitmotif in the Gospel of John.* Contributions to Biblical Exegesis and Theology 79. Leuven: Peeters, 2016.

Humphries, Rolfe. *The Aenead of Virgil.* New York: Charles Scribner's Son, 1951.

Hunt, Andrew, and David Thomas. *The Pragmatic Programmer: From Journeyman to Master.* Reading, MA: Addison-Wesley, 2000.

Hurtado, Larry W. *Lord Jesus Christ: Devotion to Jesus in Earliest Christianity.* Grand Rapids: Eerdmans, 2010.

Hyman, Arthur, and James J. Walsh, eds. *Philosophy in the Middle Ages.* Indianapolis: Hackett, 1973.

Ibba, G. "John the Baptist and the Purity Laws of Leviticus 11–16." *Jeevadhara* 36 (2006) 435–44.

Incigneri, Brian J. *The Gospel to the Romans: The Setting and Rhetoric of Mark's Gospel.* Biblical Interpretation Series 65. Leiden: Brill, 2003.

Irenaeus of Lyon. *Against Heresies.* Edited by Alexander Roberts and James Donaldson. The Ante-Nicene Fathers 1. Reprint. Peabody, MA: Hendrickson, 1994.

Jacobs, Daniel. *Jerusalem: Mini Rough Guide*. London: Penguin, 1999.

Jamieson, Kathleen M. Hall. "Generic Constraints and the Rhetorical Situation." *Philosophy and Rhetoric* 6 (1973) 162–70.

Janes, Regina. "Why the Daughter of Herodias Must Dance (Mark 6.14-29)." *Journal for the Study of the New Testament* 28 (2006) 443–67.

Jeffrey, Peter. "Philo's Impact on Christian Psalmody." In *Psalms in Community: Jewish and Christian Textual, Liturgical, and Artistic Traditions*, edited by Harold W. Attridge and Margot E. Fassler, 147–88. Leiden: Brill, 2004.

Jeremias, Joachim. *The Unknown Sayings of Jesus*. Translated by Reginald H. Fuller. Reprint. Eugene, OR: Wipf & Stock, 2008.

Jerome. *Life of Paul the First Hermit*. Edited by Philip Schaff and Henry Wace. A Select Library of Nicene and Post-Nicene Fathers of the Christian Church Second Series 6. Reprint. Grand Rapids: Eerdmans, 1983.

———. *Lives of Illustrious Men*. Edited by Philip Schaff and Henry Wace. The Nicene and Post-Nicene Fathers Second Series 3. Reprint. Grand Rapids: Eerdmans, 1982.

John of Damascus. *Saint John of Damascus, Writings*. Translated by Frederic H. Chase. N.p.: Ex Fontibus, 2015.

Johnson, Marshall D. *The Purpose of the Biblical Genealogies*. 2nd ed. Eugene, OR: Wipf & Stock, 2002.

Johnson, Maxwell E., ed. *Sacraments and Worship: The Sources of Christian Theology*. Louisville, KY: Westminster John Knox, 2012.

Jones, D. W. "The Betrothal View of Divorce and Remarriage." *Bibliotheca Sacra* 165 (2008) 68–85.

Josephus. *Antiquities*. 9 vols. Translated by H. St. Thackeray. Loeb Classical Library. Cambridge, MA: Harvard University Press, 1926–1965.

———. *The Jewish War*. 3 vols. Translated by H. St. Thackeray. Loeb Classical Library. Cambridge, MA: Harvard University Press, 1997.

———. *The Life, Against Apion*. Translated by H. St. Thackeray. Loeb Classical Library. Cambridge, MA: Harvard University Press, 1997.

Just, Arthur A., ed. *Luke*. Ancient Christian Commentary on Scripture. Downers Grove, IL: InterVarsity, 2003.

Justin Martyr. *The Apologies of Justin Martyr*. Edited by A. W. F. Blunt. Cambridge: Cambridge University Press, 1911.

———. *The First Apology*. Edited by Alexander Roberts and James Donaldson. The Ante-Nicene Fathers 1. Reprint. Peabody, MA: Hendrickson, 1994.

———. *Dialogue with Trypho, Jew*. Edited by Alexander Roberts and James Donaldson. The Ante-Nicene Fathers 1. Reprint. Peabody, MA: Hendrickson, 1994.

———. *S. Justini Philosophi et Martyris cum Tryphone Judaeo Dialogus*. 2 vols. Edited by W. Trollope. Cambridge: Cambridge University Press, 1890.

———. *The Second Apology*. Edited by Alexander Roberts and James Donaldson. The Ante-Nicene Fathers 1. Reprint. Peabody, MA: Hendrickson, 1994.

Kadushin, M. *The Rabbinic Mind*. Binghampton, NY: Global, 2001.

Kähler, Martin. *The So-Called Historical Jesus and Historic Biblical Christ*. Translated by C. E. Braaten. Philadelphia: Fortress, 1964.

Kaplan, C. "The Generation Schemes in Matthew I:1-17, Luke III:24ff." *Bibliotheca Sacra* (1930) 465–71.

Kärkkäinen, Veli-Matti. *The Doctrine of God: A Global Introduction*. Grand Rapids: Baker Academic, 2004.

Kasser, Rudolphe, et al., eds. *The Gospel of Judas*. Washington, DC: National Geographic, 2006.

Kavanaugh, Kieran, ed. *John of the Cross: Selected Writings*. Mahwah, NJ: Paulist, 1987.

Keefer, Kyle. *The Branches of the Gospel of John: The Reception of the Fourth Gospel in the Early Church*. New York: Bloomsbury T. & T. Clark, 2006.

Keener, Craig S. "'Brood of Vipers' (Matthew 3.7; 12.34; 23.33)." *Journal for the Study of the New Testament* 28 (2005) 3–11.

———. *The Gospel of John*. 2 vols. Peabody, MA: Hendrickson, 2003.

———. *The Historical Jesus of the Gospels*. Grand Rapids: Eerdmans, 2009.

———. *The IVP Bible Background Commentary: New Testament*. 2nd ed. Downers Grove, IL: InterVarsity, 2014.

———. *Matthew: A Socio-Rhetorical Commentary*. Grand Rapids; Cambridge: Eerdmans, 2009.

———. *The Spirit in the Gospels and Acts: Divine Purity and Power*. Peabody, MA: Hendrickson, 1997.

Kennedy, George A., ed. *The Cambridge History of Literary Criticism*. 9 vols. Cambridge: Cambridge University Press, 1997.

———. *Progymnasmata: Greek Textbooks of Prose Composition and Rhetoric*. Leiden: Brill, 2003.

Kidger, Mark. *The Star of Bethlehem: An Astronomer's View*. Princeton: Princeton University Press, 1999.

Kim, Sang-Hoon. *Sourcebook of the Structures and Styles in John 1–10: The Johannine Parallelism and Chiasms*. Eugene, OR: Wipf and Stock, 2014.

Kim, Sean Seongik. *The Spirituality of Following Jesus in John's Gospel: An Investigation of Akolouthein and Correlated Motifs*. Eugene, OR: Pickwick, 2017.

Kim, Seyoon. *Christ and Caesar: The Gospel and the Roman Empire in the Writings of Paul and Luke*. Grand Rapids: Eerdmans, 2008.

Kingsbury, Jack D. *The Christology of Mark's Gospel*. Minneapolis: Fortress, 1983.

———. *Conflict in Luke: Jesus, Authorities, Disciples*. Minneapolis: Fortress, 1991.

———. *Matthew: Structure, Christology, Kingdom*. 2nd ed. Minneapolis: Fortress, 1989.

Kirchhofer, Johannes. *Quellensammlung zur Geschichte des Neutestamentlichen Kanons bis auf Hieronymus*. Zürich: Meyer and Zeller, 1844.

Klawans, J. "Moral and Ritual Purity." In *Jesus in Context*, edited by Amy-Jill Levine et al., 266–84. Princeton: Princeton University Press, 2006.

Knust, Jennifer, and Tommy Wasserman. "The Biblical Odes and the Text of the Christian Bible: A Reconsideration of the Impact of Liturgical Singing on the Transmission of the Gospel of Luke." *Journal of Biblical Literature* 133 (2014) 341–65.

Koester, Craig R. *Revelation*. New Haven, CT: Yale University Press, 2014.

Koester, Helmut. *Ancient Christian Gospels: Their History and Development*. Harrisburg, PA: Trinity, 1990.

Köstenberger, Andreas J. *John*. Baker Exegetical Commentary on the New Testament. Grand Rapids: Baker Academic, 2004.

Kraemer, Ross Shepherd, ed. *Women's Religions in the Greco-Roman World: A Source Book*. Oxford: Oxford University Press, 2004.

Krueger, Derek. "Scripture and Liturgy in The *Life of Mary of Egypt.*" In *Education and Religion in Late Antique Christianity: Reflections, Social Contexts, and Genres,* edited by Peter Gemeinhardt et al., 131–43. New York: Routledge, 2016.

Kysar, Robert. *Voyages with John: Charting the Fourth Gospel.* Waco, TX: Baylor University Press, 2005.

Kytzler, Bernard. "Imitatio und aemulatio in der Thebais des Statius." *Hermes* 97 (1969) 209–32.

Lagrange, M.-J. "JÉRUSALEM D'APRÈS LA MOSAÏQUE DE MADABA." *Revue Biblique* 6 (1897) 450–58.

Laird, Martin. *Into the Silent Land.* Oxford: Oxford University Press, 2006.

Lam, Joseph. *Patterns of Sin in the Hebrew Bible: Metaphor, Culture, and the Making of a Religious Concept.* Oxford: Oxford University Press, 2016.

Lao-Tzu. *Te-Tao Ching.* Translated by Robert G. Henricks. New York: Ballantine, 1989.

Larsen, Kasper Bro, ed. *The Gospel of John as Genre Mosaic.* Studia Aarhusiana Neotestamentica 3. Göttingen: Vandenhoeck & Ruprecht, 2015.

Larsen, Matthew D. C. *Gospels before the Book.* Oxford: Oxford University Press, 2018.

Lee, Doug. *Pagans and Christians in Late Antiquity: A Sourcebook.* 2nd ed. New York: Routledge, 2016.

Lee, Yongbom. *The Son of Man as the Last Adam: The Early Church Tradition as a Source of Paul's Adam Christology.* Eugene, OR: Pickwick, 2012.

Leithart, Peter J. *Deep Exegesis: The Mystery of Reading Scripture.* Waco, TX: Baylor University Press, 2009.

———. "The Quadriga or Something Like It." In *Ancient Faith for the Church's Future,* edited by Mark Husbands and Jeffrey P. Greenman, 110–25. Downers Grove: InterVarsity, 2008.

Levine, Madeline. *The Price of Privilege: How Parental Pressure and Material Advantage are Creating a Generation of Disconnected and Unhappy Kids.* New York: Harper Collins, 2009.

Lewis, Karoline M. *John.* Minneapolis: Fortress, 2014.

Lieu, Judith. *Marcion and the Making of a Heretic: God and Scripture in the Second Century.* Cambridge: Cambridge University Press, 2015.

Lightfoot, Robert H. *The Gospel of St. Mark.* Oxford: Clarendon, 1950.

Lincoln, Andrew T. *Born of a Virgin? Reconceiving Jesus in the Bible, Tradition, and Theology.* Grand Rapids: Eerdmans, 2013.

———. *The Gospel According to Saint John.* Black's New Testament Commentary. London: Continuum, 2005.

Lindsey, Robert L. "A New Approach to the Synoptic Gospels." *Mishkan* 17 (1992) 87–106.

———. "A Modified Two-Document Theory of the Synoptic Dependence and Interdependence." *Novum Testamentum* 6 (1963) 239–63.

Litwak, Kenneth Duncan. *Echoes of Scripture in Luke-Acts: Telling the History of God's People Intertextually.* London: T. & T. Clark, 2005.

Llewelyn, S. R. *New Documents Illustrating Early Christianity. Vol. 7. A Review of the Greek Inscriptions and Papyrii Published in 1982-83.* Grand Rapids: Eerdmans, 1994.

Lockwood, Richard. *The Reader's Figure: Epideictic Rhetoric in Plato, Aristotle, Boussuet, Racinr and Pascal.* Geneva: Droz, 1996.

Longenecker, Bruce W. "A Humorous Jesus? Orality, Structure and Characterisation in Luke 14:15-24, and Beyond." *Interpretation* 16 (2008) 179–204.

Lonsdale, David. *Eyes to See, Ears to Hear: An Introduction to Ignatian Spirituality*. Maryknoll, NY: Orbis, 2000.

Lüdemann, Gerd. *Virgin Birth: The Real Story of Mary and Her Son Jesus*. Philadelphia: Trinity, 1998.

Ludolph of Saxony. *The Life of Christ, Part One*. Translated by Milton T. Walsh. Collegeville, MN: Liturgical, 2018.

Luomanen, Petri. *Entering the Kingdom of Heaven: A study on the structure of Matthew's view of salvation*. Wissenschaftliche Untersuchungen zum Neuen Testament 101. Tübingen: Mohr Siebeck, 1998.

Lupieri, E. "'The Law and the Prophets were until John': John the Baptist between Jewish Halakhot and Christian history of salvation." *Neotestamentica* 35 (2001) 49–56.

MacDonald, Dennis R. *The Homeric Epics and the Gospel of Mark*. New Haven, CT: Yale University Press, 2000.

Mack, Burton L. *The Lost Gospel: The Book of Q and Christian Origins*. San Francisco: Harper SanFrancisco, 1993.

Mackay, Ian D. *John's Relationship with Mark: An Analysis of John 6 in Light of Mark 6–8*. Wissenschaftliche Untersuchungen zum Neuen Testament 2/182. Tübingen: Mohr Siebeck, 2004.

Mahieu, Bieke. *Between Rome and Jerusalem: Herod the Great and His Sons in Their Struggle for Recognition*. Orientalia louvaniensia analecta 208. Leuven: Peeters, 2012.

Maimonides, Moses. *The Guide for the Perplexed*. Translated by M. Friedländer. New York: Barnes & Noble, 2004.

Malik, Peter. "The Earliest Corrections in Codex Sinaiticus: A Test Case from the Gospel of Mark." *Bulletin of the American Society of Papyrologists* 50 (2013) 207–54.

Mallen, Peter. *The Reading and Transformation of Isaiah in Luke-Acts*. New York: Bloomsbury T. & T. Clark, 2008.

Maloney, Francis. *Mark: Storyteller, Interpreter, Evangelist*. Peabody, MA: Hendrickson, 2004.

Maloney, R. P. "The Genealogy of Jesus. Shadows and Lights in His Past." *America* 197 (2007) 20–21.

Mannerma, Tuomo. *Christ Present in Faith: Luther's View of Justification*. Minneapolis: Augsburg, 2005.

Manney, Jim. *The Prayer That Changes Everything: Discovering the Power of St. Ignatius Loyola's Examen*. Chicago: Loyola, 2011.

Marcus, Joel. *Mark*. 2 vols. Anchor Bible Commentary. New York: Doubleday, 1999, 2000.

Maritain, Jacque. *Art and Scholasticism and The Frontiers of Poetry*. Translated by Joseph W. Evans. New York: Charles Scribner's and Sons, 1962.

Marshall, I. Howard. *The Gospel of Luke: A Commentary on the Greek Text*. The New International Greek Testament Commentary. Grand Rapids: Eerdmans, 1978.

Marshall, William. *The Cross of Christ, the Christian's Glory: A sermon preached before the University of Cambridge on Sunday, January 27, 1828*. London: George Wilson, 1828.

Martens, Peter W. *Origen and Scripture: The Contours of an Exegetical Life*. Oxford: Oxford University Press, 2012.

Martiínez, Florentino, et al., eds. *The Dead Sea Scrolls: Study Edition*. 2 vols. Grand Rapids; Leiden: Eerdmans; Brill, 1998.

Martos, Joseph. *Doors to the Sacred: A Historical Introduction to Sacraments in the Catholic Church*. Liguori, MO: Triumph, 2001.

Mason, Steve. *Josephus and the New Testament*. 2nd ed. Peabody, MA: Hendrickson, 2003.

———. "Priesthood in Josephus and the "Pharisaic Revolution." *Journal of Biblical Literature* 107 (1988) 657–61.

Massaux, Edouard. *The Influence of the Gospel of Saint Matthew on Christian Literature before Saint Irenaeus*. Edited by Arthur J. Bellinzoni. Macon, GA: Mercer University Press, 1993.

Matson, Mark A. *In Dialogue with Another Gospel? The Influence of the Fourth Gospel on the Passion Narrative of the Gospel of Luke*. Society of Biblical Literature Dissertation Series 178. Atlanta: Society of Biblical Literature, 2001.

Matt, Daniel C. *The Essential Kabbalah*. New York: Quality Paperback Book Club, 1995.

Mays, James L. *Psalms*. Louisville, KY: Westminster John Knox Press, 2011.

McCarthy, Carmel. *Saint Ephrem's Commentary on Tatian's Diatessaron: An English Translation of Chester Beatty Syriac MA 709 with Introduction and Notes*. Oxford: Oxford University Press, 1993.

McCracken, George E., ed. *Early Medieval Theology*. Louisville, KY: Westminster John Knox, 2006.

McDaniel, Karl. *Experiencing Irony in the First Gospel: Suspense, Surprise and Curiosity*. Library of New Testament Studies 488. New York: Bloomsbury T. & T. Clark, 2013.

McDonald, James I. H. *Kerygma and Didache: The Articulation and Structure of the Earliest Christian Message*. Society for New Testament Studies Monograph Series 37. Cambridge: Cambridge University Press, 1980.

McDonald, Suzanne. *Reimaging Election: Divine Election as Representing God to Others and Others to God*. Grand Rapids: Eerdmans, 2010.

McGinn, Bernard. *The Essential Writings of Christian Mysticism*. New York: Modern Library, 2006.

———. "Joachim of Fiore in the History of Western Culture." In *A Companion to Joachim of Fiore*, edited by Matthias Riedl, 1–19. Brill's Companions to the Christian Tradition 75. Leiden; Boston, MA: Brill, 2018.

McGrath, Allister E. "Newman on Justification: An Evangelical Anglican Evaluation." In *Newman and the Word*, edited by Terence Merrigan and Ian T. Ker, 91–108. Louvain: Peeters, 2000.

McGreal, Ian P. *Great Thinkers of the Western World*. New York: HarperCollins, 1992.

McIver, Robert K. "Eyewitnesses as Guarantors of the Accuracy of the Gospel Traditions in the Light of Psychological Research." *Journal of Biblical Literature* 131 (2012) 529–46.

McLynn, Frank. *Marcus Aurelius: A Life*. Philadelphia: De Capo, 2009.

Meeks, Wayne A. *The Prophet King: Moses Traditions and the Johannine Christology*. Leiden: Brill, 1967.

Meier, John P. *A Marginal Jew: Rethinking the Historical Jesus*. 5 vols. New York: Doubleday, 1991–2016.

Menzies, R. E., et al., eds. *Curing the Dread of Death: Theory, Research and Practice*. Samford Valley: Australian Academic Press, 2018.

Merton, Thomas. *Life and Holiness*. New York: Image, 1963.

Metzger, Bruce M. *The Canon of the New Testament.* Oxford: Clarendon, 1997.

———. *A Textual Commentary on the Greek New Testament.* 2nd ed. Stuttgart: Deutsche Bibelgesellschaft, 1994.

Metzger, Bruce M., and Michael D. Coogan, eds. *The Oxford Companion to the Bible.* Oxford: Oxford University Press, 1993.

Meyer, Marvin. *The Gospel of Thomas: The Hidden Sayings of Jesus.* San Francisco: HarperSanFrancisco, 1992.

Michaels, J. Ramsey. *The Gospel of John.* The New International Commentary on the New Testament. Grand Rapids: Eerdmans, 2010.

Miles, Gary B. "The *Aeneid* as Foundation Story." In *Reading Vergil's Aeneid: An Interpretive Guide*, edited by Christine G. Perkell, 231–50. Norman, OK: University of Oklahoma Press, 1999.

Miller, Amanda C. *Rumors of Resistance: Status Reversals and Hidden Transcripts in the Gospel of Luke.* Emerging Scholars. Minneapolis: Fortress, 2014.

Miller, Ed. L. "The Logos of Heraclitus: Updating the Report." *Harvard Theological Review* (1981) 161–76.

Miller, Joseph Hillis. *The Disappearance of God.* Cambridge, MA: Harvard University Press, 1963.

Miller, Stuart S. *At the Intersection of Texts and Material Finds: Stepped Pools, Stone Vessels, and Ritual Purity among the Jews of Roman Galilee.* Journal of Ancient Judaism Supplements 16. Göttingen: Vandenhoeck & Ruprecht, 2015.

Minear, Paul S. "Luke's Use of the Birth Stories." In *Studies in Luke-Acts*, edited by L. E. Keck and J. Louis Martyn, 111–30. Minneapolis: Fortress, 1980.

Morison, E. F. *St. Basil and His Rule.* Oxford: Oxford University Press, 1912.

Morton, M. J. "The Genealogy of Jesus." *Studia Evangelica* 87 (1964) 219–24.

Muers, Rachel. *Testimony: Quakerism and Theological Ethics.* London: SCM, 2015.

Muldoon, Tim. *Longing to Love: A Memoir of Desire, Relationships, and Spiritual Transformation.* Chicago: Loyola, 2012.

Nault, Jean-Charles. *The Noonday Devil: Acedia, the Unnamed Evil of Our Times.* San Francisco: Ignatius, 2015.

Nes, Solrunn. *The Mystical Language of Icons.* Grand Rapids: Eerdmans, 2004.

Netzer, Ehud. *The Architecture of Herod, the Great Builder.* Tübingen: Mohr Siebeck, 2006.

Neufeld, Dietmar. *Mockery and Secretism in the Social World of Mark's Gospel.* New York: Bloomsbury, 2014.

Neusner, Jacob. *The Mishnah.* New Haven, CT: Yale University Press, 1988.

Newberg, Andrew, and Mark Robert Waldman. *How God Changes Your Brain: Breakthrough Findings from a Leading Neuroscientist.* New York: Ballantine, 2010.

Newbigin, Lesslie. *The Gospel in a Pluralist Society.* Grand Rapids: Eerdmans, 1989.

———. *Missionary Theologian: A Reader.* Edited by Paul Weston. Grand Rapids: Eerdmans, 2006.

Newman, Jay. *Competition in Religious Life.* Waterloo, ON: Wilfred Laurier University Press, 1989.

Neyrey, Jerome H. *Honor and Shame in the Gospel of Matthew.* Louisville, KY: Westminster John Knox, 1998.

Nicholls, William. *Christian Antisemitism: A History of Hate.* Lanham, MD: Rowman and Littlefield, 1993.

Nicholson, Reynold A. *The Mystics of Islam.* London: Penguin, 1989.

Nickelsburg, George W. E., and James C. Vanderkam. *1 Enoch: A New Translation.* Minneapolis: Fortress, 2004.

Nicol, Thomas. *The Four Gospels in the Earliest Church History.* London: William Blackwood & Sons, 1908.

Noble, Thomas F. X., and Thomas Head, eds. *Soldiers of Christ: Saints and Saints' Lives from Late Antiquity and the Early Middle Ages.* University Park, PA: The Pennsylvania State University Press, 1995.

Nodet, É. "Pas un *yod,* pas un *waw* (Mt 5,18)." *Revue Biblique* 117 (2010) 614–16.

Nolland, John. *The Gospel of Matthew.* The New International Greek Testament Commentary. Grand Rapids; Cambridge: Eerdmans, 2005.

Norden, Eduard. *Agnostos Theos. Untersuchungen zur Formengeschichte Religiöser Rede.* Teubner: Leipzig-Berline, 1913.

Nordenfalk, Carl. *Die spätantiken Kanontafeln: Kunstgeschichtliche Studien über die eusebianische Evangelien-Konkordanz in den vier ersten Jahrhunderten ihrer Geschichte.* 2 vols. Göteborg: Oscar Isacsons Boktyckeri, 1938.

Norris, Kathleen. *Acedia and Me: A Marriage, Monks, and a Writer's Life.* New York: Riverhead, 2008.

Nouwen, Henri, et al. *Spiritual Direction: Wisdom for the Long Walk of Faith.* New York: HarperCollins, 2006.

Oden, Thomas. *The African Memory of Mark: Reassessing Early Church Tradition.* Downers Grove, IL: InterVarsity, 2011.

———. *The Justification Reader.* Grand Rapids: Eerdmans, 2002.

Oeming, Manfred, and Konrad Schmid. *Job's Journey: Stations of Suffering.* Critical Studies in the Hebrew Bible 7. Winona Lake, IN: Eisenbrauns, 2015.

Okihiro, Gary Y. *Margins and Mainstreams: Asians in American History and Culture.* Seattle: University of Washington Press, 2014.

Olivelle, Patrick, ed. *Upanishads.* Oxford: Oxford University Press, 1998.

Oliver, Harold H. "The Epistle of Eusebius to Carpianus: Textual Tradition and Translation." *Novum Testamentum* 3 (1959) 138–45.

Origen. *Contra Celsum.* Translated by Henry Chadwick. Cambridge: Cambridge University Press, 1953.

———. *The Song of Songs. Commentary and Homilies.* Translated by R. P. Lawson. New York: Paulist, 1957.

Oropeza, B. J. "The Expectation of Grace: Paul on Benefaction and the Corinthians' Ingratitude (2 Corinthians 6:1)." *Bulletin for Biblical Research* 24 (2014) 207–26.

Oswalt, John. *The Bible among the Myths: Unique Revelation or Just Ancient Literature?* Grand Rapids: Zondervan, 2009.

Otto, R. E. "Baptism and the *Munus Triplex.*" *Evangelical Quarterly* 76 (2004) 217–25.

Ounsworth, Richard. *Joshua Typology in the New Testament.* Wissenschaftliche Untersuchungen zum Neuen Testament 324. Tübingen: Mohr Siebeck, 2012.

Palmer, Martin. *The Jesus Sutras: Rediscovering the Lost Scrolls of Taoist Christianity.* New York: Ballantine, 2001.

Park, Andrew Sung. "A Theology of *Tao* (Way): Han, *Sin and Evil.*" In *Realizing the America of Our Hearts: Theological Voices of Asian Americans,* edited by Fumitaka Matsuoka and Eleazar S. Fernandez, 41–54. St. Louis, MO: Chalice, 2003.

Parker, P. "Luke and the Fourth Evangelist." *New Testament Studies* 9 (1963) 317–36.

Pate, C. Marvin. *The Writings of John: A Survey of the Gospel, Epistles, and Apocalypse.* Grand Rapids: Zondervan, 2011.

Patella, Michael. *Lord of the Cosmos: Mithras, Paul, and the Gospel of Mark*. New York: T. & T. Clark, 2006.

———. *Word and Image: The Hermeneutics of the Saint John's Bible*. Collegeville, MN: Liturgical, 2013.

Pausanias. *Description of Greece*. Translated by W. H. S. Jones et al. 3 vols. LCL. Cambridge: Harvard University Press, 1926.

Penner, Jeremy. *Patterns of Second Temple Prayer in Second Temple Period Judaism*. Leiden: Brill, 2012.

Pennington, Basil. *Centering Prayer*. New York: Image, 1982.

———. *True Self/False Self*. New York: Crossroad, 2000.

Pentiuc, Eugene J. *The Old Testament in Eastern Orthodox Tradition*. Oxford: Oxford University Press, 2014.

Perkell, Christine G. *Reading Vergil's Aeneid: An Interpretive Guide*. Norman, OK: University of Oklahoma Press, 1999.

Perry, Alfred M. "Is John an Alexandrian Gospel?" *Journal of Biblical Literature* 63 (1944) 99–106.

Petersen, William L. *Tatian's Diatessaron: Its Creation, Dissemination, Significance, and History in Scholarship*. Supplements to Vigilae Christianae 25; Leiden: Brill, 1994.

Peterson, Brian Neil. *John's Use of Ezekiel: Understanding the Unique Perspective of the Fourth Gospel*. Minneapolis: Fortress, 2015.

Peyriguère, Albert. *Voice from the Desert*. Translated by Agnes M. Forsyth and Ann Marie de Commaille. New York: Sheed and Ward, 1967.

Pharis, Stephen. *The Hymns of Luke's Infancy Narrative: Their Origin, Meaning, and Significance*. New York: Bloomsbury, 1985.

Philo. *Philo of Alexandria: The Contemplative Life, The Giants, and Selections*. Translated by David Winston. New York: Paulist, 1981.

———. *Who is the Heir?* Translated by F. H. Colson et al. 11 vols. LCL. Cambridge: Harvard University Press, 1929–1953.

———. *The Works of Philo*. Translated by C. D. Yonge. Peabody, MA: Hendrickson, 1993.

Plato. *The Collected Dialogues of Plato*. Edited by Edith Hamilton and Huntington Cairns. Princeton: Princeton University Press, 1999.

Pliny the Elder. *Natural History: A Selection*. Translated by John F. Healy. London: Penguin, 1991.

Plutarch. *Lives*. Translated by Bernadotte Perrin. Loeb Classical Library. Cambridge, MA: Harvard University Press, 1919.

Poirier, John, and Jeffrey Peterson, eds. *Marcan Priority without Q: Explorations in the Farrer Hypothesis*. Library of New Testament Studies 455. London: T. & T. Clark, 2015.

Pollard, Justin, and Howard Reid. *The Rise and Fall of Alexandria: Birthplace of the Modern World*. New York: Penguin, 2006.

Pollard, T. E. *Johannine Christology and the Early Church*. Society for New Testament Studies Monograph Series 13. Cambridge: Cambridge University Press, 1970.

Postell, Seth D. *Adam as Israel: Genesis 1–3 as the Introduction to the Torah and Tanakh*. Cambridge: James Clarke, 2012.

Powell, Mark Allan. *Fortress Introduction to the Gospels*. Minneapolis: Fortress, 1998.

———. *What Is Narrative Criticism?* Minneapolis: Fortress, 1990.

Powery, Emerson B. *Jesus Reads Scripture: The Function of Jesus's Use of Scripture in the Synoptic Gospels.* Leiden: Brill, 2003.

Poythress, Vern. *Inerrancy and the Gospels: A God-Centered Approach to the Challenges of Harmonization.* Wheaton, IL: Crossway, 2012.

Prabhu, George M. Soares. *The Formula Quotations in the Infancy Narrative of Matthew.* Rome: Biblical Institute, 1976.

Propp, William H. "Wilderness." In *The Oxford Companion to the Bible,* edited by Bruce M. Metzger and Michael D. Coogan, 798–99. Oxford: Oxford University Press, 1993.

Przybylski, Benno. *Righteousness in Matthew and His World of Thought.* Cambridge: Cambridge University Press, 1980.

Puéch, E. "4Q525 et la péricope des Béatitudes en Ben Sira et Matthieu." *Revue Biblique* 98 (1991) 80–106.

Quarles, Charles L. "Matthew 27:51–53: Meaning, Genre, Intertextuality, Theology, and Reception History." *Journal of the Evangelical Theological Society* 59 (2016) 271–86.

Rahner, Karl. *Theological Investigations.* 23 volumes. Translated by various. New York: Crossroad: 1961–1992.

Ramsdell, Thomas J. "The Kingdom of Heaven in the Gospel of Matthew." *The Biblical World* 4 (1894) 124–33.

Ratzinger, Joseph. *Journey to Easter: Spiritual Reflections for the Lenten Season.* New York: Crossroad, 1987.

Reasoner, Mark. *Roman Imperial Texts: A Sourcebook.* Minneapolis: Fortress, 2013.

Reicke, Bo. *The Roots of the Synoptic Gospels.* Philadelphia: Fortress, 1986.

Renan, Ernest. *Les Evangiles et la secunde generation chrétienne.* Paris: Calmann Lévy, 1877.

———. *Life of Jesus.* Translated by Charles Edwin Wilbour. New York: Carleton, 1863.

Rice, Peter H. *Behold, Your House Is Left to You: The Theological and Narrative Place of the Jerusalem Temple in Luke's Gospel.* Eugene, OR: Pickwick, 2016.

Richardson, K. C. *Early Christian Care for the Poor.* Eugene, OR: Cascade, 2018.

Rindge, Matthew S. "Reconfiguring the Akedah and Recasting God: Lament and Divine Abandonment in Mark." *Journal of Biblical Literature* 131 (2012) 755–74.

Rist, John M. *On the Independence of Matthew and Mark.* Society for New Testament Studies Monograph Series 32. Cambridge: Cambridge University Press, 1978.

Roberts, W. R. *Greek Rhetoric and Literary Criticism.* London: George C. Harrup, 1928.

Robinson, James M., ed. *The Nag Hammadi Library in English.* San Francisco: HarperSanFrancisico, 1988.

Rogers, Robert Samuel. "The Neronian Comets." *Transactions and Proceedings of the American Philological Association* 84 (1953) 237–49.

Romanides, John S. "Justin Martyr and the Fourth Gospel." *The Greek Orthodox Theological Review* 4 (1958) 115–34.

Ropes, James H. *The Synoptic Gospels.* Cambridge, MA: Harvard University Press, 1934.

Rosewell, Roger. *The Medieval Monastery.* Oxford: Shire, 2012.

Ross, Howard J. *Everyday Bias: Identifying and Navigating Unconscious Judgment in Our Daily Lives.* Lanham, MD: Rowman and Littlefield, 2014.

Roth, Dieter T. *The Text of Marcion's Gospel.* New Testament Tools, Studies and Documents 49. Leiden: Brill, 2015.

Royse, James Ronald. *Scribal Habits in Early Greek New Testament Papyri*. Leiden: Brill, 2008.

Runes, Dagobert D. *Treasury of Philosophy*. New York: Philosophical Library, 1955.

Runia, David T. *Philo in Early Christian Literature: A Survey*. Netherlands: Van Gorcum and Comp., 1993.

Saban, Marie Noonan. *The Gospel According to Mark*. Collegeville, MN: Liturgical, 2006.

Sanders, E. P. *Jesus and Judaism*. Philadelphia: Fortress, 1985.

———. *Judaism: Practice and Belief 63 BCE–66 CE*. Philadelphia: Trinity, 1992.

Sandmell, Samuel. *Philo of Alexandria: An Introduction*. New York: Oxford University Press, 1979.

Sanzo, Joseph E. *Scriptural Incipits on Amulets from Late Antique Egypt: Text, Typology, and Theory*. Studien und Texte zu Antike und Christentum 84. Tübingen: Mohr Siebeck, 2014.

Sayers, Dorothy L. *Man Born to Be King: A Play-Cycle on the Life of Our Lord and Saviour Jesus Christ*. San Francisco, CA: Ignatius, 1943.

Scazzero, Peter. *The Emotionally Healthy Church: A Strategy for Discipleship that Actually Changes Lives*. Grand Rapids: Zondervan, 2010.

Schmid, Ulrich B. "The Diatessaron of Tatian." In *The Text of the New Testament in Contemporary Research: Essays on the Status Quaestionis*, edited by Bart D. Ehrman and Michael W. Holmes, 115–42. Leiden: Brill, 2013.

Schmidt, Karl Ludwig. *The Place of the Gospels in the General History of Literature*. Translated by Byron R. McCane. Columbia, SC: University of South Carolina Press, 2002.

Schneemelcher, Wilhelm, and R. McL. Wilson, eds. *New Testament Apocrypha*. 2 vols. 2nd ed. Louisville, KY: James Clarke, 1990.

Schniewind, Julius. *Parallelperikopen bei Johannes und Lukas*. Hildesheim: G. Olms, 1958.

Scholem, Gershom. *On the Kabbalah and its Symbolism*. Translated by Ralph Manheim. New York: Schocken Books, 1965.

Schreiber, Johannes. "Die Christologie des Markusevangeliums." *Zeitschrift für Theologie und Kirche* 58 (1961) 154–83.

———. *Die Markuspassion. Eine redaktionsgeschichtliche Untersuchung*. Beihefte zur Zeitschrift für die neutestamentliche Wissenschaft 68. Berlin: de Gruyter, 1993.

Schubert, Paul. "The Structure and Significance of Luke 24." In *Neutestamentlichen Studien für Rudolph Bultmann*, edited by W. Eltester, 165–186. Berlin: Alfred Töpelman, 1954.

Schwartz, Daniel R. *Reading the First Century: On Reading Josephus and Studying Jewish History of the First Century*. Wissenschaftliche Untersuchungen zum Neuen Testament 1/300. Tübingen: Mohr Siebeck, 2013.

Schwartz, Howard. *Reimagining the Bible: The Storytelling of the Rabbis*. Oxford: Oxford University Press, 1998.

Scott, M. Philip. "Chiastic Structure: A Key to the Interpretation of Mark's Gospel." *Biblical Theology Bulletin* 15 (1985) 17–26.

Scrivener, Frederick Henry. *A Plain Introduction to the Criticism of the New Testament*. Cambridge: Cambridge University Press, 1861.

Segal, Alan. *Two Powers in Heaven: Early Rabbinic Reports about Christianity and Gnosticism*. Leiden: Brill, 2002.

Shaku, Soyen. *Zen for Americans.* Translated by Daisetz Teitaro Suzuki. New York: Dorset, 1913.

Shedinger, Robert F. "Must the Greek Text Always Be Preferred? Versional and Patristic Witnesses to the Text of Matthew 4:16." *Journal of Biblical Literature* 123 (2004) 449–66.

Shellard, Barbara. *New Light on Luke: Its Purpose, Sources, and Literary Context.* London: Sheffield Academic Press, 2002.

Shelton, W. B. "An Ancient Israelite Pattern of Kingly Accession in the Life of Christ." *Trinity Journal* 25 (2004) 61–73.

Shepherd, Sheri Rose. *Your Heart's Desire: 14 Truths that Will Forever Change the Way you Love and Are Loved.* Wheaton, IL: Tyndale Momentum, 2012.

Shiner, Whitney Taylor. *Proclaiming the Gospel: First-century Performance of Mark.* Harrisburg, PA: Trinity, 2003.

Simpson, A. B. *The Four-Fold Gospel.* New York: The Word, Work & World, 1888.

Skarsaune, Oskar, and Reidar Hvalvik, eds. *Jewish Believers in Jesus.* Peabody, MA: Hendrickson, 2007.

Skeat, T. C. "A Codicological Analysis of the Chester Beatty Papyrus Codex of the Gospels and Acts (P45)." *Hermathena* 155 (1993) 27–43.

———. "Irenaeus and the Four-Gospel Canon." *Novum Testamentum* 34 (1992) 194–99.

Skinner, Christopher W. *Reading John.* Cascade Companions. Eugene, OR: Cascade, 2015.

———. "'Son of God' or 'God's Chosen One' (John 1:34)? A Narrative-Critical Solution to a Text-Critical Problem." *Bulletin for Biblical Research* 25 (2015) 341–57.

Smart, Ninian. *World Philosophies.* New York: Routledge, 2000.

Smith, Barry D. *The Indescribable God: Divine Otherness in Christian Theology.* Eugene, OR: Pickwick, 2010.

Smith, Christopher R. "Literary Evidence of Fivefold Structure in the Gospel of Matthew." *New Testament Studies* 43 (1997) 540–51.

Smith, David Oliver. *Matthew, Mark, Luke, and Paul: The Influence of the Epistles on the Synoptic Gospels.* Eugene, OR: Resource, 2011.

Smith, Justin Marc. *Why βίος? On the Relationship between Gospel Genre and Implied Audience.* New York: Bloomsbury T. & T. Clark, 2015.

Solomon, Norman, ed. *The Talmud: A Selection.* London: Penguin, 2009.

Squillace, Robert, ed. *The Odyssey.* Translated by George Herbert Palmer. New York: Barnes and Noble, 2003.

Stanton, Graham N. *Jesus and Gospel.* Cambridge: Cambridge University Press, 2004.

Starr, Chester G. *A History of the Ancient World.* Oxford: Oxford University Press, 1965.

Stedman, Rick. *31 Surprising Reasons to Believe in God: How Superheroes, Art, Environmentalism, and Science Point toward Faith.* Eugene, OR: Harvest House, 2017.

Stemberger, Günter. *Jewish Contemporaries of Jesus: Pharisees, Sadducees, Essenes.* Translated by Alan W. Mahnke. Minneapolis: Fortress, 1995.

Stein, Robert H. *The Synoptic Problem: An Introduction.* Grand Rapids: Baker, 1987.

Steinmetz, David C. "The Superiority of Pre-Critical Exegesis." *Theology Today* 37 (1980) 27–38.

Stendahl, Krister. *The School of St. Matthew and Its Use of the Old Testament.* 2nd ed. Lund: Gleerup, 1968.

Stevens, Anthony. *Archetype Revisited: An Updated Natural History of the Self.* London: Brunner-Routledge, 2002.

Stevenson, Peter K., and Stephen I. Wright. *Preaching the Incarnation.* Louisville, KY: Westminster John Knox, 2010.

Stewart, Columba. *Prayer and Community: The Benedictine Tradition.* Maryknoll, NY: Orbis, 1998.

Stewart, Ewert. "The Fourfold Sense of Scripture in Christian Mysticism." In *Mysticism and Sacred Scripture,* edited by Steven T. Katz, 118–37. Oxford: Oxford University Press, 2000.

Stowers, Stanley Kent. *A Rereading of Romans: Justice, Jews, and Gentiles.* New Haven, CT: Yale University Press, 1994.

Strauss, Mark L. *Mark.* Exegetical Commentary on the New Testament. Grand Rapids: Zondervan, 2014.

Streeter, Burnett Hillman. *The Four Gospels: A Study in Origins.* New York: Macmillan, 1961.

Strickert, F. "Rachel on the Way: A Model of Faith in Times of Transition." *Currents in Theology and Mission* 34 (2007) 444–52.

Stumpf, Samuel Enoch. *Socrates to Sartres: A History of Philosophy.* New York: McGraw-Hill, 1966.

Sugirtharajah, R. S. *Postcolonial Reconfigurations: An Alternative Way of Reading the Bible and Doing Theology.* London: SCM, 2003.

Swanwick, Keith. *A Developing Discourse in Music Education: The Selected Works of Keith Swanwick.* New York: Routledge, 2016.

Swartley, Willard M. *The Love of Enemy and Nonretaliation in the New Testament.* Louisville, KY: Westminster John Knox, 1992.

Sweat, Laura C. *The Theological Role of Paradox in the Gospel of Mark.* New York: Bloomsbury T. & T. Clark, 2013.

Symington, Scott. *Freedom From Anxious Thoughts and Feelings: A Two-step Mindfulness Approach for Moving Beyond Fear and Worry.* Oakland, CA: New Harbinger, 2019.

Tam, Josaphat C. *Apprehension of Jesus in the Gospel of John.* Wissenschaftliche Untersuchungen zum Neuen Testament 2/399. Tübingen: Mohr Siebeck, 2015.

Tannehill, Robert. "The Magnificat as Poem." *Journal of Biblical Literature* 93 (1974) 263–75.

———. *The Narrative Unity of Luke-Acts: A Literary Interpretation.* Minneapolis: Fortress, 1994.

Tanner, Norman P., ed. *Decrees of the Ecumenical Councils.* 2 vols. Washington, DC: Georgetown University Press, 1990.

Taylor, Joan. *The Immerser: John The Baptist within Second Temple Judaism.* Grand Rapids; Cambridge: Eerdmans, 1997.

Teresa of Ávila. *The Interior Castle.* Translated by Mirabai Starr. New York: Riverhead, 2003.

Theodore the Studite. *On the Holy Icons.* Translated by Catherine P. Roth. Crestwood, NY: St. Vladimir's Seminary Press, 1981.

Theophilos, Michael P. *The Abomination of Desolation in Matthew 24.15.* New York: Bloomsbury T. & T. Clark, 2012.

Thiede, Carsten Peter. *Rekindling the Word: In Search of Gospel Truth.* Valley Forge, PA: Trinity, 1995.

Thompson, Kurt. *The Anatomy of the Soul.* Carol Stream, IL: Tyndale, 2010.

Triebel, J. "Das koranische Evangelium. Kritische Ammerkungen zur koranischen Darstellung der Person und Botschaft Jesus." *Theologische Beiträge* 38 (2007) 269–82.

Tuckett, Christopher, ed. *From the Sayings to the Gospels*. Wissenschaftliche Untersuchungen zum Neuen Testament 328. Tübingen: Mohr Siebeck, 2014.

Turner, David L. *Matthew*. Baker Exegetical Commentary on the New Testament Grand Rapids: Baker Academic, 2008.

van Balthasar, Hans Urs, ed. *Origen: Spirit and Fire*. Washington, DC: The Catholic University of America Press, 1984.

Van Der Kolk, Bessel. *The Body Keeps the Score: Brain, Mind, and Body in the Healing of Trauma*. New York: Penguin, 2014.

van der Watt, Jan, ed. *The Quest for the Real Jesus: Radboud Prestige Lectures by Prof. Dr. Michael Wolter*. Biblical Interpretation Series 120. Leiden: Brill, 2013.

van Liere, Frans. *An Introduction to the Medieval Bible*. Cambridge: Cambridge University Press, 2014.

van Oyen, Geert. *Reading the Gospel of Mark as a Novel*. Translated by Leslie Robert Keylock. Eugene, OR: Cascade, 2014.

van Ruiten, Jacques T. A. G. "The Book of Jubilees as Paratextual Literature." In *In the Second Degree: Paratextual Literature in Ancient Near Eastern and Ancient Mediterranean Culture and Its Reflections in Medieval Literature*, edited by Philip S. Alexander et al., 65–95. Leiden: Brill, 2010.

Van Tilborg, Sjef, and Patrick Chatelion Counet. *Jesus' Appearances and Disappearances in Luke 24*. Leiden: Brill, 2000.

Vande Kappelle, Robert P. *Wisdom Revealed: The Message of Biblical Wisdom Literature—Then and Now*. Eugene, OR: Wipf & Stock, 2014.

Vermes, Geza. *The Complete Dead Sea Scrolls in English*. New York: Penguin, 1998.

Veyne, Paul, ed. *A History of Private Life: From Pagan Rome to Byzantium*. Translated by Arthur Goldhammer. Cambridge, MA: Harvard University Press, 1987.

Viljoen, F. P. "Fulfillment in Matthew." *Verbum et Ecclesia* 28 (2007) 301–24.

Viviano, Benedict. "John's use of Matthew: Beyond Tweaking." *Revue Biblique* 111 (2004) 209–37.

———. "The Movement of the Star, Matt 2:9 and Num 9:17." *Revue Biblique* 103 (1996) 58–64.

Voelz, James W. *Mark 1:1—8:26*. Concordia Commentary Series. St. Louis: Concordia, 2014.

von Harnack, Adolf. *Marcion: das Evangelium vom Fremden Gott; eine Monographie zur Geschichte der Grundlegung der katholischen Kirche*. 2nd ed. Leipzig: Hinrichs, 1924.

von Heijne, Camille Hélena. *The Messenger of the Lord in Early Jewish Interpretations of Genesis*. Berlin: Walter de Gruyter, 2010.

von Wahlde, Urban C. "The Relationship between Pharisees and Chief Priests: Some Observations on the Texts in Matthew, John, and Josephus." *New Testament Studies* 42 (1996) 506–22.

Waheeb, Mohammad. "The Discovery of Bethany Beyond the Jordan River (Wadi Al-Kharrar)." *Dirasat* 35 (2008) 115–26.

Wakefield, Gordon S. *Groundwork of Christian Spirituality*. Peterborough, UK: Epworth, 2001.

Wallace, Daniel B. *Greek Grammar Beyond the Basics: An Exegetical Syntax of the New Testament.* Grand Rapids: Zondervan, 1996.

Wallis, Glenn. *The Dhammapada: Verses on the Way.* New York: Modern Library, 2007.

Walters, Patricia. *The Assumed Authorial Unity of Luke and Acts: A Reassessment of the Evidence.* Society for New Testament Studies Monograph Series 145. Cambridge: Cambridge University Press, 2009.

Ward, Benedicta. *The Lives of the Desert Fathers.* Translated by Norman Russell. Kalamazoo, MI: Cistercian, 1981.

———. *The Sayings of the Desert Fathers: The Alphabetical Collection.* Oxford; Kalamazoo, MI: Cistercian, 1975.

Ward, Keith. *God: A Guide for the Perplexed.* UK: Oneworld, 2003.

Wasserman, Tommy, and Peter J. Gurry. *A New Approach to Textual Criticism: An Introduction to the Coherence-Based Genealogical Method.* Stuttgart; Atlanta: Deutsche Bibel Gesellschaft; Society of Biblical Literature, 2017.

Watson, Francis. *The Fourfold Gospel: A Theological Reading of the New Testament Portraits of Jesus.* Grand Rapids: Baker Academic, 2016.

Webb, Robert L. "John the Baptist and his Relationship to Jesus." In *Studying the Historical Jesus: Evaluations of the State of Current Research,* edited by Bruce Chilton and Craig A. Evans, 179–230. Leiden: Brill, 1998.

Weisse, Christian Hermann. *Die evangelische Geschichte, kritisch und philosophisch bearbeitet.* 2 vols. Leipzig: Breitkopf und Härtel, 1838.

Wellhausen, Julius. *The Pharisees and the Sadducees: An Examination of Internal Jewish History.* Translated by Mark E. Biddle. Mason, GA: Mercer University Press, 2001.

Wendland, Paul. *Die hellenistisch-römische Kultur in ihren Beziehungen zu Judentum und Christentum. Die urchristlichen Literaturformen.* Handbuch zum Neuen Testament 1.2. Tübingen: Mohr, 1912.

Wenham, Gordon J. *Psalms as Torah: Reading Biblical Song Ethically.* Studies in Theological Intepretation. Grand Rapids: Baker Academic, 2012.

Werman, Cana. "Levi and Levites in the Second Temple Period." *Dead Sea Discoveries* 4 (1997) 211–25.

Westcott, B. F. *A General Survey of the History of the Canon of the New Testament.* 5th ed. London: Macmillan, 1881.

Westerholm, Stephen. *Understanding Matthew: The Early Christian Worldview of the First Gospel.* Grand Rapids: Baker Academic, 2006.

Wiles, Maurice F. *The Spiritual Gospel: The Interpretation of the Fourth Gospel in the Early Church.* Cambridge: Cambridge University Press, 1960.

Wilken, Robert Louis. *The Christians as the Romans Saw Them.* New Haven, CT: Yale University Press, 2004.

———. *The Spirit of Early Christian Thought: Seeking the Face of God.* New Haven, CT: Yale University Press, 2003.

Wilkins, Michael J. *Matthew.* NIV Application Commentary. Grand Rapids: Zondervan, 2004.

Williams, Peter J. *Can We Trust the Gospels?* Wheaton, IL: Crossway, 2018.

Williams, Rowan. *The Wound of Knowledge: Christian Spirituality from the New Testament to Saint John of the Cross.* Cambridge, MA: Cowley, 1990.

Wimbush, Vincent L. *Ascetic Behavior in Greco-Roman Antiquity: A Sourcebook.* Minneapolis: Fortress, 1990.

Wink, Walter. *John the Baptist in the Gospel Tradition.* Society for New Testament Studies Monograph Series 7. Cambridge: Cambridge University Press, 1968.

Winn, Adam, ed. *An Introduction to Empire in the New Testament.* Resources for Biblical Study 84. Atlanta: Society of Biblical Literature, 2016.

Witherington, Ben, III. *Jesus, the Sage: The Pilgrimage of Wisdom.* Minneapolis: Fortress, 2000.

———. *Women in the Earliest Churches.* Cambridge: Cambridge University Press, 1988.

Wolf, Maryann. *Proust and the Squid: The Story and Science of the Reading Brain.* New York: Harper Perennial, 2007.

Wolff, Pierre. *The Spiritual Exercises of Saint Ignatius: A New Translation for the Authorized Latin Text.* Liguori, MA: Triumph, 1997.

Wood, Susan K. *Spiritual Exegesis and the Church in the Theology of Henri de Lubac.* Eugene, OR: Wipf & Stock, 1998.

Worley, Taylor. "The Splendor of Holiness: The Church as the Theatre of Divine Beauty." In *Marking the Church: Essays in Ecclesiology,* edited by Greg Peters and Matt Jenson, 63–75. Eugene, OR: Pickwick, 2016.

Wright, N. T. *Who Was Jesus?* Grand Rapids: Eerdmans, 1992.

Yoder, John Howard. *The Politics of Jesus.* Grand Rapids: Eerdmans, 1972.

Zaas, P. "Matthew's Birth Story: An Early Mile Post in the History of Jewish Marriage Law." *Biblical Theology Bulletin* 39 (2009) 125–28.

Zelyck, Lorne. R. *The Egerton Gospels (Egerton Papyrus 2 + Papyrus Köln vi 255.* Leiden; Boston, MA: Brill, 2019.

———. *John among the Other Gospels.* Wissenschaftliche Untersuchungen zum Neuen Testament 2/347. Tübingen: Mohr Siebeck, 2013.

Zizioulas, John. *Being As Communion: Studies in Personhood and the Church.* Yonkers, NY: St. Vladamir's Seminary Press, 1997.

Zsengellér, József, ed., *Rewritten Bible after Fifty Years: Texts, Terms, or Techniques? A Last Dialogue with Geza Vermes.* Supplements to the Journal for the Study of Judaism 166. Leiden: Brill, 2014.

Subject Index

Modern Author Index

Ancient Document Index

Old Testament/ Hebrew Bible

Genesis

Exodus

Leviticus

Numbers

Deuteronomy

Joshua

Judges

Ruth

1 Samuel

2 Samuel

1 Kings

2 Kings

1 Chronicles

2 Chronicles

Ezra

Job

Psalms

Proverbs

Ecclesiastes

Song of Songs

Isaiah

Isaiah *(continued)*

Jeremiah

Lamentations

Ezekiel

Daniel

Hosea

Joel

Amos

Micah

Nahum

Zephaniah

Haggai

Zechariah

Malachi

Apocrypha

Tobit

Judith

Wisdom of Solomon

Sirach

Prayer of Azariah

Song of the Three Young Men

Bel and the Dragon

25 (Theodotion)

36 (Theodotion)

1 Maccabees

Prayer of Manasseh

4 Maccabees

Pseudepigrapha

3 Baruch

1 Enoch

Mark

Luke

Luke *(continued)*

John

Acts

Romans

1 Corinthians

2 Corinthians

Galatians

Ephesians

Greco-Roman Writings

Jewish Antiquities

Jewish Wars

The Life

Lucian

Demonax

How To Write History

Pausanias

Description of Greece

Philo

Against Flaccus

On the Confusion of Tongues

On the Contemplative Life

On the Posterity of Cain

On the Special Laws

Epiphanius

Panarion

Eusebius of Caesarea

Ecclesiastical History

Preparation for the Gospel

1 Clement

Gregory of Nyssa

Life of Macrina

Life of Moses

Gregory the Great

Dialogues

Ignatius of Antioch

To the Ephesians

To the Smyrnaeans

Irenaeus of Lyon

Against Heresies

Jacob of Serugh

Homily on Epiphany

Jerome

Adversus Pelagianos dialogi III

Commentarium in Isaiam libri XVIII

Commentarium in Matthaeum libri IV

Commentarium in Michaeum libri II

De viris illustribus

John Cassian

Conferences

John Chrysostom

Homilae in Joannem

Homilae in Matthaeum

John of Damascus

Orthodox Faith

Justin Martyr

First Apology

Second Apology

Dialogue with Trypho

Origen

Commentarius in Canticum

Commentarii in evangelium Joannis